Major Psychological Assessment Instruments

Second Edition

Charles S. Newmark

EDITOR

Allyn and Bacon
Boston   London   Toronto   Sydney   Tokyo   Singapore

DEDICATED TO MY PASSIONS IN LIFE:

My family, babies, dogs,
University of North Carolina basketball,
Minnesota Viking football, and Las Vegas

Copyright 1996, 1985 by Allyn & Bacon
A Simon & Schuster Company
Needham Heights, Massachusetts 02194

Library of Congress Cataloging-in-Publication Data

Major psychological assessment instruments / Charles S. Newmark,
   editor. — 2nd ed.
     p. cm.
   Includes bibliographical references and index.
   ISBN 0-205-16869-8
   1. Psychological tests.   I. Newmark, Charles S.
BF176.M35   1996
150'.28'7—dc20   95-40858
                                         CIP

Printed in the United States of America
10 9 8 7 6 5   00 99 98

Contents

Preface

The first edition of *Major Psychological Assessment Instruments* was published in 1985. Not long after the book appeared, some people said that I should do a second book that would include tests not covered in the first one. I heeded that advice and the second book on major instruments was published in 1989. That book was called Volume II. Both books together constituted an efficient source of information about the most widely used tests in current psychological practice. More than just a compilation of how-to manuals, these two books offered the reader easy access to information concerning the introduction, construction, administration, interpretation, and status of major tests. The intent was to present the core clinical knowledge necessary for the competent use of these instruments.

Favorable book reviews, positive feedback from clinicians as well as colleagues and students, relatively high sales volume, and the need to recognize the significant changes that have occurred with regard to these tests provided the impetus for this second edition of the original book. In addition to updating all information about the tests, two new chapters have been added on the Minnesota Multiphasic Personality Inventory-Adolescent (MMPI-A) and on the Millon Clinical Multiaxial Inventory (MCMI-III). Because of the relationship between the figure drawing tests, those tests are now covered in one chapter. All of the tests are discussed in terms of their basic underlying assumptions, strategies, and issues, and each is accompanied by an illustrative case example. This work should serve as an invaluable reference not only for school, clinical, and counseling psychologists but also for anyone in the mental health field.

I am extremely appreciative of the authors' significant contributions. Working with such a dedicated, responsible, and reliable group of professionals has been a rewarding experience and made the editorial duties relatively easy. All of the authors have published extensively and are nationally recognized authorities in their respective areas.

Appreciation must be extended to Georgye Woody and Linda Newmark for their assistance in typing and proofreading the manuscript. Additionally, I am most fortunate to have worked with Mylan Jaixen, editor at Allyn and Bacon. His confidence, encouragement, and many helpful comments and suggestions are testimony to his dedicated and responsible publishing expertise.

Thank you also to Susan Hutchinson, editorial assistant, for helping to coordinate this project. I am grateful, too, to Gary L. Arthur, Georgia State University, for his thorough and insightful review.

Finally, I am thankful for many comments and criticisms of the previous volumes that have been offered by students and colleagues and I hope that this second edition has benefitted from their input in the way it was intended.

About the Editor

Charles S. Newmark, Ph.D., is a clinical psychologist in private practice in Chapel Hill, North Carolina. Formerly, he was the director of the Clinical Psychology Training Program and an associate professor of Psychology in the Department of Psychiatry at the University of North Carolina School of Medicine in Chapel Hill. Dr. Newmark received the doctorate in clinical psychology in 1971 from the University of Alabama. In 1977, he was awarded the Diplomate in Clinical Psychology (ABPP). He is a consulting editor for the *Journal of Personality Assessment* and an associate editor for *Psychological Reports.* His credentials include more than 80 articles as well as book and book chapters on the MMPI and related issues in personality assessment. Dr. Newmark is coeditor of *Short-Forms of the MMPI* (1978) and is editor of *MMPI: Clinical and Research Trends* (1980), *Major Psychological Assessment Instruments* (1985), and *Major Psychological Assessment Instruments, Volume 2* (1989). Additionally, he has conducted approximately 100 workshops on MMPI interpretation at various universities, hospitals, mental health centers, forensic organizations, and correctional settings.

About the Contributors

Robert P. Archer is the director of the psychology division at Eastern Virginia Medical School. He is editor of *Assessment* and associate editor of the *Journal of Personality Assessment.* He is author of *Using the MMPI With Adolescents* (1987), *MMPI-A: Assessing Adolescent Psychopathology* (1992), and *MMPI-A Case Book* (1994).

Jeffrey T. Barth holds the diplomate certification from the *American Board of Professional Psychology/American Board of Clinical Neuropsychology* and is a fellow of the National Academy of Neuropsychology in Division 40 of APA. He holds the position of chief of psychology/neuropsychology and professor in the departments of psychiatric medicine and neurological surgery.

Kristee A. Beres is an adjunct professor and assistant director of psychoeducational assessment services at the California School of Professional Psychology in San Diego, California.

Arthur Canter is professor emeritus and former chief of the division of clinical psychology in the department of psychiatry at the University of Iowa Hospitals in Iowa City, Iowa.

Richard H. Dana retired from the University of Arkansas in 1988 as emeritus university professor and now specializes in assessment and intervention with multicultural populations. He has a courtesy appointment as research professor at the regional research institute at Portland State University.

Roger D. Davis is a graduate student in the department of psychology at the University of Miami in Coral Gables, Florida.

Philip Erdberg is a diplomate in clinical psychology and in private practice in Corte Mederia, California. He is associated with Rorschach workshops and was past president of the Society for Personality Assessment.

A. J. Finch, Jr. is a diplomate in clinical psychology and currently is head and professor of psychology at The Citadel.

Leonard Handler is director of clinical psychology training program, University of Tennessee, Knoxville, Tennessee. He is on the editorial board of several psychology journals and has published extensively in the area of projective drawings.

Alvin E. House is an associate professor of psychology at Illinois State University in Normal, Illinois. He also maintains a private practice with an emphasis on psychological evaluations.

R. W. Kamphaus is professor of psychology in the department of educational psychology at the University of Georgia in Athens, Georgia. His recent books include *Clinical Assessment of Children's Intelligence: A Handbook for Professional Practice* and *Clinical Assessment of Child and Adolescent Personality and Behavior.*

Alan S. Kaufman is senior research scientist for Psychological Assessment Resources Inc. (PAR) in Odessa, Florida. He is the primary author of *The Kaufman Assessment Battery for Children (K-ABC)* and his most recent book is entitled *Assessing Adolescent and Adult Intelligence.*

Nadeen L. Kaufman is assistant professor and director of psychoeducational assessment services at the California School of Professional Psychology in San Diego, California.

Radhika Krishnamurthy is assistant professor in the school of psychology at Florida Tech. She is coauthor of *MMPI-A Casebook* (1994) and also serves as a reviewer for manuscripts for *Assessment* and the *Journal of Personality Assessment.*

Stephen N. Macciocchi is associate professor in the departments of physical medicine and psychiatric medicine at the University of Virginia Medical School. He also is the director of the division of the rehabilitation psychology and neurology in the department of physical medicine.

David M. McCord is associate professor of psychology, department of psychology, Western Carolina University, Cullowhee, North Carolina.

Theodore Millon is professor in the department of psychology at the University of Miami in Coral Gables, Florida. He is author of the Millon Clinical Inventories and the major presenter at the Millon Clinical Inventories workshops.

P. Michael Politano is associate professor of psychology and coordinator of the graduate program in school psychology at The Citadel.

1

The Minnesota Multiphasic Personality Inventory-2 (MMPI-2)

Charles S. Newmark
David M. McCord

DEVELOPMENT

Development of the Original MMPI

The original Minnesota Multiphasic Personality Inventory (MMPI) was developed in the late 1930s and has been historically the most widely used personality assessment instrument and the most extensively researched of all psychological tests. Its first and only revision, the MMPI-2, was published in 1989 and is now widely accepted in psychological practice. The unparalleled success of the MMPI is attributable primarily to three aspects of its development: the "multiphasic" nature of the test, the inclusion of formal measures of test-taking attitude, and the empirical basis for item selection. Most existing objective personality tests of the 1920s and 1930s were singular or limited in focus, measuring such characteristics as "neuroticism" (e.g., Woodworth, 1920) or small sets of personality characteristics such as dominance or introversion (e.g., Bernreuter, 1933). The ability to assess a wide range of psychopathology with a single instrument was quite attractive to real-world practitioners. Virtually none of the early instruments included measures of test-taking attitude, making them vulnerable to intentional or unintentional distortion.

The authors of the MMPI were most concerned about distorting effects of a patient's tendency to underreport pathology ("faking good") or to overreport pathology ("faking bad"), and specific validity scales were developed to as-

1

sess these tendencies. The early personality inventories (1918–1930) were comprised of test items that were rationally derived based on the theoretical notions of the test author. Although these instruments appeared to have good face and construct validity, they fared poorly under research scrutiny. Thus, the use of an empirical method of item selection, which had been developed earlier by E. B. Strong, Jr., distinguished the MMPI from its competitors and is likely the single most important reason behind its success.

The primary author of the MMPI, Starke Hathaway, Ph.D., was trained formally as a physiological psychologist. Because academic appointments were quite difficult to obtain in the mid-1930s, Hathaway accepted a position as a research psychologist in the Department of Neurology at the University of Minnesota Hospitals. The second author of the test, Jovian Charnley McKinley, M.D., was a neurologist and the department head to whom Hathaway reported. One of the very few somatic treatments available for psychiatric patients of that day was insulin coma therapy, and, because there were few alternatives, it was used with a wide variety of patients. Hathaway proposed a research project designed to assess the differential response to insulin treatment by specific diagnostic groups, and McKinley approved the project. The first task was to develop an efficient, reliable, valid method of assigning a diagnosis to the patients in the study, and it was this need that prompted the development of the MMPI.

Hathaway and McKinley collected more than 1,000 items from a variety of sources, including psychiatric textbooks, other personality tests, interviews and discussions with other clinicians, and their own clinical experience. After deleting duplicate items and those they determined were insignificant or irrelevant for their purposes, they arrived at a set of 504 items. These items were presented as first-person declarative statements, mostly in the affirmative, to which the subject responded either true or false. Next, the authors specified the major psychopathological syndromes to be assessed by the instrument. Diagnostic practice of the day utilized Kraepelinian terminology and reflected major neurotic conditions, psychotic conditions, and severe characterological disorders. Not well recognized were more subtle personality disorders, substance abuse disorders, adjustment disorders, and marital problems.

The eight specific diagnostic groups on which the authors' original efforts focused, and for which scales were developed, were labeled Hypochondriasis, Depression, Hysteria, Psychopathic Deviate, Paranoia, Psychasthenia, Schizophrenia, and Hypomania. Subsequently, the Masculinity-Femininity and Social Introversion scales were added and included on the standard test profile form. The MMPI scales were developed by contrasting the responses to the 504 items of a group of "normals" with those of a carefully identified group of patients within a specific diagnostic group. For example, in developing the Hypochondriasis scale, Hathaway identified 50 patients exhibiting relatively pure and uncomplicated hypochondriasis who did not meet criteria for any other diagnosis. For each of the 504 items, the proportion of true versus false responses given by the patient group was compared to the proportion of true versus false responses given by a sample of "normal" individuals. Using a Z-test for the significance of the difference between two independent proportions, Hathaway selected items that were significant at the .05 level or better. In addition to the primary norm group of 724 visitors to the University of Minnesota Hospitals, Hathaway developed four additional, smaller comparison groups for cross-validation purposes. To remain on the scale, an item had to discriminate not only between the diagnostic group and the primary norm group but it also had to survive cross-validation. After selecting the items for the eight primary clinical scales, each scale was normed by calculating its mean and standard deviation in the primary norm group.

The Masculinity-Femininity scale and the Social Introversion scale were developed later and somewhat differently. Because few of the original 504 items reflected sexual orientation or gender interest patterns, 55 items reflecting these issues were added to the item pool.* Because individuals in the original norm group (the "Minnesota normals") had not responded to these items, they could not be used for item selection procedures. Thus, the identified group of male homosexuals were compared to a group of 54 male soldiers. Actually, very few items discriminated between these two groups, and items from the original pool were added to the scale if they discriminated between men and women in the standardization sample. Drake (1946) developed the Social Introversion scale by selecting MMPI items that discriminated between students scoring above the 65th percentile with those scoring below the 35th percentile on the Minnesota T-S-E, a test of social introversion-extraversion.

Finally, four standard validity scales were developed. The ? scale (Cannot Say) indicates omitted or double-marked items. The L scale measures more obvious or blatant efforts to present oneself in an unrealistically favorable manner. The F scale is comprised of items endorsed only rarely by "normal" individuals and elevated scores may reflect confusion, poor reading ability, psychotic states, or exaggeration of pathology. The K scale reflects more subtle or sophisticated defensiveness or positive self-presentation. Table 1–1 lists the four standard validity scales and the 10 basic scales on the original MMPI. Included are the standard abbreviations for the scales as well as their scale number. Several new validity scales have been developed with the MMPI-2 and will be presented later in this chapter. It is now common practice to refer to the scales by number rather than by name. This reflects an effort to avoid the often misleading connotations of the scale names, several of which are obsolete.

---

*The 55 additional items added to the original 504 results in 559 items. However, the final form of the MMPI contained only 550 unique items (16 items were repeated in order to facilitate mechanical scoring, resulting in the familiar 566-item format). The fate of the 9 missing items is not known.

Table 1–1   MMPI Validity and Clinical Scales

Traditional Scale Name	Abbreviation	Number
Validity		
Cannot Say	?	
Lie	L	
Frequency	F	
Correction	K	
Clinical		
Hypochondriasis	Hs	1
Depression	D	2
Hysteria	Hy	3
Psychopathic Deviate	Pd	4
Masculinity-Femininity	Mf	5
Paranoia	Pa	6
Psychasthenia	Pt	7
Schizophrenia	Sc	8
Hypomania	Ma	9
Social Introversion	Si	0

Development of the MMPI-2

The MMPI gained popularity very rapidly, and, as noted earlier, has been the most widely used personality test in history. Hathaway's test development procedures represented a trail-blazing effort at the time and are still very much respected today. In particular, the great care he exerted in forming his diagnostic groups resulted in minimally contaminated subject samples. His extensive cross-validation efforts set a standard for test development. One major shortcoming, though, has been the composition of the original standardization group. The 724 "Minnesota normals" were all white, primarily of rural background, primarily farmers or blue-collar workers or their spouses, almost all Protestant, many of Scandinavian descent, with an average age of 35 and an average education level of 8th grade (Graham, 1990). While this group may have been reasonably representative of the Minnesota population in the late 1930s, it certainly does not reflect the broader U.S. culture of today. Furthermore, many of the original items contain content that is obsolete, offensive, or politically incorrect. Thus, after years of discussion and debate, restandardization of the MMPI was completed in 1989 (Butcher, Dahlstrom, Graham, Tellegen, & Kaemmer, 1989).

Briefly, the restandardization committee eliminated 13 items from the standard clinical and validity scales as well as the 16 duplicate items. They reworded 141 items to increase understandability and to eliminate sexist or outdated language. They then added 154 items reflecting areas not fully considered in the original item set, such as substance abuse and marital relationship issues, resulting in an experimental set of 704 items that were administered to the new standardization sample. The committee eventually eliminated 77 additional items from the original set, included 68 of the 141 rewritten items, and included 107 of the 154 new items. The result is the 567-item MMPI-2 currently in use. A listing of MMPI and MMPI-2 items, including the items rewritten, deleted, and added, is available in Pope, Butcher, and Seelen (1993).

The standardization sample for the MMPI-2 consisted of individuals between the ages of 18 and 90 from seven states (California, Minnesota, North Carolina, Ohio, Pennsylvania, Virginia, and Washington), an Indian reservation in Washington, and several military bases. Over 2,900 individuals were tested; after excluding incomplete or invalid test records, a standardization sample of 2,600 remained (1,138 males and 1,462 females). The sample compares reasonably well with U.S. census data with regard to ethnic composition, though Hispanics and Asian Americans may be somewhat underrepresented. The sample compares well with census data regarding age, marital status, and income level. However, the standardization sample has a much higher education level and corresponding bias toward professional occupational status than does the U.S. population as a whole.

On the original MMPI, results were expressed as T scores with a mean of 50 and a standard deviation of 10. Scores over 70 were interpreted as clinically significant. Examination of the raw score distributions revealed that most were positively skewed, and there was considerable variability among scales. Thus, a T score of 75 on one scale might represent a very different percentile rank than the same T score on another scale. To correct this problem, the restandardization committee chose to express results in the form of "uniform" T scores (Butcher et al., 1989). Briefly, uniform T scores have a distribution that represents the average or typical T score distribution for the MMPI-2 scales, based on a composite of 16 distributions (male and female raw score distributions on the eight basic scales, excluding scales 5 and 0). Using uniform T scores results in greater internal consistency for the inventory so that similar T scores on two different scales represent about the same degree of departure from the mean on those scales. At least partly because of the use of uniform T scores, scale elevations on the MMPI-2 tend to be about 5 points lower than scores on the original MMPI. Thus, the restandardization committee has recommended that the cutoff score of 65 be used to reflect clinical significance, replacing the traditional cutoff score of 70.

ADMINISTRATION AND SCORING

Administration

In general, administration of the MMPI-2 is straightforward and easy, adequately managed by an appropriately trained psychometrist or psychological assistant. The test is extraordinarily robust, and research over several decades has demonstrated that valid results may be obtained using a wide variety of administration formats, including standard paper and pencil forms, presentation of items, card sort forms (one item per card), audiotape, computer-administered items with response via keyboard, group administration, and even reading items aloud to the subjects (e.g., Cottle, 1950; Honaker, 1988; MacDonald, 1952; Moreland, 1985; Roper, Ben-Porath, & Butcher, 1991; Wiener, 1947).

Despite the ease of administration and robustness of the test, it should certainly be presented to the patient as a serious and important task. In order to maximize cooperation, instructional set is critical. Patients should be informed why the MMPI-2 is being administered. For example, in a psychiatric inpatient setting, the clinician may explain that the psychotherapist specifically requested psychological testing to learn more about the patient so appropriate treatment strategies can be formulated. Effectively explaining to the patient that the testing is for his or her benefit will help immeasurably in enlisting full cooperation. If additional reassurance or further clarification of the intended use of the results is needed, a frank approach should be used. Furthermore, it is crucial the patient receive feedback regarding the results.

Some patients seek advice or request clarification of the items. Since the success of the instrument in documenting personality differences is based on the different ways patients interpret and answer the statements, the clinician should avoid providing direct help. For example, patients may have concerns regarding the word *frequently,* such as in the item "I frequently have headaches." The clinician must emphasize a response to this item based on the patient's interpretation of frequently. That is, if a patient has one headache a week and thinks that is frequently, then True should be checked. On the other hand, if the patient has 10 headaches a week, but does not view this as frequently, then False should be checked. Some patients will have questions about the time frame they should consider in answering the test items. For example, they may say that they would answer an item one way now but differently six months ago. Emphasize that they should answer the items in a way that reflects their *current thoughts, feelings, behaviors, and experiences.*

The standard instructions in the test booklet state that if the item does not apply to the patient, no marks should be made on the answer sheet. However, the instructions state twice that the patient is to try to respond to every item. Omitted items cannot be scored and obviously have the effect of lowering the scale scores. Thus, the clinician administering the test should emphasize that the patient should answer every item. A vast majority will comply with this request and will omit very few or no items. It is good practice for the clinician to examine the answer sheet immediately after completion of the test. If more than two or three items are omitted, return the test to the patient and offer a carefully phrased request that he or she consider the omitted items.

The original MMPI was used with patients as young as age 14—even 13, given above-average intelligence and reading ability (separate adolescent norms had been developed). The revision process has included development of a new form of the test specifically for adolescents, the MMPI-A (see Chapter

2). Thus, the MMPI-2 is recommended for use with patients 18 years of age and older. There is no upper age limit, given adequate reading ability. Butcher and colleagues (1989) suggest that most patients with at least eight years of education can take the test because most of the items reflect sixth-through eighth-grade reading levels. Poor reading ability is the single biggest cause of inconsistent responding (Greene, 1991), so this issue must receive serious consideration. If there are any doubts about the patients' reading ability, a reading achievement test is recommended.

Test completion time is typically 60 to 90 minutes, though less intelligent patients and those with other complicating factors may take two hours or more. Results obtained in less than 60 minutes should be evaluated with some degree of suspicion. Most patients are able to complete the test in one session. However, multiple sessions may be required by those with marginal reading ability and/or with certain psychiatric conditions, such as attention deficit disorder, mania, or severe depression.

Test Forms

The most commonly used form of the MMPI-2 is the reusable test booklet containing the 567 items (referred to in ordering materials as the "Software Test Booklet") with separate answer sheet. Several different answer sheets are available, depending on the method of scoring to be utilized (hand scoring versus scanning, local versus mail in, etc.). An alternative spiral-bound hardcover booklet is also available ("Hardcover Test Booklet"). The specialized answer sheet is mounted inside the back cover of the booklet, and pages are successively shorter so that each item lines up directly with the appropriate blank on the answer sheet. This "step-down" hardcover form is useful in settings such as hospitals where tables or desks may not be readily available.

Other forms of the MMPI-2 include a Spanish version, an audiotaped presentation of items, and software for computer-administrated testing. Unlike the original MMPI, all forms of the MMPI-2 contain the 567 items in identical order. All items included on the standard validity and clinical scales are included in the first 370 items. In general, the use of short forms of the MMPI-2 is discouraged. In most settings, patients who can complete 370 items are able to complete the remaining items as well, providing the opportunity to score a variety of additional validity and supplementary scales. However, there may be some research settings and even some clinical settings where only the standard validity and basic clinical scales are needed. Materials may be obtained from National Computer Systems, Inc. (NCS), P.O. Box 1416, Minneapolis, Minnesota 55440.

Scoring

As indicated earlier, both hand-scoring and computer-scoring methods are available for the MMPI-2. Hand scoring involves the use of semi-transparent plastic templates that are placed over the answer sheet. Sets of templates are available separately for the basic scales, the supplementary scales, the content scales, the Harris-Lingoes subscales, and the subtle-obvious scales. Hand-scoring users will also need to purchase profile sheets for any of these five scale sets they wish to score. Answer sheets should be separated by sex, since separate templates are used for scale 5 (Mf) for males and females. Next, the answer sheet should be visually examined for omitted and double-marked items and these should be circled, or otherwise marked, and counted. The total number of omitted or double-marked items becomes the raw score for the Cannot Say (?) scale and should be entered in the appropriate blank on the Basic Scales profile sheet. The other three traditional validity scales and 10 basic scales are scored by placing the scoring templates over the answer sheet and counting the number of responses appearing in the target boxes on the template. The total number of items endorsed becomes the raw score for the scale and is entered in the appropriate raw score blank on the profile sheet. It should be noted that all profile sheets are two-sided, with male norms incorporated on one side and female on the other. Thus, it is very important to use the proper side of the profile form when entering data.

Note that the Cannot Say scale is treated as a raw score only and is not plotted on the profile. For each of the other three traditional validity scales— L, F, and K—a mark should be made at the elevation reflecting the raw score for that scale. Within each column on the profile sheet, a dash represents a raw score increment of 1; increments of 5 are labeled and indicated with a longer dash. The marks indicating elevations for L, F, and K should be connected with a continuous line.

Before plotting the basic clinical scales, attention should be paid to the row under the raw scores labeled "K to be added." Five of the basic scales (1, 4, 7, 8, and 9) require a correction to the raw score before they are plotted, with the correction being a specific proportion of the raw score for the K scale. The bottom row on the profile sheet, labeled "Raw Score with K," contains blanks for the corrected raw score, and it is this value that should be marked and plotted above. The proportion of K to be added to each of the five scales is printed next to the scale name, above the scale number, at the top and bottom of the plotting grid on the profile sheet. For example, .5 K should be added to the raw score for scale 1, and the sum ("Raw Score with K") should be plotted on the grid. Scales 4 and 9 require adding .4 K and .2 K, respectively, whereas scales 7 and 8 require adding the full K raw score. For convenience, a table is provided on the far left side of the profile sheet with .5 K, .4 K, and .2 K already calculated for the full range of K raw scores. The scorer should circle the row including the K raw score and use the proportional values along that row. Briefly, the K-correction has been found to increase the discriminatory power of these five scales, while the uncorrected raw score is most effective with the other scales. A complete discussion of the rationale for and relative merits of the use of the K-correction can be found elsewhere (e.g., Graham, 1990; Greene, 1991; Hsu, 1986). Special profile sheets for plotting noncorrected scores are available from NCS. Because the norms are incorporated into the plotting grid, K-corrections must be used with the standard profile sheet.

Once the elevations for the 10 basic scales are marked on the profile sheet, these should be connected with a line. Note that the 3 validity scales are connected with a line and the 10 clinical scales are connected with a second line. Uniform T scores are on the far left and far right columns.

Computer scoring may be accomplished in several different ways. NCS provides a comprehensive software system to be installed in the clinician's microcomputer that allows for the administration, scoring, and interpretations of the MMPI-2 and MMPI-A. A "hardware key" is installed on the parallel port of the computer to count the number of administrations used. Additional administrations may be ordered by phone, and the clinician is given a code to enter via keyboard that resets the counter. A second option, suitable for lower-volume usage, is to use a modem and any communications software package to connect to the NCS host computer. The patient's test responses are keyed in via keyboard, and results (profile and interpretation if requested) are downloaded to the remote computer. Scannable answer sheets are available for both of these scoring services. Finally, scannable answer sheets may be mailed to NCS for scoring, with overnight delivery options available.

Coding the Profile

Hathaway's original expectation was that a patient's MMPI profile would include a single elevation or "spike" that would indicate the diagnosis. From the very beginning, though, it was clear that most profiles are best seen as a *configuration* of scale elevations. Relevant in interpretation are the absolute elevations of the scales as well as their positions relative to each other. To facilitate interpretation and to reduce the very large number of potential profiles to a more reasonable number, a coding system was developed to record in an efficient and concise manner the most important aspects of a profile. Generally, scales, represented by their number (1, 2, etc.), are arranged from most elevated to least elevated, with each number followed by a symbol (*, -, /, etc.) representing its elevation. Hathaway himself developed the original coding system (Hathaway, 1947), though the more elaborate system developed by Welsh (1948) has been the predominant coding method used for the past 40 years. The MMPI-2 manual (Butcher et al., 1989) recommends the use of the Welsh coding system with the MMPI-2. However, because a T score of 65 is now clinically significant, a slight modification has been proposed by Butcher and Williams (1992) and is recommended by Graham (1990) as well as the present authors. Following are steps to construct a modified Welsh code from an MMPI-2 profile:

Step 1. Write down the 10 numbers representing the basic clinical scales, with the scale with the highest T score elevation on the left, followed by the next highest, and so forth. Following these 10 numbers, separated by some space, list the three validity scales (L, F, and K) in order from highest to lowest. The Cannot Say scale is not included in the coding system, nor are any supplementary scales, content scales, or subscales.

Step 2.   When adjacent scales are within one T score point from each other, underline the two scale numbers. If two scales have exactly the same T score, list them in the order they appear on the profile sheet and then underline them.

Step 3.   Insert the appropriate symbols after scale numbers:

120 and above	!!
110–119	!
100–109	**
90–99	*
80–89	"
70–79	'
60–69	-
50–59	/
40–49	:
30–39	#
29 and less	the right of #

Traditionally, it is not necessary to include the symbol to the left of the highest scale or to the right of the lowest scale. However, within the profile all symbols should be included, even if there is no score within that range. Code the validity scales similarly. An example of a modified Welsh code, representing the profile of the case example at the end of this chapter, is 5"742'89603-/1:F'-/KL:

INTRODUCTION TO INTERPRETATION

The MMPI-2 includes several new validity scales and numerous supplementary scales, content scales, and subscales. However, experienced clinicians rely most heavily on the 3 traditional validity scales and the 10 basic clinical scales appearing on the standard profile form. Indeed, an extreme position, supported by a number of empirical analyses, is that information provided by supplementary scales is redundant with that provided by the basic scales. The present authors take a more moderate stance, suggesting that the supplementary and content scales may add some helpful information in some cases, but the primary focus should certainly be on the basic scales.

As noted earlier, many of the MMPI-2 basic scale names are obsolete or misleading, and standard practice is to refer to them by their number on the profile sheet. The validity scales are referred to by name or by their one-letter abbreviation.

In approaching an MMPI-2 profile, the first step is to consider the test-taking attitude of the patient. The configuration of validity scales provides the primary information in this regard, but the basic scales should be considered as well. Once some determination has been made regarding test-taking attitude and profile validity, the basic scales are examined for clinical meaning. The MMPI-2 was developed to identify problems, and high scores reflect the presence of the problem the scale was designed to measure. For most purposes, a T score of 65 or greater should be considered a high score. When this is not the case, more precise information will be presented. In general, the higher the score, the more likely the behavioral correlates of that scale will apply to the patient. Usually, T scores below 40 are considered low. Much less information is available regarding the meaning of low scores, and for many scales low scores just reflect the absence of the characteristics associated with high scores. In some configurations, though, the presence of very low scores on some scales alters the implications of the pattern as a whole.

The following section discusses the traditional validity scales, the new validity scales, and the 10 basic clinical scales; subsequent sections will address configural interpretation. In all cases, the information provided refers to psychiatric patients. To present this information in a cogent yet parsimonious manner, references for each statement will be omitted. Most of the interpretive information presented has been extracted, distilled, and compiled from the following sources: Butcher (1990), Dahlstrom, Welsh, and Dahlstrom (1972), Fowler (1966), Golden (1979), Graham (1990), Greene (1991), Lachar (1977), Meyer (1983), and Webb and McNamara (1979). The selection, integration, and augmentation of materials from these sources is based on the first author's (Newmark) extensive experience interpreting over 10,000 MMPI and MMPI-2 profiles of psychiatric patients.

TRADITIONAL VALIDITY SCALES

? (Cannot Say) Scale

The ? scale is not actually a scale but is simply the number of test items either omitted or double-marked. The effect of omitted or double-marked items is to lower the score of any scales on which the item occurs. Despite careful administration procedures, it is not uncommon for patients to omit some items. The recommended procedure in this case is to return the answer sheet to the patient and request that all items be answered.

The traditional assumption is that over 30 omissions invalidates a profile. Although this may be a good rule in many cases, it is certainly an oversimplification. For example, if all omissions occurred after item 370, the traditional validity and basic clinical scales can all be scored. On the other hand, even a much lower number of omissions (e.g., 10 to 12) may have a distorting effect on the profile if all omitted items occurred on the same scale or within the same content area. Thus, the pattern of omissions and the content of the omitted items should be examined before making a judgment regarding profile validity.

Most sources agree that profiles with more than 30 omissions are probably invalid, whereas those with 10 or fewer are most likely valid. Profiles with omissions between 10 and 30 should be treated with increasing caution as the number of omissions approaches 30. In most cases, omitted items are randomly distributed. Some reasons for omitted or double-marked items and the resultant elevations on this scale include:

1. Insufficient reading level
2. Carelessness
3. Confusion and/or the presence of psychotic manifestations
4. Severe obsessive-compulsive tendencies or ruminative components so the patient is indecisive regarding an answer.
5. The patient does not possess the information or experience necessary for a meaningful response.
6. The question does not apply to the patient. For example, on the question, "I love my mother," the patient may never have known his or her mother.

It is Newmark's experience that items are usually not omitted as a defensive ploy. Omitting or double-marking draws attention to those items. Therefore, it seems logical that if a patient wants to be defensive, he or she will just deny rather than omit.

L (Lie) Scale

The L scale was originally constructed to detect a deliberate and rather unsophisticated attempt to present oneself in a favorable light. In contrast to all other MMPI scales, the 15 items on the L scale were selected *rationally* to identify individuals who were deliberately attempting to avoid answering the MMPI frankly and honestly. The items reflect attitudes and behaviors that are admirable in U.S. culture but are actually found only in the most conscientious individuals.

Examples of L scale items with the scorable response included in parentheses are:

"Once in a while I think of things too bad to talk about." (F)
"I do not read every editorial in the newspaper every day." (F)
"If I could get into a movie without paying and be sure I was not seen I would probably do it." (F)*

Over 95 percent of the population, if they were being honest and nondefensive, would answer True to these items. However, of the 15 items, many "normals" do endorse a few. The mean raw score on the L-scale within the standardization group was 4.

Research has revealed that better educated, brighter, more sophisticated patients from higher social classes tend to obtain lower scores on the L scale. Thus, such variables must be considered when deciding if a score is high. For example, a borderline-IQ black female with a sixth-grade education from rural North Carolina may score high on this scale in order to present herself in a favorable light so that she will be accepted by those evaluating her. This test-taking attitude does not necessarily invalidate the profile, but it does mean that denial may be a prominent defense mechanism. Indeed, high L scores rarely invalidate the profile. This is simply a measure of denial and blatant, naive defensiveness.

High scores are sometimes obtained from members of the clergy, who may be trying to convince themselves that they do indeed lead impeccably virtuous lives. High scores may also be obtained from job applicants with limited social awareness who are naive enough to think that a favorable impression can be made by answering negatively. Sociopathic individuals who lack a clear understanding of how they are seen by others may also take this very naive, unsophisticated approach to impression management.

High scores (60 or greater in this case) reflect an attempt by patients to present themselves in an unrealistically positive light concerning their self-control, moral values, and freedom from common human frailties. A general lack of flexibility, limited insight, denial, and poor tolerance for stress and pressure are strongly suggested. Low scores (below 45) suggest that the patient responded frankly to the items and was comfortable enough to be able to admit to minor faults and shortcomings.

F (Infrequency) Scale

Unlike most other scales, The F scale was not derived by comparing a criterion group with "Minnesota normals." Instead, these 60 items were those answered in the scored direction by fewer than 10 percent of a normal population (actually, a subsample of the original "Minnesota normal" group). Hathaway's original intent was to develop a scale that would easily reflect inadequate reading ability. His reasoning was that individuals who answered a large number of items only infrequently endorsed by the standardization group must not be able to read the items well. Because of this original purpose, the resulting scale was named "Feeblemindedness" (hence the abbreviation F). Although limited reading ability is a possible cause of elevated F scores, there are many other possibilities, including severe confusion and various forms of psychopathology. Thus, it is best to think of this scale as a measure of rarely endorsed items. In current terminology, F is referred to as the "Frequency" or "Infrequency" scale.

This scale taps a wide variety of content areas, including bizarre sensations, strange thoughts, peculiar experiences, feelings of alienation, and a

number of contradictory or unlikely beliefs, expectations, and self-descrip-
tions. Examples of F scale items with the deviant answer in parentheses are:

"Evil spirits possess me at times." (T)
"When I am with people, I am bothered by hearing very strange things."
 (T)
"I believe I am being plotted against." (T)*

Elevations on F (65 and above) may be produced by a number of different factors, including:

1. Scoring errors
2. Poor reading ability
3. A deliberate attempt to look bad by endorsing those items reflecting significant pathology (F is usually greater than 95 in these cases)
4. Confusion, delusional thinking, or other psychotic processes
5. A cry for help by a patient who is exaggerating symptoms
6. In adolescents and prisoners, the expression of defiance, hostility, and
   negativism

T scores in the range from 70 to 95 generally reflect the most significant
psychopathology. T scores above 95 suggest that the profile may be invalid
due to poor reading ability or to an inability to understand the questions, random responding, or a deliberate attempt to fake bad. These attempts to exag-
gerate psychopathology usually involve patients who have something to gain
from a poor impression, such as those involved in court cases, disability applicants, patients attempting to use an insanity plea, or patients who want to
use hospitalization as an escape from life. Most psychotic patients score in the
range from 70 to 95. Patients with a T score over 105 are rarely diagnosed as
psychotic, as their awareness of those items that reflected significant pathology suggests a clarity of thinking not consistent with a psychotic state.

Low scores on F suggest an absence of bizarre or unusual thinking. Very
low scores are sometimes associated with an attempt to "fake good." Of the 60
items, "normal" adults endorse only 2 to 8.

K (Correction) Scale

The K scale was added to the MMPI in an attempt to detect more subtle or
sophisticated attempts to deny faults and present oneself favorably than were
measured by the L scale. This scale consists of 30 items that were helpful in
discriminating between the "Minnesota normals" and a group of patients with

known psychopathology who produced normal-appearing MMPI profiles. Thus, K is a measure of defensiveness as a test-taking attitude. Examples of K scale items with the scorable answer in parentheses are:

"People often disappoint me." (F)
"I think nearly anyone would tell a lie to keep out of trouble." (F)
"I have very few quarrels with members of my family." (T)*

K scale items cover several different content areas in which patients can deny problems (e.g., hostility, suspiciousness, family turmoil, lack of self-confidence). The items tend to be much more subtle than items on the L scale, so it is less likely that a defensive patient will be able to avoid detection.

High K scores are not correlated with specific behaviors but instead reflect a reluctance to admit to psychopathology. Patients with T scores over 65 are very guarded and defensive and show a marked resistance to psychological probing and assessment. They tend to minimize and overlook faults in themselves, their families, and their circumstances. Therefore, in such cases, an elevation greater than 65 on the K scale results in a invalid profile due to excessive defensiveness. One exception includes various types of histrionic patients for whom an elevated K is expected.

Low scores, unless the result of a deliberate effort to fake bad, suggest that a patient's characteristic defenses are not working effectively or have deteriorated. When defenses are down, a patient is likely to be rather self-critical and to overendorse pathological items, but usually not those reflecting psychotic manifestations. Such a patient will probably not score over 95 on any of the clinical scales but will likely have significant elevations on a 2 and 7. Psychotic patients usually score between 75 and 95 on scales F, 6, and 8. More specific criteria for assessing the presence of psychotic manifestations will be discussed later in the chapter, under Special Issues.

K scale scores are influenced by setting, socioeconomic status, and education level. For example, an elevated K is expected in child custody cases and in personnel selection or job interview settings. Well-educated patients and those with high socioeconomic status tend to obtain higher scores on K as well. Among normal adults, K is not so much a measure of defensiveness as it is personality integration and adjustment, with higher scores reflecting healthy adjustment.

As noted earlier, the K scale was used to develop a correction factor for five of the basic clinical scales. Hathaway and McKinley reasoned that if the effect of a defensive test-taking attitude as reflected by a high K is to lower scores on the clinical scales, perhaps they could determine the extent to which the scores should be raised in order to reflect more accurately a patient's behavior. By comparing the efficiency of each clinical scale with various portions of K added as a correction factor, these authors and colleagues determined the appropriate weighting of the K scale score for each clinical scale to correct for the defensiveness indicated by K. Scales 1, 4, 7, 8, and 9 have proportions of K added ranging from .2 to 1.0, while scales 2, 3, 5, 6, and 0 are not K- corrected because the simple raw score on these scales seemed to produce the most accurate prediction.

NEW VALIDITY SCALES

F_B (Back F) Scale

When the MMPI was revised, most of the F scale items occurred in the first half of the 704-item experimental form of the test booklet. The restandardization committee felt that it would be useful to have a similar measure covering the second half of the test. Thus, they identified items in the second half of the test responded to in a given direction by less than 10 percent of the standardization sample, 40 of which make up the current F_B scale. Because this experimental form of the test utilized a two-sided answer sheet and the items under consideration were all answered on the back of the answer sheet, the scale was named the "Back-Page Infrequency" or simply the Back F scale.

MMPI-2 test administration requires a considerable amount of time—over an hour in most cases—and it is conceivable that a patient's test-taking approach might shift over the course of testing. It would be possible to produce a set of results with a normal-range F scale and an elevated F_B. This would suggest that the patient responded in a valid manner to the first half of the test items but responded inconsistently to the remainder of the items. Thus, F and F_B together provide a way to assess task approach over the course of time. If, in fact, F is within the normal range and F_B is elevated, the basic clinical scales, which fall within the first 370 items, could still be interpreted. As of yet, little research is available concerning F_B, and cautious use is recommended.

TRIN (True Response Inconsistency) Scale

The TRIN scale is one of two new measures for the MMPI-2 based on the internal consistency of the patient's response pattern. This scale consists of 23 pairs of items that have contradictory or opposite content. For example, the following pair of items is included on TRIN:

> 3. "I wake up fresh and rested most mornings."
> 39. "My sleep is fitful and disturbed."*

*Source: Minnesota Multiphasic Personality Inventory-2. Copyright © 1942, 1943 (renewed 1970), 1989 THE REGENTS OF THE UNIVERSITY OF MINNESOTA. All rights reserved. "MMPI-2" and "Minnesota Multiphasic Personality Inventory-2" are trademarks owned by the University of Minnesota.

If a patient responded True to both of these items, inconsistency is reflected, and they would receive one point on the TRIN scale. Of the 23 pairs, 14 are scored if both items are answered True, and 9 are scored if both items are answered False. The final TRIN score is computed by adding one point for each of the 14 "true" pairs when both are answered True, subtracting one point for each of the 9 "false" pairs when both are answered False, and then adding 9 to the total to avoid negative numbers. Despite its name, TRIN should not be interpreted as reflecting the patient's consistency of responding. Instead, high scores indicate an acquiescent or "yea-saying" response set, whereas low scores represent a nonacquiescent or "nay-saying" response set. A raw score of 9 corresponds to a T score of 50. Raw scores both above and below 9 are transformed to T scores greater than 50 and plotted on the profile with a "T" or an "F" to reflect yea-saying or nay-saying. The MMPI-2 manual suggests that a T score cutoff of 80 be used with this new scale to determine profile invalidity. As is the case with F_B, little research is currently available on TRIN.

VRIN (Variable Response Inconsistency) Scale

The VRIN scale consists of 67 pairs of items that are either similar or opposite in content. The patient receives one point on the VRIN scale for each air answered inconsistently. For example, the 3/39 pair just presented also occurs on the VRIN scale. Because these items have contradictory content, if both are answered True, one point is added to the VRIN scale. An example of the second type of item on the VRIN scale is:

> 6. "My father is a good man, or (if your father is dead) my father was a good man."
> 90. "I love my father, or (if your father is dead) I loved my father."*

Because these items share similar content, if one is answered True and the other False, one point is added to the VRIN scale. Still other items with dissimilar content are scored on the VRIN scale if both are answered False.

An example of the potential usefulness of VRIN would be a profile with an elevated F. If VRIN were also elevated, one would lean toward interpreting the F as reflecting confusion, random responding, or poor reading ability. On the other hand, if VRIN were not elevated, interpretations might focus on deliberate efforts to fake bad or serious but nonpsychotic psychopathology.

As in the case with TRIN, because this is a new scale with very little research available, the test manual suggests that a conservative cutoff score of T = 80 be used to determine profile invalidity due to inconsistent responding. Both TRIN and VRIN are complicated to score by hand, and great care should be taken if this is attempted. The advantages of computer scoring are quite obvious with these scales.

Determining Profile Invalidity

In addition to the behavioral characteristics associated with elevations of the validity scales, the configuration of validity scales provides important information regarding test-taking attitude, response set, and response bias. In many cases, the difference between a valid and invalid profile is not readily apparent. The determination of profile invalidity can be difficult and requires close scrutiny, not only of the validity scales but also of the clinical scales.

A traditional rule of thumb was to discard as invalid any profile with an elevation of 70 or greater (65 on the MMPI-2) on scales L, F, or K or a raw score of 30 or greater on the Cannot Say scale. This is an extremely conservative and very oversimplified approach that would result in discarding many valid profiles. For example, as discussed earlier, if the 30 or more omissions occurred past item 370, the basic clinical and validity scales are still interpretable. Similarly, most psychotic patients will produce an elevation greater than 65 on scale F, whereas patients with hysterical disorders may score above 65 on scale K and elevations on scale L may occur among members of the clergy and very naive individuals of lower socioeconomic status.

Of these traditional criteria, the most generally accepted is that in most cases when K is greater than 65, the profile should be regarded with suspicion. The K elevation may not reflect a deliberate attempt to fake good, but it does suggest that the patient was so defensive, guarded, and uncooperative that the clinical profile may not be valid. However, it should be emphasized that before discarding a profile as invalid, the clinical scales should be examined for consistency with other data, including other test results, demographic and historical information, and interview impressions. If the profile is indeed consistent with other data, it may be interpreted as valid, regardless of the validity scale pattern.

In determining profile invalidity, it is important to be aware of and recognize typical response patterns associated with invalid profiles. For example, the answer sheet itself should be examined for all-true or all-false responding. However, a random response pattern is not readily evident. Random responding should be considered when both scales F and 8 have T scores over 105, VRIN is over 80, and L plus all the clinical scales are elevated above 55. Such a profile is distinguishable from a highly psychotic profile having T scores on scales F and 8 between 75 and 95 and usually a low score on K.

Two other response sets that are important to consider in interpreting MMPI-2 profiles have been referred to traditionally as the "fake bad" and "fake good" approaches. Greene (1991) prefers to use the terms *overreporting* and *underreporting psychopathology*. The term *fake* implies a conscious, deliberate attempt at distortion, whereas the actual motivation underlying a particular response set may or may not be conscious. Overreporting pathology usually results in T scores over 95 on F and T scores over 85 on 6, 7, and 8 with L and K below 45. In addition, these patients typically endorse a large number of critical items (see Critical Items).

In contrast, patients who are underreporting pathology are attempting, consciously or not, to deny or minimize their problems. The resulting profile is characterized by a K greater than 65 and most clinical scales and F below 45. The L scale score will be inversely related to education and psychological sophistication. In detecting both "fake good" and "fake bad" responses, the motivation for responding in such a manner should be determined if possible.

When the issue of profile invalidity is discussed in the MMPI literature, mention is usually made of the so-called F minus K index (F–K). Gough (1950) originally suggested taking the difference between the raw F and the raw K scores (F–K), with a result greater than 9 indicating faking bad and a score less than –9 indicating faking good. Subsequent research and clinical experience revealed that the use of these cutoff scores excluded a significant number of valid profiles. For example, most schizophrenics produce an F–K greater than 9. Ziskin (1981) provided data supporting the use of F–K with a much higher cutoff (15) in forensic settings. It must be noted, however, that all research with F–K has been conducted using the original MMPI. On the MMPI-2, the number of F items has been reduced from 64 to 60, while K remained the same at 30 items. Thus, the present authors discourage the use of the F–K index with the MMPI-2.

THE CLINICAL SCALES

Several factors must be kept in mind when evaluating the importance of each clinical scale in a profile. First, the meaning of a scale elevation is relative to the rest of the profile. A score that is both elevated (greater than 65) and higher than all other scales has much more interpretive significance than a high score that is fifth or sixth highest. Similarly, a score between 60 and 65 assumes much greater significance if it is the highest score in the profile. The lowest score or scores on the profile should also be noted.

A second significant factor is to recognize that several scales share significant overlap in item content. For example, scales 1 and 3 share many items, as do scales F and 8, and thus will tend to move up or down together. The extent to which one is high and the other low often suggests specific interpretations important to the scale and pattern analysis. Third, the test-taking attitude reflected by the validity scales must be considered when interpreting the clinical scales. Interpretations should be adjusted according to whether the patient is minimizing, exaggerating, or responding openly and honestly. Finally, the influence of key demographic variables must be considered in modifying the interpretation. The effects of age and race will be discussed under Special Issues, and other important demographic variables will be discussed within each clinical scale description.

Scale 1 (Hs) Hypochondriasis

This 32-item scale is a direct measure of the degree of concern regarding body functioning. The items are obvious in content and span a wide variety of vague somatic complaints. Scale 1 is the most clearly unidimensional of all basic scales and is characterized by the denial of good health and the admission of numerous physical symptoms. Examples of scale 1 items with the scored response in parentheses are:

"I have a good appetite." (F)
"My hands and feet are usually warm enough." (F)
"I am troubled by attacks of nausea and vomiting." (T)*

High scorers on this scale endorse an excessively large number of somatic complaints and show prominent concern with body functions. Scale elevations suggest not only that the patients utilize somatization as a defense mechanism but also that this defense mechanism is not working effectively. These patients often appear to be contradictorily asking, even pleading, for care, while at the same time rejecting the possibility of treatment. A rather sour, whiny, and complaining attitude is characteristic, and a great deal of hostility and cynicism may be expressed in this indirect manner. These traits may intensify into a rather paranoid posture when the patient feels threatened.

Because of the wide variety of physical complaints contained on scale 1, elevations above 75 indicate that patients are endorsing items reflecting virtually every organ system. Indeed, some of these patients have developed remarkable skills for frustrating physicians. Passivity is pronounced, dependency readily apparent, and there is the almost child-like expectation that others should take care of them. Medical patients with legitimate physical problems generally obtain somewhat lower scores on this scale (55 to 65) than psychiatric somatization reactions. These medical patients will endorse their legitimate physical symptoms, but they will not endorse the entire gamut of complaints tapped by scale 1. Low scorers tend to be much the opposite of high scorers (cheerful, optimistic, etc.), but they are a rather heterogeneous group as their common characteristic is the nonendorsement of somatic complaints.

Scale 2 (D) Depression

Scale 2 is comprised of 57 items measuring symptomatic depression, a general attitude characterized by poor morale, lack of hope for the future, and a general dissatisfaction with life. The items deal with various aspects of depression, such as denial of happiness and personal worth, psychomotor retardation, lack of interest, social withdrawal, physical complaints, and excessive worry. Scale 2 tends to be more of a state measure and thus usually reflects situational depression. Examples of scale 2 items with scored responses in parentheses are:

"I wish I could be as happy as others seem to be." (T)
"I am certainly lacking in self-confidence." (T)
"I usually feel that life is worthwhile." (F)*

High scorers are described as depressed, worried, pessimistic, and are likely to show a great deal of indecision, doubt, and vacillation as well as withdrawal. The depression is likely to be expressed as feelings of hopelessness and futility and may be accompanied by suicidal ideation. Marked feelings of insecurity, inadequacy, and inferiority exist. The depression may not be confined to subjective experiences and may extend to a motor retardation accompanied by a loss of interest, initiative, and involvement. These patients have difficulty expressing emotions in a modulated, adaptive way, and instead will internalize many of their feelings to the point that overcontrol is likely. They will attempt to avoid unpleasantness and will make concessions in order to avoid confrontations.

The exact interpretations of scale 2 vary markedly depending on other scale elevations (see Code Types). When scale 2 is the only elevated scale in the profile, this usually reflects a reactive depression in an individual who has experienced some type of situational stress, such as the death of a close relative. Indeed, temporary scale 2 elevations typically occur in response to such situations.

Low scores on scale 2 generally reflect a lack of depression, worry, pessimism, and a tendency to feel comfortable with life. That is, these patients generally show an absence of the traits and behaviors characteristic of high scale 2 patients. Very low scale 2 scores (below 35) are associated with an unrelenting cheerfulness, buoyancy, and optimism that may strike others as rather obnoxious.

In order to achieve consistency in clinical practice, Newmark has adopted a routine subjective system for labeling the degree of depression. Scale 2 T scores from 60 to 69 are labeled mild depression, 70 to 79 are labeled moderate depression, and scores of 80 or greater are labeled severe depression. Depression of psychotic proportions can only be inferred based on the entire profile (see Special Issues). Also, low scores on a scale 9 tend to accentuate the amount of depression indicated by scale 2.

Scale 3 (Hy) Hysteria

The 60 items on scale 3 tap two broad areas: specific somatic complaints and denial of psychological or emotional problems and of discomfort in social situations. While these two groupings of items are negatively correlated or unrelated in "normal" subjects, they are closely associated in patients utilizing the defensive pattern historically labeled hysterical. Examples of scale 3 items with scored responses in parentheses are:

> "Much of the time my head seems to hurt all over." (T)
> "I have never had a fainting spell." (F)
> "I find it hard to make talk when I meet new people." (F)*

Patients who score high on this scale are generally immature, egocentric, and demanding, with histrionic characteristics and repressive defenses. They tend to be rather vain, liable, lacking in insight, and dependently demanding in social interactions. When they do not receive the necessary attention and affection desired, hostility and resentment occur. However, these feelings will be denied and not expressed overtly. Although usually gregarious, interpersonal relationships are maintained on a rather shallow, superficial level. These patients may act out sexually, often behaving in a seductive manner toward those of the opposite sex.

When an elevation on scale 3 is also accompanied by an elevation over 65 on scale 1, then the scale is tapping more of the conversion reaction. These patients are described as prone to develop any of a variety of circumscribed conversion symptoms. While the symptoms may be based in some actual organic pathology, they generally arise after protracted periods of tension in patients with a history of insecurity, immaturity, and a well-established proclivity to physical complaints. Thus, before a conversion reaction can be noted, some evidence of somatic complaints is needed. Additionally, it is crucial never to state that the somatic complaints are totally functional (or psychological) in nature. Even if an organic cause has not been identified, it is best to emphasize that the reaction *may* be based on some actual organic pathology.

Low scorers on scale 3 are described as being constricted, conforming, overly conventional, suspicious, and with a narrow range of interests and restricted emotional expression. Nevertheless, they tend to be realistic, logical, and level headed in their approach to problems and are not likely to make impulsive decisions. They seem to be quite content with what others might judge to be a dull, uneventful life situation.

Scale 4 (Pd) Psychopathic Deviate

Scale 4 contains 50 items that reflect a primary dimension ranging from constricted social conformity to antisocial acting-out impulses. In this respect, it is directly related to the tendency to express or inhibit aggressive and hostile impulses. Scale 4, like scale 3, is a characterological scale and tends to assess general maladjustment, the absence of strongly pleasant experiences, a failure to appreciate the interpersonal side of life, complaints about family and authority figures in general, social alienation, and an emotional shallowness toward others. Examples of scale 4 items with scored responses in parentheses are:

> "I am sure I get a raw deal from life." (T)
> "No one seems to understand me." (T)
> "I have never been in trouble because of my sex behavior." (F)*

Patients scoring high on scale 4 are characterized by angry disidentification with recognized conventions and norms. Impulse control problems are prevalent as they exhibit an apparent inability to plan ahead, if not a reckless disregard of the consequences of their actions. They may justify their disregard of convention on the basis of being above mere propriety, reflecting the high value that many place on themselves. They are likely to show diminished affective reactions and have difficulty sustaining an affectionate relationship due to their inability to express tender feelings as well as their impaired ability to empathize and put others first. Indeed, patients characteristically exhibit a disregard and even disdain for the rights and feelings of other people. Consequently, marital and/or family conflicts are likely. They tend to view interpersonal relationships as opportunities for exploitation and self-gratification. They are unwilling to accept the responsibility for their behaviors and tend to use projection as a primary defense. Sexual acting out and substance abuse are not uncommon. Frustration tolerance is limited, judgment poor, and there seems to be minimal benefit from experience. Immaturity and narcissism are rather pronounced.

Patients who obtain low scores on this scale tend to be overly conventional, conforming, and moralistic, with low levels of drive and heterosexual aggressiveness. They feel uncomfortable in situations demanding anger, originality, or strength, and they tend to avoid competitive situations and may have strong guilt feelings over minor infractions.

The specific interpretation of scale 4 in any particular profile is dependent on relations with other scales as well as the incorporation of demographic

---

data, especially age. For example, accompanying elevations on scale 3 appear to inhibit the potential for direct impulse expression suggested by scale 4, whereas an accompanying elevation on scale 9 often provides increased impetus to acting out, antisocial behaviors (see Code Types).

Scale 5 (Mf) Masculinity-Femininity

This 56-item scale measures the extent to which the patient endorses or identifies with culturally stereotype masculine or feminine interest patterns as well as vocational choices, aesthetic interests, and an activity-passivity dimension. Most of the items are obvious in content and can be easily faked without detection. Examples of scale 5 items include:

> "I think I would like the work of a librarian." (T)
> "I like poetry." (T)
> "I enjoy reading love stories." (T)*

Note that the responses to these items are scored when they reflect feminity in men and masculinity in women. Scale 5 is the only MMPI-2 scale scored differently for males and females. That is, the T score conversions are reversed as a function of sex. On the profile sheet, a high raw score for males is transformed to a high T score, whereas a high raw score for females is transformed to a low T score. The result is that a high T score for either sex is indicative of deviation.

By itself, the scale is an inadequate estimate of tendencies toward overt or latent homosexuality. Male patients who are so overtly homosexual as to show extreme elevations on scale 5 could just as easily be identified by asking them directly. Nevertheless, the possibility of homoerotic trends, homosexual behavior, and/or effeminate qualities should be considered when extreme elevations are obtained, particularly if the scores deviate markedly from expectations based on various demographic variables. That is, brighter, better educated, and higher social class males obtain higher scores. Male college students and male college graduates often obtain T scores in the 60 to 70 range.

There is no established relationship between scores on scale 5 for female patients and either homosexual ideas and behaviors or demographic characteristics such as intelligence, education, and social class. Most female patients obtain scores below 50 on this scale.

Males with high scores tend to be rather passive, dependent, ambitious, sensitive, and interested in cultural and aesthetic pursuits. They lack interest in sterotypically masculine pursuits and may be experiencing fundamental and disturbing questions concerning their own sexual identity.

Low-scoring males tend to adhere to the cultural stereotype of masculinity and place great emphasis on traditionally masculine behaviors. They may appear somewhat crude, coarse, or even vulgar and may need to demonstrate their virility in order to camouflage underlying doubts about their masculinity.

Females with high scores (greater than 55 to 60) are rare but seem to have rejected many of the aspects of their traditional feminine role. They are described as active, aggressive, assertive, competitive, uninhibited, and domineering. They have strong interests in the so-called masculine areas of sports, work, and hobbies. Many of these women see themselves in active competition with men, attempting to prove they are equal or better.

Females with low scores on scale 5 are described as being passive, submissive, yielding, and demure, sometimes to the point of being caricatures of the cultural stereotype of femininity. They are highly constricted, self-pitying, and may have significant doubts regarding their own adequacy as females.

Scale 6 (Pa) Paranoia

Scale 6 contains 40 items ranging from obviously psychotic content, such as delusions of persecution and ideas of reference, to interpersonal hypersensitivity, suspiciousness, and moral self-righteousness. Because of the obvious content of most of the items, this scale is easier to fake than most. Thus, there are few false positives (high scores by nonparanoid patients) but some false negatives (low scores by paranoid patients). Examples of scale 6 items with scored responses in parenthesis are:

"If people had not had it in for me, I would have been much more successful." (T)

"I believe I am being plotted against." (T)

"At times I hear so well it bothers me." (T)*

Patients who obtain high scores on scale 6 can be divided into two groups. The first involves T scores in the range of 60 to 70 and even approaching 75. This indicates heightened sensitivity to criticism, a basic mistrust of the motives of others, a tendency to brood and harbor grudges, feelings of being discriminated against, a tendency to use rationalization and projection as primary defenses, and considerable anger and hostility regarding their difficulties. In other words, these are traits and behaviors suggesting paranoid tendencies and/or a paranoid personality disorder. With regard to the second group, as the T score becomes elevated beyond 70 and 75, the possibility of psychotic manifestations becomes more likely. These include ideas of reference, feelings of external influence, feelings of persecution, as well as a variety of delusions resulting in impaired reality testing. Anger, hostility, and resentment are readily apparent and likely to be expressed overtly.

The T score ranges presented here are general guidelines and it is sometimes quite difficult to differentiate the paranoid personality from paranoid psychosis. Occasionally, the paranoid personality will obtain a T score greater than 75 and the patient with paranoid delusions may obtain a T score of less than 70. Therefore, it is important to examine the profile for other information. First, the elevation on F can be helpful. If the F scale is elevated over 70, there is an increasing possibility the items reflecting more serious psychotic pathology were endorsed, whereas if F is below 70, there is an increasing possibility the nonpsychotic items were endorsed. Additionally, examination of the critical items (see Critical Items) can prove informative. If several critical items reflecting paranoid psychotic ideation is endorsed, this lends support to an interpretation reflecting the psychotic thinking. If few or none of these items is endorsed, this increases the likelihood the elevation on scale 6 reflects paranoid personality traits.

Three groups of patients obtain low scores (below 35) on scale 6. The first and most common are those described as self-centered, stubborn, easily irritated, unaware, and insightless in their dealings with others. The second group of patients blatantly deny any interpersonal sensitivity and attempt to present themselves as rather cold and callous. This appears to be a reaction formation against extreme interpersonal sensitivity and a basic mistrust of the motives of others. The paranoid symptomatology is well ingrained and there is sufficient reality testing to avoid endorsing the obvious content items on scale 6. Finally, a T score below 35 may also indicate a patient who is overtly paranoid, delusional, defensive, and evasive. It is these latter qualities that result in their denying symptomatology.

Scale 7 (Pt) Psychasthenia

Scale 7 consists of 48 items reflecting chronic or trait anxiety, general dissatisfaction with life, indecisiveness, difficulty with concentration, self-doubt, rumination and agitated concern about self, and the obsessional aspects of the obsessive-compulsive personality. More compulsive patterns of coping may not be reflected in high elevations if such compulsive mechanisms are effective in reducing anxiety. This scale is a good index of psychological turmoil and discomfort. The original diagnostic label is antiquated and the scale now seems more related to obsessive-compulsive traits. Examples of scale 7 items with scored responses in parentheses are:

"I find it hard to keep my mind on a task or job." (T)
"I feel anxiety about something or someone almost all the time." (T)
"Life is a strain for me much of the time." (T)*

Patients with high scores on this scale are described as rigid, meticulous, moralistic, and intensely dissatisfied with their present life situation. Anxiety is rather pronounced and likely to be manifest clinically. They tend to be ruminatively introspective, self-analytical, and are overly ideational in their approach to solving emotional problems. However, their ideas are rarely translated into constructive behavior. Indecision, doubt, and vacillation as well as inefficiency in living are likely as these patients rely heavily on intellectualization, isolation, and rationalization as primary defenses. They may show some difficulty in concentration and thinking, and in recognizing environmental cues that could rationally reduce their anxiety. They are guilt ridden, intropunitive, and seem to have established for themselves unattainable goals and high levels of aspiration. Generalized physical complaints, such as fatigue, are common.

Patients who obtain low scores on scale 7 show an absence of the traits and behaviors characteristics of high scale 7 patients. Patients in an emergency room having just experienced a crisis situation appear overtly anxious with motor tension and heightened autonomic activity. However, administration of the MMPI-2 may not result in an elevated scale 7. This occurs because the anxiety precipitated by a crisis is usually situational in nature, different from the more chronic type of anxiety measured by scale 7. Other methods of assessing state anxiety will be discussed under Special Scales.

Scale 7 has been described as the "obsessional glue" that keeps potentially psychotic patients relatively intact. Whenever scale 7 is equal to or greater than scale 8, it is rarely a psychotic disorder, but more likely a patient whose defenses are tenuous and who, under stress, will deteriorate into a psychosis. Following the deterioration, there usually is a decrease in the elevation on scale 7 and an increase in the elevation on scale 8.

Scale 8 (Sc) Schizophrenia

Scale 8, the longest scale on the MMPI-2 with 78 items, taps dimensions of schizoid mentation, feelings of being different, feelings of isolation, bizarre thought processes and peculiar perceptions, poor family relationships, sexual identity concerns, and a tendency to withdraw into wish-fulfilling fantasy. Consequently, the scale appears to measure a general dimension of ego intactness to ego deterioration. Examples of scale 8 items with the scored responses in parentheses are:

"At times I have fits of laughing and crying that I cannot control." (T)
"I have had very peculiar and strange experiences." (T)
"Most anytime I would rather sit and daydream than do anything else."
    (T)*

As with scale 6, the patients who score high on this scale can be divided into two groups, not necessarily mutually exclusive. One group shows disturbances in thought that are marked by alterations of concept formation, loose associations, and poor judgment, which may lead to misinterpretations of reality. Corollary mood changes include ambivalent, constricted, and inappropriate emotional responsiveness and loss of empathy with others. These patients almost always receive a diagnosis of schizophrenia. The other group, who are not psychotic, tend to feel lonely, alienated, isolated, misunderstood, and not a part of the general social environment. They have fundamental and disturbing questions concerning their own sexual identity and worth, and they appear confused about how to cope with everyday stresses. Therefore, under stress they are likely to withdraw and occupy themselves with wish-fulfilling fantasies. This usually reflects a rather schizoid lifestyle.

When interpreting the MMPI-2, it is very important to differentiate the schizophrenic from the more schizoid adjustment. The differentiation process is quite similar to what occurs with scale 6. That is, if scale F is equal to or greater than a T score of 70, then bizarre and unusual thinking is likely and the possibility of a schizoiphrenic disorder should be further explored. But if F is less than a T score of 70, psychosis is much less likely, and other interpretations are more applicable. Also helpful in this differentiation process is an examination of the critical items. Schizophrenics tend to endorse many critical items, especially those related to thought disturbance, feelings of derealization, and other psychotic processes. If only a few of these items are endorsed, the likelihood is increased that scale 8 reflects a schizoid adjustment rather than the schizophrenic process.

As elevations on scale 8 increase beyond 95, several possibilities occur. These include an attempt to look bad, a plea for help, or an acutely disturbed patient. As noted earlier, it is unusual for a schizophrenic to produce an elevation in this range. The fact that the patient was aware that those items reflect the most serious pathology and was able to selectively endorse them as applicable tends to preclude a psychotic diagnosis, as this awareness implies clear thinking and most likely reality contact.

Patients who obtain low scores on scale 8 show an interest in people and practical matters to the exclusion of theoretical and philosophical concerns. Nevertheless, interpersonally they appear compliant, submissive, and overly accepting of authority. They rarely devise creative solutions to their difficulties as pragmatic and concrete thinking is characteristic.

Scale 9 (Ma) Hypomania

The 46 items comprising scale 9 are a direct measure of energy level, a continuum ranging from low energy through optimum energy, with further elevations suggesting hypomanic symptomatology, including flight of ideas, elevated mood, increased motor activity, expansiveness, and grandiosity. Examples of scale 9 items with scored responses in parentheses are:

"I am an important person." (T)

"At times my thoughts have raced ahead faster than I could speak them." (T)

"I have periods of such great restlessness that I cannot sit long in a chair." (T)*

T scores on scale 9 greater than 85 may be suggestive of a manic disorder in a patient who is characterized by expansiveness, easy distractibility, hyperactivity, flight of ideas, and delusions of grandeur resulting in impaired reality testing. However, most manics are too hyperactive and agitated to sit still to take the test. Therefore, psychotropic medication frequently needs to be given before the MMPI-2 is administered. As a result of this medication, the majority of manic patients obtain scores between 70 and 85 on scale 9.

Certain nonpsychotic patients also obtain scores between 70 and 85 on scale 9. They are described as restless, enthusiastic, impatient, energetic, gregarious, and having an exaggerated sense of self-worth and importance. They are competitive, have difficulty in any enterprise requiring sustained effort, and often show irritability and ready anger at minor obstacles and frustrations. These symptoms are suggestive of the possible diagnosis of hypomania or attention deficit disorder in adults.

The differentiation among a manic psychosis, hypomania, attention disorder, and high energy level cannot be made simply on the basis of the scale 9 elevation. Manic patients are relatively easily identified behaviorally, and case history information will usually clarify the other diagnostic considerations.

Some manic patients obtain MMPI-2 profiles that are essentially within normal limits except for an elevated scale 9. This is a reflection of the manic's grandiosity and implies that everything is fine. Most notable on this type of profile will be low scores on scales 2 and 7, suggesting a lack of psychological distress and a lack of concern regarding their actual difficulties.

There is one group, however, for whom the elevation on scale 9 has other implications. These are women between 40 and 50 years of age who are experiencing what is referred to as the "empty nest syndrome." They have dedicated their lives to raising their children and now that the children have left home, these women become depressed and lonely. They rechannel their energies and become overly involved in a variety of activities—such as civic, church, or community endeavors—in order to distract themselves from their depression and sense of loss. This sudden change in behavior is readily apparent to friends and family, who are likely to request a psychiatric consultation. The elevated scale 9 thus reflects a defense against depression, namely their overinvolvement and efforts to distract themselves from their distress. Brief psychotherapeutic intervention is usually very effective in these cases.

Patients who obtain low scores on scale 9 (especially below 40) are described as being listless, lethargic, low in drive, and difficult to motivate. They lack interest, initiative, and involvement, and are likely to show chronic fatigue and even physical exhaustion. In many cases, this reflects the psychomotor retardation seen in some types of depressive disorders. A low score on scale 9 tends to accentuate elevations on scale 2, as this reflects the more behavioral manifestations of depression, while scale 2 is a reflection of the mood or affective state. Low scorers on scale 9 also tend to be somewhat reserved, withdrawn, overly controlled, and reluctant to express emotions overtly.

Scale 0 (Si) Social Introversion

Scale 0 consist of 69 items assessing the introversion-extroversion dimension, with high scores indicative of introversion. As noted earlier, this scale was developed later than the eight basic clinical scales, and it has not attracted much research interest. Thus, the clinical lore for this scale is somewhat limited. Examples of scale 0 items with scored responses in parentheses are:

"I wish I could be as happy as others seem to be." (T)
"It makes me uncomfortable to put on a stunt at a party even when others are doing the same sorts of things." (T)
"I am a very sociable person." (F)*

Patients who score high on this scale tend to be introverted, shy, socially inept, and have a tendency to withdraw from others as well as from competitive situations. They lack self-confidence, are threatened by intimacy, feel uncomfortable—especially around members of the opposite sex, and are overly sensitive to what others think of them. Their approach to problem solving tends to be cautious, conventional, and unoriginal. Elevations above 70 may reflect a schizoid withdrawal from interpersonal relationships, especially when combined with an elevated scale 8.

Patients who obtain T scores in the range of 55 to 64 tend to be slightly introverted and may prefer to be alone or with a small group of friends. Although they do have adequate social skills, they generally prefer to keep their interactions to a minimum. Patients who obtain T scores in the 45 to 55 range tend to have an average balance between extroverted and introverted attitudes and behaviors.

Patients who obtain low T-scores on scale 0 appear quite adept at making initial social contacts and are viewed as extremely gregarious, extroverted, confident, and the life of the party. However, close examination of their behavior reveals superficial and flighty social techniques and social relationships that are maintained on a rather shallow, insincere level. They are reluctant to discuss emotionally laden topics, are quite threatened by intimacy, and may manipulate others for their own advantage. The potential for engaging in self-indulgent behaviors is high.

TWO-POINT CODE TYPES

In the last section, interpretive data were provided for each of the validity and clinical scales. It should be obvious, though, that the original scales were grossly deficient as measures of the diagnostic categories their scale names imply. In fact, the original test manual and related publications now caution against literal interpretations of the clinical scales. Instead, it is believed the relationships between the various scales provide extremely important information. This led to the development of profile analysis (i.e., code types) as the main interpretive mechanism of MMPI-2 data.

Furthermore, on many occasions, especially with psychiatric patients, more than one scale is elevated. The standard procedure is to interpret profiles according to the two highest clinical scales above a T score of 65, provided both scales are within 10 T points of each other. A code type is referred to by writing the number of the two scales involved with the most elevated one first. For example, if the patient obtained a T score of 85 on scale 4 and a T score of 81 on scale 8, then you have a 4-8 code type. There are 110 possible two-point code types on the MMPI-2 following this procedure.

Behavioral correlates of the 22 most prominent (most frequent and most investigated) code types will be presented in this section. Please note that the individual scale correlates still may apply, but combining into code types yields some unique interpretive materials. The order of scales within the code type will not be differentiated unless empirical evidence indicates the correlates of the code type change depending on which scale is elevated higher. Also, it must be emphazied that each interpretive statement, while applying to most patients, does not apply to every patient who obtains that code type. Each interpretive statement is a probability statement that may or may not apply to a specific patient.

When multiple code types are interpreted in a single profile, the highest two-point code type receives more weight than any lower pairs if there are any contradictions. Another difficulty may occur when three scales are all elevated above 65 and all are within a few T points of each other. In such situations, it is best to divide the profile into as many two-point code types as possible. For example, if scales 2, 6, and 7 all were elevated at approximately a T score of 70, it would be best to divide this into a 2-6 and 2-7 code type. This is done because a 6-7 code type occurs infrequently, and little is documented in the literature regarding the behavioral correlates other than the information that can be obtained by individual scale interpretations.

1-2/2-1

These patients tend to experience depression, worry, and pessimism, and endorse a large number of somatic complaints accompanied by a marked preoccupation with body functions. Symptoms are likely to involve pain, weakness, and easy fatigability, and are most pronounced during periods of stress. They may present multiple somatic complaints or the symptoms may be restricted to one particular system. There is difficulty externalizing emotions and therefore patients feel uncomfortable in situations demanding anger, originality, or strength. Many of their angry and hostile feelings become introjected, resulting in an increase in heightened physiological reactivity. They tend to be passive-dependent in relationships and may harbor hostility toward others who are perceived as not offering enough attention or support. A history of drug and/or alcohol abuse should be considered. A rather sour, whiny, and complaining attitude is likely accompanied by skepticism and a great deal of cynicism regarding treatment. Patients' motivation for change is quite weak, as they have learned to tolerate high levels of discomfort and because they refuse to consider physiological symptoms as signs of psychological stress. These patients consistently will seek medical attention in order to substantiate their somatic concerns. Although insight is likely to be quite limited, judgment usually is intact.

1-3/3-1

These patients are generally immature, egocentric, and demanding, with hysteroid characteristics and repressive defenses. If there are elevations on scale 2, then this implies these repressive defenses are not working effectively. Patients are prone to develop any of a variety of circumscribed conversion symptoms. Although these symptoms may be based in some actual organic pathology, they generally arise after protracted periods of tension in patients with a history of insecurity, immaturity and well-established proclivity to physical complaints. They are likely to be quite demanding of attention and affection and will attempt to receive this through unobtrusively manipulative means. Rarely are such patients seen as psychotic. Denial is a major defense, as they manifest an overly optimistic and Pollyannaish view of their situation and of the world in general, and they may not show appropriate concern about their symptoms. Overcontrol is likely, as they will go to great lengths to inhibit the expression of hostile and aggressive feelings. This internalization of impulses occurs in almost every area except with the possibility of sexual acting-out behaviors. Many of these patients are especially vulnerable to narcissistic injury in heterosexual relationships. In psychotherapy, they want immediate concrete solutions to their difficulties and will terminate prematurely when the therapist fails to respond to their excessive demands for attention. They lack insight into the nature of their behaviors and are very resistant to interpretations that could imply psychological explanations of their physical difficulties.

1-8/8-1

When there is an elevated F associated with this profile, one possible diagnosis is schizophrenia. These patients are described as having difficulty handling stress and may show clearly delusional thinking regarding bodily functions and bodily illnesses. They harbor feelings of anger and hostility, but are unable to express these overtly for fear of retaliation from others. They either inhibit expression—almost completely resulting in the feeling of being "bottled up"—or they are overly belligerent, abrasive, and caustic in speech. Internalization of feelings may be represented via numerous somatic complaints and heightened physiological reactivity. Trust appears to be a crucial issue, resulting in limited social contacts and subsequent feelings of loneliness, alienation, isolation, and rejection. These patients have fundamental and disturbing questions concerning their own sexual identity and worth, and feel generally misunderstood and not a part of the general social environment. The possibility of some type of prepsychotic disorder also should be considered.

1-9/9-1

These patients are described as being rather tense, anxious, and experiencing a great deal of emotional turmoil. They expect a high level of achievement from themselves but lack clear and definitive goals. Much of their frustration occurs due to their inability to obtain their rather high levels of aspiration. The elevation on scale 1 may be considered an indicator of basic passivity and strong needs for dependency which are being struggled against in counterphobic denial fashion by hyperactivity and tremendous efforts to produce. They are basically passive-dependent individuals who are trying to compensate for their perceived inadequacies. This code type also may be found among individuals with brain damage who are experiencing difficulty coping with their limitations and deficits. However, the diagnosis of cerebral dysfunction never should be made based on MMPI-2 code types.

2-3/3-2

Somewhat similar to the 2-1 code type, these patients typically show greater immaturity, feelings of inadequacy and insecurity, and inefficiency in living. Depression as well as lowered activity levels, feelings of helplessness, and self-doubt are evident. Initiative is lacking in these patients and they are likely to rely on others to take care of them. They are viewed by others as rather passive, docile, and dependent. Feelings of social inadequacy are evident, resulting in a tendency to keep social contacts to a minimum. They especially avoid competitive situations where failure might occur. They also are quite uncomfortable with members of the opposite sex, and sexual maladjustment, including frigidity and impotence, is common. Nevertheless, they do elicit nurturant and helpful attitudes from others. Overcontrol is pronounced, as there is difficulty expressing angry and hostile feelings in a modulated, adaptive way. Instead, these patients deny experiencing these unacceptable feelings, but feel anxious and guilty when this denial fails. Somatic symptoms are present but often are inconsistent and changing. The prognosis in psychotherapy is guarded because these patients have learned to adjust to their somewhat chronic problems and have continued to function at low levels of efficiency for prolonged periods of time. Thus, their motivation for change typically is weak.

2-4/4-2

This code type is characteristic of two different types of patients. The most common is psychopathic individuals who have been caught in some illicit or illegal behavior and are subsequently being evaluated. The depression is a reaction to the constraints being placed on their behavior, such as being put in prison or in a hospital. This depression abates when escape from stress is effected or when the constraints are removed. Nevertheless, the presence of even this situational depression results in a slightly better prognosis than for individuals in similar circumstances who do not admit this affect. The most valid interpretation for these psychopathic patients would use primarily the correlates of scale 4.

Other patients obtaining this code type are described as being extremely hostile, angry, and resentful. Marital and/or family turmoil is prevalent, resulting in intense dissatisfaction with their present life situation. Patients are immature, dependent, egocentric, and often vacillate between pitying themselves and blaming others for their difficulties. Impulse control problems are quite prevalent, as they exhibit an apparent inability to plan ahead if not a reckless disregard of the consequences of their behaviors. They may react to stress with excessive alcohol comsumption and/or drug abuse. They experience a failure to appreciate the interpersonal side of life, have difficulty showing warmth, tend to resent authority figures and demands imposed on them, and may misinterpret the meaning of social events and relationships. Psychotherapeutic intervention will prove difficult, as numerous characterological difficulties exist, and the depressive features are chronic in nature and deeply ingrained into the character structure.

2-6/6-2

This code type suggests the probability of an early stage of a psychosis in a patient who may be experiencing more severe emotional difficulties than the profile ordinarily would suggest. There is a reservoir of anger and hostility present that is not entirely masked by the depressed feelings. Unlike most depressed patients who are unable to express their anger overtly, these patients usually are openly hostile, aggressive, and resentful toward others. They adopt a chip-on-the-shoulder attitude in an attempt to reject others before they are rejected. Also, they read malevolent meaning into neutral situations and jump to conclusions on the basis of insufficient data. Paranoid trends are rather pronounced, sometimes to the point where paranoid ideation is psychotic in nature.

2-7/7-2

This code type is the most common among psychiatric patients and suggests depression, worry, and pessimism with accompanying anxiety, tension, nervousness, and a pervading lack of self-confidence. Psychic conflicts may be represented in hypochondriacal tendencies and somatic complaints. These patients are guilt ridden, intropunitive, generally fearful, and obsessively preoccupied with their personal deficiencies. The latter is in disturbing conflict with their typically perfectionistic and meticulous attitude and their strong motive for personal achievement and recognition. They have high expectations for themselves and feel rather guilty when they fail to achieve their goals. Patients respond to frustration with considerable self-blame and guilt. They worry excessively, are vulnerable to both real and imagined threat, and anticipate problems before they occur. Socially, they tend to be rather docile and dependent, and find it difficult to be assertive when appropriate. The prognosis in psychotherapy is excellent, as these individuals appear motivated for help. However, if the elevation on scale 2 or 7 is greater than a T score of 80, then the distress may be incapacitating. In such cases, psychopharmacological treatment should be instituted before psychotherapy is attempted. The most likely diagnosis is some type of depressive and/or anxiety disorder.

2-8/8-2

This code type suggests depression with accompanying anxiety and agitation leading to a fear of loss of control of hostile and aggressive impulses. Suicidal ideation is likely and the potential for self-destructive behaviors is high. These patients exhibit a marked psychological deficit as evidenced by a general loss of efficiency, periods of confusion, a retarded stream of thought, a stereotyped approach to problem solving, and noticeable difficulties with concentration. Occasionally, the clinical picture may include hysterically determined somatic symptoms of an atypical variety. Unlike the hysteric, however, these patients typically are unsociable, interpersonally sensitive, and suspicious. They complain of concentration and thinking difficulties and may show a formal thought disorder consistent with a schizophrenic disorder. The potential inherent in intimacy for subsequent rejection results in their reluctance to become involved with others. This lack of meaningful involvement increases their feelings of despair, worthlessness, and low self-esteem. This code type represents a chronic level of adjustment of marginal quality so that the prognosis for intervention and subsequent change is poor. Most of these patients receive a diagnosis of either major depression, schizophrenia or schizoaffective disorder.

2-9/9-2

This code type often reflects an agitated depression in which tension is discharged through heightened motor activity. These patients are overly expressive affectively, are extremely narcissistic, and ruminate expressively regarding their self-worth. Although they may express concern about achieving at a high level, it often appears that they set themselves up for failure. Another interpretation is that these patients are denying underlying feelings of inadequacy and worthlessness and may be attempting to use a variety of manic mechanisms—such as hyperactivity, denial of poor morale, and overinvolvement with others—to avoid focusing on their depression. In other words, these patients are experiencing a hypomanic process that is no longer sufficient to obscure their depressive features, at least on the MMPI-2. Both types of patients will appear tense and restless and will show irritability and ready anger at minor obstacles and frustrations.

In younger patients, this code type may be suggestive of an identity crisis characterized by a lack of personal and vocational direction as well as numerous existential concerns. In older patients, this code type may be a reaction to physical disability or reflect a melancholic depression.

3-4/4-3

Patients with a 3-4 code type have been found to display different behaviors from patients with a 4-3 code type. The relationship between scales 3 and 4 serves as an index of whether patients will overtly express or inhibit their socially unacceptable impulses—particularly anger, aggression, and hostility. If 3 is higher than 4, then a rather passive-aggressive expression of anger is likely. When aggressive actions do occur, these patients deny hostile intent and show a striking lack of insight. If 4 is higher than 3, these patients are likely to appear overcontrolled and bottle up their anger for long periods of time. They then explode in a rage, periodically committing violent behaviors.

The 3-4/4-3 code type reflects patients experiencing a chronic and stable character disorder and tending to be extrapunitive in their reaction to stress and frustration. They handle conflicts by utilizing provocation, manipulation, as well as blame, projection, and attempts at domination. Some of these patients are free of disabling anxiety and depression, but somatic complaints may occur. These patients typically experience marital disharmony, sexual maladjustment, and alcoholism. Interpersonal relationships usually are tenuous, though many establish enduring, though turbulent, relationships with marginal, acting-out individuals, thereby vicariously gratifying their own antisocial tendencies. Psychotherapeutic intervention proves difficult because such patients are apt to use psychotherapy for voicing complaints about others instead of concentrating on their own problems. Their motivation for help is typically weak and of questionable sincerity. Personality disorder diagnoses are most commonly associated with this code type.

3-6/6-3

Patients with this code type are seen as angry, bitter individuals who are repressing their own hostile and aggressive impulses. They tend to deny any suspicious attitudes and comfort themselves with a naive and rosy acceptance of things as they are. They perceive their relationships in positive terms and have difficulty understanding why others react to them the way they do. This no doubt contributes to significant marital turmoil. Their chronic feelings of hostility usually are directed toward members of the immediate family. Whenever this anger and hostility are recognized, these patients tend to rationalize so that these feelings appear reasonable, warranted, and justified. They are hypersensitive to criticism, experience considerable anxiety and tension, and frequently have somatic complaints. When scale 6 is higher than scale 3 by five or more T points, such patients strive for social power and prestige, even to the point of ruthless power manipulations. The possibility of paranoid or psychotic features should be evaluated in the latter group, even though such traits are relatively unusual for this code type. The prognosis for significant change is poor.

3-8/8-3

Patients obtaining this code type typically have major thought disturbances (if F is greater than or equal to 70) to the point of disorientation, difficulty with concentration, and lapses of memory. Regression and autistic overideation may be present, and thinking may become delusional in nature. Feelings of unreality and emotional inappropriateness are likely. Also evident is a moderate degree of psychic distress that may be discharged into somatic complaints, especially headaches and insomnia. These patients are generally fearful, emotionally vulnerable, immature, and possess schizoid characteristics. They have an exaggerated need for attention and affection from others, but are quite threatened by intimacy and dependent relationships. They display intropunitive reactions to frustration and approach problems in a stereotyped manner. The most common diagnosis is schizophrenia, but somatoform as well as hysterical disorders also should be considered. Supportive psychotherapy seems to have some limited impact.

4-5/5-4

This code type is most common among men, and it suggests a chronic character disorder in patients appearing to experience minimal psychic distress. Any occurring depression or anxiety usually is situational in nature. These patients have nonconforming and defiant attitudes and values as well as aggressive and antisocial tendencies. They exhibit emotional passivity and poorly recognized desires for dependency. Dependency conflicts may be acted out and create masculine protest types of behaviors as well as a variety of conduct disturbances. The guilt feelings and remorse about such actions may temporarily prevent further expression. However, their strong tendency to narcissistically indulge themselves and their lack of frustration tolerance probably will determine their behaviors. They have sexual identity concerns and may, in fact, be preoccupied regarding homoerotic impulses. There is a fear of female domination. Females obtaining this code type usually are rebelling against cultural stereotype of femininity and although they have strong needs for dependency, they fear domination by significant others.

4-6/6-4

Patients obtaining this code type are likely to accentuate their complaints by a tendency to be self-dramatic and hysteroid. They can be expected to be chronically hostile and resentful and to use projection and acting out as preferred defense mechanisms. Impulse control is likely to be deficient and ineffective, and difficulty will be encountered in any enterprise requiring sustained effort. These patients tend to be narcissistic, dependent, and quite demanding of attention and sympathy, yet they will not reciprocate and resent demands imposed on them. They are extremely sensitive to criticism, mistrust the motives of others, tend to brood and harbor grudges, and feel they are not receiving the appropriate treatment they deserve. A history of social maladjustment is likely. These patients are often seen as irritable, sullen, argumentative, and obnoxious. Serious sexual and marital maladjustment is likely as well as excessive alcohol consumption and/or drug abuse. While the most likely diagnosis is some type of character disorder, the possibility of a borderline or psychotic disorder should be considered, especially if scale 8 also is elevated. These patients have difficulty in psychotherapy because denial is prominent and their basic mistrust of the motives of others precludes their acceptance of constructive criticism and attempts to help them. Furthermore, they will be reluctant to discuss emotionally laden topics for fear that dire consequences may follow if they reveal themselves in any way.

4-7/7-4

Patients obtaining this code type show numerous characterological difficulties as well as cyclical patterns of acting out followed by periods of guilt, regret, and remorse for having done so. This guilt usually is out of proportion to the actual acting-out behavior and frequently is accompanied by somatic complaints. While these patients appear to be overcontrolled, these controls are not sufficient to prevent recurrences of acting-out behaviors and gross insensitivity to the consequences. Episodes of acting out may include excessive alcohol consumption, drug abuse, and sexual promiscuity. These patients find rules, regulations, and limits imposed by others to be quite irritating and anxiety provoking. Though quite concerned with their own feelings and problems, they are markedly callous and indifferent to the needs and feelings of others.

Psychotherapy initially may prove effective, as these patients seek help when guilt is most pronounced. However, the long-term prognosis is guarded.

4-8/8-4

Patients obtaining this code type are experiencing considerable distress in addition to irritability, hostility, suspiciousness, and even possibly ideas of reference. Projection and acting out in asocial ways are primary defenses. Whenever they commit crimes, they tend to be vicious, senseless, poorly planned, and poorly executed. The personality type is schizoid and these patients appear socially isolated and avoid close relationships because of fear of emotional involvement. Social intelligence is likely to be limited and serious difficulties can be expected in the areas of empathy and communication abilities. They are moody, emotionally inappropriate, and cannot express emotions in a modulated, adaptive way. In their behavior, these patients are unpredictable, changeable, and nonconforming. Their educational and occupational histories are noted by underachievement, marginal adjustment, and uneven performance. Serious sexual identity concerns are present and excessive alcohol consumption and/or drug abuse likely. Judgment tends to be poor and insight is extremely limited. Suicide attempts are relatively common in these patients, who are viewed by others as rather odd, peculiar, different, and who do not seem to fit into the environment. The diagnostic possibilities include a borderline disorder, schizoid personality, or schizophrenia. The latter is most likely when scales 4 and 8 become elevated above a T score of 75. According to Butcher (1990), psychotherapy is likely to be unproductive at worst and difficult at best.

4-9/9-4

Patients with this code type show numerous characterological difficulties and are described as being impulsive and irresponsible in their behavior, and trustworthy, shallow, and superficial in relation to others. They have easy morals, are narcissistic and hedonistic, but temporarily may create a favorable impression because they are internally comfortable and free from inhibiting anxiety, worry, and guilt. However, they are actually quite deficient in their role-taking ability. Judgment is likely to be poor and they do not seem to benefit from past experiences. Their limited ability to intuitively sense the feelings of others persistently handicaps their development of an effective adult role. These patients have fluctuating ethical values and are prone to continue activities so long that they exceed proprieties, neglect other obligations, and alienate others. They possess a marked disregard for social rules and convention, and engage in behaviors with little or no forethought. Alcoholism, legal difficulties, marital problems, and sexually acting-out behaviors are common. These patients are unwilling to accept responsibility for their own behavior and construct emotionally satisfying but irrational explanations for their difficulties. They will rarely become involved in psychotherapy. The most likely diagnosis appears to be some type of character disorder, with antisocial personality the most common.

6-8/8-6

Patients obtaining this code type usually show evidence of a formal thought disorder and paranoid ideation compatible with a paranoid schizophrenic reaction (if F is greater than or equal to 70). They can be expected to suffer from moderate psychological distress, to be pervadingly hostile and suspicious, and to experience delusions of persecution and/or grandeur and hallucinations. Regression, disorganization, and autistic associations are likely. Such patients are often preoccupied with abstract or theoretical matters to the exclusion of specific concrete aspects of their life. General apathy may be pronounced, affect seems blunted, and established defenses are lacking. Under stress, they are likely to withdraw and occupy themselves with secretive autistic fantasy accompanied by loss of capacity to recognize reality. These patients are quite resentful of demands imposed on them and are described as moody, irritable, unfriendly, and negativistic. Conflicts regarding sexuality are evident. When this code type does not meet traditional MMPI-2 criteria for schizophrenia, then the most likely diagnosis involves a paranoid psychosis or schizoid personality. Psychotropic medications usually are the treatment of choice.

6-9/9-6

Patients with this code type are tense, anxious, and usually react to even minor obstacles and frustrations with irritability, jumpiness, and ineffective excitability. They respond to environmental stimuli in an emotional way and have difficulty with thinking and concentration. Grandiosity is a prominent feature and disorientation, feelings of perplexity, and confusion are noted. They suffer from ideas of reference and a pervading suspiciousness, which at times may take the form of paranoid mentation and even delusions. These patients tend to ruminate and obsess but rarely translate their ideas into constructive behaviors. Also evident is considerable difficulty externalizing their obvious anger and hostility in a socially acceptable way. Periodic undercontrolled emotional outburst will alternate with excessive restraint and control. If scales F and 8 also are elevated, then a schizophrenic disorder is a possibility. Otherwise, some type of manic disorder, acute psychotic episode, or drug-induced psychosis should be considered. Medications appear to be the treatment of choice.

7-8/8-7

Patients obtaining this code type show chronic personality difficulties characterized by excessive worry, introspection, and overideational rumination.

Passivity is pronounced and difficulty will be encountered in situations demanding anger, originality, and strength. Dependency is evident in these patients and they suffer from feelings of insecurity, inferiority, and inadequacy. They lack established defense patterns and tend to be quite nervous around others. A history with few rewarding social experiences is evident, as they lack poise, assurance, and dominance. Judgment is likely to be poor and some confusion evident as their actions and planning reveal a lack of common sense. Rich fantasy lives are suggested, especially with regard to sexual matters, and they spend much time daydreaming. Serious sexual identity concerns exist as these patients feel inadequate in their traditional sex role and in heterosexual relations. They complain of concentration and thinking difficulties, suffer from excessive indecision, doubt, and vacillation, and may show a formal thought disorder. Psychological interventions are difficult because of the chronic ingrained nature of their conflicts and because of the difficulty in forming interpersonal relationships. The relative elevations of scales 7 and 8 are crucial in differential diagnosis, especially with regard to schizophrenia.

8-9/9-8

The majority of patients with this code type show evidence of paranoid mentation and a formal thought disorder. Onset is typically acute and accompanied by excitement, disorientation, and general feelings of perplexity. Well-established autistic trends, delusions, and hallucinations are likely. Regression is manifested by retarded and stereotyped thinking and by emotional inappropriateness. Such patients tend to be narcissistic and infantile in their expectations of others, and become extremely resentful and hostile when their demands for attention are not met. They appear hyperactive, easily distractible, labile, and show grandiose thinking. They are quite unpredictable in their behavior and may act out unexpectedly. Psychotherapeutic intervention may prove extremely difficult because these patients are rather vague and evasive and tend to shift rapidly from topic to topic, so that addressing a specific issue is difficult. While the modal diagnosis is schizophrenia, manic disorders and drug-induced psychoses also should be considered.

SUPPLEMENTAL SCALES AND CRITICAL ITEMS

In addition to the validity scales assessing test-taking attitude and the 10 clinical scales identifying common types of abnormal behavior, numerous supplemental MMPI-2 scales have been constructed. Some of these specialized scales have been constructed to measure common personality dimensions, such as dominance, while others have been developed to identify specific patterns of abnormal behaviors, such as alcoholism, that are not assessed directly by any of the standard clinical scales. Scoring keys for the scales discussed next are available from the test publisher. It should be noted that the popular Wiggins (1969) content scales were eliminated following the revision due to item deletion. Furthermore, the Wiggins scales did not represent adequately the new content dimensions induced into the MMPI-2 by the addition of new items (Graham, 1990). Instead, 15 new content scales were developed by Butcher, Graham, Williams, and Ben-Porath (1990) via a combination of rational and statistical procedures. Because the validity data for these scales are limited at this time and only tentative interpretive inferences are available, a decision was made to exclude their listing in this section. A brief discussion of critical items, though, has been included. The supplemental scales are summarized as follows, with a more detail presentation available in Graham (1990).

Welsh's Anxiety (A)

High scorers on this scale tend to be anxious, tense, nervous, uncomfortable, unemotional, excitable, overcontrolled, accepting of authority, conforming, and conventional in their behavior. These patients have a slow personal tempo, lack self-esteem, and lack poise in social situations. Constructive coping abilities are limited when stressed. The anxiety assessed by this scale reflects situational (state) anxiety rather than chronic (trait) anxiety, as assessed by scale 7. All of the original 39 items have been maintained in the MMPI-2 version.

Welsh's Repression (R)

High scorers on this scale tend to be rather submissive, unexcitable, and conventional, and have a rather careful and cautious lifestyle. Affects are internalized and not expressed directly for fear of initiating a conflict situation that subsequently could overwhelm them. These patients are unwilling to discuss emotionally laden topics which may reflect conscious suppression or actual repression and denial. Any difficulties will be rationalized. Although their thinking is clear, their insight is limited. Of the original 40 items, 37 have been maintained in the MMPI-2 version of the scale.

Ego Strength (Es)

This scale was developed to predict the response of neurotic patients in individual dynamically oriented psychotherapy. However, it is not useful for predicting response to other kinds of treatment or for other kinds of patients. The scale seems to be related to emotional adjustment and may indicate strength of psychological resources available for dealing effectively with stress. Many patients scoring high on this scale possess the capacity to initiate deliberate and constructive actions in most coping situations. Patients who score low on this scale lack established defense patterns and may experience serious psychopathology. Coping devices and emotional resources are limited and they suffer from marked feelings of insecurity, inferiority, and inadequacy. Of the original 68 items, 52 are included in the MMPI-2 version of this scale.

Overcontrolled-Hostility Scale (OH)

This scale was developed to detect patients with the potential for committing extreme physical aggression. They have a history of chronic overcontrol and rigid inhibitions against the expression of any form of aggression. Most patients scoring high on this scale do not respond appropriately to even extreme provocation, but tend to let their angry, hostile feelings accumulate to the point that an unexpected violent and destructive outburst may occur. These patients are described as rigid, socially alienated, and reluctant to admit to any forms of psychological difficulties. The OH scale is highly correlated with the 3-4/4-3 code type. Cutoff scores for predicting violence must be established separately in each setting where the scale is used. Of the original 31 items, 28 were retained in the MMPI-2 version of this scale.

The MacAndrew Alcoholism Scale-Revised (MAC-R)

Initial research with this scale has shown consistently that the MAC will differentiate alcoholics from nonalcoholics in a variety of psychiatric settings. Subsequent research, however, has documented that the MAC is much more a measure of addiction proneness to either alcohol or drugs rather than just a specific measure of alcohol abuse. High scorers on this scale are described as having a significantly high potential for substance abuse and other addictive problems. They are impulsive, energetic, nonconforming, uninhibited, and gregarious. However, social relationships usually are maintained on a shallow superficial level. Four of the original MAC items were eliminated from the MMPI-2 because of the objectional content. These items were replaced with 4 new items selected because they differentiated alcoholic from nonalcoholic males.

Dominance Scale (DO)

High scorers on this scale view themselves as assertive, rarely intimidated, poised, self-assured, and self-confident. Perseverance, resoluteness, and leadership abilities also are prominent. Of the original 28 items, 25 are included in the MMPI-2 version of this scale.

Social Responsibility Scale (RE)

High scorers on this scale are willing to accept responsibility for their behaviors and are viewed by others as dependable, reliable, trustworthy, and responsible. They have high ethical and moral standards and value honesty and justice. Of the original 32 items, 30 have been included in the MMPI-2 version of this scale.

College Maladjustment (Mt)

This scale was developed to discriminate between emotionally well-adjusted and maladjusted college students. Students scoring high on this scale are apt to be easily overwhelmed by stress, lack adequate coping devices and emotional resources, and are apt to be poorly adjusted. Of the original 43 items, 41 have been maintained on the MMPI-2 version of this scale.

Masculine Gender Role (GM) and Feminine Gender Role (GF)

These new scales have been developed by Peterson (1989) for inclusion in the MMPI-2 as separate measures of the masculine and feminine components in the bipolar Masculinity-Femininity (MF) scale of the original MMPI. Unfortunately, though, because of their recent development, very limited validity data are available and it is difficult to generate interpretive statements that can be applied with confidence to high and low scores on these scales (Graham, 1990).

Posttraumatic Stress Disorder Scales (PK & PS)

The PK scale (Keane, Malloy, & Fairbank, 1984) is designed primarily to evaluate whether veterans are experiencing considerable emotional turmoil, are feeling guilty, depressed, and anxious, and are experiencing disturbing intensive thoughts. In contrast, few investigations have been conducted on the 60 items of the PS scale. Consequently, at this time it is not clear which personality dimensions or specific patterns of abnormal behavior are being identified.

CRITICAL ITEMS

Critical items are frequently used as "stop items" in screening patients. These are items that might have face validity for the presence of significant psychopathology. Endorsement of any of the critical items may indicate areas of major concern to the patients, but due to their obvious face validity the failure to endorse may not indicate the absence of these concerns.

The original set of items was developed intuitively by Grayson (1951) and included a number of blatantly psychotic behaviors and attitudes as well as items reflecting substance abuse, antisocial attitudes, family conflicts, sexual concerns, and somatic complaints. Although no empirical validation of these items has occurred, they have been accepted as an important source of content information on the original MMPI. Since these original 38 items, which overlap considerably with scales F and 8, various others have developed their own set of critical items, either on a rational (Caldwell, 1969) or on an empirical (Koss & Butcher, 1973; Lachar & Wrobel, 1979) basis to identify severe psychopathology. The Koss-Butcher Critical Item list was expanded in the MMPI-2 to incorporate new item content of importance in the assessment of two major problems, namely substance abuse and suicidal threats (Butcher, 1990). The Lachar-Wrobel Critical Item List was not revised for the MMPI-2 but four of the original items were deleted. It has not been determined empirically which of the critical item lists are most useful for which populations. In any case, these items supposedly have the greatest degree of discriminative validity, as the endorsement frequencies for "normals" usually are less than 10 percent. Examples of critical items appearing on several of the lists mentioned here include:

"I commonly hear voices without knowing where they come from."
"At times I have a strong urge to do something harmful or shocking."
"Someone has been trying to poison me."

Endorsement of any of the critical items should not be accepted as valid because an error or misunderstanding could have occurred. Therefore, the general consensus is to use the endorsement of the critical items as an entrée or an interview with the patient, and then obtain clarification.

Finally, as mentioned throughout, examination of the critical items list can be helpful in determining whether the interpretations on scales F, 6, and 8 reflect psychotic manifestations, since many of the items reflecting bizarre and unusual thinking on the critical items also appear on these scales. If these three scales or some combination are elevated and numerous critical items from this area are endorsed, then scale interpretations reflecting psychotic manifestations are most applicable. On the other hand, if none or only a few of these critical items are endorsed, then alternative interpretations for these scale elevations should be considered. In all cases, caution should be exercised when using critical items since single items are extremely unreliable indicators of psychopathology.

SPECIAL ISSUES

A number of special concerns frequently arise in the interpretation of an MMPI-2 profile. This section will attempt to address some of the more prominent as well as the utility of this revised instrument with adolescents, blacks, and the aged.

Acting-Out Behavior

Acting-out behavior refers to those behaviors that range from verbal hostility to physical assault. It is the latter that obviously is most important to predict. As Graham (1990) has emphasized, it is crucial to differentiate two types of potentially physically assaultive patients. First, there is the undercontrolled patient who has failed to learn to inhibit the expression of hostile and aggressive impulses, and reacts impulsively in response to external forms of provocation, until finally these affects accumulate to the point that a series of trivial events may result in acting out in an extremely destructive manner. The 4-3/3-4 code type and the OH scale, which have been associated with violent, assaultive behaviors, tend to reflect those patients described as over-controlled.

Scales on the MMPI-2 can be divided into exciter or lack of impulse controls scales (namely, 4, 6, 8, and 9) and inhibiter or control scales (namely, 1, 2, 3, 5, 7, and 0). Depending on whether the exciter or inhibiter scales are elevated, problems with impulse control can be predicted. When both are elevated, then passive-aggressive behaviors are likely.

Although the 4-9/9-4 code type typically has been associated with difficulties with impulse control problems, it should be noted that such a code type also is the most common for college students, attorneys, and psychologists. The crucial variable in determining acting out in such cases is level of intellectual functioning (Heilbrun, 1979). That is, the 4-9/9-4 code type is predictive of impulse control problems including violence, but only with less intelligent patients. The higher the level of intellectual functioning, the less likely there will be overt acting-out behaviors.

Suicide

Clopton (1979), in his comprehensive review of the literature on the MMPI and suicide, concluded that neither standard MMPI scales, MMPI profile analysis, nor specific MMPI items are reliable in predicting suicide at significant levels. Attempts to develop a special MMPI suicide scale or validate the accuracy of particular MMPI items as suicide predictors also have been unsuccessful. However, elevations on scale 2 and 7 are suggestive of depression and dissatisfaction with life that can precipitate suicidal ideation. When elevations on these two scales are accompanied by elevations on the exciter scales, then the likelihood of a suicide attempt increases. This occurs because an elevation on scale 4 suggests poor impulse control, an elevation on scale 8 indicates poor judgment, and an elevation on scale 9 implies adequate energy level to act on the suicidal ideation. However, these data must be integrated with all the demographic variables and related situational variables in order to increase the predictive accuracy.

Two critical items—namely, "Most of the time I wish I were dead" and "The future seems hopeless to me"—although not necessarily correlated with suicide attempts, may reflect desperation and a plea for help. Often it is quite beneficial to interview these patients and discuss with them the reasons for endorsing these items.

Psychotic Manifestations

Attempts to use the MMPI to diagnose schizophrenia via individual scale elevations, especially on scale 8, have proven futile. Consequently, emphasis shifted from interpretation and diagnosis on a single high point to a careful examination of more complex patterns of scales in the standard profile. These subsequent approaches ranged from coding of pattern and elevation data and constructing sets of profile rules to using various regression analyses for discriminant functions. Unfortunately, these approaches are either quite cumbersome and time consuming or have not proven particularly accurate.

Newmark and colleagues (1978) developed a set of criteria for the detection of schizophrenia that include: T score on scale 8 greater than or equal to 80 less than or equal to 100; total raw score on scale 8 consists of not more than 35 percent K items; T score on scale F greater than or equal to 75 less than or equal to 95; and T score on scale 7 less than or equal to scale 8. Approximately 72 percent of patients reliably diagnosed as schizophrenics were detected on the MMPI via this set of criteria. Thus, a crucial relationship emerged between scale 7 and scale 8. If scale 8 is greater than scale 7, a psychosis is more likely than if the reverse is true. When scale 7 is greater than or equal to scale 8, the patient may be prepsychotic or experiencing some type of borderline state. In any case, scale 7 is viewed as the obsessional glue that is maintaining the integrity of the patient's defense system. Unfortunately, though, no effort has been made to assess the utility of the Newmark criteria with the MMPI-2. If one attempts to do so, it is important to remember that scale elevations on the MMPI-2 tend to be approximately five points lower than scores on the original MMPI. Therefore, the T scores noted in the Newmark criteria also should be reduced approximately five points.

The MMPI-2 appears to have some utility in diagnosing functional psychoses due to cognitive impairment. A major weakness of both the original and the MMPI-2 involves diagnosing functional psychoses due to major affective states. As mentioned earlier, it is difficult to diagnose a manic disorder because most manics are not able to sit still long enough to complete the test. Therefore, the test results will be confounded by the effects of psychotropic medications, usually Lithium. This obviously will reduce the elevation on scale 9, making it difficult to differentiate a manic disorder from a hypomanic state from an energetic, exuberant, and restless individual.

Diagnostic difficulties also occur with major depressive disorders. Specifically, it is often difficult to determine if a depression is of psychotic proportions. In many cases, accompanying elevations on scales F and 8 will occur, suggesting some cognitive disturbance due to the presence of depression. However, some depressive reactions may be severe and incapacitating yet cognitive functions remain relatively intact. Unfortunately, there are not sufficient indicators on the MMPI-2 to detect these psychoses.

Alcohol and Drug Abuse

The original MMPI item pool has been used to develop a number of scales for identifying alcoholics. Most of these scales effectively discriminate alcoholics from nonalcoholic controls, but do not differentiate alcoholic from nonalcoholic psychiatric patients. However, one alcoholism scale discussed earlier, developed by MacAndrew (1965), can make this distinction and was revised for inclusion in the MMPI-2. Subsequent investigations have found this scale to more accurately reflect a general measure of addiction proneness.

Substance abuse, in general, is discussed as if there were a single personality type or trait common to all. Composite MMPI profiles presented by Penk (1981) contradict this notion. Instead, it appears that many different types of personality organizations contribute to substance abuse. Such heterogeneity in MMPI-2 profiles not only is revealed when well-defined groups are compared with averaged composite profiles but it also is evident when frequency distributions of individually coded profiles are compiled. Various MMPI-2 code types that have been associated with alcoholism and/or drug abuse include the 2-7-4, 2-4, 4-7, 4-8, 4-9, 6-8, 8-9, 1-3-9, and elevated 4 or 9. The 4-9, 4-8, and 8-9 code types are the most frequent of drug addicts. This suggests that many addicts tend to be impulsive, socially nonconforming, rejecting of traditional values and restrictions, and show poor judgment.

The 8-9 code type deserves special mention. College students who appear in an emergency room with some confused and delusional thinking, feelings of perplexity, and even hallucinations, may obtain this MMPI-2 profile. Because psychotic manifestations are readily apparent, it often is assumed that this profile reflects a schizophrenic disorder. However, drug-induced psychoses often are accompanied by elevations on scale 1. The latter occurs due to the physical effects induced by the substances.

Prognosis

Many of the code types discussed earlier have prognostic statements associated with them. In this section, prognostic implications will be summarized for each MMPI-2 scale as discussed by Graham (1990) and Butcher (1990). It is assumed that each scale is elevated above a T score of 65.

Scale K.   These patients may be reluctant to discuss emotionally laden topics and will censor their answers for fear of too much self-disclosure. They become rigidly defended and threatened whenever their inadequacies are noted. They respond best to a pragmatic, problem-solving type of psychotherapy that focuses on changing behavior to solve current problems and avoids exploration of underlying feelings, motivations, and dynamics.

Scale 1.   These patients are not responsive to traditional psychotherapy. They lack insight into the nature and causes of their difficulties and are reluctant to accept the psychological interpretations of their problems. Instead, they will focus on the soma and will refuse to consider these physiological symptoms as signs of psychological stress. They will terminate therapy quickly if the therapist is perceived as not providing sufficient support and attention. Medication abuse is common.

Scale 2. When the elevation on this scale is between a T score of 65 and 80, these patients show a good prognosis and usually are motivated for psychotherapy. However, as the elevation on this scale increases over 80, then the depression may be overwhelming and incapacitating. Some type of psychotropic medication is needed before psychotherapeutic intervention can be effective. Some elevation on this scale with any diagnostic entity improves the prognostic picture.

Scale 3. These patients initially are quite enthusiastic about psychotherapy because of strong needs for acceptance, affection, and affiliation. However, they are slow to gain insight into the underlying causes of their behaviors and will resist psychological interpretations of their conflicts. Unless they remain involved in long-term treatment, the prognosis is guarded.

Scale 4. Many of these patients are perceived initially as good candidates for psychotherapy due to smooth social skills. However, they are unwilling to accept responsibility for their difficulties, as projection is a primary defense. Many enter treatment in order to avoid something more unpleasant (e.g., incarceration, divorce, etc.). Their motivation for change is of questionable sincerity. Their propensity to abuse medications is well documented, so caution should be exercised in recommending psychopharmacologic agents.

Scale 5. Although Butcher (1990) provides some hypotheses to consider with regard to psychotherapy prognosis, there is little consensus regarding the prognostic significance of elevations on this scale for either males or females.

Scale 6. These patients are likely to show a basic mistrust of the motives of others, precluding their acceptance of constructive criticism and attempts to help them. They have difficulty forming trusting relationships and will establish obstacles in order to assess the therapist's acceptance. Their attitudes and habits are deeply ingrained and pervade the entire fabric of functioning. Modest inroads are possible, but the prognosis generally is quite guarded.

Scale 7. As with scale 2, when the elevation on this scale is between a T score of 65 and 80, these patients usually are motivated for psychotherapy and show a favorable prognosis. However, as the elevation on this scale increases over 80, the anxiety may be overwhelming and incapacitating. Some type of psychotropic medication is needed before psychotherapeutic intervention can be effective. These patients tend to rationalize, intellectualize, ruminate, and have difficulty translating gained insights into constructive behaviors. Insight-oriented approaches may be unproductive by encouraging discussion about their problems without implementation of newly learned adaptive behaviors. Although these patients usually remain in psychotherapy longer than most, they show steady but slow progress.

Scale 8.   These patients show poor judgment and a schizoid adjustment, and will have difficulty relating to the therapist in a meaningful way. There is difficulty expressing emotions in a modulated, adaptive way and a reluctance to sustain their efforts. Clearer and more focused styles of thinking may be fostered by employing careful and well-reasoned therapeutic communications. The long-standing, chronic nature of their problems results in a rather guarded prognosis.

Scale 9.   These patients tend to terminate psychotherapy prematurely because they are impatient, want immediate concrete solutions to their difficulties, and do not want to become dependent on the therapist. Denial and minimization will occur in order to avoid self-exploration. The relationship with the therapist usually will be maintained on a shallow, superficial level, resulting in only minimal progress.

Utility with Adolescents

The previous information with regard to behavioral correlates of individual scales and code types for the MMPI-2 applies to individuals 18 years of age or older. Consequently, in 1989, the MMPI Adolescent Project Committee was appointed by the University of Minnesota Press to develop the MMPI-A. This new instrument was derived from the original MMPI, not the MMPI-2, with adolescent-specific items, scales, and norms. Chapter 2 in this book provides a cogent yet concise discussion of the MMPI-A. Additionally, Archer (1992), in his volume on the "MMPI-A: Assessing Adolescent Psychopathology," offers a comprehensive discussion of the development, administration and scoring, validity scales and validity assessment interpretation, clinical scales and code type correlates, content and supplementary scale interpretation, as well as interpretive strategies. This must-read volume acknowledges that the MMPI-A is in its infancy and considerable clinical and research investigations need to be conducted to understand comprehensively this test instrument. A manual for the administration, scoring, and interpretation of the MMPI-A is available from the University of Minnesota Press via distribution through National Computer Systems. Also, an interesting but detailed table comparing the psychometric properties of the MMPI, MMPI-A, and MMPI-2 is available (Pope, Butcher, & Seelen, 1993).

Utility with the Aged

Only a paucity of investigations have assessed the performance of the "normal" aged on the original MMPI. It seems the aged scored at least 10 T points higher on scales 1, 2, and 3, at least 5 T points higher on 8 and 0, and at least

5 T points lower on scale 9. Additionally, males tend to score at least 5 T points higher on scale 5. The rationale for many of these norms is fairly obvious; for example, the higher scores on scale 1 reflect appropriate preoccupation with bodily functions and legitimate physical concerns. Unfortunately, there is little published research on how to interpret an MMPI profile based on aged norms (Greene, 1980).

Less than 6 percent of the subjects in the MMPI-2 restandardization sample were 70 years of age or older. Thus, caution should be heeded when attempting to extend the utility of this instrument with this elderly age group. Although the norms for the MMPI-2 are more representative of the population of the United States than were those for the original MMPI, little is known about the use of this instrument with the aged.

Utility with Blacks

The controversial issue of racial bias in the MMPI remains unresolved. Numerous methodological difficulties are apparent in many investigations tending to preclude any definitive results. Although black-white differences on the MMPI may be statistically significant, they have limited clinical applications because of the small mean differences. This is not surprising because the standardization sample for the original MMPI did not include any black subjects. Nevertheless, it is generally assumed that blacks are overpathologized using standard MMPI interpretive criteria. In general, blacks tend to score at least five T points higher on scales F, 4, 6, 8, and 9.

Minimal data have been published concerning the MMPI-2 performance of black and white subjects. However, the investigators involved in revising the MMPI analyzed normative data separately for various ethnic groups and concluded that differences between the groups were small and did not justify separate norms for the ethnic groups included in the normative samples (Graham, 1990). One recent study (Timbrook & Graham, 1994) provides some support for this conclusion.

CASE EXAMPLE OF PROFILE INTERPRETATION

Several issues need to be emphasized before attempting to interpret an MMPI-2 profile. First, the interpretive process never should be done blind—that is, without any additional source of data about the patient. It is important to consider a wide range of demographic data having some potential influence on the test profile. These data include age, education, occupation, race, socioeconomic status, religion, marital status, and cultural background. For example, similar profiles obtained from a 45-year-old black male in rural Alabama and a 19-year-old white male in New York City obviously have different implications. Also, a sudden dramatic spike on scale 8 is frequently seen in prisoners at the time of their incarceration; blind interpretation might well suggest a psychotic condition. In most cases, however, the scale

8 elevation declines notably, and within two weeks the profile does not have any psychotic characteristics.

Second, a thorough knowledge of psychopathology definitely is needed. For example, a 65-year-old white female admitted to a psychiatric hospital for the first time obtains criteria compatible with schizophrenia on the MMPI-2. Because this is her first psychiatric admission and because there is no previous history of mental illness, it is doubtful this is a schizophrenic process. Alternative interpretation for these scales should be considered. Finally, while patients may endorse items that reflect significant psychopathology, such as "I believe I am being followed" or "I constantly hear things that others don't hear," it is important whenever possible to assess the accuracy of these statements. For example, this latter item was endorsed by a 60-year-old farmer in North Carolina who lives in an isolated rural area. Information obtained from a subsequent interview verified real noises did occur at night that are typical for isolated and wooded rural areas.

Therefore, it is important to integrate all available demographic data, historical data, presenting complaints, interviews, and observational behavior with the MMPI-2 data. Such a procedure will increase significantly the accuracy of the interpretation.

The patient is a 29-year-old divorced white male from an extremely wealthy southern family who received a high school general equivalency diploma (GED) and attended college for brief periods on several occasions. He was referred as an outpatient by his family in order to assist in developing viable career options and a general life plan. The patient works as an entertainer in avant-garde clubs and theaters. After intense involvement with drugs, fundamental religion, and counterculture lifestyles, the patient now is expressing a desire to "get my life together." The patient acknowledges bouts of depression, continued marijuana use, episodic alcohol abuse, homosexual as well as heterosexual behaviors, and painfully intense and highly conflictual interactions with his family, particularly his father. He has been in psychoanalytically oriented therapy in the past, and presently is being seen by a psychomotor therapist.

In order to make the interpretive process more readily understandable, each statement or group of statements will be followed in parentheses by the individual scale numbers, code types, and/or contextual information from which the statements came. If there are several successive statements without identifying numbers in parentheses, the next identifying scale numbers and/or code types then apply to that entire group of statements.

The patient was open and honest in his approach to the test and seemed to be making a sincere effort to cooperate (L, K, 75-minute administration time). Although there was a slight tendency to overendorse pathology, perhaps exaggerating some symptoms in an effort to be sure that his distress is acknowledged, the profile remains valid (F). He is experiencing a relatively high degree of general psychological distress (F, 2, 7) and feels defenseless and incapable of coping with his present difficulties (F, K). The predominant symptom picture is likely to include moderate depression, worry, pessimism

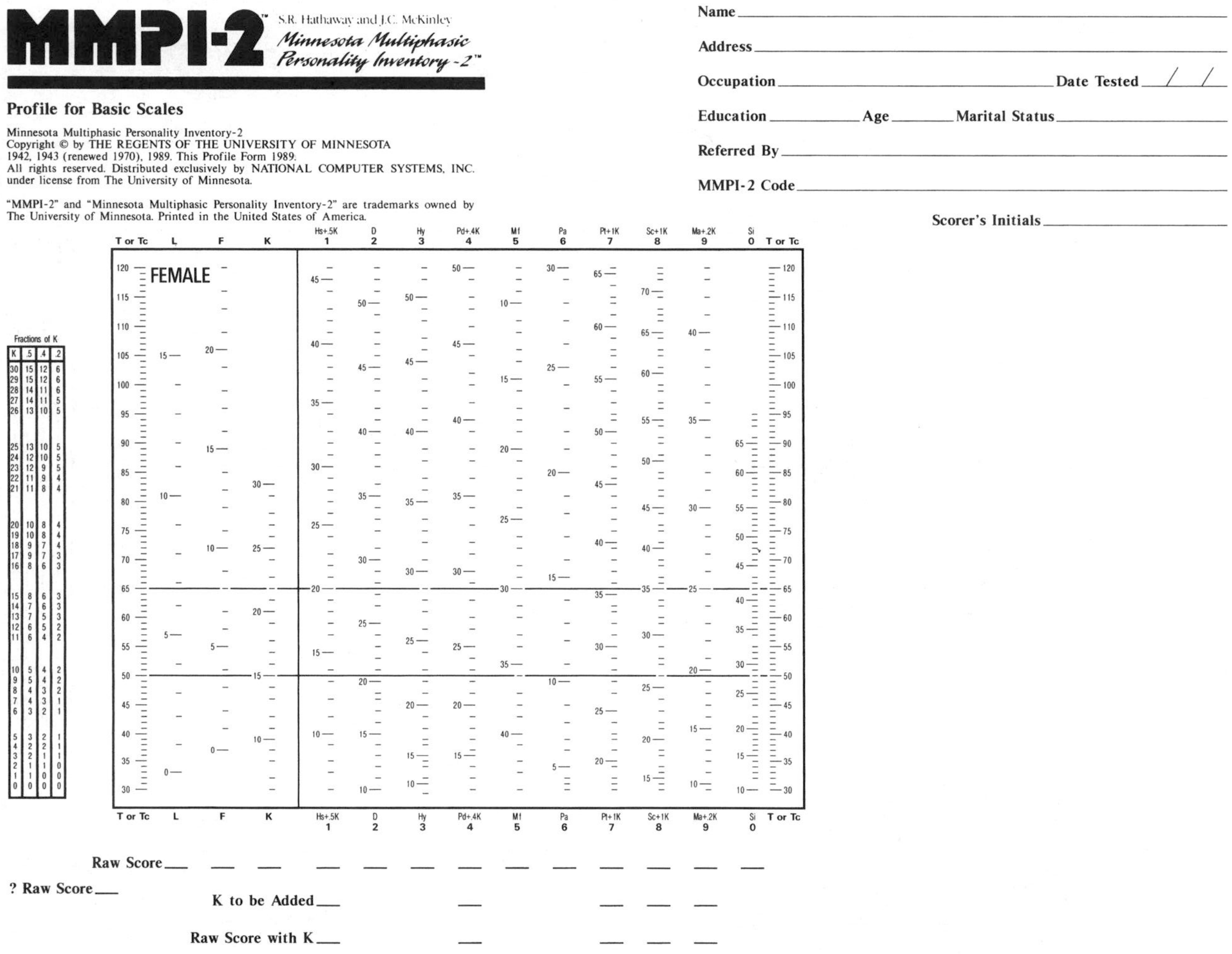

Figure 1–1 Profile for Basic Validity and Clinical Scales

MMPI-2™

S.R. Hathaway and J.C. McKinley

Minnesota Multiphasic Personality Inventory -2™

Profile for Basic Scales

Name Caucasion male outpatient

Address large southeastern city

Occupation musician/performer   Date Tested

Education 13 yrs. Age 29 Marital Status Divorced

Referred By

MMPI-2 Code 5"742'89+603-/1 F''+/KL

Scorer's Initials

MALE

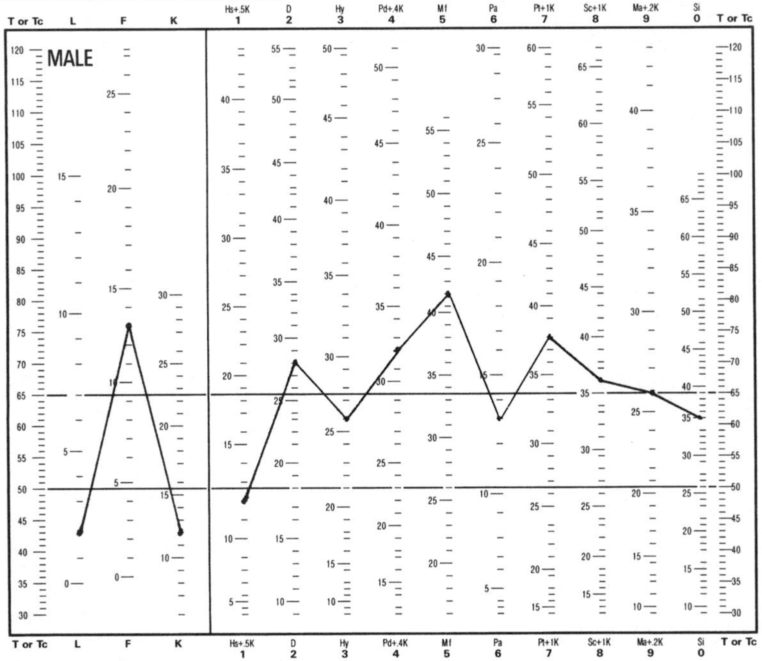

	L	F	K	Hs+.5K 1	D 2	Hy 3	Pd+.4K 4	Mf 5	Pa 6	Pt+1K 7	Sc+1K 8	Ma+.2K 9	Si 0
Raw Score	2	13	12	6	28	26	27	42	13	26	24	24	35
K to be Added				6			5			12	12	2	
Raw Score with K				12			32			38	36	26	

? Raw Score

Figure 1-1 Continued

with accompanying anxiety, tension, nervousness, and agitation (2-7 code type). The patient suffers from indecision, doubt, and vacillation, and is likely to be obsessive, ruminative, and introspective (7). Also noteworthy is a cyclical pattern of acting out, including substance abuse and sexual promiscuity, followed by periods of guilt, regret, and remorse for having done so. These latter feelings, though, are only temporary and have limited effectiveness in inhibiting future episodes of acting out (4-7 code type). During periods of remorse and self-condemnation, feelings of hopelessness and helplessness are likely and will be accompanied by suicidal ideation (2, critical items). This potential is enhanced by frequent lapses in impulse control, poor judgment, and at least adequate energy level (4, 8, 9).

Impulse control problems are prevalent as the patient exhibits an apparent inability to plan ahead if not a reckless disregard of the consequences of his actions. He experiences a failure to appreciate the interpersonal side of life, has difficulty showing warmth, tends to resent authority figures and demands imposed on him, and does not seem effectively governed by societal rules, laws, and behavioral expectations (4, 2-4 code type). The patient is quite concerned with his own feelings and problems, but can be markedly callous and indifferent to the needs and feelings of others (4-7 code type).

The patient feels different, alienated, misunderstood, and not a part of the general social environment (8). There appears to be some qualities in his thinking that are unconventional, perhaps highly original or idiosyncratic in nature, with occasional periods of confusion. At times, he is likely to experience a sense of loss of control over cognitive functioning, but there is no evidence of overtly psychotic features (8, F, critical items). He tends to be plagued by self-doubt, personal dissatisfaction, and feelings of inferiority and inadequacy (7). The patient has high needs for achievement, but tends to avoid competitive situations due to a fear of failure (7, 8, 2-7 code type). Therefore, he will give up immediately whenever difficulty occurs and withdraw (8).

The very high elevation on Scale 5 can be attributable in part to the patient's profession as an artist and performer and his orientation toward cultural and aesthetic pursuits. However, elevations of this magnitude also tend to reflect fundamental and disturbing questions concerning his own sexual identity and worth as well as experiencing homosexual thoughts and impulses. He is likely to exhibit emotional passivity and poorly recognized desires for dependency. These dependency conflicts may be acted out (4-5 code type). Finally, although the patient feels somewhat defenseless and without adequate psychological resources at this time (K, 7), he appears to have adequate energy to pursue a plan of action if one is developed for him (9). Furthermore, he appears able and willing to interact regularly and on a meaningful level with other people in his environment. He would prefer, though, to have social contacts limited to small groups (0).

Patients obtaining similar MMPI-2 profiles usually receive a diagnosis of some type of anxiety or depressive disorder superimposed on an Axis II diagnosis. The latter includes borderline, antisocial, and narcissistic features as well as possible dependent and passive-aggressive traits. Although reality testing usually seems adequate, psychotic manifestations related to a major affective disorder, while unlikely, cannot be totally ignored.

Due to the presence of moderate psychological distress, the patient is likely to be motivated for change and at least initially receptive to psychotherapy (2-7 code type). If the depression and anxiety appear to be incapacitating, then psychotropic medications should be considered in order to reduce this distress to a more tolerable level. The presence of deeply ingrained character traits clouds the prognostic picture (4, 4-5 code type). Insight-oriented approaches are likely to have limited impact, but supportive approaches may be of value in establishing rapport, whereas cognitive methods of reorientation may be useful in exploring misconceptions and channeling more constructive behaviors. Behavior modification procedures may help extinguish certain repugnant forms of acting out, although their effectiveness in similar cases has not been sufficiently documented. Treatment for substance abuse should involve not only relapse prevention but also education regarding addiction and disease. Group treatment methods in a controlled setting also may produce some therapeutic gains (Butcher, 1990). It is not likely, though, that this patient will be willing to sustain his effort in treatment.

SUMMARY

A desperately needed major revision of the MMPI apparently has been a success. Since publication of the MMPI-2, numerous articles have been published regarding this new instrument (e.g., Clavelle, 1992). The majority have supported its utility and practical value resulting in escalating popularity among practicing clinicians and researchers. Unfortunately, though, as with the original MMPI, some clinicians assume that interpretation is a rather simplistic, routine procedure. Anyone familiar with this instrument has realizations to the contrary. The MMPI-2 is an excellent tool for the skilled clinician who has mastered its intricacies and has a due appreciation of the relevant statistical concepts. However, it can be highly dangerous in the hands of the casual user who has seized it as one of the most reputable personality tests and one free of the problems of subjective scoring (Adcock, 1965; Newmark, 1985).

REFERENCES

Adcock, C. J. (1965). Review of the MMPI. In O. K. Burros (Ed.), *The sixth mental measurement yearbook*. Highland Park, N.J.: Gryphon Press.

Archer, R. P. (1992). *MMPI-A: Assessing adolescent psychopathology* Hillsdale, N.J.: Erlbaum Associates.

Bernreuter, R. G. (1933). The theory and construction of the personality inventory. *Journal of Social Psychology, 4,* 387–405.

Butcher, J. N. (1990). *The MMPI-2 in psychological treatment.* New York: Oxford University Press.

Butcher, J. N., Dahlstrom, W. G., Graham, J. R., Tellegen, A., & Kaemmer, B. (1989). *Minnesota Multiphasic Personality Inventory-2 (MMPI-2): Manual for administration and scoring.* Minneapolis: University of Minnesota Press.

Butcher, J. N., Graham, J. R., Williams, C. L., & Ben-Porath, Y. S. (1990). *Development and use of the MMPI-2 Content Scales.* Minneapolis: University of Minnesota Press.

Butcher, J. N., & Williams, C. L. (1992). *Essentials of MMPI-2 and MMPI-A interpretation.* Minneapolis: University of Minnesota Press.

Caldwell, A. D. (1969). *MMPI critical items.* Unpublished mimeograph. (Available from Caldwell Roberts, 3122 Santa Monica Boulevard, Santa Monica, California 90404.)

Clavelle, P. R. (1992). Clinicians' perception of the comparability of the MMPI and MMPI-2. *Psychological Assessment, 4,* 466–472.

Clopton, J. R.(1979). *The MMPI and suicide.* In C.S. Newmark (Ed.), *MMPI: Clinical and research trends.* New York: Praeger Publishers.

Cottle, W. C. (1950). Card verus booklet forms of the MMPI. *Journal of Applied Psychology, 34,* 255–259.

Dahlstrom, W. G., Welsh, G. S., & Dahlstrom, L. E. (1972). *An MMPI handbook. Vol. 1. Clinical interpretations (rev. ed.).* Minneapolis: University of Minnesota Press.

Drake, L. E. (1946). A social I-E scale for the MMPI. *Journal of Applied Psychology, 30,* 51–54.

Fowler, R. D. (1966). *The MMPI notebook: A guide to the clinical use of the automated MMPI.* Roche Psychiatric Service Institute, Nutley, N.J.

Golden, C. J. (1979). *Clinical interpretation of objective psychological tests.* New York: Grune & Stratton, Inc.

Gough, H. G. (1950). The F-K dissimulation index for the MMPI. *Journal of Consulting Psychology, 14,* 408–413.

Graham, J. R. (1990). *MMPI-2: Assessing personality and psychopathology (2nd ed.).* New York: Oxford.

Grayson, H. M. (1951). *A psychological admission's testing program and manual.* Los Angeles: VA Center, Neuropsychiatric Hospital.

Greene, R. L. (1991). *The MMPI-2/MMPI: An interpretive manual.* Boston: Allyn and Bacon.

Hathaway, S. R. (1947). A coding system for MMPI profiles. *Journal of Consulting Psychology, 11,* 334–337.

Heilbrun, A. D. (1979). Psychopathy and violent crime. *Journal of Consulting Psychology, 47,* 509–516.

Honaker, L. M. (1988). The equivalency of computerized and conventional MMPI administration: A critical review. *Clinical Psychology Review, 8,* 561–577.

Hsu, L. M. (1986). Implications of differences in elevations of K-corrected and non-K-corrected MMPI T scores. *Consulting and Clinical Psychology, 54,* 552–557.

Keane, T. M., Malloy, P. F., & Fairbank, J. A. (1984). Empirical development of an MMPI subscale for the assessing of combat-related posttraumatic stress disorder. *Journal of Consulting and Clinical Psychology, 52,* 888–891.

Koss, N. P., & Butcher, J. N. (1973). A comparison of psychiatric patients' self-report with other sources of clinical information. *Journal of Research in Personality, 7,* 225–236.

Lachar, D. (1977). *The MMPI: Clinical assessment and automated interpretation.* Los Angeles: Western Psychological Services.

Lachar, D., & Wrobel, T. A. (1979). Validating clinician's hunches: Construction of a new MMPI critical item set. *Journal of Consulting and Clinical Psychology, 47,* 277–284.

MacAndrew, C. (1965). The differentiation of male alcoholic outpatients from non-alcoholic psychiatric outpatients by means of the MMPI. *Quarterly Journal of Studies on Alcohol, 26,* 238–246.

MacDonald, G. L. (1952). A study of the shortened group and individual forms of the MMPI. *Journal of Clinical Psychology, 8,* 309–311.

Meyer, R. G. (1983). *The clinician's handbook.* Boston: Allyn and Bacon.

Moreland, K. L. (1985). Computer-assisted psychological assessment in 1986: A practical guide. *Computers in Human Behavior, 1,* 221–223.

Newmark, C. S. (1985). The MMPI. In C. S. Newmark (Ed.), *Major psychological assessment instruments* (pp. 11–64). Boston: Allyn and Bacon.

Newmark, C. S., Gentry, L., Simpson, M., & Jones, T. (1978). MMPI criteria for diagnosing schizophrenia. *Journal of Personality Assessment, 42,* 366–373.

Penk, W. E. (1981). Assessing the substance abuser with the MMPI. In *Clinical notes on the MMPI.* Nutley, N.J.: Hoffmann-LaRoche.

Peterson, C. D. (1989). *Masculinity and femininity as independent dimensions on the MMPI.* Unpublished doctoral dissertation, University of North Carolina, Chapel Hill.

Pope, K. S., Butcher, J. N., & Seelen, J. (1993). *The MMPI, MMPI-2 & MMPI-A in court,* Washington, D.C.: American Psychological Association.

Roper, B. L., Ben-Porath, Y. S., & Butcher, J. N. (1991). Comparability of computerized adaptive and conventional testing with the MMPI-2. *Journal of Personality Assessment, 57,* 278–290.

Timbrook, R. E., & Graham, J. R. (1994). Ethnic differences on the MMPI-2? *Psychological Assessment, 6,* 212–217.

Webb, J. T., & McNamara, K. M. (1979). Configural interpretation of the MMPI. In C. S. Newmark (Ed.), *MMPI: Clinical and research trends.* New York: Praeger Publishers.

Welsh, G. S. (1948). An extension of Hathaway's MMPI profile coding system. *Journal of Consulting Psychology, 12,* 343–344.

Wiener, D. N. (1947). Differences between the individual and group forms of the MMPI. *Journal of Consulting Psychology, 11,* 104–106.

Wiggins, J. S. (1969). Content dimensions in the MMPI. In J. N. Butcher (Ed.), *MMPI: Research developments and clinical applications* (pp. 127–180). New York: McGraw-Hill.

Woodworth, R. S. (1920). *Personal data sheet.* Chicago: Stoelting.

Ziskin, J. (1981). Use of the MMPI in forensic settings. In *Clinical notes on the MMPI.* Nutley, N.J.: Hoffman-LaRoche.

2

The Minnesota Multiphasic Personality Inventory-Adolescent (MMPI-A)

Robert P. Archer
Radhika Krishnamurthy

INTRODUCTION

The Minnesota Multiphasic Personality Inventory (MMPI; Hathaway & McKinley, 1943) has a long history of use with adolescents. The original normative sample for the MMPI included subjects as young as 16 years old, and the test authors clearly felt that the MMPI was suitable for assessing personality characteristics in adolescents (Hathaway & McKinley, 1940). Research on applications of the MMPI with adolescents was begun as early as 1941, preceding the release of the final form of the inventory. A pioneering study by Dora Capwell demonstrated that several clinical scales of the MMPI, particularly scale 4, discriminated between delinquent and nondelinquent girls (Capwell, 1945). Early studies conducted by Monachesi (1948, 1950) also supported the effectiveness of scale 4 in accurately identifying delinquent boys.

Hathaway's investment in the application of the MMPI to adolescents is evident in his undertaking the largest prospective study ever conducted with the MMPI. Between 1947 and 1954, Hathaway and Monachesi collected extensive MMPI data from two large samples of ninth-grade adolescents, resulting in a combined sample exceeding 15,000 subjects. The MMPI was readministered in 1956–1957 to a subsample of approximately 4,000 adolescents when they entered the twelfth grade. These data were gathered in a longitudinal study conducted to identify personality characteristics that would predict delinquency. Thus, a broad range of additional information was also obtained for these subjects from school records, teacher reports, and test scores, and follow-up data were collected, including information from police records and court files (Hathaway & Monachesi, 1963). The valuable and enduring contributions of Hathaway and Monachesi in evaluating adolescents with the original MMPI are best reflected in two texts: their 1961 text entitled *An Atlas of Juvenile MMPI Profiles,* which is an extensive compendium of case histories associated with a variety of MMPI codes, and their 1963 text, *Adolescent Personality and Behavior: MMPI Patterns of Normal, Delinquent, Dropout, and Other Outcomes,* which presents research findings based on their longitudinal study of MMPI markers of adolescents' future adjustment.

Hathaway and Monchesi's (1961, 1963) research findings were of considerable importance for several reasons. First, their research provided detailed empirical information on the MMPI as used with adolescents. For example, they reported data on the differences in MMPI item endorsements between adolescents and adults and between male and female adolescents, identified test-retest differences reflecting personality changes that occurred between middle and late adolescence, and generated valuable external correlate information related to high and low scores on the 10 basic clinical scales. Second, this research established the validity of the MMPI in predicting the important behavioral domain of delinquency. Third, Hathaway and Monachesi's data served as the foundation for the subsequent development of adolescent norms (i.e., Gottesman, Hanson, Kroeker, & Briggs, 1987; Marks & Briggs, 1972) and for several follow-up investigations of this sample (e.g., Hanson, Gottesman, & Heston, 1990).

While Hathaway and Monachesi's data were subsequently used in developing adolescent norms, it should be noted that they did not develop or recommend the use of adolescent norms for the MMPI (Hathaway & Monachesi, 1963). However, evidence of unique profile characteristics among adolescents and differences in scale correlates for adults and adolescents (Hathaway & Dahlstrom, 1974) eventually led to the development of adolescent norms. For example, several later studies (e.g., Archer, 1984; Klinge & Strauss, 1976; Lachar, Klinge, & Grissell, 1976) demonstrated that adolescents responses produced marked elevations when adult norms were employed, particularly on scales F, 4, and 8. These findings indicated that adult norms were not applicable to an adolescent population. The Marks and Briggs (1972) norms came to be the most frequently used adolescent norm set for the original form of the MMPI, and provided the impetus for a number of clinical correlate studies to facilitate interpretation of patterns of code types (Marks, Seeman, & Haller, 1974; Williams & Butcher, 1989b) and single-scale elevations (Archer, Gordon, Gianetti, & Singles, 1988; Williams & Butcher, 1989a).

The research initiated by Hathaway and Monachesi (1961, 1963), and extended by other researchers, led to the widespread use of the MMPI with adolescents. This popularity of the MMPI was reflected in findings from a recent national survey of clinicians working with adolescents concerning their use of contemporary assessment instruments (Archer, Maruish, Imhof, & Piotrowski, 1991). Archer and colleagues' (1991) survey data revealed that the MMPI was the third most frequently mentioned test measure (after the Wechsler scales and the Rorschach) and ranked sixth in frequency of psychological test usage with adolescents. Further, the MMPI was the most frequently used objective personality assessment in this survey, and the only objective measure found among the 10 most widely used tests. The MMPI was also found to be included by approximately half of the survey respondents in their standard test batteries employed with adolescents.

Development of the MMPI-A

Despite the widespread popularity and use of the MMPI with adolescents, a number of problems were identified with the original test by researchers and clinicians. A central concern related to the limitations of the available adolescent norm sets. The Marks and Briggs (1972) norms were substantially dated, having been based on data collected in the 1940s through the 1960s. Further, the use of these norms produced a large number of false-negative MMPIs among adolescents evaluated in clinical settings (Archer, 1987). The Gottesman (Gottesman et al., 1987) norms were a reanalysis of Hathaway and Monachesi data collected in the 1940s and 1950s and did not reflect contemporary adolescents response patterns (Butcher & Williams, 1992a).

A third set of adolescent norms, developed by Colligan and Offord (1989), were based on a geographically and ethnically restricted sample, and their norms tended to attenuate T scores in the clinical range of elevation (Archer, Pancoast, & Klinefelter, 1989; Butcher & Williams, 1992a). Other concerns, reflected in the findings from Archer and associates' (1991) survey of clinicians, included issues related to the length of the test, the relatively high reading level required to comprehend test items, and the presence of inappropriate or outdated language. Finally, the item pool of the original MMPI was subjected to criticism in terms of the inclusion of some items that were inappropriate to adolescents, while also lacking items relating specifically to important adolescent experiences such as school-related problems, drug use, and eating disorders (Archer, 1992a, Butcher et al., 1992).

In response to these issues and concerns, the University of Minnesota Press appointed the MMPI Adolescent Project Committee—consisting of James N. Butcher, Beverly Kaemmer, Auke Tellegen, and Robert P. Archer—on July 1, 1989. The committee was asked to offer a recommendation on the feasibility of creating an adolescent form of the MMPI and to identify those elements that should be incorporated into the new form of the test instrument. This committee provided oversight for the development of the MMPI-A and established guidelines for normative criteria, item and scale construction, and profile development (Archer, 1992, Fall). Identified goals included developing contemporary norms based on a national representative sample, shortening the length of the inventory without losing important clinical information, retaining the standard validity and clinical scales to ensure continuity with the original test instrument, modifying and improving existing scales and developing new items and scales relevant to adolescent issues, and standardizing and refining assessment practices with adolescents (Archer, 1992a).

CONSTRUCTION

Experimental Booklet (Form TX)

The development of the MMPI-A began with the creation of an experimental test booklet (labeled MMPI Form TX) comprised of 704 items used in normative data collection and preliminary analyses. Form TX contained the original 550 MMPI items and a pool of 154 new items. Approximately 13 percent of the original MMPI items appeared in a reworded or modified form designed to improve content and wording, and the 16 repeated items appearing on the MMPI were dropped from Form TX. Research by Archer and Gordon (1994) has shown that the item modifications that occurred in the MMPI-A did not result in significant changes in response patterns for these items.

Normative Sample

MMPI-A normative data collection was conducted in eight states, including Minnesota, Ohio, California, Virginia, Pennsylvania, New York, North Carolina, and Washington. Adolescents were solicited through junior and senior high schools selected in each data collection site, and approximately 2,500 subjects were tested in group sessions typically conducted within the school setting. In addition to Form TX, subjects in the normative sample were administered a 16-item Biographical Information Form containing questions related to age, ethnicity, family characteristics, parental education and occupation, and academic history. Further, subjects completed a 74-item Life Events Form that solicited information concerning the occurrence and effects of significant life events. Following the application of various exclusion criteria (e.g., omission of >35 TX Form items), the MMPI-A normative sample was reduced to 805 males and 815 females, with mean ages of 15.5 and 15.6, respectively. All subjects were in the seventh- to twelfth-grade level at the time of testing and between the ages of 14 through 18, inclusive. An additional sample of 225 13-year-old adolescents was collected in Norfolk, Virginia, and served as the basis for the MMPI-A norms for this age group, which appear in Appendix C of Archer's (1992a) text.

The data collection sites for the MMPI-A normative sample were selected with the goal of achieving ethnic heterogeneity and providing considerably more diversity than the normative samples for the original instrument. The ethnic distribution of the MMPI-A normative sample consists of approximately 76 percent Caucasians, 12 percent African Americans, 2 percent Hispanics, and 10 percent of subjects from "other" ethnic groups. This ethnic distribution was reasonably congruent with U.S. Census data, with the exception of Hispanic groups, which were underrepresented in the MMPI-A normative sample.

Information concerning the living situation of the normative subjects indicated that approximately 66 percent of the subjects reported living with both parents, and approximately 30 percent lived with a single biological parent. With reference to parental education, biographical data findings indicated that higher educational levels were overrepresented in the normative sample's parents compared to 1980 U.S. Census figures. Specifically, approximately 50 percent of the fathers and 40 percent of the mothers of normative subjects were college graduates or had postgraduate education, in comparison to 20 percent of men and 13 percent of women who reported similar educational levels in the 1980 census. Similarly, professional and managerial occupations were found more frequently among normative subjects' parents, in contrast with lower occupational frequencies in the categories of unskilled laborers, homemakers, and unemployed individuals. The higher socioeconomic status and educational background represented in the families of the normative sample appears related to the data collection procedure of soliciting volunteers as subjects, which typically elicits greater participation from individuals and families with higher education and income levels. Further details concerning the characteristics of the normative sample are provided in the MMPI-A test manual (Butcher et al., 1992) and in Archer's (1992a) text.

Clinical Sample

Form TX was also employed in the collection of a clinical sample used to generate empirical descriptors of the standard clinical scales and to develop the MMPI-A content scales (Williams & Butcher, 1989a, 1989b; Williams, Butcher, Ben-Porath, & Graham, 1992). This clinical sample was composed of 492 boys and 352 girls who were receiving treatment in inpatient psychiatric and substance abuse facilities, day treatment centers, and special school settings. The majority of the clinical sample was derived from treatment facilities in Minnesota. The age range and grade levels represented in the clinical sample were similar to those for the normative sample, but clinical subjects had a higher likelihood of disrupted family backgrounds. The ethnic distribution of the clinical sample tended to be more representative of Minnesota than of other U.S. geographic regions.

Subjects in the clinical sample were administered Form TX and the two questionnaires (Biographical Information Form and Life Events Form) that were also completed by the normative sample. Additionally, data from several criterion measures were collected, including behavioral ratings obtained from clinical subjects' parents and treatment staff using standardized rating scales, self-report data, and record review information. These data were used to generate MMPI-A scale descriptors. The clinical scale profiles produced by the MMPI-A clinical sample were found to be similar to those of the adolescents in Marks and colleagues' (1974) clinical sample (Butcher et al., 1992).

Structure of the MMPI-A

The final form of the MMPI-A contains 478 items. This instrument has 69 scales and subscales that are presented on three profile sheets for basic scales, content and supplementary scales, and Harris-Lingoes and Si subscales, respectively. The standard validity scales (i.e., scales L, F, and K) and clinical scales (i.e., scales Hs through Si) of the MMPI are retained in the MMPI-A to preserve the continuity of this instrument with the original test, although some modifications have been made at the item level. Item changes include the deletion of 58 basic scale items, primarily from scales F, Mf, and Si. Specifically, scale F underwent substantial revision because the original F scale was inappropriate for adolescents, as reflected in frequent elevations found for adolescents without external evidence of significant psychopathology (e.g., Archer, 1984). Scales Mf and Si were shortened to reduce the overall length of the test instrument.

In general, the item-level changes implemented for the MMPI-A included the removal of selected items related to religion (e.g., "I believe there is a God"), bodily functions (e.g., "I have diarrhea once a month or more"), and sexual preferences (e.g., "I am very strongly attracted by members of my own sex"), as well as deletion of items inappropriate to adolescent life experiences (e.g., "Sometimes at elections I vote for men about whom I know very little"). Item additions were designed to provide increased content coverage related to alcohol and drug use, family conflicts, school/achievement difficulties, eating disorders, and identity problems, thus increasing the relevance of the test for adolescents.

Table 2–1 presents an overview of the MMPI-A scales and subscales, organized by profile sheets.

Basic Scales.   In addition to the traditional validity scales, which are re-ordered as F, L, and K on the MMPI-A, there are four new validity scales for this instrument: the Variable Response Inconsistency Scale (VRIN), True Response Inconsistency Scale (TRIN), F_1, and F_2. VRIN and TRIN are measures of response consistency that are counterparts of the similarly labeled scales on the Minnesota Multiphasic Personality Inventory-2 (MMPI-2; Butcher, Dahlstrom, Graham, Tellegen, & Kaemmer, 1989). The VRIN scale enables identification of indiscriminate or random responding, and TRIN facilitates detection of indiscriminate responding in either an acquiescent or a nay-saying direction. Scales F_1 and F_2 are subscales of F that provide information concerning the validity of the subject's responses to the initial and later stages of the test booklet, respectively. F_1 contains 33 items occurring in the first 240 items of the MMPI-A, whereas all of the 33 F_2 items occur after item 241. A comparison of the scores on these subscales helps to detect changes in the test-taking approach that may have occurred between the two halves of the test.

The 10 basic clinical scales for the MMPI-A appear in the same order as they do on the MMPI. These scales include scale 1: Hypochondriasis (Hs); scale 2: Depression (D); scale 3: Hysteria (Hy); scale 4: Psychopathic Deviate (Pd); scale 5: Masculinity-Femininity (Mf); scale 6: Paranoia (Pa); scale 7: Psychasthenia (Pt); scale 8: Schizophrenia (Sc); scale 9: Hypomania (Ma); and scale 0: Social Introversion (Si).

Supplementary Scales.   The MMPI-A contains six supplementary scales. Three of these scales, Welsh's (1956) Anxiety (A) and Repression (R) scales and the MacAndrew Alcoholism Scale-Revised (MAC-R; MacAndrew, 1965), are modified versions of the scales used previously with the MMPI. New

Table 2–1 Overview of the MMPI-A Scales and Subscales

Basic Profile Scales (17 Scales)

Validity Scales (7)
VRIN (Variable Response Inconsistency)
TRIN (True Response Inconsistency)
F_1
F_2
F   (Infrequency)
L   (Lie)
K   (Defensiveness)

Clinical Scales (10)
1/Hs   (Hypochondriasis)
2/D   (Depression)
3/Hy   (Hysteria)
4/Pd   (Psychopathic Deviate)
5/Mf   (Masculinity-Femininity)
6/Pa   (Paranoia)
7/Pt   (Psychasthenia)
8/Sc   (Schizophrenia)
9/Ma   (Mania)
0/Si   (Social Introversion)

Content and Supplementary Scales (21 Scales)

Content Scales (15)
A-anx (Anxiety)
A-obs (Obsessiveness)
A-dep (Depression)
A-hea (Health Concerns)
A-aln (Alienation)
A-biz (Bizarre Mentation)
A-ang (Anger)
A-cyn (Cynicism)
A-con (Conduct Problems)
A-lse (Low Self-Esteem)
A-las (Low Aspirations)
A-sod (Social Discomfort)

A-fam (Family Problems)
A-sch (School Problems)
A-trt (Negative Treatment Indicators)

Supplementary Scales (6)
MAC-R (MacAndrew Alcoholism-Revised)
ACK   (Alcohol/Drug Problem Acknowledgement)
PRO   (Alcohol/Drug Problem Proneness)
IMM   (Immaturity)
A   (Anxiety)
R   (Repression)

Harris-Lingoes and Si Subscales (31 Subscales)

Harris-Lingoes Subscales (28)
D_1 (Subjective Depression)
D_2 (Psychomotor Retardation)
D_3 (Physical Malfunctioning)
D_4 (Mental Dullness)
D_5 (Brooding)
Hy_1 (Denial of Social Anxiety)
Hy_2 (Need for Affection)
Hy_3 (Lassitude-Malaise)
Hy_4 (Somatic Complaints)
Hy_5 (Inhibition of Aggression)
Pd_1 (Familial Discord)
Pd_2 (Authority Problems)
Pd_3 (Social Imperturbability)
Pd_4 (Social Alienation)
Pd_5 (Self-Alienation)
Pa_1 (Persecutory Ideas)
Pa_2 (Poignancy)

Pa_3 (Naivete)
Sc_1 (Social Alienation)
Sc_2 (Emotional Alienation)
Sc_3 (Lack of Ego Mastery, Cognitive)
Sc_4 (Lack of Ego Mastery, Conative)
Sc_5 (Lack of Ego Mastery, Defective Inhibition)
Sc_6 (Bizarre Sensory Experiences)
Ma_1 (Amorality)
Ma_2 (Psychomotor Acceleration)
Ma_3 (Imperturbability)
Ma_4 (Ego Inflation)

Si Subscales (3)
Si_1 (Shyness/Self-Consciousness)
Si_2 (Social Avoidance)
Si_3 (Alienation-Self and Others)

Source: From *MMPI-A: Assessing Adolescent Psychopathology* (pp. 59–60) by R. P. Archer, 1992a, Hillsdale, NJ: Lawrence Erlbaum. Copyright © 1992 by Lawrence Erlbaum. Adapted by permission.

supplementary scales developed specifically for the MMPI-A include the Immaturity (IMM) scale, the Alcohol/Drug Problems Acknowledgment (ACK) scale, and the Alcohol/Drug Problems Proneness (PRO) scale.

The original A scale was developed to assess the first dimension found in factor-analytic studies of the MMPI involving general maladjustment and distress, and the R scale was created to measure the second factor, repression. Both scales have been slightly reduced in length on the MMPI-A. Among the substance abuse scales, the MAC-R and PRO scales are empirically derived measures, whereas the ACK scale was constructed using a combination of rational and statistical procedures. Items on all three scales have been shown to differentiate between adolescents with and without alcohol and drug problems. The 43-item IMM scale was developed by Archer, Pancoast, and Gordon (1994) using a combined rational-statistical procedure of scale development, for the purpose of assessing psychological maturation during adolescence. Scale items address content areas related to insecurity, lack of insight and introspection, externalization of blame, interpersonal and social discomfort and alienation, lack of future planning, egocentricity and self-centeredness, and presence of hostile and antisocial/asocial attitudes.

Content Scales. The 15 content scales for the MMPI-A were developed using a five-stage, multimethod approach involving both rational and statistical procedures. The first stage involved selecting MMPI-2 content scales for adaptation to the MMPI-A, identifying new adolescent-specific content areas, and determining scale membership of the items. The judgments of independent raters were used in the process of developing the preliminary list of content scales and their items. Stage two involved statistical methods to evaluate and improve the reliability and validity of the initial set of content scales. The third stage consisted of a rational review of the content dimensions to evaluate item relevance. Stage four involved further statistical refinement, including computation of the final reliability and validity coefficients. In the fifth and final stage, narrative descriptions were written for each content scale utilizing a combination of rational inferences and empirically derived descriptors (Williams et al., 1992).

The MMPI-A content scales measure aspects of psychopathology and maladjustment that may be directly inferred from the scale labels. Correlate information for these scales are provided in the MMPI-A manual (Butcher et al., 1992) and in texts by Archer (1992a), Butcher and Williams (1992a), and Williams and associates (1992). The Adolescent-Anxiety (A-anx) scale is comprised of items relating to tension, worry, dread, and perceptions of being overwhelmed by stress. The Adolescent-Obsessiveness (A-obs) scale involves symptoms of excessive rumination, difficulty making decisions, intrusive thoughts, and compulsive actions. The Adolescent-Depression (A-dep) scale items are related to depressive symptoms, including sadness, self-deprecation, crying spells, fatigue, hopelessness, and loneliness. The Adolescent-Health Concerns (A-hea) scale measures a range of physical symptoms, encompassing gastrointestinal, neurological, sensory, cardiovascular, and respiratory problems, as well as tendencies to worry about health issues. The Adolescent-Alienation (A-aln) reflects experiences of social isolation, alienation, and withdrawal. The Adolescent-Bizarre Mentation (A-biz) scale involves strange experiences, including hallucinations, paranoid ideation, and delusional beliefs.

The Adolescent-Anger (A-ang), Adolescent-Cynicism (A-cyn), and Adolescent-Conduct Problems (A-con) scales measure problems of anger control, distrust, and delinquent or antisocial attitudes and behaviors, respectively. The Adolescent-Low Self-Esteem (A-lse) scale identifies issues of low self-confidence, feelings of inadequacy, and negative self-perceptions. Items on the Adolescent-Low Aspirations (A-las) scale relate to a lack of interest in, and expectation of, success. The Adolescent-Social Discomfort (A-sod) scale measures introversion and interpersonal discomfort. The Adolescent-Family Problems (A-fam) scale concerns issues related to family conflict, whereas difficulties related to poor school performance, negative attitudes toward school, and learning difficulties are measured by the Adolescent-School Problems (A-sch) scale. Finally, the Adolescent-Negative Treatment Indicators (A-trt) scale involves items reflecting both negative attitudes toward mental health treatment and pessimism concerning one's ability to be helped. Scores on the MMPI-A content scales are susceptible to distortion by means of underreporting or overreporting symptomatology due to the face validity of the items, and therefore require a careful evaluation of profile validity prior to interpretation (Archer, 1992a).

Subscales.   The 28 Harris-Lingoes scales (Harris & Lingoes, 1955) developed for the MMPI are carried over to the MMPI-A with minimal item changes. These subscales were originally developed to facilitate identification of the content areas producing elevations on MMPI basic scales 2, 3, 4, 6, 8, and 9. The Si subscales (Ben-Porath, Hostetler, Butcher, & Graham, 1989) developed for the MMPI-2 are also available for the MMPI-A. These subscales differentiate issues of shyness and self-consciousness from social avoidance and alienation. The Si subscales appear together with the Harris-Lingoes subscales on the third profile sheet for the MMPI-A.

MMPI-A Structural Summary.   In comparison to the original MMPI, the MMPI-A presents a much larger number of standardly used scales and subscales that require careful integration of extensive information derived from the three profile sheets in the course of test interpretation. The interpretive process is further complicated by the observation that there are substantial intercorrelations between the MMPI-A basic and content scales (Butcher et al., 1992) and among the content scales (Archer, 1992a). Indeed, some of these intercorrelational values are so high ($r \geq .85$) that several scales provide what is essentially redundant information concerning the respondent's personality and psychopathology. The Structural Summary approach for the MMPI-A was developed by Archer and Krishnamurthy (1994a, 1994b) and represents a potentially useful method of organizing MMPI-A data to facilitate test interpretation. This approach is based on the factor structure underlying clusters of MMPI-A scales and subscales, and permits a more systematic method of data compilation and integration by cutting across the largely arbitrary distinctions between MMPI-A basic scales and subscales, content scales, and supplementary scales.

In a recent factor-analytic study of the MMPI-A (Archer, Belevich, & Elkins, 1994), eight primary scale-level factors were identified using a principal factor-analysis procedure. These eight factors accounted for 94 percent of the total scale score variance for the 1,620 adolescents in the MMPI-A normative sample. The eight factors were labeled General Maladjustment, Immaturity, Disinhibition/Excitatory Potential, Social Comfort, Health Concerns, Naivete, Familial Alienation, and Psychoticism. The MMPI-A Structural Summary (Archer & Krishnamurthy, 1994b) is organized around these factor groupings and is therefore derived purely from empirical findings regarding the relationships between, and underlying dimensions of, the MMPI-A scales. This approach could be contrasted to the use of a theoretical or conceptual model to identify important dimensions of test content. Figure 2–1 presents the MMPI-A Structural Summary.

The first section of the Structural Summary concerns the validity of the MMPI-A, evaluated along three dimensions, including the number of item omissions, indices of the consistency of item endorsement, and indices of the accuracy of item endorsement. The remainder of the Structural Summary contains clusters of MMPI-A scales and subscales organized around the eight factor groupings. The scales subsumed under each factor cluster are organized logically in terms of basic scales, content scales, supplementary scales, and subscale groups. Within these subgroups, the scales appear in descending order from scales having the highest to the lowest correlation with the respective factor. With very few exceptions, the scales presented on the Structural Summary form correlate $\geq .60$ or $\leq -.60$ with the assigned factor.

The factor grouping labels are identical to those in Archer and associates' (1994) study, with the exception of factor 4, which is labeled Social Discomfort on the Structural Summary form. This reversal was done to make this dimension consistent with the remaining factors in measuring aspects of psychopathology. The scoring direction of the scales defining this factor grouping are correspondingly reversed such that elevations in the critical direction reflect difficulties in social adjustment. The Structural Summary form also presents spaces at the bottom of each factor grouping to derive the total number or percentage of scales that show critical values (i.e., $T \geq 60$ or $T \leq 40$ depending on the expected direction) for a specific factor.

The empirical correlates of the MMPI-A Structural Summary factors have been provided by Archer and Krishnamurthy (1994b), based on data concerning salient behaviors, life events, and presenting problems (as applicable) obtained from the 1,620 adolescents in the MMPI-A normative sample and an inpatient sample of 122 adolescents. A comprehensive presentation of all significant external correlates of the Structural Summary factors for normative and clinical sample subjects is provided in Appendix C of the *MMPI-A Casebook* by Archer, Krishnamurthy, and Jacobson (1994). Table 2–2 presents a

MMPI-A Structural Summary

Robert P. Archer and Radhika Krishnamurthy

Name: _____   Date: _____

Age: _____   Grade: _____

Gender: _____   School: _____

Test-Taking Attitudes

1. Omissions (raw score total)

_____ ? (Cannot Say scale)

2. Consistency (T-score values)

_____ VRIN

_____ TRIN

_____ F_1 vs. _____ F_2

3. Accuracy (check if condition present)

Overreport

_____ F scale T score ≥ 90

_____ All clinical scales except 5 and $0 \geq 60$

Underreport

_____ High L ($T \geq 65$)

_____ High K ($T \geq 65$)

_____ All clinical scales except 5 and $0 < 60$

Factor Groupings
(enter T-score data)

1. General Maladjustment

_____ Welsh's A

_____ Scale 7

_____ Scale 8

_____ Scale 2

_____ Scale 4

_____ D_1 (Subjective Depression)

_____ D_4 (Mental Dullness)

_____ D_5 (Brooding)

_____ Hy_3 (Lassitude-Malaise)

_____ Sc_1 (Social Alienation)

_____ Sc_2 (Emotional Alienation)

_____ Sc_3 (Lack of Ego Mastery – Cognitive)

_____ Sc_4 (Lack of Ego Mastery – Conative)

_____ Si_3 (Alienation)

_____ Pd_4 (Social Alienation)

_____ Pd_5 (Self-Alienation)

_____ Pa_2 (Poignancy)

_____ A-dep

_____ A-anx

_____ A-lse

_____ A-aln

_____ A-obs

_____ A-trt

__/23 Number of scales with $T \geq 60$

2. Immaturity

_____ IMM

_____ Scale F

_____ Scale 8

_____ Scale 6

_____ ACK

_____ MAC-R

_____ Pa_1 (Persecutory Ideas)

_____ Sc_2 (Emotional Alienation)

_____ Sc_6 (Bizarre Sensory Experiences)

_____ A-sch

_____ A-biz

_____ A-aln

_____ A-con

_____ A-fam

_____ A-trt

__/15 Number of scales with $T \geq 60$

Figure 2–1   MMPI-A Structural Summary

Source: Reproduced by special permission of Psychological Assessment Resources, Inc., from the MMPI-A Structural Summary by Robert P. Archer, Ph.D., Copyright 1994. Further reproduction is prohibited without permission from PAR, Inc.

3. Disinhibition/Excitatory Potential

_____ Scale 9

_____ Ma_2 (Psychomotor Acceleration)

_____ Ma_4 (Ego Inflation)

_____ Sc_5 (Lack of Ego Mastery, Defective Inhibition)

_____ D_2 (Psychomotor Retardation) (low score)*

_____ Welsh's R (low score)*

_____ Scale K (low score)*

_____ Scale L (low score)*

_____ A-ang

_____ A-cyn

_____ A-con

_____ MAC-R

_____/12 Number of scales with $T \geq 60$ or ≤ 40 for scales with asterisk

4. Social Discomfort

_____ Scale 0

_____ Si_1 (Shyness/Self-Consciousness)

_____ Hy_1 (Denial of Social Anxiety) (low score)*

_____ Pd_3 (Social Imperturbability) (low score)*

_____ Ma_3 (Imperturbability) (low scores)*

_____ A-sod

_____ A-lse

_____ Scale 7

_____/8 Number of scales with $T \geq 60$ or $T \leq 40$ for scales with asterisk

5. Health Concerns

_____ Scale 1

_____ Scale 3

_____ A-hea

_____ Hy_4 (Somatic Complaints)

_____ Hy_3 (Lassitude-Malaise)

_____ D_3 (Physical Malfunctioning)

_____/6 Number of scales with $T \geq 60$

6. Naivete

_____ A-cyn (low score)*

_____ Pa_3 (Naivete)

_____ Hy_2 (Need for Affection)

_____ Si_3 (Alienation–Self and Others) (low score)*

_____ Scale K

_____/5 Number of scales with $T \geq 60$ or $T \leq 40$ for scales with asterisk

7. Familial Alienation

_____ Pd_1 (Familial Discord)

_____ A-fam

_____ Scale 4

_____ PRO

_____/4 Number of scales with $T \geq 60$

8. Psychoticism

_____ Pa_1 (Persecutory Ideas)

_____ Scale 6

_____ A-biz

_____ Sc_6 (Bizarre Sensory Experiences)

_____/4 Number of scales with $T \geq 60$

Note. The presentation of scales under each factor label is generally organized in a descending order from the best to the least effective marker. Within this overall approach, scales are grouped logically in terms of basic clinical scales, Harris-Lingoes and *Si* subscales, and content scales. The majority of scales included in this summary sheet were correlated $\geq .60$ or $\leq -.60$ with the relevant factor for the MMPI-A normative sample.

PAR Psychological Assessment Resources, Inc.
P.O. Box 998/Odessa, Florida 33556/Toll-Free 1-800-331-TEST

9 8 7 6 5 4 3 2 1   Reorder #RO-2698   Printed in the U.S.A.

This form is printed in blue ink on white paper. Any other version is unauthorized.

Figure 2–1 *Continued*

Table 2–2   Description of the MMPI-A Structural Summary Factors

Factor	Description
General Maladjustment (23 scales or subscales)	This factor is associated with substantial emotional distress and maladjustment. Adolescents who score high on this dimension experience significant problems in adjustment at home and school and feel different from other teenagers. They are likely to be self-conscious, socially withdrawn, timid, unpopular, dependent on adults, ruminative, subject to sudden mood changes, and to feel sad or depressed. They are viewed as less competent in social activities and as avoiding competitive situations with peers. These adolescents are more likely than other teenagers to report symptoms of tiredness or fatigue, sleep difficulties, and suicidal thoughts, and to be referred for counseling or psychotherapy. Academic problems including low marks and course failures are common.
Immaturity (15 scales or subscales)	The Immaturity dimension reflects attitudes and behaviors involving egocentricity and self-centeredness, limited self-awareness and insight, poor judgment and impulse control, and disturbed interpersonal relationships. Adolescents who obtain high scores on this factor often have problems in the school setting involving disobedience, suspensions, and histories of poor school performance. Their interpersonal relationships are marked by cruelty, bullying, and threats, and they often associate with peers who get in trouble. These adolescents act without thinking and display little remorse for their actions. Familial relationships are frequently strained, with an increased occurrence of arguments with parents. Their family lives are also often marked by instability that may include parental separation or divorce. High-scoring boys are more likely to exhibit hyperactive and immature behaviors, whereas girls are prone to display aggressive and delinquent conduct.
Disinhibition/Excitatory Potential (12 scales or subscales)	High scores in this dimension involve attitudes and behaviors related to disinhibition and poor impulse control. Adolescents who score high on this factor display significant impulsivity, disciplinary problems, and conflicts with parents and peers. They are perceived as boastful, excessively talkative, unusually loud, and attention-seeking. They display increased levels of heterosexual interest and require frequent supervision in peer contacts. High-scoring adolescents typically have histories of poor school work and failing grades, truancy, disciplinary actions including suspensions, school drop-out, and violations of social norms in the home, school, and social environment. Their interpersonal relationships tend to be dominant and aggressive, and they quickly become negative or resistant with authority figures. These adolescents are likely to engage in alcohol/drug use or abuse. Their behavioral problems include stealing, lying, cheating, obscene language, verbal abuse, fighting, serious disagreements with parents, and running away from home. In general, they may be expected to use externalization as a primary defense mechanism.

Continued

Table 2–2 *Continued*

Factor	Description
Social Discomfort (8 scales or subscales)	Adolescents who elevate the scales involved in this dimension are likely to feel withdrawn, self-conscious, and uncertain in social situations, and display a variety of internalizing behaviors. They are frequently bossed or dominated by peers and tend to be fringe participants in social activities. These adolescents are typically perfectionistic and avoid competition with peers. They are viewed by others as fearful, timid, passive or docile, and acting young for their age. They may present complaints of tiredness, apathy, loneliness, suicidal ideation, and somatic complaints. These adolescents have a low probability of acting-out behaviors including disobedience, alcohol or drug use, stealing, or behavioral problems in school.
Health Concerns (6 scales or subscales)	Adolescents who obtain high scores on the Health Concerns dimension are seen by others as dependent, socially isolated, shy, sad, and unhappy. They are prone to tire quickly and have relatively low levels of endurance. They may display a history of weight loss and report sleep difficulties, crying spells, suicidal ideation, and academic problems. A history of sexual abuse may be present. High-scoring boys are likely to be viewed as exhibiting schizoid withdrawal whereas high-scoring girls are primarily seen as somatizers. These adolescents typically display lower levels of social competence in the school setting. They are unlikely to be involved in antisocial behaviors or have histories of arrests.
Naivete (5 scales or subscales)	High scores on the Naivete factor are produced by adolescents who tend to deny the presence of hostile or negative impulses and present themselves in a trusting, optimistic, and socially conforming manner. They may be described as less likely to be involved in impulsive, argumentative, or socially inappropriate behaviors, and are more often seen as presenting in an age-appropriate manner. They have a low probability of experiencing internalizing symptoms such as nervousness, fearfulness, nightmares, and feelings of worthlessness, or of acting-out and provocative behaviors including lying or cheating, disobedience, and obscene language.
Familial Alienation (4 scales or subscales)	Adolescents who score high on scales or subscales related to this dimension are more likely to be seen by their parents as hostile, delinquent, or aggressive, and as utilizing externalizing defenses. They are also viewed as being loud, verbally abusive, threatening, and disobedient at home. These adolescents tend to have poor parental relationships involving frequent and serious conflicts with their parents. Presenting problems in psychiatric settings may include histories of running away from home, sexual abuse, and alcohol/drug use. In addition to family conflicts, high-scoring adolescents are also more likely to have disciplinary problems at school resulting in suspensions and probationary actions.

Table 2–2 *Continued*

Factor	Description
Psychoticism (4 scales or subscales)	Adolescents who produce elevations on the Psychoticism factor are more likely to be seen by others as obsessive, socially disengaged, and disliked by peers. They may feel that others are out to get them, and are more likely to be teased and rejected by their peer group. Sudden mood changes and poorly modulated expressions of anger are likely. They may also exhibit disordered behaviors including cruelty to animals, property destruction, and fighting, and are likely to have histories of poor academic achievement.

Source: The factor descriptions are based on Archer and Krishnamurthy's (1994b) findings concerning the empirical correlates of the MMPI-A Structural Summary factors. Reproduced by special permission of Psychological Assessment Resources, Inc., from the MMPI-A Casebook by Robert P. Archer, Ph.D., and Radhika Krishnamurthy, Copyright 1994. Further reproduction is prohibited without permission from PAR, Inc.

summary of the descriptions of the Structural Summary factors based on correlate findings.

TEST ADMINISTRATION

Because of the continuity between the MMPI, MMPI-2, and MMPI-A, clinicians who have experience with the original test and the revised form for adults should have a relatively firm foundation in becoming familiar with administering and scoring the MMPI-A. However, there are several unique features on the MMPI-A, including new scales, the reordering of previously existing validity scales, and unique MMPI-A profile sheets, which require all test users to acquaint themselves with this instrument. Clinicians using the MMPI-A should also be reasonably well versed in the areas of test theory and psychometrics, adolescent development, personality and behavior, and psychodiagnostics and psychopathology.

Further, test users should review the MMPI-A manual prior to undertaking personality assessment with this instrument. MMPI-A testing should always be conducted under the supervision of an examiner, and the test booklet should not be taken home by respondents to complete in an unsupervised setting. This issue is particularly crucial in evaluating adolescents, in contrast to adults, because there is a greater probability of threats to test validity associated with reading or comprehension problems with this population. The MMPI-A administration may, however, be separated into two or more testing sessions if the adolescent is distractible, hyperactive, impulsive, or becomes fatigued. In general, problems with noncompliance or resistance to testing can usually be minimized by establishing sufficient rapport with the subject prior to testing, explaining the purposes of the evaluation, ensuring that the testing environment is relatively free of noise and interruptions, providing clear test instructions, and offering an opportunity for the adolescent to receive test feedback.

Age Criteria

The MMPI-A is designed to evaluate psychopathology in adolescents ages 14 through 18 years. Given that the normative samples for both the MMPI-A and the MMPI-2 include 18-year-olds, this age group may potentially be assessed with either instrument. The general guideline for the selection of test form provided in the MMPI-A manual (Butcher et al., 1992) is to administer the MMPI-A to 18-year-olds who are attending high school and/or living at home, and to use the MMPI-2 with 18-year-olds who are in college, employed, or otherwise leading a more independent adult lifestyle.

At the other end of the age continuum, the MMPI-A manual notes that the test may be selectively administered to 12- and 13-year-olds following careful consideration of their appropriateness for evaluation with this instrument. Specifically, they should have adequate reading ability, life experience, and cognitive and social maturity to undergo MMPI-A assessment. The norms for 13-year-old adolescents provided in Archer (1992a) may be utilized for these adolescents in conjunction with the standard MMPI-A norms. Profile interpretation should be based primarily on the standard norms, and the normative information specific to 13-year-old adolescents may be used to gain an appreciation of the degree to which developmental influences affect the standard profile (Archer, 1992a).

Reading Level

MMPI-A profile validity depends partly on the respondent's ability to read and comprehend test items. A higher frequency of item omissions is found among adolescents who have difficulties with reading the test items (Archer, 1992a). Similarly, inadequate comprehension of the meaning of items may result in inconsistent responding and elevated F scale scores. The MMPI-A manual (Butcher et al., 1992) recommends that a seventh-grade reading level would generally be required for this instrument. It should be noted, however, that reading difficulty level for the MMPI-A item set ranges from the first- to the sixteenth-grade level (Archer, 1992a).

Dahlstrom, Archer, Hopkins, Jackson, and Dahlstrom (1994) recently evaluated the average reading difficulty of the MMPI, MMPI-2, and MMPI-A using various indices, including a Reading Ease Index and the Lexile Index. Their major conclusions were as follows:

1. The average difficulty level of all three forms of the MMPI is approximately the sixth-grade level.
2. Although the MMPI-A requires less reading mastery than the MMPI-2 and the original form of the MMPI, the differences tend to be small.

3. On average, the most difficult items appear on scale 9, whereas scale 5 contains the easiest items.
4. The number of years of education completed by subjects is an unreliable index of their reading competence level.

Dahlstrom and colleagues (1994) also reported, based on the Reading Ease Index, that approximately 6 percent of the MMPI-A items require a tenth-grade reading level or higher.

The best supported recommendation concerning reading requirements for the MMPI-A is to employ the criterion of seventh-grade reading level. In addition, Archer (1992a) and Dahlstrom and colleagues (1994) recommend administering a reading test prior to MMPI-A testing when the adolescent's reading comprehension level is questionable and/or requiring the respondent to read aloud and explain a sample of the more difficult items in the test booklet. Further, reading comprehension difficulties may be identified by the use of two experimental subscales for the MMPI-A: the Items-Easy (Ie) and Items-Difficult (Id) scales, developed by Krakauer, Archer, and Gordon (1993). These subscales assist in detecting deficient reading ability among MMPI-A test-takers in terms of examining their pattern of responses to easy and difficult items. The audiocassette version of the MMPI-A may prove helpful in evaluating adolescents with learning disabilities in the reading or language skill areas. However, the MMPI-A should not be administered in any form to adolescents with IQs lower than 70 and reading levels below the fourth grade, as indicated by results of standardized testing (Archer, 1992a).

Short Forms/Abbreviated Assessments

The original form of the MMPI had at least two commonly used short forms: the Mini-Mult (Kincannon, 1968) and the MMPI–168 (Overall & Gomez-Mont, 1974). These forms were developed in attempts to accommodate time constraints surrounding test administration. MMPI short forms present a reduced number of test items and involve shortening the length of the scales. Therefore, this procedure also serves to reduce the overall reliability of these scales. Further, a significant amount of test-based information is lost because the scale profile or pattern resulting from the short-form administration will often differ from the pattern based on a full-length administration. Based on the negative effects noted here, use of MMPI or MMPI-A short forms is not recommended.

In contrast to short-form administrations, an abbreviated administration of the MMPI involves limiting the number of test items by presenting only those items that load on selected scales. The length of the basic scales remain unaltered in an abbreviated assessment and the basic scale pattern is unaffected by this procedure. The MMPI-A clinical scales and validity scales F_1, L, and K may be scored by administering the first 350 items of the test. Although this option may be necessary under certain circumstances, the information derived from the test is incomplete because the content and several supplementary scales, as well as the validity scales VRIN, TRIN, F, and F_2, cannot be scored (Archer, 1992a). An abbreviated MMPI-A assessment should consequently be limited to rare situations that impose unavoidable time restrictions.

Test Formats

The MMPI-A is available in booklet and audiocassette formats, both being suitable for either individual or group administration. Unlike the original form of the MMPI, items in all formats of the MMPI-A are in identical order to facilitate scoring. The booklet format may be purchased in either soft-cover or hard-cover forms, and a separate answer sheet is provided for subjects to record their responses. Audiocassette administration of the MMPI-A takes approximately an hour and a half, which includes test instructions and two readings of each item. This format is particularly useful for children who are visually impaired and reading disabled. A computerized administration of the MMPI-A is another available option, whereby test items are presented on a video screen and responses are entered by the subject through use of a keyboard.

SCORING

MMPI-A scoring may be accomplished through either hand-scoring or computer-scoring procedures. Prior to undertaking scoring, the answer sheet should be examined to ensure that a substantial number of items were not omitted or marked both True and False. A careful survey of the answer sheet may also reveal the presence of all-true or all-false response sets (e.g., an entire column marked True) or random responding (e.g., sequential alternation between True and False responses throughout the answer sheet).

Hand Scoring

Hand scoring the MMPI-A involves the use of scoring keys to obtain the raw scores for each of the 69 MMPI-A scales and subscales. Each scoring key is placed over the answer sheet and lined up appropriately, and the responses endorsed for the particular scale are counted to obtain the raw score. The raw scores are then transferred to the spaces on the bottom row of the MMPI-A profile sheets, and raw score data points are recorded on the profile to obtain the corresponding T scores. The total number of omitted and double-marked items is entered as a raw score value on the space for the Cannot Say (?) score on the bottom left corner of the Profile for Basic Scales.

This hand-scoring procedure is applicable for all scales except VRIN and TRIN, which require some additional steps and use of separate recording grids. The VRIN scale is composed of 50 item pairs reflecting content areas that require endorsement in either a similar direction (e.g., item 20: "No one seems to understand me" and item 211: "My way of doing things is apt to be misunderstood by others") or a different direction (e.g., item 60: "My feelings are not easily hurt" and item 121: "Criticism or scolding hurts me terribly") to be consistent. The VRIN raw score reflects the total number of item pairs that received inconsistent responses. For some item pairs, responding True to one item and False to the other results in a point added to the total score. Other item pairs receive a score when the adolescent responds True to both items, and a third set of items elevate the VRIN score when endorsed in the False direction.

The TRIN scale contains 24 item sets, including 21 standard item pairs and 3 repeated item pairs scored in a different direction. All TRIN item pairs are comprised of items that are opposite in content (e.g., item 46: "I am a very sociable person" and item 475: "I am usually very quiet around other people"). A point is added to TRIN when the adolescent responds True to both items within certain pairs, and a point is subtracted when False responses are provided to both items within other pairs. An elevated TRIN raw score therefore reflects indiscriminate responding using an acquiescent response set, and a very low raw score reflects inconsistent responding using a nay-saying response set.

Hand scoring the MMPI-A is rather time consuming and requires focused and sustained attention to minimize scoring errors. Greene (1980) reported that hand scoring of the MMPI produced one or more errors in 30 percent of hand-scored answer sheets for two samples evaluated, in contrast to a 0 percent error rate for computer scoring. Typical sources of error mentioned by Greene (1980) included miscounting the number of deviant responses and failing to use the appropriate, gender-specific scoring key for scale 5. Although scoring errors are typically not large enough to alter the test findings significantly, every effort should be made to recheck scoring prior to undertaking interpretation.

MMPI-A hand-scoring procedures require attention to two additional factors. First, it should be noted that K-correction (standardly used with the MMPI-2) is not performed in obtaining T score values for the MMPI-A. Second, there are separate profile sheets for male and female adolescents, and care should be taken to ensure that the raw scores are transferred to the appropriate profile sheet. The MMPI-A norms are broken down only by gender and not by age. This can be contrasted with the Marks and Briggs (1972) adolescent norms for the original MMPI that were presented separately for age groups 17, 16, 15, and 14 and below, and required use of age-specific profile sheets. Further, the Marks and Briggs (1972) norms involved use of a linear transformation procedure to convert raw scores to T scores. In contrast, a uniform T score transformation procedure is used with eight MMPI-A basic scales, excluding scales 5 and 0, and all the 15 content scales in order to achieve greater percentile equivalence across these scales (i.e., to ensure that a given T score will produce a similar percentile value on each scale).

Scoring procedures on the original form of the MMPI included use of a Welsh code (Welsh, 1948) to summarize T-score elevations on the basic scale profile. A modified version of the Welsh code may be utilized for the MMPI-A traditional validity and clinical scales. The scales are first arranged in descending order from left to right based on scale elevations, and the following symbols are used to denote degrees of T score elevation:

**	100 and above
*	90–99
"	80–89
'	70–79
+	65–69
-	60–64
/	50–59
:	40–49
#	30–39

Scales with T scores of 29 or below are recorded to the right of the # symbol, and the MMPI-A manual notes further optional code symbols that may be used to denote T scores above 109 (!) and 119 (!!). Scales that are within one T score point of each other are linked together by an underline. Examples of Welsh coding are provided in the MMPI-A manual (Butcher et al., 1992) and in Archer (1992a).

Norm Tables

Adolescent norm tables to be utilized in deriving T scores for the MMPI-A are provided in Appendix A of the MMPI-A manual (Butcher et al., 1992) and are reprinted in Appendix D of Archer's (1992a) text. Both texts also provide T score conversion tables that make it possible to score an adolescent's MMPI-A protocol using the original MMPI norms, and enables comparisons of the scale elevations obtained with the two sets of norms. These T score conversion tables present linear T scores for the MMPI-A basic scales separately for ages 17, 16, 15, and 14 and below, based on the original adolescent norms developed by Marks and Briggs (1972) for the MMPI.

Converting MMPI-A raw scores to estimates of the corresponding Marks and Briggs adolescent norm values is often important because the profile (in terms of elevations and the resulting codetype patterns) may differ across the two instruments. These differences occur primarily due to differences in the mean raw scores obtained by the Marks and Briggs and the MMPI-A normative samples, and, to a lesser extent, because of differences in T score transformation procedures between the two instruments. The advantage of scoring the MMPI-A on both sets of norms is that the convergence or divergence between the profiles may be examined on a case-by-case basis. This procedure, in turn, enhances the clinician's understanding of the changes associated with the MMPI-A and informs him or her of the extent to which the research accumulated on the MMPI is generalizable to the MMPI-A. The disadvantages of employing this strategy are that it is time consuming and may interfere with adaptation to the new instrument (Archer, 1992a, 1994). Finally, as previously noted, norms for 13-year-old adolescents for the MMPI-A basic, content, and supplementary scales are provided in Archer's (1992a) text.

Computer Scoring

Alternative scoring methods for the MMPI-A available through National Computer Systems (NCS) include computer scoring, mail-in scoring, and scoring by means of fax services. Computer-scoring approaches may involve either on-line test administration or transcribing the test-taker's item responses from the answer sheet to the computer. Mail-in scoring requires the responses to be entered on an optical-scan answer sheet that is mailed to NCS for scoring. The third option involves faxing the answer sheet to NCS using a toll-free telephone number. Because the MMPI-A is a copyrighted test and NCS serves as the official test distributor, consumers are prohibited from developing their own scoring programs for use on their personal computers (Butcher & Williams, 1992a).

INTERPRETATION

MMPI-A profile interpretation is best conducted by integrating a broad range of test-based data, including findings concerning profile validity, individual scale features, and profile characteristics, with background information, interview data, and findings from other tests. A variety of approaches to test interpretation are available, including the interpretation of single-scale elevations, the interpretation of code types, and the use of Caldwell's A-B-C-D paradigm to interpret multiscale elevations. The clinician may adopt any one of these approaches, or a combination of interpretive strategies, to obtain valid information concerning the nature and extent of the adolescent's psychopathology. MMPI-A profile data permit the examiner to derive diagnostic impressions and formulate hypotheses concerning the adolescent's adjustment, defensive operations, symptom picture, level of distress, nature and quality of interpersonal relationships, and probable initial responsiveness to psychological interventions (Archer, 1992a). Table 2–3 presents an outline of an interpretive approach suggested by Archer (1992a) and elaborated by Archer and colleagues (1994).

Contextual Factors

Consideration of the context in which the testing is undertaken is important for two reasons. First, elevated scores on specific MMPI-A scales may be partially accounted for by the circumstances in which the testing occurs. For example, adolescents evaluated in medical clinic or hospital environments may often produce marginal range (T = 60 to 64) elevations on scales Hs, Hy, and A-hea, and teenagers with histories of learning disabilities or communication

Table 2–3   Steps in MMPI-A Profile Interpretation

1. Setting in which the MMPI-A is administered
   a. Clinical/psychological/psychiatric
   b. School/academic evaluation
   c. Medical
   d. Neuropsychological
   e. Forensic
   f. Alcohol/drug treatment
2. History and background of patient
   a. Cooperativeness/motivation for treatment or evaluation
   b. Cognitive ability
   c. History of psychological adjustment
   d. History of stress factors
   e. History of academic performance
   f. History of interpersonal relationships
   g. Family history and characteristics
3. Validity Assessment
   a. Omissions
   b. Consistency
   c. Accuracy
4. Codetype (provides main features of interpretation)
   a. Degree of match with prototype
      (1) Degree of elevation
      (2) Degree of definition
      (3) Caldwell's A-B-C-D paradigm for multiple high-points
   b. Low-point scales
   c. Note elevation of scales 2 (D) and 7 (Pt)
5. Supplementary scales (supplement and confirm interpretation)
   a. Factor 1 and Factor 2 issues
      (1) Welsh A and R
   b. Substance abuse scales
      (1) MAC-R and PRO
      (2) ACK
   c. Psychological maturation
      (1) IMM scale
6. Content scales
   a. Supplement, refine, and confirm basic scale data
   b. Interpersonal functioning (A-fam, A-cyn, A-aln), treatment recommendations (A-trt), and academic difficulties (A-sch and A-las)
   c. Consider effects of overreporting/underreporting
7. Review of Harris-Lingoes subscales and critical item content
   a. Items endorsed can assist in understanding reasons for elevation of basic scales
8. Structural Summary (factor approach)
   a. Identify factor dimensions most relevant in describing adolescent psychopathology
   b. Use to confirm and refine traditional interpretation
   c. Consider effects of overreporting/underreporting on factor patterns

Source: Reproduced by special permission of Psychological Assessment Resources, Inc., from the MMPI-A Casebook by Robert P. Archer, Ph.D., and Radhika Krishnamurthy, Copyright 1994. Further reproduction is prohibited without permission from PAR, Inc.

disorders may produce some elevation on the content scales of A-sch and A-las. Awareness of the context reduces the possibility of overinterpreting or misconstruing the test findings.

Second, consideration of the setting enables the clinician to orient test-derived conclusions and recommendations to the specific questions that prompted the evaluation and to the particular needs of the adolescent and the referral agency. Similarly, knowledge of the adolescent's history and background should be used to enrich the interpretation of the MMPI-A profile. For example, awareness of an abusive family background may facilitate a deeper understanding of elevations on various distress-related scales as well as content scales including A-fam, A-cyn, and A-aln. Further, knowledge of an adolescent's substance abuse history permits the test interpreter to rule out psychoticism when scale 8 is moderately elevated in the absence of observable psychotic symptoms, and to focus attention more fully on MAC-R, ACK, and PRO scores. Although "blind" interpretations of MMPI-A profiles may frequently yield useful and accurate information, the resulting inferences are always more tentative than interpretations integrated with an understanding of the history and background of the adolescent, and this latter interpretation process permits a much more comprehensive description of the adolescent's functioning.

Validity Assessment

Greene (1991) has provided a useful model for evaluating MMPI-2 validity that may be applied to MMPI-A validity assessment. Using this model, evaluation of the technical validity of the MMPI-A profile first involves examining the number of omitted and/or double-marked items, indicated by the Cannot Say (?) score on the basic scale profile sheet. Most adolescents will omit fewer than 10 test items. Omissions in excess of 10 items are relatively uncommon and may reflect intellectual deficits, difficulties in reading comprehension, or carelessness and inattention. Item omissions of 30 or more items should result in a judgment that the MMPI-A profile is invalid and not subject to meaningful interpretation. In these circumstances, the adolescent should be encouraged to complete the items left unanswered, if he or she is capable of adequately reading and comprehending the test items (Archer, 1992a).

The next step in validity assessment consists of evaluating the consistency of item endorsement, based on examining the pattern of scores on VRIN, TRIN, F_1, and F_2. As noted earlier, an elevated VRIN score is suggestive of random responding that may result from either lack of attention, active resistance to testing, or the presence of significant reading difficulties. In contrast, a TRIN scale elevation is associated with the use of a yea-saying or nay-saying response set. It should be noted that the TRIN scale T score may fall within an acceptable range under conditions of random responding. A rough guideline provided by Archer (1992a) for interpreting

VRIN and TRIN is to view T scores in the 70 to 79 range as indicative of marginal levels of response consistency; T scores $\geq$ 80 reflect sufficient inconsistency to invalidate the profile.

Identification of response inconsistency is also facilitated by a comparison of F_1 and F_2 subscale T scores. In general, a difference of 20 or more T score points between F_1 and F_2 suggests the need for caution in interpreting the MMPI-A profile. For example, a marked elevation on F_2, when F_1 is within the normal range, suggests a change in the test-taking approach that occurred during the latter half of the test administration. This type of change may reflect boredom or inattention, and is frequently associated with random responding. The F_2 elevation interferes with accurate interpretation of the content and supplementary scales since many of the items on these scales appear on the second half of the MMPI-A booklet. However, the basic clinical scales may be interpreted if an acceptable F_1 score is produced. Finally, it may be noted that the VRIN scale may be used in combination with scale F to refine validity interpretation. For example, T score elevations $\geq$ 90 on scale F accompanied by a markedly elevated VRIN scale indicate an inconsistent and probably random response set problem, whereas a high F scale score and an acceptable VRIN scale score is more likely associated with significant psychopathology in a valid test protocol or with a consistent but symptom overreport pattern.

The third step in evaluating technical validity concerns assessing the accuracy of item endorsement. This step involves the use of the F-, L-, and K-scale configuration to detect tendencies to underreport or overreport symptomatology. A validity scale configuration in which the F-scale T score is higher than L and K scores is considered "open" in terms of the adolescent's willingness to report symptoms. The more pronounced the F-scale elevation, relative to L and K, the greater the likelihood that the adolescent is overreporting symptoms. An overreporting response set is clearly apparent when F is in the T $\geq$ 90 range and a "floating profile" is obtained characterized by all clinical scales (except Mf and Si) falling in the $\geq$ 60 T score range. In contrast, a "closed" profile involving conscious or unconscious minimization or denial of psychological problems is characterized by elevated L- and K-scale scores relative to the elevation on F. A tendency to underreport symptoms is evident when the T score difference between scale F and scales L and K is marked. Specifically, an underreporting response set is suggested when L- and K-scale T scores are $\geq$ 65 and all clinical scale T scores are in the $\leq$ 60 range for an adolescent with current psychiatric symptomatology (Archer, 1992a).

Determining an MMPI-A profile to be valid for interpretation also requires ruling out other response sets, including the all-true, all-false, and random response patterns. An all-true response set results in extremely low L and K scores and marked elevations on F, F_1, F_2, and TRIN. The VRIN scale score does not elevate under these circumstances. The all-false response set involves an elevated TRIN score associated with a nay-saying response style, a normal range VRIN score, and extreme elevations on L and K. Use of a random response set may produce a wide variety of clinical scale patterns, but is associated with elevation of the VRIN scale and an unusual validity scale pattern in which scale F and its subscales are elevated in conjunction with scale L (Archer, 1992a; Butcher & Williams, 1992a).

Basic Scale Interpretation

A central aspect of interpreting the MMPI-A basic scale profile involves determining the two-point code type for the profile based on the two most elevated clinical scales. This process first requires noting the number of scales that are elevated above a T score of 60 and the magnitude of these elevations. The greater the elevation on a particular scale, the greater the likelihood that the scale descriptors would describe accurately the adolescent's functioning. It should be noted that clinical range elevations on the MMPI-A are represented by T scores ≥ 65. Further, a unique feature on the MMPI-A involves the demarcation of a "gray" zone denoting marginal or transitional range elevations. The gray zone was developed to reflect the ambiguity of the boundary between normalcy and psychopathology in adolescents, and encompasses T scores in the 60 to 64 range.

Another issue relevant to basic scale code-type interpretation concerns the degree of correspondence between the specific adolescent's profile configuration and the prototypic profile associated with a particular code type. This comparison assists in determining the degree of confidence that can be placed in the code-type description for the adolescent being evaluated. The computerized interpretive system for the MMPI-A developed by Archer (1992b) provides a coefficient of fit representing the Pearson Product-Moment correlation between the adolescent's T scores on the 10 basic scales and corresponding scale T scores for the prototypic code type profile based on the available research findings. Finally, the degree to which the code type is well defined should be evaluated. Definition of a two-point code type refers to the magnitude of T score difference between the second-and third-highest scale elevation in the basic scale profile. A code type is considered well defined when there is at least a five-point T score difference between the pertinent scales. To illustrate this point, a profile in which T scores for scales 2 and 4 are 71 and 69, respectively, is denoted as a 2-4/4-2 code type. This code type would be said to have sufficient definition if the next highest scale is no higher than a T score of 64. Code-type descriptors are generally more accurate when the two-point code type is clearly defined.

The code-type interpretive approach furnishes a wealth of descriptive information based on extensive correlate data accumulated through empirical investigations of clinical correlate patterns for the original form of the MMPI, the MMPI-2, and the MMPI-A. The scales appearing in the two-point code type are typically interchangeable in terms of the descriptors derived from the code type, unless exceptions are noted in the code-type literature. For example, a profile in which the two most elevated scales are scales 2 and 7, respectively, is described as a 2-7/7-2 code type, and the same descriptors are provided regardless of whether scale 2 or scale 7 has the higher T score elevation. Code-type correlates for the MMPI-A basic scales are provided in Archer's (1992a) text. The most frequent code type for adolescent males evaluated with either the MMPI or the MMPI-A is the 4-9 code. Other frequently appearing MMPI-A code types for boys include the 4-6, 2-4, 3-4, 6-8, and 4-8 codes, respectively. The most frequent MMPI-A code types for girls include the 1-3, 2-3, 4-6, and 4-9 codes, respectively.

The code-type interpretation approach, although widely used with adolescents and adults, has not received unequivocal support for use with adolescents (Butcher & Williams, 1989b). Further, rates of code-type congruence between the original form of the MMPI (on which the current code-type literature is based) and the MMPI-A are reduced substantially when the MMPI-A profile lacks sufficient definition. Consequently, care is advised in the use of code type data in interpreting MMPI-A profiles.

An alternative approach to MMPI-A interpretation advocated by Butcher and Williams (1992a) and by Archer (1992a) involves use of single or individual scale descriptors for the clinically elevated scales in the profile. Thus, an MMPI-A profile containing elevations on scales 1, 3, and 0 would be interpreted by combining information from each of the individual scales to obtain an overall picture of the adolescent's functioning.

A third interpretive strategy involves the application of Caldwell's A-B-C-D paradigm to interpret profiles with multiple clinical-range elevations. In this approach, the pertinent scales are arranged in descending order in terms of degree of elevation and are assigned a letter of the alphabet. For example, a profile characterized by elevations on scales 4, 8, 9, and 6, respectively, would be coded as 4 = A, 8 = B, 9 = C, and 6 = D. The profile would then be divided into all possible two-point combinations (i.e., A-B, A-C, A-D, B-C, B-D, and C-D), and descriptors for each code type would be integrated to develop a composite picture of the individual's personality and psychopathology. Primary code types, particularly the A-B (or 4-8) code type, receive the greatest emphasis in this approach, especially when discrepant information is generated from the various combinations. The A-B-C-D paradigm is described more fully in Friedman, Webb, and Lewak's (1989) text and in Archer (1992a) and Archer and associates (1994). Detailed illustrations of the single scale, code-type, and multiscale interpretive strategies for the MMPI-A are provided in Archer and associates (1994).

Interpreting the MMPI-A basic scale profile is completed by incorporating descriptors derived from low-point scales in the profile. For example, a low score on scale 9, defined as a T score ≤ 40, provides important information concerning the extent of the adolescent's depression and accompanying psychomotor slowing when evaluated in conjunction with the elevation on scale 2. Consideration of profile configurations, including both elevated and low-range scores, represent a more sophisticated approach to MMPI-A interpretation,which should be typically utilized only by the more experienced test user.

Integration of Additional Scales

The fifth, sixth, and seventh steps of profile interpretation summarized in Table 2–3 involve the processes of augmenting and refining basic scale information with findings from the content scales, supplementary scales, Harris-Lingoes and Si subscales, and individual item content. Supplementary scales A and R furnish valuable data concerning the adolescent's overall maladjustment and use of primary defense mechanisms involving repression. MAC-R, ACK, and PRO allow for a more direct evaluation of substance abuse problems that may have been suggested indirectly by elevations on scales 4, 8, and 9. The IMM scale permits an estimate of the adolescent's psychological maturation, which has important prognostic value. The content scales also help to clarify the basic scale elevations. For example, consideration of scale A-anx together with scale 7, A-dep with scale 2, A-biz with scale 8, and A-con, A-fam, and A-ang with scale 4 is frequently useful to evaluate the specific domains of anxiety, depression, psychotic processes, and social adjustment, respectively. The clinician should bear in mind, however, that many content scales are highly intercorrelated with basic scales. For example, correlations of .91 between A-hea and scale 1 and .84 between A-anx and scale 7 have been reported for the MMPI-A normative sample (Butcher et al., 1992). Consequently, caution should be exerted to avoid simplistically viewing the content scales as confirming the basic scale findings.

Further, as noted previously, content scale items are obvious in nature and the endorsement of these items may be easily influenced by response biases. The Harris-Lingoes and Si subscales may be used to elaborate basic scale interpretations when the basic scale scores fall within an intermediate range of elevation (i.e., are neither subclinical nor markedly elevated) (Archer, 1992a). Subscale interpretation should be conservative, as these scales have not been validated in adolescent populations. Finally, MMPI interpretation has typically involved a review of responses to critical items to identify crisis-related issues such as suicidal ideation, acute anxiety, or loss of reality testing. However, critical items are frequently endorsed by normal adolescents at higher rates than are found among normal adults, and should consequently be used with substantial caution (Archer & Jacobson, 1993).

Use of the Structural Summary

The MMPI-A Structural Summary (Archer & Krishnamurthy, 1994a, 1994b) facilitates integration and organization of the extensive information derived from the 69 scales and subscales of the MMPI-A into meaningful categories reflecting broad underlying dimensions of psychological functioning. The advantages of this approach include its parsimony, breadth of scope, empirical foundations, and utilization of the redundancy associated with the intercorrelations between various MMPI-A scales. Further, the data concerning the empirical correlates of the Structural Summary factors facilitate the formulation of interpretive statements. A survey of the adolescent's scores on the

Structural Summary dimensions enables the clinician to separate the central components of the adolescent's psychopathology from less salient issues. Use of the Structural Summary is demonstrated in the clinical case example that follows.

Computer-Based Test Interpretation

The MMPI-A may be interpreted using either or both of the two currently available computer-based test interpretation (CBTI) packages: (1) the MMPI-A Interpretive System, developed by Archer (1992b) and distributed by Psychological Assessment Resources (PAR); and (2) the Minnesota Report: Adolescent Interpretive System developed by Butcher and Williams (1992b) and distributed by National Computer Systems (NCS). The PAR report is a software product that can be purchased for unlimited usage and requires entry of MMPI-A scale T score values, whereas the NCS report is a test interpretation service accessed by furnishing item responses to NCS for processing.

The information presented in the two narrative reports is organized in different manners. The PAR product provides configural validity scale interpretations and basic scale code-type interpretations followed by a scale-by-scale summary for all MMPI-A scales and subscales. An additional feature consists of a Profile Matches and Scores section that provides a coefficient of fit between the prototypic code type and the specific adolescent's profile, and furnishes other data, including the degree of code-type definition, mean clinical scale elevation, and mean excitatory scale elevation. The NCS report organizes interpretive statements into the categories of validity considerations, symptomatic behaviors, interpersonal relations, behavioral stability, and diagnostic and treatment considerations. Guidelines for evaluating the assets and liabilities of CBTI products are provided in texts by Archer (1992a), Butcher (1987), and Butcher and Williams (1992a).

The narrative reports obtained from both CBTI systems are based on combinations of actuarial data and expert clinical judgment, and are not intended to represent finished psychological reports. Rather, they constitute summaries of symptoms, personality characteristics, and psychological difficulties, and present hypotheses related to diagnoses and treatment response. The test user retains the responsibility of determining the accuracy of the CBTI interpretive statements as applied to the individual's unique characteristics, incorporating information concerning the subject's history and background, and integrating the CBTI output into a psychological report.

CLINICAL CASE EXAMPLE

The case presented here is selected to underscore the point that a variety of interpretive approaches may be utilized with the MMPI-A, each yielding valid and meaningful findings. Further, this case example allows for discussion of the sometimes complex issues involved in the selection of the MMPI-A versus the MMPI-2, and the utility of the Structural Summary approach in identifying salient aspects of the adolescent's psychopathology.

Background Information

Alice was an 18-year-old African-American female who was brought to the emergency room of a medical/surgical hospital by her mother because she had been "acting different" for three days. She was described as appearing bewildered and preoccupied, and was reported as recently unable to perform daily activities, including bathing and dressing. Parental reports further indicated that Alice had abruptly withdrawn from others and spent most of her time reading and reciting the Bible, interspersed with sudden, unprovoked verbal outbursts involving randomly accusing her family and friends of criminal behavior. The precipitating event for Alice's regressive and disorganized behaviors consisted of her watching a television program concerning child abuse, which reportedly triggered memories of her own sexual abuse at age 7. Another event that was proximally connected to the onset of Alice's psychiatric symptoms involved her giving birth to a child two months earlier. She was unmarried and had been abandoned by the father of her child when he discovered she was pregnant. Conflicted feelings toward her child were suggested by Alice's admission that she drank heavily on one occasion during her pregnancy with the expressed goal of aborting the fetus.

Alice lived with her mother and was in the eleventh grade in school. She denied substance abuse problems or any other "wrongdoings," and stated that she was recently "saved" as a result of discussions with a pastor. During the emergency room evaluation, Alice reported suicidal ideation, insomnia, and loss of appetite, and stated that people were constantly proclaiming that "the devil was going to get her." Upon admission to the hospital's acute psychiatric unit, she displayed labile affect ranging from elation to weeping. Initial diagnoses included Psychotic Disorder NOS, with the provision to rule out Bipolar Disorder and Dissociative Disorder. Alice did not have a previous history of psychiatric evaluation or treatment. She was described as even-tempered, acquiescent, and psychologically uninsightful or naive. The psychological evaluation was undertaken to facilitate diagnostic determination, treatment planning, and discharge recommendations.

Alice was administered a battery of psychological tests that included the MMPI-A, Rorschach, and Thematic Apperception Test (TAT). Her Rorschach protocol revealed the presence of substantial stress, impulsive affect, lack of psychological sophistication, perceptual distortions, idiosyncratic thought processes, and negative self-esteem. Her specific verbalizations reflected a preoccupation with religiosity, struggles between good and evil, and elements of fear, guilt, and apprehension juxtapositioned with percepts of beauty, tranquility, and salvation. Her TAT responses similarly conveyed a sense of threat and retreat into a fantasy accompanied by euphoric and grandiose themes involving special religious powers or missions.

MMPI-A Interpretation

Prior to interpreting the MMPI-A profile, it should be noted that Alice may have been evaluated with either the MMPI-A or the MMPI-2. The normative and clinical samples for both measures include 18-year-old individuals. Utilizing the guidelines provided in the MMPI-A manual (Butcher et al., 1992), the clinician's decision concerning test selection should depend on the background of each individual case. Alice was tested with the MMPI-A because she lived at home, attended high school, and was not gainfully employed. On the other hand, an argument could be made for the use of the MMPI-2, given that she was the parent of a two-month old child. In general, the psychosocial information provided in her psychiatric record suggested that the MMPI-A item content would be more relevant to Alice's life experiences and developmental stage.

Figure 2–2 presents Alice's profile for the basic scales. Validity assessment may be undertaken by examining the (?) score on the bottom left of the profile sheet and the T score elevations on the left side of the basic scale profile that present validity scale results. Alice omitted only three items, well within the acceptable limit of item omissions. The next step involves evaluation of the consistency of item endorsement. Alice's scores on VRIN and TRIN indicate no significant problems with response consistency, given that questions about inconsistent responding are raised only when T score values for these scales equal or exceed 70. Further, her F_1 and F_2 scores differ only by two T score points, indicating that she responded with similar frequency to F-scale items in the first and latter halves of the test booklet. With reference to the accuracy of item endorsement, the F-L-K configuration reflects willingness to report psychiatric symptomatology and is consistent with the pattern expected for an inpatient admission. There are no indications of significant accuracy problems involving the use of an overreporting or underreporting response set. In summary, Alice's MMPI-A profile meets all standard criteria for profile validity and is suitable for interpretation.

The basic scale profile for this adolescent has a marked elevation on scale 6 (T = 82), a moderate clinical-range elevation on scale 8 (T = 68), and marginal-range elevations (T ≥ 60 and ≤ 64) on scales 9, 4, and 2. One potentially useful interpretive approach would involve basing the profile interpretation on the two-point code type. However, the use of this approach should be tempered by the observation that the 6-8/8-6 code type is not clearly defined in this profile because the third highest elevation, scale 9, is only four T score points lower than scale 8. Further, the Profile Matches and Scores section of Archer's (1992b) computer interpretive program indicates that the 6-8/8-6 code type for this profile correlates at only r = .63 with the prototypic 6-8/8-6 code. An alternative or additional approach would be to interpret this as a Spike 6 profile, augmented by interpretive statements concerning scales 8, 9, 4, and 2. A third approach would be to use a A-B-C-D paradigm with scale 6 = A, 8 = B, 9 = C, and 4 = D. The 6-8 code would serve as the anchor for the interpretation, supplemented with available information concerning the

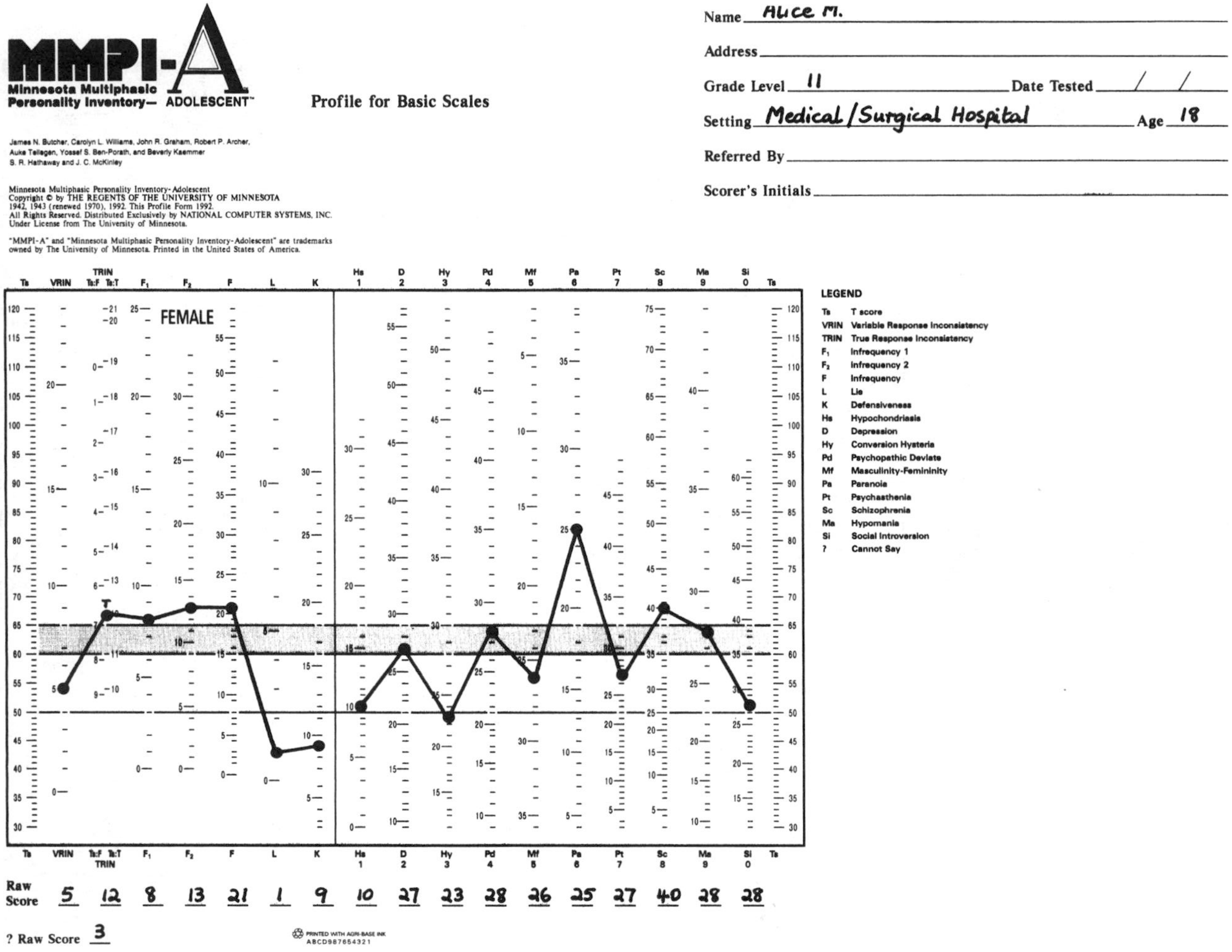

Figure 2–2 MMPI-A Basic Scale Profile for the Clinical Case Example: Alice

Source: Copyright © the Regents of the University of Minnesota, 1942, 1943 (renewed 1970), 1992. This profile form 1992. Reproduced by permission of the publisher. "Minnesota Multiphasic Peresonality Inventory-Adolescent" and "MMPI-A" are trademarks owned by the University of Minnesota.

MMPI-A

Minnesota Multiphasic Personality Inventory— ADOLESCENT

James N. Butcher, Carolyn L. Williams, John R. Graham, Robert P. Archer,
Auke Tellegen, Yossef S. Ben-Porath, and Beverly Kaemmer
S. R. Hathaway and J. C. McKinley

Minnesota Multiphasic Personality Inventory-Adolescent
Copyright © by THE REGENTS OF THE UNIVERSITY OF MINNESOTA
1942, 1943 (renewed 1970), 1992. This Profile Form 1992.
All Rights Reserved. Distributed Exclusively by NATIONAL COMPUTER SYSTEMS, INC.
Under License from The University of Minnesota.

"MMPI-A" and "Minnesota Multiphasic Personality Inventory-Adolescent" are trademarks
owned by The University of Minnesota. Printed in the United States of America.

Profile for Basic Scales

Name _____

Address _____

Grade Level _____ Date Tested ___/___/___

Setting _____ Age _____

Referred By _____

Scorer's Initials _____

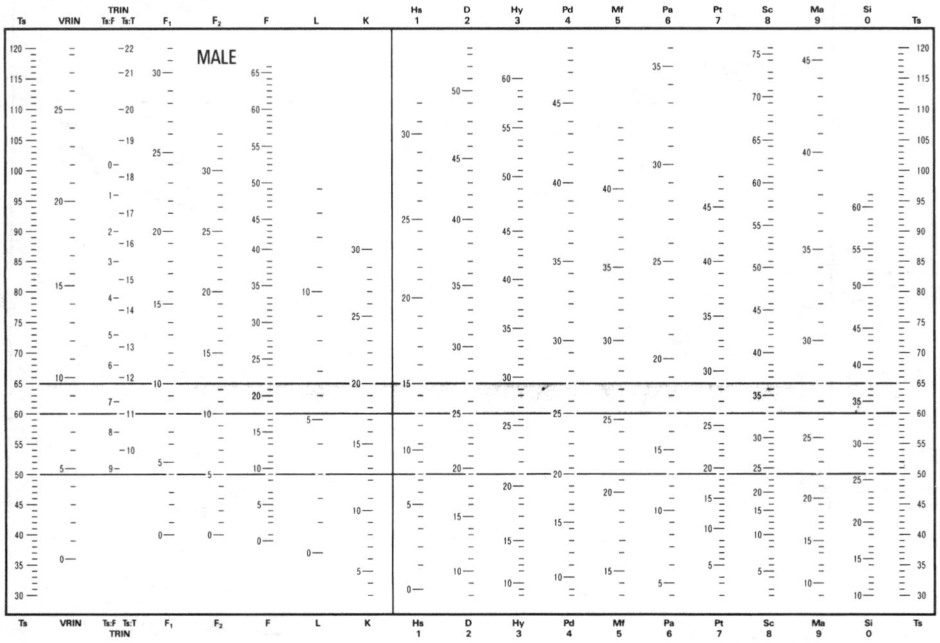

MALE

PRINTED WITH NON-READ INK
A B C D 9 8 7 6 5 4 3 2 1

LEGEND

Ts	T score
VRIN	Variable Response Inconsistency
TRIN	True Response Inconsistency
F₁	Infrequency 1
F₂	Infrequency 2
F	Infrequency
L	Lie
K	Defensiveness
Hs	Hypochondriasis
D	Depression
Hy	Conversion Hysteria
Pd	Psychopathic Deviate
Mf	Masculinity-Femininity
Pa	Paranoia
Pt	Psychasthenia
Sc	Schizophrenia
Ma	Hypomania
Si	Social Introversion
?	Cannot Say

Raw Score

? Raw Score

Figure 2-2 *Continued*

remaining two-point code-type combinations. Given space limitations, we will illustrate the use of the code-type and individual scale approaches in the following paragraphs, but note that the A-B-C-D paradigm could also be applied to the current case example.

The code-type literature indicates that the 6-8/8-6 code type is associated with serious psychopathology in both adolescents and adults. This code type reflects paranoid symptomatology, including grandiose and persecutory ideas, hallucinations, and outbursts of hostility. Individuals with this code type tend to display inappropriate and unpredictable behavior and exhibit problems with thought processes ranging from poor concentration to bizarre thinking. Fantasy and reality are frequently merged by these individuals, and they may withdraw into autistic fantasy in stressful situations. Adolescents with a 6-8/8-6 code type are often disliked and teased by peers and are likely to be socially isolated. Their predominant forms of affective distress include moderate depression and feelings of guilt and shame. Primary defense mechanisms employed by these adolescents include projection and denial, and they display little insight into their psychological problems (Archer, 1992a, 1992b).

A review of the single-scale descriptors for scale 6 indicates an increased likelihood of paranoid symptoms at the marked elevation produced by Alice. Other possible symptoms include excessive sensitivity to the actions and opinions of others, interpersonal guardedness, hostility and resentment, and inflexibility. An examination of the Harris-Lingoes subscales, presented later in this case example, facilitates identification of the specific content areas producing the scale 6 elevation. It should be noted that relatively few descriptors for scale 6 are available for adolescent girls in the MMPI-A manual (Butcher et al., 1992). The correlates of scale 8 include confusion and disorganization, unconventionality, poor reality testing, alienation, frustration and unhappiness, emotional vulnerability, poor school adjustment, and reluctance to engage in interpersonal relationships (Archer, 1992a). Elevated scale 8 scores were found to be associated with a history of sexual abuse in the MMPI-A clinical sample (Butcher & Williams, 1992a). Scale 9 elevations involve characteristics of restlessness, impulsiveness, egocentricity, emotional lability, flight of ideas, and grandiose self-perceptions. Scale 4 elevations may reflect a variety of behavioral problems, impulsivity, family conflict, rebelliousness, social alienation, and substance abuse problems. Scale 2 descriptors involve symptoms of depression, isolation, and overall distress.

Again, the data provided by the Harris-Lingoes subscales should prove useful in identifying which content areas of scales 8, 9, 4, and 2 were actually endorsed by this adolescent. A comparison of the code type and single scale descriptors reveals overlapping content related to paranoid symptoms, thought disturbance, social isolation, behavioral instability, and depressed affect, supporting the view that both approaches yield valid, useful, and consistent information.

The content and supplementary scale profile, shown in Figure 2–3, furnishes additional information concerning Alice's psychopathology. Prominent elevations on the content scale profile are seen on the A-lse (T = 73), A-obs

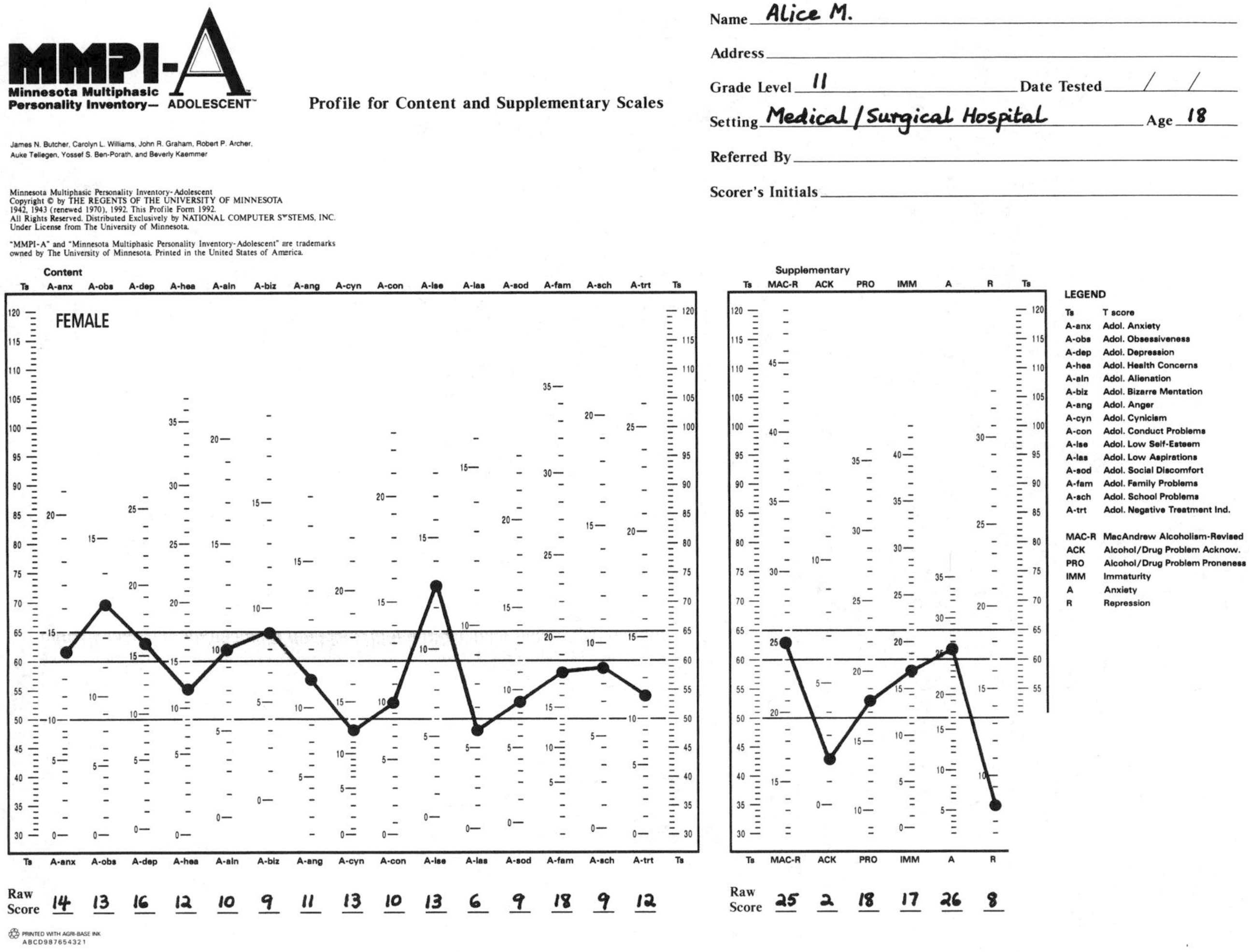

Figure 2-3 MMPI-A Content and Supplementary Scale Profile for the Clinical Case Example: Alice

Source: Copyright © the Regents of the University of Minnesota, 1942, 1943 (renewed 1970), 1992. This profile form 1992. Reproduced by permission of the publisher. "Minnesota Multiphasic Personality Inventory-Adolescent" and "MMPI-A" are trademarks owned by the University of Minnesota.

MMPI-A

Minnesota Multiphasic Personality Inventory— ADOLESCENT

Profile for Content and Supplementary Scales

James N. Butcher, Carolyn L. Williams, John R. Graham, Robert P. Archer,
Auke Tellegen, Yossef S. Ben-Porath, and Beverly Kaemmer

Name

Address

Grade Level _____ Date Tested __/__/__

Setting _____ Age _____

Referred By

Scorer's Initials

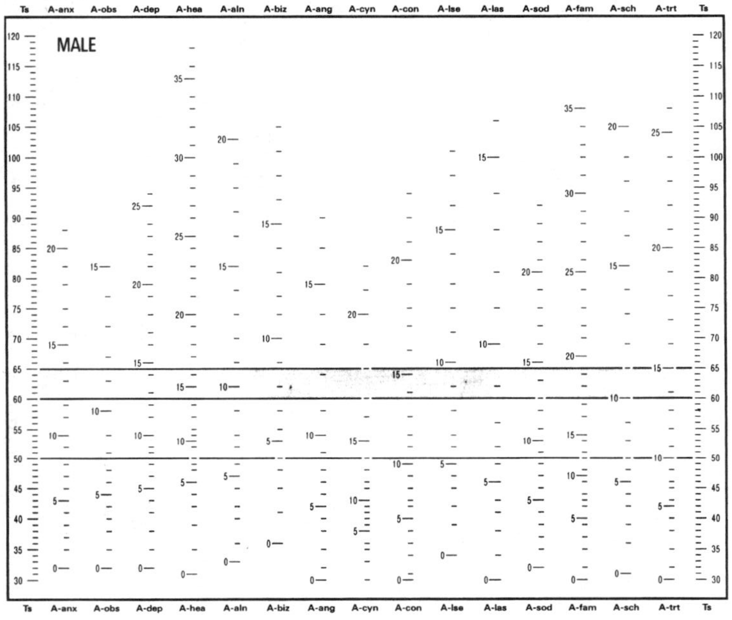

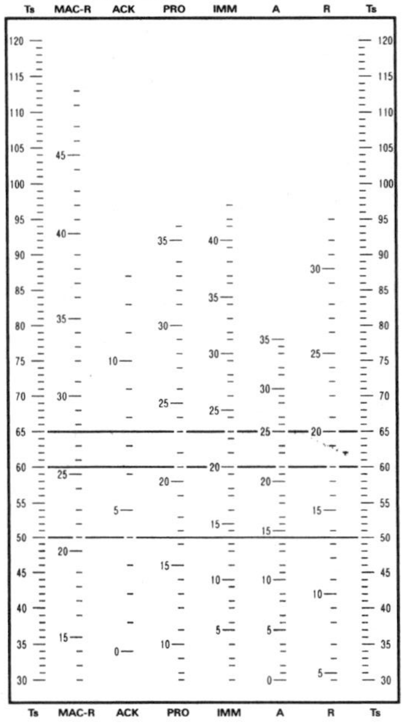

Content

MALE

Supplementary

Raw Score

LEGEND

	T score
Ts	
A-anx	Adol Anxiety
A-obs	Adol Obsessiveness
A-dep	Adol Depression
A-hea	Adol Health Concerns
A-aln	Adol Alienation
A-biz	Adol Bizarre Mentation
A-ang	Adol Anger
A-cyn	Adol Cynicism
A-con	Adol Conduct Problems
A-lse	Adol Low Self-Esteem
A-las	Adol Low Aspirations
A-sod	Adol Social Discomfort
A-fam	Adol Family Problems
A-sch	Adol School Problems
A-trt	Adol Negative Treatment Ind.
MAC-R	MacAndrew Alcoholism–Revised
ACK	Alcohol/Drug Problem Acknow.
PRO	Alcohol/Drug Problem Proneness
IMM	Immaturity
A	Anxiety
R	Repression

PRINTED WITH AGPASSE INK

Figure 2-3 *Continued*

(T = 70), and A-biz (T = 65) scales. Elevations on A-lse are typically produced by adolescents who feel inadequate, incompetent, flawed, and disrespected or rejected by others. High A-lse scores for girls in clinical settings have also been related to depression. High scores on A-obs are associated with excessive worry and rumination, intrusive thoughts, and difficulty in making decisions. Elevations on A-biz reflect psychotic thought processes, particularly symptoms related to paranoid beliefs. The preceding symptom descriptions derived from Alice's content scale elevations are quite consistent with her basic scale profile findings. Readers are reminded, however, that this should not be surprising in that many content scales have substantial correlations with basic scales.

Scale A-biz, for example, correlates .77 with scale 8 and .64 with scale 6 (Butcher et al., 1992). Alice's marginal-range elevations on scales A-aln, A-dep, and A-anx suggest problems related to interpersonal isolation and alienation, sadness and hopelessness that may include suicidal ideation, and a sense of being overwhelmed by stress. Difficulties related to overall maladjustment and ineffectiveness are indicated by the marginal-range elevation on the A-scale in the supplementary scale profile. The MAC-R scale score, while elevated in the midrange of the transitional zone, is still below the raw score value of 28 or greater recommended by Archer (1992a) to identify adolescents at risk for substance abuse problems. The MAC-R scale is unique among MMPI scales in that interpretation of this measure has traditionally been based on raw score, rather than T score, elevation. Alice's scores on the other two substance abuse related scales (ACK and PRO) are also clearly within normal limits and are consistent with her apparently negative history of alcohol or drug problems.

Alice's profile for the Harris-Lingoes and Si subscales is shown in Figure 2–4. The test interpreter would focus attention primarily on the subscales for basic scales 8, 9, 4, and 2 which, are in the T = 60 to T = 70 marginal-to-moderate range of elevation, with a secondary interest in the subscales for the markedly elevated (T $\geq$ 80) scale 6. Harris-Lingoes subscales would not be used to interpret basic scales that show T score elevations $\leq$ 59. Further, regardless of the degree of elevation on the basic scales, the Harris-Lingoes scales would not be interpreted if they fall in the T $\leq$ 64 range.

Using this approach, we find that the scale 8 elevation in Alice's profile results from a sense of being misunderstood and alienated from others (Sc_1: Social Alienation), feelings of despair and pessimism (Sc_2: Emotional Alienation), and a sense of psychological vulnerability and inertia (Sc_4: Lack of Ego Mastery-Conative), suggesting that Alice is socially withdrawn, psychologically fragile, and despondent. Although the Sc_3 (Lack of Ego Mastery-Cognitive) score is not quite clinically elevated, the A-biz content scales informs us of Alice's problems with disturbed thinking. The elevation on Ma_4 (Ego Inflation) is consistent with the grandiosity expressed in Alice's verbal responses to the TAT and Rorschach. The elevated Pd_5 (Self-Alienation) score reveals her emotional discomfort and possible feelings of guilt, and the Within-Normal-Limit scores found for other Pd subscales indicate that her

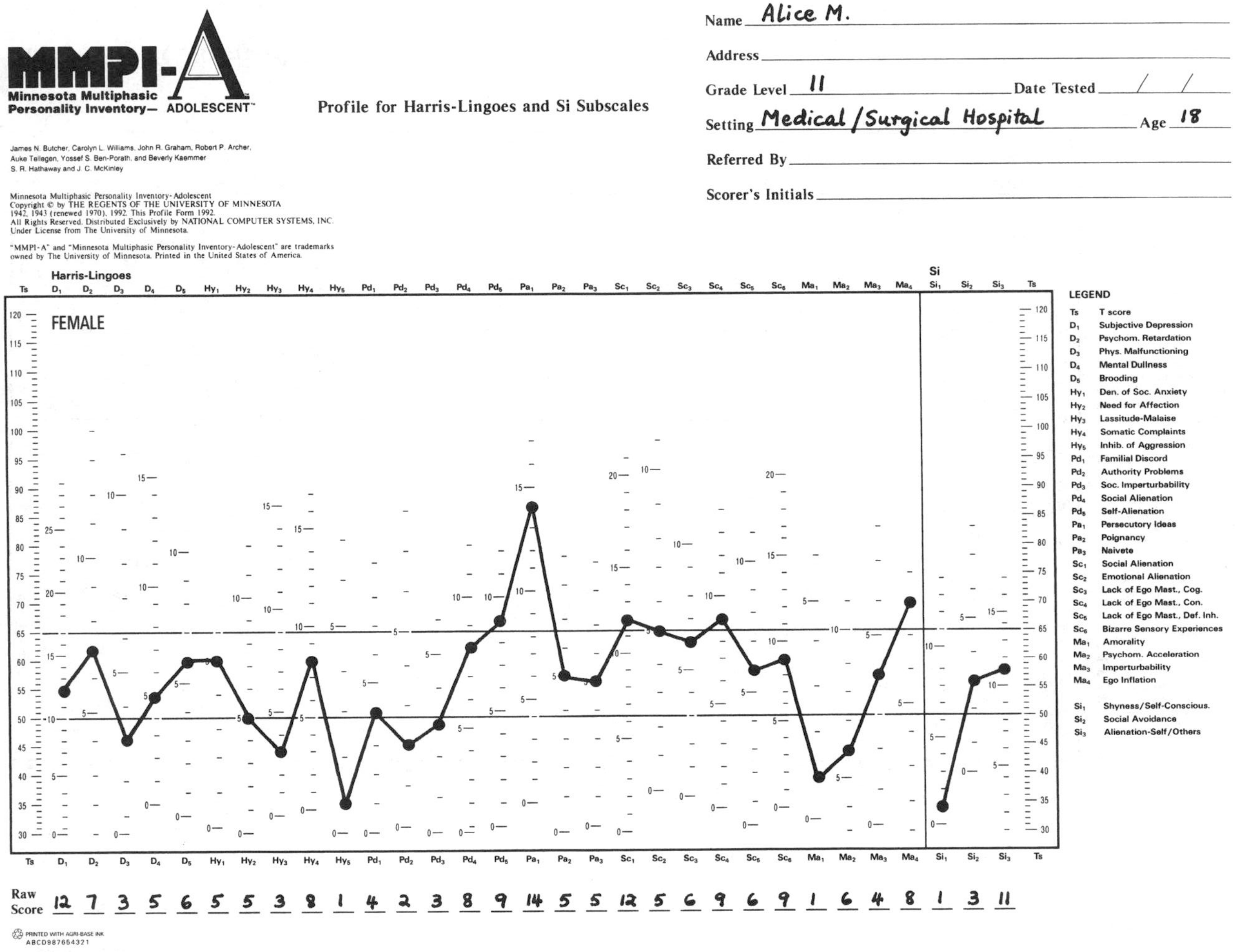

Figure 2–4 MMPI-A Harris-Lingoes and Si Subscale Profile for the Clinical Case Example: Alice

Source: Copyright © the Regents of the University of Minnesota, 1942, 1943 (renewed 1970), 1992. This profile form 1992. Reproduced by permission of the publisher. "Minnesota Multiphasic Personality Inventory-Adolescent" and "MMPI-A" are trademarks owned by the University of Minnesota.

MMPI-A
Minnesota Multiphasic Personality Inventory— ADOLESCENT™

Profile for Harris-Lingoes and Si Subscales

James N. Butcher, Carolyn L. Williams, John R. Graham, Robert P. Archer,
Auke Tellegen, Yossef S. Ben-Porath, and Beverly Kaemmer
S. R. Hathaway and J. C. McKinley

Name ____________________

Address ____________________

Grade Level ____________ Date Tested ___/___/___

Setting ____________________ Age ________

Referred By ____________________

Scorer's Initials ____________________

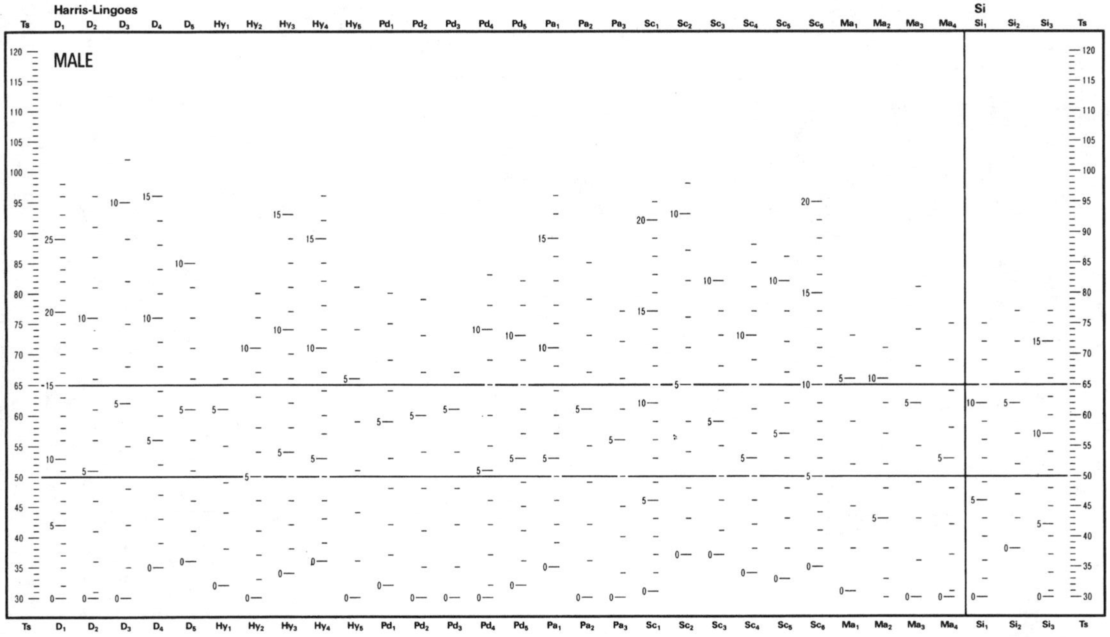

LEGEND

Ts	T score
D_1	Subjective Depression
D_2	Psychom. Retardation
D_3	Phys. Malfunctioning
D_4	Mental Dullness
D_5	Brooding
Hy_1	Den. of Soc. Anxiety
Hy_2	Need for Affection
Hy_3	Lassitude-Malaise
Hy_4	Somatic Complaints
Hy_5	Inhib. of Aggression
Pd_1	Familial Discord
Pd_2	Authority Problems
Pd_3	Soc. Imperturbability
Pd_4	Social Alienation
Pd_5	Self-Alienation
Pa_1	Persecutory Ideas
Pa_2	Poignancy
Pa_3	Naivete
Sc_1	Social Alienation
Sc_2	Emotional Alienation
Sc_3	Lack of Ego Mast., Cog.
Sc_4	Lack of Ego Mast., Con.
Sc_5	Lack of Ego Mast., Def. Inh.
Sc_6	Bizarre Sensory Experiences
Ma_1	Amorality
Ma_2	Psychom. Acceleration
Ma_3	Imperturbability
Ma_4	Ego Inflation
Si_1	Shyness/Self-Conscious.
Si_2	Social Avoidance
Si_3	Alienation-Self/Others

Raw Score __

PRINTED WITH AGRI-BASE INK
ABCD987654321

Figure 2–4 ***Continued***

scale 4 elevation is not due to antisocial behaviors, familial discord, or denial of social anxiety. The absence of significant subscale elevations for scale 2 reflect the very marginal nature of Alice's elevation (T = 61) on this basic scale. Finally, Alice's quite marked elevation on Pa_1 (Persecutory Ideas) underscores her use of projection as a primary defense and the possibility of delusional thinking.

The information derived from the three MMPI-A profile sheets may be summarized from the perspective of the Structural Summary presented in Figure 2–5. The first section of the Structural Summary concerns test-taking attitudes. This section presents the data, summarized earlier, that provide evidence of the technical validity of this MMPI-A profile. In surveying Alice's scores from each of the eight factor groupings, it is evident that her psychopathology is best represented by three factors: Psychoticism, General Maladjustment, and Immaturity, respectively.

Alice's scores exceed the T score criterion of $\geq$ 60 on all four scales loading on the Psychoticism factor. The correlate data for this factor emphasize characteristics of sudden mood changes, poorly modulated expressions of anger, obsessiveness, and social disengagement. Within the General Maladjustment dimension, 16 of the 23 (i.e., 70 percent) scales loading on this factor are elevated in Alice's MMPI-A profile. This result reflects the presence of substantial emotional distress and problems in adjustment at home and school. Adolescents who elevate this factor feel different from other teenagers, are more likely to report fatigue and suicidal thoughts, and are frequently referred for psychotherapy. A review of the individual scales and subscales that meet the T score criterion on this dimension indicates that the most salient aspects of Alice's distress include anxiety, obsessiveness, low self-esteem, and both social and self-alienation. Finally, the Immaturity factor in Alice's MMPI-A Structural Summary is characterized by elevations on 9 of 15 scales (60 percent), reflecting limited self-awareness and insight, poor judgment, and disturbed interpersonal relationships. Adolescents who obtain elevated scores on scales of this factor often have histories of poor school performance and family lives marked by substantial instability.

Case Summary

The MMPI-A record presented in this case example, supported by other test findings and background information, suggests that Alice is an alienated, confused, and distressed adolescent whose overideational, ruminative, and emotionally labile response style is currently accompanied by a breakdown in reality testing. Test findings point to the development of a psychotic reaction that includes delusional thoughts structured around her recently developed religious preoccupation. The MMPI-A data also suggest that Alice's symptom picture, including her interpersonal distrust and lack of insight into her problems, would present initial barriers to developing a therapeutic alliance. The identification of a possible thought disorder further suggests consideration of the use of psychotropic medication to achieve stabilization of functioning.

MMPI-A Structural Summary

Robert P. Archer and Radhika Krishnamurthy

Name: _Alice M._

Age: _18_   Grade: _11_

Gender: _Female_   School: _____

Test-Taking Attitudes

1. Omissions (raw score total)

   _3_ ? (Cannot Say scale)

2. Consistency (T-score values)

   _54_ VRIN

   _67T_ TRIN

   _66_ F_1 vs. _68_ F_2

3. Accuracy (check if condition present)

Overreport

_____ F scale T score ≥ 90

_____ All clinical scales except 5 and 0 ≥ 60

Underreport

_____ High L ($T \geq 65$)

_____ High K ($T \geq 65$)

_____ All clinical scales except 5 and 0 < 60

Factor Groupings
(enter *T*-score data)

1. General Maladjustment

   _62_ Welsh's A

   _56_ Scale 7

   _68_ Scale 8

   _61_ Scale 2

   _64_ Scale 4

   _55_ D_1 (Subjective Depression)

   _54_ D_4 (Mental Dullness)

   _60_ D_5 (Brooding)

   _44_ Hy_3 (Lassitude-Malaise)

   _67_ Sc_1 (Social Alienation)

   _65_ Sc_2 (Emotional Alienation)

   _63_ Sc_3 (Lack of Ego Mastery – Cognitive)

   _67_ Sc_4 (Lack of Ego Mastery – Conative)

   _58_ Si_3 (Alienation)

   _62_ Pd_4 (Social Alienation)

   _67_ Pd_5 (Self-Alienation)

   _57_ Pa_2 (Poignancy)

   _63_ A-dep

   _61_ A-anx

   _73_ A-lse

   _62_ A-aln

   _70_ A-obs

   _54_ A-trt

   _16_ /23 Number of scales with $T \geq 60$

2. Immaturity

   _58_ IMM

   _68_ Scale F

   _68_ Scale 8

   _82_ Scale 6

   _43_ ACK

   _63_ MAC-R

   _87_ Pa_1 (Persecutory Ideas)

   _65_ Sc_2 (Emotional Alienation)

   _60_ Sc_6 (Bizarre Sensory Experiences)

   _59_ A-sch

   _65_ A-biz

   _62_ A-aln

   _53_ A-con

   _58_ A-fam

   _54_ A-trt

   _9_ /15 Number of scales with $T \geq 60$

Figure 2–5 MMPI-A Structural Summary for the Clinical Case Example: Alice

3. Disinhibition/Excitatory Potential

_____ Scale 9

_____ Ma_2 (Psychomotor Acceleration)

_____ Ma_4 (Ego Inflation)

_____ Sc_5 (Lack of Ego Mastery, Defective Inhibition)

_____ D_2 (Psychomotor Retardation) (low score)*

_____ Welsh's R (low score)*

_____ Scale K (low score)*

_____ Scale L (low score)*

_____ A-ang

_____ A-cyn

_____ A-con

_____ MAC-R

____/12 Number of scales with $T \geq 60$ or ≤ 40 for scales with asterisk

4. Social Discomfort

_____ Scale 0

_____ Si_1 (Shyness/Self-Consciousness)

_____ Hy_1 (Denial of Social Anxiety) (low score)*

_____ Pd_3 (Social Imperturbability) (low score)*

_____ Ma_3 (Imperturbability) (low scores)*

_____ A-sod

_____ A-lse

_____ Scale 7

____/8 Number of scales with $T \geq 60$ or $T \leq 40$ for scales with asterisk

5. Health Concerns

_____ Scale 1

_____ Scale 3

_____ A-hea

_____ Hy_4 (Somatic Complaints)

_____ Hy_3 (Lassitude-Malaise)

_____ D_3 (Physical Malfunctioning)

____/6 Number of scales with $T \geq 60$

6. Naivete

_____ A-cyn (low score)*

_____ Pa_3 (Naivete)

_____ Hy_2 (Need for Affection)

_____ Si_3 (Alienation–Self and Others) (low score)*

_____ Scale K

____/5 Number of scales with $T \geq 60$ or $T \leq 40$ for scales with asterisk

7. Familial Alienation

_____ Pd_1 (Familial Discord)

_____ A-fam

_____ Scale 4

_____ PRO

____/4 Number of scales with $T \geq 60$

8. Psychoticism

_____ Pa_1 (Persecutory Ideas)

_____ Scale 6

_____ A-biz

_____ Sc_6 (Bizarre Sensory Experiences)

____/4 Number of scales with $T \geq 60$

Note. The presentation of scales under each factor label is generally organized in a descending order from the best to the least effective marker. Within this overall approach, scales are grouped logically in terms of basic clinical scales, Harris-Lingoes and *Si* subscales, and content scales. The majority of scales included in this summary sheet were correlated $\geq .60$ or $\leq -.60$ with the relevant factor for the MMPI-A normative sample.

PAR Psychological Assessment Resources, Inc.
P.O. Box 998/Odessa, Florida 33556/Toll-Free 1-800-331-TEST

9 8 7 6 5 4 3 2 1   Reorder #RO-2698   Printed in the U.S.A.

This form is printed in blue ink on white paper. Any other version is unauthorized.

Figure 2–5 *Continued*

MMPI-A Structural Summary

Robert P. Archer and Radhika Krishnamurthy

Name: _____   Date: _____

Age: _____   Grade: _____

Gender: _____   School: _____

Test-Taking Attitudes

1. Omissions (raw score total)

_____ ? (Cannot Say scale)

2. Consistency (T-score values)

_____ VRIN

_____ TRIN

_____ F_1 vs. _____ F_2

3. Accuracy (check if condition present)

Overreport

_____ F scale T score ≥ 90

_____ All clinical scales except 5 and 0 ≥ 60

Underreport

_____ High L $(T \geq 65)$

_____ High K $(T \geq 65)$

_____ All clinical scales except 5 and 0 < 60

Factor Groupings
(enter T-score data)

1. General Maladjustment

_____ Welsh's A

_____ Scale 7

_____ Scale 8

_____ Scale 2

_____ Scale 4

_____ D_1 (Subjective Depression)

_____ D_4 (Mental Dullness)

_____ D_5 (Brooding)

_____ Hy_3 (Lassitude-Malaise)

_____ Sc_1 (Social Alienation)

_____ Sc_2 (Emotional Alienation)

_____ Sc_3 (Lack of Ego Mastery – Cognitive)

_____ Sc_4 (Lack of Ego Mastery – Conative)

_____ Si_3 (Alienation)

_____ Pd_4 (Social Alienation)

_____ Pd_5 (Self-Alienation)

_____ Pa_2 (Poignancy)

_____ A-dep

_____ A-anx

_____ A-lse

_____ A-aln

_____ A-obs

_____ A-trt

_____ /23 Number of scales with $T \geq 60$

2. Immaturity

_____ IMM

_____ Scale F

_____ Scale 8

_____ Scale 6

_____ ACK

_____ MAC-R

_____ Pa_1 (Persecutory Ideas)

_____ Sc_2 (Emotional Alienation)

_____ Sc_6 (Bizarre Sensory Experiences)

_____ A-sch

_____ A-biz

_____ A-aln

_____ A-con

_____ A-fam

_____ A-trt

_____ /15 Number of scales with $T \geq 60$

Figure 2–5 *Continued*

3. Disinhibition/Excitatory Potential

- **64** Scale 9
- **44** Ma_2 (Psychomotor Acceleration)
- **70** Ma_4 (Ego Inflation)
- **58** Sc_5 (Lack of Ego Mastery, Defective Inhibition)
- **62** D_2 (Psychomotor Retardation) (low score)*
- **35** Welsh's R (low score)*
- **44** Scale K (low score)*
- **43** Scale L (low score)*
- **57** A-ang
- **48** A-cyn
- **53** A-con
- **63** MAC-R

5 /12 Number of scales with $T \geq 60$ or ≤ 40 for scales with asterisk

4. Social Discomfort

- **51** Scale 0
- **34** Si_1 (Shyness/Self-Consciousness)
- **60** Hy_1 (Denial of Social Anxiety) (low score)*
- **49** Pd_3 (Social Imperturbability) (low score)*
- **57** Ma_3 (Imperturbability) (low scores)*
- **53** A-sod
- **73** A-lse
- **56** Scale 7

1 /8 Number of scales with $T \geq 60$ or $T \leq 40$ for scales with asterisk

5. Health Concerns

- **51** Scale 1
- **49** Scale 3
- **55** A-hea
- **60** Hy_4 (Somatic Complaints)
- **44** Hy_3 (Lassitude-Malaise)
- **46** D_3 (Physical Malfunctioning)

1 /6 Number of scales with $T \geq 60$

6. Naivete

- **48** A-cyn (low score)*
- **56** Pa_3 (Naivete)
- **50** Hy_2 (Need for Affection)
- **58** Si_3 (Alienation–Self and Others) (low score)*
- **44** Scale K

0 /5 Number of scales with $T \geq 60$ or $T \leq 40$ for scales with asterisk

7. Familial Alienation

- **51** Pd_1 (Familial Discord)
- **58** A-fam
- **64** Scale 4
- **53** PRO

1 /4 Number of scales with $T \geq 60$

8. Psychoticism

- **87** Pa_1 (Persecutory Ideas)
- **82** Scale 6
- **65** A-biz
- **60** Sc_6 (Bizarre Sensory Experiences)

4 /4 Number of scales with $T \geq 60$

Note. The presentation of scales under each factor label is generally organized in a descending order from the best to the least effective marker. Within this overall approach, scales are grouped logically in terms of basic clinical scales, Harris-Lingoes and *Si* subscales, and content scales. The majority of scales included in this summary sheet were correlated $\geq .60$ or $\leq -.60$ with the relevant factor for the MMPI-A normative sample.

PAR Psychological Assessment Resources, Inc.
P.O. Box 998/Odessa, Florida 33556/Toll-Free 1-800-331-TEST

Figure 2–5 *Continued*

Alice's inpatient admission was followed by an exacerbation of symptoms involving active and recurring hallucinations, incoherence, and marked behavioral disorganization. She received short-term treatment primarily involving psychopharmacologic interventions and supportive individual therapy, and was referred to the local community mental health center for medication management and individual psychotherapy following her hospital discharge.

ASSETS AND LIMITATIONS OF THE MMPI-A

The MMPI, an empirically derived test developed over five decades ago, has received greater research attention and clinical application than any other objective personality assessment instrument. The MMPI-A is a contemporary, developmentally sensitive adaptation of this instrument designed specifically for use with adolescents. The basic continuity between this adolescent-specific instrument and its more broadly applied predecessor permits the accumulated MMPI literature to retain much of its relevance and utility as applied to the MMPI-A. Although the MMPI and MMPI-A are not psychometrically equivalent forms, these instruments do share a very substantial psychometric overlap and common heritage. While seeking to retain the strengths of the MMPI, the authors of the MMPI-A have also attempted to address several of the limitations associated with the original test instrument, including its length, awkward wording, and areas of objectionable content. Perhaps most importantly, development of the MMPI-A has appropriately facilitated the perspective that a single instrument is not equally applicable to adolescents and adults, and that the unique, developmentally related features of adolescence require an instrument adapted and standardized for use with this age group.

The MMPI-A is a broad-band measure that provides a comprehensive assessment of psychopathology in adolescents and presents a rich source of information concerning psychological functioning. Use of this instrument can consequently contribute significantly to treatment planning and to the assessment of treatment progress and outcome (Archer, 1994). The additional set of scales available for standard use with the MMPI-A, in conjunction with the traditional or basic scales, generates a vast amount of descriptive data and allows for greater refinement of interpretive hypotheses than was formerly possible with the original MMPI.

Specific advantages of the MMPI-A presented in this chapter include:

1. Retention of the basic validity and clinical scales to maintain continuity with the original instrument
2. Development of contemporary norms based on a representative national sample
3. Reduction of the overall test length without loss of significant psychometric information

4. Addition of adolescent-specific content areas
5. Derivation of new scale descriptors for the basic, content, and supplementary scales based on MMPI-A normative and clinical samples
6. Utilization of a developmental perspective in test construction of the MMPI-A
7. Provision of improved and expanded methods for assessing profile validity
8. Use of uniform T score procedures to increase percentile equivalence within basic and content scale categories (Archer, 1992a; Butcher & Williams, 1992a)

While the MMPI-A represents an improvement over the MMPI in the assessment of adolescents, it also presents several limitations, including the continuation of some problems that existed with the original instrument. Despite the reduction of the test length from 556 items to 478 items, the MMPI-A still presents a lengthy item pool and demands considerable time and sustained attention from the adolescent in order to achieve a successful administration. The reading requirements for the MMPI-A continue to be demanding, which may limit its use with many adolescents in treatment settings and will certainly prohibit usage with the many 12- and 13-year-old adolescents who do not read at a seventh-grade level. Further, the wording of the MMPI-A items, while often improved in comparison to the MMPI, still manifest occasional awkwardness and the presence of some inappropriately difficult terms (e.g., "I *brood* a great deal").

In our opinion, the central problem related to the use of the MMPI-A concerns potential limitations in test sensitivity or the ability to accurately detect the presence of psychopathology. As noted previously, the original MMPI, when used with the Marks and Briggs (1972) adolescent norms, frequently resulted in normal-range profiles for adolescents with known psychopathology. The MMPI-A will typically yield even lower basic scale T score values and has the risk of producing a relatively high rate of false-negative profiles (i.e., normal-range profiles produced by psychologically disturbed adolescents). This problem has been partially addressed in the creation of the MMPI-A by lowering the T score value defining clinical-range elevations from 70 to 65 and by delineating a transitional range of elevation in the 60 to 64 T score range. However, the degree to which these adjustments adequately compensate for lower T score values in promoting test sensitivity remains to be evaluated in systematic research projects.

Another potential limitation of the MMPI-A relates to the issue of the code-type congruence between the MMPI and MMPI-A—that is, the degree to which the profiles produced using the MMPI-A are comparable to adolescents' profiles based on the MMPI. This issue, in turn, concerns the degree to which the research based on the MMPI is applicable to the MMPI-A. The two-point code-type congruence rate reported in the MMPI-A manual (Butcher et al., 1992) is 95.2 percent for boys and 81.8 percent for girls in the normative sample for well-defined profiles (i.e., profiles showing at least five T score points difference in elevation between the second and third highest clinical scales). These congruence figures diminish to 67.8 percent for boys and 55.8 percent for girls when the profile convergence is calculated based on all profiles in the normative sample, regardless of code-type definition. Similarly, lower rates of code-type congruence are also found in clinical samples (69.5 percent for boys and 67.2 percent for girls) when code-type definition requirements are not used in selecting profiles for congruence estimates.

It should also be noted that the generalizability of MMPI research data to the MMPI-A essentially stops with the traditional 13 basic scales and the 3 previous established supplementary scales (A, R, and MAC-R) and does not extend to the numerous newly created MMPI-A scales. These new scales will require substantial validity research to identify their clinical correlates and to fully understand the most reliable and efficient methods of interpreting these measures. Until such research is accomplished, relatively greater caution will be necessary in the use of these more innovative features of the MMPI-A.

A final limitation relates to the potential instability of MMPI-A profile features and code types over relatively short time periods. The typical standard error of measurement for the MMPI-A basic scales is reported in the test manual (Butcher et al., 1992) to be approximately four to six T score points. This indicates that an adolescent's T score values would be expected to fall within a range of about five T score points above, to about five points below, the original score only 50 percent of the time if retesting occurred immediately and without significant changes in the psychological status of the adolescent. Test-retest reliability is decreased further when longer time periods intervene between test administrations, with the added effects of possible changes in the adolescent's psychiatric status.

While the standard error of measurement for the MMPI-A is similar to those reported for the MMPI and MMPI-2, the inherent limitations in the reliability of MMPI-A test scores, combined with the dramatic and sudden changes in psychological features often shown by adolescents, suggest that the MMPI-A is best used to provide a "snapshot" of the adolescent's psychological functioning at a given moment in time. Like all other measures of adolescent personality or psychopathology, the MMPI-A is not well suited to making long-range predictions of personality functioning (Archer, 1992, Fall; 1994).

CONCLUSIONS

Although the MMPI-A has a promising beginning and a proud heritage, much research remains to be done to evaluate the utility of this instrument in the assessment of adolescents. These research needs include carefully executed evaluations of the clinical correlates of MMPI-A basic scale code types, and investigations of the correlates derived for the MMPI content scales and the new supplementary scales. In particular, the ability of the content and supplementary scales to provide additional or incremental information, beyond that provided by the basic scales in identifying and describing psychiatric symptomatology among adolescents, requires careful evaluation.

The Harris-Lingoes and Si subscales would also benefit from validation studies undertaken in adolescent populations. As previously noted, the sensitivity and specificity of the MMPI-A in accurately identifying adolescents with and without psychiatric disorders should also be comprehensively investigated. Finally, a promising area of research relates to the utility of the MMPI-A Structural Summary in augmenting and refining traditional interpretive strategies, and playing an organizing role in the test interpretation process. The future popularity and utility of the MMPI-A will ultimately depend largely on establishing systematic and ongoing research efforts generated in the spirit of the rich empirical tradition associated with the MMPI.

REFERENCES

Archer, R. P. (1984). Use of the MMPI with adolescents: A review of salient issues. *Clinical Psychology Review*, *4*, 241–251.

Archer, R. P. (1987). *Using the MMPI with adolescents*. Hillsdale, NJ: Erlbaum.

Archer, R. P. (1992a). *MMPI-A: Assessing adolescent psychopathology*. Hillsdale, NJ: Erlbaum.

Archer, R. P. (1992b). *MMPI-A interpretive system* [Computer program]. Odessa, FL: Psychological Assessment Resources.

Archer, R. P. (1992, Fall). Issues in the development and use of the MMPI-A. *SPA Exchange*, *2*, 1–3, 12.

Archer, R. P. (1994). Minnesota Multiphasic Personality Inventory-Adolescent. In M. E. Maruish (Ed.), *The use of psychological testing for treatment planning and outcome assessment* (pp. 423–452). Hillsdale, NJ: Erlbaum.

Archer, R. P., Belevich, J. K. S., & Elkins, D. E. (1994). Item-level and scale-level factor structures of the MMPI-A. *Journal of Personality Assessment*, *62*, 332–345.

Archer, R. P., & Gordon, R. (1994). Psychometric stability of MMPI-A item modifications. *Journal of Personality Assessment*, *62*, 416–426.

Archer, R. P., Gordon, R. A., Gianetti, R., & Singles, J. (1988). MMPI special scale clinical correlates for adolescent inpatients. *Journal of Personality Assessment*, *52*, 707–721.

Archer, R. P., & Jacobson, J. M. (1993). Are critical items "critical" for the MMPI-A? *Journal of Personality Assessment*, *61*, 547–556.

Archer, R. P., & Krishnamurthy, R. (1994a). *MMPI-A structural summary* [Summary form]. Odessa, FL: Psychological Assessment Resources.

Archer, R. P., & Krishnamurthy, R. (1994a). A structural summary approach for the MMPI-A: Development and empirical correlates. *Journal of Personality Assessment*, *63*, 554–573.

Archer, R. P., Krishnamurthy, R., & Jacobson, J. M. (1994). *MMPI-A casebook*. Odessa, FL: Psychological Assessment Resources.

Archer, R. P., Maruish, M., Imhof, E. A., & Piotrowski, C. (1991). Psychological test usage with adolescent clients: 1990 survey findings. *Professional Psychology: Research and Practice*, *22*, 247–252.

Archer, R. P., Pancoast, D. L., & Gordon, R. A. (1994). The development of the MMPI-A Immaturity (IMM) scale: Findings for normal and clinical samples. *Journal of Personality Assessment*, *62*, 145–156.

Archer, R. P., Pancoast, D. L., & Klinefelter, D. (1989). A comparison of MMPI code types produced by traditional and recent adolescent norms. *Psychological Assessment: A Journal of Consulting and Clinical Psychology, 1,* 23–29.

Ben-Porath, Y. S., Hostetler, K., Butcher, J. N., & Graham, J. R. (1989). New subscales for the MMPI-2 Social Introversion (Si) Scale. *Psychological Assessment: A Journal of Consulting and Clinical Psychology, 1,* 169–174.

Butcher, J. N. (1987). *Computerized psychological assessment: A practitioner's guide.* New York: Basic Books.

Butcher, J. N., Dahlstrom, W. G., Graham, J. R., Tellegen, A., & Kaemmer, B. (1989). *MMPI-2 (Minnesota Multiphasic Personality Inventory-2): Manual for administration and scoring.* Minneapolis: University of Minnesota Press.

Butcher, J. N., & Williams, C. L. (1992a). *Essentials of MMPI-2 and MMPI-A interpretation.* Minneapolis: University of Minnesota Press.

Butcher J. N., & Williams, C. L. (1992b). *The Minnesota report: Adolescent interpretive system* [Computer program]. Minneapolis: National Computer Systems.

Butcher, J. N., Williams, C. L., Graham, J. R., Archer, R. P., Tellegen, A., Ben-Porath, Y. S., & Kaemmer, B. (1992). *MMPI-A (Minnesota Multiphasic Personality Inventory-Adolescent): Manual for administration, scoring, and interpretation.* Minneapolis: University of Minnesota Press.

Capwell, D. F. (1945) Personality patterns of adolescent girls. II. Delinquents and nondelinquents. *Journal of Applied Psychology, 29,* 284–297.

Colligan, R. C., & Offord, K. P. (1989). The aging MMPI: Contemporary norms for contemporary teenagers. *Mayo Clinic Proceedings, 64,* 3–27.

Dahlstrom, W. G., Archer, R. P., Hopkins, D. G., Jackson, E., & Dahlstrom, L. E. (1994). *Assessing the readability of the Minnesota Multiphasic Personality Inventory instruments—The MMPI, MMPI-2, MMPI-A* (MMPI-2/MMPI-A Test Reports No. 2). Minneapolis: University of Minnesota Press.

Friedman, A. F., Webb, J. T., & Lewak, R. (1989). *Psychological assessment with the MMPI.* Hillsdale, NJ: Erlbaum.

Gottesman, I. I., Hanson, D. R., Kroeker, T. A., & Briggs, P. F. (1987). New MMPI normative data and power-transformed T-score tables for the Hathaway-Monachesi Minnesota Cohort of 14,019 15-year-olds and 3,674 18-year-olds. In R. P. Archer, (Ed.), *Using the MMPI with adolescents* (pp. 241–297). Hillsdale, NJ: Erlbaum.

Greene, R. L. (1980). *The MMPI: An interpretive manual.* New York: Grune & Stratton.

Greene, R. L. (1991). *The MMPI-2/MMPI: An interpretive manual.* Boston: Allyn and Bacon.

Hanson, D. R., Gottesman, I. I., & Heston, L. L. (1990). Long-range schizophrenic forecasting: Many a slip twixt cup and lip. In J. E. Rolf, A. S. Masten, D. Cicchetti, K. N. Nuechterlein, & S. Weintraub (Eds.), *Risk and protective factors in the development of psychopathology* (pp. 424–444). New York: Cambridge University Press.

Harris, R. E., & Lingoes, J. C. (1955). *Subscales for the MMPI: An end to profile interpretation.* Unpublished manuscript, University of California, Los Angeles.

Hathaway, S. R., & Dahlstrom, W. G. (1974). Foreword to the revised edition. In P. A. Marks, W. Seeman, & D. L. Haller, (Eds.), *The actuarial use of the MMPI with adolescents and adults* (pp. vii–x). New York: Oxford University Press.

Hathaway, S. R., & McKinley, J. C. (1940). A multiphasic personality schedule (Minnesota): I. Construction of the schedule. *Journal of Psychology, 10,* 249–254.

Hathaway, S. R., & McKinley, J. C. (1943). *The Minnesota Multiphasic Personality Inventory* (rev. ed.). Minneapolis: University of Minnesota Press.

Hathaway, S. R., & Monachesi, E. D. (1961). *An atlas of juvenile MMPI profiles.* Minneapolis: University of Minnesota Press.

Hathaway, S. R., & Monachesi, E. D. (1963). *Adolescent personality and behavior: MMPI patterns of normal, delinquent, dropout, and other outcomes.* Minneapolis: University of Minnesota Press.

Kincannon, J. C. (1968). Prediction of the standard scales scores from 71 items: The mini-mult. *Journal of Consulting and Clinical Psychology*, *32*, 319–325.

Klinge, V., & Strauss, M. E. (1976). Effects of scoring norms on adolescent psychiatric patients' MMPI profiles. *Journal of Personality Assessment*, *40*, 13–17.

Krakauer, S. Y., Archer, R. P., & Gordon, R. A. (1993). The development of the Items-Easy (Ie) and Items-Difficult (Id) subscales for the MMPI-A. *Journal of Personality Assessment*, *60*, 561–571.

Lachar, D., Klinge, V., & Grissell, J. L. (1976). Relative accuracy of automated MMPI narratives generated from adult norm and adolescent norm profiles. *Journal of Consulting and Clinical Psychology*, *44*, 20–24.

MacAndrew, C. (1965). The differentiation of male alcoholic outpatients from non-alcoholic psychiatric outpatients by means of the MMPI. *Quarterly Journal of Studies on Alcohol*, *26*, 238–246.

Marks, P. A., & Briggs, P. F. (1972). Adolescent norm tables for the MMPI. In W. G. Dahlstrom, G. S. Welsh, & L. E. Dahlstrom, (Eds.), *An MMPI handbook. Vol. I. Clinical interpretation* (rev. ed., pp. 388–399). Minneapolis: University of Minnesota Press.

Marks, P. A., Seeman, W., & Haller, D. L. (1974). *The actuarial use of the MMPI with adolescents and adults*. Baltimore: Williams & Wilkins.

Monachesi, E. D. (1948). Some personality characteristics of delinquents and non-delinquents. *Journal of Criminal Law and Criminology*, *38*, 487–500.

Monachesi, E. D. (1950). Personality characteristics of institutionalized and non-institutionalized male delinquents. *Journal of Criminal Law and Criminology*, *41*, 167–179.

Overall, J. E., & Gomez-Mont, F. (1974). The MMPI–168 for psychiatric screening. *Educational and Psychological Measurement*, *34*, 315–319.

Welsh, G. S. (1948). An extension of Hathaway's MMPI profile coding. *Journal of Consulting Psychology*, *12*, 343–344.

Welsh, G. S. (1956). Factor dimensions A and R. In G. S. Welsh & W. G. Dahlstrom (Eds.), *Basic readings on the MMPI in psychology and medicine* (pp. 264–281). Minneapolis: University of Minnesota Press.

Williams, C. L., & Butcher, J. N. (1989a). An MMPI study of adolescents: I. Empirical validity of standard scales. *Psychological Assessment: A Journal of Consulting and Clinical Psychology*, *1*, 251–259.

Williams, C. L., & Butcher, J. N. (1989b). An MMPI study of adolescents: II. Verification and limitations of code type classifications. *Psychological Assessment: A Journal of Consulting and Clinical Psychology*, *1*, 260–265.

Williams, C. L., Butcher, J. N., Ben-Porath, Y. S., & Graham, J. R. (1992). *MMPI-A content scales: Assessing psychopathology in adolescents*. Minneapolis: University of Minnesota Press.

3

The Millon Clinical Multiaxial Inventory-III (MCMI-III)

Theodore Millon
Roger D. Davis

Assessment instruments are typically created and refined through multiple stages of validation, using large samples of subjects, often numbering in the thousands. Arguments for their validity rest on sample-based statistics, such as distribution properties, internal consistency, retest reliability, concurrent validity, and operating characteristics. Through these and similar statistics, text authors ensure that the intervening variables they have created and refined—whether self-report scale, checklist, or structured interview—bear as much fidelity to their respective hypothetical constructs as possible.

In contrast, clinicians are usually concerned with one patient at a time. Once the client's symptoms (Axis I) have been identified, the question with which the clinician is challenged is: Why? This question is explanatory, not merely descriptive in nature, and it is the clinician's presumed ability to confront this question directly that makes psychology a clinical, rather than merely a natural or observational, science. With the multiaxial model, first adopted in the *DSM-III,* personality disorders (Axis II) and the psychosocial environment (Axis IV) have been assigned contextual roles. The multiaxial model has been deliberately constructed such that the Axis I symptoms seek their reason for being the context of the client's larger personality style and its interaction with the current social milieu: The transaction between Axes II and IV produces Axis I.

What is being assessed, then, are not diseases, but contexts that transform the meaning of what might more properly be thought of as diseases, of the existing Axis I symptomatology. An anxiety disorder in a dependent individual is different from an anxiety disorder in a negativistic individual. Were this not true, were there an independence between clinical syndrome and personality style, there would be no reason for the multiaxial model to exist at all, for then personality and psychopathology would exist as completely separate phenomena, to be separately treated. Instead, personality and psychopathology are inextricably intertwined. The most important question an integrative assessment must answer is: Why this set of symptoms rather than some other? Obviously, any answer to this question goes beyond the level of description of either the symptoms or the client's personality alone, but instead draws the two together into a single, coherent, logical formulation. If the assessment achieves its purpose, then it has achieved what we refer to here as *idiographic validity*—that is, the case conceptualization of an intervening variable, and like any intervening variable, it stands in place of the person just as a scale stands in place of the construct it presumably measures.

The question is: How can clinicians go from population-based measures to idiographic validity? Paradoxically, the methodology through which assessment instruments are created is, in spirit, opposed to the goal that directs their use. In tapping dimensions of individual differences, only those dimensions taken as being common or fundamental to most persons are abstracted. Rich biographical specificities, the very thing that many would argue makes each individual, are left behind as residual variance, effectively aggregated out of the analysis.

First, some corpus of generalities is created—that is, persons are aggregated over in order to test or specify a portion of a nomological network, and then these generalities are *generalized back* to any individual who becomes a clinical focus. Profiles, for example, are profiles of population-based dimensions, refined through clinical samples, and then considered conjointly as a means of finding the individual in the instrument. The circle completes itself as a synthesis: From (1) rich idiographic individuality (all that the person is), we abstract (2) certain nomothetic commonalities, which in turn inform the individual assessment, giving rise to a kind of (3) nomothetic individuality. The fractionated person—the person who lies dispersed across many dimensions and content areas—is put back together again as the organic whole it once was. The scale scores that once were each an intervening variable for a population-based hypothetical construct now become personality profiles. The personality profile in turn becomes an intervening variable for the individual's entire personality. This kind of reflexivity in the clinical process is reminiscent of Loevinger's (1957) integrated process model of validity, and it argues for the process character of the validity in the individual assessment as well.

Although undoubtedly biased in our appraisal, we believe that no other inventory offers as potentially complete an integrative assessment of problematic personality styles and classical psychiatric disorders and as the Millon Clinical Multiaxial Inventory-II (MCMI-II). Moreover, perhaps no other instrument is both as coordinated with the official *DSM* taxonomy of personality disorders as conceptually consonant with the logic of the multiaxial model. As an objective psychodiagnostic instrument, it is designed for use with psychiatric patients who are undergoing clinical evaluation or are

involved in psychotherapy. The 175 true-false items of the MCMI are organized into 24 clinical scales and three modifier indices (see Table 3–1); 14 of
these scales are coordinated both to the personality disorders that make up
Axis II of the *DSM-III-R* and *DSM-IV* (American Psychiatric Association,
1987, 1994) and to the generative evolutionary theory elaborated by Millon
(1990). These 14 are further subdivided into the basic clinical personality
patterns, represented by 11 scales, and the more severe personality patterns, represented by the borderline, paranoid, and schizotypal. Of the remaining 24 scales, 7 represent common clinical syndromes of Axis I; 3 oth-

Table 3–1 MCMI-III Scales

Scale	Name
Clinical Personality Patterns	
1	Schizoid
2A	Avoidant
2B	Depressive
3	Dependent
4	Histrionic
5	Narcissistic
6A	Antisocial
6B	Aggressive (Sadistic)
7	Compulsive
8A	Passive-Aggressive (Negativistic)
8B	Self-Defeating
Severe Personality Pathology	
S	Schizotypal
C	Borderline
P	Paranoid
Clinical Syndromes	
A	Anxiety
H	Somatoform
N	Bipolar: Manic
D	Dysthymia
B	Alcohol Dependence
T	Drug Dependence
R	Post Traumatic Stress Disorder
Severe Syndromes	
SS	Thought Disorder
CC	Major Depression
PP	Delusional Disorder
Modifying Indices	
X	Disclosure
Y	Desirability
Z	Debasement
V	Validity

ers assess the more severe Axis I syndromes of Thought Disorder, Major Depression, and Delusional Disorder.

CONSTRUCTION I: THEORETICAL BASIS FOR SCALE SELECTION

Rather than developing independently and being left to stand as an unconnected body of structures and functions, a truly mature, integrated clinical science must embody and coordinate the following: (1) theories (i.e., explanatory and heuristic conceptual schemas that are consistent with established knowledge in both their own and related sciences, from which reasonably accurate propositions concerning pathological conditions can be both deduced and understood). Theories enable the development of a (2) formal nosology (i.e., a taxonomic classification of disorders that has been derived logically from the theory and arranged to provide a cohesive organization within which its major categories can be grouped and differentiated). Nosology permits the development of coordinated (3) instruments (i.e., tools that are empirically grounded and sufficiently sensitive quantitatively to allow the theory's propositions and hypotheses to be adequately investigated and evaluated, and the constructs comprising its nosology to be dimensionalized and measured). These instruments specify target areas for (4) planned interventions (i.e., strategies and techniques of therapy, designed in accord with the theory and oriented to modify problematic clinical characteristics in a manner consonant with professional standards and social responsibilities).

Philosophers of science are agreed that it is theory that provides the conceptual glue that binds a nosology together. A good theory not only summarizes and incorporates extant knowledge but it also possesses systematic import, in that it originates and develops new observations and new methods. In setting out a theory of personality prototypes, what is desired is not merely a descriptive list of disorders and their correlated attributes, but an explanatory derivation based on theoretical principles. The categories or dimensions of a taxonomy must account for themselves in some way. To address this question, a taxonomy must seek a theoretical schema that "carves nature at its joints," so to speak. The philosopher of science Carl Hempel (1965) clearly distinguished between natural and artificial classification systems. The difference, according to Hempel, is that natural classifications possess "systematic import." Hempel wrote:

> Distinctions between "natural" and "artificial" classifications may well be explicated as referring to the difference between classifications that are scientifically fruitful and those that are not: in a classification of the former kind, those characteristics of the elements which serve as criteria of membership in a given class are associated, universally or with high-probability, with more or less extensive clusters of other characteristics. . . . A classification of this sort should be viewed as somehow having objective existence in nature, as "carving nature at the joints." (pp. 146–147)

The biological sexes, male and female, and the periodic table of elements are both examples of classifications schemes that can be viewed as possessing "objective" existence in nature. To achieve such an end, the systems of kinds that undergird any domain of inquiry must itself be answerable to the question that forms the very point of departure for the scientific enterprise: Why does nature take this particular form rather than some other? Just as the clinician must ask Why these particular symptoms rather than others? The scientist must ask Why these particular personality disorders rather than others? The goal of science is to explain the objects and events we find in the world, and among the objects we find in the world are classification systems for objects themselves. Applied to a taxonomy, the question is thus rephrased: Why this particular system of kinds rather than some other? Theory and taxonomy, then, are intimately intertwined.

Is such a taxonomy possible? The stakes are nothing less than whether Axis II should be viewed as a semi-autonomous field possessing its own intrinsic taxonomy, or simply as an aggregation of diagnostic entities established according to behaviors that extrinsic cultural conventions deem problematic. Perhaps we live in a more enlightened age, but was it not so long ago that Sullivan proposed the "homosexual personality"—or that the Masochistic personality came under fire as being prejudicial against women? If particular characteristics or attributes are not to be spuriously elevated to a taxonic level, some set of logical principles will be required to assist in making this distinction. Although the *DSM* was deliberately and appropriately formulated to be atheoretical (but see Faust & Miner, 1986) in order not to alienate special interest groups among psychological consumers, ultimately one will require some way of culling the wheat from the chaff, which depends on the generativity of scientific theory.

In contrast to committee procedures, the deductive approach generates a true taxonomy to replace the primitive aggregation of taxons which preceded it, thus forming a true diagnostic schema. This generative power is what Hempel (1965) meant by the "systematic import" of a scientific classification. Meehl (1978) has noted that theoretical systems comprise related assertions, shared terms, and coordinated propositions that provide fertile grounds for deducing and deriving new empirical and clinical observations. What is elaborated and refined in theory is understanding—an ability to see relations more clearly, to conceptualize categories more accurately, and to create greater overall coherence in a subject (i.e., integrate its elements in a more logical, consistent, and intelligible fashion). Pretheoretic taxonomic boundaries that were set according to clinical intuition and empirical research can now be affirmed or refined by critically examining the disorders in relation to fundamental undergirding principles or polarities. Entirely new diagnostic categories may be generated, as was the case with the Avoidant personality, derived from Millon's system (1969). These polarities lend the model a holistic, cohesive structure that facilitates the comparison and contrast of groups along basic axes of content, not only sharpening the meanings of the taxonomic constructs derived but also protecting them from the construct drift incumbent to single perspective formulations (e.g., narcissism from a psychodynamic perspective) and the vicissitudes of diagnostic faddishness.

The theoretical model that follows is grounded in evolutionary theory. In essence, it seeks to explicate the structure and styles of personality with reference to deficient, imbalanced, or conflicted modes of ecological adaptation and reproductive strategy. The proposition that the development and function of personologic traits may be usefully explored through the lens of evolutionary principles has a long, if yet unfulfilled, tradition. Spencer (1870) and Huxley (1870) offered suggestions of this nature shortly after Darwin's seminal *Origins* was published. In more recent times, we have seen the emergence of sociobiology, an interdisciplinary science that explores the interface between human social functioning and evolutionary biology (Wilson, 1975, 1978).

Four domains or spheres in which evolutionary principles are demonstrated are labeled as existence, adaptation, replication, and abstraction. Existence relates the serendipitous transformation of random or less organized states into those possessing distinct structures of greater organization. Adaptation refers to homeostatic processes employed to sustain survival in open ecosystems. Replication pertains to reproduction styles that maximize the diversification and selection of ecologically effective attributes. Abstraction concerns the emergence of competencies that foster anticipatory planning and reasoned decision making. Polarities derived from the first three phases (pleasure-pain, passive-active, other-self) are used to construct a theoretically embedded classification system of personality disorders.

The first phase, existence, concerns the maintenance of integrative phenomena—whether nuclear particle, virus, or human being—against the background of entropic decompensation. Evolutionary mechanisms derived from this stage regard life enhancement and life preservation. The former are concerned with orienting individuals toward improvement in the quality of life; the latter are concerned with orienting individuals away from actions or environments that decrease the quality of life, or even jeopardize existence itself. These may be called *existential aims.* At the highest level of abstraction, such mechanisms form, phenomenologically or metaphorically expressed, a pleasure-pain polarity. Some individuals are conflicted in regard to these existential aims (e.g., the sadistic), which other possess deficits in these crucial substrates (e.g., the schizoid). In terms of neuropsychological growth stages (Millon, 1969, 1981), the pleasure-pain polarity is recapitulated in a "sensory-attachment" phase, the purpose of which is the largely innate and rather mechanical discrimination of pain and pleasure signals.

Existence, however, is but an initial phase. Once an integrative structure exists, it must maintain its existence through exchanges of energy and information with its environment. The second evolutionary stage relates to what is termed the *modes of adaptation;* it is also framed as a two-part polarity, a passive orientation, a tendency to accommodate to one's ecological niche, versus an active orientation, a tendency to modify or intervene in one's surrounds. These modes of adaptation differ from the first phase of evolution, in that they regard how that which is, endures. Unlike pleasure-pain and self-other, the active-passive polarity is truly unidimensional—one cannot be both active and passive at the same time. In terms of neurophysiological growth stages, these modes are recapitulated in a sensorimotor-autonomy phase, during which the child either progresses to active disposition toward his or her physical and social context or perpetuates the dependent mode of prenatal and infantile existence.

Although organisms may adapt well to their environments, the existence of any life form is time limited. To circumvent this limitation, organisms have developed *replicatory strategies* by which to leave progeny. These strategies regard what biologists have referred to as an r (or self-propagating) strategy at one polar extreme, and a K (or other-nurturing) strategy at the second extreme. Psychologically, the former strategy is disposed toward actions that are egotistic, insensitive, inconsiderate, and uncaring; whereas the latter is disposed toward actions that are affiliative, intimate, protective, and solicitous (Gilligan, 1982; Rushton, 1985; Wilson, 1978). Like pleasure-pain, the self-other polarity is not truly unidimensional. Some personality disorders are conflicted on this polarity, such as the compulsive and passive-aggressive. A very brief description of each of the derived personality patterns follows.

Deriving the Axis II Personality Styles from the Polarity Model

Some personalities exhibit a reasonable balance on one or other of the polarity pairs. Not all individuals fall at the center, of course. Individual differences in both personality features and overall style will reflect the relative positions and strengths of each polarity component. Personalities we have termed deficient lack the capacity to experience or to enact certain aspects of the three polarities (e.g., the schizoid has a faulty substrate for both "pleasure" and "pain"); those spoken of as imbalanced lean strongly toward one or another extreme of a polarity (e.g., the dependent is oriented almost exclusively to receiving the support and nurturance of "others"); and those we judge conflicted or reversed struggle with ambivalences toward opposing ends of a bipolarity (e.g., the negativistic vacillates between adhering to the expectancies of "others" versus enacting what is wished for one's "self"). In the explications that follow, it is suggested that the reader not only attend to the trait content of the various patterns but particularly to their embeddedness in the polarity model from which they are derivable (see Figure 3–1). Consistent with integrative logic, this theoretical foundation will prove important both in MCMI interpretation and in intervention.

Basic Personality Patterns

The following descriptions of the Axis II constructs focus on ways of functioning that are characteristic of these personality patterns even under normal circumstances. They reflect those enduring and pervasive traits that represent patient styles of behaving, perceiving, thinking, feeling, and relating to others. Although patients in crisis exhibit more distinctive pathological

	Existential Aim		Replication Strategy		
	Life Enhancement	Life Preservation	Reproductive Propagation	Reproductive Nurturance	
Deficiency, Imbalance, Conflict	Pleasure - Pain		Self - Other		
	Pleasure-Pain - +	Pleasure-Pain (Reversal)	Self - Other +	Self + Other -	Self-Other (Reversal)
Adaptation Mode	DSM Personality Disorders				
Passive: Accommodation	Schizoid / Depressive	Masochistic	Dependent	Narcissistic	Compulsive
Active: Modification	Avoidant	Sadistic	Histrionic	Antisocial	Negativistic
Structural Pathology	Schizotypal	Borderline, Paranoid	Borderline	Paranoid	Borderline, Paranoid

Figure 3–1   **Polarity Model and its Personality Disorder Derivatives**

symptoms, the features noted refer to their premorbid characterological pattern. They are listed in accord with the scales developed in the MCMI-III to record the degree to which these features are represented on the inventory.

Scale 1: Schizoid Personality (16 items). These patients are noted by their lack of desire and their inability to experience deeply either pleasure or pain. They tend to be apathetic, listless, distant, and asocial. Needs for affection as well as emotional feelings are minimal. The individual is typically a passive observer, detached from the rewards as well as from the demands of human relationships.

Scale 2A: Avoidant Personality (16 items). These patients experience few positive reinforcements from either self or others, are perennially on guard, and are disposed to distance themselves from what they feel will be life's painful experiences. Their adaptive strategy reflects a deeply ingrained fear and mistrust of others. Despite desires to relate, they have learned that it is best to deny these feelings and maintain a good measure of interpersonal distance.

Scale 2B: Depressive Personality (15 items). Both avoidant and depressive personalities have in common a diminished ability to experience pleasure and a comparable tendency to be overly sensitive to pain—that is, events of a foreboding, disquieting, and anguishing character. However, avoidants have learned to anticipate these troublesome events, taking proactive steps to distance from them, to decrease their occurrence by minimizing involvements with others, and by aspiring to want or possess little, lest it be unattainable or quickly withdrawn. Depressives are notably more passive that the anxiously proactive avoidant. They permit themselves to be stuck in the mire of feeling helpless and hopeless, do little to eschew pain, and simply give in to what they feel is life's inevitable helplessness. With nothing that can be done to alter their circumstances, depressives either sit immobile, feeling incompetent, sorrowful, useless and unworthy, or simply cry out in painful misery.

Scale 3: Dependent Personality (16 items).   Dependent individuals have learned not only to turn to others as their source of nurturance and security but also to wait passively for others to take the initiative. They are typified by a search for relationships in which they can lean on others for affection, security, and guidance. As a function of life's experiences, they have simply learned the comforts of assuming a passive role in interpersonal relations, accepting what kindness and support they may find, and willingly submitting to the wishes of others in order to maintain their affection and support.

Scale 4. Histrionic Personality (17 items).   Although, like the Dependent personality, these individuals turn toward others, they appear on the surface to be quite *unlike* their passive counterparts. This difference owes to the active-dependent's facile and enterprising manipulations to maximize the attention and favor of others, as well as to avoid their indifference. They often show an insatiable, if not indiscriminate, search for stimulation and affection. Beneath a guise of confidence and self-assurance lies a fear of genuine independence and a constant need for signs of acceptance and approval.

Scale 5: Narcissistic Personality (24 items).   These individuals are noted for their egotistic self-involvement in which they experience significant pleasure by simply focusing on themselves. Early experience has taught them to have a high degree of self-esteem, but this confidence may be founded on false premises. Nevertheless, they assume that others will recognize their special qualities, and they benignly exploit others for their own advantage. Although the tributes of others are both welcome and encouraged, their sense of superiority requires little confirmation through genuine accomplishments or social approval. The belief that things simply will work out well for them undermines what little incentive they may have to engage in the reciprocal give and take of social life.

Scale 6A: Antisocial Personality (17 items).   These individuals anticipate pain and suffering at the hands of others and act forcefully to counteract it through duplicitous and illegal behaviors designed to exploit others for self-gain. They are skeptical concerning the motives of others, have a strong desire to maintain their autonomy, and wish revenge for what they judge the injustices of the past. Often irresponsible and impulsive, they see their behaviors as justified because others are considered harmful and untrustworthy; their own ruthlessness is only a means to head off abuse and victimization.

Scale 6B: Sadistic (Aggressive) Personality (20 items). The orientation incorporates the sadistic personality disorder listed in the appendix of the *DSM-III-R,* recognizing the clinical features of individuals who are not publicly antisocial, but whose behaviors abuse and humiliate others, no less violate their rights and feelings. Termed *aggressive* personalities in the theory (Millon, 1986a, 1986b), they are generally hostile and combative, and are indifferent to, if not pleased by, the negative consequences of their abusive and brutal behaviors. Although they may cloak or sublimate their more malicious and power-oriented tendencies in socially approved vocations, they are seen in private as dominating and antagonistic persons.

Scale 7: Compulsive Personality (17 items). These individuals have been shaped into accepting the reinforcements imposed on them by others. Their prudent and perfectionistic ways derive from a conflict between hostility toward others and a strong fear of social disapproval. They resolve this ambivalence by overconforming behaviors that suppress their strong resentments and by placing high demands on themselves. Self-restraint serves to control their intense oppositional feelings, resulting in an overt passivity and public compliance. Lurking behind this front of propriety and constraint, however, are intense oppositional feelings that occasionally break through their controls.

Scale 8A: Negativistic (Passive-Aggressive) Personality (16 items). These individuals struggle between following the rewards offered by others as opposed to those desired by themselves. This dilemma represents an inability to resolve struggles similar to those of passive-ambivalents (compulsives); however, the conflicts of the active-ambivalent personality remain on the surface and intrude into everyday life. These patients get themselves caught up in endless wrangles and disappointments as they vacillate between deferential behavior and obedience one time, and defiance and negativism the next. They display an erratic pattern of explosive anger or stubbornness intermingled with periods of guilt and contrition.

Scale 8B: Self-Defeating (Masochistic) Personality (15 items). Relating to others in a self-sacrificing manner, these persons allow, if not encourage, others to take advantage of them. Focusing on their very worst features, many feel that they deserve being shamed and humbled. To compound their pain and anguish, states they experience as familiar, they actively and repetitively recall their past misfortunes and transform otherwise fortunate circumstances into potentially problematic ones. Typically acting in an unassuming and self-denigrating way, they will often magnify their flaws and place themselves in an inferior light or abject position.

Structural Personality Pathologies

Three more decompensated patterns of personality pathology in the *DSM* are perceived in the theory as elaborations of the more basic personality styles that display severe structural defects owing to the press of persistent or intense adversity. No matter how severe or maladaptive these structural defects may be, they are distortions in the underlying organization of personality that are consistent with one of the basic styles of personality. For example, the schizotypal personality, assessed on MCMI-III scale S, represents a structurally defective variant among patients characterized usually by one of the two basic detached personality styles, the schizoid or the avoidant. Similarly, the *DSM-IV* borderline personality, assessed on scale C, is seen as a structurally disturbed variant of several personality styles—for example, the ambivalent patterns, such as the passive-aggressive and self-defeating styles. The paranoid personality, noted on scale P, is a structurally problematic form, usually of the two independent personality styles, the narcissistic and the antisocial.

Scale S: Schizotypal Personality (16 items).   The *DSM* schizotypal personality disorder represents a poorly integrated and dysfunctionally detached individual. These patients prefer social isolation, with few, if any, personal attachments and obligations. Inclined to be either autistic or cognitively confused, they think tangentially and often seem self-absorbed and ruminative. Behavioral eccentricities are notable, and the patients are often seen as strange or different. Depending on whether their pattern has basically been active or passive, there will be either an anxious wariness and hypersensitivity or an emotional flattening and lack of affect.

Scale C: Borderline Personality (16 items).   The *DSM* borderline personality disorder can occur with a wide number of the theory's milder personality styles. Structurally defective, borderlines experience extreme endogenous moods, with recurring periods of dejection and apathy, often interspersed with spells of anger, anxiety, or euphoria. What distinguishes them most clearly from the two other more severe personalities, the schizotypal and the paranoid, is the constant shifting of moods, seen most clearly in the instability and lability of their affect. Many share recurring self-mutilating and suicidal thoughts, appear overly preoccupied with securing affection, have difficulty maintaining a sense of identity, and display a cognitive affective ambivalence.

Scale P: Paranoid Personality (17 items).   The *DSM* paranoid personality disorder covaries most frequently with three of the theory's personality styles—the narcissistic, antisocial, and aggressive-sadistic types. Here one sees a vigilant mistrust of others and a defensiveness against imagined or anticipated criticism and deception. There is an abrasive irritability and a tendency to precipitate exasperation and anger in others. There is a fear of losing independence, leading these patients to resist external influence and control vigorously.

Clinical Syndromes (Axis I Scales)

Although the *DSM* Axis II personality patterns have been derived deductively from a theoretical model, those of Axis I have not. The Axis I categories scaled by the MCMI have been included because of their prevalence and relevance to clinical work. Typical of those of moderate severity that are assessed on the MCMI are Anxiety, Somatoform, Bipolar-Manic, Dysthymia, PTSD, Alcohol abuse, and Drug abuse; three more severe disorders—Psychotic Thinking, Major Depression, and Delusion Disorders—are tapped as well. Although certain clinical syndromes arise most frequently among particular personality styles, each of these symptom conditions occurs in several patterns. For example, Dysthymia (scale D) occurs most often among avoidant, dependent, passive-aggressive, and self-defeating personalities, whereas Drug Dependence (scale T) is found primarily among histrionic, narcissistic, and antisocial styles.

In contrast to the personality disorders (Axis II), the clinical syndrome disorders making up Axis I are often best seen as extensions or distortions of the patient's basic personality patterns. These Axis I clinical syndromes tend to stand out distinctly or to be transient states, waxing and waning over time, depending on the impact of stressful situations. Typically, they are exaggerations of the patient's basic personality.

Most of the clinical syndromes described in this section are of the reactive kind and are of briefer duration than the personality disorders. They usually represent states in which an active pathological process is clearly manifested. Many of these symptoms are precipitated by external events. Typically, they appear in somewhat striking or dramatic form, often accentuating or intensifying the patients' more routine features. During periods of active pathology, it is not uncommon for several symptoms to covary at any time and to change over time in their degrees of prominence. Scales A, H, N, D, B, and T represent disorders of moderate severity; scales SS, CC, and PP reflect disorders of marked severity.

Scale A: Anxiety (14 items). Patients achieving high scores often report feeling either apprehensive or specifically phobic; they are typically tense, indecisive, and restless and often complain of a variety of physical discomforts, such as tightness, excessive perspiration, ill-defined muscular aches, and nausea. A review of the specific items on the scale will aid in determining whether the patient is primarily phobic. Most, however, give evidence of a generalized state of tension, manifested by an inability to relax, a fidgety quality to movements, and a readiness to overreact and be easily startled.

Somatic discomforts—for example, clammy hands or upset stomach—are also characteristic. Also notable is an apprehensive sense that problems are imminent, a hyperalertness to one's environment, an edginess, and a generalized touchiness.

Scale H: Somatoform (12 items).   Here we see psychological difficulties expressed through somatic channels, persistent periods of fatigue and weakness, and a preoccupation with ill health and a variety of often dramatic but largely nonspecific pains in different and unrelated regions of the body. Some patients demonstrate a primary somatization disorder that is manifested by recurrent, multiple somatic complaints, often presented in a dramatic, vague, or exaggerated way. Others have a history that may be best considered hypochondriacal, since they interpret minor physical discomforts or sensations as signifying a serious ailment. If diseases are factually present, they tend to be overinterpreted, despite medical reassurance. Typically, these somatic complaints are employed to gain attention.

Scale N: Bipolar: Manic (13 items).   This high-scoring patient evidences periods of restless overactivity and distractibility, pressured speech, impulsiveness, and irritability. Also evident may be an unselective enthusiasm; planning for unrealistic goals; an intrusive, pressured, and demanding quality to interpersonal relations; decreased need for sleep; flights of ideas; and rapid and labile shifts of mood. Very high scores may signify psychotic processes, including delusions or hallucinations.

Scale D: Dysthymia (14 items).   The high-scoring patient remains involved in everyday life but has been concerned over a period of two or more years with feelings of discouragement or guilt, a lack of initiative and behavioral apathy, low self-esteem, and frequently voiced futility and self-deprecatory comments. During these periods of dejection, there may be a tearfulness, suicidal ideation, a pessimistic outlook toward the future, social withdrawal, poor appetite or overeating, chronic fatigue, poor concentration, a loss of interest in pleasurable activities, and a decreased effectiveness in fulfilling ordinary and routine life tasks. Unless scale CC (Major Depression) is also elevated, there is little likelihood that psychotic features will be evident. Close examination of the specific components of the patient's high score should enable the clinician to discern the nature of the dysthymic mood (e.g., low self-esteem or hopelessness).

Scale B: Alcohol Dependence (15 items).   The high-scoring patient probably has a history of alcoholism; may have made efforts to overcome the difficulty, with minimal success; and, as a consequence, experiences considerable discomfort in both family and work settings. What is of value in this and the subsequent scale (Drug Dependence) is the opportunity to understand the problem within the context of the patient's overall personality style.

Scale T: Drug Dependence (14 items). The high-scoring individual is likely to have had a recurrent or recent history of drug abuse. There is likely to be difficulty in restraining impulses or keeping them within conventional social limits, as well as an inability to manage the personal consequences of these behaviors. Comprising many subtle and indirect items, this scale may be helpful in identifying those with problems of drug abuse who are not readily disposed to admit their difficulties.

Scale R: Post-traumatic Stress Disorder (16 items). PTSD is the result of an event that involved a threat to the patient's life and caused intense fear or feelings of helplessness. Images and emotions associated with the trauma result in distressing recollections and nightmares that reactivate the feelings generated by the original event. Symptoms of anxious arousal (e.g., startle response, hypervigilance) persist, and the patient avoids circumstances associated with the trauma.

Severe Syndromes

Scale SS: Thought Disorder (17 items). Depending on the length and course of the problem, these patients are usually classified as schizophrenic, schizophreniform, or brief reactive psychosis. They may periodically exhibit incongruous, disorganized, or regressive behavior; often appear confused and disoriented; and occasionally display inappropriate affect, scattered hallucinations, and unsystematic delusions. Their thinking may be fragmented or bizarre, their feelings may be blunted, and they may have a pervasive sense of being isolated and misunderstood by others. Withdrawn, seclusive, and secretive behavior may be notable.

Scale CC: Major Depression (17 items). These patients are usually incapable of functioning within their normal environment; they are severely depressed and express a dread of the future, suicidal ideation, and a sense of hopeless resignation. Some exhibit marked motor retardation, whereas others display an agitated quality, incessantly pacing about and bemoaning their sorry state. Several somatic processes are often disturbed during these periods—notably, there may be a decreased or increased appetite, fatigue, weight loss or gain, insomnia, or early rising. Problems of concentration are common, as are feelings of worthlessness and/or guilt. Repetitive fearfulness and brooding are frequently in evidence. Depending on the underlying personality style, there may be a shy, introverted, and seclusive pattern; a sluggish immobility; or an irritable, complaining, and whining tone.

Scale PP: Delusional Disorder (13 items). This high-scoring patient, often considered acutely paranoid, may become intermittently belligerent, voicing irrational but interconnected sets of delusions of a jealous, persecutory, or grandiose nature. Depending on the constellation of other concurrent syndromes, there may be clear-cut signs of disturbed thinking and ideas of reference. Moods usually are hostile, and feelings of being picked on and mistreated are expressed. A tense undercurrent of suspiciousness, vigilance, and an alertness of possible betrayal are typical concomitants.

Modifier Indices

The literature is replete with studies suggesting factors that may distort the results of various self-report inventories. These distortions may produce test data that either require adjustments to increase their validity or are so awry that they are totally unusable for either measurement or interpretive purposes. However, evidence for the importance of these confounding factors is mixed. Deliberate misrepresentation or random responding on personality or clinical inventories is much less common than often thought. Similarly, the role of response styles as a source of distortion seems to be a minor factor in comparison to the content of substantive scales. Inventories whose scoring is substantially determined by external-criterion research are only minimally affected by problems of stylistic or intentional distortion; potentially confounding items either fail to correlate with external criteria and are thereby removed, or prove to be predictive of these criteria.

As evident from our efforts to appraise and control for these factors, the preceding argument has not been interpreted as a rationale for dismissing the potential impact of problematic test-taking attitudes. The first of the gauges to be appraised are the four highly unusual items that make up the *validity index*. On the machine-scored profile printout, index scores of 2 or more are identified as invalid; a score of 0 is recorded as valid; and a score of 1 on the index is noted by the statement "questionable validity." The automated interpretive report advises readers to be cautious in accepting the interpretations of protocols with a validity index score of 1; it records protocols as invalid and terminates the report when two or more index items are marked. Despite its brevity, the validity index has proved to be highly sensitive to careless, confused, or random responding.

The *disclosure level,* labeled scale X, is the second of the indices that may signify problematic response behaviors, notably whether the patient was inclined to freely reveal self, on the one hand, or to be reticent and secretive, on the other.

Calculated by the degree of positive or negative deviation from the midrange of an adjusted composite raw score total of 10 basic personality scales, it is further transformed into a base-rate (BR) score equivalent. Corrections are made only if the adjusted composite raw score is greater than 400 or less than 250. If the composite sum is less than 145 or greater than 590, however, the results should be considered invalid, and are so indicated on the profile page of the interpretive report. Viewed on its own as a single measure, a low BR score on scale X indicates either a general hesitancy and reserve or a broad unwillingness to be candid about one's psychological feelings and problems. Conversely, a high BR score on scale X suggests an unusually open and self-revealing attitude, not only while completing the inventory but probably also in discussing one's emotional difficulties with others.

The *desirability gauge,* referred to as scale Y, seeks to identify the degree to which the results may have been affected by the patient's inclination to appear socially attractive, morally virtuous, and/or emotionally well composed. High BR scores on scale Y signify the tendency to place oneself in a favorable light; the higher the score, the greater the care that must be given to discovering what the patient may be concealing about his or her psychological or interpersonal difficulties.

Scale Z, the *debasement measure,* reflects tendencies opposite to those of scale Y, although on occasion both indexes are high, especially among patients who are unusually self-disclosing (scale X). In general, high BR scores on scale Z suggest inclinations to depreciate or devalue oneself by presenting emotional and personal difficulties in stronger terms than are likely to be uncovered upon objective review. Especially high scores deserve closer examination than usual, not only for purposes of gaining a more accurate assessment of what might prove to be a distorted level of psychological severity but also to inquire whether the responses signify a call for help—a drawing of attention by a patient experiencing an especially distressing degree of emotional turmoil.

The computer-based interpretive report provides an analysis of the likely meaning of the configuration of scales X, Y, and Z. For example, a low BR on scales X and Y, with a high score on scale Z, suggests a moderate exaggeration of current emotional problems that is likely to have been sufficiently corrected so as to retain the MCMI-III's interpretive validity.

CONSTRUCTION II: ITEM SELECTION AND SCALE CONSTRUCTION

This section will discuss how new items were generated and how clinicians were recruited to participate in the development project. The information obtained from clinicians will be described, as will the procedures used to evaluate the new items and develop the MCMI-III scales.

Item Development

The revision process began with the selection of 150 new items from a large item pool. These new items were written (1) to sample the domains of two new scales, Depressive (scale 2B) and Post-Traumatic Stress Disorder (scale R), and (2) to ensure that all MCMI-III scales paralleled the diagnostic criteria proposed for the *DSM-IV* (American Psychiatric Association, 1993).

In generating new items, the goal was to produce statements that were congruent with the instrument's guiding theoretical system (discussed above) and with official diagnostic. To achieve this goal, the *DSM-IV* criteria were rephrased to make them understandable as inventory items and to reflect personality attributes consonant with the theory. For example, the second *DSM-IV* schizoid criterion is "almost always chooses solitary activities." The comparable text item (item 27) is "When I have a choice, I prefer to do things alone." The third schizoid *DSM-IV* criterion is "has little, if any, interest in having sexual experiences with another person." In the test, this is phrased "I've always had less interest in sex than most people do" (item 46). The fourth *DSM-IV* criterion is "takes pleasure in few, if any, activities." In the test, this became "Few things in life give me pleasure" (item 148). The first *DSM-IV* criterion for the paranoid personality, "suspects, without sufficient basis, that others are exploiting, harming, or deceiving him or her," is represented as "Sneaky people often try to get the credit for things I have done or thought of" (item 103). *DSM-IV* paranoid criterion 5 is "persistently bears grudges, i.e., is unforgiving of insults, injuries, or slights." An analogous test item is "I never forgive an insult or forget an embarrassment that someone caused me" (item 42). A complete criterion-item correspondence is given in Appendix A of the MCMI-III manual. All items that met theoretical-structural goals (Millon, 1987a) were added to the 175 items of the MCMI-II. The resulting 325-item form was called the MCMI-II Research Form (MCMI-II-R).

Research Participants

Several hundred clinicians who regularly use the MCMI-II for evaluating and treating adult clients were asked to participate in the revision research. Between June 1992 and February 1993, data were collected from 1,079 subjects in 26 states and Canada. Each subject was administered the MCMI-II-R. In addition, clinicians rated the subjects on several clinical characteristics.

Subjects also completed at least one of the following collateral tests: (1) the Beck Depression Inventory (BDI; Beck & Steer, 1987), (2) the General Behavior Inventory (GBI; Depue et al., 1981), (3) the Impact of Events Scale (IOES; Horowitz, Wilner, & Alvarez, 1979), (4) the Michigan Alcoholism Screening Test (MAST; Selzer, 1971), (5) the MMPI-2 (Butcher, Dahlstrom, Graham, Tellegen, & Kaemmer, 1991), (6) the State-Trait Anxiety Inventory (STAI; Spielberger, 1983), and (7) the Symptom Checklist-90-Revised (SCL-90-R; Derogatis, 1994).

All subjects signed informed consent forms. The subjects were not paid; clinicians received National Computer Systems (NCS) credits for amounts that approximated the cost of an automated interpretive report. Clinicians were also able to generate separate MCMI-II scores and interpretive reports from the participants' responses on the MCMI-II-R. From the original pool of 1,079 clinical subjects, 998 subjects were retained for analyses and divided into two groups. One (n = 600) was used to define the MCMI-III scales and to develop base rate scores, and the other (n = 398) was used for cross-validation. Demographic and clinical information for the two subject groups is presented in Tables 2a and 2b of the MCMI-III manual. Some 87 subjects were administered the MCMI-III-R again 5 to 14 days after the first administration. Data from the second administration were used to estimate retest stability of the MCMI-III scales.

Clinician Ratings

Clinicians completed a brief Clinician's Form for MCMI-II-R that required a variety of ratings for each participating subject. This form included a description of 11 personality patterns and 3 severe personality patterns. For each of his or her subjects, the clinician was asked to indicate the first, second, and third most prominent personality patterns displayed. Clinicians also indicated which of these were traits and which were extreme enough to possibly qualify as personality disorders. Similar ratings were made for the three severe personality patterns. Clinicians also indicated their level of confidence in these ratings. Formal diagnostic interviews were not included as part of the MCMI-III development project. Also included on the form was a list of 10 presenting problems or syndromes. Clinicians were asked to indicate which problem was the most prominent and which was the second most prominent (i.e., notably present but not as prominent as the first).

Development of the Clinical Scales

The scale development phase, which was conducted using the 600 subjects in the development sample, began by examining the endorsement rates for the 325 items. Any item with a particularly low or high endorsement rate was evaluated to ensure that the rate was not unexpected given the item content. Items with unexpectedly high or low endorsement rates were eliminated from consideration. Each item that remained after the first screening was assigned to one MCMI-III scale on the basis of item content. These items, defined as the prototype items for each scale, were assigned a scoring weight of 2 when the scale scores were computed.

After these preliminary scales (i.e., scales containing only prototype items) were constructed, the following statistics were computed: internal consistency reliability (coefficient alpha); corrected item-total correlations (i.e., correlations between each item and its scale score calculated without that item); correlations between item responses and scores on other preliminary MCMI-III scales, clinician ratings, and collateral test scores; and correlations between scale scores and other preliminary MCMI-III scale scores, MCMI-II scale scores, clinician ratings, and collateral test scores.

Development of the final MCMI-III scales was an iterative process in which all of the statistics listed above were recomputed and reevaluated as items were added to or removed from scales. For each iteration, each item was required to appear as a prototype on exactly one scale. After the first iteration, most items also appeared as nonprototype items on other scales, where they were assigned a weight of 1. Test length decreased after each iteration as items were dropped from consideration. At the end of the scale development phase, 175 of the original 325 items remained on at least one of the 28 scales (including 24 clinical scales, 3 modifying indices, and the validity scale).

Development of the Modifying Indices

For the MCMI-II, the three modifying indices (scales X, Y, and Z) were empirically derived by asking students to take the test while keeping a particular response set in mind (e.g., trying to put one's best foot forward and to appear as psychologically healthy as possible for the Desirability index). For the MCMI-III, such empirical studies were not conducted. Instead, all items that appeared on MCMI-II scales X, Y, and Z and that were retained on the MCMI-III clinical scales were assigned to the appropriate MCMI-III modifying index. Items from the MCMI-II modifying indices that were not included on the MCMI-III were replaced with items with similar content.

Base-Rate Scores

The traditional procedure of transforming raw scores into standard scores is inappropriate under certain circumstances. Standard scores assume normal distributions or frequency spreads that are equivalent for the traits or dimensions being measured. This assumption is not met when a set of scales is designed to represent personality or clinical syndromes, since neither is normally distributed or of equal prevalence in populations of patients. In addition, a clinical instrument is not designed to place a patient at a point on a frequency distribution but, rather, is intended to indicate whether the patient belongs in a particular diagnostic category. Transformation scores for such instruments that are more directly meaningful and useful than conventional standard scores need to be constructed (Meehl & Rosen, 1955).

For the MCMI, raw scores have been transformed into base-rate (BR) scores, a conversion determined by personality and diagnostic prevalence estimates. In these studies, clinicians were asked to diagnose their patients with reference to the *DSM* criteria for each MCMI-III related personality disorder and clinical syndrome. These investigations produced estimates of the prevalence data, which were then considered in relation to other prevalence studies and settings in which the MCMI-III might be used to produce the final prevalence estimates. Both the BR scores and the more familiar T score or percentile rank are transformations of the raw scores, and each has the purpose of putting the raw scores on a common metric. Unlike T scores or percentile ranks, however, the BR scores are created such that the percentage of the clinical population deemed diagnosable with a particular disorder falls either (1) at or above a common threshold (clinical scales) or (2) at a particular rank order in the profile (personality scales). Thus, if 5 percent of the clinical population is deemed to possess a schizoid pattern as its primary personality style, and another 2 percent the schizoid pattern as a secondary feature, then the raw scores have been transformed so that the normative sample reflects these *prevalence* or *base* rates.

Obviously, the BR score implies that we are not so much interested in the "absolute quantity" of a particular trait as in the implications of that quantity for psychological functioning. While a certain level of narcissism is considered healthy in our society, the same level of antisocial behavior may not be; we might treat the second, but not the first. Thus, the BR concept recognizes that equal quantities of a trait or characteristic have differential pathological implications, and the intention of the transformation is to equate the scales in terms of the implications of a particular quantity for psychological functioning. The base-rate score simply represents the most direct way of getting at such considerations.

ADMINISTRATION AND SCORING

Administration of the MCMI-II follows a procedure similar to that of most self-report inventories. Test directions, a patient information chart, an identification grid, and special coding sections for clinicians are printed on the front page. True and false bubbles are printed next to each of the 175 item statements. This increases the accuracy of patient markings and allows the clinician to scan individual item responses. In addition, although some clients may require supervision, the MCMI can be administered routinely by office or hospital personnel with a minimum of training. The examiner should scan the test booklet for double markings and excessive omissions when it is returned; examinees should be gently encouraged to resolve such ambiguities. A Spanish-language version is available.

A principal goal in constructing the MCMI was to keep the total number of items small enough to encourage use in diverse diagnostic and treatment settings, yet large enough to permit the assessment of a wide range of clinically relevant behaviors. At 175 items, the final form is much shorter than comparable instruments. Potentially objectionable items were screened out, and terminology was geared to an eighth-grade reading level. The majority of clients can complete the MCMI in 20 to 30 minutes, facilitating relatively simple and rapid administration, and minimizing client resistance and fatigue.

Computer scoring is the fastest and most convenient method for obtaining MCMI profiles. The MCMI interpretive report, available from National Computer Systems, consists of a computer plotted Profile Report and a theoretically and empirically based narrative that integrates clients' primary Axis II personality styles and Axis I symptom features. These reports can be obtained from NCS in several ways. Mail-in scoring provides 24-hour turnaround. Alternately, results can be keyed in item by item through teleprocessing technology. By far the most popular, however, is computer administration through the MICROTEST™ assessment software. Here, the traditional paper and pencil format is bypassed completely in favor of computer administration and scoring. Results can be printed on most popular printers. Although item-weighting, modifying indices, and look-up tables greatly complicate hand-scoring (research indicates that most scorers make one or more errors, sometimes severe enough to change the resulting profile), scoring templates have been made available primarily for students, researchers, and public agencies.

INTERPRETATION OF MCMI PROFILES

The MCMI offers several layers or levels of interpretation. Consistent with integrative logic, each level subsumes the previous one in an explanatory hierarchy, demanding a higher order of complexity and integration. At the first level, the personality and clinical syndrome scales are simply examined for single-scale elevations. If these scales are sufficiently elevated, a diagnosis of personality disorder may be warranted. Although this level of interpretation is usually necessary when writing clinical reports, where the patient typically receives diagnoses listed by axis, this is the weakest layer of clinical interpretation, and should never be a stopping point, if only because it raises more questions than it answers. As noted near the beginning of this chapter, it is the transaction between Axes II and IV produces Axis I. In the *DSM*, personality and clinical symptoms have been separated, but only for heuristic purposes. Real individuals do not exist as axes, but rather as entities. Descriptive validity in the individual case—that is, identifying the facts or symptoms of the case—is only the beginning. A genuinely integrative assessment must account for the existence of a particular set of traits and symptoms, and be prepared to argue why this particular set exists rather than some other. The ability to address this question is what differentiates a clinical science from one that is merely observational. To illustrate this process, the following case is presented.

Case Study

Ken, a 29-year-old Caucasian male, formerly majoring in accounting, presented at the outpatient center of a large psychiatric hospital complaining of suicidal thoughts and paranoid ideation. A 10-year psychiatric history revealed that Ken had been treated by numerous mental health professionals and had received almost as many diagnoses, including PTSD, manic depression, and paranoid schizophrenia.

Ken responded easily during the interview, presenting himself as helpless and overcome. He readily offered psychologically salient information, noting that his problems began with a "nervous breakdown." 10 years previous, when the male companion with whom he was in the process of breaking up was diagnosed with terminal lung cancer. He admitted that it was the first real relationship that he has ever had. His companion was substantially older and established, and was, at that time, considered a relatively powerful political figure in their community. He had always taken care of Ken. However, in the week before receiving the unfortunate diagnosis, Ken finally decided that he needed to end the relationship in order to pursue a heterosexual lifestyle. He was already moving his belongings out of their apartment when the announcement came.

Further explorations revealed that Ken's father had abandoned the family for "the lady across the street," a close friend of his mother's, when Ken was 12 years old. Although support payments were regularly made, the father was never again emotionally close to his only son, but instead adopted the new wife's children as his own. In addition, his father was an alcoholic. Following the dissolution of the family, Ken's mother was devastated and turned to her son for emotional support. To his shame, Ken did not know how to deal with his mother's emotions, wanting, but feeling incapable, or nurturing her. His grades, which had previously been in the high-average range, plummeted, and by the age of 15 he was abusing alcohol and smoking an ounce of marijuana a week. During this time he also became involved in homosexual relationships. These, he felt, explained why "my social skills didn't develop." His substance abuse was rationalized as an attempt at self-medication so that he could feel comfortable around people.

Diagnostic testing revealed a WAIS-R Verbal IQ of 106 and a Performance IQ of 103 with a relative weakness in digit span, with a scaled score of 5. In the absence of other information, this was attributed to chronic drug use. The Rorschach Inkblot Test, scored according to the Comprehensive System, revealed a positive Schizophrenia Index, many Level 1 Deviant Verbalizations, and a high X-minus percent, indicating numerous violations of the contours of the blots. Stories told to the Thematic Apperception Test repeatedly featured a more powerful figure taking an interest in and rescuing a more helpless one.

Ken's MCMI-III profile is presented in Figure 3–2. Note that elevations are recorded on a BR scale ranging from 0 to 115. The BR score is intended to suggest positive characteristics of psychopathology. In Ken's case, three personality disorders clearly spike higher than the others: the Avoidant, Dependent, and Paranoid. While it has become traditional to view BR 75 as indicating the presence of either a significant personality trait or a personality disorder, there are, as with every test, always false positives and false negatives. In the absence of auxiliary confirmatory evidence, there is always a possibility of interpretive error in diagnosing a personality disorder, or worse, multiple personality disorders, wherever base rate scores equal or exceed a certain threshold. In a false-negative result, a test indicates the presence of pathology where pathology does not exist. In a false-negative result, a test indicates the absence of pathology where pathology in fact exists. As with most tests, false positives and false negatives derive principally from the insensitivity of any rigorous procedure, whether self-report, interview, or physiological measure, to contextual factors. Such factors must always be taken into consideration—a function of trained clinical judgment. In the featured

Millon Clinical Multiaxial Inventory - III
CONFIDENTIAL INFORMATION FOR PROFESSIONAL USE ONLY

CATEGORY		SCORE RAW	SCORE BR	PROFILE OF BR SCORES	DIAGNOSTIC SCALES
MODIFYING INDICES	X	140	90		DISCLOSURE
	Y	4	20		DESIRABILITY
	Z	16	97		DEBASEMENT
CLINICAL PERSONALITY PATTERNS	1	15	78		SCHIZOID
	2A	19	98		AVOIDANT
	2B	18	70		DEPRESSIVE
	3	10	67		DEPENDENT
	4	5	16		HISTRIONIC
	5	12	55		NARCISSISTIC
	6A	8	59		ANTISOCIAL
	6B	15	67		AGGRESSIVE (SADISTIC)
	7	16	56		COMPULSIVE
	8A	12	65		NEGATIVISTIC
	8B	14	63		MASOCHISTIC
SEVERE PERSONALITY PATHOLOGY	S	9	65		SCHIZOTYPAL
	C	4	57		BORDERLINE
	P	11	82		PARANOID
CLINICAL SYNDROMES	A	13	72		ANXIETY DISORDER
	H	6	47		SOMATOFORM DISORDER
	N	3	32		BIPOLAR: MANIC DISORDER
	D	12	77		DYSTHYMIC DISORDER
	B	8	66		ALCOHOL DEPENDENCE
	T	5	60		DRUG DEPENDENCE
	R	6	73		POST-TRAUMATIC STRESS
SEVERE SYNDROMES	SS	6	47		THOUGHT DISORDER
	CC	11	68		MAJOR DEPRESSION
	PP	10	21		DELUSIONAL DISORDER

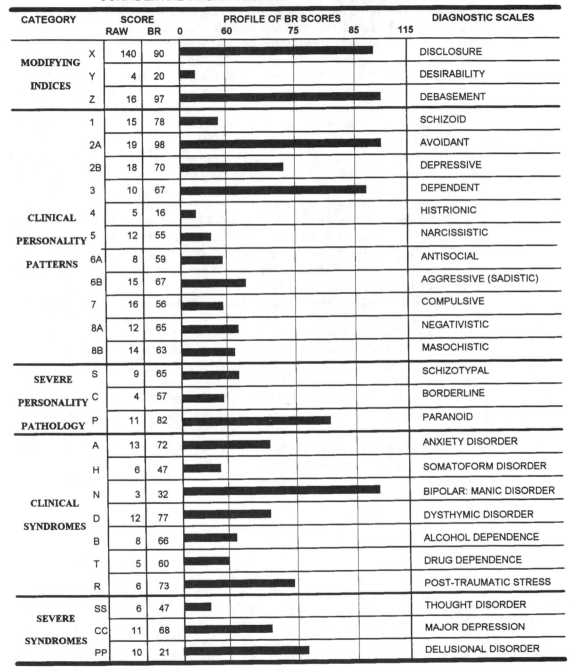

Figure 3–2   Ken's MCMI Profile

case, we have no reason to believe that any other Axis II disorders might be applicable. Our attitude for the current case, then, is one of culling the true positives from the set of all positives. In the current case, the avoidant and dependent diagnoses clearly seem clinically relevant.

The paranoid diagnosis, however, might be viewed more in a more skeptical light. We might want to ask whether the paranoid disorder in fact reflects a personality disorder or an Axis I condition. Personality disorders are related to Axis I disorders in several ways, as originally noted by Paykel, Klerman, and Prusoff (1976). Figure 3–3 schematizes what are referred as the predisposition or vulnerability model, the complication model, the spectrum model, and the pathoplasty model. According to the *vulnerability model,* personality disorders work to dispose the individual to the development of an Axis I disorder. When coping responses are limited or impoverished, the probability of developing an Axis I disorder such as anxiety or depression is greatly increased. The vulnerability model is particularly appropriate for personality disorder patients, who often evoke the very stressors under which these disorders will be developed. Interpersonally, for example, they may become involved in vicious circles which perpetuate stressful conditions and so function to keep their "immune systems" chronically weakened–that is, disposed to the development of more severe clinical conditions.

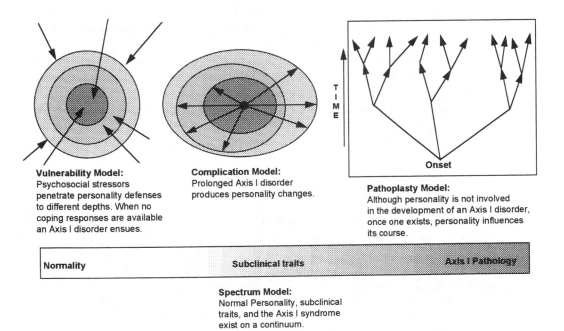

Vulnerability Model:
Psychosocial stressors penetrate personality defenses to different depths. When no coping responses are available an Axis I disorder ensues.

Complication Model:
Prolonged Axis I disorder produces personality changes.

Pathoplasty Model:
Although personality is not involved in the development of an Axis I disorder, once one exists, personality influences its course.

Spectrum Model:
Normal Personality, subclinical traits, and the Axis I syndrome exist on a continuum.

Figure 3–3   Possible Relationships between Axis II Personality Styles and Axis I Disorders

In the *complication model,* the causality of the vulnerability model is reversed, so that Axis I conditions, however initiated, create a distortion of the underlying personality matrix, changing the personality. Axis I conditions that are long lasting and resistant to treatment may encrust themselves as enduring traits that reflect the more florid disorder while caricaturing the individual. Alternately, these traits may be reactive in nature, as when an individual whose disorder has a strong genetic basis accepts the disorder but becomes helpless and depressive.

In contrast to the vulnerability and complication models, which conceptualize Axis I and Axis II conditions as interacting but distinct, personality disorders, Axis I conditions may be seen as developing from out of the same constitutional soil and therefore as existing on a continuum, as in the *spectrum model.* Here, biologically based subclinical traits so preempt the development of other more adaptive characteristics that they effectively become the organizing principle for the entire personality. Given the appropriate circumstances, a genetic predisposition toward an Axis I condition may be amplified into a full-blown disorder. Kraepelin and Kretschmer were both of this persuasion, as is Akiskal (1980) today.

In contrast to the above models, which see Axis I and Axis II conditions as either directly causally related or derived from the same "third variable" of constitution, the *pathoplasty model* holds that personality influences the course of an Axis I disorder, but does not in itself dispose toward the development of the disorder. If the form of particular Axis I conditions is related to personality, it is only because the course of the disorder tends to be canalized by certain personality features.

All of these models are possible and likely to be true to some extent in different individuals. In fact, it is not impossible that all might be applicable within a single individual to some degree. In Ken's case, for example, the vulnerability model might argue for a developmental double-whammy. First, his relationship with his older male companion appears to be related to an attempt to bond with and find nurturance from an absent and abandoning father. Paradoxically, the fact that it was Ken who was ending the relationship when his companion was diagnosed symbolically casts Ken in the role of the abandoner, and his companion in Ken's own role as a child. How can Ken do to someone else what was done to him? To stay in the relationship would be to sacrifice his own self-development, yet to leave would be to step into the shoes of someone he despised. Second, there is the memory of his emotionally devastated mother, his inability to nurture her, and the associated guilt. Thus, if Ken leaves the relationship, he is forced into an alliance with his father against the lonely child inside him and against his companion, but if he stays, he is almost certainly forced to relive his past empathic inefficacies, since ultimately he cannot save someone who is certain to die.

For Ken, the only solution to this paradox was a psychotic withdrawal. On the basis of his symptoms, he was first diagnosed as paranoid schizophrenic, then later as manic-depressive, and still later as PTSD. The PTSD diagnosis is not unreasonable, since the diagnosis of one's companion with terminal cancer can certainly be seen as a traumatic event outside the range of normal human experience. The MCMI did in fact pick some of this up, albeit at a subthreshold BR = 73. Not surprisingly, the Delusional Disorder scale is also in the disordered range, at BR = 77.

Given the long-lasting nature of Ken's problems, the complication model also warrant examination. In the complication model, the question is: How has Ken's Axis I condition affected his personality? Earlier, we noted that the Paranoid PD score might be viewed suspiciously. The issue was framed as if this elevation should be viewed either as a true positive or as the false positive reflection of an Axis I disorder—that is, in terms of choices that were mutually exclusive. One value of the complication (and spectrum) model is that it approaches Ken as a whole being, not merely as an aggregation of axes. Framed in this manner, the paranoid elevation may *validly* be seen as the result of an Axis I condition with socioperceptual distortions so intense, enduring, and pervasive that the underlying premorbid personality matrix, rather than retaining the capacity to snap back into shape at the diminishment of torsional forces, was instead coopted, caricatured, and changed essentially. From the perspective of the complication model, what is at issue is the degree to which the organism has been changed, not if it has been changed. In Ken, the unresolvable object paradoxes that originally led to a paranoid decompensation appear to have insinuated as secondary effects more crystallized paranoid qualities which now may validly be considered as personality traits.

Configural Interpretation of MCMI Personality Scales

The quality of information that can be deduced from the profile analysis of a test is a function of several factors, including the adequacy and generativity of the theory that provides the logic underlying its various scales, the overall empirical validity of the inventory, its internal consistency and scale generalizability, and, of course, other auxiliary information that might be fertile ground for clinical hypotheses, such as the patient's history. An interpretation that mirrors the client's characteristic style of functioning as well as his or her current problems depends ultimately on the clinician's skill in weighing the degree to which a variety of client variables interact in order to corroborate, moderate, or even disqualify straightforward hypotheses, as well as suggest ones that are more subtle. As noted by Wetzler and Marlowe (1992), even the best inventory is only as good as the clinician interpreting it. Perfect construct validity and generalizability will not make up for inadequate knowledge of the theory undergirding an inventory or ignorance of fundamental principles of psychopathology.

Although examining the elevation of single scale may be useful for making diagnostic assignments, the interpretive value is, as we have touched on above, greatly amplified when viewed in the context of the remaining profile. Why? The short answer is that the process of profile interpretation is similar to that of knowledge building in the integrative world view. In Ken's case, the test results already suggest several diagnoses and other characteristics, each being a hypothesis about the nature of his pathology. As the complication model makes clear, such integrative configural logic is inherently nonlinear or nonmechanistic. Although it asks for a level of sophistication, in return it breaks the pattern of labeling clients and fitting them to discrete diagnostic categories. Instead, diagnostic constructs are viewed as the beginning of an assessment rather than its endpoint. Putting the assessment in a perspective that makes sense in light of the client's history argues that beyond the logic of the disorders themselves, this is the logic of the case, which explains how the relationship of the individual's clinical symptoms relate to his or her personality and unique history.

Moderate versus Severe Personality Scales

In making configural personality interpretations, a separation should be made between those scales pertaining to the *basic* clinical personality pattern (1–8B) and those pointing to the presence of more *severe* Axis II pathology: the borderline (C), schizotypal (S), and paranoid (P). These structural pathologies differ from the other clinical personality patterns by several criteria, notably deficits in social competence and frequent, but reversible, psychotic episodes. Less integrated in terms of their personality organization and less effective in coping than their milder counterparts, they are especially vulnerable to decompensation when confronted with the strains of everyday life. In terms of the theoretical model, these patterns are significantly less adaptable in the face of ecological trials. They are dysfunctional variants of the more moderately pathological patterns. Consequently, the overall elevation of S, C, and P may be used as a rough index of the degree to which the client's basic personality pattern has become structurally compromised. If, for example, a client receives BR 105 on the narcissistic scale, but S, C, and P are low, then structurally the personality appears to be fundamentally intact, despite the elevated BR score. If, on the other hand, a client receives BR 80 on the narcissistic scale, but scale P is also at BR 85, this suggests a basic narcissistic pattern with paranoid tendencies, and considerable structural pathology as well. The additional difficulties posed by structural pathology was certainly evident in Ken, whose paranoid tendencies had taken on a life of their own, thus further amplifying his problems and perpetuating his difficulties.

Generating Domain Hypotheses

A single diagnostic label rarely if ever provides information specific and comprehensive enough to serve as a sound basis for intervention efforts. Not only do clients differ with respect to the magnitude of their pathology within a diagnostic class, they also differ in the features with which they approximate the class. Whether diagnostic taxons are derived through clinical observation, mathematical analyses, or theoretical deduction, clients differ in how they meet taxonic requirements, a fact institutionalized in *DMS-III* with the adoption of the polythetic model. In and of itself, then, a diagnosis alone represents an underspecification of psychopathology. Especially on Axis II, the vast majority of clients are so-called mixed types. In moving toward nomothetic individuality, we ask "what part of the mix" is relevant to interpreting the individual case.

One option is to systematically investigate characteristics associated with each MCMI suggested personality prototype in a domain-oriented fashion. These characteristics or clinical domains have been usefully organized in a manner similar to distinctions drawn in the biological realm—that is, by dividing them into *structural* and *functional* attributes. Functional characteristics represent dynamic processes that transpire within the intrapsychic world and between the individual's self and psychosocial environment. They represent "expressive modes of regulatory action." Structural attributes represent a deeply embedded and relatively enduring template of imprinted memories, attitudes, needs, fears, conflicts, and so on, which guide experience and transform the nature of ongoing events to accord with preformed characteristics.

Several criteria were used to select and develop the clinical domains that comprise this assessment schema: (1) that they be varied in the features they embody—that is, not be limited just to behaviors or cognitions, but to encompass a full range of clinically relevant characteristics; (2) that they parallel, if not correspond, to many of our profession's current therapeutic modalities; and (3) that they not only be coordinated to the official *DSM* schema of personality disorder prototypes, as well as its guiding model of evolutionary polarities, but also that each disorder be characterized by a distinctive feature within each clinical domain. Brief descriptions of these functional and structural domains have been given in several publications (e.g., Millon, 1990) and are printed in the MCMI manual as well. In Table 3–2, these domains are schematized according to their respective data level, reflecting the four historic approaches that have characterized the study of psychopathology— namely, the biophysical, intrapsychic, phenomenological, and behavioral.

In the context of the individual case, the question then becomes: Which functional processes and structural attributes are (1) necessary for the client's personality pattern to exist as the organic whole represented by the code type and (2) converge with or make sense on the basis of auxiliary information, such

Table 3–2   Functional and Structural Domains of Personality

(F) Functional Domains	(S) Structural Domains
Behavioral Level	**Intrapsychic Level**
(F) Expressive Acts	(F) Regulatory Mechanisms
(F) Interpersonal Conduct	(S) Morphologic Organization
Phenomenological Level	**Biophysical Level**
(F) Cognitive Style	(S) Mood/Temperament
(S) Object Representations	
(S) Self-Image	

as the individual's family and clinical history? If the personality assessment is to be exhaustive, then, with the guidance of the code type, at least a brief description of the client in each clinical domain should be formulated. Each domain description represents a "within-domain" hypothesis about client functioning in that circumscribed area, and this hypothesis should be evaluated and amended as needed until it converges with other available data. Because the domains exist at a level of specificity that is not directly assessed by the MCMI itself, it is necessary to supplement the code type with other sources of information when making personality descriptions below the syndrome level. Given a two- or three-point code, client functioning may be prototypal of the domain description for the primary code, prototypal of the domain description for the secondary code, or lie somewhere in between.

With the aid of domain hypotheses and auxiliary evidence to bear on their validity, we are now in a position to construct a remarkably detailed picture of the individual. Structural attributes and functional processes relevant to the avoidant, dependent, and paranoid patterns are reprinted in Table 3–3. We simply move down the chart from domain to domain, asking ourselves which description the client most resembles, synthesizing and alternating these descriptions when the evidence requires. Behaviorally, Ken's presentation during diagnostic testing strongly suggested a dependent-avoidant behavioral style characterized by passivity, docility, immaturity, and guarded awareness of other's reactions. Interpersonally, Ken had shown himself to be submissive to potentially nurturing figures, as evidence in the persistent TAT theme of an older figure taking interest in and rescuing a weaker and unfortunate one. Nevertheless, he admitted that he could be quarrelsome and argumentative at times, a feature characteristic of more independent styles and inconsistent with that of the dependent. Cognitively, Ken was both distracted (as evidenced perhaps from the low digit span score) and suspicious. The later trait, in particular, is consistent with his Axis I disorder, and may support the complication model. In terms of defense mechanisms, Ken's basic premorbid matrix seemed oriented primarily toward a dependent's introjection. Nevertheless, he often appeared to attribute his own shortcomings and failings to others, a paranoid characteristic, perhaps as a means of gaining some relief from long-standing guilt feelings. Not surprisingly, Ken's self-image was one of self-alienation (avoidant) and ineptness (dependent), a combination squarely consistent with the object paradox described earlier.

Because the specificity of the domain in relation to the broad-band clinical syndromes, the yield of domain hypotheses will almost inevitably be much richer than can be practically evaluated with data internal to the MCMI. As seen above, we have drawn on TAT and WAIS-R data, as well as the interpersonal impressions of the examiner. Some domain hypotheses will be thoroughly corroborated, as, for example, by a therapist's own clinical observations. Other hypotheses will only partially be corroborated, perhaps because the evidence simply suggests something else, but more often because not enough data exist to make an informed judgment. Evaluation of such hypotheses must await the accrual of extra-MCMI data, whether through

Table 3–3 Functional and Structural Domains of the Avoidant, Dependent, and Paranoid Prototypes

Avoidant Personality	Dependent Personality	Paranoid Personality
(F) Expressively Fretful (e.g., conveys personal unease and disquiet, a constant timorous, hesitant and restive state; overreacts to innocuous events and anxiously judges them to signify ridicule, criticism, and disapproval).	**(F) Expressively Incompetent** (e.g., withdraws from adult responsibilities by acting helpless and seeking nurturance from others; is docile and passive, lacks functional competencies, and avoids self-assertion).	**(F) Expressively Defensive** (e.g., is vigilantly guarded, alert to anticipate and ward off expected derogation, malice, and deception; is tenacious and firmly resistant to sources of external influence and control).
(F) Interpersonally Aversive (e.g., distances from activities that involve intimate personal relationships and reports extensive history of social pananxiety and distrust; seeks acceptance, but is unwilling to get involved unless certain to be liked, maintaining distance and privacy to avoid being shamed and humiliated).	**(F) Interpersonally Submissive** (e.g., needs excessive advice and reassurance, as well as subordinates self to stronger, nurturing figure, without whom may feel anxiously alone and helpless; is compliant, conciliatory, and placating, fearing being left to care for oneself).	**(F) Interpersonally Provocative** (e.g.,not only bears grudges and is unforgiving of those of the past, but displays a quarrelsome, fractious, and abrasive attitude with recent acquaintances; precipitates exasperation and anger by a testing of loyalties and an intrusive and searching preoccupation with hidden motives).
(F) Cognitively Distracted (e.g., warily scans environment for potential threats and is preoccupied by intrusive and disruptive random thoughts and observations; an upwelling from within of irrelevant ideation upsets thought continuity and interferes with social communications and accurate appraisals).	**(F) Cognitively Naive** (e.g., rarely disagrees with others and is easily persuaded, unsuspicious and gullible; reveals a Pollyanna attitude toward interpersonal difficulties, watering down objective problems and smoothing over troubling events).	**(F) Cognitively Suspicious** (e.g., is unwarrantedly skeptical, cynical and mistrustful of the motives of others, including relatives, friends, and associates, construing innocuous events as signifying hidden or conspiratorial intent; reveals tendency to read hidden meanings into benign matters and to magnify tangential or minor difficulties into proofs of duplicity and treachery, especially regarding the fidelity and trustworthiness of a spouse or intimate friend).
(S) Alienated Self-Image (e.g., sees self as socially inept, inadequate, and inferior, justifying thereby his or her isolation and rejection by others; feels personally unappealing, devalues self-achievements, and reports persistent sense of aloneness and emptiness).	**(S) Inept Self-Image** (e.g., views self as weak, fragile, and inadequate; exhibits lack of self-confidence by belittling own attitudes and competencies, and hence not capable of doing things on one's own).	**(S) Inviolable Self-Image** (e.g., has persistent ideas of self importance and self-reference, perceiving attacks on one's character not apparent to others, asserting as personally derogatory and scurrilous, if not libelous, entirely innocuous actions and events; is pridefully independent, reluctant to confide in others, highly insular, experiencing intense fears, however, of losing identity, status, and powers of self-determination).

Continued

Table 3–3 *Continued*

Avoidant Personality	Dependent Personality	Paranoid Personality
(S) Vexatious Objects (e.g., internalized representations are composed of readily reactivated, intense and conflict-ridden memories of problematic early relations; limited avenues for experiencing or recalling gratification, and few mechanisms to channel needs, bind impulses, resolve conflicts, or deflect external stressors).	**(S) Immature Objects** (e.g., internalized representations are composed of infantile impressions of others, unsophisticated ideas, incomplete recollections, rudimentary drives and childlike impulses, as well as minimal competencies to manage and resolve stressors).	**(S) Unalterable Objects** (e.g., internalized representations of significant early relationships are a fixed and implacable configuration of deeply held beliefs and attitudes, as well as driven by unyielding convictions which, in turn, are aligned in an idiosyncratic manner with a fixed hierarchy of tenaciously held but unwarranted assumptions, fears, and conjectures).
(F) Fantasy Mechanism (e.g., depends excessively on imagination to achieve need gratification, confidence building, and conflict resolution; withdraws into reveries as a means of safely discharging frustrated affectionate, as well as angry impulses).	**(F) Introjection Mechanism** (e.g., is firmly devoted to another to strengthen the belief that an inseparable bond exists between them; jettisons independent views in favor of those of others to preclude conflicts and threats to relationship).	**(F) Projection Mechanism** (e.g., actively disowns undesirable personal traits and motives, and attributes them to others; remains blind to one's own unattractive behaviors and characteristics, yet is overalert to, and hypercritical of, similar features in others).
(S) Fragile Organization (e.g., a precarious complex of tortuous emotions depend almost exclusively on a single modality for its resolution and discharge, that of avoidance, escape and fantasy and, hence, when faced with personal risks, new opportunities, or unanticipated stress, few morphologic structures are available to deploy and few back-up positions can be reverted to, short of regressive decompensation).	**(S) Inchoate Organization** (e.g., owing to entrusting others with the responsibility to fulfill needs and to cope with adult tasks, there is both a deficient morphologic structure and a lack of diversity in internal regulatory controls, leaving a miscellany of relatively undeveloped and undifferentiated adaptive abilities, as well as an elementary system for functioning independently).	**(S) Inelastic Organization** (e.g., systemic constriction and inflexibility of undergirding morphologic structures, as well as rigidly fixed channels of defensive coping, conflict mediation and need gratification, create an overstrung and taut frame that is so uncompromising in its accommodation to changing circumstances that unanticipated stressors are likely to precipitate either explosive outbursts or inner shatterings).
(S) Anguished Mood (e.g., describes constant and confusing undercurrent of tension, sadness, and anger; vacillates between desire for affection, fear of rebuff, embarrassment, and numbness of feeling).	**(S) Pacific Mood** (e.g., is characteristically warm, tender, and noncompetitive; timidly avoids social tension and interpersonal conflicts).	**(S) Irascible Mood** (e.g., displays a cold, sullen, churlish, and humorless demeanor; attempts to appear unemotional and objective, but is edgy, envious, jealous, quick to take personal offense, and react angrily).

additional testing or experience with the client during therapy itself. As with any form of clinical inference, the combination of various gauges from diverse settings provide the data aggregates (Epstein, 1979, 1983) necessary to increase the likelihood of drawing correct inferences, especially when coupled with multimethod approaches (Campbell & Fiske, 1959).

Putting Symptoms in Perspective

Over the course of arriving at an integrative formulation of the patient's problem, the logic of the case comes more and more into the foreground, and diagnoses become more and more trivial. In fact, as more integrative formulations are achieved—that is, as the limit of the series is reached in the necessary theory of the client, one that ties up all the loose ends—this theory becomes eminently more suitable for treatment planning than is a list of diagnoses alone. The proper question, in understanding each individual's pathology is not a "whether" but a "how"—how the interaction of individual characteristics and contextual factors (the interaction of Axis II and Axis IV) produces Axis I, classical psychiatric symptomatology. In the featured case, it was Ken's fear of not being able to deal with the terminal illness of a companion who symbolized his own self, thus exacerbating and confirming a guilt he already shouldered, that was his psychic undoing. This, in turn, produced its own secondary effects, which over time became crystallized as traits in their own right.

Frequent Scale Covariations

With the first subsection of the profile, that pertaining to basic personality pattern, clinicians are likely to find a higher proportion of the two- and three-point combinations that are listed in Table 3–4. These combinations may make up nearly 70 percent of all MCMI-III profiles in a diverse patient

Table 3–4   Frequent Clinical Personality Pattern (Scales 1 through 8B) and High-Point Configural Combinations

High-Point Scale	Frequent Clinical Personality Pattern Configural Combinations
1	1-2B-3, 1-2A-3, 1-2A-6B, 1-2A-8A, 1-2B-8B, 1-3
2A	2A-1-3, 2A-1-8B, 2A-3-8B, 2A-8A-8B, 2A-8B-1, 2A-8B-3, 2A-8B-8A
2B	2B-1-3, 2B-1-8A, 2B-2A-3, 2B-2A-8B, 2B-3-8B, 2B-8A-8B
3	3-1-7, 3-2B-1, 3-2B-8B, 3-4-5, 3-4-8B, 3-7-1, 3-7-4, 3-8B-2B
4	4-3-5, 4-3-7, 4-5-6A, 4-5-6B, 4-5-8A, 4-8A-6B
5	5-4-6B, 5-4-7, 5-6A-4, 5-6A-6B
6A	6A-6B-5, 6A-8A-5, 6A-8A-6B
6B	6B-5-4, 6B-5-6A, 6B-8A-2A, 6B-8A-5, 6B-8A-6A
7	7-1, 7-3-4, 7-4, 7-5-4, 7-5-6B
8A	8A-2A, 8A-2A-8B, 8A-3-8B, 8A-4, 8A-6B-6A
8B	8B-2B-3, 8B-3-2B, 8B-8A-2B, 8B-8A3

Table 3–5   Covariation of Basic Clinical Personality High-Point Configuratons (Scales 1 through 8B) and High BR Clinical Syndrome Scales (A through PP)

High BR Clinical Syndrome Scales	Frequent Covariant Two-Point Basic Clinical Personality Configurations
A	1-2A, 2A-1, 2B-3, 2A-8A, 2A-8B, 3-1, 3-2A, 3-8A, 3-8B, 4-8A, 8A-2A, 8A-3, 8B-2A
H	3-2A, 4-3, 4-8A, 8A-2A, 8B-2B
N	3-4, 4-3, 4-5, 5-4
D	1-2B, 2B-3, 2B-8A, 2B-8B, 3-1, 3-2B, 3-8A, 3-8B, 4-8A, 8A-2B, 8B-2B
B	2A-8A, 2A-8B, 4-3, 4-5, 4-6A, 4-6B, 5-4, 5-6A, 5-6B, 6-A4, 6-A5, 6A-6B, 6-B5, 6B-6A, 6B-8A
T	4-5, 4-6A, 4-6B, 5-4, 5-6A, 5-6B, 6A-4, 6-A5, 6A-6B, 6A-8A, 6B-6A, 6B-8A
R	1-2A, 2A-1, 2A-8A, 2A-8B, 3-2A, 3-8A, 3-8B, 6A-2A, 8A-2A, 8A-3, 8B-2A
SS	1-2A, 2-A1, 2A-3, 2A-8B, 3-2A, 3-8B, 8B-2A
CC	2B-8A, 2B-8B, 3-2B, 3-8A, 3-8B, 8A-2B, 8A-3, 8B-2B, 8B-3
PP	2A-8A, 5-6A, 5-6B, 6A-2A, 6A-6B, 6B-6A, 8A-6A, 8A-6B

population. Of equal value is Table 3–5, which lists the most frequent covariations between the Axis II personality code combinations and high BR scores on the nine Axis I clinical syndrome scales (A through PP).

Typical Two-Point Codes

In the following sections, a number of interpretive features of three of the more typical MCMI-III two-point codes will be presented. These are only a small number of the interpretive possibilities for the MCMI-III. Important differences may be deduced and demonstrated empirically between a matched pair of high-point codes, depending on which of the pair is higher. For example, a significant difference may be shown to exist between a 3-2A and a 2A-3 high-point code. In the former case, patients are likely to control their social aversiveness sufficiently to become comfortably dependent on institutional, if not personal, sources of support. In the latter example, distrust is likely to overtake the individual, and needed sources of support may be tolerated, but only tentatively and with much discomfort. It is often clinically useful also to record the third highest in a profile code series. This reflects the fact that certain scales are notably "penetrant" and/or "expressive" even when ranking somewhat down in the profile configuration. For example, scales 6A and 8A frequently alter the clinical meaning of a profile when they are the third highest scale. Thus, a 3-2A-1 code suggests a pattern substantively different from a 3-2A-8A. In the former case, the patient is likely to have become accustomed to an inadequate and dependent state with chronic flattening of affect; in patients with the latter profile, however, we often see displays of stubbornness, passive-aggressive behavior, and periodic irritable outbursts.

As with the single-scale interpretive guidelines presented previously, the three illustrative two-point code descriptions furnished in the following sections represent prototypes. Because of the effects of moderator variables, the uniqueness of each case, and the inevitable limitations of any psychometric technique, what follows is by no means infallible as a guide to depicting every patient who exhibits a particular profile code.

Code 3-4: Dependent and Histrionic. The behavior of these patients is best characterized by their submissiveness, dependency, and deficits in competent assertiveness. Fears of losing emotional support often lead them to be overcompliant and obliging. Behaving in a superficially charming manner, they may seek attention through self-dramatizing behaviors. Many are quite naive about worldly matters and avoid taking everyday positions of responsibility. Their thinking is often unreflective and scattered. When faced with interpersonal tensions, they attempt to maintain an air of buoyancy and to deny disturbing thoughts or acknowledge inner tensions.

These patients are likely to be highly accommodating and responsive to the needs of others. Having learned to accept an inferior role, they allow others to assume the role of being more competent than themselves. An active soliciting of praise, a marketing of appeal, and a tendency to be entertaining are also apparent. They seek harmony with others, often without regard to their own values and beliefs. Unassertive and lacking in confidence, they avoid situations that may involve personal conflict.

Despite their efforts to control any oppositional feelings, their repressed angers and frustrations may break out into the open at times. Their resentments stem in part from their awareness that they have little or no identity apart from others. Instead of valuing themselves, they submerge in favor of others. However, they no longer believe that these relationships will fulfill their needs or even protect them against loss. Despite their growing disillusion with others, they are still alert to signs of potential hostility and rejection and seek to minimize the dangers of indifference and disapproval. By paying close attention to the desires of others, they are able to shape their behaviors to conform to others' wishes and needs.

Despite a growing desire to assert their independence, these patients feel helpless when faced with responsibilities that demand assertiveness and initiative. The loss of the central source of emotional support and guidance often prompts severe dejection, and they may begin openly to solicit signs of reassurance. Guilt, illness, anxiety, and depression are used to deflect serious criticism and to transform threats of disapproval into expressions of support and empathy. More extreme reactions, such as a severe depression or a brief manic period or even a most uncharacteristic hostility, may spill forth when the security of their dependency is genuinely threatened.

Code 5-6A: Narcissistic and Antisocial. These patients characteristically display an overbearing and arrogant sense of self-worth, an indifference to the welfare of others, and an intimidating interpersonal manner. Tendencies to exploit others and to expect special recognition and consideration without assuming reciprocal responsibility are notable. Actions that raise questions of personal integrity may indicate a deficient social conscience, as they show little regard for the rights of others.

These patients attempt to maintain an image of cool strength, arrogance, fearlessness, self-reliance, sentimentality, and hard-boiled competitiveness. They also may display a rash willingness to risk harm, and are notably fearless in the face of threats and even punitive action. Indeed, punishment may only reinforce their rebellious and hostile feelings. Malicious tendencies seen in others are used to justify their own aggressive inclinations and may lead to frequent personal and family difficulties, as well as to occasional legal entanglements. Antisocial behavior and alcohol or drug problems may be prominent reasons for referral.

When matters are well under control, these patients may be skilled in the ways of social influence and adept at exploiting the good will of others. More commonly, they are envious of others, are wary of their motives, feel unfairly treated, and are easily provoked to anger. Their thin façade of sociability can quickly give way to angry or caustic comments. A marked suspicion of those in authority leads these patients to feel secure only when they possess power.

Lacking deep feelings of loyalty and displaying an indifference to truth, they may successfully scheme beneath a veneer of civility. Their guiding principle is that one must outwit others, controlling and exploiting them before they gain control. Displaying a chip-on-the-shoulder attitude, they often exhibit a readiness to attack those whom they distrust. If they are unsuccessful in channeling their ever-present aggressive impulses, resentment may mount into acts of brutal hostility.

Code 4-8A-C: Histrionic, Negativistic (Passive-Aggressive), and Borderline. These patients' behavior is typified by a thin veneer of sociability and maturity. Beneath this façade, however, lies an intense fear of true autonomy, a need to present a favorable public front, and a pained submission to the expectancies of others. These individuals' front of social propriety and self-assurance covers deep and increasingly intense, but generally suppressed, antagonisms and feelings of worthlessness. There is a struggle to control these oppositional tendencies through discipline and a socially agreeable affability, with moments of dramatic conviviality. These patients engage in a wide variety of interpersonal maneuvers designed to elicit favorable attention and social approval. There is a long-standing pattern of being deferential and ingratiating with superiors, going to great lengths to demonstrate efficiency and serious-mindedness while completing all tasks regardless of the fairness of the demands.

Recent failures to evoke this approval may have led to depressive periods and chronic anxiety. At this point, patients are high-strung and moody, seeking to express attitudes contrary to inner feelings of tension, anger, and dejection. In an effort to avoid these discomforts, these individuals have become increasingly sensitive to the moods and expectations of others. The extreme other-directedness used in achieving approval has resulted in a lifestyle characterized by its high adaptability. These patients have also learned to be alert to signs of potential hostility and rejection, and usually avoid disapproval by adapting their behaviors to conform to the desires of others. This preoccupation with external approval, however, has resulted in a growing sense of personal impotence and social dependency.

These patients deny awareness of inner deficiencies, since awareness would point up the discrepancy between the overt impressions created and the patient's inner feelings of sterility and emotional poverty, coupled with an unwillingness to accept blame. This tendency to seal off and deny the elements of inner life further intensifies dependence on others. Increasingly, deep resentments have begun to emerge toward those to whom these patients conform and on whom they depend. These antagonisms have periodically broken through surface constraints to erupt in outbursts of guilt and contrition. These vacillations in behavior between periods of submissive compliance and sullen negativism compound discomforts. Such public displays of inconsistency and impulse expression contrast markedly with self-image. There are bitter complaints about being treated unfairly; about expecting to be disappointed and disapproved of by others; and about no longer being appreciated for one's diligence, sociability, and respectability. With the persistence of these ambivalent feelings, these patients have begun to suffer somatic discomforts and voice growing distress about a wide range of physical symptoms.

LIMITATIONS AND QUALIFICATIONS

Despite its coordination both with theory and the *DSM-IV,* the MCMI-III is, like all tests, a less than perfect diagnostic tool. Neither does it reflect precisely its theoretical foundation of clinical constructs nor mirror all facets of the syndromal disorders fashioned for the *DSM.*

As illustrated above, the MCMI-III is a remarkably rich source of clinical hypotheses. Whenever possible, however, these hypotheses should be sustained through convergence with other data sources. The MCMI-III interpretive report states that the narrative text "should be evaluated in conjunction with additional clinical data" (e.g., current life circumstances, observed behavior, biographic history, interview responses, demographic data, and information from other tests). As is the case with any self-report measure, the accuracy and richness of the test is enhanced when its findings are appraised in the context of other clinical information. Not only does the combination of various gauges from diverse settings provide the data aggregates that increase the likelihood of drawing correct inferences (Epstein, 1979, 1983), but multi-method approaches (Campbell & Fiske, 1959) provide both the experienced and the novice clinician with an optimal base for deciphering the features that characterize each patient.

The MCMI-III is not a general personality instrument to be used for normal populations or for any purpose other than diagnostic screening or clinical assessment. Normative data and transformation scores for the MCMI-III are based entirely on clinical samples and are applicable only to individuals who evidence psychological problems or who are engaged in a program of professional psychotherapy or psychodiagnostic evaluation. Assessments for forensic purposes—such as child custody, criminal competency, and personal injury evaluations—are appropriate, owing to the presence of many such cases in the MCMI-III normative sample. To use the MCMI-III for a wider range of problems or class of subjects (such as those found in business and industry), or to diagnose neurological problems, or to assess general personality traits among college students is to apply the instrument to settings and samples for which it is neither intended nor appropriate.

Important implications for evaluating MCMI-III results stem from the fact that certain personality disorder scales are sensitive to the current affective state of a patient. All self-report inventory scales, whether personality oriented (Axis II) or syndrome oriented (Axis 1), reflect in varying degrees both "traits" and "states." Despite methodologic and psychometric procedures to distinguish enduring personality characteristics from clinical features of a more transient nature, every scale reflects a mix of predisposing and generalizing attributes as well as those of a more situational or acute nature. Noteworthy are the partial blurring effects of depressive and anxiety states on specific personality disorder scales (Hirschfeld et al., 1983). These results stem in part from shared scale items (Wiggins, 1982), but the level of covariation is appreciably greater than can be accounted for by item overlap alone (Lumsden, 1987). Experience with earlier versions of the MCMI indicates that the presence of dysthymic and anxious states accentuates scores on the personality scales while diminishing those obtained on the other scales—a view that is consistent with research by Shea, Glass, Pilkonis, Watkins, and Doherty (1987).

The MCMI-III's diagnostic scale cutoffs and profile interpretations are oriented to the majority of patients who take the inventory—that is, to those displaying psychic disturbances in the midranges of severity rather than to those whose difficulties are either close to normal (e.g., some workers compensation litigants, clients in marital therapy) or of manifest clinical severity (e.g., acute psychotics, chronic schizophrenics). To optimize diagnostic and interpretive validity, narratives have been written to focus on moderate levels of pathology; this results in a slightly diminished degree of diagnostic and interpretive accuracy among patients in both the least and the most severe ranges of psychological disturbance—a fact that users of the interpretive reports should bear in mind. Narrative analyses of patients who are experiencing ordinary life difficulties or minor adjustment disorders will tend to appear

more troubled than they really are, and those with the most serious pathologies will often appear less troubled than they really are.

For these and other reasons, this interpretive guide should be considered
only a brief introduction to the MCMI-III. Normative data and interpretive
deductions made from the MCMI are based entirely on clinical samples;
hence, the test should be administered exclusively to persons who exhibit psychological symptoms or who are actively involved in programs of professional
psychodiagnosis, forensic evaluations, or psychotherapy. It is inappropriate to
employ and interpret MCMI-III results with other problems or subjects.

CONCLUSION

Assessment instruments are typically created and refined through multiple
stages of validation, using large samples of subjects, often numbering in the
thousands. In contrast, clinicians are usually concerned with one patient at a
time. The clinician's ability to address why the patient is as he or she makes
psychology a clinical rather than merely a descriptive science. The question
is: How can clinicians go from population-based measures to interpretations
that have validity for the individual?

Not only is the MCMI based in a generative evolutionary theory of
human behavior but it also seeks to be coordinated to the *DSM-IV*. All the personality disorders of the *DSM-IV* have been included, and their validity is
supported by the theory. In addition, both more moderate (e.g., Anxiety and
Depression) and more severe (e.g., Delusional Disorder) Axis I conditions are
assessed, including Post-Traumatic Stress Disorder. A number of modifier indices are available to detect deviate test-taking attitudes or agendas. Of
course, these indices are often interpretable on their own terms.

The MCMI revision process began with the selection of new items from
a large pool. In generating new items, the goal was to produce statements that
were congruent both with the instruments guiding theoretical system and
with *DSM-IV* diagnostic criteria. Several hundred clinicians who regularly
use the MCMI for evaluating and treating adult clients participated in revision research. Subjects were administered the MCMI-II-R research form, as
well as any of a number of collateral instruments. The final pool of 998 subjects was divided into development and cross-validation samples. Items were
assigned to their respective scales, according to both the *DSM* criteria with
which they were coordinated as well as theoretical considerations. The final
scales were produced through an iterative process that emphasized the internal consistency of the scales. Base rates were estimated on the basis of clinicians' ratings and other extant prevalence studies. The BR transformed
scores range from 0 to 115.

The MCMI offers several levels of interpretation. The simplest examines
scale elevations in conjunction with some cutoff score, traditionally BR=75.
The ultimate purpose of a multiaxial assessment, however, is to explain the
nature of the Axis I symptoms and their connection to psychosocial stressors

and the patient's personality. Achieving such integrative formulations requires profile interpretation, supplemented by the generation of more specific "domain" hypotheses. Each prominent scale in the code type is examined as it is expressed across each of the eight clinical domains. These descriptions are amended or synthesized on the basis of all available data until they best reflect client characteristics. Like all tests, the MCMI is a less than perfect tool, and it suffers the limitations common to all self-report inventories. Nevertheless, the MCMI offers a rich source of personality and clinical hypotheses for the integrative assessment.

REFERENCES

American Psychiatric Association. (1987). *Diagnostic and statistical manual of mental disorders* (3rd ed., revised). (DSM-III-R). Washington, DC: Author.

American Psychiatric Association. (1993). *DSM-IV draft criteria.* Washington, DC: Author.

American Psychiatric Association. (1994). *Diagnostic and statistical manual of mental disorders.* (4th ed.). (DSM-IV). Washington, DC: Author.

Beck, A. T., & Steer, R. A. (1987). *Beck Depression Inventory manual.* San Antonio, TX: The Psychological Corporation.

Campbell, D. T., & Fiske, D. W. (1959). Convergent and discriminant validation by the multitrait-multimethod matrix. *Psychological Bulletin, 56,* 81–105.

Depue, R. A., Slater, J. F., Wolfstetter-Kausch, D. K., Klein, D., Goplerud, E., & Farr, D. (1981). A behavioral paradigm for identifying persons at risk for bipolar depressive disorder: A conceptual framework and five validation studies. *Journal of Abnormal Psychology Monograph, 90*(5), 381–437.

Derogatis, L. R. (1994). *SCL-90-R administration, scoring, and procedures manual* (3rd ed.). Minneapolis: National Computer Systems.

Epstein, S. (1979). The stability of behavior: 1. On predicting most of the people much of the time. *Journal of Personality and Social Psychology, 37,* 1097–1126.

Epstein, S. (1983). Aggregation and beyond: Some basic issues on the prediction of behavior. *Journal of Personality, 51,* 360–392.

Faust, D., & Miner, R. A. (1986). The empiricist and his new clothes: DSM-III in perspective. *American Journal of Psychiatry, 143,* 962–967.

Gilligan, C. (1981). *In a different voice.* Cambridge. MA: Harvard University Press.

Hempel, C. G. (1965). *Aspects of scientific explanation.* New York: Free Press.

Horowitz, M., Wilner, N., & Alvarez, W. (1979). Impact of Events Scale: A measure of subjective stress. *Psychosomatic Medicine, 41*(3), 209–218.

Loevinger, J. (1957). Objective tests as instruments of psychological theory. *Psychological Reports, 3,* 635–694.

Lumsden, E. A. (1987). The impact of shared items on the internal-structural validity of the MCMI. In C. Green (Ed.), *Conference on the Millon clinical inventories (MCMI, MBHI, MAPI)* (pp. 325–333). Minneapolis: National Computer Systems.

Meehl, P. (1978). Theoretical risks and tabular asterisks: Sir Karl, Sir Ronald, and the slow progress of soft psychology. *Journal of Consulting and Clinical Psychology, 46,* 806–834.

Meehl, P. E., & Rosen, A. (1955). Antecedent probability and the efficiency of psychometric signs, patterns, or cutting scores. *Psychological Bulletin, 52,* 194–216.

Millon, T. (1969/1983). *Modern psychopathology: A biosocial approach to maladaptive learning and functioning.* Philadelphia: Saunders (Reprinted: Prospect Heights, IL: Waveland Press).

Millon, T. (1981). *Disorders of personality: DSM-III, Axis II.* New York: John Wiley.

Millon, T. (1986a). Personality prototypes and their diagnostic criteria. In T. Millon & G. L. Klerman (Eds.), *Contemporary directions in psychopathology: Toward the DSM-IV* (pp. 671–712). New York: Guilford.

Millon, T. (1986b). A theoretical derivation of pathological personalities. In T. Millon & G. L. Klerman (Eds.), *Contemporary directions in psychopathology: Toward the DSM-IV* (pp. 639–670). New York: Guilford.

Millon, T. (1987a). *Manual for the Millon Clinical Multiaxial Inventory-II (MCMI-II)* (2nd ed.). Minneapolis: National Computer Systems.

Millon, T. (1990). *Toward a new personology.* New York: John Wiley.

Paykel, E. S., Klerman, G. L., & Prusoff, B. A. (1976). Personality and symptom pattern in depression. *British Journal of Psychiatry, 129,* 327–334.

Selzer, M. L. (1971). The Michigan Alcoholism Screening Test: A quest for a new diagnostic instrument. *American Journal of Psychiatry, 127*(12), 1653–1658.

Shea, M. T., Glass, D. R., Pilkonis, P. A., Watkins, J., & Docherty, J. P. (1987). Frequency and complications of personality disorders in a sample of depressed outpatients. *Journal of Personality Disorders, 1,* 27–42.

Spielberger, C. D. (1983). *Manual for the Stait-Trait Anxiety Inventory.* Palo Alto: CA: Consulting Psychologists Press.

Wetzler, S., & Marlowe, D. (1992). What they don't tell you in test manuals: A response to Millon. *Journal of Counseling and Development, 70,* 327–428.

Wiggins, J. (1982). Circumplex models of interpersonal behavior in clinical psychology. In P. Kendall & J. N. Butcher (Eds.), *Handbook of research methods in clinical psychology* (pp. 183–222). New York: John Wiley.

Wilson, E. O. (1975). *Sociobiology: The new synthesis.* Cambridge, MA: Harvard University Press.

Wilson, E. O. (1978). *On human nature.* Cambridge, MA: Harvard University Press.

4

The Rorschach

Philip Erdberg

INTRODUCTION

If you were to choose some people at random, show them the words *personality test,* and ask them to tell you their first thought, many of them would respond with something about the Rorschach or inkblots. The Rorschach is an old and widely used instrument, and in the popular mind it is often synonymous with psychological testing. If you then let your subjects turn the tables and ask you a question, chances are many of them would be curious about how the Rorschach works. They would want to know how psychologists take a person's responses about some inkblots and come up with an extensive personality description. The purpose of this chapter is to answer that question. In the process, we'll discuss many aspects of the Rorschach, but our emphasis throughout will be on understanding how the test accomplishes its goal of describing people.

SOME RORSCHACH BASICS

The Rorschach is a personality test that psychologists use with children as young as age 5 and with adults throughout the lifespan. It consists of 10 inkblots, 5 of which are black or some shade of gray and 5 of which have other colors as well, all on white backgrounds. The blots were developed by a Swiss psychiatrist, Hermann Rorschach, who first described his work in 1921 in his monograph, *Psychodiagnostik.* Earlier researchers had used inkblots to study imagination, but Rorschach moved beyond a focus solely on content to come up with a unique contribution—the idea that observing the strategies people use in formulating responses to inkblots could allow descriptions of how they are likely to handle a variety of real-world situations. As an example, imagine a person who brings a great deal of action and organization to her Rorschach percepts ("Two people dancing around a Maypole with streamers flying and capes blowing in the wind, like at a celebration," as opposed to "Two people sitting down"). We might hypothesize that that person would take an active and integrative approach to problems if he or she were serving as a member of a planning committee. Concurrent validity studies that associated different organizing approaches on the Rorschach with different real-world problem-solving styles would provide support for our hypotheses and allow personality descriptions.

Rorschach died in 1922 at the age of 38, only a year after the test was published. Sadly, he was never able to develop many of the remarkable foresighted ideas he had introduced in his monograph. Some of his colleagues kept interest in the test alive, and after it was brought to the United States in 1925, five American psychologists each developed systems for its utilization. From 1936 to 1957, these five systematizers—Samuel Beck, Marguerite Hertz, Bruno Klopfer, Zygmunt Piotrowski, and David Rapaport—produced overlapping but independent approaches to the test. Although disagreement among proponents of the various systems was frequent, the research studies and training of psychologists that resulted from each ensured the survival of the Rorschach. More recently, Exner (Exner, 1991, 1993; Exner & Weiner, 1982) has combined the most useful components of the earlier approaches with his own research to develop what has now become the mostly widely used Rorschach method—the Comprehensive System. An extensive network of normative and validity studies supports the test's applicability in a variety of settings.

Using the Comprehensive System's guidelines, let's describe how a psychologist would administer the Rorschach. The examiner, who is seated by the patient's side so as to minimize the body language communication that might occur if they were face to face, begins the *response phase* by presenting the first blot with the simple question, "What might this be?" If the patient asks for more information about how to formulate answers ("May I turn the card sideways?"), the examiner responds in a nondirective way ("It's up to you"). When all 10 blots have been presented, the examiner starts the *inquiry phase*. She explains to the patient that they will go back through the responses and that she will be asking questions to find out the exact location of each percept and to ascertain which variables, such as the form or color of the blot, played a part in producing the answer. The data developed during the response and inquiry phases later allow the examiner to *code* the patient's responses—a process which involves reducing responses to a series of symbols. As an example, an answer would be coded *o* (ordinary form quality) if it appeared in a Comprehensive System normative table of commonly reported percepts. After all the responses have been coded, the psychologist can calculate a series of summary scores. An example of such a summary score is the *X+%*, the percentage of a patient's answers that are normatively common. The psychologist then reviews these scores, as well as the actual content of the patient's responses, in order to formulate a personality description.

Let's put what we've said so far about how the Rorschach works in different words. It is a perceptual-cognitive task in which people respond to a series of problems consisting of moderately ambiguous visual stimuli. With little in the way of guidance from the examiner, they are asked to come up with answers to the question "What might this be?" Validity studies suggest that people often solve these inkblot problems in ways representative of strategies they use to deal with moderately ambiguous real-world situations. The perceptual part of the process occurs quickly (eye movement studies indicate that people typically scan each of the blots in less than a second). The next several seconds are devoted to a complex cognitive sequence in which habitual problem-solving styles and psychological needs come together to determine the structure of the response. We know, for example, that depressed inpatients in comparison with nondepressed individuals are more likely to use the gray-black features of the blots in formulating their answers. We code these varied approaches that individuals use in solving the Rorschach problem. Then, through a network of validity studies that link Rorschach elements with real-world behavior or membership in independently determined diagnostic categories, we attempt a description of the person. The next section is a survey of these various Rorschach elements.

THE RORSCHACH ELEMENTS

In the previous section, we described a process in which the ambiguous visual problems that are the Rorschach elicit organizing and problem-solving strategies representative of how an individual experiences and handles real-world situations. We chronicle this process by coding the various elements the person uses in producing Rorschach percepts. In this section we'll discuss these elements. We'll first describe how each is identified. Then we'll talk about relationships between that Rorschach finding and aspects of the person's real-world behavior. The elements we'll discuss are those of the Comprehensive System. You can read more about the normative and validity data supporting them in the works by Exner cited earlier.

Location

The first element the psychologist codes in describing a Rorschach percept is its location—how much of the blot was used to produce the answer. If the person uses the entire blot, the location is coded *W* (whole). If he chooses a part that normative tables indicate is frequently seen, the location is *D* (common detail). If he uses an area that is not often reported, the location is *Dd* (uncommon detail). If the white background space (S) makes up part of the percept, the coding is *WS, DS,* or *DdS,* depending on whether the overall location is the whole blot or a common or uncommon detail area.

The use of the entire blot (W) appears to be associated with ability and motivation to interact extensively with the environment. That is particularly true if these W percepts organize different parts of the blot into a whole or if they occur on some of the more fragmented blots whose configurations make such responses difficult. Adults have more of these complex Ws than do children. Within the adult population, individuals with no psychiatric history have more complex Ws than do schizophrenics or neurotics.

Common details (D) are also related to efficient function, and they are the most frequent location choice made by nonpatient adults. They probably involve a less energy-consuming integrative approach than does W, indicating instead a more conservative, matter-of-fact response to the obvious aspects of the environment. Adult nonpatients give about one and one-half times as many Ds as they give Ws.

Uncommon details (Dd) account for about 5 percent of the location choices nonpatient adults make in their Rorschachs. If the percentage goes much higher than that, normative data tell us that our patient has responded to one aspect of the test—the locations he used to formulate answers—quite differently from the way most people do. Inpatient schizophrenics, for example, have notably higher proportions (21 percent) of Dd percepts in their records. Our concern would be that the individual with a disproportionate number of Dd answers focuses on unusual aspects of his environment in gathering the data necessary for solving problems.

Rorschach and most of the other systematizers viewed the use of the white space (S) areas as associated with an oppositional or negative style, although it was suggested that this attribute could also be associated with autonomy and uniqueness. There are S areas in 6 percent of the location choices on average for a group of nonpatient adults. S occurs somewhat more frequently (10 percent) in an outpatient character disorder group, and suicidal and paranoid individuals also have more S in their records than the nonpatient sample. It would appear that, in low proportions, S represents a "healthy" ability to differentiate oneself from the world. Higher numbers on this finding tend to be associated with a variety of syndromes that are characterized by a sense of alienation.

Determinants

After coding the percept's location, the psychologist next turns to the question of what aspects of the blot, such as color, have been used in producing the response. Psychologists call this element the *determinant.* It may involve color or shading, the shape of the area chosen, some attribution of movement, or a combination of these possibilities (blends). These determinants provide a major source of interpretive data. We'll discuss each of them in some detail.

Chromatic Color.   The first determinant we'll describe is chromatic color. We code it when the person uses the reds, blues, greens, or other nongray, black, or white colors to help formulate the percept. When this happens, the examiner must ascertain whether the shape of the blot was also involved. This is done during the inquiry phase. For example, if an individual reported the percept "blood" in the response phase, during the inquiry the examiner would ask him to explain what about the blot made it look like that. If he said, "It's all red, just like blood," the coding would be C. The percept "flower," explained during the inquiry as "It has that reddish color and these might be the petals," would be scored CF. That would indicate that color was the primary determinant but that there was also some use of the shape or form (F) features. If the same percept was explained as "Here are the petals and the stem with a shape like a rose and it has a pinkish color," the coding would be FC. That would mean that form was the primary determinant but that color was secondarily involved. This decision as to whether form is totally absent, secondary, or primary is made in coding determinants that involve achromatic color and shading as well.

A number of validity studies link chromatic color on the Rorschach with an interactive responsiveness to other parts of the environment. Individuals who give more chromatic color are more susceptible to distraction, more apt to alter their judgments in the face of persuasion, and more likely to give words related to the environment in a free association task.

Chromatic color appears to be associated with interaction with the environment; our next question is how well controlled this interaction is. The balance of FC to CF and C provides some data about this question. FC is associated with greater ability to maintain well-modulated behavior at times when emotion plays a part in its formulation. Normative studies indicate that children have more CF and C in their records than $FC,$ with this balance shifting at about age 14 as their ability to modulate interaction with the world increases. Adults who are able to delay their responses in a problem-solving task have more FC than CF and C in their records. A shift from CF and C to FC is associated with ratings of treatment progress and lowered probability of relapse for a variety of patient groups.

Human Movement.   The second determinant to be discussed is human movement. M is the symbol used to indicate this way of producing a percept. It is coded for any sort of human activity, either active ("Two people dancing") or passive ("A man sitting down").

The M determinant appears associated with the use of internal resources as a way of solving problems. Validity studies have linked M with cognitive operations, abstract thinking, and a less interactive, more ideational style. When a problem comes up, the individual whose Rorschach contains a lot of M is more likely to go off for a walk to think it through than to seek out a friend with whom to talk it through.

The two problem-solving styles associated with chromatic color and human movement are quite different, stylistically. Rorschach called this contrast the *Erlebnistypus* (EB) and suggested that it described a fundamental aspect of psychological function. Individuals with a preponderance of chromatic color in their Rorschachs (*extratensives*) tend to deal with stressful situations by interacting with the environment. Individuals whose EB is significantly in the *M* direction (*introversives*) are more apt to delay behavior while they bring their ideational resources to bear on the situation. Test-retest and neurophysiological studies suggest that Rorschach was right in identifying the EB as a basic and enduring characteristic that is typically well entrenched by midadolescence.

Although the two problem-solving styles categorized by the EB are different behaviorally, they are equally effective in coming up with solutions. In problem-solving studies, for example, extratensives are more likely to take a trial-and-error approach, whereas introversives often operate more slowly and systematically. But if we use time to solution as our criterion, typically there are not significant differences between these two stylistically very different groups. The results are suggestive both of clear-cut differences—extratensives use more environmental feedback and introversives depend more on internal processes—and good efficiency for both styles. Most people are able to use both approaches, with their EB direction predicting which one is likely in most situations. A summary score, the Experience Actual (EA), totals the introversive and extratensive sides of the EB to provide a single measure of the person's ability to operate in an organized, task-oriented manner.

Some people, however, have Rorschachs in which the amount of chromatic color and the amount of human movement responses are nearly equal. These individuals, *ambitents* in Rorschach terminology, are characterized by less consistent, often inefficient problem-solving approaches. Other individuals have Rorschach findings in which either human movement of chromatic color far outweighs the other determinant. These super-introversives and super-extratensives are often inflexible in their problem-solving approach. A super-extratensive individual might, for example, continue to use an extratensive approach in a situation in which he would be well served by shifting to a more introversive style.

The next several determinants we'll discuss are associated with less well-organized psychological processes than those we have described so far. Although stylistically different, chromatic color and human movement both involve organized, task-oriented approaches to solving problems. The next determinants appear associated with experiences in which ideation or emotion impinges on the person in unpredictable, nonvolitional ways, making it difficult to solve problems efficiently.

Animal Movement.   This determinant is coded *FM* and is reserved for animals in activities appropriate for their species. "A tiger poised to leap" or "A seahorse swimming through the water" would be examples of percepts we would code with an *FM* determinant.

Interpretively, *FM* appears associated with the experience of some sort of drive state that has the ability to intrude into consciousness, disrupt concentration and task-oriented activities, and sometimes provoke behavior. While *M* involves the deliberate decision to use thinking as a way of solving problems, *FM* is need-state ideation that impinges in nonpredictable ways. If *FM* is greater than *M,* the probability of relapse after hospitalization is greater for psychiatric patients. *FM* may drive inappropriate and sometimes impulsive behavior, whereas *M* is associated with a greater likelihood of thinking carefully about stressful situations. Two studies suggest that *FM* increases in juvenile offenders with indeterminate sentences and in overweight individuals hospitalized on a liquid-only diet—two groups we would expect to be in high-need states.

Inanimate Movement.   The coding for this determinant is *m.* It involves inanimate objects that are described as being in motion. An example of *m* would be "a rocket ship blasting off."

While *FM* appears to be associated with internal need states, *m* is linked with the awareness of pressure coming from outside. *m* increases significantly in individuals who are under situational stress in settings where they have little control over the circumstances. Trainees on the day before their first parachute jump, patients on the day before surgery, and Navy personnel during severe storm conditions all show increases in the amount of *m* in their records. Test-retest studies indicate that *m* shows a good deal of fluctuation over time, reflecting day-to-day variations in a person's level of situational stress.

Shading.   This is the first of the determinants we'll discuss in which people use variations in ink saturation to produce their answers. The ink distribution is not uniform across each blot, and there is a substantial amount of light-to-dark variation on many of them. If the shape of the percept is primary and the use of the light-dark variation is secondary, the coding would be *FY.* An example would be the response "an x-ray of an arm bone" with an inquiry that explained the percept by noting, "It's sort of long, like an arm, and some parts are darker like in an x-ray." If the shading variation is primary and shape plays a secondary role in creating the percept ("It has darker and lighter parts like a storm cloud, and it has that shape too"), the coding would be *YF.* If there is no use of form at all ("It's just lighter and darker smoke"), the coding would be *Y.*

The presence of shading in the record is associated with the unpleasant emotional experience of helplessness in the face of stressful situations. Although anxiety may be involved, we are probably talking more specifically about the feeling of not having the necessary resources to master problems. This determinant occurs with greater frequency in depressed inpatients, alcoholics, and recent heart attack victims. People who are able to terminate psychotherapy at 18 months show decreases in the amount of shading determinants in their Rorschachs. Those who are not ready to terminate have about the same amount of shading as they did in their pretreatment records.

Texture.   This determinant involves using the light-dark variation to give a sense of texture, as if the blot were a tactile instead of a visual stimulus. An example would be a response of "bearskin rug" explained during the inquiry as "Some parts are lighter and some parts are darker, like it would feel furry." The coding is *FT, TF,* or *T,* depending on whether the shape of the blot is the dominant determinant with texture secondary, whether shape is secondary, or whether there is no use of shape at all.

Texture seems to be associated with a need for emotional contact with others. It shows up with greater frequency in people who have had recent interpersonal disruptions, such as adults who have just been separated or divorced or children who have recently been placed in a foster home for the first time because of parental loss. However, if interpersonal resources are taken away very early or were never present, as with children who have been in many brief foster placements, there may be no texture in the record at all. This finding is suggestive of a "burnt child" syndrome.

Most nonpatients have one texture response in their Rorschachs. Studies of a variety of patient groups suggest that they are characterized either by more than one texture response or records that have none at all. What we may be seeing with these groups is either an inordinate wish for emotional contact or the denial of any need for this sort of experience. Studies demonstrating a shift toward the modal one-texture-response Rorschach for patients in a variety of different kinds of psychotherapy underscore the fundamental importance of the relationship in therapeutic change.

Vista.   This determinant is coded when variations in ink saturation are used to give a sense of depth or three dimensionality. As with the other shading determinants, the coding is *FV, VF,* or *V,* depending on whether shape is primary, secondary, or not used at all. An example of an *FV* percept would be the response of "a tunnel," elaborated during the inquiry as "The lighter part makes it look like it goes back into the distance."

Vista is a relatively infrequent determinant. It appears to be associated with thinking about oneself in an unremittingly negative light. It is related to painful, unrealistic introspection that maximizes and distorts deficiencies, often in a guilt-ridden way. This determinant occurs more frequently in the Rorschachs of chronically depressed and suicidal individuals.

Achromatic Color.   A percept that included the gray, white, or black features of the blot would be coded *FC'*, *C'F,* or *C'* depending on whether form was primary, secondary, or not used at all. The response "a black bat," explained during the inquiry as "Here are the wings and the antennae and it's black like a bat," would be an example of *FC'*.

From an interpretive standpoint, it appears that significant amounts of achromatic color in someone's Rorschach can be associated with emotional constraint. This holding in of feelings is a disruptive process. Patients with psychosomatic problems, obsessive-compulsives, and schizoid individuals have more achromatic color in their records than people who are better able to let others know about their emotions. Inpatient depressives show marked decreases in achromatic color when their discharge Rorschachs are compared with the ones they took before treatment began.

Although animal and inanimate movement, shading, texture, vista, and achromatic color depict widely different sorts of experiences, they are all disruptive and nonvolitional. These determinants are associated with ideas or emotions that impinge on the person in unpredictable ways, interfering with task-oriented function. The Experienced Stimulation (*es*) is a measure that quantifies these disruptive psychological processes. It is calculated as the total of these "intrusive" determinants. If we compare a person's *EA*, the total of his organized psychological resources, with his *es*, we can predict the likelihood of his being able to direct his behavior toward identified goals. If the unorganized material (*es*) is significantly greater than the task-oriented functions associated with *EA*, the potential for disrupted behavior controlled by need states and intrusive emotionality goes up.

Pure Form and Lambda.   All of the determinants we've discussed so far, whether indicative of task-oriented or intrusive processes, involve people bringing complex aspects of their psychology into the production of their percepts. There is another determinant, pure form (*F*), that is qualitatively different in that it reflects more objective operation. Along with a derivative measure, Lambda, the pure form determinant provides information about the person's tendency to simplify versus his potential for more intricately elaborated involvement with the world.

From a coding standpoint, we assign the determinant *F* when the individual uses only the shape or form of the blot in creating a percept. An example would be the response "butterfly" with an inquiry that explained the percept by saying, "Here are the wings and here is the head and here's the tail with that shape just like a swallowtail butterfly." The person has used only the form of the blot, with no articulation of color, movement, or shading. This is the most common determinant on the Rorschach. Nonpatient adults typically give pure form as the only determinant for about 35 percent of their responses.

As we noted, pure form is the most "objective" way to approach the Rorschach. The person responds to the task by searching through his database about the shapes of objects. He then comes up with a best fit in the same way that a computer with optical scanning capability might. The person's psychological complexity doesn't play much of a part in producing the percept. Instead, this approach employs rational, affect-free operation.

An important question is how much of the time the individual operates in the simplifying way reflected by the pure form determinant. Lambda is a summary score that provides a useful measure of the balance between the pure form style and more complex engagement with the world. It is calculated as the number of answers using only pure form divided by all the other kinds of answers in the record. Some examples may be helpful in understanding the use of this index. In a 20-response Rorschach with 5 pure form answers and 15 answers involving other determinants, Lambda would be 5 divided by 15, or .33. Lambda for adults is typically around .60, so this finding would suggest that the individual has substantially less than the normative proportion of pure form answers. He is likely to find his own psychology frequently impinging, making it difficult to operate in a matter-of-fact way. On the other hand, if the person has 15 pure form responses and only 5 with other kinds of determinants, his Lambda would be 15 divided by 5, or 3.0, well above what we would have expected. This person would be apt to simplify situations, not allowing either his own complexity or the nuances of the circumstance to play much of a part in formulating responses.

Form Quality

After the psychologist has coded the answer's determinant, she next evaluates it for perceptual convergence or form quality. She starts by using tables that provide data about the objects many people have reported for the various blot areas. Form quality evaluated in this way becomes, to some extent, a normative concept. If many people have reported a particular percept for a blot area, it is coded as ordinary (o) form quality. If the answer is normatively uncommon but easily seen once reported, it is coded unusual (u). If the percept involves a gross distortion of the blot area, it is coded minus (−) to indicate that it can't be easily seen by others. By calculating percentages for the amount of ordinary, unusual, and minus form quality in a person's Rorschach ($X+\%$, $Xu\%$, $X-\%$), we can assess whether psychological difficulties are interfering with what should be a relatively easy perceptual-cognitive task.

We expect that about 80 percent of a person's answers will be coded o. This is a very stable finding that characterizes individuals throughout the lifespan. If the percentage drops significantly below 70 percent, particularly if several answers with − form quality appear, we become concerned that disruptive factors are intruding on the person's easy ability to operate convergently. The content of some responses is normatively so common that they are coded as Populars. These answers make up about 30 percent of most records. If the percentage of Populars drops markedly below this figure, we can raise concerns about conventionality. Inpatient schizophrenics, for example, give Popular content in only about 20 percent of their answers.

Self-Focus Measures

Several Rorschach elements provide data about the amount and quality of time a person spends in self-focus activities. These indicators allow a description of the proportion and intensity of attention devoted to self versus that concentrated on others.

The use of pairs ("two ladies") and reflections ("A bear looking at himself in the water") appears to be related to self-focus. These kinds of responses occur more frequently in individuals who give more self-oriented answers on incomplete sentences tests, those who spend more time looking in a mirror while waiting for an interview, and those who make more use of the pronoun *I* during an interview. Many psychiatric patients are either higher or lower than the normal range for the number of pair and reflection percepts they produce. A shift toward the norm tends to be associated with improvement for these patients.

A weighted measure, the Egocentricity Index, relates the number of pair and reflection answers a person gives to his total number of percepts. Findings that are much higher or lower than the norm for a person's age suggest possible difficulties in maintaining a developmentally appropriate balance between emphasis on self and others. High Egocentricity Index findings, particularly when reflection responses are involved, suggest an egocentric stance. Low findings suggest that the person isn't sufficiently self-centered.

Another element associated with self-focus is a determinant we haven't discussed yet, form dimensionality (*FD*). This is coded when the person uses the shape of the blot to give a sense of perspective. An example would be "A monster looking down at you," explained during the inquiry by "His head looks small, like it's a long way up, and his feet are gigantic." A number of studies suggest that this determinant is associated with a thoughtful sort of introspection, the ability to put positive and negative aspects of oneself in perspective. This more even-handed approach to thinking about oneself contrasts with the intensely negative self-focus associated with the presence of Vista determinants.

Active-Passive Ratio

All of the movement determinants—human, animal, and inanimate—can be coded for whether the movement is active or passive. An example of active movement would be "A man banging on a drum," whereas "A bear lying down and resting" would be coded as passive movement. By cumulating the number of active versus passive movement percepts in the record, we can produce an index called the active-passive ratio. Nonpatients tend to have a balance of active and passive answers. Normatively this involves about twice as many active as passive percepts.

A wide variety of patient groups show very skewed active-passive ratios, either with more than three times as many active percepts or with passive greater than active by more than one answer. This sort of skewed profile may be associated with cognitive and interpersonal rigidity, making it difficult for the person to move easily between obtaining information and acting on it. Patients rated as improved show a change toward a more normative active-passive ratio during their treatment. Those individuals who are not rated as improved tend to stay about the same on this variable.

Organizational Activity

Another element that the psychologist codes is the amount of organization that goes into a Rorschach response. In the percept "Two people cooking soup in a kettle outdoors as a bird flies by," the individual has done a substantial amount of organizing. He has taken different blot areas and formulated relationships among them. That is a very different approach than "Two people," a response that does not create links among different components. Percepts that involve organization and most Whole responses are more energy consuming than single detail percepts. Normatively, about half of the answers nonpatient adults give involve this more complex sort of organizational activity. If the person is much higher or lower than that percentage in organizational attempts on the Rorschach, we may want to focus on the extent of organizational complexity he brings to daily life.

Regardless of how frequently the person organizes his world, another important question concerns the efficiency of each organizational effort. For any given number of responses involving organization, we know about how many details a nonpatient sample typically processes. We can compare an individual's responses against that norm with a variable called the *Zd*. If he has brought in many more details than most people do for a given number of organizational attempts, we say that he is an *over-incorporator*. Over-incorporators deal very extensively with their worlds, needing to account for every detail. Although frequently useful, sometimes this very cautious style can immobilize behavior, since often it is necessary to act with less than complete data. On the other hand, *under-incorporators* bring in fewer details per organizational effort than most people do. They may miss important elements in their environment because they scan too quickly. Their approach is characterized by fast speed but many errors. Sometimes under-incorporators behave inappropriately because they have not processed all the elements necessary to make a thoughtful decision.

Affective Ratio

The last three inkblots (card VIII, IX, and X) are fully chromatic, with many hues of blue, green, yellow, pink, and brown. The other seven cards are either solely gray and black (I, IV, V, VI, and VII) or only partially chromatic (II and III), with just some red areas in addition to the gray/black parts. The Affective Ratio, the number of answers to the three fully chromatic cards compared to the number of answers to the other seven cards, provides some data about willingness to process affective aspects of the world. Most people give about 40 percent of their answers to these last three cards. If the individual's percentage is much higher or lower than that, a number of studies suggest that he may be either very receptive to the emotional parts of his world or someone who is very uncomfortable about emotionally charged situations.

Extratensives give somewhat more responses to the fully chromatic cards than do introversives, although there is a good deal of overlap between the groups. This finding is consistent with the characterization of extratensives as people who interact more readily with their environment. Younger children are also higher on the Affective Ratio, consistent with observations about their openness to emotion. As has been the case with some of the other Rorschach elements we've discussed, patient groups tend to be at the extremes on the affective ratio. These individuals manifest either too much or too little responsiveness to the emotional parts of their experience. A shift toward a more normative Affective Ratio is often associated with treatment progress.

Content

The final element the psychologist evaluates is the actual content of the percepts. Normatively, answers with animal and human content are frequent. We expect that about 45 percent of a person's responses will involve animals and about 20 percent will involve humans. If an individual's percentages deviate significantly from these averages, we can analyze the findings in terms of interest in interpersonal activities.

Another group of content categories—including plant life, maps, and natural phenomena such as clouds or mountains—appears to be associated with a rather isolated interpersonal stance. If these responses make up more than a quarter of the person's Rorschach content, the correlation with measures of social isolation is significant.

Sometimes individuals elaborate on their percepts, describing objects or living things as damaged or dead or portraying humans or animals as involved in aggressive or cooperative interactions. If the elaboration includes a description of death, damage, injury, or a dysphoric characteristic such as sadness, we code the percept as *Morbid* content. Depressed children and adults give more of these answers than nonpatients do, and they also occur more frequently in suicidal individuals. Morbid content answers correlate with lower findings on the Egocentricity Index, suggesting poor self-concept. As the number of Morbid content answers goes up, validity studies suggest the likelihood that the person's stance is a pessimistic, self-depreciating one.

Percepts in which interactions are described as aggressive are coded *AG*. Individuals whose Rorschachs are significantly above the norm for *AG* answers may manifest more verbal and nonverbal aggressiveness and are more likely to see the interpersonal world in negative, hostile terms. If the person elaborates percepts with descriptions of positive, productive interactions ("Two people setting a table for a formal dinner together"), the coding is *COP*. These answers are associated with a view of the interpersonal world as pleasant and cooperative. Individuals with more than two *COP* elaborations are likely to be perceived positively by peers. Clinically, the presence of *COP* is associated with more active involvement in group therapy sessions and with successful treatment outcome.

RORSCHACH INTERPRETATION: A CLINICAL EXAMPLE

Psychologists work with all the elements we've discussed to produce comprehensive descriptions of the people they test. A good way to observe this process—and at the same time to review some of the Rorschach elements—is by taking a sample set of Rorschach data to generate a personality description. We'll consider the elements in the order they were presented in the last section, using the normative data provided by Exner (1991) to guide our interpretation. Our subject is a 46-year-old male, Mr. H, who came for counseling because of interpersonal and family difficulties.

Location

W = 10; D = 5; Dd = 1; Space = 0. The most noteworthy finding in Mr. H's choice of locations for his percepts is that he uses many more Wholes (*W*) than we would expect. He has twice as many *W*s as common details (*D*), nearly opposite of what normative data would lead us to predict. This finding has both positive and negative aspects. His use of the Whole location, particularly since many of his *W*s involve complex organizational activity, indicates an active approach to the environment. The relative scarcity of *D* in the record suggests that he may run into difficulty when he must shift from his energetic, integrative style to a more detail-oriented one. His one uncommon detail location (*Dd*) is normative. We do not want to overinterpret Mr. H's complete absence of white space (*S*) locations, because such a finding occurs in about 14 percent of nonpatients. It may suggest some tendency toward a rather conventional style.

Determinants

M = 4; Chromatic Color = 4.5; FM = 1; m = 1; C' = 1; V = 1; T = 2; Y = 5; F = 1; Lambda = .07; Blends = 10. We begin our analysis of the determinants Mr. H chose for his percepts by noting that his use of chromatic color and human movement (*M*) are nearly equal. Mr. H is an ambitent. He does not have a clear-cut problem-solving style. His approach when faced with stressful situations may involve oscillation between interacting with the environment and trying to think the problem through. The approach that ambitents use is less efficient than either an introversive or an extratensive style, both of which allow more decisive resolutions in shorter times.

We next look at the sum of Mr. H's human movement (*M*) and chromatic color (his *EA* is 8.5) in comparison with the sum of his shading and achromatic color determinants (his *es* is 16). The *EA* represents the totality of a person's organized coping strategies, whereas *es* reflects unorganized, disruptive psychological material. At present, Mr. H has substantially more unorganized material impinging on him than he has available coping resources. He is about two standard deviations below the adult mean in this regard. It is no wonder that he has sought counseling at this time. A first therapeutic intervention must address his present overload.

In order to understand the specific nature of Mr. H's disruptive overload, we look at the actual determinants making up his *es*. He has nearly twice the normative number of animal movement (*FM*) determinants. This finding suggests a lot of ideational intrusion, often associated with need states, that has the ability to disrupt concentration. He has one more texture (*T*) determinant than we would expect, indicating some greater than usual need for emotional contact with others. The presence of even his one vista (*V*) determinant is of concern. It raises the possibility that Mr. H is spending some time in painful introspection, thinking about himself and coming up with negative material. Mr. H has substantially more than the normative amount of the shading determinant (*Y*), suggesting that he currently is likely feeling helpless about dealing with the stress he is experiencing.

Mr. H's Lambda of .07 is far below the adult male mean (.56)—a finding that tells us that he has used the pure form (*F*) determinant much less frequently than most people do. *F* is associated with relatively affect-free operation, in which the individual deals with situations in an objective, matter-of-fact way. When Lambda is as low as Mr. H's is, we can say that his ideational turmoil is likely to be involved in much of his behavior.

Mr. H is a complicated person. He used more than one determinant in more than 60 percent of his answers (blends), as opposed to the 23 percent we would expect normatively. Several of his answers involved three-determinant blends. Although blends do reflect psychological energy and richness, the excessive number and complexity of Mr. H's responses may suggest a level of overengagement that could become immobilizing.

Form Quality

X+% = 81%; Xu% = 19%; X–% = 0%; Populars = 6. Mr. H's form quality findings are normative. He converges on commonly seen percepts effortlessly. Although some of the earlier findings we've discussed suggest that this is a difficult time for him, these difficulties are not interfering with his ability to read the world accurately.

Self-Focus Measures

Egocentricity Index = .44; Reflections = 1; FD = 1. Mr. H's Egocentricity Index is edging toward the upper end of the normative range and it includes a reflection response, normatively infrequent for adults. We can say that he may spend somewhat more time in self-focus activities than most people and that some of this activity may be quite intense. We have already mentioned that Mr. H has a Vista response, suggesting that some of his introspection may be painful. The presence of a form dimensionality (*FD*) answer is a positive finding, suggesting that he also has the ability to view himself in a more even-handed way.

Active-Passive Ratio

Active-Passive Ratio = 8:3. Mr. H's active-passive ratio is within the normative range. He is able to maintain an appropriate active versus receptive balance.

Organizational Activity

Z-Frequency = 13; Zd = +6.5. Mr. H brought a great deal of organizational effort to his solution of the Rorschach task. He either used the Whole blot or he formulated relationships among different components for 13 of his 16 answers. Normatively, we would have expected this sort of organizational activity in only about half of his percepts. For many of those organizational efforts, Mr. H integrated more components than the norm. His *Zd* of +6.5 suggests that he is an over-incorporator. He scans his world very extensively. This finding, in combination with Mr. H's use of Whole locations and disproportionately infrequent pure form (*F*) determinants, describes a man whose engagement of the world's complexity is active and substantial. As we've noted, although often positive, this style can be immobilizing in situations that require a "reasonable best guess" when less than total information is available. As an example, Mr. H might have trouble with projects that involve deadlines.

Affective Ratio

Affective Ratio = .33. Mr. H's Affective Ratio is low, a surprising finding in light of all that we've said so far about his extensive engagement of the world's complexity. Remember, however, that the Affective Ratio provides a measure of how responsive a person is to *emotion.* Mr. H may not be comfortable when interactions involve feelings as well as information.

Content

Total Human Content = 5; Total Animal Content = 9; Morbid = 0; COP = 2; AG = 0. Mr. H is interested in the interpersonal world and views it as a place where positive, productive collaborations can occur. The specific content of his percepts did not indicate the likelihood of disturbing themes and, if anything, suggested a rather conventional outlook.

Treatment Implications

As we integrate the various Rorschach elements, Mr. H emerges as a man who is presently in an overload condition, experiencing more disruption than his organized resources can handle. His concentration and ability to handle situations in a task-oriented, objective manner are significantly compromised. He does not have a well-practiced way of solving problems, and he often feels helpless as he tries to make his situation better. A complicated and thought-ful man, he sometimes has difficulty getting beyond his deliberations. He is spending substantial time in rather intense self-focus, sometimes with painful results.

Since his presenting problem included family difficulties, it will be help-ful to think about the interpersonal implications of some of his Rorschach findings. His broadly conceptual style could make it hard for Mr. H to deal with day-to-day details. Other family members may see him as impractical and perfectionistic in his expectations and perhaps as overly conventional in his values. On the other hand, when they want to talk with him about emo-tional issues, his response may be to "back off," making him appear cold and uninterested. But Mr. H *is* interested in others and would like closer rela-tionships. His difficulty in talking about these needs with the people who might be able to satisfy them is likely to be an important therapeutic target.

Let's consolidate these Rorschach findings into an intervention ap-proach for Mr. H. His current state of overload must be our first target, since his stress level is substantial. It will be crucial to talk with Mr. H about his present situation so as to develop some short-range techniques to deal with the problems about which he feels so helpless. Our assessment has also iden-tified two sets of issues that will be important on a long-range basis.

From an individual standpoint, we've noted that Mr. H's problem-solv-ing style is highly conceptual and sometimes vacillating. Helping him develop an approach that allows timely, decisive resolutions while still taking advan-tage of his substantial integrative abilities would likely relieve stress and his sense of helplessness.

From an interpersonal standpoint, the combination of Mr. H's perfec-tionistic style and his discomfort with emotions likely makes family life diffi-cult and unsatisfying for everyone. After Mr. H has had a chance to think these issues through, he and his family might benefit from discussing them in some conjoint sessions.

Our assessment has identified a variety of important issues and helped place them in perspective. We can suggest that an approach that involves some immediate, problem-oriented intervention and then some longer-range individual and conjoint therapy would serve Mr. H and his family well.

SUMMARY

What the Rorschach does best is to provide descriptions of people—their prob-lem-solving capacities, emotional operations, interpersonal function, and self-concept. We use these descriptions to plan treatment approaches and to mon-itor how well the intervention is going. As research efforts generate data about how individuals with various syndromes respond to the Rorschach, we can provide hypotheses about diagnostic questions as well. The Rorschach's ability to continue a history of clinical usefulness that is now well into its second half-century depends on the acquisition of more and more validity data linking test findings with behavior.

REFERENCES

Exner, J. E. (1993). *The Rorschach: A Comprehensive System. Volume 1: Basic foundations* (3rd ed.). New York: Wiley.

Exner, J. E. (1991). *The Rorschach: A Comprehensive System. Volume 2: Interpretation* (2nd ed.). New York: Wiley.

Exner, J. E., & Weiner, I. B. (1982). *The Rorschach: A Comprehensive System. Volume 3: Assessment of children and adolescents.* New York: Wiley.

Rorschach, H. (1921). *Psychodiagnostik.* Bern: Bircher (Trans. Hans Huber Verlag, 1942).

The Thematic Apperception Test (TAT)

Richard H. Dana

INTRODUCTION

The Thematic Apperception Test (TAT) was developed in the 1930s to provide a vehicle for applying the need-press personality theory developed by Henry Murray (1938) to individuals. Murray assumed that the TAT elicited fantasy as a result of projecting past experience and present needs in response to ambiguous picture stimuli. The TAT provides a sample of oral behavior—storytelling—that is structured by directions, focused, time limited, and repetitive across picture stimuli. The protocol data are presumed to provide an adequate representation of personality contents. However, these contents are also responsive to culture, the clinician, and the purpose for assessment.

This chapter presents an approach to the analysis of TAT storytelling with historic roots in the clinical methodology of first-generation clinical psychologists, the structural approach developed by Silvan Tomkins (1947), and an attention to research literature for potential ingredients for TAT dimensions analogous to Rorschach locations, determinants, and content (see Dana, 1986).

Since this chapter originally appeared, the TAT has not only remained a primary instrument for personality description but it also has been enriched by continuing research on objective scoring and applications to racial/ethnic groups. This chapter will be primarily concerned with understanding the TAT as used for personality description. The first section will describe construction, administration, and stimulus characteristics. The nature of the picture stimuli will be considered in detail, using story examples from two college students. This section conveys some sense of the relationship between hypothesis development and card stimuli. The second section on principles of interpretation will synthesize literature to provide a context for the two reports whose stories were examined in the card stimuli section. These reports were discussed with the assessees as part of informed consent since complete feedback, including the written report, is an essential ingredient of responsible TAT practice (Dana, 1985) that has been incorporated into routine assessment practice by Finn (e.g., Finn & Tonsager, 1992). The third section introduces an assessment model for multicultural assessment using the TAT as an example with stories from a well-functioning American-Indian woman.[1] Working notes and a completed report provide an example of the author's usual approach. Finally, a favorable prognosis for an expanded TAT usage within the current assessment context is suggested.

CONSTRUCTION

There are 31 pictures that include 11 for adult men and women over 14 years of age (1, 2, 4, 5, 10, 11, 13, 14, 15, 19, 20); 7 of these are for adult males (BM cards) and adult women (GF cards) and for boys and girls from 7 to 14 years of age. There is one card for adult males (12M), one for adult women (12F), one for children of either sex (12BG), one for male children (13B), one for female children (13G), and a blank card (16) for all clients. Each picture contains a dramatic event or critical situation and a person with whom the client can identify (Morgan & Murray, 1935). The cards were intended to be a standard set and comprehensive in the sense of including the gamut of life situations. Murray believed that the first 10 cards evoked everyday situations while the second 10 could provide more unusual, dramatic, and bizarre fantasy. The manual acknowledges suggestions for specific pictures and artists (Murray, 1943). Picture 20 is a reproduction of an unknown original.

ADMINISTRATION

Murray instructed clients to sit with their backs to the clinician to facilitate free association, as in early psychoanalysis. Clients are now seated in a conventional manner, face to face across a table or at the corner of a desk. The original directions stressed that the TAT was a test of fantasy, creative, or literary imagination as a form of intelligence (Murray, 1943). All 20 cards for men or women were administered in standard order (1 through 10 and 11 through 20) during two separate sessions. The stories were dictated to an examiner for verbatim recording. An inquiry was provided to elicit responses to omitted parts of the stimulus. However, the majority of subsequent clients were not Murray's Harvard undergraduates and directions now exclude referents to imagination or intelligence.

A typical set of directions asks for a story that includes describing the cards, explaining what the characters are doing, what they have done in the past or what led up to the situation, and what they may do in the future. Feelings and thoughts of the characters are requested. An outcome is also asked for whenever there is one. Unlike the Rorschach, which apparently tolerates varied directions, it does make a difference in the TAT whether or not standard directions are used. Blatant directions with loaded words have produced distress in a number of studies. Similarly, research indicates that the traditional oral story will differ markedly from a written or dictated story given by the same individual. Group thematic responses also differ from those to an individual administration (see Dana, 1982, pp. 113–115).

Verbatim recording is used because it is the only safeguard for probity of the data. Clinicians are usually convinced individually that they seldom (if ever) lapse from the professional propriety of this deceptively simple task. Nonetheless, verbatim recording often does not occur. In teaching projective techniques, it is helpful for students to have audio and/or video exemplars of their TAT administrations for comparison with their own presumably verbatim recordings.

STIMULUS CHARACTERISTICS

Assessors have consistently used short forms composed of selected cards (Dana, 1982, see pp. 120–121, 139–149, 380, 383), although there are 31 cards to be administered in standard order as numbered during two sessions. The practice of using short forms can be justified only when stimulus and response characteristics are known to be equivalent between the short form and the entire set of cards. In fact, whenever the TAT is the only assessment instrument used, it is unethical to omit cards in the standard series. However, unless the assessor can anticipate court proceedings involving testimony based on the use of the TAT, a short form as part of a test battery is an acceptable practice. Whenever short forms are used, it is preferable to administer cards in their original numbered order, although Murstein (1963) has suggested, on the basis of several studies, that stimulus properties may overshadow order effects. In composing short forms, cards of medium ambiguity are most useful in eliciting relevant personality data from college students; cards 2, 3BM, 4, 6 (BM or GF), 7 (BM or GF), and 13MF meet this criterion. In addition, cards 11, 19 and 16 may elicit personalized stories laden with psychodynamics and/or psychopathology indicants in spite of their relative ambiguity. For short form sets composed of less than 10 cards, the cards listed above are preferred. Short forms have been developed primarily for use with college students, although there is one form for psychiatric patients (Newmark & Flouranzano, 1977).

The remainder of this section will describe the stimulus potential of each card for male and female assessees. Discussion of each card begins with the original Murray (1943) description in parenthesis after the card number. For each card, reference is made to the Eron (1950, 1953) norms for major themes as well as to more recent research. Two sets of verbatim stories from male and female college students are provided as examples. The man was a 23-year-old senior from a small-town working-class family in the south and had three male siblings. The woman was a 22-year-old senior from an upper middle-class family in a small southern city and had one younger sister. For sake of anonymity, these students will be called John and Amy. Although I prefer to omit any inquiry, most assessors do use an inquiry. Accordingly, (?) indicates at what points in the stories requests were made for additional content or specific questions were asked. These two stories per card are compared with stimulus characteristics and normative expectations for development of interpretive hypotheses. For each MF card, John's story will be presented first.

Card 1 (A young boy is contemplating a violin which rests on a table in front of him.)
This picture is the prototype for all achievement dramas, at least within middle-class U.S. culture. The violin and learning to play it are symbolic of achievement in anything. The fact that it is a child in the picture means that clients may project a personal childhood achievement dilemma. The absence of others in the picture permits the client to include early family surroundings, especially as pertinent to the atmosphere of support, indifference, or censure for the child's efforts. A story is expected that relates to achievement. The child plays or does not play the violin and the reasons for this behavior are usually stated. There are generally both immediate and long-term consequences of the child's degree of achievement with the violin. The 1950s norms indicated that nearly 50 percent of normal males produced aspiration themes, while women and hospitalized males were less likely to do so. Parental pressure for achievement is a dominant theme for both sexes. Occupational concerns for women were salient, perhaps due to Eron's selected sample.

John: OK. This boy is taking violin lessons and he's been taking them for a couple of weeks and he's tried and tried to get this thing down—and he's realized that this is not for him—and he's pondering how to tell his folks that he is not cut out to be a violinist. And he's pretty right to be worried about it because his parents are not going to be happy when they hear what he has to say.

Commentary.   It should be noted that many stories recognize that years or a lifetime of practice may be necessary for achievement. Here, the decision is made quickly by the child. There is awareness of responsibility to parents and awareness of their feelings as well. Internalized values and insight in the client may be inferred from such awareness by the character in the story. Although there is no active or long-term conflict with parents as a result of the decision, there is anticipation of their negative reaction, even though this prediction does not change the outcome. At another level, the client may be suggesting that conventional achievement of any kind is not for him.

Amy: (What if I have two stories?) This looks like he either wants to learn how to play the violin or he's frustrated—been participating—I can see in his eyes he doesn't hate it—or it could have belonged to someone who was very dear to him.

Commentary.   Either/or, dual themes suggest the quality of thinking with rapid fluctuation of ideas and feelings. There is a hint of family concern with achievement in past ownership of violin. She may not want achievement, but it does not happen, at least in the context of family concern, and frustration ensues. Facial expression is used as an indicant of feelings.

Card 2 (Country scene: In the foreground is a young woman with books in her hand; in the background a man is working in the fields and an older woman is looking on.)
This farm scene usually evokes a story concerning family relationships and quality of life. The young girl in the foreground may be leaving home for an independent life with whatever emotions this change entails. One-third of Eron's males focused on occupational concern and aspiration, while aspiration was the dominant theme for the women. What is being relinquished and the belief in what is coming to pass are salient.

John: (John almost rejected the card; pressure from the clinician was required to elicit the story.) (I don't get any clear sense of what's happening with these people or where they might be headed.) (Wanted to go to next card.) (? to stretch imagination.) I can see man and woman in foreground as maybe newlyweds—woman against tree . . . mother-in-law. Three of them trying to eke out an existence. Woman is schoolteacher, man with horse getting ready to plow this field. Woman against tree looks pretty grim—wondering where their sustenance is going to come from—maybe own a mortgage on their farm or something.

Commentary.   Instead of the usual focus on the girl in the foreground, the emphasis is on the couple who are designated as newlyweds, a unique label in this instance. The quality of family life is depicted as bleak and marginal. The grimness may stem from turmoil, poor family relationships, lack of love—all potential equivalents of sustenance. Somehow the picture has confused the client and the result is a reversal of the usual relationships, perhaps because the client sees himself as mired in the family drama and unable to extricate himself. These hypotheses stem from departures from normative expectations.

Amy: Well, in one sense, I see this as kinda the development of man: have animal there, beast of burden used to plow fields—man very muscular—woman who is pregnant—development on to the girl who pursues intellectual things—holding the books. She looks like she is reflecting on all this—not sure if she sees herself different from woman who is pregnant—man in the fields. I think she might. All looking in this direction—may be toward the future and this is past. Or could be parents—real simple—woman concerned with having babies and man out working—divided by this barrier of rocks because she's different dressed nicely (?). I would say that she's gonna take all this into account—anxious, apprehensive about the future—kinda cradling these books—knowledge—guess she's got that to back her up—guess she's just gonna go out in the world.

Commentary. The "development of man" is an intellectualized screen that initially prevents a more personal story by use of card description. "Reflecting" constitutes an anxious concern regarding her own continuity and identity with family, especially her mother. She is not certain that she is different from her family, but she is detached from them by a barrier. The barrier may be something tangible, an event, or a personal characteristic. The anxiety extends to her personal future. Mother is "simple"—conventional, sex-role stereotyped—but she is not. The "cradling" is of books instead of being "pregnant/having babies." Knowledge may be "cradled" for her—handled tenderly, nurtured, loved, supported, although the reasons for this are unclear.

> *Card 3BM (On the floor against a couch is the huddled form of a boy with his head bowed on his right arm. Beside him on the floor is a revolver.)*

Card 3BM is frequently used for both men and women. This card is considered to pull for central value, or whatever is sufficiently important to account for the posture of the figure and the implied dysphoric affect. Most stories may be analyzed in this manner and the central value becomes whatever provided the impetus for suicide or emotional disturbance in normatively high-frequency stories. Inclusion or omission of the gun on the floor is indicative of acceptance and/or denial of hostile feelings. The gun may also be misperceived as scissors, a knife, or even an innocuous object such as keys. The figure is reported as male or female with equal frequency by males and females and no special interpretation is made from the sex of this figure.

John: This is a woman just in existential despair—she's just on the brink of suicide . . . I don't know why she wants to commit suicide, but she feels like an abject failure, defeated by everything she has tried. She feels nobody has any empathy for situation or true understanding of her internal life. Object on floor is a knife. Weeping against this piece of furniture because she feels deep contempt for herself because she lacks the courage to end her own misery.

Commentary. This story labels the condition of the central figure, notes the cause, attributes insensitivity and neglect to others, but accepts ultimate responsibility. In telling this story, the client feels sorry for himself, simultaneously blames others for lack of understanding and himself for conspicuous lack of courage. The intensity of feelings is betrayed by the use of words and phrases like "brink," "abject," and "deep contempt." The story seems to follow from Card 1, in which the hero does not really try to persevere. Here, "defeated in everything she has tried" evokes the idea that he has dabbled with life opportunities in search of meaning, probably with notions of some self-fulfilling career objective. While there is anger turned inward and directed out at significant others, these feelings are also dissipated by being intellectualized. As a result, there is a portrait of despair in which the lament is louder than any destructive action so that failure of resolve is experienced once again in an unending cycle of ontological guilt, anger, and self-immolation. These interpretive statements stem from the vividness of language, the intensity of feeling, and the reiteration of existential process. After three stories, there is already an impression of a young man who is enmeshed for personal reasons with family and loved ones. He struggles half-heartedly with vocation as a purveyor of meaning and/or purpose, but is not steadfast either in goal definition or means-end process for reasons as yet undisclosed.

Amy: Hmm. This girl is either very, very tired and she's resting on this bench or she's contemplating suicide or she's already killed herself. Gun under hand—might have dropped it. Not in position for someone who has shot herself—might have tried, threw herself in this position, dropped the gun. Don't know where she would be, have a bench like that—have them in churches (?). She looks frustrated—maybe she feels she can't do anything about her life situation—can't even kill herself—correlated to one of stories—probably has no control over life as she sees it.

Commentary.   3BM was originally administered after 3GF. Initial defensiveness renders a blatant stimulus innocuous, but the client then deals with a suicide/gun theme. After intense affect, she retreats to card description, and questions "bench" with religious infusion again. Has she lost her religion? Frustration as in Card 1, but makes reference to a "life situation" that may be beyond her control. Use of "correlate" is an intellectual support.

Card 3GF (A young woman is standing with downcast head, her face covered with her right hand. Her left arm is stretched forward against a wooden door.)
This card elicits no predominant theme in Eron's normative data with relatively equal frequencies for themes of a child's death/illness, pressure from a partner, an unrequited woman, parental pressure, and guilt. The quality of affect, as on 3BM, is predominantly dysphoric.

Amy: This woman—she's really—she's upset—more than upset—can't exactly think what she's upset about—clutching the door—see muscles in right had holding her face. Probably would be crying—I can't tell if she's gonna open the door—or just opened the door—and is seeing something that caused her great anxiety and she's turned around. . . . Also another interpretation might be panels on door form a cross, might be really repenting for what she's done—holding on to this door and her head is down. Also she has on a long white dress—sort of formal (?). I don't know. Looks like someone might have died.

Commentary. Amy responds to the card-pull with "upset" and uses physical cues throughout the story. A second theme is religious and the "cross" is almost fabricated. Her own mental images are unremittingly vivid. The reason, event, or act to be repented for is not suggested. Death as an explanation for the position/upset was elicited by a question. There is no real story, but alternation between story components and use of physical cues that do not necessarily cohere with the story.

> *Card 4 (A woman is clutching the shoulders of a man whose face and body are averted as if he were trying to pull away from her.)*

This card usually evokes themes related to the balance of power in male-female relationships. Attitudes toward oneself and toward the opposite sex are displayed prominently. For males, pressure from partner is the major theme, while women provide themes of succor from partner. However, such themes for women may now differ markedly from these norms of the 1950s. In addition, there are opportunities for a romantic triangle by inclusion of the poster content in the background.

John: This reminds me of a 1940s movie of some sort with swashbuckling hero—Rhett Butler character—Dietrich or somebody saying, "Don't go! Don't go!" "But I have to." Sort of like *High Noon* or something. So he'll go take care of the bad guys coming in on the train and he and she will go off in the sunset together and live happily ever after.

Commentary. This story provides distance from the client and a tongue-in-cheek vision of stereotyped roles for men and women. An honest, sincere, self-searching young man should not deal with this critical card in such casual terms. The matters portrayed here appear to be of central importance and it is possible to wonder whether or not he feels that relationships and romantic love are beyond his grasp.

Amy: This woman wants this man's attention and, well, she wants it in a physical way—not sure if necessarily sexual—might be because of eyes half-closed, veiling. He's looking away, not looking at anything in picture—fact of picture on wall behind head, he's thinking of another woman. . . . I can't even think of a situation that could lead up to this. He's not being very responsive to her, not doing it intentionally to get her to act that way. Doesn't care either way—what she does. She obviously cares more about him than he does about her from the picture—but you can't tell. Or think I've decided that she wants some kind of sexual contact with this man. That's why he's turned his head away—thinking of someone else, or doesn't know how to tell her that he doesn't feel the same way.

Commentary. A single theme is repeated here. Sexual focus with physical cues again—"eyes . . . veiling." Man rejects woman because of "thinking" about another woman with resultant lack of responsiveness. Her caring is unrequited. The use of "I" indicates a loss of distance, signaling the intensely personal nature of this story.

Card 5 (A middle-aged woman is standing on the threshold of a half-opened door looking into a room.)
This infrequently used picture yields themes of curiosity and parental pressure. It may also tap attitudes of suspicion and distrust between parents and children. A focal issue concerns what is discovered when the woman opens the door. Since the card is essentially innocuous, themes that are extravagant in presenting a blatant situation are potentially more interpretable than themes more congruent with the neutral picture.

John: OK. This is a lady—a mother—peeking into the parlor where her daughter and her date are necking on the couch. Kind of a comical situation, but mother is not able to see the humor of the situation, but she probably will later on—a few years later on. Right now, she'll just tell the kid to go home and she'll speak to her daughter for a few minutes, but it's not going to be a major blow-up.

Commentary.   This neutral story has two notable exceptions from expectations. First, the mother is intruding on a daughter rather than a son. This reversal is similar to the focus on a couple in Card 2 rather than the young woman with the books in the foreground. Second, the absence of humor and perspective in mother has been replaced by understanding in the future. As in Card 1, there is acute awareness and acceptance of parental displeasure over the daughter's behavior.

Amy: This woman looks middle-aged, looking into this room, and she's either checking to see whether it's still there, or could be someone in there—past the table—that she's checking on, or they've called her. At first I thought she looked questioning—whatever drew her to the door. Doesn't look like she's gonna go into the room just because of the way she's positioned—holding on to knob, looks like she's going to shut the door pretty soon. Not much in there (describes room). Flowers don't really go—room looks old and very uninteresting—flowers mean someone goes in there—also a lyre—don't know if old phonograph or piece of furniture with lyre carved on it. Maybe really subtle—all objects in this room, subtle and vague, but part of her past.

Commentary.   In this story, the checking on "it" suggests suspicion and protectiveness. There are lapses into card description and use of physical cues. As in Card 1, there is a hint of family presence or life, as symbolized by flowers among old and uninteresting artifacts. This story reaffirms a family history that is subtle and vague.

6BM (A short elderly woman stands with her back turned to a tall young man. The latter is looking downward with a perplexed expression.)

Parental pressure and departure from parents are frequent themes; marriage of child, succorance from parents, and aggression occur less often. The mother-son relationship is the primary focus. The emotional reactions to communication, or attempted communication, often provide clear evidence of the quality of relationships.

John: This one also makes me think of a 1940s era movie—something where father has died, lost mortgage on house. Mother staring out window, saying, "Where will we go? What will we do?" Young man thinking, "We'll find a way somehow." Man makes good for himself and sends a check to saintly, gray-haired mother. Usually meets a girl behind counter in candy store in process. Even though things seem bleak for them just now, I feel confident that they are going to come out all right.

Commentary.   This story is reminiscent of Card 4. The tragedy is presented by juxtaposing father's death with a lost mortgage as if to minimize the importance of the father or to relegate him to a financial resource for the family. The happy ending not only includes making good and supporting the mother financially, but also almost gratuitously introduces a girlfriend to further the fantasy.

   6GF (A young woman sitting on the edge of a sofa looks back over her shoulder at an older man with a pipe in his mouth who seems to be addressing her.)
Stories here most frequently reflect pressure from parents and less often fear/worry or ordinary activities. The emotional tone is much less frequently dysphoric than in Card 6BM.

Amy: This woman looks like she might be in a bar-nightclub. She's dressed nicely, but yet not dressed immaculately—part of collar button, material over collar, handkerchief in pocket sideways. Kind of leaning—was sitting comfortably before man walked up—either a stranger who thinks a lot of himself—trying to persuade this woman to think a lot of him, too. Looks really comfortable, relaxed, in control of this situation—way he's leaning. Or else he's an old lover of hers—seeing her out—she's kind of surprised—not letting it be known. He's self-assured about the situation, but he's caught her in an awkward position—manipulative—said something to her—she turned around. He's using that to his advantage I think. Hard to say what their relationship was or how long it lasted—she doesn't look like she's a very caring person—at least not when someone approaches her like that. Could be she is youth and he is experienced—looking down on her. She doesn't look like she's very open to his suggestions—might be doing something and he can see right through it because he is experienced, and she doesn't like that maybe.

Commentary.   Again, there is potential sexual content in a story of rejecting a self-assured man. The woman is not dressed "immaculately," suggesting self-criticism or criticism of women who reject men. A second theme hides the client's own uncaring reaction to an ex-lover who tries to catch her off balance and is "manipulative." A third theme contrasts youth versus experience and betrays fear of her own transparency to an experienced male (perhaps the test/assessor) that results in a lack of genuine cooperation.

Card 7BM (A gray-haired man is looking at a younger man who is sullenly staring into space.)
Normatively this card evokes themes of succorance from a father or older man. In addition, the quality of their relationship may suggest attitudes toward authority.

John: The fellow on the right side with dark hair—looks a little like Jimmy Stewart—*Mr. Smith Goes to Washington*—when Jimmy Stewart is waging a one-man filibuster against a piece of corrupt legislation—been up 48 hours without sleep. Mentor comes and gives me "Win one for the Gipper" speech. Even though looks dragged out, essentially young and healthy, will draw on his resources and support from elder statesman. He'll pull it off because he did in the movie.

Commentary. While the extravagant tone is similar to earlier stories, the succorance content differs. There is probably identification with the ideology of a Jimmy Stewart liberal politician, hence the use of "me." There is balance between external support and inner resources, although the outcome is marred by the reason for success—"because he did it in the movie." The bravado falters because the sources of motivation may be insufficient to the task of implementing idealism. At least there is doubt concerning his own wherewithal.

7GF (An older woman is sitting on a sofa close beside a girl, speaking or reading to her. The girl, who holds a doll in her lap, is looking away.)
One-third of Eron's themes were of parental pressure with less frequent elicitation of facts-of-life or advent-of-a-sibling talk. Again, the emotional tone is usually more positive than 7BM.

Amy: This looks like a mother and a daughter. I can't tell what the mother is holding. It looks like a book. Little girl looks like she'd rather be playing—rather be somewhere else. Holding doll—not cradling it—doesn't even want to play with it. Crowded room (furniture). Not giving full attention. Looks like Bible—maybe just doesn't like—some dogmatic type document—looks a little young. Doesn't like having something read to her that she knows she must believe. Mother's hair all the way up to top of head—in place—being restrictive/conservative. Girl's hair hanging wild, loose, out of face. Mother is aggressively trying to keep her attention. Little girl very blatant—not interested—doesn't know how to get out of situation. Mother so intent, doesn't know she's thinking about something else. Mother's eyes closed, little girl's eyes open—symbolized open-mindedness and close-mindedness to me.

Commentary. A usual story except for not cradling doll as a rejection of it, mother, Bible (religion), and being told what to believe (think). Mother is presented as restrictive, conservative, and demanding that the child conform, and is not aware that she is perceived as close-minded. The girl is wild/loose, perhaps from mother, blatant, perhaps in the sense of being nondeceptive, but simultaneously bound. Physical cues are used symbolically.

8BM (An adolescent boy looks straight out of the picture. The barrel of a rifle is visible at one side, and in the background is the dim scene of a surgical operation, like a reverie-image.)
Although the norms suggest aspiration as a frequent theme, more often there is an interplay of violence directed toward father or a father-surrogate. As in Card 3BM, there are opportunities to recognize or deny the gun and knife, although recognition is more usual since the stimulus is blatant.

John: ... This seems almost surrealistic—sort of effeminate-looking young boy in foreground seems to be remembering sort of battlefield surgery—doesn't seem to have much of effect on him—remembers it with indifference. Man on table looks to be in excruciating pain, even though they hadn't made the incision. Perhaps his father. Father killed in battle—remembers in abstract way what it must have been like for the father to have been killed in battle when he was still young boy or infant.

Commentary. This is a complex story beginning with the unusual and again gratuitous description of an "effeminate-looking boy." The indifference of the boy to the trauma and the mention of extreme pain suggest both anger and distance from father, although the personal pain may be in his remote past. Father has had little impact on his life for many years, but older males (Card 7BM are seen as helpful and mentors.

8GF (A young woman sits with her chin in her hand looking off into space.)
A frequent theme here is of reminiscence and happiness with aspiration, occupation, economic pressure, and posing accounting for a majority of other themes.

Amy: Well, this girl could be posing for an art class. Struck a pose and something draped over chair so students won't draw the chair. Classic pose or could be thinking about something—reminiscing—not analyzing it and not longing for it. Might be she's unenergetic—resting her head—might be tired—might be cleaning up her room, but I can't imagine her resting like that—must be posing—either that or so deep in thought can't feel the strain of it.

Commentary. This story of posing plus card description suggests that the client may enjoy attention at a distance because she is not required to respond. Instead, there can be reminiscence that consists of neither analysis, longing, or desire. "Longing" may be so frequent and intense that an innocuous retreat—"so deep in thought"—is powerful, fixating, and immobilizing.

9BM (Four men in overalls are lying on the grass taking it easy.)
This is probably the least frequently used card of the first 10. The range of themes is narrow. Retirement is suggested normatively, but a work break with a boy on the periphery who does not quite fit in may be more frequent.

John: This is a WPA work team and they've been planting trees all afternoon, taking a little break about three o'clock. Probably been planting trees since about 7 A.M. Probably a jug of iced tea around somewhere out of the field of view.

Commentary.   Here, expectations for a story are met with a curious precision about time, how long the men have worked, and the nicety of iced tea. The fact of a "WPA" (Works Progress Administration) work team in the 1980s suggests a social consciousness and bolsters that hypothesis for Card 7BM.

Card 9GF (A young woman with a magazine and a purse in her hand looks from behind a tree at another young woman in a party dress running along a beach.)
Themes of escape and curiosity occur with relative frequency, followed by jealousy and fear/worry. The emotional tone is characteristically sad.

Amy: (turns card) Well, first of all, can't imagine what these two women are doing out—river, trees, rock—not dressed for outdoors. Lower one looks like she's angry, trying to move fast, dress held up on one side, determined look on face. Other leaning on a tree looking down, might be had an argument—sees how angry other woman is—doesn't know how to deal with it—so irrational and strong. She's moving, too, going to go after her—not going to run—or totally different is that way it's divided—same woman looking at self; calm on top—life just divided by black edge—looking at self—mild-mannered, somewhat passive—other side of her—exact opposite.

Commentary.   One theme concerns parts of the client's self. An initial physical description is followed by anger in a strong but irrational woman juxtaposed with a calm, mild-mannered, somewhat passive woman. She may be suggesting something of the woman she could become if a stronger more intense submerged self were united with the present surface self. The "black edge" is an internal equivalent of the barrier in story 2.

Card 10 (A young woman's head against a man's shoulder.)
Themes of contentment from both men and women are frequent, especially in the context of an older couple holding each other closely or dancing and reminiscing about their good life together. Tenderness, sensitivity, and responsivity in a heterosexual context may also occur.

John: . . . This could be a young couple, just embracing in an intimate moment, or could be a young couple after of moment of tragedy, some disaster, trying to console one another. They're not terribly young—probably late thirties, early forties, but seems kinda like an ambiguous picture—I have a hard time deciding what is going on.

Commentary.   John reverses the usual age expectations. It is possible that he does not perceive old people—especially parents—as having harmonious relationships, and thus younger persons are described. That the picture is difficult and ambiguous raises the question of what is disturbing to him—heterosexual intimacy, young and/or old figures, or the hint of tragedy?

Amy: Well, I can't really tell—can't be sure of their sex—lower one looks like a woman but also looks like a man. Top one looks like a man, could be a woman. What's going on—not sexual. I think it's affection—holding each other close. Both got eyes closed. I think both thinking about other one.

Commentary.   It is unusual to be ambivalent about the gender of figures here. There is a double denial of homosexual activity in inclusion of affection and comfort. The use of physical cues and thinking occur instead of any sexuality.

   Card 11 (A road skirting a deep chasm between high cliffs. On the road in the distance are obscure figures. Protruding from the rocky wall on one side is the long head and neck of a dragon.)
Impersonal aggression is the normative theme. However, the ambiguity of the figures permits either human or animal figures to be recognized. Clients with well-developed abstract and conceptual intelligence are more likely to discover human figures. Often, the figures are fleeing across the bridge to sanctuary, with the dragon in pursuit. The embellishment, process, and outcome all provide cues that often pertain to a present life crisis. Expression may be in a symbolized form, such as a struggle between good and evil. This dragon is an aggressive figure akin to the weapons in Cards 3BM and 8BM.

John: OK. This is a medieval quest. This is a band of journeyers on their way to a castle—swords and sorcery situations—dragon just made a pass at them, trying to get over bridge into cover—before dragon makes a second pass. There's a variety of travelers in this band. In addition to the usual knights, elves, I can see a roc and cloak of a magician whose magic is probably going to be critical to the success of the travel.

Commentary.   Although there is distance here expressed by the time period of the story, linkage to the present occurs by the "swords and sorcery" game referent. "Roc" was carefully spelled out for the examiner in order to emphasize the significance of this special journeyer. To say that magic is critical to the success of life's voyage is to place a premium on the unknown and unexpected, while negating the impact of the conventional means-end sequences of events. When juxtaposition is made with the ready abandonment of the drudgery of achievement in Card 1, it is clear that it is not whimsey, laziness, or impulsivity, but merely a matter of belief in the credibility of other routes to desired outcomes.

Amy: This looks like prehistoric times—all the rocks and the height of the walls. Well, it could be . . . this dinosaur looks like a phallic symbol—could be, might be, whole picture symbol of intercourse. Inside is inside of woman. It's vast and there is one way to enter it, which this dinosaur has—whatever the creature is. It's a whole other world in there. Dinosaur didn't expect it, even another little creature in there, too.

Commentary.   "Prehistoric" implies great distance and permits equation of dinosaur with male sexuality and symbolized intercourse. Suggests that for this client male sexuality may be dangerous, archaic, primitive, obsolete. There is preoccupation with her own sexuality. The reason for including "another little creature" is not clear.

Card 12M (A young man is lying on a couch with his eyes closed. Leaning over him is the gaunt form of an elderly man, his hand stretched out above the face of the reclining figure.)
While hypnotism is the most frequent normative theme, religion, emotional disturbance, and death or illness also occur with some frequency. Stories to this card have been used to predict responses to psychotherapy as well as susceptibility to hypnosis.

John: OK. This is a physician leaning over a male in his twenties. Physician is recoiling a little bit, just taken hand away from lad's neck where he was feeling his pulse. Just realized boy is not breathing—unexpected—didn't realize that the kid was dead.

Commentary.   Without fanfare, without overstatement, this story describes the loss of faith in physicians, psychologists, authoritarian healers, and gurus of all persuasions. The tone is matter of fact. The hypothesis is that the client has lost faith in conventional goals, conventional explanations, and conventional resolutions to life's problems.

Card 12F (The portrait of a young woman. A weird old woman with a shawl over her head is grimacing in the background.)
Disappointment in parent(s) and parental pressure are conventional themes within an emotional context that is relatively neutral.

Amy: Well, this character on left could be a man and could be a woman—real androgynous-looking person. Way eyebrow is—almost a smile—thinking about something pleasant. Woman behind is much older, doesn't seem to think about things. . . . Woman is kinda reproachful, society manifestation in androgynous person's mind. Older woman doesn't know enough about it to understand—not very powerful about it—got so many male and female characteristics—so maybe older one is not very intelligent. Could not say if younger person thinking about future, or older person about when she was young—way positioned—first interpretation.

Commentary. As in Card 10, sexual identity is again confused with androgyny labeling and the use of physical cues. The older woman may represent society as well as a mother who is negative, reproachful, dull, and neither knowledgeable nor understanding. Thoughts regarding the future do not stimulate any action, although apprehensiveness in Card 2 did lead to action.

Card 13MF (A young man is standing with downcast head buried in his arm. Behind him is the figure of a woman lying in a bed.)
For men, guilt, remorse, death, illness, and illicit sex top the list of normative themes, while women produce death and/or illness themes more frequently and remorse themes less frequently. Affect is predominantly sad, negative, and dysphoric.

John: . . . OK. I see this being about 6 A.M.—sun's just coming up and the fellow is wiping brow—whew! What a night! And the woman in the bed is still asleep. I think they are probably college students—hardly any furniture in there—bed looks like made by putting your mattress on the floor. This is a fairly strapping young man—can see muscles—pecs—through shirt. These two people have some affection for each other but I don't think their relationship is going to last any length of time.

Commentary. The departure from conventional storytelling here is the physical description of the young man. The "Whew! What a night!" and the emphasis on physique may constitute a protest that the storyteller is really a lusty, robust male—even macho in the sense of proving or demonstrating male sexual prowess. The other side of the coin, however, is recognition that satisfying a woman sexually (and otherwise as well) is no easy task. The fragility of the relationship in this story and the potential independence of affection from sexuality suggest that in his own perceptions, at least, the necessary conditions for an enduring relationship are not present.

Amy: Well, this looks like she's nude. She's in a one-person, single bed. Man looks like he's turned away—sort of anxiety. He's fully dressed. Might be he walked in and saw her undressed. Maybe she wants to have sex with him. Maybe he doesn't want to with her. He's being very dramatic, looks away, putting hands over his eyes. He's in a dilemma. I can't figure out why the bed is so close to ground. Looks like it's a single bed. Looks like she might be touching his leg with her hand. Might be he's telling her something that he's ashamed of—can't understand why she would be laying there nude if they were having such a serious conversation about something else.

Commentary.   The response is immediate here: a nude woman who wants sex and an anxious man who rejects her. There is physical description of the card and a misinterpretation of "touching his leg" that suggests loss of distance and personalization. The client appears critical, bewildered, and confused about the picture and her interpretation.

   Card 14 (The silhouette of a man (or woman) against a bright window. The rest of the picture is totally black.)
Frequent themes for both men and woman include curiosity and aspiration. There is opportunity for looking out or looking in as well as for accompanying feelings of joy or despair, although dysphoric themes are rare. The silhouette figure may be interpreted as male or female.

John: Ah—this could equally well be right at dawn on farm—fellow throws up window and looks out—here's the promise of a new day. I can just about hear all animal noises on farm. Or else could equally well be fellow in urban setting—city—looking out window at night-time sky. Looking at sky—cold, clear winter's night. First I thought he was standing with foot up on stool—window section—decided he's not by himself in the room—person sitting in chair in foreground—two images have combined to make a single silhouette. (Points to corner of chair and other person's head.) Line of stomach not fall like that. So he's probably sitting up late at night talking to somebody—philosophical meaning-of-life talk.

Commentary.   Contrasts and vistas of alternative futures are presented, perhaps for himself, but these perspectives are immediately short-circuited by focus and preoccupation on what is happening in the room. Since these events and the other person are literally conjured up from the dark ink, they serve to forestall any further planning. In addition, since the stimulus does not yield these story components, there is distortion required to produce them. The action has been transferred (again) from a possible means-end sequence to an internal dialogue. This present problem is a perennial conflict that interferes with planning for the future. The elaborate transition to a conjured figure in the darkness, the combination of images into a single silhouette, and the apparently innocent "philosophical meaning-of-life talk" strongly suggest the ingredients for something that is actively inhibiting future plans.

Amy: Well, this man is looking upward and out this window and it's the only light. It could be symbolic of the future: looking upward, outward, and toward the light. Everything else about him could be dark, vague, ambiguous—window is only outlet to direct, clear, unambiguous situation.

Commentary. The symbolism here indicates that the present is dark, vague, and ambiguous, while in Card 5, the past was vague and subtle. Only the future is more clear. The unstated content here may refer to the client's own sexual identity and androgyny.

   Card 15 (A gaunt man with clenched hands is standing among gravestones.)
Normative themes for both sexes include death and/or illness of partner or peer, religion, or some supernatural event with the most sad/dysphoric emotional tone. Additionally, women produce themes of emotional disturbance, loneliness, guilt, and acquisition. In fact, this stimulus is so foreboding that the story should reflect gloom, despondency, or reactive depression.

John: This makes me think of Charles Dickens—not any particular story. This man is a very rigid, inflexible, austere person. Probably a miser—never really done anybody much harm but has never done much good for anybody either. He's come to visit the grave of a business partner—who's also the only person he had any real dealings with. He's beginning to wonder if he's lived his life in a proper way. I think as a result of this visit that he's going to undergo a character change and turn over a new leaf.

Commentary. Initially, there is distance by evoking an historic fiction writer. A hint of the Scrooge theme, repentance upon confrontation with the grave occupied by the only person "he had any real dealings with." The message is that just getting along is not sufficient for a proper life, since the description is not of an evil man but simply an average citizen who could even be anyone's father. He wants to achieve a different kind of life, one that makes a difference to others and one that is described in other stories, particularly 7BM. However, there is a hint in his most ebullient and secret fantasy that themes in Cards 4 and 6BM are not as repugnant as their casual presentation suggests.

Amy: It has on a dress, but I don't think it's a woman . . . in a graveyard, crosses, makes me think of religion and death. Hands on the figure are cuffed together. May be mankind chained to ideas about life and death and religion—Christianity.

Commentary. Male is "it," has dress, but is not a woman. Christianity and death are now associated with an ambiguous sexual identity and the misinterpretation of "hands cuffed together" (see Cards 3GF, 5). The cuffing may be related to the client's sex-role stereotyped activities instead of androgyny. Suggests she may be stifled, inhibited in movement (as is the conservative mother in 7GF and the reproachful/negative society in 12GF).

   Card 16 (Blank card.)
This card almost always evokes themes of either an ideal life situation or a current problem. Usually the ideal life situation contains either family or

loved ones sharing some pleasant activity or depicts a person contemplating nature or otherwise enjoying some solitude. A review suggests that the usefulness of this card has been underestimated (Kahn, 1984) and recommends presenting it last in any series of cards, as was done with John.

John: OK. (This is—not sure—fair or not—short story idea. Can't decide how it's going to come out.) There's this character named Atman and she's kinda of a maverick—not very conforming kind of person and she's trying to figure out—kinda struggling with questions of theology—whether or not God exists—if exists is good, or even actively evil and she's either training in psychology or undergoing psychological services—haven't decided yet. Keeps coming up against this philosophy that psychologists are always doing things to people, saying it is in their own best interests—wonder whether that same thought applies to God—because religions say that world is made as is because have eventually best result for human beings—really made for human beings or for God and his convenience? Eventually strain and strife of all of her conflicts with psychological establishment leads her to be hospitalized—electroshock therapy and all sorts of violent things, repugnant to her and person she is being made into. Throws herself out of tall building—commits suicide—when dies discovers she was never a person at all—a computer simulation created by team of psychologists to try to solve questions about approaches to therapy. Rationale: More humane than trying this on flesh ad blood people. "What about me? Ethical to use me this way? How many times do I live this life you have made for me just so you can find answers to your questions?" Psychologist says, "As many as it takes."

Commentary.   In fact, this was a capsule presentation of a short story idea, but emergence here suggests strong personal significance. If the interpretation is focused on a current problem, then identification of the problem is the first task. John related that Atman was from the Hindu word for self or ego, so the personal relevance is unmistakable. The central character is female. In Cards 2, 3BM, and 5, there was also some alteration in sex of the character with whom identification is expected. In Card 16, psychologists are manipulating Atman and their motives are suspect. At one level, the client may be impugning the motives of the clinician by suggesting that feedback is of less consequence than the data to include in this chapter. This notion is generalized to a loss of faith in all authorities, including God. There is a cynical core to this convoluted tale that begins with the self (Atman), and progresses to include psychologists, the clinician, and ultimately God. John can be separated from his story by labeling the conflict as an obsessive concern with the ramifications of all actions. This hypothesis accounts for the absence of means-end, enduring, goal-oriented behaviors in spite of the requisite intelligence, internalized values, and adequacy of work habits to be a coherent person. In addition, there is a nagging doubt with regard to identity, and the question "Who am I?" is further broken down into sexual identity, work identity, religious identity, and even human identity. Such rumination, even when attenuated by fictional plots that might well become cogent short stories in their own right, does dampen, inhibit, and restrain his decision making in the present and future.

Amy: If I was going to make a picture—use symbols for all the general flux of things, all perceptions. Probably be just an entangled mess. Symbols for good, evil, knowledge, ignorance, male and female . . . and love and hate, and warm and cold, mind and body, day and night. Then it would have all sorts of little intricate connectors—couldn't single out any one without having touched all the rest of them. I don't think I've named all symbols. Middle of picture have round symbol-like Platonic ideal of soul—where all these opposites come together. Don't think have a name—this center of picture. Would be some transcendent thing. Probably a mess.

Commentary.   It is unusual and infrequent to omit people here. Perhaps symbols are safer, or primary?—a Jungian entourage of opposites/dichotomies that are really continuous or "intricate connections"? The client juxtaposes "mess" with "transcendent thing." This suggests that her intellectual armormentarium (bravado, defenses against world of conventional, middle-class standards, people, parents, etc.) is a "mess" and a poor substitute for life, strong emotional attachments to males, and a personal future.

Card 17BM (A naked man is clinging to a rope. He is in the act of climbing up or down.)
This card elicits themes of self-esteem, exhibition, competition, and escape. Hidden in these themes are achievement, narcissism, adulation, and physical prowess concerns. This card is ranked lowest for sadness and dysphoria.

John: Olympics coming up next spring—hard not to think of Olympics. I see it as gymnast training for Olympics—probably worried whether or not they're going to find the steroids in his blood.

Commentary.   The story begins as the normal combination of achievement and/or athletic prowess, but it does not include any future or any outcome. The gymnast apparently becomes bogged down by rumination and the story ends at this point. There is some concern that a secret may be discovered that will vitiate the client's masculinity and/or social acceptability.

Card 17GF (A bridge over water. A female figure leans over the railing. In the background are tall buildings and small figures of men.)
Suicide is a frequent theme, but so are ordinary activities and curiosity. The potential for dysphoric emotional tone is in the middle for the entire set of cards.

Amy: This looks like slavery. One guy in charge, all rest humped over carrying big packages of something—fruit of vegetable. Odd because sun is black, yet it is still shining. Might be black because of slavery. Woman on top of bridge—looking other way—may mean slavery is common knowledge to her or ignoring it—looking into river.

Commentary.   Similar to cards 11 and 13MF is the blatancy of the situation—the "slavery." The black sun is a misperception. The story uses paradox and symbolism. There is no outcome for the woman who, by looking without action, is hiding in the present tense. She doesn't reach out and extrude herself and is thus neither recognized nor understood. She takes her social conscience for granted ("turns away") as part of her level of development.

Card 18BM (A man is clutched from behind by three hands. The figures of his antagonists are invisible.)
While themes of drunkenness predominate, peer succorance, pressure, and emotional disturbance are also frequent. This card is not often used in short forms.

John: These all make me think of a 1940s movie. Denouement where Edward G. Robinson has been nabbed and police lieutenant is saying, "The gig is up, Rocky." Going to take him off to the pokey. Probably standing on rooftop in city where he has been chased and there is nowhere left to run.

Commentary.   The distance of another movie plot permits a story without a positive outcome, even though the chief character is probably not an idealized folk-hero for John. There are none of the extravagant statements present in other renditions of movie plots. This one is serious and it is possible to infer that the storyteller believes there is literally "nowhere left to run."

Card 18GF (A woman has her hands squeezed around the throat of another woman whom she appears to be pushing backwards across the banister of a stairway.)
This card elicits themes of parental succorance or pressure, death/illness of child or sibling, aggression to a peer or from a parent or the environment, and behavior disorders. The emotional tone is uniformly sad.

Amy: Again, there are two women. One is really upset—can't see her face—fallen on floor—maybe talking . . . sobbing on floor. Other has picked her up. Disgust in face also compassion—leaning her on staircase. Might be other woman just really upset about something—really in pitiful state—other woman doesn't know what to do, just looking at her.

Commentary.   In Card 3GF, death, an interpersonal cause for "upset," has to be elicited by a question, but no cause is provided here for distress. However, "disgust" is an unusual reaction to "fallen on floor" unless "fallen" means degraded by unacceptable behavior/ideation. This disgust is moderated by "compassion." There is no outcome. She is immobilized in the present, "just looking at her."

Card 19 (A weird picture of cloud formations overhanging a snow-covered cabin in the country.)
Impersonal aggression is the predominant theme for both sexes. Forces of nature threaten whoever is within the cabin. Contentment within the dwelling and invocation of supernatural forces are secondary themes. The critical content of these stories has to do with whatever happens within the house and there may be a description of family dynamics in response to an external danger.

John: OK. There's a video game called Donkey Kong[2] and these little tiny flames that look like spooks chase your character around the screen. Just like the top of his head peeking out from behind. Igloo has chimney and a couple of little windows. Might be got tired of being spook—decided to go live on North Pole.

Commentary.   There is a playfulness to this story—a rapid alternation of focus and a lack of sustained effort that results in abandonment of the game. John has produced a second computer simulation person (see Card 16 for first one) who, instead of being trapped in an unending succession of manipulated lives, has the option of leaving for distant and unknown places. The transformation of video game flame into "spooks" with the capacity for voluntary, self-directed action is noteworthy here. The difference between these two stories is that in Card 16, the grim reality of the client's life is presented—the entrapment of a pseudo-person in unending manipulations by others—while in Card 19, the hope of breaking out of the diurnal ritual appears. Only by assuming control of his own destiny can John do what he wants to do.

Amy: Either a child's drawing of house . . . in a snowstorm—or a submarine—or kinda looks like the Loch Ness monster or a whale. If a house, there's a glow around the windows—kinda like eyes—inside very warm—outside it's cold, wind blowing. Looks like a dream image—not very well defined, sky got all those other objects (?). I think they'd be having a pleasant time—two or three people—sitting and talking—glad to be inside together because so windy and cold—almost scary.

Commentary.   The client avoids the house initially by having many stories, but returns to it, perhaps being forced into the house by the assessor's question. It is unusual to find three persons in the house unless labeled as family. She avoids intimacy/family dynamics and chooses not to be revealing, although we wonder about the identities of the people.

Card 20 (The dimly illumined figure of a man (or woman) in the dead of night leaning against a lamp post.)

The predominant theme for men is vacillation; economic pressure is secondary. For women, vacillation and loneliness occur with moderate frequency. Themes of waiting for someone or something to happen are also frequent.

John: OK. This is equally one or two things. Could be Humphrey Bogart hanging out in front of Rick's Place in *Casablanca* or could be Jimmy Stewart leaning against his street lamp in *Harvey,* waiting for his rabbit to come visit.

Commentary. These ordinary themes are embellished by two movie characters who presumably represent separate but equal sides of the fantasy. The tough honest guy who takes what he wants is contrasted with the idealistic social reformer (see also Card 7BM) who attends an imaginary companion (see Card 14) albeit a companion whom he loves and cherishes.

Amy: This looks like a soldier overseas standing under a street lamp—maybe in London—looks foggy. He's reflecting or thinking—it's not cold. He's just casually leaning. He's not waiting for someone, looking for anyone. Maybe he had a couple of beers, just walking around the street, just stopped to think.

Commentary. In this extended picture description, the hero is alone and does not wait for anyone. One can infer that thinking may be more important and certainly safer than contact with people.

SCORING

Some form of coding the raw story data usually occurs prior to either scoring or interpretation. This may be done informally by notes, hypotheses, and themes, or more formally by writing a synopsis or restatement of each story, as has been done in the third TAT example later in this chapter. However, as Shneidman (1951) has indicated in his summary of interpretive methods, there are scoring systems that quantify the story data into psychograms, profiles, ratios, patterns, and scores to be compared with norms. Frequency and intensity of these variables can then be obtained. Some of these scoring systems have been used for clinical diagnosis (e.g., Dana, 1959). Scoring systems like Murray (1938), Tomkins (1947), and Henry (1956) are elaborate attempts to sensitize neophyte assessors to the richness of data provided by TAT stories and are valuable reading for this purpose. None of these systems has received any widespread usage for personality description or diagnosis of personality.

INTERPRETATION

Interpretation is based on verbatim recording, a few mechanical steps to organize and render portions of the stories salient, immersion in the stories by reading and rereading them, and an attitude requiring identification of and testing of hypotheses. Examples of this process may be found elsewhere (Dana, 1982). Essentially, however, TAT interpretation remains intuitive and creative. However, it is trained intuition and disciplined creativity. Training consists of a general clinical exposure to procedures permitting systematic, empirically grounded, and normatively relevant use of stories as data. Prior experience with many clients who have told stories to these same picture stimuli is required, but it is the use of implicit normative data within a hypothesis-testing frame of reference that contributes to consensus in interpretation.

Initially, the mechanical steps include a synopsis of each story as it stems from the particular card stimulus. There is subsequent cross-referencing for similar themes, conflicts, persons, settings, and so on. Frequencies of occurrence and the particular cards involved are noted. Finally, recording is made of relative emphasis, importance, or personalization of thematic contents.

Each TAT analyst has a set of interpretive guidelines, usually implicit, that can be applied systematically as a series of questions that are asked of the summarized story data. Several such guidelines will be suggested and will constitute a synthesis of literature and experience with interpretation. These guidelines include congruence of stories with picture stimuli and directions, distance of story content from client life experiences, the presence and intensity of conflict, and the literalness of story content.

Congruence with Picture Stimuli

Typical and expected themes, at least for the early 1950s, were noted earlier in the descriptions of separate cards. However, in the absence of published normative thematic data that are representative and of recent origin, departures from expectations are only notable whenever the theme is blatantly discordant with the stimulus such as a bland story to Card 13MF or a violent story to Card 5. Infrequent themes may also be personally relevant. Some assessors will want to use the Arnold (1949) classification for themes that include parent-child situations, heterosexual situations, same-sex situations, and single-person situations.

Card hypotheses similar to Rorschach plate IV, father-authority, may also be evoked, such as achievement (Cards 1, 14, 17BM), central value (Card 3BM for both sexes), ideal life situation versus present conflict (Card 16), depression (Card 15), and response to psychotherapy (Card 12M). Caution should be exercised in using card hypotheses since only for 3BM and 16 are these hypotheses comparable in research credibility to Rorschach plate IV.

Conformity with Directions

The ordinary seven-part directions constitute another framework of implicit normative expectations Dana (1959). Adequate representation of these directions in stories, or ego sufficiency, suggests that omission of direction components not only relates to personality organization but to adequacy of functioning as well (for construct validity review, see Dana & Cunningham, 1983).

Application is made by recording the relative conformity with directions across cards and noting omitted components by card. For example, if there are no endings in stories from cards stimulating achievement themes, or if feeling is omitted from stories to cards relating to one or both parents, relevant hypotheses can be formulated. Additional violations of directions are found in any attempt, successful or otherwise, to reject a card (for example, Card 2 for John), inconsistent latencies between card presentation and the beginning of a story (similar to Rorschach reaction times), or in the relative length of stories across cards.

Distance

Physical, psychological, and geographic distance in stories from the client's actual life are evidences of remoteness from awareness (see Tomkins, 1947, pp. 78–82; Piotrowski, 1950, "Rules"). These distance indicators should be related to the story content from specific cards. As a result of distancing, personal content can be more readily revealed. Although preoccupation with card description may mask genuine drives, Piotrowski has suggested that whenever the client and TAT figures are similar, the action in the story will be more acceptable. Less acceptable drives occur in stories that contain characters who differ from the client in age, gender, race, or social status. Social attitudes may be directly reflected by the behaviors and personality characteristics of TAT figures who differ from the client.

Conflict

The conflicts expressed in TAT stories may be similar across cards or vary from one card to another. Conflict strengths may be estimated by tallying the presence of similar conflicts in different cards and computing the percentages of the total number of cards administered that evidence each conflict (Tomkins, 1947). This provides indices of the amount of energy expended by each conflict. When conflicts are dissimilar across cards, but frequent in occurrence, poor functioning and anxiety may be inferred (Piotrowski, 1950). In addition, the intensity of conflict or accompanying emotionality, especially where expression is not congruent with card stimulus demand or hypothesis, may indicate the presence of distress in a single instance.

Literal Story Content

Central to interpretation is the recognition of instances in which story content is considered to be a literal statement of the client's subjective experience and/or life events. It is known that TAT imagery stabilizes over long periods of time and is correlated with behavior. The problem is to identify the portions of the TAT protocol that can be accepted at face value.

When stories are considered as free associations, then any alterations in the process of storytelling are evidence of personal relevance. Voice inflection, rate of speech, groupings of words, out of place phrases, changes in affect, misplaced concreteness, and concurrent behavior—all become indicators.

PREPARATION OF REPORTS

This section will present the reports for John and Amy. These reports were prepared to be read and discussed with the assessees. First-person styles are used for illustrative purposes.

Report for John

Your TAT stories depict a young man with an exacerbated awareness and sensitivity to himself and to others. You are still enmeshed in a family drama containing turmoil, a certain bleak perdurability, and little appreciation for your differentness from other family members. You harbor some anger at your father for being distant and unable to provide you with emotional support and any reaffirmation of your own identity. Your love and understanding of family members prevents you from any extrication from family or your own feelings about them.

You are engaged in a quest for meaning that will enable you to understand who you are. When you implicitly ask "who am I?" you are querying with regard to identity—sexual, religious, work, and even human identity. This quest falters because you have experienced a loss of faith and only intermittent and unsteady motivation. You have lost faith in the credibility of conventional goals, conventional aspirations, and conventional resolutions to life problems. You have lost faith in the traditional sources of knowledge—both in persons and institutions. As a result of being aware of the great disparity between institutional goals and human needs, you often feel alienated and manipulated in a series of life experiences you cannot control.

Your reiterated question "Who am I?" is especially poignant in areas of work and love. You struggle with vocational choice and with the means-end preparation for any career. You dabble with opportunities and avenues for meaningful occupation that are consonant with your values, ideals, and a creative, unorthodox approach to problem solving, but you cannot persevere in any sustained direction.

You have a strong inclination toward romantic love and idealized love relationships. You yearn for an enduring relationship with a woman who is intelligent, sensitive, compassionate, and shares your view of the world, but discover only momentary sexual liaisons and disappointment.

Because you are so attuned to an inner landscape and nurtured by your own fantasy, you wonder if you are sufficiently masculine, perhaps as an explanation for failure to maintain a love relationship with a woman. You experience an awareness of your own submerged femininity (anima) almost as a secret part of yourself that you are hesitant to share with others. Not only do you fear social censure for being more human than macho but you also feel incursions upon your self-concept as well. Your masculinity is an issue.

While you accept responsibility (albeit with a little squirming and self-pity), you experience conflict and paralysis of action as a direct result of your internal dialogue. You know resolution of your dilemma ultimately requires will (and guts) and voluntary self-initiated, self-directed, and self-sustained actions. However, you cannot act in a self-consistent goal-directed manner in order to affirm individuality, assert integrity, and confirm identity. Instead, you experience ontological guilt, anger, self-immolation, and a short-circuiting of action. Your acute awareness enables you to foreclose on all possible outcomes before they can be translated into behavior. Since knowledge is not sufficient and the sources of the continuing human support that you sorely need are suspect, you struggle to maintain equilibrium. In this process, you present yourself as an honest, engaging, idealistic person who usually displays good cheer and belief in the positive outcome of his quest. However, when it is hardest to cope with the immensity and apparent futility of your dilemma, you express genuine distress in the form of uncontrolled anxiety that sometimes interferes with daily activities.

Feedback.   John expressed concern about two apparent departures from verbatim recording during the TAT administration. In Card 7BM, he affirmed that although he recalled an *m* sound, he did not use the word *me,* which signaled the literal nature of this story for the clinician. Although there are other cues in this story from the idealistic nature of the original movie, this slight variation in recording could have led to accepting a story at face value as being highly personal that did not, in fact, reflect his own motives and behaviors. In Card 14, a potentially more serious difference in perceptions pertained to John's memory that the two versions were looking out in daytime and looking into the room at night. The difference here is between an either/or construction of alternative themes and a reversal of figure-ground, which would document a facile creativity in dealing with card stimuli and an important addition for subsequent interpretation.

Finally, a more substantive matter pertains to the interpretation of Card 16. Remember that John had a previously formulated plot for a short story that was convenient for him to relate in this context, presumably due to recency and saliency of content. To what extent does this fact of story origin mitigate the interpretive hypotheses? First, the choice of the name, Atman, refers additionally to *essence of youness* so that there is a choice of interpretation between gender and self-revelatory implications, or both. Second, and more important, the feelings directed at psychologists (and attributed here as directed toward the clinician as well) were not experienced as emerging from this assessment proceeding, but from a recent suicide of a friend who had been consistently mistreated by the psychology establishment and ultimately was coercively socialized as a mental patient. These memories were still present, raw, and unverbalized, persistently nagging at him, flooding him with feelings and unanswered questions. Thus, the choice of story was dictated by his own feelings of confusion and/or helplessness and by anger at the ostensible failure of area mental health services to prevent a tragedy.

When John read the report, he denied awareness of anger toward his father, although recognized occasional anger directed at his mother. He was also concerned with the description "feels alienated and manipulated" and wanted to be clear that he did not experience a conspiracy or personalize his reactions. However, as an antidote for these feelings, he does choose to take issue, to stand up and be heard in jousts with the establishment over matters of ideology, morality, or humanity. In addition, he wanted to affirm that six months after the TAT administration, he is finding an ability to sustain endeavor, particularly in the academic area, and is experiencing a productive and rewarding semester—the first one in several years.

Report for Amy

In consenting to this TAT assessment and feedback, you were genuinely curious, almost intrigued by the possibility of genuine self-scrutiny, but nonetheless your usual stance is to be somewhat guarded with other persons not to reveal your emotions and reactions easily (as the woman in 6GF). As a result, few people know you well and intimately. You entered this situation nondefensively with no intention to dissemble or withhold yourself. However, the use of symbolism, the creative (albeit highly personal) misinterpretations or misperceptions of card stimuli, and the complexity of themes do provide some protection and this formidable intellectual display may serve to distance you from other persons. Thus, although you were comfortable during the assessment process, you did not really anticipate being understood.

You are still in process of emancipation from family, but it is not an easy transition in spite of long-standing differences between your values and behaviors and their expectations for you. It appears you are emerging from a family that has clear expectations for children, close working relationships, and a mother, especially, who has a strong influence on your life. Your mother is depicted in these stories as family and child preoccupied. Your mother may share some of the characteristics of mothers in your stories: religious, conservative, dogmatic, restrictive, dominant, even suspicious, and, to use your own word, close-minded. In your stories, the mother also symbolized society with reproachful and negative attitudes toward you, your behavior, and your differences.

While you feel frustrated by demands and/or expectations from family and recognize their waning power over you—especially for conformity to a middle-class lifestyle, conventionality, religiosity, and sex-role stereotype—this is not the major source of concern. Rather, it is the person you are becoming that is the major focus of your attention, energy, and apprehensiveness. You want to become whole in the sense of putting submerged parts of your identity together. You want to integrate strength that is expressed in capacity for anger and irrationality with calmness, mild manners, and passivity. You would like to be able to be truly androgynous—able to express equally female and male archetypes in your behavior.

Sexuality is part of your internal pressure toward an androgynous lifestyle. Your sexual needs are strong. You see yourself as capable of being wild and even loose, and yet you are critical (or ambivalent) toward a woman who actively looks for sex. In a sense, attention and sexual attention from males have not been clearly distinguished. However, you have had some rejection experiences with men who cared less than you did. As a result, there is some derogation of males and male sexuality as if to suggest that, ultimately, males may be unnecessary for your sexual satisfaction and well-being.

However, you are remarkably uneasy about any transition toward androgyny. You deny active homosexuality and express disgust and compassion for a fallen woman. The result of this turmoil is crisis in the present, a muddle in which books are substituted for babies, for proper (expected) sex-role identity, and an intellectual sanctuary is erected to permit control of your own thought processes and hence of your own life. But the present is dark, vague, ambiguous, even a mess, while you have pious hopes that in the future you will be direct, clear, and unambiguous in your sexual identity.

Sometimes you are so deep in thought as to be oblivious of your surroundings (internal and external) and even to accept aloneness. You have been asking persistent questions about yourself that invade consciousness—questions pertaining to identity, sexuality, future—and are immobilizing. Some experience is intellectualized and you hope your intelligence will suffice and prevail and even substitute for genuine intimacy. Affection, sexuality, engagement of curiosity, and especially intellectual pursuits have become substitutes for intimacy and development of long-standing relationships. Nonetheless, at some level you do label this mess—this panoply of intellect, of symbol, of personal understandings—as deficient and are aware that there can be no substitutes for loving, intimate, enduring relationships.

Some of this interpretation is dramatized and overstated in the attempt to capture the quality of experience. Nonetheless, the consequences of divesting yourself of a valuable family heritage in order to be a person in your own right—one who is whole and human and uses her intelligence in constructive, growth-oriented ways—is certainly your preoccupation. There is no hint in these stories of what the future will bring, since you are still looking over your shoulder at a subtle, vague, and confusing past while you attempt to forge a meaningful identity in the present.

Feedback.   During the feedback hours, the client was intent upon understanding the logic of the inference process. She described the report as "very accurate," cited particular contents as examples, and did not take exception to any interpretive statement.

CROSS-CULTURAL TAT USE

The use of picture-story tests with persons in many cultures all over the globe, including American Indians, has a history in anthropological research. The TAT, especially with modified pictures, is believed to provide an adequate sample of personality data in cultures with oral traditions and interest in pictorial content. The availability of special cards for culturally diverse populations, although necessary for easier identification with figures and contexts, is not sufficient in the absence of assessor cultural competence. There are few culture-specific picture-story measures that meet rigorous standards for multicultural assessment, but the Tell-Me-A-Story (TEMAS) picture-story test is an exception (Costantino, Malgady, & Rogler, 1988).

Cultural competence in assessment requires knowledge of the client's culture and a systematic approach to assessment employing this knowledge to understand clients as cultural beings. Many standard tests have constraints on their usage with multicultural clients because of content, administration procedures, normative data, and Anglo-American interpretive procedures, to name a few. The continued use of these tests has necessitated alterations that may compromise their validity in order to avoid inadvertent bias, incorrect interpretation, or pathologization (Dana, submitted). Moreover, in order to decide whether or not standard tests are appropriate, it is necessary to know whether a client's cultural orientation is assimilated, bicultural, marginal, or traditional (Dana, 1992). This information can be gained by test or interview (see Dana, 1993, Chapter 7).

Learning to administer and interpret thematic tests for use with multicultural populations is extraordinarily difficult for Anglo-American middle-class assessors, since adequate training is available in only a few programs. As a result, assessors providing assessment services for these populations are ethically obligated to avail themselves of relevant information and special skills as stipulated the 1992 APA Ethical Code (Dana, in press).

Culturally different persons often expect the worst possible outcomes from assessment provided by an Anglo-American middle-class clinician. This expectation is fueled by the history of cross-cultural contact in which American Indians may bring with them into the assessment setting an implicit knowledge that genocide has been at issue historically. These less tangible matters may need to be addressed by the assessor prior to assessment by using a culture-specific service-delivery style, or social etiquette that is recognized by the client as appropriate. For example, American Indians, especially traditional persons, may not be comfortable with immediate eye contact or a style that does not permit a relaxed and slow process of relationship development based on mutual acquaintances, shared experiences, and assessor knowledge of the client's tribal history. Sometimes it is not feasible to do any testing whatsoever for several meetings, especially if the clinician does not live in the community or have a preexisting social relationship with the client. Even then, many American-Indian clients will appear to be task oriented and provide a minimal response process that the assessor believes constitutes an adequate data set. Treatment of the protocol as a guarded record may then result in overinterpretation or pathologization and subsequent disservice to the client. Moreover, there are few guidelines for interpretation, although John Monopoli has provided cues for Hopi, Navajo, and Zuni TAT protocols of acculturated and traditional persons (see Dana, 1993, pp. 152–155).

As an example of minimum background for the example to follow, this clinician had several summers of assessment experience with Sioux Indians for clinical and research purposes. Moreover, there had been time for getting to know them in a variety of social settings. Ethnographies and other tribe-related materials had been examined carefully, although reservation residents had a poor opinion of these documents. More specifically, several informal conversations with the client had preceded asking for her cooperation. She wanted to understand the entire process of test administration, interpretation, and feedback before agreeing to participate.

American-Indian TAT Example

The stories for this TAT interpretation were obtained from a 33-year-old Navajo-Sioux woman (called Ms. C) who is the eldest of four children raised by grandparents in a medium-sized midwestern city. She has also lived on two reservations and in several major cities in different parts of the country. She is married, has three children, and is employed by a mental health facility serving an American-Indian reservation community. She completed high school and started junior college and beautician school. The TAT stories were obtained soon after a trip to a nearby city, an exciting fun-filled junket with a co-worker, and some of the let-down experienced in the return to more mundane activities is apparent in the stories. The TAT stories and working notes follow in tabular form. Card 16 was administered after Card 20.

TAT Stories and Working Notes: An American-Indian Woman

Card/Story

1. What does this look like? Looks like a little boy looking at a violin. He doesn't look too happy about it. I don't know. (directions repeated) Looks like he wants to play the violin—other side—looking at violin and just can't play it—wants to and doesn't want to—maybe thinking to self if he really tries he can play it (Enough? Or do you want more?) (Continues spontaneously) Either taking lessons and can't master it or looking at violin wanting to play it— just sitting there wishing that he

Notes

Cautious repetition of directions to provide more structure. Very important to do what is expected. Card description and immediate brief emotional reaction, then elaboration. Ambivalent about achievement and own abilities. Does not achieve and uses fantasy-wish-fulfillment. No future included.

Card/Story

Notes

could—dreaming about him being one of those guys that really play real good.

2. That looks like a young girl, father, mother, and background. Her mother looks pregnant—looks peaceful and happy. She doesn't want that kind of life—probably wants to learn more—go on to school or college—got back turned to her father and mother. (That's about it.)

Card description. Sibling. Pregnancy associated with good feelings—contentment in being woman and mother. Rejects family lifestyle but does not leave, wants different life but cannot have it. No future—just desire. No good communication with parents—her choice.

3BM. That is a woman and she's not happy about something. Looks like she's in a lot of pain—hurts a lot. Looks like something on side—scissors or knife or something. Only way out—then couldn't go through with it—sitting there crying.

Pain-suicide solution not feasible. Hurt without surcease, without behavioral solution. Can only suffer and hurt, cannot avoid life.

3GF. Now this looks like a person that just came through the door and she must be ashamed or something or something must have hurt her—crying—or not something in eye (laughs) or maybe somebody died. That's what it looks like—maybe she heard somebody died and going into her bedroom to figure out death—and that person she's feeling bad about.

Responsive to social pressure, sense of humor, tries to make light of tragedy but death must be dealth with and pain experienced. Reaction to loss is internalization/solitude.

4. This looks like Gary Cooper movie—I don't know which movie though—then again looks like man that wants to do something and woman is holding him back. (That's about it.) Does look like Gary Cooper, though, and Ida Lupino.

More description: labeling. No outcome in male-female relations, just stasis in present.

5. This reminds me of my grandma—coming in—tell us kids to go to bed. Then again reminds me of my mother when I had a boyfriend coming over—every now and then peek—to see if they are doing anything—peek in—check up on me.

Grandmother first influence in early life. Mother is controlling, suspicious.

Card/Story	**Notes**
6GF. Those look like old movie characters—seems like he's asking her some questions and she's just been accused or something. He looks like a lawyer. Might be a movie where he's trying to find out if she had anything to do with murder. (That's all.)	Movie: description, murder as theme, accusatory.
7GF. That reminds me of grandmother! Playing dolls—got that doll in her hand. Looks like grandma trying to tell her how she should raise her baby when she grows up. (My grandma did a lot of that—tell me how to raise babies and where they came from. My mother didn't tell me that stuff.)	Grandmother instructs—very much personalized—contrast to mother.
8GF. That looks like a poor, married woman that's bored and just staring out the window (laughs) thinking of how things might have been—only if—for a lot of reasons. Either that or she's daydreaming about something that happened to her that she was happy about.	Poor—feels sorry for herself, but self-perspective in laughter; nostalgia, romanticization, fantasy, daydream.
9GF. (long pause) (Geez. Can I say it just looks like two women running to something?) Reminds me of a movie—I don't know what the name of the movie is. (That's all I can think about this.) Maybe a boat just came in.	Movie: excitement-seeking, running toward and running away from. Wish fulfillment.
10. This looks like my grandma and grandpa—cause they're together for 61 years now—still alive—always together. (That's all.) They love each other—they're old—either old or they're dancing. (Raised me until I was about eleven.)	Venerates age and own grandparents. Personalized (7GF).

Card/Story

11. That looks like a monster movie and some—what is name—gargoyles or something like that—monster coming out of its hole on ledge—old monster movie—cause they don't make them anymore.

12GF. That reminds me of Snow White and Seven Dwarfs. Older woman in back looks like the witch—looks evil—doesn't look very nice. Other woman looks like Snow White. (She don't look anything like my grandma.)

13MF. (long pause) Well, there's a naked lady laying there. There's this guy but he's got his clothes on. Maybe he came home and found his wife drunk and he feels bad for her being drunk. Either that or he's just killed her.

14. That reminds me of a book I read—I read a lot of books. In Italy—gone there to get training art—peeking out at night—because he misses the United States—thinking about Big Apple, hot dogs, baseball—probably his family and his friends. Then again he could be saying to himself, Italy is really pretty place—look at street lights and water.

15. Oh, reminds me of *Christmas Carol*—what's his name—Scrooge—graveyard. He looks evil. That's about it. Then again he might be a poor old man who is lonesome for someone who just died—probably wishes he was with them because he looks miserable.

Notes

Movie: sheer threat without outcome.

Movie: evil and personalization (loss of distance) and clear distinctions—dichotomous thinking.

Sympathy with drunkenness, atypical theme, or murder. Drunkenness is frequent and forgiven on reservation.

Personalization—books as escape. Solace for eloneliness is nostalgia and a sensuous enjoyment of immediate present.

Story: evil-either/or—two stories but what passes for evil is only someone lonesome and miserable.

Card/Story

Notes

16. I'd like to see real pretty mountains—like in Arizona—sand and desert, mountains and trees, and a stream. I could just smell it—just animals and kids playing. Everything nice and clean. Like anymore all of the pictures you have—sorta wish it could be like it was a long time ago before all this civilization came, I guess. Everything was nice and clean—no bottle, no cars, nothing. When life was just simple—you see a house, hogan, teepee, whatever, no signs, beer bottles. Pampers. Kids playing, happy, everybody doing their own thing—father working in garden, mother—something. That's about it.

Ultimate wish fulfillment: Land is source for family—nostalgia for earlier times—with clean and simpler life. Theme: things were better in good old days. Nostalgia for Arizona—for Navajos.

17GF. (Tell a story about this?) This sorta reminds me of that one movie—*Escape from New York*—cause it's got a big wall. Can't make up no story about this—just plain. There's this guy—looks like he's waiting for this girl to come down. Maybe she's running off from someplace and they're gonna escape. Then again, it looks like a girl standing on a bridge looking over—maybe she wants to jump.

Movie: escape/suicide are equivalent themes.

18GF. This don't look like anything—except for woman that collapsed or something—other woman trying to help her, see if she's alright. Reminds me of movie—*Gone with the Wind*—Scarlet taking care of her—woman fainted, sick, or something.

Movie: helpful—nonjudgmental—fainted or sick.

19. This looks like it's in Alaska—snowy—it's a blizzard. Looks like hogan—Navajo hogan in a way. That's it. I could look at it longer and longer and say something evil is

Navajo origins: ambivalence. Hogan in Alaska not seen as inconsistent. She is also superstitious. Evil spirits are equivalent to being consumed/destroyed.

Card/Story	Notes

trying to creep up on house(?). I don't know—probably like a big monster story—eat them up—or maybe get possessed by evil spirits. First guess—hogan in wintertime something evil trying to get it, take over. Navajos are really superstitious.

20. This reminds me of *Thin Man* movie—guy always standing on street and theme song comes on. That's all (repeats). He walks across the street, stands in doorway, lights up a cigarette, looks into a camera, and they say, "Thin Man." (Hams it up.)

Loner tries to embellish the present.

Organization of Notes, Report, and Discussion of Feedback

To summarize, 10 stories have themes from movies or books, 4 stories contain themes of suffering/death/sorrow, 3 stories contain grandparents or grandmother, and 2 stories demonstrate ambivalence.

Report. Ms. C approached the storytelling cautiously, wanting to please and do it exactly the right way. Life as experienced is extraordinarily difficult. Suffering and pain, hurt, alcohol, murder, death are everyday occurrences. Life can also be boring and lacking in excitement. Pleasant experiences are infrequent. She is ambivalent regarding her own ability and likelihood of achievement. She is also ambivalent regarding where she belongs—with her family or away from her family, on the reservation or elsewhere. She is literally frozen in day-to-day activities and can see little change over time. Although she was a ready sense of humor, compassion for others, and perspective on her life situation, she sometimes feels sorry for herself and uses fantasy to remove herself from the daily events of her life. Books and movies provide nourishment, but the salient content of these escapist activities is remarkably similar to her own life experiences: themes of being bogged down in the present, threats, murder, sickness, and evil. She honors her grandparents as models for human relationships involving love, devotion, and caring for others. She imagines being like her grandmother, growing old, and experiencing the pleasures of her grandchildren. An ideal life for her constitutes a family in a rural setting before "all this civilization came." There is nostalgia but no real hope for change or surcease from the pain of living. She endures with good humor and good feelings for others, but she aches for a daily life that contains more than work, tragedy, and escapes into fantasy.

Feedback.   During the feedback process, Ms. C expressed discomfort about the report. First, she noted that most of the pictures seemed designed to yield negative emotions and did not present scenes that are particularly relevant for American Indians. Second, she felt that there was some overstatement in the report. For example, her own life has not been "extraordinarily difficult." She had a good family life with the exception of alcoholism in the family. Nor are pleasant experiences necessarily infrequent. She cites time spent with her children, work, gardening, and visiting as examples of pleasant everyday experiences. In addition, her exposure as a counselor and mental health worker to the tragedy in human life may have served to select negative experiences for inclusion in these stories.

It should be emphasized, however, that reservation life is characteristically punctuated by a high incidence of the kinds of negative events occurring in her stories and reports of stress by many persons on this same reservation consistently emphasize an extraordinary concatenation of negative life experiences (Dana, Hornby, & Hoffman, 1984). Finally, she demurs regarding the final sentence in the report, suggesting she desires more from life than work, tragedy, and escapist fantasy. Here, the overstatement in the report may approach distortion because, in fact, her life is more tranquil and more rewarding than is typical for this reservation.

ASSETS AND LIABILITIES

The TAT is a more difficult instrument than the Rorschach to interpret competently due to the absence of consensual scoring. However, a half dozen approaches to scoring are still taught in graduate assessment courses (Vane, 1981), including Murray's system. Moreover, interpretation is vulnerable to eisegesis or faulty interpretation via projection of clinician-related contents (see Dana, 1966). Interpretation requires caution, an adequate time commitment, and a systematic approach that includes feedback from clients and more experienced assessors (Dana, 1982). Formal training for use of the TAT is generally inadequate and requires supplementation by clinical method (e.g., Rapaport, 1945) and sensitization acquired from immersion in formal scoring systems (e.g., Henry, 1956; Murray, 1938; Tomkins, 1947).

The TAT was once the second most frequently recommended projective technique by clinical psychologists (Wade, Baker, Morton, & Baker, 1978) and one of the most frequently mentioned projective techniques by clinical psychology training and internship directors (Durand, Blanchard, & Mindell, 1988). By the late 1980s, however, the TAT was fifth in usage by outpatient mental health facilities (Piotrowski & Heller, 1989) and was no longer even cited by health psychologists (Piotrowski & Lubin, 1990)—a trend discerned earlier in clinical assessment training preferences (Durand et al., 1988). A reported decline in TAT research (Polyson, Norris, & Ott, 1985) was soon followed by the conclusion that the TAT was now obsolete as a result of insufficient validity due to poor stimuli and procedures, apparently as a result of preference for more systematically developed sets of picture-story test stimuli (Keiser & Prather, 1990). These newer sets of picture-story stimuli, especially the Tell-Me-A-Story (TEMAS) and Apperceptive Personality Test (Costantino et al., 1988; Karp, Holstrom, & Silber, 1990), have developed scoring systems that more adequately reflect TAT research history (e.g., Buros, 1978).

Story-telling continues to have a central role in the life of human beings (Howard, 1991). A fifth edition of Bellak (1993) and a new book by Teglasi (1993) provide evidence for a continuing tradition of clinical skill used for interpretation of stories to pictorial stimuli. Formal scoring procedures have not diminished in what they contribute to knowledge of TAT assessment (e.g., Smith, Atkinson, McClelland, & Veroff, 1992).

The TAT continues to be useful for personality description and for clinical diagnosis. For example, Shneidman (1951) synthesized 16 approaches to interpretation and found that 14.5 percent of the 802 statements contained in reports from one set of TAT stories were related to symptoms, diagnoses, and etiology, while the remainder of the content was germane to personality description. The personality areas elucidated were affects, feelings, emotions (13 percent), personality defenses and mechanisms (12 percent), interpersonal and object relations (12 percent), sexual thoughts and behavior (9 percent), and outlook, attitudes, beliefs (8 percent).

Interpretation of TAT records from culturally diverse clients must be contextualized in a knowledge of the particular culture as well as those interactive and social role/social etiquette behaviors that are specific to the assessment setting. Special attention to ethical issues with these clients is mandatory (Dana, in press).

SUMMARY

The TAT continues to be used in assessment practice because of the potential richness of the protocol data for personality study. The major TAT limitations include unsystematic card stimuli, lack of standard directions and administration procedures, use of various short forms, absence of consensual scoring, and a paucity of adequate training, particularly for use with multicultural populations. In order for the TAT to regain more widespread and competent use, a scoring system that adequately codes the entire response process is required. Since the TAT protocol is a combination of structure and content, the fact that such scoring has not been developed may be due to disinterest rather than the magnitude of the task. In spite of these deficits, that TAT does rival the Rorschach for description of personality and even for clinical diagnosis. TAT-like cards designed for particular populations acknowledge the impact of relevant card stimuli and make for easier identification with figures and settings, although they have not as yet developed a substantive research basis for applications.

The TAT can be used in a unique fashion to delineate and understand a human developmental process containing both individuality and interrelatedness, a conceptualization that has been neglected in Western societies (Guisinger & Blatt, 1994). In this way, the TAT can help to redirect psychologists' expertise toward health and behavioral problems in addition to mental illness, as Fox (1994) has recommended.

ENDNOTES

1. Grateful acknowledgment is made to the three anonymous persons who contributed their TAT data and graciously permitted the working notes and written reports to be included.

2. Donkey Kong is a trademark and copyright of Nintendo, 1981.

REFERENCES

Arnold, M. B. (1949). A demonstration analysis of the TAT in a clinical setting. *Journal of Abnormal and Social Psychology, 44,* 97–111.

Bellak, L. (1993). *The T.A.T., C.A.T., and S.A.T. in clinical use.* (5th ed.). Boston: Allyn and Bacon.

Buros, O. K. (Ed.). (1978). *Mental measurements yearbook.* Highland Park, NJ: Gryphon Press.

Costantino, G., Malgady, R. G., & Rogler, L. H. (1988). *Tell-Me-A-Story (TEMAS) manual.* Los Angeles, CA: Western Psychological Services.

Dana, R. H. (1959). Proposal for objective scoring of the TAT. *Perceptual and Motor Skills, 10,* 27–43.

Dana, R. H. (1966). Eisegesis and assessment. *Journal of Projective Techniques and Personality Assessment, 32,* 215–222.

Dana, R. H. (1982). *A human science model for personality assessment with projective techniques.* Springfield, IL: Charles C. Thomas.

Dana, R. H. (1985). A service-delivery paradigm for personality assessment. *Journal of Personality Assessment, 49,* 598–604.

Dana, R. H. (1986). Thematic Apperception Test used with adolescents. In A. I. Rabin (Ed.), *Projective techniques for children and adolescents* (pp. 14–36). New York: Springer.

Dana, R. H. (1992). Assessment of cultural orientation. *SPA Exchange, 2*(2), 14–15.

Dana, R. H. (1993). *Multicultural assessment perspectives for professional psychology.* Boston: Allyn and Bacon.

Dana, R. H. (in press). Testing and assessment for all persons: A beginning and an agenda. *Professional Psychology: Research and Practice.*

Dana, R. H. (submitted). Cultural competence in assessment: Advantages and limitations of using "corrections" for culture. *Hispanic Journal of Behavioral Sciences.*

Dana, R. H., & Cunningham, K. M. (1983). Convergent validity of Rorschach and Thematic Apperception Test ego strength measures. *Perceptual and Motor Skills, 57,* 1101–1102.

Dana, R. H., Hornby, R., & Hoffmann, T. (1984). The Rosebud Sioux: Personality assessment using local normative data. *White Cloud Journal, 3*(2), 19–25.

Durand, V. M., Blanchard, E. B., & Mindell, J. A. (1988). Training in projective testing: Survey of clinical training directors and internship directors. *Professional Psychology: Research and Practice, 19,* 236–238.

Eron, L. D. (Ed.). (1950). A normative study of the Thematic Apperception Test. *Psychological Monographs, 64*(9, Whole No. 15).

Eron, L. D. (1953). Responses of women to the Thematic Apperception Test. *Journal of Consulting Psychology, 17,* 269–282.

Finn, S. E., & Tonsager, M. E. (1992). Therapeutic effects of providing MMPI-2 test feedback to college students awaiting therapy. *Psychological Assessment, 4,* 278–287.

Fox, R. E. (1994). Training professional psychologists for the twenty-first century. *American Psychologist, 49,* 200–206.

Guisinger, S., & Blatt, S. J. (1994). Individuality and relatedness: Evolution of a fundamental dialectic. *American Psychologist, 49,* 104–111.

Henry, W. E. (1956). *The analysis of fantasy.* New York: Wiley.

Howard, G. S. (1991). Culture tales: A narrative approach to thinking, cross-cultural psychology, and psychotherapy. *American Psychologist, 46,* 187–197.

Kahn, M. (1984). The usefulness of the TAT blank card in clinical practice. *Psychotherapy in Private Practice, 2*(2), 43–50.

Karp, S. A., Holstrom, R. W., & Silber, D. E. (1990). *Apperceptive Personality Test manual.* Orlando Park, IL: International Diagnostic Systems.

Keiser, R. E., & Prather, E. N. (1990). What is the TAT? A review of ten years of research. *Journal of Personality Assessment, 55*(3–4), 800–803.

Morgan, C. D., & Murray, H. A. (1935). A method for investigating fantasies. *AMA Archives of Neurology and Psychiatry, 34,* 389–406.

Murray, H. A. (1938). *Explorations in personality.* New York: Oxford University Press.

Murray, H. A. (1943). *Thematic Apperception Test manual.* Cambridge, MA: Harvard University Press.

Murstein, B. I. (1963). *Theory and research in projective techniques.* New York: Wiley.

Newmark, C. S., & Flouranzano, F. (1977). Replication of an empirically derived TAT set with hospitalized psychiatric patients. *Journal of Personality Assessment, 37,* 340–341.

Piotrowski, C., & Heller, J. W. (1989). Psychological testing in outpatient mental health facilities: A national study. *Professional Psychology: Research and Practice, 20,* 423–425.

Piotrowski, C., & Lubin, B. (1990). Assessment practices of health psychologists: Survey of APA Division 38 clinicians. *Professional Psychology: Research and Practice, 21,* 99–106.

Piotrowski, Z. A. (1950). A new evaluation of the Thematic Apperception Test. *Psychoanalytic Review, 37,* 101–127.

Polyson, J., Norris, D., & Ott, E. (1985). The recent decline in TAT research. *Professional Psychology: Research and Practice, 16,* 26–28.

Rapaport, D. (1945). *Diagnostic psychological testing* (Vol. 2). Chicago: Yearbook Medical Publishers.

Shneidman, E. S. (1951). *Thematic test analysis.* New York: Grune & Stratton.

Smith, C. P., Atkinson, J. W., McClelland, D. C., & Veroff, J. (Eds.). (1992). *Motivation and personality: Handbook of thematic apperception test content.* Cambridge: Cambridge University Press.

Teglasi, H. (1993). *Clinical use of story telling: Emphasizing the TAT with children and adolescents.* Boston: Allyn and Bacon.

Tomkins, S. S. (1947). *The Thematic Apperception Test.* New York: Grune & Stratton.

Vane, J. R. (1981). The Thematic Apperception Test: A review. *Clinical Psychology Review, 1,* 319–336.

Wade, T. C., Baker, T. B., Morton, T. L., & Baker, L. J. (1978). The status of psychological testing in clinical psychology: Relationships between test use and professional activities and orientations. *Journal of Personality Assessment, 42,* 3–11.

The Clinical Use of Drawings

Draw-A-Person, House-Tree-Person, and Kinetic Family Drawings

Leonard Handler

INTRODUCTION

Even members of various ancient societies consistently recognized that artists project themselves into their artistic productions. For example, the Paleolithic cave paintings in the Trois Frères cave in France depict a man wrapped in an animal hide, playing a primitive flute, as if he meant to put a spell on the animals or attract them to him. Jaffé (1964) describes another painting in the same cave: "a dancing human being, with antlers, a horse's head, and bear's paws . . . unquestionably the 'Lord of the Animals'" (p. 235). The painting symbolizes the artist's control of the animals—by incorporating all their strengths. It long ago became obvious that all art reflects some aspects of the artist's personality, his or her style of life, and his or her approach to the world. Hammer (1958) quotes Elbert Hubbard, an artist who stated, "when an artist paints a portrait, he paints two, himself and the sitter," (p. 8) and another artist who stated, "The artist does not see things as they are, but as he is" (p. 8).

The creation of the artistic production involves the expression of the unconscious through symbolism, as well as the expression of the artist's style and approach. A variety of conflicts may also be symbolized in the artist's production. The style of approach to the paper or canvas may be typical of the artist's approach to the world in general. One artist may draw with bold,

The author wishes to gratefully acknowledge Chris Kite, Justin R. Padawer, and Rupal Patel for their help in the preparation of this book chapter.

colorful strokes on a large canvas, while another draws tiny, "tight" figures, in muted colors, on a small canvas.

Many people recognize the symbolic content of the art they view in countless museums around the world, and they continue to speculate freely about the personalities of the various artists whose works they view and admire. Yet, they are often reluctant to take the same intuitive, subjective approach in the interpretation of drawings. This chapter will review three types of drawing tests often used in personality assessment—the Draw-A-Person Test (DAP), the House-Tree-Person Drawing Technique (H-T-P), and the Kinetic Family Drawing Technique (K-F-D)—and will describe several approaches to interpretation. An effort will be made to describe ways in which the clinician can interpret the drawings in the same holistic manner in which one interprets art work in a museum. Also note that all three drawing techniques may be used with children, adolescents, and adults, although many clinicians use the H-T-P and the K-F-D primarily with children and adolescents.

THE DRAW-A-PERSON TEST (DAP)

In 1926, Florence Goodenough developed and standardized an intelligence scale that was based on the drawing of a man. This test, which came to be called the Goodenough Draw-A-Man Test (DAP), was based mostly on the quality of the drawing and the amount of detail in it. Clinicians (such as Hammer, Karen Machover, and even Goodenough herself) soon became aware that although the Draw-A-Man Test was supposed to be a test of intelligence, the drawings also tapped a variety of personality variables.

Since 1926, the clinical use of the DAP has increased dramatically. Indeed, in 1961, Sundberg reported that the DAP was the second most frequently used psychological test in hospitals, clinics, and counseling centers throughout the country. Other surveys of psychological testing practices (Crenshaw, Bohn, Hoffman, Matheus, & Offenbach, 1968; Lubin, Wallis, & Paine, 1971) indicate that the DAP continues to be used with a majority of cases in a variety of clinical settings and it is among the five most frequently used projective tests in research situations. Even more recent surveys indicate that the DAP consistently ranks among the most frequently used tests by psychologists in clinical practice (Lubin, Larsen, & Matarazzo, 1984; Piotrowski, Sherry, & Keller, 1985). Piotrowski and Zalewski (1993) asked directors of doctoral programs in clinical psychology to specify with which projective instruments the clinical doctoral candidate should be familiar. The DAP/H-T-P ranked fourth, both in a 1982 survey and in a 1991 survey. Projective drawings (the DAP, the H-T-P, and the K-F-D) are also among the most frequently used tests in school settings with children who are referred for suspected social and/or emotional problems (Eklund, Huebner, Groman, & Michael, 1980; Fuller & Goh, 1983; Goh, Teslow, & Fuller, 1981; Prout, 1983; Vukovich, 1983).

Just what is there about the drawing of a human figure that makes it a good indicator of personality patterns and conflicts? Perhaps it is because graphic representation and drawing are both early developmental skills. Indeed, Hammer (1958) emphasizes that children draw before they can write. Drawings are therefore capable of tapping early, primitive layers of personality, set down before a great deal of intellectual control has taken over. The artist expresses symbolically many hidden aspects of personality that people have typically come to control and modulate. Thus, Hammer (1958) states:

> The drawing page . . . serves as a canvas upon which the subject may sketch a glimpse of his inner world, his traits and attitudes, his behavioral characteristics, his personality strengths and weaknesses including the degree to which he can mobilize his inner resources to handle his psychodynamic conflicts, both interpersonal and intrapsychic. (p. 6)

Advantages of the DAP

Advantages include the following:

1. The DAP is a simple, easy task for most patients. Children, especially young children, like it and will usually cooperate quite readily. They are often more fluent graphically than they are verbally.

2. Children with certain internalized disorders (e.g., depression and anxiety disorders) often do not demonstrate these problems in their overt behavior. Therefore, they sometimes go unnoticed by parents and teachers, and occasionally by psychologists who sometimes do not look beyond overt behavior. Even when they are interviewed, children do not typically communicate their problems directly because they often lack the ability to express their emotional discomfort. Most children, especially younger ones, lack the ability to use language that labels or describes these emotions. The DAP (and other similar drawing procedures) offer a window into their experienced subjective discomfort.

3. The DAP is quick and easy to administer; it is typically completed within 5 to 10 minutes, and it requires few materials.

4. The DAP is one of the few graphic tests in the assessment battery. Therefore, it offers expression in a modality that is novel, and one that also may offer clues concerning conceptual and motor development.

5. The DAP is the only test in the battery that has no external stimulus or structure. There are no designs to copy and no vague forms from which to produce associations. Therefore, the clinician has the opportunity to observe the patient's functioning on a relatively unstructured task; the structure must come completely from within. The patient's functioning under these task conditions should be compared with functioning on more structured tests in order to determine the degree to which he or she needs external structure in order to function, and to determine the qualitative and quantitative effects of functioning when external structure is absent. Is the internal structure (the self) sufficient to allow the patient to produce a well-integrated drawing? The data generated from the DAP, compared with other tests, can frequently answer this question. In situations where there is not adequate functioning, an analysis of the style and content of the drawing will often offer clues concerning the specific conflict areas that might be responsible for poor self-integration. For example, a poorly integrated drawing that shows a great deal of distortion in the sexual areas might indicate that the ego disturbance is focused around sexual conflict.

6. The DAP often yields a great deal of information concerning self-concept, as well as information concerning personality style, orientation, and conflict areas.

7. The DAP has few age and intelligence limitations. It can be used with very young children (sometimes as early as age 3), and it generates valuable data even when the patient is of limited intelligence.

8. The DAP is often welcomed by inhibited and nontalkative patients. It is a relatively nonverbal test (the only verbal material is contained in the thematic associations to the drawings) and therefore it is useful when language is a problem (e.g., with the patient who is poorly educated, the patient who is mentally defective, the patient who does not speak English, the patient who is mute, the patient who is shy or withdrawn, the patient from an underprivileged background who feels insecure about verbal ability, the patient who is disabled or reading disabled and who sometimes develops emotional blocks in verbal areas, all of which frequently interfere with productivity on the more verbal tests).

9. The DAP is a useful test with patients who are evasive and/or guarded. These patients give barren verbal records in tests where they are able to exercise more control over their verbal expression. But in the DAP, these patients express themselves in a more revealing manner. Such guarded patients seem more aware of what they might be expressing in the verbal tests, but they are less certain of what their graphic expression might reveal about them and they can perhaps utilize less control over this more primitive mode of expression. Concrete, primitive personalities often produce richer DAP records, compared with their Rorschach records, whereas verbal, intellectual patients often produce richer Rorschach and TAT records compared with their DAP protocols (Fox, 1952; Hammer, 1954).

10. Since the DAP is quick and easy to administer, it lends itself well as an instrument to measure change in psychotherapy. For example, Figure 6–1, taken from Harrower (1965), represents the before-and-after therapy drawings of a female patient rated as maximally improved. Note the improvement in overall drawing quality, the more sophisticated presentation of the head and body, and the disappearance of the transparency. Robins, Blatt, and Ford (1991) present examples from patients in long-term inpatient treatment at the Austen Riggs Center. They found significant changes in the quality of the drawings when the patient was rated as improved. Figures 6–2 and 6–3 il-

Figure 6–1   Illustrates the Before-and-After Therapy Drawings of a Female Patient Rated as Maximally Improved

Source: From *Psychological Testing: An Empirical Approach* by M. Harrower, 1965, Springfield, IL: Charles C. Thomas. Reprinted by permission of the author.

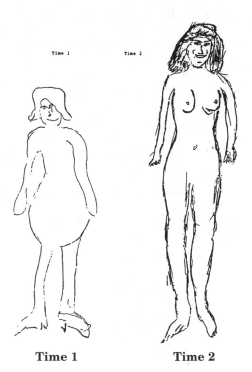

Time 1   Time 2

Figure 6–2   Before-and-After Therapy Female Drawings of a 24-Year-Old Male Patient

Source: From "Changes in Human Figure Drawings during Intensive Treatment" by C. Robins, S. Blatt, and R. Ford, 1991, *Journal of Personality Assessment, 57* (3). Copyright 1991 by Lawrence Erlbaum Associates, Inc. Reprinted by permission.

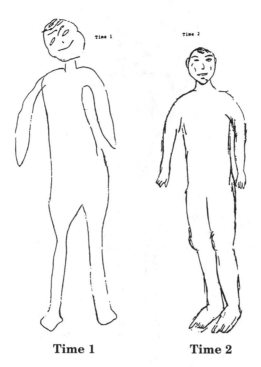

Time 1   **Time 2**

Figure 6–3   Before-and-After Therapy Male Drawings of a 24-Year-Old Male Patient

Source: From "Changes in Human Figure Drawings during Intensive Treatment" by C. Robins, S. Blatt, and R. Ford, 1991, *Journal of Personality Assessment, 57* (3). Copyright 1991 by Lawrence Erlbaum Associates, Inc. Reprinted by permission.

lustrate the changes in drawing quality in a 24-year-old male patient. Note the distortion in the before-therapy drawings; they are devoid of details and lack well-defined boundaries.

11. The DAP is often an excellent springboard for discussion of specific conflict areas. Here, the patient may be asked to associate to the drawing just completed. Repeated administration allows the clinician to see changes that have taken place, and to identify problem areas that still need attention. Hammer (1968) cites the case of a 25-year-old school teacher who had a problem relating to men and a block against getting married (see Figure 6–4). Hammer sensed that the teacher's moderate obesity might be a defense against males:

> After . . . a year-and-a-half of treatment, she was able to reduce, had begun going out, and had established a "going steady" relationship with one young man. One day, she came to the therapy session, proudly showed an engagement ring, and announced jubilantly that she was to be married.
>
> Feeling that she had accomplished her goals in therapy, but also having some marginal doubts, she asked if she might re-take the H-T-P to compare it

Figure 6–4   Drawing by a 25-Year-Old School Teacher After Becoming Engaged, Suggesting Sexual Panic at Impending Marriage

Source: From E. Hammer in *Projective Techniques in Personality Assessment* (p. 369) by A. Rabin (Ed.), 1968, New York: Springer. Copyright 1968 Springer Publishing Company, Inc. New York 10012. Used by permission.

with the one she had initially taken upon entering treatment. . . . The drawing of a female she now produced (Figure 6–4) was better integrated, prettier, more feminine and certainly no longer the representation of the obese woman it had been. The figure, like the earlier one, still stood on phallic feet, however, and the hands were now drawn into a position of "pelvic defense." Both hands, in spite of the ring now conspicuous on the third finger of one of them, were drawn to a position of guarding the genital area. Whereas noteworthy gains in self-image were apparent, the projective drawing cried out with the problem of fear of intercourse and some underlying masculine identification still unresolved. (p. 370)

12. The DAP is more sensitive to psychopathology compared with other projective tests (Calden, 1954; Zucker, 1948). Zucker found that the DAP was the first test in the battery to show incipient psychopathology. Thus, it is a good prognostic indicator. However, Zucker also found that the DAP was the last test to show improvement.

13. A number of clinicians have begun to utilize the DAP as a measure of progress and outcome in therapy for sexual disorders (Hartman & Fithian, 1972; Sarrel & Sarrel, 1979). Sarrel, Sarrel, and Berman (1981), in a remarkable paper, describe the major ways in which the DAP is useful in sex therapy: assessing the individual (including psychopathology, body image, sexual orientation and/or gender identity, sexual response and behavior, organic disease, motivation, and personality style); assessing interpersonal issues; and assessing change during the course of sex therapy. Concerning the use of the DAP in interpersonal issues, clinicians use the drawing to determine feelings about the opposite sex and feelings specific to the couple's relationships (the psychological bonding between the couple), and to assess changes in the couple's relationship during the course of sex therapy. The DAP is also used to assess such differences as global body image problems, body penetration anxiety, body boundary problems, and anxiety about the genitals or other parts of the body. Figure 6–5 illustrates the initial drawings done by a 26-year-old woman who disliked sex and had never had an orgasm. The patient felt rejected by her father, who told her at age 16 that she was "as sexy as a wet dishrag." Figure 6–6 was done at the completion of therapy. Note the dramatic change in body image.

The DAP can be used to monitor changes in the individual's personality dynamics as well as changes in a couple's interpersonal dynamics. Figure 6–7 was drawn by a 32-year-old impotent male who was extremely fearful and severely disturbed. The first drawing was done before therapy, the second drawing was done when the patient began to have early successful erections, and the third drawing was done at the end of therapy. "The first drawing," the patient remarked, "was a hermaphrodite." Note the tiny size of the figure, the lack of definition of the body, and the discontinuity in the line—all indicators of severe pathology.

The last illustrations (Figure 6–8) are the drawings of a sexually dysfunctional, inhibited woman who began to emerge as an assertive, sexual woman. In turn, her initially confident husband became frightened and sexually dysfunctional. The woman's drawings are on the left and her husband's drawings are on the right. Note the immature and child-like self-image projected by the woman in the first drawing. The subsequent drawings show her

Figure 6–5   Drawing by a 26-Year-Old Woman Before Sex Therapy

Source: From "Using the Draw-A-Person (DAP) Test in Sex Therapy" by P. Sarrel, L. Sarrel, and S. Berman, 1981, *Journal of Sex & Marital Therapy, 7.* Copyright 1981 by Plenum Publishing Corporation. Reprinted by permission.

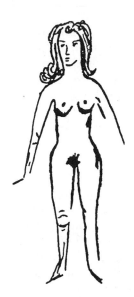

Figure 6–6   Drawing by a 26-Year-Old Woman After Sex Therapy

Source: From "Using the Draw-A-Person (DAP) Test in Sex Therapy" by P. Sarrel, L. Sarrel, and S. Berman, 1981, *Journal of Sex & Marital Therapy, 7.* Copyright 1981 by Plenum Publishing Corporation. Reprinted by permission.

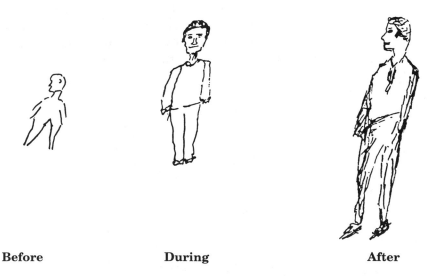

Before   **During**   **After**

Figure 6–7   Drawings by a 32-Year-Old Male Before, During, and After Sex Therapy

Source: From "Using the Draw-A-Person (DAP) Test in Sex Therapy" by P. Sarrel, L. Sarrel, and S. Berman, 1981, *Journal of Sex & Marital Therapy, 7.* Copyright 1981 by Plenum Publishing Corporation. Reprinted by permission.

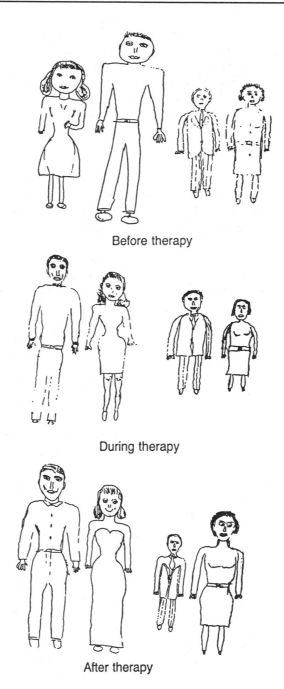

Before therapy

During therapy

After therapy

Figure 6–8   Drawings of a Sexually Dysfunctional, Inhibited Woman and Her Husband Before, During, and After Sex Therapy

Source: From "Using the Draw-A-Person (DAP) Test in Sex Therapy" by P. Sarrel, L. Sarrel, and S. Berman, 1981, *Journal of Sex & Marital Therapy, 7.* Copyright 1981 by Plenum Publishing Corporation. Reprinted by permission.

increasing self-confidence and her husband's increasing anxiety. As therapy progressed, the husband could not ejaculate. He feared losing control of himself and hurting his wife. The authors note that his pictures indicate "increasing levels of repressed anger . . . and genital anxiety" (Sarrel, Sarrel, & Berman, 1981, p. 180).

Instructions

The clinician should have a supply of 8½ × 11-inch unlined paper and some well-sharpened #2 pencils with erasers. The drawing surface beneath the paper should be flat and smooth and there should be sufficient illumination. The patient should be seated comfortably with enough room for their arms and legs, and should be able to rest their arms comfortably on the drawing surface.

One sheet of paper should be placed in front of the patient in a vertical position, along with one pencil. The patient should be told: "I would like you to draw a picture of a person." The clinician should give the patient little more guidance than that, despite the fact that the patient often asks a variety of questions in order to get the examiner to structure the situation more clearly. However, since this is a projective test, the clinician should resist adding any additional instructions that will interfere with unencumbered, free performance. For example, patients often ask, "What kind of figure should I draw?" "Should I draw the head only?" "Should I draw the whole person?" or "Is a stick figure OK?" In response to these and other such questions, the clinician should respond, "Do it any way you like; it's up to you." Sometimes the patient responds with comments indicating concern about his or her ability to perform adequately, such as "I was never a good artist," or "I can't do this because I can't draw." To such comments as these, the examiner should respond, "This is not a test of artistic ability. I'm not concerned with how good an artist you are. Just do the best you can and don't worry." Should the patient draw merely the head, the head and shoulders, or a stick figure, he or she should be given another sheet of paper and should then be told, "This time I'd like you to draw the entire person (or, a nonstick figure person)."

When the first complete drawing is finished, the clinician should put another sheet of paper in front of the patient and state, "Now I'd like you to draw a person of the opposite sex." If the patient being tested is a child, the clinician should say, "You drew a boy (man); now draw a girl or a woman," or "You drew a girl (woman); now draw a boy or a man." When this task has been completed satisfactorily, the patient should be asked to sign each drawing. The clinician should then date each drawing, either on the front or on the back. In addition, the clinician should indicate which drawing was done first, which was done second, and so on.

The clinician should then present the first complete drawing to the patient and should request that the patient make up a story about the person drawn: "Now I'd like you to make up a story about the person you've drawn. Look at it and make up a story, and I'll write it down." The story should be recorded verbatim because interpretation often depends on the manner in which the words are phrased and expressed. Sometimes it is necessary to urge or encourage the patient. Should the patient be unable to make up a story, it will then be necessary to ask specific questions about the drawing—for example: "How old is the person?" "What does the person do for a living?" "How does the person feel?" "What is he (she) thinking about?" "What will happen to him (her) in the future?" "What fears does he (she) have?" "What gets him (her) angry?" "How does he (she) get along with his (her) wife (husband, mother, father, etc.)?" For a more detailed set of questions for an adult and a separate set for a child, see Machover (1951). The clinician should use any questions he or she feels will help the patient associate to the drawing.

A third approach in obtaining verbal associations is to ask the patient to examine the drawings and to then associate to them. The patient should be asked to describe the person he or she has drawn and to tell what comes to mind when the drawing is examined, or the examiner might ask, "Tell me about this person; what is he/she like?" Sarrel, Sarrel, and Berman (1981) ask the patient to "Look at the finished pictures . . . and write down any observations or feelings that occur to you as you look at the pictures" (p. 165).

In recent years there has been a shift in psychoanalytic theory from a metapsychological approach stressed by the ego psychologists to an approach that is more phenomenological and that stresses the experience of the patient. As part of this movement there has been an increased interest in the concept of object relations, which includes self-representation (the experiential symbolization of the self and the associated emotions [Kissen, 1986]), object representation ("the . . . modes by which the individual symbolizes an experiential image of a significant other and its associated affects" [Kissen, 1986, p. 177]), and the patient's ego state ("more complex and relatively differentiated units of self and object representation and their associated affects" [Kissen, 1986, p. 177]).

Kissen (1986) describes an important modification of the verbal association phase, based on an object-relations approach, that, he feels, enhances the "psychodynamic potentiality" of the DAP. He encourages the patient to "adopt an attitude of naivete and curiosity" toward his or her own figure drawings, and he invites the patient to "explore psychologically some of the salient expressive characteristics of the human figures produced" (pp. 43–44). The patient becomes a consultant, thereby joining the resistance. This role reversal "allows the patient to become spontaneous and open to inner experiential states" (p. 44).

After the patient completes both figures, the clinician states: "I would like you to look at your first drawing as though it were drawn by somebody else. From the physical characteristics of the drawing, facial expression, posture, style of clothing—what sort of person comes through to you? What personal characteristics come to mind?" (p. 45).

The clinician asks the patient to describe how the male person in the drawing relates to other males, how the female relates to other females, and how the person in the drawing relates to peers of the opposite sex. Kissen also asks the patient to describe an animal that seems most like the person in the drawing, and then he draws a cartoon balloon coming from the mouth of the figure and asks the patient to "write in the balloon a statement that you can imagine the person you have described making. Write a typical statement that is characteristic of this sort of person" (pp. 45–46). The same procedure is used for the second drawing.

During the drawing task itself, it is important for the clinician to observe the drawing sequence. For example, although most of patients draw the head first, a recent patient began with the feet and ended with the head. Since this pattern is quite atypical and may indicate severe pathology, it is important that the clinician observe and record such variations in approach to the drawing task. A patient drew a mouth with a frown, erased, it, and replaced it with a heavily overworked grin. An adolescent male first drew a male with small, narrow shoulders, only to erase them and replace them with extremely broad compensatory shoulders. In still another example, the patient went back over a light, tentative line and reinforced it to give the drawing a superficial look of confidence and adequacy.

Although the DAP is one of the easiest tests in the battery for most patients, the clinician should be aware that the task of drawing a person is difficult for some patients, especially in the anxiety-provoking testing situation. Although a good clinician will help the patient manage and deal with anxiety concerning the testing situation and the anxiety concerning personal self-revelation, the testing situation is sometimes tension filled and the patient has little knowledge concerning the adequacy of their performance. Therefore, the remarks made by the patient, the style of approach to the task, and the adequacy of attempts to manage the task appropriately despite the pressure of the testing situation should all be observed and noted. For example, Does the patient stop to erase and fix a poorly drawn spot? Does the patient verbalize any defensive responses (e.g., "I can't draw too well, I never studied art in school")? Does the patient verbalize an evaluation of the drawing (e.g., "This man looks angry")?

It is important to note how the patient orients to the relatively unstructured drawing situation. Does the patient ask for direction, either verbally or nonverbally, or does he or she seem comfortable and self-assured? Is the patient's approach to the task quick and impulsive, careful, or overly cautious and uncertain? Does the patient express doubts about his or her ability? Each aspect of approach to the task tells the clinician a great deal about adaptation in the environment, self-concept, methods of dealing with stressful situations, conflicts, and personality style.

The Patient's Experience

What is the experience of the patient when asked to draw a person? How does a patient begin to organize the task, to pick and choose what he or she will draw? Of course, previous drawing experience may provide a guide, but experience alone is probably not enough to produce an integrated drawing. The patient must in some way refer to all of the images of himself or herself and of other persons that crowd his or her mind, drawing on the visual perception of other people, both past and present, as well as the emotional experiences that go with these perceptions. There is also the patient's visual perception of his or her body image, which is a product of experience, identifications, projections, and introjections.

The composite DAP image is intimately tied to the self. In the process of creating the figure, conscious and unconscious determinants guide patients; images of cultural and social stereotypes contribute to body image conception. Thus, tall, thin, asthenic people are associated with certain psychological attributes in patients' minds, while other types of body builds are identified with other temperaments. Strong arms, thick necks, and long noses often have stereotyped social meanings. For example, Dick Tracy's square jaw symbolizes strength, virtue, and determination, whereas Elmer Fudd's short, round body, and bald head symbolize bumbling inadequacy and ineffectualness. Combined with these social images are those that arise from private experience. Added to this list are the more universal symbols of psychoanalysis and folklore. All of these images intermingle to produce the subtle and complex projections of the self.

It is clear, then, that the task of drawing the human figure is a creative one. The pencil is guided by unconscious forces asking for expression and by stylistic patterns of expressive behavior that are typical of the patient in a variety of situations. The figure the patient draws is himself or herself in many respects, and the page upon which the patient draws is his or her world. The end product is a drawing of self-experience in the patient's world.

The Drawing as a Representation of the Self

Perhaps the preceding paragraph describes why human beings do not typically draw what they look like or how they are built, but instead draw a figure that reflects how they feel about themselves and how they feel as a person experiencing their environment. For example, a burly and powerful lumberjack or construction worker might draw a tiny, uncertain-looking man, while a thin, frail, and effeminate-looking man might draw a large, virile male in an attempt to live out a fantasy. The body image projected on the paper may refer to deep, unconscious wishes, to a frank acknowledgment of physical or psychological impairment, to conscious or unconscious compensation for a physical or a psychological defect, or to a combination of all of these factors.

The drawing that a patient makes of a human figure represents the self in the environment. The actual presentation of the self may reflect the patient's deepest wishes; it may reflect and expose a painful physical or emotional defect; it may be a vigorous compensation for this defect; or a combination of all these factors. The drawing may represent an ego ideal or a hero figure, as, for example, the drawing of a fierce and muscular warrior drawn by a recent patient—a short, chubby 11-year-old Filipino boy. However, this approach may be seen as an attempt to present the self in a more admired manner. The patient seems to be saying, "Right now I feel small in a much larger adult world, but when I grow up I'm going to be a big, strong, brave man like this!" Perhaps during the experience of drawing, which seemed quite pleasurable to the boy, he was also saying, "Right now I *am* big; I *am* that strong, brave warrior!"

Patients sometimes attempt to express an ideal self rather than the real self, but the underlying basis for this expression may also be seen in the drawing, thereby giving the clinician a picture of both the real self and the ideal self. Occasionally, the patient draws in such a manner as to illustrate his or her attitudes toward life and society in general. The drawing may be a conscious expression of these feelings or it may include deeply disguised and unconscious information, expressed indirectly through symbolism.

Some clinicians (Levy, 1950) feel that the drawing might also represent a projection of attitudes toward someone else in the environment (e.g., the patient's feelings about his or her father or mother), a projection of an ideal self-image, or an expression of the patient's attitude toward life and toward the world in general. This writer feels that these other possible representations constitute or relate to some aspect of the self-concept. For example, the patient's attitude about a parent or feelings about the world are directly related to how the patient feels about himself or herself.

Some observers have indicated that the DAP is invalid because people do not represent themselves as they appear physically, and therefore the DAP does not represent a true picture of the self. These critics do not understand the principle of symbolic representation, where the material is presented in a disguised or symbolically transformed manner. For example, Hammer (1958) illustrates a drawing produced by a man with a missing left arm and hand. The left arm and hand are present in the drawing, but they appear withered and much smaller than the right arm and hand.

Several other examples come from the work of Schildkrout, Shenker, and Sonnenblick (1972). The drawing in Figure 6–9 was done by a 15-year-old girl with exaggerated concern about a mild facial acne and irregular menses. She eradicates her acne by becoming totally faceless. The next drawing (Figure 6–10) was done by a 12-year-old girl with a congenital heart defect, about which she verbalized no concern. Notice that she symbolized her underlying concern about her heart problem by the heart-shaped body she drew.

Normative Data

The typical drawing of a person consists of a head, which is drawn first; facial features (eyes, nose, mouth, ears, hair); legs; feet; arms; hands; fingers; neck; shoulders; and trunk. The typical drawing also includes such additional details as a belt and clothing of some type (skirt, dress, trousers, shirt, jacket). It is placed approximately in the middle of the page and is about six to seven inches in size.

There are relatively few studies concerning the quality of the typical adult drawing. Here is a short summary of these findings: The head, trunk,

Figure 6–9   Drawing by a 15-Year-Old Girl with Exaggerated Concern about Mild Facial Acne and Irregular Menses

Source: From *Human Figure Drawings in Adolescence* (page 87) by M. S. Schildkrout, I. R. Shenker, and M. Sonnenblick, 1972, New York: Brunner/Mazel. Copyright 1972 and reprinted with permission from Brunner/Mazel, Inc.

Figure 6–10   Drawing by a 12-Year-Old Girl with a Congenital Heart Defect about Which She Seemed Unconcerned

Source: From *Human Figure Drawings in Adolescence* (page 68) by M. S. Schildkrout, I. R. Shenker, and M. Sonnenblick, 1972, New York: Brunner/Mazel. Copyright 1972 and reprinted with permission from Brunner/Mazel, Inc.

arms, and legs are typically in proportion, with relative symmetry, spontaneity, movement, or animation. The line quality is typically consistent. The head is more oval than round, and some attempt is made to draw the facial features in a realistic manner (e.g., eyes are almond shaped, not round circles or dots; lips are indicated by a double line). The body is lifelike, with a three-dimensional quality. The head sits well on the neck and shoulders. Secondary sex characteristics are included, so that the male and female drawings may be distinguished from each other (Jones & Thomas, 1964; Thomas, 1966; Urban, 1963; Wagner & Schubert, 1955).

Drawings by children must be judged by other criteria, since the style and quality of the drawing will vary with age and with developmental status. Unless the clinician knows the developmental drawing norms, he or she is liable to make an interpretation based on developmental or maturational issues. For example, the omission of the neck or the feet on the DAP are not unusual for the typical 5-year-old boy, and therefore they do not have clinical significance. It is also important to note that drawings done by children and adults from other cultures and other countries should not be evaluated with the same criteria, since cultural factors affect drawing style and quality in some dramatic ways.

Table 6–1, which summarizes the expected drawing items (present in 85–100 percent of the drawings) and the exceptional items (present in 15 percent or less of the drawings) for boys and girls, 5 to 12 years old, is taken from Koppitz (1968). The exceptional items are found only in drawings of children with above-average mental maturity. This table may be used to rate the developmental quality of the drawing to distinguish developmental factors from emotional factors. For example, a 5-year-old boy can be expected to include hands, eyes, nose, mouth, body, and legs in his drawing. Omission of one or more of these items is said by Koppitz to be clinically significant. Groves and Fried (1991) validated these norms on a Canadian sample. They also include norms for 3- and 4-year-old boys and girls, utilizing Koppitz's categories.

Koppitz has validated a series of emotional indicators, listed in Table 6–2, along with the ages at which they become clinically valid for boys and girls. Note, for example, that Koppitz finds that shading of the body and/or limbs is normal for young children and therefore it does not become an indicator of conflict until the boy is 9 years old and the girl is 8 years old. In a later publication, Koppitz (1984) lists the emotional indicators for use with middle school pupils. They are said to occur significantly more often, but not exclusively, on figure drawings of children with serious emotional problems, compared with the drawings of well-adjusted children. Koppitz points out that the presence of only one or two of these indices does not reflect severe psychopathology. The indicators include those which are said to reflect the following:

1. *Impulsivity:* poor integration of body parts; gross asymmetry of limbs; transparencies; figure larger than nine inches; omission of the neck

Table 6-1 Expected and Exceptional Items on Human Figure Drawings of Boys and Girls Age 5 to 12

	Age 5		Age 6		Age 7		Age 8		Age 9		Age 10		Age 11 & 12	
	Boys	*Girls*	*Boys*	*Girls*	*Boys*	*Girls*	*Boys*	*Girls*	*Boys*	*Girls*	*Boys*	*Girls*	*Boys*	*Girls*
N	*128*	*128*	*131*	*133*	*134*	*125*	*138*	*130*	*134*	*134*	*109*	*108*	*157*	*167*
Expected Items														
Head	X	X	X	X	X	X	X	X	X	X	X	X	X	X
Eyes	X	X	X	X	X	X	X	X	X	X	X	X	X	X
Nose	X	X	X	X	X	X	X	X	X	X	X	X	X	X
Mouth	X	X	X	X	X	X	X	X	X	X	X	X	X	X
Body	X	X	X	X	X	X	X	X	X	X	X	X	X	X
Legs	X	X	X	X	X	X	X	X	X	X	X	X	X	X
Arms		X	X	X	X	X	X	X	X	X	X	X	X	X
Feet			X	X	X	X	X	X	X	X	X	X	X	X
Arms 2 dimension					X	X	X	X	X	X	X	X	X	X
Legs 2 dimension						X		X		X	X	X	X	X
Hair						X		X		X	X	X	X	X
Neck				X						X	X	X	X	X
Arm down													X	X
Arms at shoulder														X
2 clothing items												X		X
Exceptional Items														
Knee	X	X	X	X	X	X	X	X	X	X	X	X	X	X
Profile	X	X	X	X	X	X	X	X	X	X		X		
Elbow	X	X	X	X	X	X	X	X	X					
Two lips	X	X	X	X	X	X	X	X	X					
Nostrils	X	X	X	X	X		X		X		X			
Proportions	X	X	X	X	X									
Arms at shoulder	X	X	X	X										
4 clothing items	X	X	X											
Feet 2 dimension	X	X												
Five fingers	X	X												
Pupils	X													

Source: Psychological evaluation of children's human figure drawings by E. Koppitz, 1968, Orlando, FL: The Psychological Corporation. © 1968 by Grune & Stratton. Reprinted by permission.

Table 6–2   Emotional Indicators on Human Figure Drawings of Children

Poor integration of parts of figure (Boys 7, Girls 6)

Shading of face

Shading of body and/or limbs (Boys 9, Girls 8)

Shading of hands and/or neck (Boys 8, Girls 7)

Gross asymmentry of limbs

Slanting figure, axis of figure tilted by 15° or more

Tiny figure, two inches high or less

Big figure, nine inches or more in height (Boys and Girls 8)

Transparancies

Tiny head, head less than 1/10th of total figure in height

Crossed eyes, both eyes turned in or out

Teeth

Short arms, arms not long enough to reach waistline

Long arms, arms long enough to reach knee line

Arms clinging to sides of body

Big hands, hands as large or larger than face of figure

Hands cut off, arms without hands or fingers (hidden hands not scored)

Legs pressed together

Genitals

Monster or grotesque figure

Three or more figures spontaneously drawn

Clouds, rain, snow

Omissions: Eyes; Nose (Boys 6, Girls 5); Mouth; Body; Arms (Boys 6, Girls 5); Legs; Feet (Boys 9, Girls 7); Neck (Boys 10, Girls 9)

Note: All of the Emotional Indicators are considered valid for boys and girls age 5–12, unless otherwise indicated.

Source: Psychological evaluation of children's human figure drawings by E. Koppitz, 1968, Orlando, FL: The Psychological Corporation. © 1968 by Grune & Stratton. Reprinted by permission.

2. *Insecurity/Inadequacy:* slanting figure, tiny head; hands cut off; monster or grotesque figure; omission of arms and/or legs and/or feet
3. *Anxiety:* shading of the face, body and/or limbs, hands and/or neck; legs pressed together; omission of eyes; inclusion of clouds, rain, or flying birds
4. *Shyness/Timidity:* tiny figure; short arms; arms clinging to the body; omission of the nose and/or mouth
5. *Anger/Aggressiveness:* crossed eyes; presence of teeth; long arms; big hands; nude figure and/or presence of genitals

Koppitz (1984) found significantly more impulsivity, insecurity, and anger/assertiveness indices in drawings of 11- to 14-year-olds with learning disabilities, compared with a matched group of regular public school children.

Koppitz (1984) reports that there is no direct relationship between her list of emotional indicators and the child's overt behavior. Each drawing sign can have multiple meanings. For example, a big head may be interpreted as meaning ambition, striving for success, concern over poor achievement and mental inadequacy, an indication of migraine headaches, brain disease or brain injury, or mental retardation, but there are additional possibilities for this sign, as there are with other signs. For example, a large head may also be an indication of an intellectualizing approach or an overemphasis on cognition or fantasy.

One might decide that these many possibilities make interpretation of this and other multidetermined factors rather difficult because there are so many different possibilities. However, the child's history, the context of other drawing factors, and data from other tests all help the interpreter choose from among these many possibilities. In addition, normative findings are also helpful in differential interpretation.

Machover (1960) offers normative DAP data from middle-class white boys and girls, ages 5 through 12. She correlates the normative findings with sex, age, and stage-related psychodynamic patterns and cultural epochs (e.g., the Oedipal and latency periods). Selected drawings are included here (Figure 6–11) to illustrate the beginning development of the body concept.

Schildkrout and colleagues (1972) emphasize that drawings done by normal adolescents typically reflect their predominant age- and stage-related problems and conflicts. For example, the early adolescent (ages 12 through 15) is said to have an overpowering urge to return to dependency on the infantile mother image. The teenager directs his or her efforts against this regressive tendency and toward an object of affection outside the family.

> The dependency upon the parent is seen commonly in drawings of both boys and girls in the form of obvious midline emphasis numerous buttons, and belt buckles. Efforts to control impulses in the face of weakening superego and ego are reflected in the frequent use of stripes, plaids, dots, and other designs covering much of the body. . . . The use of body shading and emphasis in sexual regions, reflect(s) the anxiety experienced over the dramatic physical changes which are taking place. (p. 6)

Schildkrout and colleagues (1972) discussed the typical conflicts of the middle and the late adolescent, and their reflection in the drawing. For example, the drawings of the middle adolescent often appear grandiose by depicting an idealized physical image because of the resolution of the Oedipus conflict through identification with the parent of the same sex and the establishment of a male or female role. The authors state, "The sixteen-year-old girl may draw a seductive, fashionably dressed female while the boy may portray a male of obvious athletic prowess" (p. 7).

Saarni and Azara (1977) compiled two categories of anxiety indices—an aggressive-hostile category (scars, gross asymmetry of limbs, oversize figures, crossed eyes, teeth present, transparencies, disproportionately long arms and

Figure 6–11   Male and Female Figure Drawings Produced by Boys and Girls 4 to 12 Years of Age: (a) 4-Year-Olds; (b) 5-Year-Olds; (c) 6-Year-Olds; (d) 7-Year-Olds

Source: From "Sex Differences in the Developmental Pattern of Children as Seen in Human Figure Drawings" by K. Machover in *Projective Techiniques with Children* by A. Rabin and M. Haworth (Eds.), 1960, New York: Grune & Stratton. Copyright 1960 by Grune & Stratton. Reprinted by permission.

Figure 6–11 *Continued:* **(e) 8-Year-Olds; (f) 9-Year-Olds; (g) 10-Year-Olds; (h) 11-Year-Olds**

Male I

Female II

Twelve year old boy

Female I

Male II

Twelve year old girl

Figure 6–11 *Continued:* **(i) 12-Year-Olds**

hands, omission of arms, genitals present) and an insecure-labile category (vertical slant more than 15 degrees; undifferentiated shading of face, neck; disproportionately short arms; arms clinging to sides of body; no hands, fingers, eyes, mouth, legs, feet, neck; tiny figure; baseline under figure; excessive midline detailing; and faint, scribbly-scratchy lines). They theorized that a developmental comparison of adolescents, young adults, and aged adults would reveal different patterns of aggressive-hostile signs and insecure-labile signs. They found that relative to females, males revealed significantly more aggressive-hostile indices. High school girls obtained a mean number of insecure-labile indices that were almost twice those of the young adult females. Insecure-labile indices were not sex typed, as the authors had predicted, but the incidence of bizarre figures appeared to be a male sex-typed DAP characteristic, whereas ambiguous, child-like figures were somewhat more typical in the female DAP.

The results of this study strongly suggest that it is important, in the analysis of an individual DAP, to be aware of normative findings. There are apparently some DAP variables that are related primarily to personality factors, those that are primarily related to sociocultural factors, and those that reflect both personality and sociocultural variables, as they interact. Gilbert and Hall (1962) indicate that as people get older, there is an increasing tendency for their drawings to become absurd, incongruous, fragmented, and primitive; they found a marked similarity between the drawings of young and middle-age schizophrenics and normal elderly people. If additional studies support such a surprising finding, it will be necessary to generate an extensive set of age-related norms.

Social and Cultural Factors.   Social and cultural variables can vastly influence the results of the drawings obtained from both children and adults (see Dennis, 1966; Gardiner, 1974; Kelpsch & Logie, 1982; Handler & Habenicht, 1994; Meili-Dworetzki, 1982; Smart & Smart, 1975; Koppitz, 1984; Zardi, 1979). Koppitz and deMoreau (1968) found significant cultural differences on 10 emotional indicators. For example, 14 percent of Mexican pupils drew slanted figures, compared with only 7 percent of U.S. pupils. The findings for "tiny figure" were 27 percent and 5 percent, respectively, and the corresponding percentages for "shading hands/neck" were 2 percent and 15 percent, respectively. In general, the findings were consistent with the view of the Mexican youths as more shy, but less anxious and aggressive, compared with U.S. pupils. Differences were also found between the drawings of Argentinean and U.S. children (Koppitz & Casullo, 1983).

Dennis (1966) illustrates the vast differences in drawing skill among children of various cultures, indicating that the expectancies for U.S. children are typically quite different from those of other cultures. The clinician who wants to utilize the DAP (or other drawing tests) with children or adults from other cultures or subcultures should first attempt to compare those drawings to those obtained from normative samples from that culture or subculture. In addition, a more thorough understanding of the particular culture or subculture will undoubtedly help to understand which differences are primarily cultural and which differences are due to individual variation. See Handler and Habenicht (1994) for a description of the cultural influences on the K-F-D.

The Problem of Artistic Ability

A major problem in the use of the DAP concerns the relationship between drawing signs and artistic ability. It has been determined that clinicians often make clinical interpretations based on the artistic ability of the patient and not on actual personality variables (Levy, Lomax, & Minsky, 1963; Lewinsohn & May, 1963; Nichols & Stumpfer, 1962; Sherman, 1958; Stumpfer & Nichols, 1962; Whitmyre, 1953). This finding has been utilized by research-oriented clinical psychologists to discredit the clinical use of the DAP. However, more applied clinicians have continued to use figure drawings because they believe that the test has clinical merit. While the researcher typically believes that the applied clinician is deluding himself or herself, the applied clinician believes that the researcher is being entirely too rigid and conservative. And so the battle continues on, with each side merely reaffirming what it already believes.

In an effort to resolve this controversy, this writer decided to investigate the incorporation of research-oriented methodology into the clinical interpretive process. He reasoned that if the DAP interpreters confused artistic ability with emotional problems, a control figure was needed to determine, for each patient, how much of the variation in performance was due to artistic ability and how much was due to emotional problems as they were portrayed in the drawing. This writer reasoned that if artistic ability was a large factor in a patient's drawing, then a neutral control figure of equal task difficulty could be utilized in the interpretive process to partial out the differential effects of emotional factors and artistic ability.

Several different types of drawings were considered and were ruled out as possibilities for a variety of reasons. This writer finally decided to use the drawing of an automobile as the control figure. In a series of pilot studies with males and females who drew a man, woman, and an automobile, it was determined that drawing an automobile was equal in task difficulty, compared with drawing a man or woman; both men and women felt it was as easy (or as difficult) to draw an automobile as it was to draw a person. The automobile drawing was then subject to a series of validation studies to determine whether it could be used as a neutral control figure. In a series of studies, it was found that externally induced stress significantly increased manifestations of anxiety on all three figures; the automobile drawing reflected significantly less anxiety compared with the male and female drawings (Handler & Reyher, 1964; Jacobson & Handler, 1967).

In several other studies (Handler & Reyher, 1966; Nordquist & Handler, 1969), subjects were asked to draw a man, woman, and an automobile while autonomic measures (heart rate or GSR) were obtained. A huge difference was found in the degree of anxiety reflected in the three drawings; the automobile drawings had the fewest number of anxiety indices. Exactly the same results were obtained when the autonomic measures were analyzed. Since the automobile was found to be a relatively neutral drawing of equal task difficulty, this writer concluded that it was possible to use it as a control figure. If the automobile drawing is done poorly, and the people drawings are also done poorly, then an interpretation of poor artistic ability should be made. However, if the people drawings are done poorly and the automobile drawing is done well, the interpretation of poor artistic ability should not be made. Instead, the poor execution of the people drawings should be taken as an indication of either intrapsychic problems, an indication of the effects of external stress (emanating from the testing situation itself or perceived stress from other external sources), or both.

Recently, it has become increasingly clear that artistic ability itself is an important factor in reflecting degree of psychopathology, rather than a source of error in DAP interpretation. Of course, the writer does not mean by this the difference between drawings of gifted artists, compared with those of ordinary artists. However, the fact that clinicians tend to attribute drawings with low overall artistic quality to poorly adjusted persons and drawings with high overall artistic quality to well-adjusted people (Cressen, 1975) may be an accurate measure of these clinicians' diagnostic acumen. The following drawing examples by psychiatric inpatients (Figure 6–12) are good examples of this relationship. These drawings demonstrate significant impairment in the ability

Figure 6–12   Drawings from Patients in a Psychiatric Hospital, Showing Major Distortion

to represent the body image accurately. The drawings demonstrate significant distortion of the body image and in reality testing, which are often significant factors in severe pathology.

Lewinsohn (1965) also demonstrated that the overall quality of the drawing was related to certain measures of patients' adjustment, and Maloney and Glasser (1982) reported that the overall quality of the drawing differentiated various client populations. Yama (1990) also found that ratings of overall artistic quality, an impressionistic rating of bizarreness of the drawn figures, and an impressionistic estimate of overall adjustment obtained from Vietnamese foster children were all related to the number of foster care placements a child had five years subsequent to the time the drawings were obtained. The frequency of these placements indicated that the child had severe emotional problems and therefore had to be moved. Thus, Yama's findings indicate that the drawing variables described here tap into "an enduring characteristic of the person; this trait, operating through time and influencing how a person adapts to his environment, is potent enough to influence the nature of a drawing, produced in one point in time in one specific setting" (p. 85). Yama is suggesting that the better drawings are produced by children who were able to adapt better to the demands of foster care placement and therefore they did not need to be moved from their placement, whereas those with problem drawings had to be moved several times.

It is important to note that an approach to the data that used a more quantitative index, the Koppitz emotional indicators, did not differentiate those with one foster home placement from those with numerous placements. Again, the superiority of an impressionistic measure proved more effective than a more quantitative drawing measure. This is not to say that the quantitative approach is not valid or useful. For example, Currie, Holtzman, and Swartz (1974) found that the number of emotional indicators present in a child's drawing predicted future adjustment of children nine years later.

Recently, a number of clinical and experimental findings have occasioned a reexamination of the artistic ability issue. It appears that the more emotionally disturbed a patient is, the more there is a disturbance in body image and in reality testing, thereby occasioning rather unusual and major distortions in the drawings of these disturbed patients. The reader can obviously see the major changes in the before-and-after therapy drawings in Figure 6–1, and the change in the drawings in Figures 6–2 and 6–3, after 15 months of therapy. The initial drawings are rather simplistic and primitive; they are grossly distorted, devoid of details, and lack well-defined boundaries. The drawings of patients who do not improve in treatment do not change much at all (see Figure 6–1), whereas those drawings of patients who improved changed significantly after successful treatment.

Robins, Blatt, and Ford indicate that the first (before inpatient therapy) drawings lack "important body parts that deal with definition of the self as well as communication with others (e.g., the face, eyes and mouth, as well as the hands and fingers" (p. 491) (see Figures 6–2 and 6–3). The first drawing of the female also lacks sexual differentiation, whereas the second female drawing has definite sexually defined body areas. The first male drawing is very similar in style to the first female drawing; it is quite primitive and infantile, with poor boundaries, poorly articulated hands and arms, and a posture that suggests passivity and dependence. Note the very significant degree of body and head distortion in the first drawing, and the lack of details. Also note the significant change in the second drawing; the posture has changed to a more assertive stance, the drawing proportions and the drawing quality have improved, all of which reflect a sense of activity and improved adequacy.

It is easy to see the marked improvement in drawing quality and the significant decrease in distortion in the drawings after 15 months of therapy. There are now clearer, more realistic facial features present and better defined hands, suggesting better ability to communicate with others. There is a sense of self-definition in the second drawing, which is not present in the first drawing. Similar differences can be seen in the before-therapy male drawing and the drawing done after 15 months of therapy, both in drawing quality and in the sense of activity, personal power, and authority the after-therapy drawing conveys about the patient. Robins, Blatt, and Ford note

> The [first] male [drawing] strikes one as an infantile "blob" doll, with poor boundaries and proportions, helpless arms ("flippers"), no hands, and a posture suggestive of passivity and dependence. The [second] male is erect, with very clear definite shape; the [drawing] shows a young man with proper form, proportion, a protruding chin, and accentuated knees, suggesting movement, activity, and assertion. The dim, unassertive line quality of [the first drawing] changes to a more forceful, defined execution [in the second drawing]. (p. 491)

How have these people developed the drawing talent and ability they seemed to lack so much in the pretreatment examples? The answer is that the body image and personality integration have improved and this is reflected in the patient's representational ability. Therefore, it is quite possible that those clinicians who seemed to be making diagnoses based on artistic ability might have been responding appropriately, at least in some cases, to the distorted drawing. This is not to say that there are not large variations in artistic ability. Rather, this writer is indicating that at least some of these poor artists are emotionally disturbed, and their poor drawings are an accurate reflection of their psychological problems.

Interpretation

Many tests lend themselves to both impressionistic interpretation and to more detailed quantified interpretation. The DAP is not an exception. For example, it is possible to investigate conflict and anxiety in a drawing by the use of an objective rating scale (e.g., Handler & Reyher, 1964, 1966; Handler, 1967) or the drawings may be interpreted more impressionistically, emphasizing the clinician's phenomenological experience of the data and related affective visceral associations. In this latter approach, the drawing is perceived in a more holistic manner; the specific drawing details are less important than the interpreter's impressions. While some researchers and interpreters decry this approach as unscientific, many others see it as a quite meaningful way of interpreting the drawings. There are a number of very old and some very recent studies that demonstrate the superiority of the empathic, intuitive approach (e.g., Schmidt & McGowan, 1959; Scribner & Handler, 1993).

More recently, Tharinger and Stark (1990) compared the ability of an objective scoring system and a holistic, qualitative approach for the DAP and the K-F-D to differentiate children with mood disorders and anxiety disorders, compared with a control group of children without disorder. With the qualitative, integrative approach, the drawings were scored on a 5-point scale, ranging from "absence of pathology" to "severe pathology," utilizing a summary rating based on the following four criteria: inhumanness of the drawing; lack of agency (the inability of the individual in the drawing to effectively interact with the world); lack of well-being of the individual in the drawing (reflected mostly in negative facial expressions); and the presence of a hollow, vacant, or stilted sense in the individual portrayed in the drawing. No significant differences were found among groups using the objective scoring system, but the intuitive-holistic approach significantly differentiated the groups, with both the DAP and the K-F-D.

Similar findings were reported by Kot, Handler, Toman, and Hilsenroth (1994) in the analysis of figure drawings obtained from a group of homeless men, compared with a group of psychiatrically hospitalized patients, and a group of subjects who had a home but who had no job (vocational rehabilitation clients). No significant differences were found in an objective analysis, where individual drawing signs were objectively scored. However, when an advanced graduate student was asked to evaluate the drawings for psychological impairment, according to four impressionistic criteria, significant differences were found. The evaluator was asked to consider the drawings in reference to the following four criteria: (1) Is the person in the drawing frightened of the world? (2) Does the person in the drawing have intact thinking? (3) Is the person in the drawing comfortable with close relationships? (4) Would you feel comfortable (safe) being with the person in the drawing?

The student was asked to summarize the four ratings, utilizing a 1–5 rating scale, where 1 = no impairment and 5 = most impaired. The drawings of the psychiatric group *all* scored in the two most impaired categories (4 and 5); the homeless group had scores in all five categories; the vocational rehabilitation group had more scores in the absence of impairment category and the mild impairment category (1 and 2) than did either group, and had more scores in category 4. This latter finding probably reflects the fact that some of the hospitalized subjects had been referred to vocational rehabilitation for job training and placement after they were released, and therefore this group contains some patients who were previously hospitalized.

In order to utilize the holistic-intuitive method, it is important for the clinician to become intimately involved with the drawing. The clinician must be able to become the person drawn to some degree, and put himself or herself in the position of the person drawn—to lose distance, so to speak. Kris (1952) has described this creative experience as "regression in the service of the ego." If clinicians can experience what it is like to be the person drawn, then they will be able to feel and understand the artist. Since the drawn person is believed to be representative of the personality of the drawer, getting in touch with the drawing gives clinicians a valuable method to understand the individual being studied. In order to accomplish this task, it is often useful for the clinician to put his or her body in the same position as that of the drawing and to imitate the facial expression as represented in the drawing. Sometimes asking the question, "What must be going on right now with this individual to produce a drawing like this?" helps to experience the patient's world as he or she experiences it.

Kris (1952) describes the reaction of a person viewing a work of art that is probably quite close to the phenomenological process of interpreting a drawing:

> Looking long enough, one tends to become aware of a kinesthetic reaction, however slight; it may be that one tries, at first imperceptibly and later consciously, to react with one's own body, or it may be that the reaction remains unconscious. We know that our ensuing emotional experience will still be colored by the reflection of the perceived posture, that our ego has in the process of perception utilized a complex apparatus, the body scheme, or . . . the image of the body. . . . On the second stage of reaction we identify ourselves with the artist's model. . . . We change imperceptibly from identification with the model into the stage in which we "imitate" the strokes and lines with which it (the drawing) was produced. To some extent we have changed roles. We started out as part of the world which the artist created; we end as co-creators: We identify ourselves with the artist. (pp. 55–56)

Sometimes it is difficult to "lose distance" and to "become" the person drawn. An alternative approach, which is an intermediate step, and which is often somewhat easier to accomplish, is for the clinician to imagine himself or herself meeting and/or interacting with the person drawn, such as asking himself or herself such questions as, "How would it be to go to dinner with this person?" "How would I feel if I were out on a date with this person?" "What would it be like to work for (or with) this person?" "What would it be like to be this person's employer (or friend, or child, or parent, sister or brother)?" Questions such as these allow the clinician to imagine how the person drawn would interact in a variety of interpersonal situations, in order to give the clinician a sense of "the other."

In a series of five classroom demonstrations over a period of five years, second-year graduate students who had no previous DAP experience were able to achieve 81 percent correct interpretations. In these demonstrations the students were given a drawing done by a patient who was in psychotherapy with a colleague, who would verify the accuracy of the interpretations generated by the graduate students. The drawing was passed around and the students were presented with the impressionistic process of interpretation as described earlier. The students were asked to become intimately involved with the drawing, to "lose distance," so to speak, and then to generate specific, detailed hypotheses concerning the patient, which were recorded on a chalkboard. Once the students generated all the hypotheses they could (typically 20 to 30), the therapist went down the list and verified each hypothesis.

The author has done a number of blind interpretations that have convinced him that the DAP can yield important clinical information about a patient. For example, a student brought in a DAP done by a patient who had applied for a weekend pass from a nearby state mental hospital. Based on a battery of test results, it was recommended that the patient should be allowed to return home and visit his wife for the weekend. The writer urged the student not to recommend the pass: "This man is dangerous; he'll hurt his wife, and perhaps try to kill her," he told the student. Unhappily, it was too late; the patient had been released the previous weekend and had slit his wife's throat and killed her! All indications of this tragic event were clear from the drawings. The male drawing reflected an angry, impulse-oriented person with sadistic tendencies and poor judgment; the woman he drew appeared frightened and helpless, and there was a strange line drawn across her neck, a clumsy exaggerated attempt to represent a collar. There, in the drawing, was even represented the method by which the patient was to kill his wife!

In another informal interpretive attempt, the writer told a student that the person who did the female drawing he had presented was an assertive, sexually manipulative woman who handled men in a rather domineering manner, and that she was an artist, recently divorced from a weak and passive husband, and was on the prowl. The student was quite surprised at first and then insisted that the writer knew the woman who had drawn the picture. When the student was finally convinced that this was not so, he requested an explanation. The writer explained that the female drawing was executed with rather large, bold strokes. The figure was drawn rather large, was attractively clothed, with a smug look of self-assurance. The seated male was nude, rather small, and his head was pointed downward, facing away from the viewer. The automobile control figure was a phallic, sleek, late-model convertible sports car. Twenty years ago, women typically did not draw such cars. Although artists typically draw the nude figure, this woman chose to draw the male without clothes rather than the female or both figures without clothes. The nude male in the seated position, exposed and unhappily turned away, certainly portrayed less adequacy and ability than the engrossing, dynamic female.

Are clinicians to conclude that because of negative research findings the DAP should be abandoned as a clinical tool? How can so many clinicians who use the technique so effectively come to grips with these negative research findings? On the other hand, how can researchers who view the DAP as unreliable and invalid come to terms with its rich and creative use in the hands of many gifted clinicians? In response to these issues and questions, it is first necessary to understand the interpretive process. For example, Schmidt and McGowan (1959) found that clinicians with an affective orientation, who used an impressionistic or feeling approach to drawings, could diagnostically sort drawings correctly, whereas a cognitive group, who evaluated the drawings in terms of specific signs, in a more scientific and intellectualized manner, could not sort the drawings correctly. Hunt (1946) recommended that "we should consider the individual clinician as a clinical instrument, and study and evaluate his performance exactly as we study a test" (p. 317), examining the validity of "the clinician as interpreter" rather than the drawing itself. A number of researchers have found that subjects with little or no experience in the interpretation of projective tests can judge figure drawings with the accuracy of skilled clinicians (Albee & Hamlin, 1950; Levenberg, 1975; Schmidt & McGowan, 1959; Scribner & Handler, 1993).

Hammer's observations concerning the differential ability of clinicians to use the DAP effectively is expressed quite picturesquely: "My own experience is that in the hands of some students projective drawings are an exquisitely sensitive tool, and in the hands of others, those employing a wooden, stilted approach, they're like disconnected phones" (1968, p. 385).

Burley and Handler (1994) attempted to determine whether there were individual differences among examiners in the accuracy of DAP interpretation. Introductory psychology students and graduate students were shown DAP protocols and were given a list of forced choice interpretations that were based on therapeutic contact with the patients. The students were asked to choose the interpretation that seemed most descriptive of the patient whose drawings they were studying. The most and least accurate undergraduates and all the graduate students were given the Remote Associates Test, as a measure of creativity and divergent production; the Myers-Briggs Type Indicator to provide a measure of intuition; and the Hogan Empathy Scale. There were significant differences found for the good interpreters versus the poor interpreters on the Hogan Empathy Scale, the Myers-Briggs, and the Remote Associates Test. The good DAP interpreter was a person who could think creatively, who was able to connect loosely associated ideas, and who was socially sensitive to subtle nuances in interpersonal behavior. Subjects who were capable of putting themselves in their patients' shoes and who were more able to utilize their preconscious and unconscious associations to the test data were found to be more accurate in their interpretations.

Scribner and Handler (1987) compared "good" and "poor" undergraduate DAP interpreters on the Leary Interpersonal System, a multilevel, interpersonal circomplex personality assessment method. They found that good interpretive skill was significantly related to an affiliative approach and poor interpretive skill was associated with a disaffiliative approach. This association was even stronger when unconscious personality levels were tapped. Some 73 percent of the subjects who were good interpreters saw themselves as responsible and cooperative in relationships with others, whereas 85 percent of subjects who were poor interpreters saw themselves as dominant and competitive in their relationships with others. The poor interpreters' approach to life emphasized power, dominance, order, and precision. Scribner and Handler concluded that the ability to "read" human figure drawings in an intuitive, impressionistic manner was consistent with an affiliative rather than with a disaffiliative orientation. However, they noted that an affiliative interpersonal orientation is necessary but not sufficient to be a good interpreter.

The findings of the Burley and Handler study, along with those reported by Scribner and Handler (1987, 1993), can be integrated to form a picture of the good qualitative DAP interpreter and to illuminate the process of accurate interpretation, utilizing a qualitative approach. The good qualitative interpreter is an open, empathic person whose thinking is flexible, a person whose openness to the drawings (and through them, to the artist) is evident as intuitiveness. Empathy involves such attributes as being perceptive to a wide range of cues, having insight into one's own motives, and having the ability to accurately evaluate the motives of others. Utilizing this approach to the interpretation of drawings requires a certain amount of affective "tuning in" to one's own feelings and to the feelings of others. Poor intuitive DAP interpreters emphasized their need to control activities and experiences, whereas the good intuitive interpreters expressed a willingness and ability to relinquish control of what they experienced and simply allowed themselves to experience fully and openly, relaxing their stance toward reality in order to permit ego regression to occur.

Using a qualitative approach, the good interpreter would be ready and willing to engage fully in order to transcend mechanistic patterns of thought. This sounds similar to the concept of psychoanalytic listening developed by Kohut (1959, 1977) as well as by other analysts. Although this process is in part similar to the concept of "adaptive regression in the service of the ego" described by Kris (1952), it goes beyond the emphasis of the dynamic aspects of regression and the primitive, immature content of thoughts and feelings. What is added here is openness in turning toward the object and the ability to approach it with freshness, spontaneity, and interest (Schachtel, 1984/1959). Introspection and self-reflection in the regressive process is probably not enough to achieve valid interpretation. What is needed, in addition, is the ability to become again reconnected, with cognitively reorganized creative understanding.

What are the elements that go into the accurate interpretation of the DAP? In addition to the variables mentioned so far, a good DAP interpreter should understand the concept of symbolism from one or more psychoanalytic and/or existential points of view, as well as understanding symbolization in culture and in folklore. It would help if the clinician studied art and understood the various approaches to symbolization used by various artists. Understanding symbolization in myth, the dream, and in other unconscious representations is a great help in allowing the drawing to communicate meaning. A thorough working knowledge of the "dream work" (Freud, 1938/1969), along with an understanding of the mechanisms of substitution, displacement, and condensation, would be of great help in allowing the clinician to see the manner in which the unconscious symbolization is transformed into graphic structures.

In approaching the interpretation of the DAP, a more impressionistic approach should be used at first. Attention should then be focused on the drawing details as they fit together to communicate a feeling tone or message. The posture of the figure and the facial expression convey a mood and tone of the figure, perhaps active and vigorous, perhaps passive and bewildered. The type of line used by the patient and the strength conveyed by the arms and legs add a great deal to the overall impression. The figure may be rigid or tense or there may be undue emphasis on symmetry. Expansiveness, constriction, daydreaming, self-involvement, depression, or anger may be the major expressive element around which the impressions crystallize.

How Conflict Is Expressed.   Conflict may be expressed in a variety of ways. First, the patient's approach to the task of drawing may indicate conflict. The patient may be reluctant to draw, he or she may omit body parts or perhaps even the entire body and may draw only the head, thereby avoiding one or more issues relating to the body. The patient may ask too many preliminary questions, attempting to delay or avoid coming to grips with the situation. Other observable conflict indicators include frequent erasure and reworking of one or more areas, usually with poor results; verbalized dissatisfaction with one or more drawn areas; and random and feverish graphic expression.

It is important to emphasize that an interpretive approach that merely lists signs observed in the drawings, coupled with their specified meanings, is in the worst tradition of both clinical and experimental psychology. Such a procedure precludes an approach that attempts to find reason and coherence in the understanding of human personality functioning. All the reasoning surrounding the many implications of the presence of such a sign is curtailed when only one specific interpretation is generated for a specific test sign. There is no attempt to try to reconstruct how a patient is thinking or how the patient approaches a task.

Therefore, the clinician should not ask what it means that, for example, the hands are drawn behind the back, but should instead ask what it *could* mean that the hands are drawn behind the back. Perhaps the patient is a poor artist, and he or she has difficulty drawing hands. Artistic ability is often a factor in the omission of hands or in hiding hands behind the back; many normal individuals indicate that drawing hands is difficult. It is therefore difficult to determine whether hands behind the back or hands otherwise hidden (e.g., in pockets) indicate a normal reaction to the performance of a difficult task under pressure (the testing situation) or whether the approach to drawing the hands represents a tendency to withdraw, or perhaps anxiety about interpersonal relationships. These hypotheses can be examined by observing the quality of the drawing and the control figure. Other data (from the DAP and other tests) can help to differentiate among a number of hypotheses concerning concealed hands that include anxiety concerning interpersonal relationships, sexual anxieties, evasiveness, or guilt feelings.

A Note of Caution.   Although many hypotheses can be generated concerning a patient's functioning, it is important to check these interpretations against other data in the test battery. There should be both a convergence of several sources of data and/or an integration of data from different sources to form a three-dimensional picture of the patient's functioning. Thus, for example, if a male patient's graphic production suggests an attempt to present himself as a smiling, friendly, and open person, but other aspects of the test battery suggest an angry aggressive person, it would probably be best to combine these two observations and suggest that although the patient attempts to present himself in a positive light, as an open, friendly, and carefree person, the underlying personality pattern is one of anger and aggression.

There are a variety of additional test signs, especially on the Rorschach or the TAT, that would indicate how likely and under what circumstances these underlying hostility patterns would surface, as well as the source of these patterns. A more detailed examination of the figure drawing for signs of hostility and aggression can also offer clues concerning the likelihood that these underlying and somewhat masked aggressive impulses would make themselves evident in a wide variety of interpersonal relationships and life situations. A more in-depth discussion of aggressive acting out is presented in a later section of this chapter.

Interpretation of Structure and Content

Ogdon (1977) has produced a handbook of interpretive hypotheses for the evaluation of the DAP (along with other tests) derived from both the clinical *and* the experimental literature. Following is a selected list of figure drawing variables and some possible interpretive hypotheses. This section should not be used as a cookbook, and the signs should not be interpreted in isolation. Ogdon cautions the user of the manual that these are "suggested interpretive hypotheses," since few if any DAP indices "have been found to be valid assessors and prognosticators when applied to individual evaluations of psychodiagnosis" and "no single sign is conclusive evidence of anything" (p. 66). The reader is referred to Ogdon's book for the sources of these interpretations, as well as for a more detailed exposition of figure drawing variables.

Drawings may be analyzed utilizing both structural variables and content variables. The structural variables concern the style in which the drawing was executed (size, pressure, line quality, placement on the page, degree of detailing, perspective, shading, erasure, and reinforcement). The content variables concern the type of person drawn, the facial expression, the postural tone, and the subtle nuances that communicate to the viewer the emotional tone of the patient who executed the drawing.

Size.   Typically, the size of the drawing tells clinicians something about the patient's self-esteem and the manner in which the patient deals with self-esteem. A patient who feels inadequate may draw a tiny figure, thereby directly indicating inadequacy feelings and perhaps responding to them by withdrawal. On the other hand, another patient may react with self-expansiveness and self-aggrandizement in order to cover up similar inadequacy feelings. In this case, the drawing may fill the entire page. Such a patient may compensate for feelings of inadequacy by resorting to compensatory action or fantasy. Other possible interpretations of small and large size are probably related to the issue of self-confidence. Unusually large drawings can be a sign of aggressive and acting-out tendencies; expansive, euphoric, or grandiose tendencies; hyperactive, emotional, manic conditions; or anxiety/conflict. Unusually small drawings are often said to indicate feelings of inferiority; inadequacy and low self-esteem; anxiety; withdrawal tendencies in inhibited, restrained, timid, shy, or constricted adults and children; depressive tendencies; regressive, dependent tendencies; constriction under stress. Each of these possibilities must be considered in light of the rest of the data collected for each patient.

Pencil Pressure.   Pencil pressure has been described as an indication of the patient's energy level. Heavy pressure has been said to indicate high energy level; light pressure has been said to indicate low energy level. Heavy pressure may also indicate extreme tension or anxiety; an approach to life which is assertive and forceful (ambition); aggressive tendencies; anxiety and constrictive behavior, particularly under stress; and possible paranoid conditions. Unusually light pressure has been said to indicate a hesitant, indecisive, timid, fearful, inhibited, and insecure personality pattern; a neurotic condition, most often with anxiety symptoms; depressive conditions, or an expansive adaptation under external stress situations.

Stroke and Line Quality.   Long pencil strokes indicate controlled behavior, perhaps even inhibition in the extreme; short strokes are said to indicate impulsive behavior and excitation. Horizontal movement emphasis may suggest fearfulness or self-protective tendencies; vertical movement could suggest assertiveness ad determination. Curved line emphasis is said to suggest flexibility; straight line emphasis may indicate assertiveness, or rigidity. Line quality that is discontinuous (e.g., many breaks in the outside boundary of the figures) has been found to indicate anxiety and/or conflict, but in the extreme it suggests that the anxiety has overwhelmed the patient. Drawings in which the outline of the figure seems to be so discontinuous that it appears as a series of disconnected dashes are often found in severely disturbed (psychotic) patients who have problems with reality contact and who are overwhelmed by confused bizarre thoughts. Straight, uninterrupted strokes have been associated with a personality style that emphasizes a quick, decisive, and assertive approach to life.

Lack of Detail.   Lack of detail indicates withdrawal tendencies with an associated reduction of energy; a typical reaction to stress experienced as external to the patient; or depression that is often associated with withdrawal tendencies and lack of energy to complete the figure. Excessive detailing is often seen in obsessive-compulsive patients. Some patients, under external stress conditions, deal with the stress by becoming increasingly obsessive; their drawings contain much detail and they are carefully and meticulously drawn.

Placement.   Placement roughly in the middle of the page is typical of most normal subjects. Placement on the right side of the page has been said to indicate stability and controlled behavior; willingness to delay satisfaction of needs and drives; preference for intellectual satisfactions compared to emotional ones; tendency to intellectualize; introversive tendencies; orientation to the future; negativism and rebellious tendencies. Placement on the left side of the page has been said to indicate impulsive acting-out behavior; a tendency toward immediate, frank, and emotional satisfaction of motives; extroversion; preoccupation with one's changing needs; a self-centered approach to life; orientation and concern with the past; possible feelings of uncertainty and apprehension.

Drawings placed high on the page have been said to indicate high drive level; high level of aspiration; striving for achievement, or striving to achieve difficult goals. The higher the drawing is on the page, the greater is the possibility that the patient feels he or she is striving with great determination; that the goal is relatively unattainable; that the patient tends to seek satisfaction in fantasy rather than in reality; or that the patient is aloof and relatively inaccessible (Hammer, 1958). Some clinicians feel that drawings placed high on the page also indicate unjustified optimism, or an aloof orientation in a patient who is psychologically or socially inaccessible. Placement low on the page is said to be an indication of insecurity and inadequacy, with resultant depression; an indication that the patient feels reality bound and tends to be concrete, rather than theoretical or abstract; or an indication of a defeatist attitude.

Placement in the upper left-hand corner may indicate regressive tendencies; feelings of insecurity and hesitancy; withdrawal; anxiety (except for children in the early elementary grades, for whom this is typical). Placement in the upper right-hand corner suggests a desire to suppress an unpleasant past, or excessive optimism about the future; placement on the bottom edge of the paper suggests the need for support associated with feelings of insecurity and low self-assurance; dependency; fear of independent action; anxiety; tendency to avoid new experiences or to remain absorbed in fantasy; or depressive conditions.

Erasure.   Excessive erasure indicates uncertainty; conflict-filled indecisiveness and restlessness; dissatisfaction with self; or anxiety/conflict. The latter is especially true if the erasure and subsequent reworking does not improve the drawing. The area(s) erased offer(s) a clue to the content of the conflict. If the redrawing improves the figure, it is probable that the conflict is being adequately contained and dealt with, and that it is not causing any problem in everyday functions.

Shading. Excessive shading indicates anxiety/conflict or agitated depression. However, Handler and Reyher (1964, 1965, 1966) indicate that some shading (and erasure) is an adaptive mechanism—an attempt to give the drawing a sense of three-dimensionality. If the shading is carefully done, and seems to enhance the drawing, it is probable that the area that is drawn *is* conflict related, *but* the conflict is being dealt with appropriately. If the shading is messy, uneven, or hurriedly done, the conflict is causing anxiety and is disturbing the person in everyday adjustment.

Distortions and Omissions. Gross distortion indicates poor reality contact or negative self-concept. Moderate distortions and omissions may indicate conflict/anxiety. The parts of the body that are omitted or distorted sometimes offer clues concerning the source of the problem. Distortions and omissions can also be an indication of severe psychopathology and/or a lack of a sense of self. This problem can be seen in the drawing examples in Figure 6–12.

Transparency. Transparency can indicate poor reality ties, except, of course, in the drawings of young children, where they are typically normal. The presence of a transparency in a drawing suggests poor reality testing; anxiety/conflict; sexual disturbance; or regressive, psychotic conditions.

Vertical Imbalance. The greater the imbalance from the vertical position, the greater the anxiety. This interpretation has been validated by Handler and Reyher (1964, 1966) and by Robins, Blatt, and Ford (1991), who found a significant decrease in vertical imbalance in the before-and-after drawings of those patients who improved in therapy.

Sex of First-Drawn Figure. Most normals draw the same-sex drawing first (estimates range from 85 percent to 95 percent). Zaback and Waehler (1994) report that people tend to draw figures that are the same sex as themselves; that men do so more than woman (94 percent vs. 64 percent); and that there is no real relationship between sex-role orientation and the figure drawn first. Some studies indicate that homosexuals frequently draw the opposite sex first, but there are other interpretations of this finding, such as confused sexual identification; strong attachment or dependence on a person of the opposite sex (e.g., spouse, mother, lover); ambivalence or conflict regarding one's sexual identification; poor self-concept; or greater interest and/or awareness of the opposite sex compared with the same sex. Differentiation among these and other possibilities can often be made by reference to other available data, either test-related data or history data. Younger children (below age 8) often make a drawing that is of the same sex as the clinician.

Male-Female Drawing Comparisons

Levy (1950) presents the following drawings (Figure 6–13) done by a male. Note that the female drawing is much larger than the male drawing. The woman's stance, her posture, and her arm position suggest an active approach

Figure 6–13   Drawings of a Man and a Woman, Done by a Male

Source: From "Figure Drawing as a Projective Test" by S. Levy in *Projective Psychology* by E. Abt and L. Bellak (Eds.), 1950, New York: Alfred A. Knopf. Reprinted by permission of L. Bellak.

to life. The male's posture and arm position suggest a passive, introverted, and somewhat dependent approach. The male figure looks like a retiring, gentle person, whereas the female looks like a firm, take-charge person. The patient appears to be a spectator rather than a "man of action." He appears to need nurturance and support from a more adequate and dynamic mother figure.

From this example the reader can see that the differences in perception of the self in relationship to the opposite sex can be seen from a comparison of the two drawings. Comparisons in size, complexity, style, and quality of execution are all clues to the respective feelings about the patient compared with the opposite sex.

Interpretations Concerning Body Parts

Head.   The head is a symbol of intellectual and fantasy activity, of impulse, and of emotional control. The head is also the site of socialization and communication. Therefore, normal subjects give a great deal of attention to the head. Unusually large heads might indicate aggressive and expansive tendencies, an inflated ego, overevaluation of the intellectual, high achievement, fantasy as a primary source of satisfaction, regression, inhibition and dependency, and possible anxiety. An unusually small head can indicate feelings of inadequacy, sexual impotence, a feeling of intellectual inadequacy, or weak ego conditions. When the head is drawn by an adult of average or better intelligence in a child-like fashion (e.g., as a circle rather than an oval, with dots or circles for eyes, ears stuck on like jug handles, and mouth as a single line), the clinician might infer that the patient is grossly immature, that the patient is regressed, or that he or she is experiencing a good deal of anxiety/conflict. An overemphasis on hair on the head (and hair emphasis on the chest or face) may indicate virility strivings; sexual preoccupation; compensation for feelings of sexual inadequacy or impotence; possible angry, aggressive, assaultive tendencies; narcissism; and possible anxiety or conflict. When hair is absent, the possible interpretations include feelings of sexual inadequacy; castration fears; a possible schizophrenic condition; and low physical vigor.

Facial Features.   When facial features are omitted, the possible interpretations include psychosis, evasiveness, superficiality in interpersonal relationships, inadequate environmental interest, or possible withdrawal tendencies. On the other hand, overemphasis of facial features has been said to indicate overconcern with outward appearances, or feelings of inadequacy and weakness that are compensated for by aggressive and socially dominant behavior. Those patients with hysteroid and/or narcissistic traits often overemphasize the face and hair, typically with large eyes and prominent lashes, and an emphasis on lips and hair.

Unusually large or strongly reinforced eyes indicate suspiciousness and other paranoid characteristics, hypersensitivity to social opinion, or socially outgoing tendencies. Unusually small or closed eyes have been said to indicate introversive tendencies, self-absorption, or contemplative, introspective tendencies. Eyes drawn with the pupils omitted (empty eyes) can indicate "an introversive, self-absorbed tendency in withdrawing persons who are not interested in perceiving their environment, or who perceive it and themselves only vaguely, a condition seen in neuroses and schizoid personalities which may be due to an inability to cope or a communications difficulty" (Ogdon, 1977, p. 76).

Nose.   The nose is sometimes said to be a phallic symbol or a symbol of a power motive. Thus, a large nose or one that is otherwise emphasized may indicate sexual difficulties, including psychosexual immaturity and/or castration fears, sexual impotency, or aggressive tendencies. When the nose is omitted, interpretations include a shy, withdrawn, or depressive personality style, or feelings of castration. Noses drawn by adults as a button or a triangle suggests immaturity, since they are often found in drawings of children; a regressive response to conflict; or anxiety in *older* children, adolescents, or adults. A sharply pointed nose strongly suggests acting-out tendencies. A shaded, dim, or truncated nose may indicate castration fear.

Mouth.   Problems in drawing the mouth are sometimes associated with feeding-eating difficulties, speech disturbances, outbursts of anger, or a dependent approach to life. Mouth emphasis indicates a possible regressive orientation; oral emphasis in the personality; possible verbal aggressiveness associated with a dependent, immature personality; possible sexual difficulties; verbal sadism; or depressive or primitive tendencies. When the mouth is omitted, the interpretations include possible conflict concerning oral aggressive tendencies; depressive conditions; difficulty or reluctance to communicate; rejection of the need for affection; in children, possible obsessions and anxiety; or a shy, withdrawn, depressed interpersonal style.

A cupid bow mouth in female figures has typically been associated with exhibitionistically inclined, sexually precocious adolescent females, whereas a single line, unsmiling mouth suggests depression. A slash line mouth suggests verbal aggression, anger, hypercriticality, or possibly sadistic tendencies. A tiny mouth suggests denial of oral dependent needs, while a mouth with a large grin in an adult suggests either forced congeniality or inappropriate affect. If an adult drawing has teeth showing, this may suggest infantile, aggressive, or sadistic tendencies.

Ears.   Large ears may indicate hypersensitivity to criticism, ideas of reference, paranoid tendencies, or possible auditory hallucinations. Ears are often omitted in drawings by normal subjects.

Chin.   An overemphasized chin suggests aggressive/dominance tendencies, possible strong drive levels, possible compensation for feelings of weakness, or possible feelings of social inadequacy. A weak chin can indicate feelings of weakness or inadequacy, especially in social situations, or feelings of either psychological or physiological impotence.

Beards/Mustaches.   The presence of beards or mustaches often symbolizes the need to enhance personal or sexual status, virility strivings, efforts to enhance masculinity, attempts to hide, aggressive tendencies, or compensation for felt adult inadequacy.

Neck.   The neck is typically regarded as the link between intellectual life (symbolized by the head) and affect (basic body impulses) symbolized by the body. The neck represents the link between ego control (head) and id impulse (body). Thus, neck emphasis typically indicates concern regarding the need to control threatening impulses. Ogdon (1977) states, "Labile affect, fear of labile affect, concern regarding acting-out tendencies, and the need to separate one's cognitive activity from one's affect life may be represented in the treatment of the neck" (p. 78).

An unusually short, thick neck could indicate tendencies to be gruff, stubborn, and rigid; impulsivity; or a desire to keep impulses from hindering intellect. An unusually long neck could indicate an attempt to separate intellectual ideas from emotions; or a cultured, socially stiff, or even formally rigid and overly moral approach to life. An exceptionally long, thin neck can indicate schizoid or psychotic problems. When the neck is omitted, impulsivity is suggested (if the patient is over 10 years of age).

Shoulders.   Well-drawn and neatly rounded shoulders have typically been said to be normal, indicating adequate, well-balanced control of impulses and behavior. Large or broad shoulders in a drawing typically indicates a need for physical power, possible aggressive, acting-out tendencies; excessive defensiveness; or in females, possible sex-role confusion or masculine protest. Absence of shoulders suggests the presence of a thought disorder. Pointed shoulders have been said to indicate acting-out tendencies, while tiny shoulders suggest inferiority feelings.

Breasts.   Unusually large breasts drawn by male patients may indicate emotional immaturity, maternal overdependence, unresolved Oedipal problems, psychosexual immaturity, or strong oral and dependency needs. Unusually large breasts drawn by females may indicate an identification with a dominant mother, exhibitionism, or narcissistic problems.

Waistline.   Ogdon (1977) notes the following concerning the waistline: "In males, the waistline separates the area of physical strength from the area of sexual functioning; in females, the upper part of the body is also related to nutritional factors and secondary activity while the lower part bears more directly on sexual and reproductive activity" (p. 80). In adults, a heavy line separating the lower body from the rest of the body can suggest acute sexual conflict. An unusually high or low waistline is said to suggest blocking and conflict regarding sexual tendencies. An excessively tight waistline (corseted appearance) may indicate precarious emotional control of body impulses, perhaps expressed by temperamental outbursts. An elaborate belt possibly indicates sexual preoccupation, control of body impulses via rationalization or sublimation, or phobic or neurotic behavior.

Trunk.   The body typically symbolizes basic drives, and therefore attitudes related to the development and integration of these drives in the personality are indicated by the manner in which the trunk is drawn. If the body is drawn in fragmented fashion, the clinician should consider this an indication of serious personality disorganization. Children typically draw the trunk as a simple oval or rectangle. If the body is represented in this manner by an adult of average or better intelligence, this could indicate a regressed state, and extremely immature personality, or the presence of severe anxiety/conflict. A large trunk may symbolize unsatisfied drives, whereas a long, narrow trunk may indicate possible schizoid tendencies. Rounded trunks are said to suggest a passive, feminine, or perhaps an infantile, regressive, personality. If the trunk is omitted by an adult, it is possible the patient is severely disturbed or has severe conflicts that center on body impulses. A small trunk suggests a denial of drives, feelings of inferiority, or both.

Genitalia.   Genitalia are rarely drawn, but when they are, they indicate severe psychopathology, overt aggression (in children), or sexual preoccupation and curiosity (adolescents). It is important to note that normal art students, persons in psychoanalysis, and patients in sex therapy often produce nude drawings that may include genitalia.

Arms.   The arms reflect the type and quality of the patient's contact with the environment and interpersonal relations. Arms drawn as relaxed and flexible are considered normal. Arms drawn akimbo might indicate narcissistic or bossy tendencies, whereas arms behind the back possibly suggest reluctance to meet people halfway; need to control aggressive, hostile feelings or behavior; or guilt feelings. Folded arms may indicate suspicious, hostile attitudes; possible rigid attempts to maintain control of violent impulses; a passive, nonassertive orientation; or unwillingness to interact socially. Frail, thin, small, or shrunken arms suggest feelings of inadequacy or a general feeling of ineffectiveness. Long, strong arms might indicate acquisitive and compensatory ambition; need for achievement or physical strength; or active, aggressive contact with the environment. Omission of arms is said to indicate guilt feelings, depression, feelings of inadequacy and ineffectiveness, dissatisfaction with the environment, strong withdrawal tendencies, or passivity. Short arms indicate a lack of ambition, feelings of inadequacy, passivity, or possible castration fears.

Hands.   Outstretched hands suggest a desire for environmental or interpersonal contact or a desire for help or affection. Hands placed behind the back might indicate an evasive interpersonal approach, guilt feelings concerning other people, guilt feelings concerning masturbation, or merely a feeling of insecurity concerning the ability to draw hands adequately. Large hands can suggest compensation for inadequacy feelings, whereas small hands may indicate feelings of insecurity and helplessness. Hands drawn as mittens might indicate repressed or suppressed aggressive tendencies, with the aggression expressed indirectly. Clenched fingers suggest aggression and rebelliousness, or conscious attempts to control anger. Fingers without hands, or large fingers in adult drawings might indicate regression or infantile aggressive/assaultive tendencies. Long fingers have been found in drawings of patients with regressive tendencies, whereas omission of the fingers indicates a feeling of difficulty in interpersonal relationships or masturbatory guilt. Talon-like fingers or spiked fingers may indicate infantile, primitive, aggressive, and hostile acting-out tendencies, sometimes associated with paranoid features.

Legs.   Legs or feet are typically symbolic of security feelings and/or feelings concerning mobility. Crossed legs indicate defensiveness against sexual approaches, long legs may suggest a strong need or striving for autonomy, and short legs could indicate feelings of immobility and constriction.

Feet.   Elongated or large feet have been associated with strong security needs and possible sexual factors (e.g., a need to demonstrate virility, castration fears). Emphasis on feet has typically been said to indicate feelings of sexual inadequacy, or possible aggressive/assaultive tendencies. Omission of feet might indicate a feeling of constriction, with a lack of independence; loss of autonomy; feelings of helplessness; or, in children, shyness, aggressiveness, or emotional disturbance. Small feet have been said to indicate insecurity, constriction, or dependence.

Profile View.   A profile may indicate evasiveness, a reluctance to face and communicate with others, reserved interpersonal style, serious withdrawal or oppositional tendencies, or paranoid tendencies.

Stance.   The stance of a figure suggests the degree of security the person feels in his or her environment. Thus, the drawing may reflect activity, assertiveness, fear of the environment, and even degree of sexual approach or activity. The position of the various parts of the body produce a drawing whose stance reflects attitudes described earlier or other attitudes concerning feelings of power and adequacy in the environment.

Exploring the Literature

Handler and Reyher (1965) reviewed and summarized 51 studies concerning anxiety/conflict. Large size, small size, heavy line, light line, omission, lack of detail, distortion, head simplification, and body simplification were found to be excellent anxiety/conflict indices. For shading, hair shading, erasure, and reinforcement, the number of studies in agreement with traditional clinical interpretation (present more frequently when anxiety is present) is balanced by an equal or greater number of findings in the opposite direction (present less frequently when anxiety is present, where increased frequency was expected) and an equal or greater number of nonsignificant findings. Although this is not quite the case for placement in the upper left-hand corner, more than half of the findings for this index did not agree with the traditional clinical interpretation. Some studies found significantly less shading, hair shading, erasure, reinforcement, placement in the upper left-hand corner, and less emphasis line in situations where more was predicted.

Although the data suggest that these traditional measures may be poor indices of conflict/anxiety, Handler and Reyher (1964) suggest an alternative interpretation: These findings indicate that the anxiety-producing characteristics of the task and/or situation may create a desire to finish the figures with a minimum of effort and to leave the situation as quickly as possible (flight). This motivation would also seem to characterize the clinical testing situation. Accordingly, there is a problem in interpreting the significance of presence (or absence) of shading, hair shading, erasure, reinforcement, and emphasis line in human figure drawings. Handler and Reyher's findings show that these indices are likely to be associated with concurrent external rather than internal sources of stress. However, traditional clinical interpretation stresses the importance of these variables as being key indicators in reflecting internal conflict or stress. To further complicate the significance of these indices, Handler and Reyher found that they sometimes seemed to indicate an adaptive response to the task, in an appropriate attempt to make the figures as true to life as possible, and to give them substance. They seemed to denote adaptiveness, flexibility, and an appropriate reaction to a reality situation.

Since the figure-drawing test itself is stressful (i.e., the diagnostic testing situation), a flight reaction may be rather frequent, thereby producing a reduction of shading, reinforcement, and so on. Thus, the presence, rather than absence of reinforcement, erasure, and shading may at times indicate a coping approach to anxiety and might be indicative of good ego strength. Handler and Reyher (1966) found that shading, erasure, reinforcement, and emphasis line correlated significantly and negatively with galvanic skin response, thereby indicating that these indices are probably more sensitive to external stress (albeit in the opposite direction) than to intrapsychic stress. Thus, the presence of shading, hair shading, erasure, and reinforcement or their conspicuous absence may indicate either the presence or absence of anxiety. The rather puzzling, conflicting findings for these variables and for emphasis line may mirror differential reactions to stress. In situations where patients are under moderate or severe anxiety, a withdrawal response might be expected. With patients whose anxiety is milder, a coping defense (and thus the presence of these indices) might be expected.

Fortunately, the proper interpretation of these indices can often be determined by comparing the figure drawings with the automobile drawing. For example, those subjects who show impoverishment on all three drawings are characterized by avoidant defenses to an anxiety-producing situation. When the patients show erasure, reinforcement, and so on in the human figure drawings, but not in the automobile drawing, the source of anxiety stems from internal sources of conflict. Since these patients use erasure, reinforcement, and the like, they seem to cope with rather than avoid threatening material (i.e., they deal directly and actively with sources of threat represented by the human figure). When the automobile is characterized by erasure, reinforcement, and so forth, and the figures are not, the interpretation of an internal source of conflict still seems proper, but the defensive style is avoidant rather than coping. If the anxiety indices are present in both the figures *and* the automobile, the anxiety is probably due to external stress. Another useful clue in differentiating internal from external stress is the quality of the line. The data suggest that both light- and heavy-line quality may indicate anxiety, but that different processes underlie their presence. Heavy line probably reflects feelings of external stress or pressure from without, whereas light line may represent a feeling of stress from within.

The degree of change in figure drawings under stress might indicate something about the quality of the patient's defenses. Those patients whose drawings changed drastically in response to stress would probably be more unstable than those whose drawings changed only moderately, in appropriate response to external threat. This suggests a modification of the DAP administration procedure: A series of drawings might be obtained as soon as the patient enters the testing room, and another series might be obtained after the patient and the clinician have had a chance to become acquainted with each other and rapport is established.

When the stress and nonstress drawings for each subject were inspected, two drawing patterns emerged under stress conditions—constriction and expansion. The constricted drawings were more often characterized by heavier lines, mechanical breaks in the line, reduced line sketchiness, detached or semidetached body parts, and decrease in size. This pattern seems to reflect increased rigidity and constriction in response to stress. Expansion was marked by increased diffusion of body boundaries, increased vagueness of body parts, extremely sketchy lines, light lines, and increased size.

Trestman, Handler, and Pollio (1993) did an analysis of the Handler conflict/anxiety indices on drawings of cancer patients. They isolated two factors: one dealt with external stress and one seemed to reflect intrapsychic stress. In general, his findings indicated that omission, distortion, head and body simplification, and delineation line absence reflect intrapsychic stress. The authors found that those patients who viewed the cancer as most powerful had the highest DAP anxiety levels.

Research Findings: Validity

A number of reviewers (e.g., Roback, 1968; Swensen, 1957, 1968) have indicated that the research literature does not support a number of clinical conclusions concerning the validity of the DAP. However, the quality of the various studies has typically not been taken into account by those who cite the negative literature. This writer believes that a careful review of the literature would reveal that a number of DAP studies seem quite poorly conceived; from their methodology it seems quite clear that there is little chance that positive results would be obtained. Hammer's (1958) comment on a study by Holzberg and Wexler (1950) is an excellent case in point. These authors found no significant difference between normals and schizophrenics drawing naked feet with toes delineated, with toenails indicated, or in the frequency of drawing internal organs—all signs of schizophrenia. Hammer correctly points out that such signs occur infrequently in drawings, but when they do, they almost invariably indicate schizophrenia. To test the validity of the signs, only instances in which the signs occurred should be included. Instead, the researchers compared a normal group with a schizophrenic group. They found low frequencies of occurrence in both groups and concluded that there was no significant difference between the groups for these variables. A better approach, Hammer emphasizes, would be to accumulate 20 such drawings and then determine the incidence of schizophrenia in the patients who made the drawings.

Another problem in research with the DAP is that in group comparison studies the extremes in each group tend to cancel each other out, and therefore no significant differences are found. For example, Handler and Reyher (1964) found that under stress conditions there were no significant size changes. However, when the data were analyzed on an individual basis, it became clear that the drawings of some individuals increased greatly in size in the stress condition, while the drawings of other individuals decreased greatly in size in the stress condition. When a mean was obtained, there was a cancellation effect, and the actual effect of stress on size was obscured.

Unfortunately, there are also problems encountered in the observations of practicing clinicians who have attempted to make public their idiosyncratic approach to DAP interpretation. For one reason or another, a particular drawing sign has become associated with a particular interpretation, and sometimes the clinician clings rigidly to such an interpretation despite the fact that other possible interpretations are conceivable for such a sign. Sometimes, context and other possible meanings are ignored. Note that such an approach does not always have to be an interpretive error. For example, in the previous illustration concerning schizophrenic signs, if one or more studies had concluded that this sign occurred exclusively with schizophrenics, then it would not be unreasonable to use this sign in clinical work. However, even in this example, context is important, and there are other possibilities. For example, the writer has obtained (infrequently) drawings from college males who attempt to inject humor into a DAP by drawing large naked feet with toes delineated. These subjects were almost invariably not schizophrenic.

The DAP and Schizophrenia

Weiner (1966) argues that fragmented drawings with broken contours reflect impaired reality sense and indefinite ego boundaries, providing that the patient has labored conscientiously on the drawing, attempting to produce his or her best effort and expresses satisfaction with the quality of the drawing. The same may be said for the second index of impaired reality sense, distorted image, provided that the distortions are relatively independent of artistic ability. Weiner emphasizes the importance of undifferentiated sexuality and physical omission as DAP indices of schizophrenia. He offers additional clarity concerning eye and ear emphasis as indications of paranoid symptomatology. Although these signs cannot discriminate accurately the paranoid schizophrenics from other personality problems, if it is first determined that the patient is schizophrenic, then the presence of eye and ear emphasis is said to indicate the presence of paranoid symptomatology.

The drawing shown in Figure 6–14, from a case study by Weiner (1966), was done by a single, 23-year-old female, school teacher whose diagnostic status was unclear before testing. Weiner indicates that she became increasingly disturbed in the weeks following testing and was later hospitalized with an overt schizophrenic reaction. Note the gaps between the lines of the trunk, arms, and legs; she fails to close the ends of the arms and legs (body contour breaks). Weiner notes: "Such clear breaks in the body contour reflect indefinite, poorly delineated ego boundaries and suggest that this young woman is

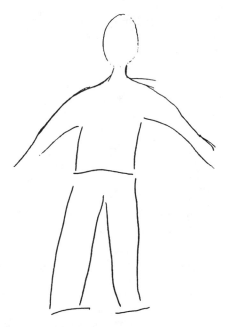

Figure 6–14   Drawings by a 23-Year-Old School Teacher Who Was Later Hospitalized with a Schizophrenic Reaction

Source: From *Psychodiagnosis in Schizophrenia* by I. Weiner, 1966, New York: John Wiley and Sons. Reprinted by permission of the author.

having marked difficulty maintaining a sense of her own reality as a single, unique and integral person" (p. 37). In addition, the patient omits body parts (hands, feet, facial features). Since her drawing is relatively well proportioned, clinicians should not interpret these omissions merely as an indication of poor artistic ability, but rather as an indication of her distorted view of her body. The reader should note the drawings in Figure 6–12 recently obtained from patients in a local state psychiatric hospital. Note the fragmentation and the broken contours, the major omissions, and the distortions reflected in the drawings, and their bizarre quality.

The DAP and Other Tests

How does the DAP compare with and relate to other tests? As mentioned previously, the DAP is more sensitive to pathology than are the other tests, even the Rorschach. For example, if the drawings are pathological and the Rorschach is relatively free of pathology, then a possible interpretation would be a negative prognosis—a future increase in psychopathology. Concerning the concurrence of themes in the DAP and the TAT, one study (Gallese & Spoerl, 1954) found between 33 and 100 percent agreement between the two tests concerning the projection of needs and conflicts (the mean percentage of agreement was 72 percent). However, Gallese and Spoerl note that the two tests illustrate the conflicts and needs quite differently. They state, "Most of the material from the Machover (DAP) was inserted on an unconscious level, and represents the more or less unadulterated basic needs" (p. 75). On the other hand, the TAT data illustrated these needs and conflicts in the total personality expression and the resulting stories were tinged and altered by the familiar techniques of defense. For example, while the DAP might contain data which suggested direct hostile feelings toward the father or the mother, the TAT stories would instead deal with indirect expression of these impulses, such as a story about "rebellion against society and its institutions, school teachers, and other dominating or superior groups or persons" (p. 76).

Shneidman (1958) cites a study by Katz who compared adult homicide or assault offenders with nonassaultive controls in the DAP and the TAT (as well as on other tests). Katz states:

> In the Thematic Apperception Test the results indicate that ability for establishing sound interpersonal relationships is severely impaired for virtually all of the assaultive subjects. . . . The drawings show indication for inconsistent motor control, a hostile view of the environment, basic inadequacy, and strong immature aggressive tensions directly expressed. . . . The essential differences in the drawing characteristics are reflected in those bodily features which are most directly related to and essential for the discharge of assaultive tensions. (pp. 622–623)

A recent study by Blatt and Ford (1994) concerning changes in personality assessment data from hospitalized patients in long-term intensive treatment at the Austen Riggs Center provides a great deal of data concerning the relationship between DAP data and data from other projective techniques, such as the Rorschach and the TAT. The authors found that the most effective psychological predictor of change was the Mutuality of Autonomy score (Urist, 1977) on the Rorschach concerning level of clinical symptoms and the quality of interpersonal relationships. The authors also found that a DAP score that measured the change in the quality of the drawing, using the Harris-Goodenough scoring system (Harris, 1963) and a measure of balance-tilt of the figure (Robins, Blatt & Ford, 1991), also indicated significant change in the after-therapy testing. The second drawings were significantly more fully articulated and differentiated and significantly more centered and organized in space, compared with the before-therapy drawings. An example of these changes was illustrated in Figures 6-2 and 6-3. These changes were relatively independent of any confounding variables, such as the level of therapist experience, the use of medication, the level of premorbid social adjustment, and even the severity of psychopathology.

Blatt and Ford also report that these changes were *not* correlated with Rorschach measures, TAT measures, or Wechsler measures. They conclude that the DAP provides *"a unique and independent dimension for assessing therapeutic change"* (italics added) (p. 133). Nevertheless, the authors add, the results of the DAP analyses "come to essentially the same conclusions about the nature of therapeutic change in seriously disturbed young adults as found with [the] other measures" (p. 133).

Other DAP Uses.   Recently, Gustafson and Waehler (1992) have indicated that the DAP may be a good indicator of the degree of concrete/literal and abstract thinking of a patient. They indicate that several DAP variables correspond to overall scores of concrete, literal, and abstract thinking: (1) lack of detail (which suggests "inattentiveness to complexity or emptiness of feeling and thought" [p. 446]); (2) the drawing of a full figure (expressing "full conception, appreciation, and representation of the human figure" [p. 446]); and (3) erasure with improvement (which conveys "a tolerable level of dissatisfaction with the representation and the ability to improve the quality of the drawing" [p. 446]). Gustafson and Waehler found that content and global-interpretive categories were found to be more differentiating than were formal scoring characteristics.

THE HOUSE-TREE-PERSON DRAWING TECHNIQUE (H-T-P)

The major credit for the invention and development of the H-T-P goes to John Buck and Emanual Hammer, who have described the technique in their extensive writings (Buck, 1948; Hammer, 1958). Much of the interpretive approach clinicians utilize with the H-T-P comes primarily from the research and clinical wisdom of these authors. John Buck (in the United States) and Emil Jucker (in Switzerland) independently discovered that the tree drawing allowed for personality projection, and Jucker's student, Charles Koch (1952), developed the tree drawing as a projective test. Buck added the house and person drawings, to form the H-T-P Technique. Hammer points out that other clinicians, Ruth Griffiths in England, and A. A. Pichon-Riviére in South America, also simultaneously identified the house as a symbolic representation of the self and of basic childhood and adult experiences. Others (e.g., Bolander, 1977) have written extensively about the tree drawing as a projective technique. Buck decided to utilize a house and a tree drawing because they were very familiar items, even to young children, and most people were quite willing to draw them. In addition, Buck found that the H-T-P drawing process stimulated free and open verbalizations, which had significant symbolic significance (Hammer, 1958).

Much of what has been said about the clinical usefulness of the DAP is also true of the H-T-P. However, there are *additional* important reasons for using the H-T-P:

1. The H-T-P reflects the patient's feelings about his or her home situation, typically represented in the house drawing.
2. The H-T-P is a less obvious test, and therefore patients are less guarded, especially when they are asked to draw a tree and a house. Therefore

they can represent self and interpersonal issues more directly and with less defensiveness.

3. The tree drawing is often able to reflect patient's emotional history and the effect of that history on the person. For example, scars or holes on the tree trunk are often said to represent specific emotional and/or physical traumas experienced by the patient, and the location of the scar or hole on the tree trunk is sometimes said to determine whether the trauma took place when the patient was younger or older.

4. The drawing of a house and a tree are very basic things children and adults enjoy drawing. They engage children and capture their interest quite easily.

5. The tree drawing, said to be a representation of the self, is said to tap deeper layers of the self than the DAP. Therefore, it is more revealing of underlying dynamic issues.

Instructions

As with the DAP, a #2 pencil with an eraser is supplied to the patient. The house drawing is requested first. The paper is held in a horizontal position. The examiner states: "I want you to draw as good a picture of a house as you can. You may draw any kind of house you wish; it's entirely up to you." The examiner then, in turn, asks the patient to draw as good a tree and as good a person as he or she can draw. If the patient hesitates or protests, he or she can be assured that this is not a test of artistic ability. The same procedure is followed for the tree and the person, except that the paper is held in the *vertical* position for these drawings. It is important to record all spontaneous comments and/or any unusual emotions expressed by the patient during the drawing procedure. Although Buck recommends timing the patient and recording the sequence of the details drawn, this writer has not found these data to be of much use in the analysis. After the patient has completed the drawings, the examiner proceeds with questions concerning the three drawings so that the patient can define, describe, and further elaborate on the drawings. A number of authors recommend various lists of questions to be asked of each subject. Such a list, modified from Buck (1966) is included in Table 6–3.

In actual practice, this writer has sometimes substituted open-ended questions for the list in Table 6–3. For example, the author typically says to the patient: "Tell me about this house (tree, person)." If the patient does not spontaneously respond, the writer then becomes more specific and he asks more directed questions. Note that Buck recommends that a chromatic H-T-P should also be administered. Here, the patient is asked to repeat the entire H-T-P, using crayons instead of a #2 pencil. The chromatic H-T-P is said to illustrate deeper layers of personality functioning. For example, one patient drew a sturdy oak tree in the achromatic phase, calling it "full-grown, stately and very solid" (Hammer, 1958, p. 229). However, beneath the surface was

Table 6–3 Selected House-Tree-Person Questions

House
1. Is that your own House? (If answer is no: Who lives in this house?)
2. Is the House strong or weak? What are its strongest and weakest parts?
3. Would you like to own that House yourself? Why?
4. What kinds of activities go on in this House?
5. If you did own that House and you could do whatever you liked with it, whom would you like to have live in that House with you?
6. What does that House make you think of, or remind you of?
7. If this House were a person, how would it feel?
8. Whom does that House make you think of? Why?
9. What does that House need most? Why?

Tree
1. What kind of Tree is that?
2. About how old is that Tree?
3. Is that Tree alive?
4. What are the weakest and strongest parts of the Tree?
5. Is any part of the Tree dead? What part? What do you think caused it to die? How long has it been dead?
6. Is that Tree by itself or is it in a group of Trees?
7. What does that Tree make you think of, or remind you of?
8. Is it a healthy Tree?
9. Is is a strong Tree?
10. What is there about it that gives you that impression?
11. What does that Tree remind you of most?
12. What does that Tree need most?

Person
1. Is that a man or a woman (or boy or girl)?
2. How old is he/she?
3. What is he/she doing? (and where is he/she doing it?)
4. What is he/she thinking about?
5. How does he/she feel? Why?
6. What does this Person make you think of, or remind you of?
7. What does he/she most (least) like to do?
8. What is there about him/her that gives you that impression?
9. Do you think you would like that Person? Why?
10. What are the best (worst) parts of his/her body?
11. Whom does this Person remind you of? Why?
12. What does this Person need most? Why?
13. What kind of clothing does this Person have on?
14. What do other people think of this person? Why?
15. What are the weakest (strongest) parts of this person?
16. What are the best and worst qualities of this person?
17. What sorts of things make this person angry (happy, sad)?

Adapted from Buck, 1966.

significant depression. His chromatic tree was a weeping willow, which he described as "weak looking."

Why does the use of color, with crayons, result in drawings that depict deeper layers of personality, allowing for projection of processes seen in the achromatic administration, but with greater emphasis? First, the introduction of color stimulates emotional responsiveness more so than the achromatic drawings. As Hammer (1986) states: "Color stimulates people, as every fine arts painter and advertising expert well knows. Asking a patient to draw in colored crayon moves us closer to being able to sample reactions to, and tolerance for, emotional situations—the very same situations in which acting out, if it is to be released, is oft to be triggered" (p. 259).

In addition to the color, the use of crayons perhaps causes individuals to regress, allowing one to move closer to earlier developmental patterns of responding. Crayons are also more difficult to use, and there is no way to erase, thereby causing more frustration for the patient in making the drawings. Thus, whatever emotion is mildly conveyed in the achromatic drawing is typically displayed more blatantly in the chromatic drawings.

Interpretation

Although Buck has put a great deal of energy into his quantitative scoring system and the use of the H-T-P as a measure of intelligence, the use of the technique in this manner has waned significantly. Instead, clinicians interpret the H-T-P in a more comprehensive manner, focusing on style and content as a personality measure. Buck has devised an elaborate *quantitative* scoring system, which has not been enthusiastically endorsed by clinicians. Instead, the H-T-P has been interpreted *qualitatively,* much like the prevailing approach to the DAP and the K-F-D. Buck suggests that the interpreter should examine the details of the drawings, the proportions (size relationships) in each drawing, and the perspective (spatial relationships, line quality), but an interpretive approach to the H-T-P that is holistic and integrative seems to be most helpful in an attempt to understand the patient. Here, as with the DAP, no single sign has only one fixed and absolute meaning.

There are a number of essential details that are typically present in each drawing. The examiner should note whether the house, tree, and person have these essential details and should discern for each patient the possible reasons for omissions. Obviously, it would be desirable if we could associate a meaning for each omission, but actually there are many possibilities for omission of these details, some of which have no relevance to personality problems or conflicts (e.g., low intelligence). The opposite approach, too many details, may also be related to the symbolization of the objects represented, but there are other possibilities, such as an obsessive and/or overinclusive stylistic approach to life.

Buck (1966) discusses the inclusion of "irrelevant details" (e.g., grass, birds, sun, clouds), which he interprets as implying "mild basic insecurity—a need to structure the situation more securely," "free floating anxiety (or conflict) in the area symbolized by the detail, or a strong withdrawal need" (p. 82). Although these are certainly possibilities, other interpretations include an overly inclusive style, or merely an attempt to produce as natural, realistic, and life-like setting as possible. As the reader will see later in this section, some clinicians interpret the inclusion of "irrelevant" details as indicating healthy relationship with their world, indicating self-actualization in a creative manner (Burns, 1987). This latter interpretation is a much more positive view, compared with the negative interpretations discussed here. The examiner must choose which type of interpretation fits best by observing this sign (and all other signs) in context.

Buck (1966) indicates that the house must have at least one door, one window, one wall, and a roof, unless it is a tropical dwelling of some type. It must also have a chimney, except where the house is heated with electricity and/or there is no fireplace. The tree must have a trunk and at least one branch. Essential standards for the person are included in the section of this chapter in which the DAP is discussed. Buck believes that the absence of even one essential detail is serious, implying some serious emotional problem. The problem is considered more serious if more essential details are missing. There are a number of details that are nonessential, but that are included to enrich the drawing (e.g., curtains, bark on trees). The elaboration of the drawings with such details is said to reflect good reality testing and good ego strength. However, the excessive use of detail suggests an approach to life marked by obsessive overconcern.

There is some disagreement concerning the symbolic meaning of the house and the tree. For example, Hammer (1968) believes that, at least with children, the house typically symbolizes attitudes concerning the home situation and the child's relationships with parents and siblings. For example, Hammer describes a house drawing done by a child who lived in a home with a "hot and turbulent emotional atmosphere" (p. 263), who drew a house with a great deal of heavily shaded smoke pouring from the chimney.

The house has also been said to be a symbol of the self or the body image. Hammer highlights the close relationship of the house drawing to the depiction of the human body in caveman drawings, as well as in the Renaissance art of the thirteenth and fourteenth centuries. It is possible to utilize both interpretations of the meaning of the house, simultaneously. For example, rather than stating that the child in the case just cited exists in a home that is emotionally turbulent and that he or she experiences this turbulence, the changed statement might go something like this: "My home is filled with turbulence and turmoil and I am troubled and angry about that." In addition, Hammer emphasizes that even for adults the childhood-related feelings about parental figures is reflected in the house drawing, and that these feelings are represented even more so in the house drawings of more disturbed patients.

Hammer (1958) believes that the tree drawing reflects the patient's somewhat deeper and more unconscious feelings about self, and he views the person drawing as "conveying the subject's closer-to-consciousness view of himself and his relationship to his environment" (p. 172). Hammer's reason for viewing the tree and person in this relationship comes from his observations that nonintensive psychotherapy typically brings about a decrease in pathological signs in the person drawing, but only extensive psychoanalytic treatment or highly significant alterations in a life situation will produce significant change in the tree drawing. He makes an additional interesting observation: It is easier to attribute negative or emotionally disturbing statements and negative traits and attitudes to the tree rather than the person, since patients are often somewhat guarded in attributing these attitudes to the person drawing, because it is "closer to home," so to speak. He believes that "the deeper or more forbidden feelings can more readily be projected onto the tree than onto the person, with less fear of revealing oneself and less need for ego-defensive maneuvering" (p. 172). Hammer emphasizes that the tree and person drawings tap what he calls "the core of personality," by which he means the body image and self-concept.

While Buck views the tree as revealing the patient's impressions of the self in relation to the environment, Bolander (1977) believes the tree drawing represents the life history of the individual, including the person's origins, experiences, hopes, and plans for the future. Bolander believes that by careful analysis of the patient's tree drawings, the clinician can achieve an overview of the patient's development through the years and can reveal biographical material. What follows is a list of interpretations concerning various house and tree parts. The reader should again be cautioned that each interpretation is only a *possibility,* and that other interpretations are also quite possible. Choosing an alternative interpretation is quite appropriate, based on other aspects of the drawing, other test data, as well as history information. The use of these *possible* interpretations as a cookbook should be studiously avoided!

Hammer emphasizes the importance of avoiding fixed sign interpretations for specific drawing areas. For example, he notes that sex offenders often display feelings of phallic inadequacy by distorting the chimney in several different ways, or by overelaboration of the chimney (Hammer, 1954), but he also notes that in well-adjusted subjects the chimney probably represents only another important detail of the house drawing and has little projective significance. Thus, the chimney is not *always* a phallic symbol in drawings, "but if a subject suffers from psychosexual conflicts, the chimney—by virtue of its structural design and its protrusion from the body of the house—is susceptible to receive the projection of the subject's inner feelings about his own phallus (Hammer, 1954, p. 170). Below is an interpretive guide for various house and tree areas.

House Drawing

Roof.   The roof is sometimes employed by some patients as a symbol of the fantasy area of life. Thus, if there are distortions or overelaborations of the roof, the possibility exists that this person is overly immersed in fantasy and is therefore withdrawn from interpersonal contact. However, one could also conceptualize the roof as a symbol of control (e.g., "he raised the roof," lost his temper), and in this case, overelaboration would suggest the patient's attempts to control emotions. As indicated earlier, which interpretation one utilizes for this sign depends, of course, on the other data collected from and about the patient. The opposite extreme—a house that is drawn with no roof, or a roof with no height—is typically seen in individuals who lack the capacity to daydream or fantasize. These people are typically concrete and constricted.

A roof that is heavily reinforced or repeatedly retraced, where this treatment was not given to the remainder of the drawing, probably signifies that the patient is attempting to defend against the threat of fantasy getting out of control. This is similar but slightly different from the interpretation which views the roof as an emotional control barrier. In that case, a reinforced roof might indicate the fear that emotions would break through and the fear of losing emotional control. Buck states that a roof drawn with eaves which overhang great deal indicates an overdefensive, somewhat suspicious attitude. Schizophrenic and schizoid patients sometimes draw a house that is *all* roof; they draw a roof outline and place the door and windows within that outline. These patients are often said to be extremely withdrawn into their fantasy world.

Walls.   Many H-T-P interpreters view walls as representing ego strength. Therefore, walls that are depicted as crumbling are often drawn by people who are fighting off an incipient psychotic process and who are making an extreme effort to maintain ego intactness. However, less extreme "shoring up" of walls possibly indicates the patient's felt need for structure and support in ego functions. Those who draw the walls with weak or faint lines are said to be similar to those who reinforce the walls, except that the former patients do not employ the compensatory efforts at containment represented in the latter group. Thus, the patient feels resigned to personality breakdown and has ceased to struggle. This group adopts an attitude of passive sufferance, rather than warding off the disintegrative forces which threaten to overwhelm the personality.

Transparent walls, where objects that ordinarily cannot be seen from outside the house are able to be seen, as if looking right through the walls, are not typically seen in drawings of houses done by adults (although children often draw with such transparencies). As with such transparencies in DAPs of *adults,* this depiction often demonstrates reality-testing problems, often seen in drawings of psychotics. However, it is also possible that the objects depicted through the walls symbolize or represent aspects of the self or home life that are so extremely disturbing that they press for more open expression, or perhaps that the person who made such a drawing feels exposed and vulnerable.

Windows.   Windows represent a way in which the person making the drawing can interact with the environment. He or she can, for example, pull the shades down and hide inside, or let people see in, or open the window and look out. Those who draw locks on windows (and doors) are perhaps fearful of intrusions from without. Such people have either been harmed by the environment or are somewhat guarded and suspicious, as in the typical paranoid orientation. Are the windows shuttered? If so, the interpreter might think of withdrawal tendencies. Are the windows open? If so, the person is probably inviting more open communication with others.

In addition, the treatment of the widows is said to be important. If is often useful to inquire of the patient about who occupies the rooms with the unusual treatment (e.g., shades, shutters, etc.) where other windows do not have such adornment. Shutters and/or curtains on the windows *could* indicate withdrawal needs or to interact with others *if* they are closed, but another or additional interpretation could be that the person has secrets that he or she is trying to hide. This is more of a possibility if one window is given such treatment when the others are not drawn as closed; Hammer (1958) indicates that windows that are drawn completely bare (without curtains, shades or cross-hatching) often occur in the drawings of those who interact in an overly blunt and direct manner, with little tact.

Typically, the living room window is drawn larger than the others, while the bathroom window is usually drawn as the smallest. When there is deviation from this expectation, the examiner might hypothesize that some strong emotional need is being expressed. While Hammer (1958) indicates that making the living room window the smallest indicates "a distinct distaste for social intercourse" (p. 177), there are other possible interpretations, such as increased symbolic importance of other windows, thereby perhaps drawing them larger. Making the bathroom window the largest is perhaps related to important events or conflictual life experiences that center around the bathroom, such as toilet training and guilt concerning various bodily functions. Usually, the windows are placed in a somewhat symmetrical fashion. Therefore, windows that are placed in disorganized fashion possibly indicate confusion and disorganizational problems typical of those with a developing thought disorder or with disorganization due to brain dysfunction.

House Levels.   Sometimes a horizontal line is drawn to indicate that the house has two levels. This treatment is said to be an attempt to compartmentalize body impulses from thought or to ward off potentially dangerous people, or to protect against potentially dangerous activities represented in either the upper or the lower floor (e.g., emotional, physical or sexual abuse).

Approach.   The approach to the house is of some interest. Sometimes the patient draws the house so that access is difficult or impossible. This treatment suggests that the person is not easily accessible, but is guarded and defensive, with reluctance to make contact with others.

Door.   The manner in which the door is drawn, and whether or not it has a handle is important because these details concern the meaning for the patient of contact with the environment. A tiny door, especially one with no doorknob, perhaps indicates reluctance to make contact with the environment or with others, or a desire to withdraw from outside relationships. Some patients place the door high above the baseline of the house and/or without any way of approaching the door, or with a barrier constructed of steep steps. Here, too, the issue is privacy and/or inaccessibility, either in terms of establishing relationships with others or in being psychologically available to another person. Thus, a person who draws in this manner may desire and attempt to achieve privacy or he or she may interact but maintain contact with others on their own terms only. Those who draw an overly large door may be expressing the opposite theme of those who draw a small door. Those in the former group may want a great deal of contact with others, perhaps because they are overly dependent on others or because they are seeking warmth from others. Some people who draw in this manner have been severely deprived and they seek nurturance and support actively and eagerly.

Perspective.   Hammer (1958) indicates that a house that is drawn as if the viewer is above it, looking down upon it (bird's eye view) indicates that the patient rejects the home situation and the values related to home. This "looking down upon" approach is said to be related to "compensatory superiority feelings with a revolt against the traditional values taught at home" and being "above the demands of convention and conformity" (p. 143). However, patients who are overly dependent on intellectualization also sometimes take this approach to drawing the house. The opposite perspective, "the worm's eye view," drawing the house (as if one were looking up at it), is said to represent feelings of poor self-worth and/or a feeling of rejection from those in the home. These people are said to feel extremely inadequate and believe that happiness in the home is unobtainable. The house presented as far away is sometimes drawn by those who want to withdraw and be inaccessible, and/or by those who feel unable to cope with situations at home.

The inquiry will often supply information that will assist the clinician in choosing appropriate interpretations of the drawings, or it will suggest alternative interpretations. For example, an open door can represent desire for warmth and support from others, but the description of the house as vacant could instead suggest that the open door indicates an extreme feeling of vulnerability and a lack of adequate ego defenses.

Groundline.   Much has been made of the meaning of the groundline in the H-T-P literature. It reflects the degree of contact with reality, and indicates that latent or borderline schizophrenics invariably have difficulty presenting their drawings in contact with reality (as represented by the groundline). Hammer indicates that they either offer a drawing "resting tenuously on a choppy or sporadically drawn groundline, . . . on an amorphous cloud-like groundline" (p. 180). An even greater break with reality is said to be reflected in the drawing that "hovers over but nowhere touches a ground-line drawn beneath it" (p. 180). While the groundline may represent issues surrounding contact with reality, it can also represent a need for security and stability. Thus, an overemphasized groundline may be drawn by someone who is saying, "I don't feel as grounded in reality as I need to be and I'm striving to attain such grounding" or "I feel insecure and I'm seeking ways in which to find a firm, secure emotional footing." Of course it is possible that both statements could be accurate for an individual.

A variety of other details are sometimes drawn along with the house. Some of these details often seem to have a great deal of symbolic importance. For example, fences are often drawn by those who need privacy or protection from a harsh environment, or who have withdrawn defensively, in a search for elusive security.

Tree Drawing

The tree, even more than the house, lends itself to rich symbolism in myth and folklore. For example, many school children learn the following line from the poem "Trees" by Joyce Kilmer: "A tree that looks at God all day, and lifts its leafy arms to pray." The myth and symbol of many countries speak of the "tree of life." Hammer (1958) indicates that in German folklore the tree "is said to have its roots in the bowels of the earth, in the nether regions of our primitive past; its trunk on the earth among the mortals; and its branches reaching into the heavens where the gods dwell and rule mankind" (p. 181). We speak, for example, of the "family tree," and the personification of the tree as the self in relation to the family is clearly symbolized by the saying, "As the twig is bent, so grows the tree." Thus, it is possible to view the branches of the tree as symbolizing the manner in which a person relates to his or her environment, the trunk as symbolizing the self, and the leaves as an indication of the degree to which the patient experiences the vigor of life and aliveness itself.

If the interpreter does not wish to symbolize the self in relation to his or her environment in this manner, which represents an intuitive leap for some, then a tree drawing is therefore merely a tree drawing and little else. However, those who are willing to allow that symbolization of the self can be represented by a tree drawing will often find startling representations of historical life relationships represented in these drawings. Thus, for example, this writer had always read that scars and holes in the trunk of the tree often represent a trauma that occurred in the life of the person who made such a drawing, and that the location of the scar or hole corresponded to the time when the event occurred. His stance about this observation many years ago, when he first started to collect tree drawings during the assessment procedure, was quite negative, and he viewed it as some clinician's "flight into fantasy." Imagine his surprise when he began to notice an extremely high correlation between significant trauma and the presence of scars and holes drawn on tree trunks, and when these scars and holes corresponded to the perceived, personally experienced (rather than actual) time when the trauma had taken place.

The trauma could be emotional, such as the early death of a parent, emotional and physical, such as a sexual assault of some type, or mostly physical, such as a severe automobile accident. Note the tree drawing in Figure 6–15, obtained from a 10-year-old child who was in a severe automobile accident when he was 7 years old. He received a moderate head injury in that accident, which left emotional scars, although the neurological ones have healed. Note also the presence of broken or stunted branches, indicating the child's subjective experience of the accident, along with his attempt at compensation for these feelings—the large size of the tree.

Figure 6–15   Tree Drawing of a 10-Year-Old Boy with Physical and Emotional Trauma Due to an Automobile Accident

Lyons (1955) found a positive correlation between an induced scar (direct instructions to place a scar on the tree) and the actual time of the worst event in the patient's life. Torem, Gilbertson and Light (1990) found a significant relationship between subjects' reports of physical, sexual, and verbal victimization and the number of scars, knotholes, and/or broken branches on the drawn trees.

Location on the Page.   Buck (1966) describes interpretations concerning vertical and horizontal axis placement. Drawings placed to the left indicate impulsive behavior, suggesting that the patient is seeking immediate emotional satisfaction, as well as overconcern with self and overconcern with the past. Placement on the right is said to indicate that the patient behaves in a stable, controlled fashion, is willing to delay satisfaction and to be more intellectual and abstract rather than frankly emotional, and to be overconcerned with the future. Drawings placed upward indicate striving for unattainable goals, seeking satisfaction in intellectualization or fantasy, and feelings of frustration; drawings placed more on the bottom are said to indicate insecurity and timidity, seeking satisfaction in reality, a relatively concrete approach to life, and a feeling of at least mild depression.

Buck (1966) describes "paper chopping," the "amputation of a part of the whole by one or more page margins"; "paper topping," defined as a situation in which "part of the whole touches the upper margin of the page, but does not appear to extend beyond it"; "paper siding," where "part . . . of the whole is extended to the page's lateral margin, but . . . does not extend beyond it"; and "paper basing," where "the bottom margin of the . . . page is the baseline of the whole" (p. 109). Paper chopping is said to indicate an unwillingness to draw what is left out, and a related unwillingness to deal with the issues these areas represent. However, a lack of ability to plan adequately, with an associated impulsive approach to the drawing task may be an alternate explanation. "Paper topping" is said to indicate an overemphasis on fantasy and ideation as sources of satisfaction; "paper siding" is said to indicate insecurity; and "paper-basing" is said to indicate either generalized insecurity or a tendency to behave in a concrete, unimaginative fashion; or depression.

Hammer (1958) indicates that a paper-based tree, in which the bottom edge of the paper becomes the groundline, with the tree resting on that edge, is a typical representation of insecure patients who feel inadequate. "They cling to the bottom of the page for compensatory security" (p. 185). Depressed patients may also represent the tree in this manner. Two-dimensional branches, drawn with unclosed distal ends, is said to imply a lack of control over the expression of impulses. A keyhole tree, depicting the trunk and foliage area as if they were drawn with one continuous line, without a line separating the crown from the trunk, is said to indicate opposition or negativism. The split tree [the sidelines of the trunk are not connected; "they extend upward, each one forming its own independent branch structure (Hammer, 1958, p. 191)] suggests "a shattering of personality, dissociation of major personality components, a breakdown in defenses and the danger of inner impulses spilling over into the outer environment. If there is any single sign in the H-T-P which can be regarded as pathognomonic of schizophrenia, it is this one" (p. 192).

In the postdrawing inquiry, the age ascribed to the tree represents the felt level of psychosexual maturity. Hammer (1954) found that a group of rapists had a mean assigned age of 24.4 years, whereas a matched group of pedophiles had an age of 10.6 years.

The tree drawing can be interpreted either in a holistic, impressionistic manner, to capture a feeling about the self, *or* the individual details of the drawing can be evaluated (trunk, branches, leaves, etc.). In the former approach, one can attempt to intuitively interpret the tree drawing in the method that was described previously in this chapter. In the latter approach, the organizing conceptual framework that often seems to work is offered by Koch, who suggests that the area of the tree from the bottom to the top, beginning with the roots, represents the patient's experience of his or her development in time, or as Hammer states, "the psychological life history" of the patient.

Roots.   Exposed roots are said to indicate the patient's need to hold too firmly to the environment, suggesting problems with reality contact. A tree with a small trunk but with an extensive branch system implies excessive satisfaction seeking without adequate ego strength, whereas the opposite, a strong trunk with little branch structure, suggests a problem in which there is an inability to satisfy strong basic needs through environmental contact, with its concomitant frustration.

Trunk.   Buck indicates that the trunk of the tree represents the patient's ego strength, his or her feelings of power, emotional strength, and adequacy. In this regard, heavily reinforced lines on the tree trunk are said to reflect the patient's felt need to maintain ego intactness. In the reinforcing effort, the patient is said to be symbolizing the use of compensatory defenses to combat feelings of disintegration. Faint or sketchy lines used for the trunk often indicate feelings of impending emotional disintegration or loss of identity, accompanied by acute anxiety.

Branches.   Buck indicates that the tree branches indicate a person's feelings of the degree of satisfaction the person is able to derive from the environment. Koch adds that the extremities of the tree branches represent the "zoned contact with the environment" (1952, p. 15). In a number of H-T-P sources (e.g., Buck, 1966), whether the branches are overemphasized on the left side of the page or on the right side of the page is said to be significant. The former is said to represent a tendency to press too strongly for immediate, frank emotional satisfaction, while the latter is said to represent a strong tendency to avoid or delay emotional satisfaction and to seek satisfaction through intellectual pursuits. Whether the branches are one dimensional or two dimensional is also said to be important, the latter suggesting better satisfaction-seeking resources, compared with the single-line branch representation. Branches drawn like clubs or fingers, and with little organization, are said to represent strong hostility. Branches drawn as dead or broken are said to represent traumatic experiences in the patient's life, which have impaired the desire and ability to seek satisfaction in the environment. It is important to emphasize that there has been little research available to validate these interpretations. Nevertheless, clinical experience has supported many of these interpretations.

Fruit.   Those who draw fruit on their trees are said to desire nurturance, although some recent clinicians see such a tree as indicating that the person feels he or she can *offer* nurturance. One can determine which interpretation is appropriate by examining the type of tree drawn. If it is barren, then the first hypothesis is preferable; if it is a bountiful and strong tree, the second hypothesis is probable.

Leaves.   Leaves are said to indicate a desire for nurturance and dependency, although it is important to point out that leaves enliven a tree in a similar way in which fruit might do the same. The interpretation here, as with the fruit, depends on the quality of the tree.

Chromatic H-T-P

The manner in which the patient uses the crayons reflects his or her personality as much as the content of the drawings. For example, a child who draws in a hesitant way, with faint lines and restricted colors, is depressed or constricted and/or interpersonally uncertain with the examiner and perhaps with most others. This approach is in direct contrast to the more open, spontaneous patient who makes firm lines with more brightly colored crayons. Another pattern, that of the excessively labile, angry patient, is often reflected by an approach in which the patient bears down very heavily with the crayons, often using a great deal of turbulent movement and a series of clashing, unharmonious, or hot colors. Hammer notes that the use of from three to five colors for the house drawing is typical, two or three for the tree, and three to five for the person drawing.

Burns (1987) has demonstrated how a modification of the theoretical approach of A. H. Maslow can be utilized in the interpretation of the H-T-P. This "need hierarchy" approach emphasizes that people cannot address higher-level relational needs if their basic needs are not satisfied. At the first level of the system, the individual is preoccupied with the issues of basic survival, or has decided he or she does not want to survive but wishes to die. In the former case, the house symbolizes a place for security and safety; entrance is barred or limited in any number of ways. The house may be drawn like a prison or fortress, the door may be small or missing, or the doorknob is missing. In the case where the patient wants to avoid life, the house may be drawn as decaying, weak or sagging, and old or crumbling.

Burns's next level (Level 2) relates to issues concerning the body. Those who "approach" in this area decorate the house with sexual and other body symbols, such as chimneys, candles, and wreaths; those who avoid body sensuality or sexuality deny such symbols by the use of "X symbols" (see Figure 6–25), by shading or by cross-hatching areas.

The next level (Level 3), "belonging to society," deals with needs for success, status, power, and respect. At this level, the house is depicted as large and stylish for those patients who have a positive view about success. Those who have a negative view of this need draw houses that are not stylish or expensive, or they indicate dissatisfaction in this area in other ways, such as a protest sign on the lawn, overgrown grass, and so forth. At the higher levels, where "self" and "not self" are seen in balance and harmony, the house is depicted with symbols of warmth, comfort, and an approach that is welcoming. Curtains are for decoration, not to hide behind; flowers, trees, and shrubs decorate an entrance; there is a nurturant quality depicted. Symbols of the world around us, such as mountains, the sun, and animals, are included.

Burns classifies tree drawings in the same manner. For example, at Level 1, the "approachers" draw trees with talon-like roots, in an attempt to "hold on"; the branches may be drawn either as thorny looking or spike-like. Those with attitudes to avoid life or who want to die draw tree trunks ending with a point, or a very narrow trunk, or a tree with no trunk at all. They also may draw a tree that is dead, or one with all the growth at the bottom and that is bare at the top. The tree may also be drawn as stunted, bent from the wind, empty, as a very small tree but with large leaves, or as a weeping willow, a typical symbol of sadness.

Trees at Level 2, "belonging to the body," are those that are drawn phallic-like or with phallic-shaped branches, or those with other sexual symbols, such as a vaginal symbol in a tire swing hanging from a branch of the tree, or with a hole or opening in the trunk. In the "avoider" approach at this level, tree branches are depicted as broken or cut off; the tree is depicted with falling or rotting fruit; or there is a knot hole or some other type of trunk injury.

A tree that "belongs to society," so to speak, is drawn as a strong, showy, or otherwise ornate specimen, whereas the avoider's trees are those with large trunks and a small branch system or those with branches but few or no leaves. At higher levels, the tree is drawn as friendly, nourishing, and/or protective. It may provide food and a home for animals. Again, harmony with the environment is often symbolized by the inclusion of mountains, flowers, and the like.

Predicting Aggressive Acting Out

The clinical prediction of acting out—that is, harming the self or others—is sometimes difficult to predict. Nevertheless, there are a number of content and stylistic signs that are highly related to acting out. The following quote by Hammer (1968) sets the stage for a discussion of the prediction of acting out using the DAP. He states:

> Generally, regarding acting-out, we may state that the stronger, the more frank, the more direct (and hence unsublimated) the expression of impulses which break through in the projective drawings, the more the defensive and adaptive operations of the ego may be presumed to be insufficient in their assimilative function, and the more the likelihood of acting-out. (p. 382)

This is an important principle in determining whether certain unconscious materials may become evident in behavior. An examination of the opposite-sex drawing may also offer clues to these questions. For example, if the female is drawn in an aggressive, hostile, negative, and/or fearful manner, it might be possible to speculate that both the source of the problem as well as the object of the negative expression may be focused on the female. An examination of the style and content of the thematic material collected with the drawings may help to support these notions, as would other thematic materials in the battery (e.g., the TAT).

Patients who portray direct acting out in their drawings are likely to act out in their everyday functioning. For example, Hammer (1986) includes a drawing of an adolescent boy who was referred for truancy, rebelliousness, and breaking school rules. He drew a picture of a man spitting on the street, next to a "No spitting" sign. Hammer states, "His adding the sign, 'No Spitting,' just so that the drawn person can disobey it, clearly parallels the subject's seeking out rules and regulations merely to break them, to prove to himself and others that they do not apply to him, that he is outside the sphere that authority encompasses, that he is bigger and better than the rules and the people who make them" (p. 244). When this adolescent was asked to draw the most unpleasant thing he could think of (the Unpleasant Concept Test), he drew a male drawing, tagged "Dad," with an angry expression, a phallic-like nose, a penis hanging out of his trousers, and a sword through the figure (Figure 6–16). It is not too difficult to understand the perceived source of this adolescent's anger.

Another illustration of direct acting out on paper is a case illustrated by Hammer (1986) of a boy who crushed baby chicks with the heel of his foot, tried to burn a cow, picked up baby pigs with a pitchfork, and released a tractor so it would roll down a hill, in an attempt to injure children. Note his tree drawing in Figure 6–17. It has spear-like branches, thorn-like leaves, and a

Figure 6–16   Angry, Acting-Out Adolescent Boy Draws "Dad" in Response to Instructions to Draw the "Most Unpleasant Thing"

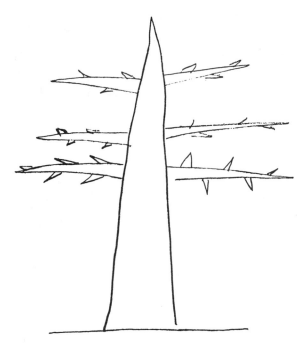

**Figure 6–17   A "Tree" by an Angry 12-Year-Old Boy Who Engaged in
Destructive Activities and Who Killed Animals**

Source: From E. Hammer in *Projective Techniques in Personality Assessment* by A. Rabin (Ed.),
1968, New York: Springer. Copyright 1968 Springer Publishing Company, Inc., New York
10012. Used by permission.

pointed trunk, all of which indicate a highly angry, aggressive stance, telling
others to stay away or be damaged.

The drawing of an adolescent boy who recently mugged a fellow student
for money is illustrated in Figure 6–18. Note the aggressively pointed shoulders, the weapons, the piercing eye and sharp nose, the primitive phallic feet,
all of which suggest that the adolescent who made the drawing is attempting
to prove himself aggressive, dangerous, and ready for violence. Note also the
vertical imbalance, described earlier in this chapter as an index of psychopathology and emotional instability.

Those H-T-P drawings that indicate extreme compulsiveness and rigidity (e.g., indicated through excessive detailing; very exact drawings; drawings
with rigid, repetitious details; drawings executed with unusual, exacting control and carefulness) are said to reflect the patient's efforts to severely overcontrol feelings of inner chaos or a similar impending feeling from the outside
world. Sometimes the body is drawn in an extremely rigid and erect position,
with legs pressed together and arms held closely at the sides. These patients
are making herculean attempts to contain impulses, and when this defensive
stance is momentarily relaxed, the underlying, overcontrolled impulses erupt

Figure 6–18   Drawing of a Man by an Adolescent Boy Who Recently Mugged a Fellow Student

Source: From E. Hammer in *Projective Techniques in Personality Assessment* by A. Rabin (Ed.), 1968, New York: Springer. Copyright 1968 Springer Publishing Company, Inc., New York 10012. Used by permission.

in an uncontrolled fashion, resulting in impulsive acting out. An example of these strained efforts to control impulses is illustrated in Figure 6–19 from a case by Hammer (1986). The 15-year-old male who completed the drawing had threatened to kill his mother. Note the strained facial expression, the head tensely pulled to one side, the efforts to restrict the hands and arms, as if they were tied together. The strained efforts to control rage suggests the probability of a fatal eruption.

Daum (1983) has attempted to differentiate between those figure-drawing characteristics that differentiate the aggressive from the withdrawn adolescent male delinquent. Of the indices that have been suggested to be related to aggression (large head, "slash-line" mouth, teeth, chin emphasis, squared shoulders, muscular reinforced arms with broad shoulders, fists, talon-like fingers, feet emphasis, pointed feet, toes on a clothed figure, wide stance) and those that are said to indicate withdrawal (omission of facial features, arms omitted, dim facial features, profile view), only squared shoulders, omission

Figure 6–19   Drawing of a 15-Year-Old-Male Who Threatened to Kill His Mother

Source: From E. Hammer in *Projective Techniques in Personality Assessment* by A. Rabin (Ed.), 1968, New York: Springer. Copyright 1968 Springer Publishing Company, Inc., New York 10012. Used by permission.

of facial features, and dim facial features discriminated between these two groups. "Slash-line" mouth differentiated the aggressive delinquent from a nondelinquent control group and omission of facial features and omission of arms differentiated the withdrawn delinquent group from the nondelinquent control group.

Hammer (1986) also discusses the presence of dissociation in figure drawings, which he argues, is one element in the prediction of acting out of aggressive, hostile impulses. Dissociation can be present in drawings in several different ways. The most pathognomonic way is in "incongruities between the graphic drawing and the verbal description of it" (p. 256). Note, for example, the following figure (Figure 6–20) drawn by a 34-year-old man who was facing a prison sentence for acting out, surprisingly, not against a person but for theft. Nevertheless, his underlying anger was easily seen in his demeanor. His denial of the anger in the drawing surprised the writer. When he was asked to describe the person he drew, the patient indicted that it was happy man. When the examiner asked him to describe the expression on the man's face, the patient indicated that he was smiling. When the examiner pressed him, the patient continued to deny that the drawing looked angry, adding that the man had a smile underneath the beard. The reader can decide for himself or herself whether the patient was dissociated from his angry feelings. In his

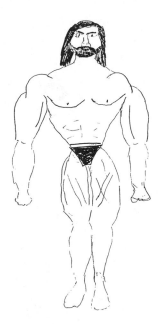

Figure 6–20   Drawing of a 34-Year-Old-Man Who Had Committed a Crime

Source: From E. Hammer in *Projective Techniques in Personality Assessment* by A. Rabin (Ed.), 1968, New York: Springer. Copyright 1968 Springer Publishing Company, Inc. New York 10012. Used by permission.

Figure 6–21   A Case of Dissociation of Hostile Impulses, in an Adolescent

Source: From E. Hammer in *Projective Techniques in Personality Assessment* by A. Rabin (Ed.), 1968, New York: Springer. Copyright 1968 Springer Publishing Company, Inc., New York 10012. Used by permission.

presentation to the examiner, he was extremely friendly and overly respectful, attempting to please in an ingratiating manner.

The drawing itself may indicate dissociation, like (Figure 6–21), where
"its massive, highly aggressive mechanical-looking hands, attached as mere
appendages at the end of the arms" (p. 258) illustrates dissociation. The au-
tomaton-like quality of this figure, depicted with distinct aggressive urges, indicates that these urges will probably be acted out automatically, because
they are not integrated with the rest of the personality.

Another way in which to predict aggressive acting out is to compare the
achromatic and chromatic drawings concerning the comparative degree of aggressiveness seen in the two sets of drawings. For example, if there is aggressiveness suggested in the achromatic drawing, which is more prominently displayed in the chromatic drawings, it is taken as a sign that the patient will act
out the aggression in emotionally charged situations. The clinician must therefore consider the social-interpersonal setting in which the patient operates in
order to be more definitive concerning the prediction of aggressive behavior.

THE KINETIC FAMILY DRAWING TECHNIQUE (K-F-D)

The use of family drawings as assessment instruments has been described
and advocated by a number of writers (Appel, 1931; DiLeo, 1970; Hammer,
1958; Hulse, 1951; Koppitz, 1968). However, a major change in approach was
taken when Burns and Kaufman (1970) introduced action instructions to the
task of drawing the family. Rather than ask the child to "draw a family" or to
"draw your family," as others (Hulse, 1951, 1952; Reznikoff & Reznikoff, 1956)
had done, Burns asked children to "draw your family doing *something*"; he
specifically asked the child to draw with "some kind of action." This seemingly
minor modification of the instructions results in surprisingly revealing data
concerning family dynamics, allowing a clearer picture to emerge of interpersonal interactions and emotional relationships among family members. Clinical comparisons of the K-F-D with the DAP or the K-F-D often reveal conflicts and difficulties when the other two procedures indicate the absence of
problems. According to Burns (Burns, 1982; Burns & Kaufman, 1970, 1972)
the K-F-D allows one to see the self as it is reflected and expressed in the family; it enables the child to depict the family as a functioning, active unit, and
allows the clinician to see the child's impressions of these interactions among
family members.

Advantages of the K-F-D

Advantages include the following:

1. The K-F-D is a very useful tool to allow the clinician to obtain a quick
understanding of the patient's view of the family and his or her position in
that family.

2. The K-F-D allows the clinician to obtain a relatively quick understanding of interaction patterns, dynamics, and relationship patterns in the family as the patient sees them.

3. The K-F-D is a useful instrument in assisting various educational, social service, and legal agencies in making decisions about the patient (e.g., custody decisions, adoption decisions, foster home placement decisions, school placement decisions, and probation decisions).

4. The K-F-D is useful in understanding the patient's symptoms in reference to family dynamics. It is often possible to understand the presenting complaint when the family dynamics are illustrated graphically on the page.

5. The K-F-D is often a very useful vehicle in communicating with the patient concerning family problems and issues. It is especially useful in focusing a discussion on self-evaluation in the family setting, the patient's perceived role in the family, and his or her view of the family problems and family assets.

6. Since the K-F-D is a concrete representation of the patient's feelings, it is often useful in allowing other family members (e.g., parents) to understand and appreciate the patient's feelings and experiences more clearly. This writer has utilized the K-F-D to inform parents of their child's view of them and of the family interactions and relationships. The graphic illustration provides concrete visual evidence of the problem. The result is that the parents are usually more cooperative in changing family relationship patterns and in attending more directly to the child's needs.

7. The K-F-D illuminates the effects of culture and subculture as they shape the family and impact the patient.

8. The K-F-D is useful in determining identification patterns within the family, as they are perceived by the patient. For example, which child stands next to which parent, which child is looking at which person, and who is drawn most like the parent (or another important family member) may be useful measures of identification within the family unit.

9. The K-F-D is useful in providing the clinician with longitudinal developmental data concerning the pattern of changes in family relationships over time.

10. The K-F-D can be used to give the clinician a view of the patient's impression.

Instructions

Since the introduction of the kinetic or movement aspects of the drawing procedure dramatically changes the drawing experience for the child, it is important to distinguish between the traditional Family Drawing Test (Hammer, 1958; Hulse, 1951, 1952; Koppitz, 1968), which asks the child to "draw a picture of your whole family; you can draw it any way you want" (Koppitz, 1983, p. 425), and the Kinetic Family Drawing Test (K-F-D), which asks the child to "draw *everyone* in your family, *including* you, doing something" (Burns, 1982; Burns & Kaufman, 1970, 1972). The difference in directions is quite important. In the Family Drawing Test (FDT) the child has more freedom, compared with the K-F-D, to draw anyone he or she wants, in any way he or she chooses; FDT instructions allow the child more freedom to show meaningful variations, especially in the area of omissions of people or of body parts, or the inclusion of nonfamily members (Koppitz, 1983). On the other hand, the K-F-D allows the clinician to get a more meaningful glimpse of the child's view of the dynamic relationships among family members and the child's adaptive and defensive responses to the forces and actions of the various family members. What may be lost in the less projective directions of the K-F-D are more than made up for by the active glimpse we get into the child's view of their family dynamics (Handler & Habenicht, 1994).

Burns suggests the following directions for K-F-D administration: "Draw a picture of everyone in your family, including you, *doing* something. Try to draw whole people, not cartoons or stick people. Remember, make everyone doing something—some kind of action" (Burns & Kaufman, 1970, pp. 19–20). As with the other drawing tasks, an 8½ × 11-inch piece of paper is placed in front of the child, typically held horizontally, to give the child more room. A #2 pencil is used, with an eraser on it.

As with other drawing techniques, it is important to record the child's verbalizations while drawing, as well as the order of the figures drawn. In addition, a postdrawing inquiry is necessary so that the examiner can learn "who is who" in the drawing and so that the activities may be explained. This author often begins by asking a general question, such as, "What's going on in this picture?" Additional questions are asked to clarify and amplify.

Burns's contention that changing the drawing instructions to add action makes the drawing task more projective and therefore more clinically useful is illustrated in the following case of a 13-year-old girl. The child was brought to the hospital for various complaints, including headaches, abdominal pain, and fainting. Figure 6–22 illustrates her family drawing using the instructions, "Draw a family." Note the relatively rigid, stylized approach, with this drawing request. When asked to draw her family "doing something" (Figure 6–23), she became visibly uneasy and asked the examiner if she could put the family members in separate rooms. She then put herself in a separate room, and enclosed her father far away from her. Father's face is turned away, and it is difficult for anyone, especially father, to reach the patient. In order to reach her, family members must move through a maze and up the winding stairs. It was later determined that the father had sexually molested all the children and was institutionalized.

Interpretation

Unfortunately, many of the formal scoring variables proposed by Burns are not well supported by research (Handler & Habenicht, 1994). For example, the style of arranging the figures on the page was said to reflect the style of defensive functioning. Burns also set up a system to interpret the symbols employed and the actions utilized by the drawn figures to communicate and to

Figure 6–22   Drawing of a 13-Year-Old Girl with Somatic Symptoms, When Asked to "Draw a Family"

Source: From *Kinetic Family Drawings* by R. Burns and S. Kaufman, 1970, New York: Brunner/Mazel. Copyright 1970 and reprinted with permission from Brunner/Mazel, Inc.

illuminate relationships. Burns's most recent scoring method (Burns, 1982) utilizes four major categories: Actions; Distances, Barriers, and Positions; Physical Characteristics of the Figures; and Styles. *Actions* refers to the content or theme of the drawing (e.g., the type of activity depicted for each figure). Burns has grouped the possible K-F-D actions into activities that symbolize cooperation, communication, masochism, narcissism, nurturance, sadism, or tension. The *Physical Characteristics* category deals with the formal aspects of the drawings (e.g., the inclusion of essential body parts, the size of each figure, the size of various body parts, facial expressions). *Distances, Barriers, and Positions* (e.g., number of barriers between mother and father, mother and child; the direction faced by each figure; the distance from one figure to another) and *Styles* refer to the organization of the figures on the page. Style variables, said by Burns to indicate psychopathology/emotional disturbance, include:

1. *Compartmentalization* (intentional separation of family figures through the use of lines)

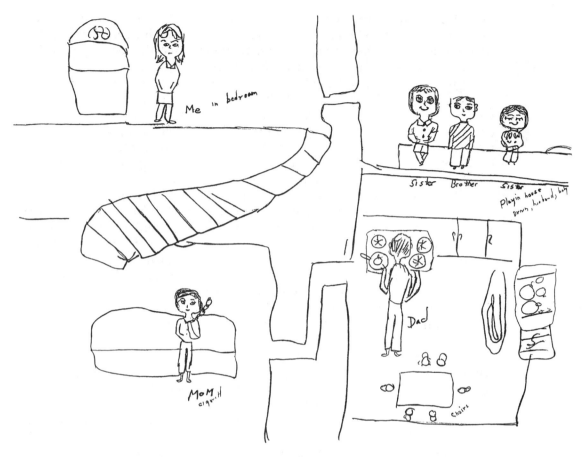

Labels within image: Me in bedroom · Sister · Brother · Sister · Playin house (mom, husband, boy) · Dad · MoM, H cigaret · Chairs

Figure 6–23 K-F-D of the Same 13-Year-Old Girl, When Asked to "Draw Your Family, Doing Something"

Source: From *Kinetic Family Drawings* by R. Burns and S. Kaufman, 1970, New York: Brunner/Mazel. Copyright 1970 and reprinted with permission from Brunner/Mazel, Inc.

2. *Edging* (placement of all family figures on the perimeter of the paper in rectangular style)
3. *Encapsulation* (encapsulating one or more figure by lines or objects)
4. *Folding Compartmentalization* (folding the paper into segments and then placing individual figures within each segment)
5. *Bottom Lining* (more than one line covering the entire bottom of the drawing)
6. *Top Lining* (more than one line covering the entire top of the drawing)
7. *Underlining Individual Figures* (lines immediately below a standing individual or individuals)
8. *Bird's Eye View* (presentation of the drawings from a bird's eye or aerial view)

Many researchers have utilized other variables in the interpretive process (e.g., distortion of body parts, line quality, and sexual differentiation). Some writers have employed variables from DAP interpretation, such as the Koppitz variables mentioned earlier in this chapter.

In order to interpret the K-F-D accurately, it is important to understand the age and sex-related changes that occur as girls and boys mature. The review of the literature by Handler and Habenicht describes these changes. For example, younger children (6 to 8 years old) pictured themselves more often interacting, whereas older children (9 to 12 years old) drew themselves not interacting. Adolescents typically draw themselves and family members in isolated situations. Thus, an interpretation of these findings that would indicate pathology, other than the typical teenage need for isolation, would be inappropriate. Although Burns and Kaufman (1970, 1972) have stated that "style" variables indicate defensiveness or psychopathology, one must see the presence of these variables in K-F-Ds of adolescents as normal techniques for coping and for survival as a teenager, and therefore as positive, adaptive indices. Perhaps this is why some researchers have found more of these so-called pathology indices in K-F-Ds of normal adolescents compared with abnormal adolescents (McPhee & Wegner, 1976; Monahan, 1986; Thompson, 1975). These findings indicate the adolescent's healthy need for individuation, independence, and separation from the family, in efforts toward self-actualization.

Children from various cultural and racial subgroups also draw somewhat differently. Handler and Habenicht (1944) review many studies in this area and describe differences in K-F-D drawings of children from a variety of groups, both in the United States and in other countries. These authors indicate that the population of the United States is composed of many cultural subgroups. The influence of culture can be observed in the K-F-Ds of the children from these cultural subgroups, reflecting different patterns of family dynamics that may be quite different from "mainstream" U.S. culture. Those who interpret K-F-Ds should be aware of these influences before they interpret a patient's K-F-D. Handler and Habenicht discuss the research in this area in an attempt to guide the clinician in his or her interpretation.

Many of the nonsignificant findings in the literature concerning the K-F-D are the result of rather poor research procedures. For example, researchers often utilize a single K-F-D variable in an attempt to correlate it with a specific behavior. The interpreter must avoid such an approach, as Reynolds (1978) cautions:

> The mere listing of clinical indicators and their possible interpretive domains is in no way sufficient to interpret the K-F-D properly. Individual signs should not be interpreted in isolation or as absolutes. The best use will be made of the K-F-D when viewed in its gestalt and interpreted in view of the family background, age, sex, intellectual level, and current behavioral status of the child at home and at school, as well as in conjunction with the other projective data. (p. 490)

Each variable must be interpreted in the context of the others. For example, the size variable has typically been seen as an indication of power and authority within the family. Thus, the relative size of the drawings is said to indicate who the child feels is more powerful and who the child feels has little power. Of course, the age of the child must be taken into account. More important, however, is that size is not necessarily related to power and authority. It could also be related to need, or to increased value or desire, as is sometimes seen in children at different ages, or perhaps to various patterns of family dynamics. In addition, to complicate matters even more, if power and authority are indeed the correct interpretation in one case, this power may be experienced as benign and protective, or as controlling and oppressive.

An examination of other variables can often help the interpreter to differentiate between these two possibilities. For example, if a child draws the mother as taller than the father, but utilizes encapsulation or compartmentalization in depicting her, the interpreter might feel more comfortable in the interpretation of larger size representing power and authority, albeit of the negative kind. Which figure is drawn next to the other figures might have something to say about the strength of the relationship. The position of the figure is also important. For example, sometimes a figure is placed in a precarious position, which is usually an indication that there is tension associated with the family member represented in that position. Sometimes a figure is omitted or it is placed on the back of the paper, representing unresolved conflicts with that family member.

This writer has come to interpret the K-F-D in a more holistic, qualitative manner rather than with a quantitative sign approach. As indicated in the DAP discussion, Tharinger and Stark (1990) found the holistic, qualitative approach superior to the quantitative approach in the identification of children with emotional disorders. In another study (Hackbarth, 1988), the objective scores did not differentiate between the K-F-Ds of sexually abused and nonsexually abused children, but a global rating of "like to live in this family" significantly differentiated the K-F-Ds of the two groups. This variable reflected the raters' impression of positive family relationships and the presence of an environment for personal growth, compared with a feeling that there was something wrong or hurtful in the family.

It is also important to understand that the K-F-D does not always represent the family as it really exists, but rather, as the child believes it to be or wishes it to be. For example, Shaw (1989) found a wide discrepancy between the number of children who reported that their fathers did not live with them and the number who drew a father in their K-F-D. A similar observation was made by Shiller (1986), who found that almost two-thirds of a group of children in sole custody of the mother depicted themselves as engaged in activity with the father, or as a member of an intact family. Thus, it is important that the clinician utilize the K-F-D with an *inquiry* concerning the figures depicted, and with a thorough family history, in order to differentiate between drawings motivated by wish fulfillment and those that represent the child's perception of the family dynamics.

Burns describes the various drawing techniques that children use to express and to deal with conflict. Figure 6–24 illustrates two such techniques,

Figure 6–24   K-F-D of a 12-Year-Old Girl Who was Raped by Her Brother, Illustrating Denial and Avoidance by Scribbling and Omission of Body Parts

Source: From *Kinetic Family Drawings* by R. Burns and S. Kaufman, 1970, New York: Brunner/Mazel. Copyright 1970 and reprinted with permission from Brunner/Mazel, Inc.

scribbling, which is said to indicate body concern and preoccupation, and omission of body parts, as an attempt at denial and avoidance. The 12-year-old girl who drew this K-F-D was raped by her brother, who she represents on the bottom, left. Note that the brother's body is cut off below the waist, by the chair, which is probably the girl's attempt to deny or repress the body area.

Compartmentalization of the figures is another method of dealing with problem relationships, through isolation. Burns also describes the "ironing board X" which the child draws as a way of negating a body area (p. 99). This is illustrated in Figure 6–25. This K-F-D was done by a 16-year-old boy who had fears of staying at home, but only at certain times. Note the shaded area below the waist on the drawings of his sister and mother, showing unusual preoccupation and tension. After obtaining the K-F-D, in a discussion with the boy, it became clear that he would become terrified when he was left alone with his seductive 11-year-old sister. Note that he symbolizes attempts to control sexual impulses in the drawing by the stop sign. Burns and Kaufman (1970) indicated that "the ironing board below the mother, with the "X" through the shaded area, is a constant theme with children attempting to control sexual impulse" (p. 98). Note that the father is depicted as leaving the family; perhaps this is why the boy needs all the external controls depicted in the drawing.

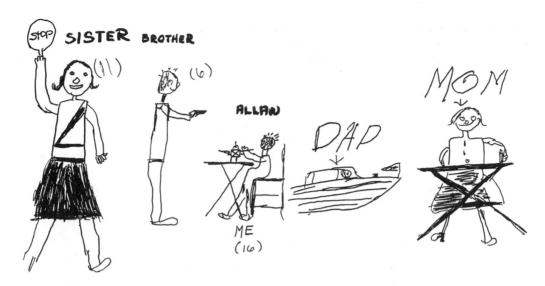

Figure 6–25   K-F-D of a 16-Year-Old Boy Illustrating the "Ironing Board X" as an Attempt to Negate a Body Area

Source: From *Kinetic Family Drawings* by R. Burns and S. Kaufman, 1970, New York: Brunner/Mazel. Copyright 1970 and reprinted with permission from Brunner/Mazel, Inc.

Figure 6–26   K-F-D of a 14-Year-Old Boy Depicting Problems of Adjustment Due to Blending of Two Families

Source: From *Kinetic Family Drawings* by R. Burns and S. Kaufman, 1970, New York: Brunner/Mazel. Copyright 1970 and reprinted with permission from Brunner/Mazel, Inc.

The next K-F-D (Figure 6–26) was done by a 14-year-old boy who recently acquired a new stepfather and two stepsisters. He was brought to treatment because he was acting out at home and in the schoolyard. Note that the two-part families are on opposite sides, as in a war; the patient is trying to defend the mother from the intruding stepfather, who seems quite capable of defending himself against the small darts, using a big shield. He has ample aggressive reserve, indicated by his big knife. The boy is rendered harmless by the stepfather's strong shield. The boy's frustration against the perceived power and virility of the stepfather is perhaps the source of his anger and frustration, expressed both at home and at school.

Burns notes that the depiction of lights and sources of heat represent the child's illustration of a need for warmth and love. This includes electric lights as well as the sun. Burns and Kaufman (1972) indicate that snow and coldness depicted in the K-F-D is associated with feelings of depression and suicidal ideation. In a later publication, Burns (1982) indicates that the moon is also a symbol of depression, typically associated with male figures as the source of the depression.

Another interesting K-F-D is the one in Figure 6–27 of a boy with an alcoholic father who had a violent temper. The father is depicted as cutting. Note the shape of his cutting "tool" and the shape of the object being cut, as well as the drawing of the self figure, with legs detached. The father appears to be cutting a penis-shaped object with his "knife," which is also shaped like a penis. The detached legs of the boy who drew the picture is perhaps symbolic of the castration fears he has. This boy has had a very difficult time competing successfully with his father.

Figure 6–27   K-F-D of a Boy Who Had an Alcoholic Father, with a Violent Temper

Source: From *Kinetic Family Drawings* by R. Burns and S. Kaufman, 1970, New York: Brunner/Mazel. Copyright 1970 and reprinted with permission from Brunner/Mazel, Inc.

Burns (1982) lists a number of K-F-D interpretations of objects and themes, along with their clinical interpretations. Many of these interpretations have been validated by clinical observation, but few have been validated experimentally. For example, Burns indicates that balloons indicate need/desire for dominance or escape, while birds are associated with sexual or depressive themes. He indicates that the inclusion of birds is common in those who seek freedom or escape, and that birds' nests are common in regressed patients who yearn for the security of "the nest." While these symbolic interpretations sound plausible, some others sound a bit strained and perhaps farfetched. For example, butterflies is said to indicate "search for elusive love and beauty," cats are said to indicate ambivalence with the mother figure, and drums are said to be a symbol of displaced anger that a child has difficulty expressing openly. Clouds are said to indicate anxiety, clowns supposedly indicate feelings of inferiority, or are a sign that the patient has taken the position of one who cheers up a depressed family. Burns indicates that garbage is found in drawings of children who are upset over the arrival of a new sibling, indicating regressive and/or competitive behavior that is motivated by jealousy.

Indications of a heat source (e.g., sun) or light (e.g., lamp) indicates a preoccupation with a need for warmth and love, whereas fire is said to indicate feelings of anger because needs for love are not being met. Motorcycles are said to be associated with depressive tendencies, as is snow, which is also said to be associated with suicidal feelings. While the drawing of the sun is typical of most young children, and is therefore said to have little diagnostic significance, in older children and adults it is said to indicate need for or insistence on emotional warmth. Burns notes that the depiction of vacuum cleaners is related to a history of oral deprivation or unmet needs. When a mother is depicted as using the vacuum cleaner, the interpretation focuses on the mother as a powerful or controlling figure. Water themes are said to reflect depressive tendencies.

Feelings or "energy" between two people can be represented in several ways—for example, who may be drawn looking at the other, or the opposite, who may be blocked or walled-off from which family member(s). Burns indicates that balls and ball playing represent a symbol of the interaction between two people, probably of a competitive nature. Underlining is said to be a sign that the person represented by the figure feels unstable in his or her environment and is attempting to create a more stable environment. The reader should remember that these hypotheses are derived either from symbolic interpretation and/or clinical observation. Alternative explanations for the variables and items discussed should always be considered.

Detection of Sexual Abuse and of Sexual Abusers

A number of studies have sought to determine whether there are any drawing indices that are specific to sexual abuse victims. In general, few have been found. Sexual abuse is not typically symbolized *directly* in drawings. Rather, the effects of such abuse are symbolized according to the individual effects of such abuse on each victim. Such effects are experienced somewhat differently for each person, and therefore one would only see general effects, such as increased tension or anxiety. In addition, the sexual abuse typically exists in a family atmosphere of tension and conflict, which is ordinarily symbolized in the drawings. Perhaps this is why Hibbard and Hartman (1990) found that although there were no significant differences for specific indicators, the drawings of abused children had significantly more emotional conflict indices, compared with those of presumably nonsexually victimized children.

Johnston and Johnston (1986) compared figure drawings of male child molesters, compared with those of a control group. They found that the overall quality of the molesters' drawings was significantly poorer than those of the control group. In addition, the molesters' drawings showed more gender confusion. The authors view these differences as indicating a sense of sexual confusion, psychosexual immaturity, and fear of women. In addition, they note that the child molesters' drawings reflect denial and evasiveness; they drew people with blank or hidden eyes, and hidden or missing hands.

German (1986) tested 40 female-adolescent incest victims, ages 12 to 18, with the K-F-D. She found that 37 of the 40 subjects drew parents not interacting; 33 of the 40 subjects drew each family member performing a different activity; 28 of the 40 drew barriers between the self and any other family members; 25 drew the self isolated or encapsulated and had anxiety indices in their drawings; 22 drawings contained aggressive indices expressed toward the father; and 21 had missing body parts. Sexual themes were present in half the drawings.

Hackbarth (1988) compared the K-F-Ds of sexually abused children (ages 6 to 13) and their mothers, with those obtained from matched control groups of children and mothers. Drawing characteristics did not differentiate among the groups, but an impressionistic score called "like to live in family" significantly differentiated the four groups. Similar findings were reported by Jordan (1985), who found only 3 of 43 objective scoring variables distinguished the K-F-Ds from abused 11- to 16-year-old female adolescents from a nonabused control group, but clinicians were able to differentiate between the two groups using their clinical judgment about the drawings. A more recent study (Rodgers, 1992) compared K-F-Ds of 81 children, ages 12 to 17, in treatment as victims or perpetrators of sexual abuse. Using a stepwise multiple regression analysis, Rodgers found that the presence of beds, the omission of torso, underclothed or naked figures, vaguely drawn hands, and objects drawn in the mouth were found more often in the drawings of the sexually abused and abusers than in the control group. The sexually abused and abuser group made drawings that were either very sexual or very asexual. They either included much detail, including sexual detail, or they drew very basic drawings, omitting most of the detail.

Howitt (1984) asked groups of clinicians, clinical psychology graduate students, and family counselors to correctly identify K-F-Ds from mothers who were alleged child abusers compared with several control group mothers. Although all the judges were not correct significantly more often than chance expectation, when the criterion of agreement by two out of three judges was used, correct classifications ranged from 80 percent for the clinicians to 92 percent correct for the clinical psychology graduate students.

It is important to note that the presence of any of the drawing variables described here *does not* indicate that the patient has been abused or is an abuser. As indicated earlier, these very same signs can also indicate other problems or patient difficulties.

SUMMARY

In a review of a book by Jonathan Miller, entitled *States of Mind,* Rosemary Dinnage (1983) comments that a primary theme in Miller's book is that the traditional picture of the mind as a mere mirror of nature has given way to a model that describes the mind as an active assimilator of various forces and experiences in all aspects of human functioning, including artistic creativity. The second major theme concerns the reawakening of interest in an unconsciousness that stresses innate skills and strategies that human beings typically utilize in daily functioning, without being aware that they are doing so. The clinical use of the DAP, the H-T-P, and the K-F-D is quite consistent with these views, as well as with the more traditional conceptualization of unconscious representation through symbolism. By observing the artist producing the drawing, by listening to the artist's comments as he or she draws, and by analyzing the artist's productions, clinicians may be able to catch a kaleidoscopic glimpse of that person in various degrees of human splendor and complexity.

Drawings of a person (and of a house and a tree) are mental images, typically of one's self, displayed graphically. Therefore, they could contain all of the richness and complexity that is themselves, given that they can effectively conceptualize themselves in this medium as a life experience. The manner in which they experience themselves, the style in which they present this experience of themselves, and feelings about such public and private representation are all reflected in their drawings. Some people are quite adept at projecting these conscious, unconscious, stylistic, and phenomenological messages.

Attitudes about the past, the present, and the future may all be involved in the drawing. The clinician can choose to focus his or her attention on any one of these aspects, but a picture of the "self-in-the world" emerges only when clinicians understand how the stylistic and symbolic representations in the drawing tell them about a person's past, how that person feels about himself or herself in the present, and his or her feelings about what the future holds.

Although DAP, H-T-P, and K-F-D research has not been as encouraging as the research-oriented psychologist would like, there are enough positive studies to encourage a researcher to seek more innovative ways of demonstrating the utility of drawings in the process of understanding people in their complexity. In fact, this writer believes that many studies are poorly conceived because they do not parallel the ways in which the drawings are used in the clinical situation. For example, the drawings are typically investigated alone, taken out of context, and individual variables and signs are analyzed rather than allowing for contextual interpretation. A research design that parallels the clinical diagnostic situation, that focuses on the clinician doing the drawing interpretation (the interpretive process) rather than on the drawing elements themselves, might be a more fruitful approach, especially since the data seem to indicate that some clinicians are quite talented in this process, while others do quite poorly. Recent findings cited in this chapter concerning an experiential approach to the interpretation of drawings are quite encouraging in this regard. Rather than test the clinical utility of the DAP, H-T-P, or K-F-D with clinicians who merely have training and/or experience, focus should instead be on excellent interpreters who demonstrate outstanding ability to interpret the drawings.

Finally, it should be noted that Burley and Handler (1994) found that empathy was necessary but not sufficient for good DAP interpretation. It is not enough to be interested, involved, and well intentioned. Cognitive flexibility and creativity are necessary in addition. Efforts on the clinician's part to facilitate the development of these skills should result in substantially better skill in the clinical interpretation of drawings.

REFERENCES

Albee, G., & Hamlin, R. (1950). An investigation of the reliability and validity judgments inferred from drawings. *Journal of Clinical Psychology, 5,* 389–392.

Appel, K. (1931). Drawings by children as aids to personality studies. *American Journal of Orthopsychiatry, 1,* 129–144.

Attkisson, C., Waidler, V., Jeffery, P., & Lambert, W. (1974). Interrater reliability of the Handler Draw-A-Person scoring. *Perceptual and Motor Skills, 38,* 567–573.

Blatt, S., & Ford, R. (1994). *Therapeutic change.* New York: Plenum Press.

Bolander, K. (1977). *Assessing personality through tree drawings.* New York: Basic Books.

Buck, J. (1948). The H-T-P. *Journal of Clinical Psychology, 4,* 151–159.

Buck, J. (1966). *The House-Tree-Person Technique, revised manual.* Los Angeles: Western Psychological Services.

Burley, T., & Handler, L. (1994). Creativity, empathy and intuition in DAP interpretation. Submitted for publication.

Burns, R. (1982). *Self-growth in families: Kinetic Family Drawings (K-F-D) research and application.* New York: Brunner/Mazel.

Burns, R. (1987). *Kinetic-House-Tree-Person Drawings (K-H-T-P).* New York: Brunner/Mazel.

Burns, R., & Kaufman, S. (1970). *Kinetic Family Drawings (K-F-D): An introduction to understanding children through kinetic drawings.* New York: Brunner/Mazel.

Burns, R., & Kaufman, S. (1972). *Actions, styles, and symbols in Kinetic Family Drawings (K-F-D).* New York: Brunner/Mazel.

Calden, G. (1954). Psychosurgery in a set of schizophrenic identical twins—A psychological study. *Journal of Projective Techniques, 18,* 316–325.

Crenshaw, D., Bohn, S., Hoffman, Matheus, J., & Offenbach, S. (1968). The use of projective methods in research: 1947–1965. *Journal of Projective Techniques and Personality Assessment, 32,* 3–9.

Cressen, R. (1975). Artistic quality of drawings and judges' evaluations of the DAP. *Journal of Personality Assessment, 39,* 132–137.

Currie, S., Holtzman, W., & Swartz, J. (1974). Early indications of personality traits viewed retrospectively. *Journal of School Psychology, 12,* 51–59.

Daum, J. (1983). Emotional indicators in drawings of aggressive and withdrawn male delinquents. *Journal of Personality Assessment, 47,* 243–249.

Dennis, W. (1966). *Group values through children's drawings.* New York: Wiley.

DiLeo, J. (1970). *Young children and their drawings.* New York: Brunner/Mazel.

Dinnage, R. (1983). Review of "States of Mind." *New York Review of Books,* August 18, 36–37.

Eklund, S., Huebner, E., Groman, C., & Michael, R. (1980, April). *The modal assessment battery used by school psychologists in the United States: 1979–1980.* Paper presented at the annual meeting of the National Association of School Psychologists, Washington, DC.

Fox, R. (1952). Psychotherapeutics of alcoholism. In G. Bychowski & J. Despert (Eds.), *Specialized techniques in psychotherapy.* New York: Basic Books.

Freud, S. (1938/1969). The interpretation of dreams. In A. H. Brill (Ed.), *The basic writings of Sigmund Freud.* New York: Modern Library.

Fuller, G., & Goh, D. (1983). Current practices in the assessment of personality and behavior by school psychologists. *School Psychology Review, 12,* 244–249.

Gallese, A., & Spoerl, D. (1954). A comparison of Machover and TAT interpretations. *Journal of Social Psychology, 43,* 73–77.

Gardiner, H. (1974). Human figure drawings as indicators of value development among Thai children. *Journal of Crosscultural Psychology, 5,* 124–130.

German, D. (1986). *The female adolescent incest victim: Personality, self-esteem, and family orientation.* Unpublished doctoral dissertation, Andrews University.

Gilbert, J., & Hall, M. (1962). Changes with age in human figure drawings. *Journal of Gerontology, 17,* 397–404.

Goh, D., Teslow, C., & Fuller, G. (1981). The practice of psychological assessment among school psychologists. *Professional Psychology, 12,* 696–706.

Goodenough, F. (1926). *Measurement of intelligence by drawings.* New York: World Book.

Groves, J., & Fried, P. (1991). Developmental items on children's human figure drawings: A replication and extension of Koppitz to younger children. *Journal of Clinical Psychology, 47,* 140–147.

Gustafson, J., & Waehler, C. (1992). Assessing concrete and abstract thinking with the Draw-A-Person Technique. *Journal of Personality Assessment, 59,* 439–447.

Hackbarth, S. (1988). *A comparison of "Kinetic Family Drawing" variables of sexually abused children, unidentified children, and their mothers.* Unpublished doctoral dissertation, East Texas State University.

Hammer, E. (1954). A comparison of H-T-P's of rapists and pedophiles. *Journal of Projective Techniques, 18,* 346–354.

Hammer, E. (Ed.). (1958). *The clinical application of projective drawings.* Springfield, IL: Charles C. Thomas.

Hammer, E. (1960). The House-Tree-Person (H-T-P) drawings as a projective technique with children. In A. Rabin & M. Haworth (Eds.), *Projective techniques with children* (pp. 258–272). New York: Grune & Stratton.

Hammer, E. (1968). Projective drawings. In A. Rabin (Ed.), *Projective techniques in personality assessment.* New York: Springer.

Hammer, E. (1986). Graphic techniques with children and adolescents. In A. Rabin (Ed.), *Projective techniques for adolescents and children.* New York: Springer.

Handler, L. (1967). Anxiety indexes in projective drawings: A scoring manual. *Journal of Projective Techniques and Personality Assessment, 31,* 46–57.

Handler, L., & Habenicht, D. (1994). The Kinetic Family Drawing technique: A review of the literature. *Journal of Personality Assessment, 63(3),* 440–464.

Handler, L., & Reyher, J. (1964). The effects of stress on the Draw-A-Person Test. *Journal of Consulting Psychology, 28,* 259–264.

Handler, L., & Reyher, J. (1965). Figure drawing anxiety indexes: A review of the literature. *Journal of Personality Assessment, 29,* 305–313.

Handler, L., & Reyher, J. (1966). Relationship between GSR and anxiety indexes in projective drawings. *Journal of Consulting and Clinical Psychology, 30,* 605–607.

Harris, D. (1963). *Children's drawings as a measure of intellectual maturity.* New York: Harcourt, Brace & World.

Harrower, M. (1965). *Psychodiagnostic testing: An empirical approach.* Springfield, IL: Charles C. Thomas.

Hartman, W., & Fithian, M. (1972). *Treatment of sexual dysfunction.* Long Beach, CA: Center for Marital and Sexual Studies.

Hibbard, R., & Hartman, G. (1990). Emotional indicators in human figure drawings of sexually victimized and nonabused children. *Journal of Clinical Psychology, 46,* 211–219.

Holzberg, J., & Wexler, M. (1950). The validity of human form drawings as a measure of personality deviation. *Journal of Projective Techniques, 14,* 343–361.

Howitt, D. (1984). *Kinetic Family Drawings and clinical judgment: An evaluation of judges' ability to differentiate between the K-F-D's of abusing, control, and concerned mothers.* Unpublished doctoral dissertation, University of Windsor.

Hulse, W. (1951). The emotionally disturbed child draws his family. *Quarterly Journal of Child Techniques, 3,* 152–174.

Hulse, W. (1952). Childhood conflict expressed through family drawings. *Journal of Projective Techniques, 16,* 66–79.

Hunt, W. (1946). The future of diagnostic testing in clinical psychology. *Journal of Clinical Psychology, 2,* 311–317.

Jacobson, J., & Handler, L. (1967). Extroversion-introversion and the effects of stress on the Draw-A-Person Test. *Journal of Consulting Psychology, 31,* 343–361.

Jaffé, A. (1964). Symbolism in the visual arts. In C. Jung (Ed.)., *Man and his symbols.* New York: Doubleday.

Johnston, F., & Johnston, S. (1986). Differences between human figure drawings of child molesters and control groups. *Journal of Clinical Psychology, 42,* 638–647.

Jones, L., & Thomas, C. (1964). Studies on figure drawings: Structural and graphic characteristics. *Psychiatric Quarterly Supplement, 38,* 76–110.

Jordan, S. (1985). *A validity study of the Kinetic Family Drawing.* Unpublished doctoral dissertation, Texas Woman's University.

Kissen, M. (1986). Object relations aspects of figure drawings. In M. Kissen (Ed.), *Assessing object relations phenomena* (pp. 175–191). Madison, CT: International Universities Press.

Klepsch, M., & Logie, L. (1982). *Children draw and tell.* New York: Brunner/Mazel.

Koch, C. (1952). *The Tree Test.* New York: Grune & Stratton.

Kohut, H. (1959). Introspection, empathy and psychoanalysis. *American Psychoanalytic Association Journal, 26,* 21–47.

Kohut, H. (1977). *The restoration of self.* New York: International Universities Press.

Koppitz, E. (1968). *Psychological evaluation of children's human figure drawings.* New York: Grune & Stratton.

Koppitz, E. (1983). Projective drawings with children and adolescents. *School Psychology Review, 12,* 421–427.

Koppitz, E. (1984). *Psychological evaluation of human figure drawings by middle school pupils.* New York: Grune & Stratton.

Koppitz, E., & Casullo, M. (1983). Exploring cultural influences on the human figure drawings of young adolescents. *Perceptual Motor Skills, 57,* 479–483.

Koppitz, E., & deMoreau, M. (1968). A comparison of emotional indicators on human figure drawings of children from Mexico and from the United States. *Revista Interamericano de Psicologià, 2,* 41–48.

Kot, J., Handler, L., Toman, K., & Hilsenroth, M. (1994, April). *The psychological assessment of homeless men.* Paper presented at the meeting of the Society for Personality Assessment, Chicago.

Kris, E. (1952). *Psychoanalytic explorations in art.* New York: International Universities Press.

Levenberg, S. (1975). Professional training, psychodiagnostic skill, and Kinetic Family Drawings. *Journal of Personality Assessment, 34,* 389–393.

Levy, S. (1950). Figure drawing as a projective test. In E. Abt & L. Ballak (Eds.), *Projective psychology.* New York: Alfred A. Knopf.

Levy, S., Lomax, J., & Minsky, R. (1963). An underlying variable in the clinical evaluation of drawings of human figures. *Journal of Consulting Psychology, 27,* 308–312.

Lewinsohn, P. (1965). Psychological correlates of overall quality of figure drawings. *Journal of Consulting Psychology, 29,* 504–512.

Lewinsohn, P., & May, J. (1963). A technique for the judgment of emotion from figure drawings. *Journal of Projective Techniques, 27,* 79–85.

Lubin, B., Larsen, R., & Matarazzo, J. (1984). Patterns of psychological test usage in the United States: 1935–1982. *American Psychologist, 39,* 451–454.

Lubin, B., Wallis, R., & Paine, C. (1971). Patterns of psychological test usage in the United States: 1935–1969. *Professional Psychology, 2,* 70–74.

Lyons, J. (1955). The scar on the H-T-P tree. *Journal of Clinical Psychology, 11,* 267–270.

Machover, K. (1949). *Personality projection in the drawing of the human figure.* Springfield, IL: Charles C. Thomas.

Machover, K. (1951). Drawing of the human figure: A method of personality investigation. In H. Anderson & G. Anderson (Eds.), *An introduction to projective techniques.* New York: Prentice-Hall.

Machover, K. (1960). Sex differences in the developmental pattern of children as seen in human figure drawings. In A. Rabin & M. Haworth (Eds.), *Projective techniques with children.* New York: Grune & Stratton.

Maloney, M., & Glasser, A. (1982). An evaluation of the clinical utility of the Draw-A-Person Test. *Journal of Clinical Psychology, 38,* 183–190.

McPhee, J., & Wegner, K. (1976). Kinetic-Family-Drawing styles and emotionally disturbed childhood behavior. *Journal of Personality Assessment, 40,* 487–491.

Meili-Dworetzki, G. (1982). *Spielarten des Menschenbildes: Ein Vergleich der Menschenzeichnungen Japanischer und schweizerischer Kinder.* Bern: Hans Huber.

Monahan, M. (1986). Situational influences on children's Kinetic Family Drawings. *Dissertation Abstracts International, 46,* 4444.

Nichols, R., & Strumpfer, D. (1962). A factor analysis of Draw-A-Person test scores. *Journal of Consulting Psychology, 26,* 156–161.

Nordquist, V., & Handler, L. (1969, April). *The relationship between heart rate and figure drawing anxiety indexes.* Paper presented at the Southeastern Psychological Association Convention, New Orleans, LA.

Ogdon, D. (1977). *Psychodiagnostics and personality assessment: A handbook* (2nd ed.). Los Angeles: Western Psychological Services.

Piotrowski, C., Sherry, D., & Keller, J. (1985). Psychodiagnostic test usage: A survey of the Society for Personality Assessment. *Journal of Personality Assessment, 49,* 115–119.

Piotrowski, C., & Zalewski, C. (1993). Training in psychodiagnostic testing in APA-approved Psy.D. and Ph.D. clinical psychology programs. *Journal of Personality Assessment, 61(2),* 394–405.

Prout, H. (1983). School psychologists and social-emotional assessment techniques: Patterns in training and use. *School Psychology Review, 12,* 35–38.

Reynolds, C. (1978). A quick scoring guide to the interpretation of children's Kinetic Family Drawings (KFD). *Psychology in the School, 15,* 489–492.

Reznikoff, M., & Reznikoff, H. (1956). The Family Drawing Test: A comparative study of children's drawings. *Journal of Clinical Psychology, 12,* 167–169.

Roback, H. (1968). Human figure drawings: Their utility in the clinical psychologist's armamentarium for personality assessment. *Psychological Bulletin, 70,* 1–19.

Robins, C., Blatt, S., & Ford, R. (1991). Changes in human figure drawings during intensive treatment. *Journal of Personality Assessment, 57,* 477–497.

Rodgers, P. (1992). *A correlational-developmental study of sexual symbols, actions, and themes in children's Kinetic Family and Human Figure Drawings.* Unpublished doctoral dissertation, Andrews University.

Saarni, C., & Azara, V. (1977). Developmental analysis of human figure drawings in adolescence, young adulthood, and middle age. *Journal of Personality Assessment, 41,* 31–38.

Sarrel, P., & Sarrel, L. (1979). *Sexual unfolding.* Boston: Little, Brown.

Sarrel, P., Sarrel, L., & Berman, S. (1981). Using the Draw-A-Person (DAP) Test in sex therapy. *Journal of Sex & Marital Therapy, 7,* 163–183.

Schachtel, E. (1984/1959). *Metamorphosis: On the development of affect, perception, attention, and memory.* New York: Da Capo Press.

Schildkrout, M., Shenker, I., & Sonnenblick, M. (1972). *Human figure drawings in adolescence.* New York: Brunner/Mazel.

Schmidt, L., & McGowan, J. (1959). The differentiation of human figure drawings. *Journal of Consulting Psychology, 23,* 129–133.

Scribner, C., & Handler, L. (1987). The interpreter's personality in Draw-A-Person interpretation: A study of interpersonal style. *Journal of Personality Assessment, 51,* 112–122.

Scribner, C., & Handler, L. (1993, March). *Intuitive DAP interpreters: An investigation of the lifestyles of good and poor interpreters.* Paper presented at the midwinter meeting of the Society for Personality Assessment, San Francisco, CA.

Shaw, J. (1989). *A developmental study on the Kinetic Family Drawing for a nonclinic, Black-child population in the Midwestern region of the United States.* Unpublished doctoral dissertation, Andrews University.

Sherman, L. (1958). The influence of artistic ability on judgments of patient and nonpatient status from human figure drawings. *Journal of Projective Techniques, 22,* 318–340.

Shiller, V. (1986). Loyalty conflicts and family relationships in latency age boys: A comparison of joint and maternal custody. *Journal of Divorce, 9,* 17–18.

Shneidman, E. (1958). Some relationships between thematic and drawing materials. In E. Hammer (Ed.), *The clinical application of projective drawings.* Springfield, IL: Charles C. Thomas.

Smart, R., & Smart, M. (1975). Group values shown in preadolescents' drawings in five English-speaking countries. *Journal of Social Psychology, 97,* 23–37.

Strumpfer, D., & Nichols, R. (1962). A study of some communicable measures for the evaluation of human figure drawings. *Journal of Projective Techniques, 26,* 342–353.

Sundberg, N. (1961). The practice of psychological testing in clinical services in the United States. *American Psychologist, 16,* 79–83.

Swensen, C. (1957). Empirical evaluations of human figure drawings. *Psychological Bulletin, 54,* 431–466.

Swensen, C. (1968). Empirical evaluations of human figure drawings: 1957–1966. *Psychological Bulletin, 70,* 20–44.

Tharinger, D., & Stark, K. (1990). A qualitative versus quantitative approach to evaluating the Draw-A-Person and Kinetic Family Drawing: study of mood- and anxiety-disorder children. *Psychological Assessment: Journal of Consulting and Clinical Psychology, 2,* 365–375.

Thomas, C. (1966). *An atlas of figure drawing variables.* Baltimore: The Johns Hopkins Press.

Thompson, L. (1975). *Kinetic Family Drawings of adolescents.* Unpublished doctoral dissertation, California School of Professional Psychology, San Francisco.

Torem, M. Gilbertson, A., & Light, V. (1990). Indications of physical, sexual, and verbal victimization in projective tree drawings. *Journal of Clinical Psychology, 46(6),* 900–906.

Trestman, R., Handler, L., & Pollio, H. (1993, March). *Anxiety indices in figure drawings of cancer patients.* Paper presented at the midwinter meeting of the Society for Personality Assessment, San Francisco, CA.

Urban, W. (1963). *The Draw-A-Person catalogue for interpretive analysis.* Los Angeles: Western Psychological Services.

Urist, J. (1977). The Rorschach test and the assessment of object relations. *Journal of Personality Assessment, 41,* 3–9.

Vukovich, D. (1983). The use of projective assessment by school psychologists. *School Psychology Review, 12,* 358–364.

Wagner, M., & Schubert, H. (1955). *DAP quality scale for late adolescents and young adults.* Kenmore, NY: Delaware Letter Shop.

Weiner, I. (1966). *Psychodiagnosis in schizophrenia.* New York: John Wiley & Sons.

Whitmyre, J. (1953). The significance of artistic excellence in the judgment of adjustment inferred from human figure drawings. *Journal of Consulting Psychology, 17,* 421–424.

Yama, M. (1990). The usefulness of human figure drawings as an index of overall adjustment. *Journal of Personality Assessment, 54,* 78–86.

Zaback, T., & Waehler, C. (1994). Sex of human figure drawings and sex role orientation. *Journal of Personality Assessment, 62(3),* 552–558.

Zaidi, S. (1979). Values expressed in Nigerian children's drawings. *International Journal of Psychology, 14,* 163–169.

Zucker, L. (1948). A case of obesity: Projective techniques before and after treatments. *Journal of Projective Techniques, 12,* 202–215.

7

The Wechsler Intelligence Scale for Children-Third Edition (WISC-III)

P. Michael Politano
A. J. Finch, Jr.

INTRODUCTION

The Wechsler Intelligence Scale for Children—Third Edition (WISC-III; Wechsler, 1991) represents the most recent version of this particular series of children's intelligence tests, following the revised version (WISC-R), published in 1974, and the initial version (WISC), published in 1949. In the intervening years since the 1949 publication, the Wechsler Intelligence Scale for Children has become a frequent integral part of psychological assessment batteries, particularly those conducted in school settings.

At its broader level, psychological assessment is geared toward three objectives: first, to determine if a problem exists; second, to evaluate the scope and magnitude of a problem if one has been determined to exist; and third, to provide information relevant to intervention and/or treatment of the identified problem. Within this broad framework, a psychological assessment should also consolidate previously existing information and highlight those areas where more information is needed.

Objective tests, such as the WISC-III, may be included in such assessment processes depending on the referral question or issues, the setting in which the assessment takes place (e.g., a school, where an intellectual measure is almost always given, versus a psychiatric clinic, where such a measure may be less frequently used), the relevance of available tests for the age of the individual being evaluated, and the type of information required, which in turn is a function of the referral question.

In any assessment process it is important to realize that one is only sampling behavior at a specific time and place. This sampling process can be generalized to the broader range of the individual's behavior only to the extent that the sampling was done accurately, objectively, and intelligently. In the assessment of children, accurate, objective, and intelligent sampling becomes even more critical given childrens' greater potential for variable behavior in response to developmental pressures and given their reduced autonomy limiting their ability to protect their own rights. These differences from adults suggest that any assessment process with children should sample behavior across as many settings and perspectives as possible.

The widespread use of intelligence tests should not be construed to suggest that such tests are accepted without question. The debate over such issues as what intelligence tests measure, the cultural and ethnic biases of such tests, and so on, are far from settled. The debate over what the tests measure and the cultural and ethnic fairness of the tests is a function, to some degree, of the extent to which the assessment method actually assesses the construct under question (e.g., whether or not such tests actually assess "intelligence" in some native form, or rather assess learning, achievement, cultural background, or a combination of all of these). The question of what is assessed is in part a function of how the construct is defined. For example, the WISC-III is based on the same definition of intelligence as was the initial version of the test, essentially the concept of *g,* derived by Wechsler in 1994 (i.e., the "capacity of the individual to act purposefully, to think rationally, and to deal effectively with his or her environment" [p. 3]). What the test assesses is also a function of the particular focus of the test (i.e., a focus on "academic" intelligence as opposed to "kinesthetic" or "social" or "artistic" intelligence).

While the debate about what intelligence tests measure has led to volumes of discourse on the subject, the relevance of the debate for the day-in-day-out practitioner becomes somewhat moot if one returns to the basic purposes of psychological assessment: to determine if a problem exists, to determine the scope and magnitude of the problem, and to plan treatment or intervention strategies. An assessment method, such as an intelligence test, that generates helpful information in such a process does not lose utility due to more esoteric discussions of the essence of the construct as long as the test has reliability and validity relevant to behavior and is used intelligently. Most intelligence tests have such reliability and validity, as attested to by the fact that they do predict, at varying levels of significance, academic achievement (Anastasi, 1982; Matarazzo, 1972; Sattler, 1988; Wechsler, 1991). As such, they serve a useful purpose in providing information relevant to intellectual abilities within academic considerations.

Additionally, in any assessment process, it is important to employ as much information as possible in making decisions that have the potential to affect an individual's life. Expanding the sources of information to include extant records (medical, educational, psychiatric, psychological), developmental history, observations of actual behavior, subjective assessment sources, and objective tests increases the likelihood of meeting the three main goals of the psychological assessment process and decreases the impact of divergence in perceptions of what essential elements constitute any particular construct. Those harmful effects that have been attributed to intelligence tests have been, too often, the result of using the test in a stand-alone format for decision making or administering the test under less than optimal conditions (e.g., not using the child's primary language if bilingual, assessing the child when the child is sick, etc.). The use of any test, for that matter, in a stand-alone format or under less than optimal conditions paves the way for limited and potentially erroneous decision making.

OVERVIEW OF THE WISC-III

Description of the Test

The WISC-III has been normed for use with children ages 6 years, 0 months, to 16 years, 11 months. It fits in the middle of the Wechsler scales, with the Wechsler Preschool and Primary Scale of Intelligence-Revised (WPPSI-R) covering 3 years, 0 months to 7 years, 3 months, and the Wechsler Adult Intelligence Scale-Revised (WAIS-R) covering 16 years, 0 months to 74 years, 11 months.

The WISC-III yields three broad measures of intelligence: the Verbal, Performance, and Full Scale IQ scores (Mean = 100, Standard Deviation = 15). The Verbal IQ score is based on five subtests—Information, Similarities, Arithmetic, Vocabulary, and Comprehension—each with a scaled-score mean of 10 and standard deviation of 3. A sixth test, Digit Span, serves as a supplemental subtest. The verbal subtests rely on verbal presentation of items and require a verbal response from the child.

The Performance IQ score is also based on a series of five subtests with the same subtest mean and standard deviation. The five Performance subtests are Picture Completion, Coding, Picture Arrangement, Block Design, and Object Assembly. The Performance section has two supplemental subtests: Mazes and Symbol Search. The Performance subtests all have verbal instructions but the actual materials are visual presentations requiring either verbal (Picture Completion) or nonverbal responses (all other Performance subtests).

Administration time tends to be from 50 to 70 minutes for the 10 basic subtests. Presentation of the optional subtests adds approximately 10 to 15 minutes to the test (Wechsler, 1991).

There are four factor scores formally available from the WISC-III that were not part of the standard scoring process on the WISC-R. Each of the factors has a mean of 100 and a standard deviation of 15. Factor I (Verbal Comprehension) is composed of the Information, Similarities, Vocabulary, and Comprehension subtests. Factor II (Perceptual Organization) is composed of the Picture Completion, Picture Arrangement, Block Design, and Object Assembly subtests. Factor III (Freedom from Distractibility) is composed of the

Arithmetic and Digit Span subtests, and Factor IV (Processing Speed) is composed of Coding and Symbol Search.

A brief description of the individual subtests, and the abilities they purport to assess, are as follows (summarized from Sattler, 1992, and Wechsler, 1991):

Verbal Scale Subtests

Information: An untimed verbal subtest, 30 items, assessing general range and fund of knowledge acquired through the child's environment

Similarities: An untimed verbal subtest, 19 items, focusing on abstract verbal classification abilities (class inclusiveness)

Arithmetic: A timed verbal subtest, 24 items, assessing numerical reasoning, attention and concentration, and long- and short-term memory

Vocabulary: An untimed verbal subtest, 30 items, assessing word knowledge, language development, and long-term memory

Comprehension: An untimed verbal subtest, 18 items, assessing social judgment and common-sense reasoning.

Digit Span: An untimed supplemental verbal subtest, administered in two trials, one forward (8 pairs of items) and one backward (7 pairs of items), assessing short-term memory, sequencing ability, and attention and concentration

Performance Scale Subtests

Picture Completion: A timed performance subtest, 30 items, assessing figure-ground discrimination and alertness to essential detail

Coding: A timed performance subtest subdivided into Part A, for ages 6 and 7 (59 items) and Part B, for ages 8 and older (119 items), assessing short-term memory and eye-hand coordination and speed

Picture Arrangement: A timed performance subtest, 14 items, assessing attention to details and visual sequencing and logic

Block Design: A timed performance subtest, 12 items, assessing visuospatial analysis and synthesis and motor coordination

Object Assembly: A timed performance subtest, 5 items, assessing visual part-whole relationship formation, spatial ability, and motor coordination

Symbol Search: A timed supplemental performance subtest subdivided into Symbol Search A, ages 6 and 7 (45 items), and Symbol Search B, ages 8 and up (45 items), which assesses perceptual discrimination, speed and accuracy, and attention and concentration

Mazes: A timed supplemental performance subtest, 10 items, assessing visual planning ability, foresight, motor coordination, and attention and concentration.

This very brief description of the abilities assessed by each subtest presents, initially, a simplified view of the test. Not addressed in the preceding descriptions are the full range of abilities measured or the overlap of abilities across subtests.

Similarities and Differences: WISC-R and WISC-III

The WISC-III retains, in original or modified form, 73 percent of the items from the WISC-R, thus providing a degree of longitudinal continuity to the tests. Thus, 27 percent of the items are new or modified. The basic subtest structure remains the same, although a new subtest, Symbol Search, has been added as a supplemental subtest. On the WISC-R, subtest order of presentation was altered between verbal and performance subtests. On the WISC-III, the alteration still exists; however, the first test presented now is a Performance subtest, hopefully making the test more immediately engaging, particularly for younger subjects. Other changes to the WISC-III include the enlargement of some of the visual stimulus material (Picture Completion) and the addition of color to stimulus materials (Picture Completion and Picture Arrangement). The factors scores, mentioned previously, have now been incorporated formally into the test with standard score conversions. Directions have been improved, expanded information added to the test protocol for administration ease, bonus points assigned to Arithmetic for the last six items based on quick accurate performance, and 8 of the standard 10 subtests have been lengthened with one shortened (Vocabulary) and one the same length (Information).

Apart from these changes, there are three very substantive changes on the WISC-III that represent a marked improvement over the WISC-R. First, the norms have been updated, thus offsetting the "upward creep" in standard scores that occurs when a test has been in use for some time (Flynn, 1984, 1987). The new norms also reflect changes in the demographics of the population since the last revision. Second, extensive efforts were made to reduce ethnic and cultural bias in the content of the WISC-III. This was done by in-depth statistical examination of WISC-R patterns across ethnic and cultural groups; statistical analyses of each item of the WISC-III for gender, ethnic, or cultural bias; and an examination of the entire test by a panel of experts in test bias.

The third change involved lowering the "floor" of the WISC-III by adding items at the lower end. To illustrate what this means, consider an "average" 9-year-old who takes the test. His or her final score will be based on some items that are easy, some items that are moderately hard, and some items that are difficult. A low-functioning or retarded 9-year-old taking the same test will have a final score based on moderately hard items and difficult items, since, for that child, there may not be any "easy" items, even at the beginning of each subtest. Lowering the floor of the test decreases the possibility of a low-functioning child obtaining a "truncated" score based on exposure to only moderate and difficult items. However, the floor has not been lowered sufficiently that one would necessarily opt for the WISC-III for use with lower-functioning individuals over other tests, such as the Stanford-Binet, Fourth

Edition (SB-FE), or the Kaufman Assessment Battery for Children, both of which were designed to assess much lower age levels than the WISC-III and which, therefore, have lower "floors."

PSYCHOMETRIC PROPERTIES OF THE WISC-III

Standardization Sample

The WISC-III was standardized on a representative sample of 2,200 children. A stratified random sampling plan was used within demographic groups based on age, gender, race/ethnicity, geographic region, and parent education according to the data from the 1988 U.S. Bureau of the Census report (Wechsler, 1991). There were 11 age groups ranging from 6 to 16 years with 200 subjects (100 males and 100 females) in each group. Race and ethnic distributions within each age group were proportional to Census Bureau data and were stratified within categories covering geographic region, gender, and parent education level (Wechsler, 1991). Sattler (1992) and Kaufman (1992) note that the standardization method used on the WISC-III is "notably superior" to the WISC-R and that the stratifications within categories represents excellent sampling methodology.

Reliability

Split-half reliability coefficients reported in the manual for the Verbal, Performance, and Full Scale IQ scores range from an average of .91 (Performance) to .96 (Full Scale), with the lowest reliability coefficient being .89 for the Performance score at age 14 and the highest .97 for the Full Scale score at age 15 (Wechsler, 1991). Subtest split-half reliabilities range from .60 (Object Assembly, age 14) to .92 (Block Design, age 15) (Wechsler, 1991). The manual offers the standard error of measurement as further evidence of reliability, with an average range from 3.20 on the Full Scale score to 4.54 on the Performance score (Wechsler, 1991).

Split-half average reliability coefficients for the four factors ranged from .85 (Processing Speed) to .94 (Verbal Comprehension; Wechsler, 1991). However, Little (1992) suggests caution in using the factor structure interpretively as some weaknesses exist, particularly in the Freedom from Distractibility factor. Likewise, the factor structure may vary with subgroups (e.g., learning disabled, mentally retarded; Politano & Tavel, 1995).

Interscorer reliabilities were assessed for those subtests requiring judgment in the assignment of a value to the response, (i.e., the Similarities, Vocabulary, Comprehension, and Mazes subtests). Interscorer reliability coefficients ranged from .92 for Mazes to .98 for Similarities and Vocabulary (Wechsler, 1991). Overall, the reliability of the WISC-III is outstanding (Kaufman, 1992; Sattler, 1992).

Standard Error of Measurement

The standard error of measurement (SEM) is a statistical technique that establishes confidence intervals around a measured score within which one's "true" score would be likely to lie. The concept is based on the idea that individuals are variable and that, on any given day, the same test could yield slightly different results. Rather than test an individual repeatedly, and then take the average of those tests to get the "best" indication of the person's intelligence, the SEM allows one to give the range within which the score would likely fall a certain percent of the time (e.g., 90 or 95 percent of the time).

To illustrate this, consider that a child has an actual measured IQ of 115 on the WISC-III. Using the tables provided in the manual (Wechsler, 1991), the child's "true" IQ would lie between 110 and 119 90 percent of the time or between 109 and 120 95 percent of the time. In other words, if the same child were tested 100 times and no test-retest effect artificially inflated scores, then 95 out of 100 times his or her measured Full Scale IQ would fall between 109 and 120.

Validity

The WISC-III Manual (Wechsler, 1991) suggests that, to the extent that the WISC-R was a valid measure of intelligence, the WISC-III must also be valid given the overlap of the two tests and given the range of correlations between the two tests (from a low of .42 on Picture Arrangement to a high of .90 on the Verbal IQ score). Data on the WISC-R do indeed support the validity of the test across issues of construct (internal), concurrent, and predictive validity (Anastasi, 1982; Kaufman, 1979; Sattler, 1982, 1988).

Factor analyses, both exploratory and confirmatory, performed on the WISC-III support a stable internal structure (Wechsler, 1991). Additional comparisons of the WISC-III with the WISC-R, the Wechsler Adult Intelligence Scale-Revised (WAIS-R), the Wechsler Preschool and Primary Scale of Intelligence-Revised (WPPSI-R), the Otis-Lennon School Ability Test, the Differential Ability Scales (DAS), selected elements of the Halstead-Reitan Neuropsychological Battery, the Wide Range Achievement Test-Revised (WRAT-R), and group achievement tests (e.g., Comprehensive Test of Basic Skills, Form U) made by the test developers yield support for convergent and/or divergent validity for the WISC-III (Wechsler, 1991).

Additional comparisons in a variety of formats using the WISC-III have been made. Specifically, the WISC-III has been compared to the Wechsler Individual Achievement Test (WIAT, Flanagan & Alfonso, 1993). A cross-comparison was made with the WISC-III and the WISC-R and Wide Range Achievement Test-Revised (WRAT-R; Foster & Politano, 1994). WISC-III short-form comparisons have been made with the WISC-R with students who are learning disabled relative to classification consistency (Dumont & Faro, 1993). The WISC-III has also been compared with the SB-FE Abbreviated

Battery (Caravajal, Hayes, Lackey, & Rathke, 1993), compared with 23 items that overlap the WPPSI-R and WISC-III (Sattler & Atkinson, 1993), and the Vocabulary of the WISC-III has been compared with the Peabody Picture Vocabulary Test-Revised (PPVT-R; Caravajal, Hayes, Miller, & Wiebe, 1993). All of these comparisons have supported the validity of the WISC-III.

In addition to comparison with existing tests, the WISC-III was correlated with school academic grades for 617 children, ages 6 through 16, with a resulting $r = .42$ (Wechsler, 1991). Additional administration of the WISC-III to children identified as gifted and mentally retarded yielded scores in the expected IQ range given the composition of the two groups (Wechsler, 1991).

Short Forms of the WISC-III

As constructed, the WISC-III allows for proration of Verbal, Performance, and Full Scale IQ scores based on administration of only four of the five Verbal and/or Performance subtests. While proration is generally used when a subtests has been invalidated for some reason, it is possible to administer 8, instead of 10, subtests and still derive scores.

Sattler (1992) suggests using the Tellegen and Briggs (1967) procedure for deriving short-form scaled scores. This procedure is described in Sattler (1992). It should be cautioned, however, that the procedure was developed on earlier forms of the scale and some caution would be in order until additional research validates short-form procedures with the WISC-III.

CLINICAL USE OF THE WISC-III

Administration

Earlier, it was mentioned that assessment needs to be accurate, objective, and conducted intelligently. Accuracy and objectivity are achieved by following the standardized administration procedures outlined in the manual (Wechsler, 1991) and elaborated on by Sattler (1988, 1992). Adherence to these standardized procedures cannot be overemphasized. The manual states that comparability of any child's individual score to the national norms presented with the WISC-III is a function of how closely the examiner adheres to the administration and scoring directions given for the WISC-III (Wechsler, 1991). How important is standardized administration? Perhaps two examples might illustrate the point of standardized administrations and answer the question of importance at the same time.

A psychology professor used to watch her students administering standardized tests, and if she found a student changing the directions, altering procedures for establishing beginning and ending points, and so on, she would demand that student's normative data for his or her version of the test just administered, often calling the test by the student's name (e.g., the Smith Intelligence Scale for Children). When the student failed to produce his or her national norms, this professor would then ask how the student intended to make any sensible interpretation of the test just given since he or she had no norms. The reader may rest assured that the degree of variation in the standardized administration procedures did not have to be large to have the test renamed in the student's honor with the subsequent demand for normative data! If the student protested that the changes were small, even tiny, and could have little impact on the applicability of the existing norms, the psychology professor would then ask for research data that demonstrated that point at which changes did or did not invalidate the existing norms.

The point of this was to impress on the student that he or she was not in a position to know how much change in standardized administration a test could sustain before invalidating the existing norms. If the student did not know, then he or she had better not make any changes because the individual who *might* suffer would be the person taking the test—the person that the student was ethically bound to serve with the highest standards possible. This professor's point was made only once with each student and made a lasting impression.

Now, as a second example, consider the timed Coding subtest. This subtest requires matching a series of symbols with specific numbers using a key. The most efficient strategy, if left to one's own devices, would be to do each number in turn (e.g., match all the 1s first, then the 2s, etc.). However, the directions require that the matching be done *in order without skipping any.* If this direction is left out (which it too often is) and the child selects the strategy described above, thus skipping items, the examiner is required to correct the child as follows: "Do them in order. Don't skip any. Do this one (pointing) next" (Wechsler, 1991, pp. 71). This correction, coupled with the pointing, takes about six seconds. A fast child can accurately match 12 items in six seconds. Thus, a child who selects the best strategy *because* directions contrariwise were not given could be penalized approximately 12 times for having selected that strategy (which represents an intelligent choice!). Depending on age, 12 items can make a difference of 4 to 5 points in the scaled score on Coding. Therefore, a child might score lower than necessary because the examiner deleted directions to start with (an examiner error with the child paying the price!). The point is this: Directions serve a purpose—deletions or changes in the directions can only harm the person taking the test.

Another important consideration in clinical administration is the establishment of rapport. Both Wechsler (1991) and Sattler (1988, 1992) discuss this process in detail. The responsibility for establishing rapport is the examiner's, particularly in working with children. Given that an assessment session is a time when children have the undivided attention of an adult who is interested in everything the child says, rapport is not difficult to establish. For reticent children, an examiner can encourage behavior by allowing the child to start with less taxing tasks, such as human figure drawings, and allowing the child to participate as a "helper" by letting the child to put away test materials, such as putting puzzle pieces back in the boxes on Object Assembly or putting away the blocks on Block Design.

Another important, but often overlooked, consideration in accurate, objective, and intelligent assessment is the standardization of examiner behavior. Over time, an examiner can build a baseline of how examinees react to the assessment situation and to the examiner *if* the examiner has standardized his or her behavior. This baseline allows for comparisons of behavior across examinees on dimensions such as appropriate-inappropriate, normal-abnormal, and so on. If, however, an examiner changes his or her behavior with each examinee, then it is difficult to establish such baselines since variations in an examinee's behaviors may well be in response to variations in examiner behavior.

Verbal Subtests

There are essentially two "classes" of responses on the Verbal subtests that need to be scored: very objective answers (such as Arithmetic and Digit Span) and somewhat more subjective answers (such as Vocabulary, Similarities, and Comprehension, in particular, and Information less so). The more subjective subtests require some degree of judgment in assigning a score and may produce some variation from one scorer to another. This is particularly true for Vocabulary, Similarities, and Comprehension, where items can be scored 0, 1, or 2. The manual provides general guidelines for classes of responses (e.g., on Vocabulary, correct use of the word in a sentence is scored 1 point) as well as examples of 0-, 1-, and 2-point responses.

When administering these subtests, vague or questionable responses can be probed by saying "What do you mean" or "Tell me more about it" (Wechsler, 1991, pp. 46). These probes are very specific and should not be modified to, for example, "What do you mean by riding a bicycle?" which may elicit a description of "riding" as opposed to the target word "bicycle." Additionally, saying "Please tell me more about it," although more polite, is a request and lacks the demand element of the appropriate query.

In addition to response inquiries, the examiner must be attentive to other factors impacting on verbal assessment—most commonly, fatigue, performance anxiety, and giving up too easily or a "don't care" attitude. Performance anxiety can be reduced by taking more time with the child, beginning with easier tasks before starting the more formal IQ assessment, explaining that the assessment is not for a "grade," and encouraging effort (but not performance). Children who fatigue during testing can be given a break and, if necessary, continued to another day, although this should be avoided if possible. Children who fatigue easily should be looked at closely for any illness that may impact on the assessment. As with performance anxiety, reticent children or children who give up too easily can be encouraged with praise for effort.

Specific suggestions that may aid testing and contribute to rapport are as follows:

Information: Because this test follows Picture Completion in the WISC-III, it presents less of a problem than on the WISC-R, where it was the first test given.

Similarities: Initial items on this test earn 1 point for either functional or abstract similarities. However, beginning with item 6, 2 points can be earned for correct abstract similarities. It is important that the examiner model correct 2-point abstractions if the child gives a correct 1-point response on either item 6 and/or item 7.

Arithmetic: This is a straightforward-appearing subtest that is quite complex. The child must remember multiple pieces of information, transpose that information, and derive an answer, all without the aid of pencil and paper. It is important that the questions are read at a slower pace to allow the child to assimilate all information. Additionally, since this is a timed subtest and bonus points can now be earned for items 19 through 24, the watch should be used from the first item to desensitize the child to being timed on content (math) that is usually anxiety provoking alone.

Vocabulary: Because items can be scored 0, 1, or 2, it is important that the examiner know the scoring criteria well enough to make judgments about responses and inquiries as he or she proceeds. The general scoring rules on pages 121 and 122 of the manual are essential to an understanding of the rationale behind the examples given for each word.

Comprehension: As with Vocabulary, responses can be scored 0, 1, or 2. Eight of the items are marked by an asterisk and require probing for an additional response if the child initially gives one scorable response. The probes involve repetition of the initial item appropriately rephrased, such as "Tell me another thing to do."

Digit Span: As a supplementary subtest, this one is often not given. However, it is quick to administer and yields important information. The child's repetition of numbers given by the examiner can be examined to see if the child is dropping numbers, adding numbers, remembering the correct numbers but getting the sequence wrong, and so on. This, plus the inclusion of Digit Span on the Freedom from Distractibility factor, make it a test worth giving.

Performance Subtests

Performance subtests, although easier to score, are more difficult to administer and require more practice. The examiner not only has to give directions accurately but also must manipulate a number of materials, such as pencil, scoring protocol, and puzzle pieces or blocks, all the while timing performances accurately with a stopwatch. Without adequate practice, examiners are likely to be so engrossed in their presentation of the materials that the child will not be observed closely.

The use of the stopwatch on these subtests requires consideration. Many children can become anxious at being timed, whereas others will want to handle and experiment with the watch as a novelty item. The examiner should handle the watch in such a way as to make it clear that the child is being timed (e.g., do not hide the watch under the table or out of view), but, at the same time, make the watch a natural and nonintrusive part of the process. Nonintrusiveness is best achieved by a simple watch that does not require extensive setting and resetting to operate and one that is quiet.

Most of the Performance subtests request that the child notify the examiner when a particular task is completed (e.g., "Tell me when you have finished"). In the process of concentrating on the task at hand, many children forget to verbally indicate that they are finished. The examiner needs to watch the child closely and stop timing when the child is obviously finished rather than waiting for a verbal indication.

There are some fairly obvious difficulties that an examiner wishes to avoid on Performance subtests. One is loss of control over materials. This is best avoided by having out only what is necessary for the task at hand, with additional materials safely out of the way and under examiner control. Another pitfall is allowing children to complete each task even when they have gone beyond the time limits. For the child that is very nearly at a correct response, a few more seconds to complete the item may be appropriate. However, additional time beyond a few additional seconds adds to the fatigue factor, may increase the child's sense of frustration, and may overexpose test materials, thus adding to any test-retest effect.

Specific considerations for the Performance subtests are as follows:

Picture Completion: This is generally a fun test for most children. Anxious children may be allowed to start with easier items below their age level as a means of reducing their anxiety. There is a 20-second limit for each picture. Children should know that they are being timed (using a wristwatch may be too subtle).

Coding: The most common error on Coding seems to be caused by the newer digital stopwatches and a lack of examiner familiarity with them. The child is permitted 2 minutes, or 120 seconds. Digital stopwatches will show 1:20 on the readout but this is not 120 seconds, it is 1 minute and 20 seconds, or 80 seconds altogether. As with the earlier WISC-R, a second Coding form may be placed to the child's right if the child is left-handed and blocks the key on their form.

Picture Arrangement: Most children arrange the picture sequence from left to right, as in reading. Arrangements from right to left, if in the correct sequence, are scored as correct but the sequence should be noted for diagnostic considerations. The examiner should pick up the cards when the child has finished, then record both time and sequence. A helpful child may pick up the cards for the examiner while the examiner is recording time and may not pick the cards up in the correct manner, thus potentially invalidating the subtest.

Block Design: The most difficult part of Block Design are the beginning items. The subtest moves progressively from building from examiner-constructed models to building from pictures of designs. Inattentiveness to directions can result in the examiner having both a design and an examiner-built model out simultaneously, which may be confusing for the child. This particular subtest invites long overextensions of time for children. It is helpful for the examiner simply to say "Let's try another one" and then move on for the child who is not close to correctly completing the design.

Object Assembly: The new shielding screen, unlike with the WISC-R, is self-supporting. This reduces a number of the problems that were present with the WISC-R, such as the child holding the screen (to involve them in the task) and trying to peek or the examiner holding the screen with one hand and putting out puzzle pieces with the other. The addition of the soccer ball adds to the length of time to administer this subtest.

Symbol Search: This is a new supplemental subtest that contributes to the Processing Speed factor. There is insufficient research or clinical applications of this subtest at this point to suggest special considerations, although the same cautions that apply to Coding with the digital stopwatch would also apply here.

Mazes: As a supplemental subtest, Mazes does not contribute to any of the factors. General practice seems to be not to give Mazes due to the time involved and the relatively low correlations of this subtest with the Verbal, Performance, and Full Scale IQ scores.

INTERPRETATION OF TEST RESULTS

Interpretation: General Considerations

Interpretation of the WISC-III basically involves three processes. One is the comparison of the child's performance to the normative sample. Another is the comparison of the child to himself or herself, looking at relative strengths and weaknesses. The other process is the integration of WISC-III data with data from other sources such as achievement tests, perceptual-motor measures, academic performance, and so on.

Interpretation of the WISC-III is not as straightforward as it may seem in that specific highs and lows on particular subtests do not correspond on a one-to-one basis with specific abilities. All of the subtests on the WISC-III assess more than one ability and most of the subtests overlap on abilities. This becomes obvious if one closely examines Table 7–1. A close look at Table 7–1 suggests that isolating specific abilities that may be strong or weak for a particular child is a complex process.

In addition to overlap of abilities, it must be remembered that, with any test, even one as "objective" as the WISC-III, one is only sampling a narrow range of an individual's behavior at a specific time and place. Therefore, it is not possible to make hard and fast statements about *what* an individual is

Table 7–1 WISC-III Abilities and Factors*

Abilities	PC	IF	CD	SM	PA	AR	BD	VO	OA	CM	DF	DB	SS	MZ
Tracking multiple pieces of info at same time					X	X						X		
Class-inclusive reasoning				X				X						
Visual/nonverbal reasoning							X							
Visual-motor speed			X										X	X
Figure-ground discrimination	X				X		X		X					
Visual-verbal reasoning	X				X				X					
General knowledge		X						X		X				
Social knowledge					X					X				
Environmental alertness		X				X		X	X	X				
Reading based learning						X		X						
Mental computation						X								
Counting						X	X				X	X		
Addition/subtraction						X					X			
Multiplication/division						X								
Social orientation					X			X		X				
Oriented to abstract				X			X							
Relational concepts				X		X							X	
Word knowledge				X				X						
G (general ability)		X		X	X		X	X	X	X				
Problem solving, verbal				X	X		X	X	X	X				
Problem solving, visual					X		X		X					

Table 7-1 *Continued*

Abilities	PC	IF	CD	SM	PA	AR	BD	VO	OA	CM	DF	DB	SS	MZ
Social norms										X				
Rote learning		X	X											
Stimulus transformation						X						X		
High concentration ability						X					X	X		
Cognitive flexibility						X						X		
Visual memory	X		X						X					
Long-term visual memory	X				X				X					
Short-term visual memory			X										X	
Object recognition	X			X	X			X		X				
Sequencing			X		X	X					X	X		
Attention			X		X	X					X	X		
Long-term auditory memory		X		X		X		X						
Short-term auditory memory											X	X		
Nonverbal reasoning	X				X		X		X					
Numerical reasoning						X	X				X	X		
Perceptual organizaation	X				X	X	X		X					
Perceptual planning					X									
Perceptual reproduction			X				X							
Perceptual abstraction							X							
Long-term memory				X										
Verbal concept formation								X						

Abilities	PC	IF	CD	SM	PA	AR	BD	VO	OA	CM	DF	DB	SS	MZ
Attention to verbal detail	X	X				X				X				
Attention to visual detail	X				X				X					
Tolerance of time presure	X		X		X	X	X		X				X	X
Factors														
Kaufman: Verbal Comprehension (WISC-R)		X		X				X		X				
Kaufman: Perceptual Organization (WISC-R)	X				X		X		X					
Kaufman: Freedom from Distractibility (WISC-R)						X					X	X		
Bannatyne: Conceptualization (WISC-R)				X				X		X				
Bannatyne: Spatial (WISC-R)	X						X		X					
Bannatyne: Sequencing (WISC-R)			X		X						X	X		
Wechsler: Verbal Comprehension (WISC-III)		X		X				X		X				
Wechsler: Perceptual Organization (WISC-III)	X				X		X		X					
Wechsler: Freedom from Distractibility (WISC-III)						X					X	X		
Wechsler: Processing Speed (WISC-III)			X										X	

*Many of these abilities have been extracted from the research over the years on the WISC-R. However, given the overlap between the WISC-R and the WISC-III, they should still have some utility for interpretation of the WISC-III pending validation through research on the new instrument.

PC = Picture Arrangement   AR = Arithmetic   DF = Digits Forwards

IF = Information   BD = Block Design   DB = Digits Backwards

CD = Coding   VO = Vocabulary   SS = Symbol Search

SM = Similarities   OA = Object Assembly   MZ = Mazes

PA = Picture Arrangement   CM = Comprehension

like. Particularly, one cannot, based on test data, offer causal interpretations of behavior (e.g., "Little Johnny is retarded due to cultural familiar deprivations during early neurological development") or predictions of future behavior (e.g., "If appropriate educational measures are not taken, little Johnny can be expected to continue to decline in his measured academic levels").

Equally important, it must be remembered that IQ tests do not measure some internal neurophysiological process. Rather, IQ tests simply quantify observed behavior. Based on this quantification, some inferences may be drawn. But those inferences should be related to the observed behavior, not to implied internal processes. For example, making the following statement is acceptable: "Although still below average, Johnny did show a relative strength in his knowledge of words and his ability to use those words to describe his environment." This describes behavior! The following statement is much less acceptable because it implies some "window into the mind" that allows one to see what is going on neurologically with the brain: "Johnny's responses indicate a verbal processing deficit." All of the following could cause a "processing" deficit: little Johnny was sick and feverish the day the test was administered; little Johnny has limited hearing in the midrange; little Johnny suffered damage to Broca's area as a result of a fall at age 3; little Johnny has an attention/concentration problem, and so on. A low score on the Vocabulary subtest does not indicate which of those reasons might be responsible for the low score—all that can be said is that little Johnny was low on that subtest and the abilities underlying the subtest at the time the test was administered.

If the WISC-III assesses overlapping abilities, and if it only samples a restricted range of behaviors, and if it does not provide hard data about causal aspects of particular behaviors, what does it do? What the WISC-III does is allow one to state plausible hypotheses about cognitive and intellectual functioning based on observed behavior. These hypotheses, then, are subject to support or modification with additional information from other sources such as achievement tests, teacher reports, observation, and the like.

Interpreting IQ scores

Actual interpretation can follow along a set pattern. Generally, it is best to proceed from macroinformation to microinformation. On the WISC-III, this means first looking at the Full Scale IQ score and what it tells about the child (see Table BC-2 in Sattler, 1992, for classifications of ranges of Full Scale IQ scores), then looking at the Verbal IQ score for the same information, then the Performance IQ score, then the Verbal-Performance split, followed by the factor scores, then the specific pattern of the Verbal subtests, followed by the specific pattern of the Performance subtests, followed by an examination of variations between Verbal and Performance subtests, followed, finally, by an examination of intra-test scatter.

To explain the interpretation process, an example is in order. These examples will illustrate both the process of hypothesis formation, interpretation sequence, and crossing of abilities using the chart in Table 7–1.

Case Example 1.   These scores were from a 14-year-old male:

Verbal IQ score = 110
Performance IQ score = 130
Full Scale IQ score = 121

Picture Completion	12	Information	10
Coding	14	Similarities	11
Picture Arrangement	18	Arithmetic	14
Block Design	12	Vocabulary	13
Object Assembly	16	Comprehension	10
(Digit Span)	(8)		

Remember, the purpose of the evaluation is to determine if a problem exists. Also remember that this would not ordinarily be done using only the WISC-III. For illustrative purposes, some license will be taken here.

As mentioned, it is usually helpful to start at a macrolevel and then proceed to a microlevel (e.g., start with the Full Scale score and then move downward to more microlevels of interpretation). Using this strategy, we find that the Full Scale score of 121 places this young man at the low end of the Superior range of IQ scores (Wechsler, 1991, Table 2.8). We might hypothesize, then, that this is a bright teenager who likely does quite well in school, all things being equal.

Next we look at the Verbal IQ score of 110. This is lower than expected if we had initially only been shown the Full Scale IQ score and asked to estimate the Verbal IQ score. This score of 110, although still slightly above average, is not in the superior range, and we might amend our earlier hypothesis about his doing quite well in school given the weight placed on verbal abilities in school settings. He may still be above average, but perhaps not at the superior level we had expected.

Now we examine the Performance IQ score of 130. This is at the higher end of Superior and the lower end of Very Superior. We can now hypothesize that his visual-spatial and nonverbal abilities (as measured by this section of the test) contribute more heavily to his Superior Full Scale IQ score than does his verbal abilities. In addition, we can also say that the difference of 20 points between the Verbal and Performance IQ scores is a significant difference—one likely to occur no more than 5 times out of 100 (Wechsler, 1991, Table B.1). So at this point, we have a young man with Superior overall abilities but with significant discrepancies between verbal and performance abilities.

Next we can examine the factor scores for those that we have and we find a Verbal Comprehension factor score of 106, a Perceptual Organization factor score of 128, and a Freedom from Distractibility score of 106. The first two scores are consistent with the Verbal and Performance Scaled scores. The 106 on Freedom from Distractibility might raise a red flag and appear to offer a solution to the discrepancies noted so far but caution is warranted. If one examines the abilities that underpin Digit Span and Arithmetic, one finds that each make use of the same abilities (Table 7–1). In fact, Arithmetic is more difficult in that it requires remembering, as well as transforming, multiple pieces of information. The score of 14 on Arithmetic versus an 8 on Digit Span suggest caution in jumping to conclusions and saying that this young man has an attention/concentration problem, although we can include that, with caution, among our potential list of hypotheses.

We next turn to the Verbal subtest scores. First, note that all subtest scores are at or above average, so, technically speaking, this young man does not have any "below-average weaknesses." His "weaknesses" are only relative to his other performances. He has strengths in Arithmetic and Vocabulary, both "taught" skills in school. He is weaker in using those "taught" skills to abstract (Similarities) and also weaker in using verbal skills in gleaning information from his general environment (Information and Comprehension). So we might hypothesize that he is using his educational environment well and is getting more from that, relatively speaking, than from his general environment.

Turning to Performance subtests, we can say that this young man does well in perceptually organizing both concrete (Picture Arrangement and Object Assembly) and abstract (Block Design) visual stimuli in his environment, although he seems to do better when the stimuli are presented in a known context (e.g., everyday situations such as Picture Arrangement).

So we would hypothesize that this is a teenager who is in the Superior range overall, relatively weaker in verbal than performance skills, who is making good use of his educational environment given basic abilities, and who may be able to use his strong visual abilities to augment his verbal abilities. Notice that no inferences have been made to neurophysiological abilities—nothing has been said about causative factors and no predictions have been made other than the suggestion that one might use strengths to augment weaknesses.

Is there any causative explanation for the hypotheses generated (e.g., a verbal Learning Disability, etc.)? The answer is yes, there is a possible explanation. From history (not test data), we know that this young man was from a military family that has just returned to the United States after a number of tours in other countries where English was not the primary language. This might explain the difference—both in terms of not being as exposed to the American culture (Comprehension and Information) as well as decreased familiarity with English. However, realize that this possible explanation is still presented as a hypothesis only!

Case Example 2. This second case illustrates several important points. The WISC-III data below is from a 15-year-old female:

Verbal IQ score = 78
Performance IQ score = 107
Full Scale IQ score = 90

Picture Completion	10	Information	9
Coding	3	Similarities	9
Picture Arrangement	12	Arithmetic	6
Block Design	11	Vocabulary	5
Object Assembly	19	Comprehension	1
(Digit Span)	(4)		
(Symbol Search)	(4)		

At first glance, this appears to contain many of the elements of the first profile—that is, some scores in the Average range and a significant split between Verbal and Performance IQ scores, but with markedly greater variation in subtest scores. A mathematical model of Learning Disabilities in which a series of questions are answered "yes" or "no" would fit this profile (Lerner, 1981): Full Scale IQ score in the low Average to above range? (yes—90); Performance IQ score 10 or more points higher than the Verbal IQ score? (yes—29 points); Highest Verbal subtest score minus lowest Verbal subtest score greater than 5 points? (yes—16 points); Highest Performance subtest score minus lowest Performance subtest score greater than 5 points? (yes—8 points); Highest Performance subtest score minus lowest Verbal subtest score greater than 7 points? (not quite—6 points); Highest Verbal subtest score minus lowest Performance subtest score greater than 7 points? (yes—18 points).

However, one must be cautious in applying "models" to profiles. Learning Disability (LD) profiles are often "mimicked" in terms of the spread of scores by profiles of individuals suffering some form of emotional upset or psychiatric disturbance. Generally, the difference between the two (LD versus emotional/psychiatric) is as follows: Subtests from an LD profile will tend to vary together in the same direction based on common underlying abilities, while emotional/psychiatric profiles generally will not.

Returning to the profile, we see that Comprehension is very low (scaled score of 1). Given underlying abilities, there should be some impact on Picture Arrangement with visual-verbal interpretation of social situations, yet Picture Arrangement is a 12. Object Assembly is a 19, yet Picture Completion, which also requires attention to detail, is a 10. Vocabulary is a 5, yet Similarities, which involves both defining and abstracting common properties between verbally presented items, is a 9. About the only subtests that are "hanging together" as might be expected are Coding, Digit Span, and Symbol Search.

Again, the question is raised as to whether there is a possible causal explanation of this profile, and again, the answer is a qualified "yes." This young lady was given this test just after admission to an inpatient psychiatric facility for severe depression and suicidal ideation. The pattern of scores probably reflects variations in energy over short periods of time, the salience of overlearned materials under stress, and the decreased concentration ability often associated with depression. Also, there is often a "shock" effect for people just hospitalized psychiatrically, which may also be adding to the variations in subtest scores.

Additional Comments on Interpretation

It is hoped that these two cases have given some indication of the complexity of interpretation of scores from the WISC-III. Add to the complexity of this single instrument the additional task of incorporating other possible tests and sources of information into a coherent picture of the individual, and the total process begins to take shape. Instruments of this complexity, used in dealing with human problems of even greater complexity, require extensive academic preparation for interpretation as well as guided practical experience.

A Final Note on Interpretation

With the WISC-R, a number of interpretation procedures were developed through research with the test—for example, significant Verbal-Performance splits were calculated as well as direction of splits relative to sample demographics; factor scores were derived; significant subtests scatter as compared to the sample as well as compared to the child's individual means across Verbal and Performance subtests; indications of individual strength and weaknesses, and so on (Kaufman, 1976, 1979). Many of these procedures have been incorporated formally with the WISC-III (e.g., factor scores, subtest deviation averages, and significance levels, etc.).

Although such statistical considerations may add to an understanding of the patterns on the WISC-III, their utility is not in the numbers themselves but in the extent to which the statistical analyses increase understanding of the child. To say that a child had a significant Verbal-Performance split at the .05 level with high to low Verbal scores ranging from 3 to 11 and high to low Performance scores ranging from 4 to 12 may accurately describe the *test* but the child gets lost somewhere in the numbers.

The essence of any evaluation is to return to the initial consideration: Is there a problem and, if so, what is it and what can be done about it? The answer to the question relies on the intelligent interpretation of test data, to include the WISC-III, wherein strengths and weakness are highlighted.

ASSETS AND LIABILITIES

It would be negligent to discuss assets and liabilities of intelligence assessment without dealing with the various issues that have been raised about intelligence testing. These issues could be organized in various ways but for our discussion we will address them in terms of legal, ethical, individual, social, and statistical issues.

Legal Issues

A number of legal cases raising issues dealing with the Fourteenth Amendment (equal protection and due process) have appeared in the courts addressing issues such as tracking minorities in school based on IQ, biases against cultural or ethnic groups inherent in the IQ tests, and so on (Bersoff & Hofer, 1990). Many of these issues have been brought to the forefront because of the consistent overrepresentation of minorities in special or low-ability classes disproportionate to their actual numbers within communities (Mercer, 1973).

An early legal test of the use of IQ tests was the *Hobson* v. *Hanson* (1967, 1969) case in which the question of the efficacy of the use of IQ tests for placement was raised. This case first raised the disproportional impact of standardized tests, called *adverse impact* in legal terms, and declared that the tests apparently did not assess innate ability but rather current skills as those skills applied to white middle-class individuals (Bersoff & Hofer 1990).

Subsequent to *Hobson* came the *Larry P.* v. *Riles* case (1984). This case, in conjunction with *PASE* v. *Hannon* (1980), has defined the legal parameters of IQ tests in particular. In the *Larry P.* case, the tests were found to be culturally biased and California was enjoined from using IQ tests for placement purposes without the expressed consent of the Court. By contrast, Judge Grady, in the *PASE* case, decided that insufficient attention had been paid by *Larry P.* to the issue of cultural biases. On his review of the Stanford-Binet, WISC, and WISC-R, Grady found some cultural bias but not enough to significantly bias final scores, particularly when the scores themselves were subject to review by a psychologist and other school personnel. He therefore did not stop the use of IQ tests.

As mentioned earlier, considerable effort was put into the WISC-III to guard against cultural and ethnic bias, both in the standardization process and in actual item content. The effectiveness of the increased representation of minorities in the standardization sample and the test content review will yet be decided by further research and, likely, further legal scrutiny.

Ethical Issues

One of the most common ethical issues that arises with assessment deals with the training and qualifications of the individuals administering the test(s). Training standards vary from program to program, even those monitored by the American Psychological Association, in terms of the number of tests that individuals may be trained to use as well as the number of times the individual may be required to administer a specific test under supervised conditions. As already suggested, results can potentially vary greatly based in examiner variations in administration with the same test.

Issues relative to training deal not only with the number of times a particular test is administered but also the degree to which the individual was trained in the appropriate use of the test as well as interpretation of the test. Based on the authors' experiences, children have been misplaced and mislabeled due to such things as administration of a nonaccepted "short form" of the Wechsler; errors in calculating the age of the child for comparison to standardization age groups; administration of the test under adverse conditions (e.g., in the library when other classes are coming and going in their use of the library); and so on.

An illustration of the ethics of testing is perhaps illustrated by *Diana* v. *State Board of Education* (1970) in which a young girl was tested with an IQ test in English when her primary language was Spanish. She was placed in special classes based on the first assessment, but when she was re-assessed in her primary language she was found to not qualify for special placement.

It should seem obvious that a person tested in a second language would not fare as well as if tested in his or her primary language. However, the lack of efficacy of this procedure should have been addressed as a part of training relative to broader issues of ethics with the idea that specific situations cannot be anticipated and one should rely on a broad-based ethical platform for resolution of such problems.

Individual Issues

There are a number of pros and cons to assessment, most dealing with the impact, positive or negative, of the "inevitable" label generated as a result of the assessment. Disadvantages to assessment are as follows: labels may be scientifically esoteric and not understood by the general public; the reliability of the classifications systems from which the labels come are suspect; assessment samples only a small range of behavior at a specific time that may not be adequate to support the label derived; labels are dehumanizing; labels predispose individuals around the labeled person toward unrealistic expectations; and labels lead to a loss of status and restricted access to equal services by the persons labeled.

Advantages to assessment are as follows: assessment and labeling allow for more consistent scientific communication and research relative to specific conditions; groups in need of services and funding are identified; legal protection is provided for labeled groups with diminished capacities of one kind or another; more intelligent approaches to treatment are provided; and through a structured and institutionalized assessment process, indiscriminant labeling is prevented.

Labeling is one of those process that tends to immediately cancel objectivity of discussants of the pros and cons of the process. To the parent(s) who finally have a name to put on their child's unusual behavior and who can now find others with the same difficulty from whom they can derive support and ideas, labels can be a blessing. To the parent(s) who have had their child mislabeled and mistreated due to an inappropriate label or inappropriate consequences to an appropriate label, labeling can be a curse. In either case, the reaction will be emotional to the issue.

Social Issues

IQ tests group individuals into ranges of cognitive ability. There are many social implications to this grouping. Wright (1960) has suggested that individuals grouped into the lower range of IQ tests have limited access to services that have a marked impact on the quality of life. The issue of the quality of life, particularly the systematic relegation of minority groups to diminished status based on grouping along IQ or other variables, whether genetically or culturally based, lies at the heart of this issue.

Statistical Issues

The WISC-III, like most modern intelligence tests, has been developed to fit the concept of the normal curve. Since Adolphe Quetelet (1796–1874) observed that the chest size of Scottish soldiers fell into a bell-shape curve, interest in measurement and plotting human characteristics has been actively pursued by psychology (Gleitman, 1991).

One of the problems endemic to the use of the bell-shaped curve is that, mathematically, a certain percentage of individuals will fall within specific ranges. With the WISC-III, slightly more than 2.27 percent of the population will fall at or below an IQ score of 70 (mentally retarded). By the same token, approximately the same percent of the population will fall at an IQ score of 130 or above.

Although the statistical distribution makes no distinction as to the "goodness" or "badness" of the excesses or deficits statistically defined by the curve, certainly values are assigned by society. IQ scores at the bottom 2.27 percent are considered "abnormal" and labeled as such. However, the extreme at the other end of the curve, even though it is just as statistically "abnormal," is value judged in a far different light!

SUMMARY

The 1991 version of the Wechsler Intelligence Scale for Children represents a considerable improvement over earlier versions, both in the sophistication of the standardization as well as the attention given to potential cultural and ethnic biases. Initial examination of reliability and validity of the WISC-III suggests little deviation of these important considerations from the WISC-R. In addition, the new version maintains sufficient overlap with the WISC-R to give some degree of "cautious continuity" to repeat testing across the two instruments, keeping the overall lowering of scores on the WISC-III in mind.

As with any statistically well-grounded instrument of this type, the utility of the information generated is a function of the skill and training of the individual using and interpreting the instrument. If used ethically and in a standardized format by a trained individual, with due concern and regard for the individual being assessed, the WISC-III adds potentially important information to the overall assessment picture.

REFERENCES

Anastasi, A. (1982). *Psychological testing* (5th ed.). New York: MacMillan.

Bersoff, D. N., & Hofer, P. T. (1990). The legal regulation of school psychology. In T. B. Gutkin & C. R. Reynolds (Eds.), *The handbook of school psychology* (2nd ed., pp. 937–961). New York: John Wiley & Sons.

Caravajal, H. H., Hayes, J. E., Lackey, K. L., & Rathke, M. L. (1993). Correlations between scores on the Wechsler Intelligence Scale for Children-III and the General Purpose Abbreviated Battery of the Stanford-Binet IV. *Psychological Reports, 72,* 1167–1170.

Caravajal, H. H., Hayes, J. E., Miller, H. R., & Wiebe, D. A. (1993). Comparison of the vocabulary scores and IQs on the Wechsler Intelligence Scale for Children-III and the Peabody Picture Vocabulary Test-Revised. *Perceptual and Motor Skills, 76,* 28–30.

Dumont, R., & Faro, C. (1993). A WISC-III short form for learning disabled students. *Psychology in the Schools, 30,* 212–219.

Flanagan, D. P., & Alfonso, V. C. (1993). WIAT subtest and composite predicted achievement values based on WISC-III verbal and performance IQs. *Psychology in the Schools, 30,* 310–320.

Flynn, J. R. (1984). The mean IQ of Americans: Massive gains 1932 to 1978. *Psychological Bulletin, 95,* 29–51.

Foster, D., & Politano, P. M. (1994). *Comparison of the WISC-R, WRAT-R, and WISC-III scores: A correlational investigation.* Paper presented at the meeting of the South Carolina Psychological Association, Myrtle Beach, SC.

Gleitman, H. (1991). *Psychology* (3rd ed.). New York: W. W. Norton & Company.

Hobson v. *Hansen,* 269 F. Supp. 401 (D. D.C. 1967).

Kaufman, A. S. (1976). A new approach to the interpretation of subtest scatter on the WISC-R. *Journal of Learning Disabilities, 9,* 160–168.

Kaufman, A. S. (1979). *Intelligent testing with the WISC-R.* New York: John Wiley & Sons.

Kaufman, A. S. (1992). Evaluation of the WISC-III and WPPSI-R for gifted children. *Roeper Review, 14,* 154–158.

Lerner, J. (1981). *Learning disabilities: Theories, diagnosis, and teaching strategies.* Geneva, IL: Houghton Mifflin.

Little, S. G. (1992). Everything old is new again. *School Psychology Quarterly, 7,* 148–154.

Matarazzo, J. D. (1972). *Wechsler's measurement and appraisal of adult intelligence.* Baltimore, MD: Williams and Wilkins.

Mercer, J. R. (1973). *Labeling the mentally retarded.* Berkeley, CA: University of California Press.

P. v. *Riles,* 343 F. Supp. 1036 (N.D. Cal. 1972).

PASE v. *Hannon,* 506 F.2d 831 (N.D. I1. 1980).

Politano, P. M., & Tavel, S. (1995). *Factor analysis of the WISC-III with emotionally handicapped school children.* Paper presented at the Annual Convention of the Southeastern Psychological Association, Savannah, GA.

Sattler, J. M. (1982). *Assessment of children's intelligence and special abilities* (2nd ed.). Boston: Allyn and Bacon.

Sattler, J. M. (1988). *Assessment of children* (3rd ed.). San Diego, CA: Jerome M. Sattler, Publisher.

Sattler, J. M. (1992). *Assessment of children: WISC-III and WPPSI-R supplement.* San Diego, CA: Jerome M. Sattler, Publisher.

Sattler, J. M., & Atkinson, L. (1993). Item equivalence across scales: The WPPSI-R and WISC-III. *Psychological Assessment, 5,* 203–206.

Tellegen, A., & Briggs, P. F. (1967). Old wine in new skins: Grouping Wechsler subtests into new scales. *Journal of Consulting Psychology, 31,* 499–506.

Wechsler, D. (1944). *The measurement of adult intelligence* (3rd ed.). Baltimore, MD: Williams and Wilkins.

Wechsler, D. (1991). *Manual: WISC-III: Wechsler Intelligence Scale for Children-Third Edition.* New York: The Psychological Corporation.

Wright, B. A. (1960). *Physical disability: A psychological approach.* New York: Harper & Row.

8

The Wechsler Adult Intelligence Scale-Revised (WAIS-R)

Alvin E. House

> Intelligence, operationally defined, is the aggregate or global capacity of the individual to act purposefully, to think rationally and to deal effectively with his environment. (David Wechsler, 1958, p. 7)

INTRODUCTION

In 1981, David Wechsler published, through the Psychological Corporation, the most recent edition of his grouping of tasks for the assessment of global intelligence in the adult individual—the Wechsler Adult Intelligence Scale-Revised (WAIS-R). This continued a tradition of mental testing that began in 1939 with the Wechsler Bellevue Intelligence Scale, Form I (W-B). The W-B was revised and reissued in 1955 as the Wechsler Adult Intelligence Scale (WAIS). Aside from relatively minor revision, updating, and replacement of items, there was essential overlap between the W-B and the WAIS in form and nature of tasks. This same consistency was preserved in the WAIS-R. Chapter 2 of the WAIS-R manual (Wechsler, 1981) detailed the modifications: (1) Gender-free language was used and representation of minority individuals introduced into the Information and Picture Completion subtests. (2) There was some substantive changes in the Comprehension and Similarities scales. (3) The Information scale received the greatest revision, with 20 items retained from the WAIS and 9 items replaced. This could be expected given the temporal and cultural specificity of Information items.

The basic structure of the Wechsler test remained the same—six verbal and five performance subtests yielding verbal, performance, and full scale intelligence quotients. Wechsler (1981) reported briefly on experimentation with two new scales as possible additions to the WAIS-R but neither were included in the final form. One potential new subtest was not sufficiently developed for inclusion and the other correlated so highly with Block Design as to add little incremental information to the test. The two most obvious changes both paralleled changes in the Wechsler Intelligence Scale for Children-Revised (WISC-R), which had been published in 1974: both trails of Digit Span were scored and the Verbal and Performance subtests were alternated in administration.

This consistency in form reflected a basic stability in Wechsler's view of the nature of human intelligence and the role of intelligence testing (Wechsler, 1958, 1975). Wechsler rejected conceptions of intelligence linked to particular abilities or attributes of the individual such as abstract reasoning, learning acuteness, or adaptability: "Intelligence is multifaceted as well as multidetermined. What it always calls for is not a particular ability but an overall competency or global capacity, which in one way or another enables a sentient individual to comprehend the world and to deal effectively with its challenges. Intelligence is a function of the personality as a whole and is responsive to other factors besides those included under the concept of cognitive abilities" (Wechsler, 1981, p. 8). Wechsler believed that intelligence tests could yield an adequate assessment of this global capacity.

Hale (1983) suggested that there seemed to be two general approaches to discussion of intellectual assessment. One is clinical, or test oriented. It presumes the reasonableness of measuring intelligence and focuses on the practical business of how to do this as well as possible given the available tools. The alternative approach is conceptual and experimental. It presumes the inadequacy of simplistic attempts to deal with complex issues and focuses on sophisticated issues of definition and analysis. Hale noted the two positions were often perceived to be in opposition and there were few attempts to integrate the contributions of each (his own paper is a notable exception).

The present discussion focuses on the applied use of the WAIS-R in adult assessment, and falls within the test-oriented tradition. Nevertheless, the reader would be well advised to periodically consider the empirical and conceptual literature upon which intellectual assessment is founded. A rather critical discussion of early development of the Wechsler scales can be found in Frank (1983). A very fine and clear discussion of the concept and empirical understanding of intelligence is available in Brody (1992). Kaufman (1990) offers an extensive discussion of the assessment of adolescent and adult intelligence using the WAIS-R and treats in detail a number of topics only touched on here.

ADMINISTRATION

Standard Administration

The basic reference for administration of the WAIS-R is the test manual (Wechsler, 1981). The Wechsler manuals are among the best written and most complete testing guides available. The WAIS-R test instructions are clearly written and well organized, the general conceptual issues underlying interpretative scoring are discussed with care, and the manual coordinates with both administration of the test stimuli and with the scoring Record Form. Working familiarity with the test manual is a prerequisite for a competent administration of the WAIS-R. The basic instructions, scoring rules, examples, and decision rules (for initiation, inquiry, and termination points) should be known to the examiner. A poorly administered instrument yields useless information. Even worse, it creates the illusion of valid knowledge and may prevent a valid and interpretable administration of the WAIS-R for several months. The psychologist loses all the advantages of a standardized evaluation that allows for interpretation of significant variation as a function of individual differences.

Clinical experience has convinced many psychologists of the value of memorizing the standard instructions. This allows the examiner to focus his or her attention on the client. For most examiners, learning the instructions is easiest within the context of actual practice administration. With or without conscious effort to memorize a set of instructions, this does tend to occur within a few sets of administrations. A conservative estimate is that by the first 50 presentations, the wording of the WAIS-R instructions and prompts of an examiner will become largely or completely routine—but not necessarily correct. If the examiner does not learn the standardized set of instructions verbatim, then over time he or she will come to memorize his or her own variations of these, which could be a source of systematic error.

Not all evaluators agree with the desirability of memorizing the instructions. Lezak (1983), for instance, believes that the possibility of systematic drift in the wording of instructions is greater if examiners attempt to memorize the commands; and she recommends continued reading of the instructions from the manual. No data are available to provide a clear answer to this disagreement. Almost all examiners would agree that it is desirable to have the test manual available throughout the testing.

Many examiners find that highlighting or underscoring portions of the instructions, administration rules, or scoring criteria in the manual is a useful exercise—especially during their initial experience with the WAIS-R. Similarly, some examiners find the use of plastic index tabs for easy turning to certain subtests or to the expanded scoring criteria for Vocabulary, Comprehension, or Similarities personally helpful. These aids and systems can be helpful in learning to administer the test and can increase confidence during the early period of use. Novice WAIS-R examiners should try at least a few practice administrations before undertaking such modifications of their manuals—lest they end up as zealous students with almost every word and page in the manual highlighted and marked with tabs or paperclips.

WAIS-R Subtests

The WAIS-R is an omnibus type of intelligence test, tapping a wide variety of tasks. Rather than shifting task requirements from item to item, such as on the classical Binet scale, the WAIS-R groups items into 11 subtests, each having roughly similar content and task requirements within the subtest. These 11 subtests have passed from the W-B to the WAIS to the present WAIS-R. Definitions and item content continue to be based on Wechsler's original conceptual analysis of intelligence. Six of the subtests are classified as Verbal: Information, Digit Span, Vocabulary, Arithmetic, Comprehension, and Similarities. Five subtests are classified as Performance (reflecting more nonverbal abilities): Picture Completion, Picture Arrangement, Block Design, Object Assembly, and Digit Symbol. Contrasting the WAIS-R with the WISC-R and the current WISC-III shows most of the subtests to be directly comparable. Digit Symbol was renamed Coding for the original Wechsler Intelligence Scale for Children (WISC). The Digit Span subtest is a supplement subtest for the WISC-R and WISC-III. Other supplemental subtests for which no adult equivalents exist are the Mazes subtest for the WISC-R and the WISC-III, and the Symbol Search subtest from the WISC-III.

The subtest scales will be discussed in the order they are usually presented to a client: Information, Picture Completion, Digit Span, Picture Arrangement, Vocabulary, Block Design, Arithmetic, Object Assembly, Comprehension, Digit Symbol, and Similarities. The reader is also referred to the discussions of the subtests in Golden, Zillmer, E., and Spiers, M. (1992), Lezak (1983), and Sprandel (1985).

Information.   The WAIS-R Information subtest consists of 29 factual inquiry questions sampling the client's general fund of knowledge. A kind of trivia test of U.S. civilization, the item content was selected to represent the sort of background information that a developmental exposure to the U.S. culture would bring within the common knowledge of most citizens. The item difficulty ranges from easy (seldom failed in an intact sample) to difficult (seldom passed in an intact sample). Information is believed by most examiners to reflect acquired knowledge and to correlate with formal education. This is certainly one source of general cultural facts, and groups with a college education tend to score higher than groups with a high school education, who in turn, score higher than populations with only a grade school education.

However, a pattern of generalized reading across diverse topics will also yield a high Information score regardless of formal education, and examiners will meet at least a few individuals who produced high Information scores despite limited education and reading. These few seemed, in informal analysis, simply to be bright individuals, who, despite limited formal training, have remained alert to knowledge throughout their lives. Doing well on the Information subtest requires not only information but also the ability to select the right information to report on. On occasion, individuals will demonstrate the inability to control their cognitive search and/or reporting—rambling on, adding unnecessary or unrelated details, and, in extreme cases, persevering in response from item to item.

Testing on Information begins with Item 5. Items 1 through 4 are passed by all but the most impaired, and these questions are given only if either Item

5 or Item 6 is failed. Scoring is relatively easy and objective—examiner judgment is required only in determining the adequacy of responses to Items 15 and 21. Some neutral probing may occasionally be necessary to elicit enough information to allow the proper scoring of the identity of the historical personalities the client is asked to identify. As with most of the subtests, it is desirable to record verbatim the client's responses. This both allows scoring to be checked and provides a good sample of the client's speech patterns, natural vocabulary, and thought processes.

Information, along with Vocabulary, is usually seen as one of the best measures of general ability among the WAIS-R subtests. For eight of the nine age groups reported in the WAIS-R standardization data, for the average intercorrelation of the tests across all nine age samples, Information has the second highest correlation with the Verbal IQ. For five of the nine age groups, Information has the second highest average correlation with Full Scale IQ across all nine age groups. It consistently loads highly on the first verbal factor identified in most common factor and principal components analyses carried out on the WAIS-R subtest intercorrelations.

Picture Completion.   Picture Completion presents the client with a series of 20 pictures from which "there is some important part missing" (Wechsler, 1981, p. 63). Testing begins with the first item, and for the first two items the correct response is identified if the client fails an item. The first time a client identifies a correct but unessential missing part, the examiner prompts, "Yes, but what is the most important thing missing?" (Wechsler, 1981, p. 63). No further help is allowed. Testing continues until five items are failed. Clients are allowed a maximum exposure of 20 seconds for each stimulus card. This is the only formally timed Verbal subtest. For three of the items, the client must identify or point to the correct location as well as label the missing part. If he or she fails to do so, the examiner must probe, "Show me where" (Wechsler, 1981, p. 64). Scoring is relatively straightforward and objective. It is useful to record verbatim the client's responses on the record blank. The WAIS-R Record Form allows adequate space for this. This permits identification of alert and perceptive individuals who correctly identify the missing part but show an impoverished vocabulary in their poor verbal labeling. Recording the response also facilitates the identification of perseverative response patterns. It may also be useful to note extremely short or long latencies, especially if the delay costs the client credit for an otherwise correct response.

Digit Span.   The Digit Span subtest actually consists of two different tasks—an immediate recall task calling for the repetition of increasing numbers of digits and a concentration span task requiring the client to repeat backwards an increasing series of numbers immediately after hearing each. Scoring is simple: The item is passed if repeated or reversed exactly correct. Two trials are given for each digit length and both count toward the raw score. Digits Forward begins with a three-digit number and proceeds until both trials of a series are failed. Digits Backwards begins with two three-digit practice items (the second administered only if the first is failed and corrected by the examiner) and proceeds with a two-digit series and continues until both trials of a series are failed. Digits Forwards has a maximum span of nine digits; Digits Backwards has a maximum span of eight digits in reverse order.

The WAIS-R Digit Span gives a rapid screening of immediate auditory recall for digits and for the more complex cognitive task of holding a digit series, "operating" on it to reverse the order, and then reporting it aloud. Lezak has humorously compared the averaging of performance on these two tasks to an orthopedic physician averaging one broken arm and three intact limbs to give a "mean orthopedic index" (Lezak, personal communication).

It is valuable, in addition to the standard scoring of Digit Span, to note the client's highest pass on both Digits Forwards and Digits Backwards separately. Lezak suggests that spans of six or better forward are clearly within normal limits, a span of five is marginal, and a span of three is defective (1983, p. 268). For Digits Backwards, Lezak suggests that spans of four or five are within normal limits, a span of three is borderline or defective, depending on the client's educational level, and a span of two is defective for individuals less than 60 years of age (1983, p. 269). Indication of concentration or memory difficulty should be followed up with more comprehensive investigation.

Picture Arrangement.   Picture Arrangement consists of 10 sets of picture cards that are presented to the client in a standard order. The client must rearrange the cards so that a sensible story is displayed from left to right. The picture series forms wordless comic strips and are humorous in content after the first. The theme of the first series is stated to the client as the pictures are presented. If the client fails the first series, the correct order is demonstrated and a second trial is administered. No further help is given. Testing continues until four consecutive errors are made (beginning with the second item) or the subtest is completely given. Scoring is determined by producing a correct order within the time limit allowed. Two sets have two sequences receiving full credit; four sets have additional sequences receiving partial credit.

Picture Arrangement is grouped within the Performance subtests but the intercorrelation patterns show it is also closely correlated with Verbal subtests. Factor loadings for Picture Arrangement in factor-analytic and principal-component analyses have yielded complex results. There is indication that the WAIS-R PA subtest is qualitatively different from the WAIS PA subtest (Broder & Oresick, 1987; Mitchell, Grandy, & Lupo, 1986; Parker, 1983; Raybourn, 1983). Neuropsychological hypotheses derived from the relationship of the WAIS PA subtest to other WAIS subtests have not been replicated for the WAIS-R PA subtest. Finally, the hypothesis that previous versions of this subtest reflect social awareness and judgment has not been supported (Lipsitz, Dworkin, & Erlenmeyer-Kimling, 1993).

Vocabulary.   The Vocabulary gives the client written and oral presentations of 35 stimulus words and asks for their meanings. Vocabulary tends to be the WAIS-R subtest requiring the most administration time and is one of the most difficult (requiring the most judgment) to score. Vocabulary tests in all forms have long been recognized as the most accurate, stable, and general measures of mental ability or intelligence. Within the WAIS-R, Vocabulary has the highest correlation with the Verbal IQ across all age groups tested in the standardization sample; for eight of the nine age groups it has the highest intercorrelation with the Full Scale IQ. This is one of the most robust subtests on the WAIS-R and is often used as an estimate of premorbid verbal and general mental ability in cases of known brain injury. Many brief forms of the WAIS-R make use of Vocabulary as one of the best single indicators of intelligence. Paradoxically, when a near full battery is given, Vocabulary is often one of the subtests omitted because of the time required for administration. It is difficult to envision a psychological evaluation without some assessment of general word use, and the WAIS-R Vocabulary subtest is an excellent measure of this verbal ability.

Block Design.   The WAIS-R Block Design subtest is a modification of the Kohs Block Design Test and is one of the best nonverbal measures of intelligence on the WAIS-R. In fact, the intercorrelation between Block Design and Verbal IQ is higher than the intercorrelation between Digit Span and the Verbal IQ across all age samples in the standardization sample. For two age groups, the Block Design/Verbal IQ intercorrelation is as high as the Arithmetic/Verbal IQ intercorrelation. The Block Design subtest is a measure of general intelligence and is often included within short forms of the WAIS-R as the Performance subtest with the highest loading on a general intellectual factor. It usually requires a significant degree of visual-spatial ability and loads heavily on the second or spatial factor identified in most factor and principal components studies.

In this subtest, the client is presented with nine cards depicting geometric designs in white and red, and with a number of identical plastic cubes each having two red, two white, and two red and white sides split on the diagonal. The task is to reproduce the design on the card with the cubes. The client's performance is timed; after the second item, additional points are awarded for rapid, errorless performance. Block Design is one of three subtests where rapid, errorless performance is rewarded (Block Design, Arithmetic, and Object Assembly), and one of five subtests where speed in an explicit factor in scoring (Block Design, Arithmetic, Object Assembly, Picture Completion, and Digit Symbol; Digit Span might be added to the list in the sense that delays are likely to be associated with failure).

The instructions explicitly identify and demonstrate that the blocks are all alike. The first design is copied by the client from a model constructed by the examiner. The second design is copied from a stimulus figure after the examiner demonstrates the correct response. For both the first and second designs, a failure by the client is followed by a second demonstration and a second trial (for half credit). In Design 2, no further help is given; the client is instructed to work as quickly as possible. The first five designs are constructed with four blocks. When Design 6 is reached, the examiner gives the client five additional blocks and instructs him or her to make the remaining designs using nine blocks. Testing continues until the series is completed or until three consecutive designs are failed (both trials of Designs 1 and 2 must be failed to be counted a failure). The final design presents a figure that is rotated 45 degrees; the client should not be allowed to turn the stimulus card to give the figure a flat base. Constructions (on any design) rotated 30 degrees or more are considered failed. The first instance of such a rotation is corrected (but scored a failure).

Block Design is often presented as a more cultural free task than subtests such as Information or Vocabulary. Unfortunately, Block Design scores can be depressed by a variety of factors, including visual or motor impairments, any kind of brain injury, and motivational influences (such as depression). A good score on Block Design tends to be more informative than a bad score, unless some of the alternative explanations for a poor performance can be ruled out. Analyzing error patterns may be informative (Kaplan, 1988; Lezak, 1983).

Arithmetic.   The Arithmetic subtest consists of 14 mathematics problems presented orally to the client (the first item requires the client to count a row of blocks) to be worked without paper or pencil. Testing begins with Item 3; the first two items are administered only if both Items 3 and 4 are failed. Testing continues until the series is completed or 4 consecutive problems are failed. All problems must be answered within a time limit for credit to be awarded; beginning with Item 10, a bonus point is awarded for rapid, correct answering. Scoring is objective and presents no difficulty. It is useful to note the response time taken by the client for the first nine problems. This may reveal a tendency for rapid, impulsive responding that the client has difficulty controlling as the problems become more difficult. It is unfortunate that the correct answer for one item on the restandardization of the WAIS-R is the same speed as the current national speed limit, since this sometimes rewards impulsive guessing. The reduction in the number of arithmetic problems from the WAIS to the WAIS-R has restricted the raw score range rather severely and two raw score points will always raise the scaled score one point and often two points. Such considerations cannot be allowed to affect the computation of the IQ, but during test interpretation such possibilities may need to be considered, especially if Arithmetic turns out to be the highest Verbal subtest.

The mathematical requirements of the Arithmetic items, even at the top of the scale, are not excessively demanding. Comparable problems would be solved within a basic high school mathematics class. However, the necessity to work the problems in one's head, the common "math anxiety" in much of the general population, and the timed nature of the test combine to make the Arithmetic test mildly stressful for many clients—especially for those aware of educational limitations or cognitive impairments. To complete the task effectively requires the ability to concentrate, analyze the nature of the problem to be solved, mentally perform the required operations (addition, subtraction, division, multiplication), and remember the partial results until the problem is solved and the answered reported. In three-factor solutions to a principal component or factor analysis of WAIS-R tests, Arithmetic is usually found to load the minor third factor along with Digit Span and sometimes Digit Symbol. This is usually interpreted as either a "memory" or a "freedom from distractibility" factor. The tasks loading on the factor seem to have in common a requirement for sustained attention and the suppression of scores by even low levels of free-floating anxiety.

Object Assembly. Object Assembly presents the client with four cardboard puzzles of common objects to be assembled as quickly as possible. All four items are presented to all clients. If the first item is not assembled correctly within the time limits, the correct solution is demonstrated. No further help is given. Bonus points are awarded for rapid perfect performances, and partial credit is given for correct assembly of portions of a figure. Scoring is relatively objective, but may require some time and study until the examiner becomes thoroughly familiar with the correct juxtapositions for each figure.

As with the other construction task, Object Assembly is sensitive to the presence of perceptual or motor disturbances. Peripheral declines in perceptual acuity or motor speed are undoubtedly the major factor accounting for the decline in raw score performance noted with advancing age for Object Assembly. The presence of perceptual or motor control difficulties must be carefully considered in interpreting the results of the test. As with the other timed tasks, concentration and sustained attention is important in obtaining a maximum score. The examiner should be alert to the client's apparent task motivation during testing. Object Assembly usually loads on the second, spatial factor in analyses of WAIS-R subtest intercorrelations. Along with Block Design, it provides an opportunity to observe how the client handles materials, deals with constructional problems, and uses perceptual cues.

The comparison of Block Design with Object Assembly is sometimes viewed as an opportunity to observe how the client deals with abstract versus concrete spatial problems. Although there is an apparent face validity to this argument, the number of items is so restricted that practical comparisons are difficult. House and Lewis have noted, along with others, that the first two stimulus figures are recognized by most clients, whereas the third and fourth figures are either not recognized or not recognized with confidence by many clients who are impaired and/or retarded. It is useful to follow testing with an inquiry to identify the objects the client was attempting to assemble. Observations of problem-solving style, the client's handling of frustration, and any preservative responses can be valuable for a qualitative interpretation.

Comprehension. Comprehension is a complex subtest consisting of 16 questions requiring explanations (as opposed to simple factual answers). Part of the complexity of the scale is that the questions are not all the same. Three of the questions ask the client to explain what he or she would do in a certain hypothetical situation. The problem solving for these problem requires judgment and what is euphemistically called common sense. Ten of the questions require a conceptual analysis of a situation and a report regarding the relevant variables pertaining to the question. These problems range from the simple and concrete to the difficult and abstract. They are different from the three judgment questions because a report of the explicit actions required by the situation is not requested. This changes, in a fundamental sense, the nature of the problem to be solved. It is not unusual to encounter clients who are high-functioning retarded who could explain the proper action needed in almost any realistic situation but could not give an adequate conceptual analysis of a simple abstract situation. Conversely, there are others who can explain quite adequately the significance of journalistic watchdogging of a central authority but who are completely incapable of suppressing their gleeful response of "Shout FIRE!" to item 7. The remaining three Comprehension items call for proverb interpretations, a highly abstract verbal task.

Probably in part due to this diversity and complexity of item content, Comprehension is a good general test of intellectual ability and correlates highly with both Verbal and Full Scale IQ. It is also a lengthy test to administer and most difficult to score. Because of the open-ended nature of the response format, a variation in client responses is possible. It would be helpful if more space could be devoted in the test manual to multiple examples of answers of different point values. Like Vocabulary and Similarities, the client's responses are scored 2, 1, or 0 points. Two items (3 and 4) require two reasons for maximum credit; if the client responds with only one reason, the clinician should ask for a second idea. This prompting is in addition to any probing needed to clarify the appropriate point value of a client's response. Part of the difficulty in administering Comprehension is that extended neutral probing may be necessary to elicit sufficient detail to allow accurate scoring of a response. The examiner must exercise care not to lead or prompt the client with the questioning, but must reach a full understanding of the ideas the client is expressing. Scoring, ultimately, requires more judgment on the part of the examiner than on any other WAIS-R subtest.

Digit Symbol. The Digit Symbol subtest is a coding task requiring the client to draw in the symbol assigned to each digit from 1 to 9 in blank boxes beneath an extended series of random selected digits. Three responses are demonstrated by the examiner and four practice responses are made. The timed administration is then begun. The client's score is the number of boxes correctly filled in within the 90-second time limit. High scoring requires sustained concentration, rapid responding, and good fine-motor control. Extreme high scoring requires that the client rapidly learn the symbols assigned to each number so that repeated looking up at the key can be eliminated and all available time is spent in filling in blanks.

Scoring is facilitated by an overlay key. Perfect reproduction of the geometric symbols in not required—any recognizable rendering of the symbol is scored as correct. The primary task of the examiner is to monitor the client's performance and halt any skipping of digits. Occasionally, despite the instructions, a client will halt at the end of a line and must be prompted to continue. The principal difficulty encountered with administration is the necessity of careful timing.

Digit Symbol performance reflects processing speed, coordination, and learning/memory. In factor-analytic three-factor solutions, Digit Symbol tends to load most heavily on the minor third factor, which is usually interpreted as memory or freedom from distractibility. A wide variety of negative influences can reduce a client's score, including any brain injury. Digit Symbol is usually viewed as one of the most brain sensitive of the Wechsler tasks. Speculation by Kaplan regarding a "warm-up" pattern of performance by older clients on Digit Symbol has not been supported (Paolo & Ryan, 1994).

Similarities.   The Similarities subtest asks the client to identify how 14 successive pairs of nouns are alike. Testing begins with the first item for all clients and proceeds throughout the series or until four consecutive failures are obtained. The clients' responses are scored 2, 1, or 0 points according to general criteria and examples are given in the test manual. Examiner judgment is required, but scoring of Similarities responses is generally the easiest of the three Verbal subtests requiring multiple-point scoring (Vocabulary, Comprehension, Similarities). If full credit (2 points) is not earned on the first item, the examiner demonstrates a two-point response. No further help is given. A large number of partial (1 point) responses and some failure (0 points) responses automatically call for an inquiry, and frequent review of the examples in the test manual is advised. A similar situation exists for Vocabulary and for Comprehension. One of the most common mistakes in WAIS-R testing is failure to question when probing is indicated. Testing should always be carried out with the assistance of the test manual (even when the instructions have been memorized).

Similarities performance loads heavily on general intelligence and on the first verbal factor identified in most factor studies. It requires abstract verbal reasoning. The test provides an opportunity to observe the client's thought processes in action, especially with the more difficult items. Emotional or behavioral disturbances of thought processes may also become evident on this test. Consider, for example, the client who responded to the stimulus pair of two directions with the response, "I haven't been around California to see if they have weather there, but Northern people have four seasons: spring, winter, autumn, summer." An informal observation is that the item order on the WAIS-R does not appear to represent evenly increasing difficulty for many groups of clients. Item 9, in particular, seems easier (more 2-point responses) for many clients with mild impairments than the four item pairs preceding it.

Order of Presentation of Subtests

The alternation of Verbal and Performance subtests on the WAIS-R was intended to maintain the client's interest and motivation, especially if a general class of activity is particularly difficult for him or her. Clinical experience has suggested this change was beneficial. Alternating between tasks that may be more and less difficult for a client can help to maintain the client's dignity as well as their task motivation. For most clients, alternating Verbal and Performance subtests in the standard order of administration produces a mixture of tasks that may be interesting. The examiner may want to modify the order of presentation if atypical circumstances are present. The order of administration of tests from any ability battery does not appear to have significant effects on a client's performance unless the length of testing is very long (Neuger, O'Leary, Fishburne, Barth, Berent, Giordani, & Boll, 1981). A very anxious client who was having obvious difficulty concentrating on the Information questions would probably do badly when Digit Span is introduced as the third subtest. Delaying the administration of Digit Span until later in the session, after the client had relaxed somewhat, could possibly yield a more informative score.

Positioning of WAIS-R Testing within a Psychological Evaluation

The WAIS-R is typically used within the context of a comprehensive examination of a client's intellectual or global functioning. It is rare to give only the WAIS-R for an evaluation of a client. This raises the question of where the WAIS-R might be optimally placed within a series of tests. Two considerations suggest that the WAIS-R be administered relatively early in the total testing. First, the order of presentation of ability measures has little effect on scores until fatigue becomes a factor. This would suggest a strategy of completing the WAIS-R early within a session while the client is fresh. Second, in more comprehensive evaluations that include personality or adjustment measures there is the possibility that clients will find these other "tests" either frustrating and irritating (e.g., lengthy personality inventories) or upsetting and provocative (e.g., inkblot tests). These emotional reactions could affect the client's cooperativeness and task motivation adversely. It seems prudent to have already completed tasks, such as the WAIS-R which requires sustained effort and cooperation.

At the other extreme, beginning an evaluation with the WAIS-R can be an intimidating and frightening experience for some clients. It is suggested that the examination begin (following initial interviewing and agreement on joint goals) with a task that would probably be more familiar in nature to a client (such as an achievement test) or easier for the client (perhaps a drawing task) than an intelligence test. The particular choice would depend on the examiner's knowledge of the client and the results of the initial inquiry and mental status assessment.

Nonstandard Supplemental Administration

In a clinical evaluation, it is often useful to incorporate a number of additional questions and inquiries into the standard administration of the WAIS-R.

None of these involves modification of the basic administration or scoring of WAIS-R subtests and items. These additions can be considered supplemental rather than modifications of the standard administration and are intended to increase the amount of useful data gained from the investigation of time in WAIS-R testing.

The WAIS-R Record Form provides space for recording basic identifying information on clients (name, marital status, race, occupation, education, birth date, test date, and place of testing). The process of completing this information provides a convenient and comfortable opportunity to carry out a mental status examination of the client. In a friendly and conversational manner, the clients are asked to provide the correct spelling of their names, their birth dates, the current full date, the day of the week, the approximate time of day, their marital status and the length of this status, their occupations or last significant occupations and how long this lasted, how far they went in school, the year they left school, and their ages when leaving school. This information is easily recorded in two or three minutes, and clients provide it comfortably and willingly. Most of the life history information can be easily checked against other information available on the client or with family members or other informants. Basic data is thus available on gross orientation and long-term memory. The day, date, and time of day allow the scoring of the Temporal Orientation Test (Benton, Hamsher, Varney, & Spreen, 1983). Any significant failure can be noted and followed with more complete investigation later. It is usually a good idea to cover the client's wristwatch before asking any temporal orientation question. Even cooperative clients may automatically glance at their watch, which often gives the date and day as well as time. This is best done with a manila folder, the Record Form, or the Object Assembly shield, rather than the examiner's hand. The use of an object for such a close body approach will be less disturbing for many clients and will not disrupt their performance with panic nor cause the examiner embarrassment.

Novice examiners often seem reluctant to systematically carry out a formal mental status examination of temporal orientation. Examiners are willing to ask grown adults to add two single-digit numbers and state the sum, but believe these same adults will be insulted if asked to state the correct date or name the city they are in or spell their names. This reflects the preconceptions and anxiety of examiners. Most clients come to a psychologist willing, even expecting, to be asked all types of silly questions. They tend to take almost all questions as a matter of course. They will take offense if the examiner communicates (often unintentionally) that the item should be offensive; and clients really become upset when examiners appear inept or treat them in a condescending or demeaning fashion.

Mental status questions are no more intrinsically upsetting than questions about arithmetic or sex or why one left his or her last job. If examiners believe these are valuable data that will be useful in order to best serve the client, then they will ask these silly questions in the same relaxed, respectful, and careful manner they ask other questions. For the very rare individual who hesitates or indicates some concern about these types of questions, a few simple, direct, and honest words of explanation are almost always sufficient. Examiners should not feel compulsively obliged to explain to every client why they ask the date. This would be a waste of the client's time. If the client finds the request puzzling, he or she will communicate this in some manner, and it is the job of the examiner to be alert to such a communication and respond appropriately. Most clients simply answer in the same manner they mentally add two single-digit numbers and give the answer—a task they are probably asked to perform in their daily lives even less often than they are asked the date.

The WAIS-R would usually be administered as part of a group of measures in order to obtain a comprehensive psychological assessment. If this is not the case, or if the other instruments will not include written responses by the client, the blank space on the lower left area of the Record Form's first page provides a good area in which clients can be asked to sign their names or produce some other brief sample of writing. In addition to a sample of writing, this provides opportunity for observation of handedness, grip, and placement in the use of a pencil. This can be compared with later pencil handling during the Digit Symbol subtest. Unusual or inconsistent grip or placement in handling a writing instrument should be noted and recorded. The Digit Symbol subtest can be influenced, among other factors, by familiarity and experience with writing instruments.

During the Information subtest, it can be useful to follow the presentation of Item 6 with an inquiry as to the name of the current president of the United States, the immediate prior president, then the president before that one, and the next prior president. Some clients who fail the standard open inquiry question are able to respond correctly, given this additional structure. Their ability to transfer this gain can be explored by repeating Information Item 6 to see if they now respond correctly (only the original response is scored). The client's general fund of knowledge can be further assessed by asking for the name of the state governor or (if the governor question is failed) the name of the state, state capital, and largest city in the state.

Lezak (1983) reports expanding the presentation of Information Item 28 by spelling the word for the client, commenting that this word is pronounced differently by many individuals. She also notes that the discontinuation rule of five consecutive failures can be discouraging for clients, especially those with limited formal education or cognitive limitation, who may believe that a normal citizen would know the answers to all or most of the items. If testing to five failures will carry the client into the top third of the scale, she will comment that he or she as done so well that they will be asked questions only a few highly educated individuals would know the answer to. She believes this may help correct a common misperception so that client is not unduly frustrated and his or her task motivation, perhaps, reduced.

A follow-up to the Information subtest that can be carried out after WAIS-R testing is to ask the client to report on a recent prominent news story. This again expands the available sample of the client's general fund of knowledge and awareness of significant environmental events. If warranted by the client's performance, it can be further informative to give the client a copy of the local daily paper and request him or her to read a brief news story to the examiner and then answer a few basic questions about the events reported in the account. There are a number of applications served by a daily newspaper during a comprehensive psychological assessment, and one can be a standard piece of the examiner's equipment.

On the Block Design subtest, it is revealing to note the client's general approach to reproducing the stimulus design. Most intact clients are able to form conceptual gestalts of the first few designs, and quickly and systematically reproduce these with the blocks. As the designs become more difficult, one can observe their problem-solving strategies in the face of frustration. With Design 6, five additional blocks are presented with the instructions: "Now make one like this, using nine blocks. Be sure to tell me when you have finished" (Wechsler, 1981, p. 74). Some clients, despite the instructional cue, never grasp the concept of a 3 by 3 array. Another point of valuable observation occurs when a client is having difficulty correctly orienting a block within a design. The instructions both inform and demonstrate that all blocks are alike. A costly error among individuals who are lower functioning and impaired is searching for the correct block among those remaining—trying block after block in hopes of finding one that correctly fits the design. If a client completes the design correctly after orientation problems, it is informative to note if, on subsequent trials, he or she recognizes the blocks are equivalent or persists in trial-and-error placement.

With any failure on Block Design, it is useful to inquire if the client believes his or her production does actually match the stimulus figure. Clients may give up any attempt to match the test figure, may recognize features in error but be unable to correct these, or may perceive their constructions as actually matching the test design. With the supposition of perceptual-motor difficulty contributing to constructional deficits, a supplemental elaboration of the Block Design subtest is to follow the standard administration by having clients use pencil and paper to copy several of the failed designs.

On the Object Assembly subtest, it is informative to have the client identify the test figure, by name, after completion of an item. Some aphasic clients can complete the object correctly but cannot verbally name it. Conversely, clients may recognize the object but be unable to solve the puzzle. The 90-degree rotation of the back of Item 4 is so common that some examiners use the notation *SE* (standard error) for this mistake.

On the Digit Symbol subtest, Lezak (1983) recommends a modification she credits to Kaplan. She notes the square reached by the client at the close of the 90-second time period, but allows the client to continue filling in squares until reaching the end of the third row. The client is then stopped, all of the page is covered except the final row (the Object Assembly shield is useful for this), and the client is asked to fill in as many symbols from memory as possible. Kaplan (cited in Lezak, 1983) reported that a correct recall of seven of the nine symbols was at the low end of the average range. This modification gives a brief measure of incidental learning after exposure to a standard number of trials (time is uncontrolled).

The overriding goal of the examiner is to learn as much as possible about the client in the time available. The WAIS-R typically requires 45 to 75 minutes to administer completely, a substantial investment of time. The justification for this time is to gain the greatest amount of data possible from the client's test performance and behavior. For selected clients, one or more of the additions discussed above may increase the information payoff.

Testing the Limits.   One of the most common supplemental modifications of the WAIS-R subtests probably involves testing the limits—continuing to present test stimuli after a client has met the discontinuation criteria in order to gain additional data about his or her capabilities and functioning. This can involve three general strategies alone or in combination: (1) the continued presentation of additional items in the standard manner after that subtest could be discontinued for the client, (2) the allowance of additional time for a client to reach a solution to a timed item, and (3) the re-presentation of a previously failed item.

It needs to be emphasized that the purpose of testing the limits is to obtain additional qualitative information from the test—it does not affect standard raw scores, computation of scaled scores, or IQ values. It may be useful to know that a client can pass the tenth item on Information after failing Items 5, 6, 7, 8, and 9; it does not add an additional raw score point to the client's Information score.

The first modification simply involves continuing to present items within a subtest after the subtest could be discontinued. The items may be presented in order until all items have been administered, until a more conservative discontinuation criterion has been met, or extended testing may involve the presentation of select items. The standard discontinuation rules were questioned for the elderly on the WAIS (Storandt, 1977) and for Canadians on the WAIS-R Information subtest (Bornstein, McLeod, McClug, & Hutchison, 1983). Both suggested administering entire scales regardless of the pass/fail pattern. An example of testing the limits on selected items would be always administering the judgment items on the Comprehension subtest even when a client reached discontinuation early in the scale.

The second modification allows the client to continue working on subtest items past the allowed time. This modification may be made for motivational purposes—giving the client who is close to a solution on a Block Design item a few additional seconds to complete the pattern to prevent discouragement—or to see if the client is capable of solving the item. This modification may be useful with populations for whom psychomotor slowing is a concern: the elderly, depressed, or heavily medicated client. This modification may be especially valuable in the evaluation of the client who is brain injured, where it is important to differentiate between the absolute loss of a mental capability and the relative loss of efficiency due to slowing in the mobilization of adaptive behavior. Similarly, qualitative insight into the competency of clients who are mentally retarded may be gained by seeing what they can do with more time.

The third modification involves re-presentation of a failed item, either for a second try (e.g., with a client believed to have suffered from performance anxiety) or with alterations of the test stimulus to clarify the nature of the problems. For example, the Arithmetic problems could be re-presented while allowing the client to use paper and pencil, or a client could be asked to copy the Block Design figures with paper and pencil to investigate apparent problems with visual-spatial construction. Lezak (1983) presents a number of valuable ideas for testing the limits with WAIS-R subtest items.

Nonstandard Modification of Administration

Attempts to increase the cost effectiveness (efficiency) of the WAIS-R have led to consideration of modifying administration to shorten testing time. Three general approaches have been taken: (1) administering fewer subtests than the standard 11, (2) altering the start and/or stop rules to reduce the number of items presented, and (3) adopting a general rule to reduce the number of items presented (e.g., giving only odd-numbered items). These modifications were discussed at length in the first edition of this text (House & Lewis, 1985). They will not be discussed here because of considerations of length, but more importantly because the author cannot recommend any of them for clinical use. Short forms of the WAIS and the WAIS-R have had their champions and their critics (see Kaufman, 1990, for a discussion). Wechsler (1958) argued against the use of brief forms on the basis of lost information. The most revealing criticism against the use of short forms was clearly stated by Zimmerman and Woo-Sam (1973) in their discussion of the WAIS—the results of a short form of the WAIS (and presumably WAIS-R) are usually reported "as a WAIS, rarely as a 'brief-WAIS' score" (p. 178). Why would one use a screening test based on the WAIS-R subtests? The answer is often to appropriate the well-established reliability and validity of the Wechsler scales—which are based on full-scale administration. If a brief screening test is acceptable to the evaluator's purpose, then several such tests are available.

INTERPRETATION

Client Characteristics Affecting Interpretation

A number of situational or state characteristics of clients may interact with the testing situation to affect WAIS-R performance. This continues to be an area which calls for further empirical investigation.

Anxiety.   Excessive tension and anxiety is believed by most experienced examiners to adversely affect WAIS-R performance on tasks such as those that require attention and concentration (e.g., Digit Span). It appears that state or situational anxiety interferes with subtests such as Arithmetic, Digit Span, and probably Digit Symbol. It remains unclear if high trait anxiety has such a clear suppressive effect.

Medication. Medication effects also remain a relative unknown in terms of differential effects on WAIS-R subtests. Any sedating medication could potentially suppress speeded motor performances. The examiner should always inquire about prescription and over-the-counter medications the client is taking, and be sensitive to possible psychomotor effects.

Sensory, Motor, and Communication Limitations. Portions of the WAIS-R can be used with some adaptation in the assessment of most individuals, including those with sensory, motor, and communication limitations. It is desirable for the examiner to remember that the WAIS-R standardization sample was probably comprised of individuals with unremarkable histories, who had enjoyed the benefits of developing with normal vision, hearing, movement, and general life experiences. The WAIS-R Verbal Intelligence results of a congenitally blind client or a client with cerebral palsy are certainly informative in a general sense, but caution would be advised in interpreting IQ scores without consideration of the individual's disability. It has not been demonstrated for most groups of individuals with some exceptional sensory, motor, or communication characteristic that the obtained IQ results with the WAIS-R have the same kind of meaning and implications that appear justified in the general population. Validity studies of the WAIS-R (and other instruments) with most exceptional populations are a continuing need. The WAIS-R Performance scales can be used as part of the assessment of clients with hearing limitations but it is strongly advised that the examiner proceed only if he or she has some skill with manual communication. In almost all cases involving evaluation of populations with significant sensory, motor, or communication impairment, it is advisable to augment WAIS-R testing with other assessment devices, including tools deliberately designed for clients with vision or hearing or motor disabilities. Sprandel (1985) discusses assessing special populations.

Deliberate Underachievement. The topic of "faking bad" is an important one that cannot be adequately addressed in the present context. Suffice it to say that the WAIS-R assumes good task motivation; it is not designed to assess client motivation. Although extreme cases of dissimulation may be apparent or suspected (usually from the client's verbal report of circumstances and the inconsistency of WAIS-R results with other behavior), there is no reason to have confidence in the examiner's ability to detect subtle manipulations. Overall, the empirical literature does not suggest that psychologists are very good at identifying deliberate faking. A good deal of humility on this topic would seem prudent.

Age Effects on the WAIS-R. The method of standardization of the WAIS-R resulted in an equal raw score earning increasing scaled score points after 35 years of age. The shifting age norms differentially reward retention of Performance task abilities, reflecting the greater decrement noted in these scales with advancing age. Sattler (1982) displayed the effects of age corrections on the raw scores needed to obtain a scaled score on 10, and the minimum raw score needed to obtain a raw score of 10 for these age groups. It is often of interpretive value to examine the age-scaled scores for the subtests in addition to the reference-group-scaled scores; this allows a comparison of the client's achievement against a cohort of similar age.

Healthy subjects over the age of 75 usually find WAIS-R testing acceptable (Paolo & Ryan, 1993). The WAIS-R manual provides norms only through the age of 74 years but alternative norms are available for older subjects (Ivnik, Malec, Smith, Tangalos, Petersen, Kokmen, & Kurland, 1992; Ryan, Paolo, & Brungardt, 1990). Psychological assessment of geriatric populations is an important area of ongoing development and the WAIS-R can be a valuable tool.

Retarded and Gifted Individuals. Most comparisons of the WAIS and the WAIS-R found that the WAIS-R yielded consistently lower IQ scores (see Kaufman, 1990, for a review). This general relationship, however, appears not to hold for clients who are mentally retarded where WAIS-R scores may be equal or even higher than WAIS scores (Ryan, Nowak, & Geisser, 1987; Spruill & Beck, 1988). In populations of mentally retarded, the WAIS-R yields higher estimates of intelligence than does the WISC-R (Rubin, Goldman, & Rosenfeld, 1990; Spitz, 1988). The examiner should be aware of interactions between client level of ability and the relationship of the WAIS-R to other instruments. Despite these complications and competition from other instruments, it appears that the WAIS-R may remain the instrument of choice for evaluating the mentally retarded (Spruill, 1991).

A rather trivial limitation of the WAIS-R is the relatively low ceiling on the IQ tables for the standardization sample, and one occasionally hears that the WAIS-R is not the best instrument for assessment of the gifted. The question of what would be a suitable instrument for measuring the capability of an individual who is probably more intelligent and creative than the examiner is an interesting one, but it seems to have limited practical merit. Truly gifted individuals usually have better things to do than worry about the accuracy of their IQ scores, and there is no indication that conventional intellectual assessments are useful in their career or life planning as adults.

Differences between WAIS-R VIQ and PIQ

Tremendous interest has been directed toward attempting to understand the meaning of differences between the Verbal and Performance IQ scores of some clients. The empirical literature is large and cannot be adequately reviewed here. A general conclusion would be that there is a high risk of overinterpretation of VIQ/PIQ disparities. The reality is that significant VIQ/PIQ differences are not uncommon in the general population. While differences in excess of 12 to 15 scaled score points are statistically significant (reliable), they are not rare and are certainly not pathognomonic of brain damage, learning disabilities, abnormal cerebral dominance, or anything else. Extreme differences (in excess of 28 to 30 points) are rare in most groups and *may* have diagnostic implications. Both caution and use of base rates tables interpretation of VIQ/PIQ differences are indicated (Matarazzo & Herman, 1985; see Kaufman, 1990, for an extensive discussion of VIQ/PIQ differences as well as the related topic of derived factor scores).

The WAIS-R as a Neuropsychological Instrument

Measures of intelligence play a central role in assessment of brain-behavior relationships. W-B and WAIS results were important supplements to the Halstead-Reitan Neuropsychological Battery (HRNB) approach developed by Ralph Reitan. Despite some concerns (Bornstein, 1987; Paniak, Silver, Finlayson, & Tuff, 1992; Reitan & Wolfson, 1990), the WAIS-R is commonly used by neuropsychologists. A recent report from Sherer, Scott, Parsons, and Adams (1994) suggested that the sensitivity of the WAIS-R to brain damage rivaled that of the HRNB.

Attempts to identify unique patterns of subtest performance on the Wechsler tests associated with brain injury or deterioration began with the W-B, Wechsler's discussion of "Hold" and "Don't Hold" subtests, and the calculation of deterioration quotients (Wechsler, 1944). These efforts have generally not been fruitful. More recent attempts to identify a WAIS-R pattern associated with cholinergic deficits and/or dementias of the Alzheimer's type (Fuld, 1984) have not proved to be either adequately sensitive or specific (Bornstein, Termeer, Longbrake, Heger, & North, 1989; Goldman, Axelrod, Tandon, & Berent, 1993; Massman & Bigler, 1993). Neither have scatter analyses proved clinically useful (Mittenberg, Hammeke, & Rao, 1989; Ryan, Paolo, & Smith, 1992).

Edith Kaplan and associates have recently published through the Psychological Corporation an expanded modification of the WAIS-R intended as a neuropsychological tool (Kaplan, Fein, Morris, & Delis, 1991). This is based on Kaplan's process approach to neuropsychological assessment (Kaplan, 1988) and may have much to offer, although little published data are available. It will need to be demonstrated how the modifications of Kaplan affect the obtained results vis-á-vis the WAIS-R original purpose of providing a measure of global intelligence.

Estimation of Premorbid Intelligence. A related topic is the attempt to estimate probable premorbid intelligence to use as a comparison with currently tested intelligence in brain injured populations. One approach has been to base estimates on current performances believed to be more resilient in the face of injury, such as oral reading in a nonaphasic population. This is a variation of the logic of Wechsler's "hold–don't hold" deterioration ratio and some of the same problems affecting that attempt could be anticipated. Use of the New Adult Reading Test-Revised for this purpose has some preliminary support but such be taken very cautiously (Berry, Carpenter, Campbell, Schmitt, Helton, & Lipke-Molby, 1994). An alternative approach is the use of demographic variables to estimate premorbid IQ (Barona, Reynolds, & Chastain, 1984; Barona & Chastain, 1986). Although this approach also has some utility, similar great caution is advised in individual application (Paolo & Ryan, 1992; Sweet, Moberg, & Tovian, 1990).

The WAIS-R as a Test of Personality

The issue of assessing personality and adjustment effects on ability performance is an interesting topic and was briefly addressed in the original edition (House & Lewis, 1985). Despite some interesting subsequent publications the overall conclusion from the available literature would be that this is not a productive use of the WAIS-R.

CASE EXAMPLE: *BEWILDERED STUDENT*

Certain demographic and nonessential features of this case may have been altered to protect the confidentiality of the client.

Bewildered Student was a 20-year-old, single, Caucasian female referred for assessment by the health service of the private college she attended. She was a junior majoring in nursing. She had graduated three years earlier from a large, public high school serving an upper middle-class neighborhood in a suburban city.

The referral came because of concern over *Bewildered*'s academic performance. It was the joint perception of *Bewildered*, her advisor, instructors, and parents that her grades did not reflect the amount of effort she put into studies. She consistently earned superior evaluations in field-based work and usually earned average grades in academic subjects from a small, liberal arts college with a reputation for high academic standards. Near failing grades in the required college mathematics course and in a pharmacy class precipitated action to evaluate the cause of her difficulties. When a physical, auditory, and visual examination at the health service failed to find any medical problems, she was referred to evaluate a possible "reading disability." *Bewildered* reported that she liked to read but frequently lost her place in reading long sentences that carried over more than one line. She also had difficulty with optical scan test forms and much preferred essay examinations.

Brief History

Bewildered reported she had always done poorly on tests but much better on class reports and papers. She said she had problems "getting things straight" when working on tests and would afterwards feel she knew the answers to problems she had missed. She reported a history of much greater difficulty in mathematics classes than in English classes. She reported enjoying public speaking and writing. She found geometry significantly more difficult than algebra in high school and doubted she would have passed without the benefit of tutoring outside of school and extensive rote learning, which she said was completely meaningless to her. Her lowest college admission score was in mathematics. She had prescription glasses for reading and her eyes had recently been checked. She reported occasional tinnitus (ringing in the ears) but a recent and through audiological examination was negative.

Observations

Bewildered was seen for two assessment appointments. She was a few minutes late to the first and reported she had difficulty finding the office. She reported often getting lost driving around town despite having lived in the city for more than two years. She was on time for her second appointment. She was neatly dressed, well groomed, and showed good social skills. She showed good task motivation.

Testing

Temporal Orientation Test
Wide Range Achievement Test-Revised (WRAT-R)
Wechsler Adult Intelligence Test-Revised (WAIS-R)
Developmental Test of Visual Motor Integration (VMI)
Reitan-Indiana Aphasia Screening Test
Nelson-Denny Reading Test
IPAT Anxiety Scale
Trail Making Test
Woodcock-Johnson Psychoeducation Battery (W-J)
   Subtest 3: Memory for Sentences
   Subtest 10: Numbers Reversed
   Subtest 15: Reading Comprehension
   Subtest 16: Calculation
   Subtest 17: Applied Problems
Benton Serial Digit Learning Test (SD9)
Benton Judgment of Line Orientation Test
Benton Facial Recognition Test
Luria-Nebraska Neuropsychological Battery, Form I (LNNB)
   C10: Memory Scale
Benton Visual Retention Test

Results of WAIS-R Testing

Bewildered obtained a Full Scale WAIS-R IQ of 105 (63rd percentile). Her Verbal IQ was 114 (83rd percentile) and her Performance IQ was 90 (25th percentile). The 95 percent confidence intervals for her VIQ was approximately 108–120 and for her PIQ 82–99; these intervals did not overlap. The 24-point difference between her VIQ and PIQ was significant beyond the 99 percent confidence interval, although a difference of this magnitude is not rare in the general population. Subtest categorization showed relatively lower scores on spatial and sequential groupings and relatively higher scores on verbal/conceptual and acquired knowledge groupings. All of her subtest scaled scores were in the average range or above. Her immediate recall was six digits forward and four digits backward. Her scaled score on Digit Span was significantly lower than her average Verbal subtest scaled score. She earned a good score on Picture Completion but her verbal responses showed one instance of Right-Left confusion. Her Block Design constructions were all systematically done as she talked herself through the design; this slowed her work and she earned no time bonuses. She failed Design 8 because of an orientation error; she corrected on follow up when asked if her design looked just like the pattern. She succeeded in Design 9 but earned no credit because she required almost twice the allowed time. She could recall all nine Digit Symbol symbols using Kaplan's supplemental assessment.

Verbal Subtest	Scaled Score	Performance Subtest	Scaled Score
Information	14	Picture Completion	12
Digit Span	8	Picture Arrangement	8
Vocabulary	15	Block Design	8
Arithmetic	11	Object Assembly	10
Comprehension	12	Digit Symbol	8
Similarities	12		

Average Verbal subtest scaled score: 12
Average Performance subtest scaled score: 9.2

Additional Test Data

The rest of the assessment supported a hypothesis that could have been generated (but certainly not concluded) from the WAIS-R results—*Bewildered* showed a consistent differential between level of performance on tasks that could be mediated verbally and tasks that demanded more visual-spatial processing. She definitely did not have a typical reading disability. Using college norms, her oral reading, recognition vocabulary, and total reading composite scores were above average; her reading comprehension was average; her reading rate was low average, as were her arithmetic skills. Her scores on brief, primarily verbal, memory scales were average, but her immediate spatial recall on the VRT was below average. Figure copying, judgment of line orientation, and facial recognition were performed at low-average levels, using general population norms. Qualitatively, her figure drawing and copy of very simple geometric forms was normal, but producing even moderately complex or composite figures yielded indications of difficulties in spatial relationships. Her copy of the key figure from the Aphasia Screening Test showed an error of the type Reitan believes is pathognomonic for constructional dyspraxia (marked asymmetry of the teeth of the key).

Impression

Based on the obtained test data, the history supplied by *Bewildered*, her parents, and the academic advisor of her college, and her academic records from elementary, junior, high school, and college, a diagnosis of an atypical specific developmental disorder (DSM-III) was made. Her test patterns closely mirrored those expected from discussion of so-called nonverbal learning disabilities, although she did not show the difficulties with social relationship and judgment some authors have suggested are often comorbid with severe visual-spatial limitations, poor arithmetic skills, and constructional problems. In addition, she showed an indication of mild test anxiety.

Recommendations and Follow Up

Bewildered and her parents were provided with feedback through both a written report and a graphical display of the disparity between her more verbal and more visual-spatial performances. It was clearly communicated that *Bewildered*'s problems were mild to moderate but very real, that the problems had nothing to do with her motivation or effort, and that she had already learned many valuable, compensatory strategies. A similar but more formal report was provided for her college, with *Bewildered*'s consent. Some accommodation for a learning problem was advised—chiefly allowing more time if multiple-choice tests were to be used as a major element in course grades, and allowing the use of a hand calculator for arithmetic calculations in quantitative courses. Recommendations were made to *Bewildered* regarding the use of reading aids such as a pencil or bookmark to "fix" the line she is reading and suggestions for good study and test-taking skills. Finally, a recommendation for brief relaxation training to counter test anxiety was made.

    Bewildered was able to graduate with her college class and earned a "respectable" class rank (very close to the middle of her cohort). She reported having made good use of all the recommendations except the relaxation training ("too boring"), but she believed that the minor accommodations made by her school had been the significant factor in making a difference. She felt the more realistic appraisal and expectations by both herself and her parents had been of benefit in reducing her test-taking anxiety. A final follow-up contact approximately one year after graduation found that *Bewildered* was employed, doing well in her clinical position (little geometry was necessary for public health nursing, although she still had problems with directions), and seemed happy with her life.

CONCLUSION

The WAIS-III

The process of revising the Wechsler Adult Intelligence Scale has begun again. According to the Psychological Corporation, the tentative publication date for the WAIS-III is sometime in 1997 ("before 1998") assuming that all goes well with the standardization trials and analysis. The goals expressed by the Psychological Corporation staff are to preserve the integrity of the WAIS and to allow for continued compatibility with previous versions. Based on this, one would not anticipate major changes in structure, although the final results remain to be seen. As with the WAIS/WAIS-R transition, the precise relationship between scales and subscales of the forthcoming WAIS-III and other scales (both previous and contemporary) will be an empirical question for a generation of researchers.

Summary

The WAIS-R has proved to be a valuable source of quantitative and qualitative information regarding clients seen in psychological evaluation. It has proved to be a fitting continuation of the line of development begun by David Wechsler. Its success and acceptance as the standard of formal adult intelligence assessment stands as a tribute to the insight and genius of Dr. Wechsler. At the same time, there continue to be many unresolved questions and issues regarding optimal use and interpretation of the WAIS-R. The practicing clinician will need to remain familiar with the empirical findings on the WAIS-R. Equally important is the need to remain attentive to clients and open to qualitative observations. The WAIS-R is an instrument—a valuable and powerful tool, but only a tool. Psychological assessment is the process of knowledgeable decision making and is ultimately not about the measurement of concepts such as intelligence but rather the understanding of another individual. The WAIS-R can play a valuable role in this process and contribute to clinicians' understanding.

REFERENCES

Barona, A., & Chastain, R. (1986). An improved estimate of premorbid IQ for blacks and whites on the WAIS-R. *International Journal of Clinical Neuropsychology*, 8, 169–173.

Barona, A., Reynolds, C.R., & Chastain, R. (1984). A demographically based index of premorbid intelligence for the WAIS-R. *Journal of Consulting and Clinical Psychology*, 885–887.

Benton, A.L., Hamsher, K., Varney, N.R., & Spreen, O. (1983). *Contributions to neuropsychological assessment*. New York: Oxford University Press.

Berry, D.T.R., Carpenter, G.S., Campbell, D.A., Schmitt, F.A., Helton, K., & Lipke-Molby, T. (1994). The New Adult Reading Test-Revised: Accuracy in estimating

WAIS-R IQ scores obtained 3.5 years earlier from normal older persons. *Archives of Clinical Neuropsychology, 9*, 239–250.

Bornstein, R.A. (1987). The WAIS-R in neuropsychological practice. Boon or bust? *Clinical Neuropsychologist, 1*, 185–190.

Bornstein, R.A., McLeod, J., McClung, E., & Hutchinson, B. (1983). Item difficulty and content bias on the WAIS-R Information subtest. *Canadian Journal of Behavioral Science, 15*, 27–34.

Bornstein, R.A., Termeer, J., Longbrake, K, Heger, M., & North, R. (1989). WAIS-R cholinergic deficit profile in depression. *Psychological Assessment, 1*, 342–344.

Broder, S.N., & Oresick, R.J. (1987). On rearranging Picture Arrangement: Data from a clinical sample. *Perceptual and Motor Skills, 64*, 1199–1202.

Brody, N. (1992). *Intelligence* (2nd ed.). San Diego, CA: Academic Press.

Craig, R.J., & Olson, R.E. (1991). Relationship between Wechsler scales and Peabody Picture Vocabulary Test-Revised scores among disability applicants. *Journal of Clinical Psychology, 47*, 420–429.

Frank, G. (1983). *The Wechsler Enterprise: An assessment of the development, structure, and use of the Wechsler tests of intelligence*. New York: Pergamon Press.

Fuld, P.A. (1984). Test profile of cholinergic dysfunction and of Alzheimer type dementia. *Journal of Clinical Neuropsychology, 6*, 380–392.

Golden, C.J., Zillmer, E., & Speirs, M. (1992). *Neuropsychological assessment and intervention*. Springfield, IL: Charles C. Thomas.

Goldman, R.S., Axelrod, B.N., Tandon, R., & Berent, S. (1993). Spurious WAIS-R cholinergic profiles in schizophrenia. *The Clinical Neuropsychologist, 7*, 171–178.

Hale, R.L. (1983). Intellectual assessment. In M. Hersen, A.E. Kazdin, & A.S. Bellack (Eds.), *The clinical psychology handbook*. New York: Pergamon Press.

House, A.E., & Lewis, M.L. (1985). Wechsler Adult Intelligence Scale-Revised. In C.S. Newmark (Ed.), *Major psychological assessment instruments*. Boston: Allyn and Bacon.

Ivnik, R.J., Malec, J.F., Smith, G.E., Tangalos, E.G., Peterson, R.C., Kokmen, E., & Kurland, L.T. (1992). Mayo's older Americans normative studies: WAIS-R norms for ages 56 to 97. *Clinical Neuropsychologist, 6*, Supplement, 1–30.

Ivnik, R.J., Smith, G.E., Malec, J.F., Tangalos, E.G., & Parisi, J.E. (1993). Comparison of Wechsler vs. Mayo summary scores in a clinical sample. *Journal of Clinical Psychology, 49*, 534–542.

Kaplan, E. (1988). A process approach to neuropsychological assessment. In T. Boll & B.K Bryant (Eds.), *Clinical neuropsychology and brain function* (pp. 129–167). Washington, D.C.: American Psychological Association.

Kaplan, E., Fein, D., Morris, R., & Delis, D.C. (1991). *WAIS-R NI Manual*. New York: Psychological Corporation.

Kaufman, A.S. (1990). *Assessing adolescent and adult intelligence*. Boston: Allyn and Bacon.

Lezak, M.D. (1983). *Neuropsychological assessment* (2nd ed.). New York: Oxford University Press.

Lipsitz, J.D., Dworkin, R.H., & Erlenmeyer-Kimling, L. (1993). Wechsler Comprehension and Picture Arrangement subtest and social adjustment. *Psychological Assessment, 5*, 430–437.

Massman, P.J., & Bigler, E.D. (1993). A quantitative review of the diagnostic utility of the WAIS-R Fuld Profile. *Archives of Clinical Neuropsychology, 8*, 417–428.

Matarazzo, J.D., & Herman, D.O. (1985). Clinical use of the WAIS-R: Base rates of differences between VIQ and PIQ in the WAIS-R standardization sample. In B.B. Wolman (Ed.), *Handbook of intelligence*. New York: John Wiley & Sons.

Mitchell, R.E., Grandy, T.G., & Lupo, J.V. (1986). Comparison of the WAIS and the WAIS-R in the upper range of IQ. *Professional Psychology: Research and Practice, 17*, 82–83.

Mittenberg, W., Hammeke, T.A., & Rao, S.M. (1989). Intratest scatter on the WAIS-R as a pathognomonic sign of brain injury. *Psychological Assessment, 1*, 273–276.

Neuger, G.J., O'Leary, D.S., Fishburne, F.J., Barth, J.T., Berent, S., Giordani, B., & Boll, T.J. (1981). Order effects on the Halstead-Reitan Neuropsychological Test Battery and allied procedures. *Journal of Consulting and Clinical Psychology, 49*, 722–730.

Paniak, C.E., Silver, K., Finlayson, M.A.J., & Tuff, L.P. (1992). How useful is the WAIS-R in closed head injury assessment? *Journal of Clinical Psychology, 48*, 219–225.

Paolo, A.M. & Ryan, J.J. (1992). Generalizability of two methods of estimating pre-morbid intelligence in the elderly. *Archives of Clinical Neuropsychology, 7*, 135–143.

Paolo, A.M., & Ryan, J.J. (1993). Is the WAIS-R an acceptable test for the elderly? Opinions of examinees 75 years and older. *Journal of Clinical Psychology, 49*, 720–723.

Paolo, A.M., & Ryan, J.J. (1994). WAIS-R Digit Symbol patterns for persons 75 years and older. *Journal of Psychoeducational Assessment, 12*, 67–75.

Parker, K. (1983). Factor analysis of the WAIS-R at nine age levels between 16 and 74 years. *Journal of Consulting and Clinical Psychology, 51*, 302–308.

Piedmont, R.L., Sokolove, R.L., & Fleming, M.Z. (1992). An evaluation of various WAIS-R factor structures in a psychiatric sample. *Journal of Clinical Psychology, 48*, 658–666.

Raybourn, R.E. (1983). The Wechsler Adult Intelligence Scale (WAIS) and the WAIS-Revised: A comparison and a caution. *Professional Psychology: Research and Practice, 14*, 357–361.

Reitan, R.M. & Wolfson, D. (1990). A consideration of the comparability of the WAIS and WAIS-R. *Clinical Neuropsychologist, 4*, 80–85.

Rubin, H., Goldman, J.J., & Rosenfeld, J.G. (1990). A follow-up comparison of WISC-R and WAIS-R IQs in a residential mentally retarded population. *Psychology in the Schools, 27*, 309–310.

Ryan, J.J. (1984). Abnormality of subtest score and Verbal-Performance IQ differences on the WAIS-R. *The International Journal of Clinical Neuropsychology, 6*, 97–98.

Ryan, J.J., Nowak, T.J., & Geisser, M.E. (1987). On the comparability of the WAIS and WAIS-R: Review of the research and implications for clinical practice. *Journal of Psychoeducational Assessment, 5*, 15–30.

Ryan, J.J., Paolo, A.M., & Brungardt, T.M. (1990). Standardization of the Wechsler Adult Intelligence Scale-Revised for persons 75 years and older. *Psychological Assessment, 2*, 404–411.

Ryan, J.J., Paolo, A.M., & Smith, A.J. (1992). Wechsler Adult Intelligence Scale-Revised intertest scatter in brain-damaged patients: A comparison with the standardization sample. *Psychological Assessment, 4*, 63–66.

Ryan, J.J. & Prifitera, A. (1990). The WAIS-R index for estimating premorbid intelligence: Accuracy in predicting short form IQ. *The International Journal of Clinical Neuropsychology, 12*, 20–23.

Sherer, M., Scott, J.G., Parsons, O.A., & Adams, R.L. (1994). Relative sensitivity of the WAIS-R subtests and selected HRNB measures to the effects of brain damage. *Archives of Clinical Neuropsychology, 9*, 427–436.

Sattler, J.M. (1982). Age effects on Wechsler Adult Intelligence Scale-Revised tests. *Journal of Consulting and Clinical Psychology, 50*, 785–786.

Spitz, H.H. (1988). Inverse relationship between the WISC-R/WAIS-R score disparity and IQ level in the lower range of intelligence. *American Journal on Mental Retardation, 92*, 376–378.

Sprandel, H.Z. (1985). *The psychoeducational uses and interpretation of the Wechsler Adult Intelligence Scale-Revised*. Springfield, IL: Charles C. Thomas.

Spruill, J. (1991). A comparison of the Wechsler Adult Intelligence Scale-Revised with the Stanford-Binet Intelligence Scale (4th Edition) for mentally retarded adults. *Psychological Assessment, 3*, 133–135.

Spruill, J., & Beck, B.L. (1988). Comparison of the WAIS and WAIS-R: Different results for different IQ groups. *Professional Psychology: Research and Practice, 19*, 31–34.

Storandt, M. (1977). Age, ability level, and method of scoring the WAIS. *Journal of Gerontology, 32*, 175–178.

Sweet, J.J., Moberg, P.J., & Tovian, S.M. (1990). Evaluation of Wechsler Adult Intelligence Scale-Revised premorbid IQ formulas in clinical populations. *Psychological Assessment, 2*, 41–44.

Thompson, A.P., & Molly, K. (1993). The stability of WAIS-R IQ for 16-year-old students retested after 3 and 8 months. *Journal of Clinical Psychology, 49*, 891–898.

Wechsler, D. (1944). *The measurement of adult intelligence* (3rd ed.). Baltimore: Williams & Wilkins.

Wechsler, D. (1958). *The measurement and appraisal of Adult intelligence* (4th ed.). Baltimore: Williams & Wilkins.

Wechsler, D. (1975). Intelligence defined and undefined. *American Psychologist, 30*, 135–139.

Wechsler, D. (1981). *Wechsler Adult Intelligence Scale-Revised: Manual*. New York: Psychological Corporation.

Zimmerman, I.L., & Woo-Sam, J.M. (1973). *Clinical interpretation of the Wechsler Adult Intelligence Scale*. New York: Grune & Stratton.

9

The Kaufman Assessment Battery for Children (K-ABC)

R. W. Kamphaus
Kristee A. Beres
Alan S. Kaufman
Nadeen L. Kaufman

The Kaufman Assessment Battery for Children (K-ABC; Kaufman & Kaufman, 1983a) has been the subject of scores of research investigations (at least several hundred). The K-ABC is also becoming a frequently used test in everyday assessment practice. In a nationwide survey of school psychologists conducted in 1987 by Obringer (1988), respondents were asked to rank the following instruments in order of their usage: Wechsler's scales, the K-ABC, and both the old and new Stanford-Binets. The Wechsler scales earned a mean rank of 2.69, followed closely by the K-ABC with a mean of 2.55; then came the old Binet (1.98) and the Stanford-Binet Fourth Edition (1.26). A more recent survey of school psychologists has confirmed these findings (Bracken, 1989). This survey revealed that 41 percent of the practitioners used the McCarthy Scales of Children's abilities with preschoolers (see Bracken, 1989, Chapter 12), 28 percent used the Binet 4, and 25 percent used the K-ABC. For ages 5 to 11 years, the WISC-R was endorsed by 82 percent, the K-ABC by 57 percent, and the Binet 4 by 39 percent of the practitioners. These results argue that child clinicians should have at least some familiarity with the K-ABC. Whether it is the novelty of the instrument (it differs from other scales in theory, organization of subtests, and other ways), its ease of use, or other factors that make it relatively popular is not clear. It does, however, appear to be around for the long haul.

This chapter is an adaptation of a chapter that appeared previously in R. Kamphaus (1993), *Clinical Assessment of Children's Intelligence* Boston: Allyn and Bacon.

From the outset, the K-ABC has been the subject of great controversy, as attested to by the strongly pro and con articles written for a special issue of the *Journal of Special Education* devoted to the K-ABC (Miller & Reynolds, 1984). Many of the controversies, especially those regarding the validity of the K-ABC theory, will likely endure unresolved for some time. In the meantime, however, a wealth of research can lead clinicians in interpreting the K-ABC because so much is known about how it correlates with other measures.

THEORETICAL FRAMEWORK

The K-ABC intelligence scales are based on a theoretical framework that differs greatly from the approach of Wechsler who emphasized the assessment of "g" (general ability). The Kaufmans put a great deal more emphasis on their subscales, Sequential and Simultaneous information processing, which relate to *how* children solve problems rather than *what* type of problems they must solve (i.e., verbal or nonverbal). Wechsler used the Verbal and Performance scales as means to an end, that end being the assessment of general intelligence. The Kaufmans, however, elevated the Sequential and Simultaneous scales so that they are the focus of interpretation rather than the overall score—the Mental Processing Composite (MPC).

The theoretical underpinnings of the Sequential and Simultaneous scales are really an updated version of a variety of theories (Kamphaus, 1990). They were gleaned from a convergence of research and theory in diverse areas, including clinical and experimental neuropsychology and cognitive psychology. The Sequential and Simultaneous theory was distilled primarily from two lines: the information processing approach of Luria (e.g., Luria, 1966) and the cerebral specialization work done by Sperry (1968, 1974), Bogen (1969), Kinsbourne (1975), and Wada, Clarke, and Hamm (1975).

Simultaneous Processing

Simultaneous processing refers to the mental ability of the child to integrate input all at once to solve a problem correctly. Simultaneous processing frequently involves spatial, analogic, or organizational abilities (Kaufman & Kaufman, 1983c; Kamphaus & Reynolds, 1987). Often, there is a visual aspect to the problem and visual imagery may be involved in solving it. The Triangles subtest on the K-ABC (an analog of Wechsler's Block Design task) is a prototypical measure of simultaneous processing. To solve these items correctly, one must mentally integrate the components of the design to "see" the whole. Such a task seems to match up nicely with Luria's qualifying statement of synthesis of separate elements (each triangle) into spatial schemes (the larger pattern of triangle, which may form squares, rectangles, or larger triangles). Whether the tasks are spatial or analogic in nature, the unifying characteristic of simultaneous processing is the mental synthesis of the stimuli to solve the problem, independent of the sensory modality of the input or the output.

Simultaneous processing is also required on the Photo Series subtest of the K-ABC. This finding is sometimes a surprise to the new user because of the similarities between this test and Wechsler's Picture Arrangement. The Photo Series test, however, is a marker test of the Simultaneous scale, as it is tied with Triangles for having the best factor loading on the Simultaneous factor (Kaufman & Kamphaus, 1984). Hence, even though the Photo Series subtest appears to have a sequential component (and the Kaufman's theorized that it was a sequential task but were surprised themselves [Kamphaus & Reynolds, 1987]), the process that most children elect to use places it on the Simultaneous scale. Evidently, the more crucial aspect of solving Photo Series items correctly involves developing a sense of the whole series of pictures and how they connect to one another. Overall, the Simultaneous Processing Scale measures all three aspects of this process, as defined by Luria: Perceptual (Magic Window, Gestalt Closure), mnestic or memory (Face Recognition, Spatial Memory), and complex intelligence (Matrix Analogies, triangles, Photo Series).

Sequential Processing

Sequential processing, on the other hand, emphasizes the arrangement of stimuli in sequential or serial order for successful problem solving. In every instance, each stimulus is linearly or temporally related to the previous one (Kaufman & Kaufman, 1983c), creating a form of serial interdependence within the stimulus. The K-ABC includes sequential processing subtests that tap a variety of modalities. The Hand Movements subtest involves visual input and a motor response; the Number Recall subtest involves auditory input with an auditory response. Word Order involves auditory input and a visual response. Therefore, the mode of presentation or mode of response is not what determines the scale placement of a task, but rather the *mental processing demands* are important (Kaufman & Kaufman, 1983c). Nor is short-term memory the single unifying feature of the scale; Face Recognition and Spatial Memory both load on the Simultaneous factor.

Achievement vs. Intelligence

One controversial aspect of the K-ABC was to take the equivalent of Wechsler's Verbal Scale and say that these types of tests are no longer intelligence tests—they are now achievement tests (Kamphaus & Reynolds, 1987). This is what the Kaufmans did by taking analogs of tests such as Information (Faces & Places), Vocabulary (Riddles and Expressive Vocabulary), and Arithmetic (Arithmetic) and putting them on their own scale as achievement tests. The K-ABC authors (Kaufman & Kaufman, 1983c) give the following rationale for this move:

Unlike the theoretically based mental processing scales, the K-ABC Achievement Scale was derived from only rational and logical considerations. . . . We see these diverse tasks as united by the demands they place on children to extract and assimilate information from their cultural and school environment. Regardless of more traditional approaches to the definition and measurement of intelligence, the K-ABC is predicated on the distinction between problem solving and knowledge of facts. The former set of skills is interpreted as intelligence; the latter is defined as achievement. This definition presents a break from other intelligence tests, where a person's acquired factual information and applied skills frequently influence greatly the obtained IQ. (p. 2)

The label *achievement* may, however, not be the best for this scale (Kamphaus & Reynolds, 1987) because of its similarity to the WISC-III Verbal Scale. In some cases, this scale may function as two measures—verbal intelligence and reading (Kamphaus & Reynolds, 1987). This division of the Achievement Scale is especially appealing in light of the factor-analytic data on the K-ABC, which suggests that the K-ABC possesses three factors that are very similar to those of the WISC-R and WISC-III.

ORGANIZATION OF THE K-ABC

The intelligence scales of the K-ABC consist of subtests that are combined to form scales of Sequential Processing, Simultaneous Processing, and the Mental Processing Composite, a summary score reflective of the Sequential and Simultaneous scales. On the separate Achievement scale, subtests are combined to form a global Achievement score. The K-ABC differs greatly from the WISC-III in its developmental focus. Instead of giving all subtests to all children, the K-ABC has subtests that are designed only for specific age groups. As a result, children at different ages not only are administered different subtests but also different numbers of subtests, with young children receiving far fewer subtests than older children.

The K-ABC also includes a special short form of the Mental Processing Composite, known as the Nonverbal scale (composed of tasks that can be administered in pantomime and that are responded to motorically) to assess the intelligence of children with speech or language problems, children with hearing impairments, and those who do not speak English. It is particularly useful as part of the assessment of children suspected of aphasias or other expressive or receptive language disorders. However, the Nonverbal scale is useful as an estimate of general intellectual level only and cannot be subdivided into Sequential or Simultaneous Processing scales.

All of the K-ABC global scales (Sequential Processing, Simultaneous Processing, Mental Processing Composite, Achievement, and Nonverbal) yield standard scores, with a mean of 100 and standard deviation of 15, to provide a commonly understood metric and to permit comparisons of mental processing with achievement for children suspected of learning disabilities. Furthermore, use of this metric allows for easy comparison of the K-ABC global scales to other major tests of intelligence and to popular individually administered tests of academic achievement. The Mental Processing subtests yield standard scores with a mean of 10 and standard deviation of 3, modeled after the familiar Wechsler scaled score. Achievement subtests, on the other hand, yield standard scores with a mean of 100 and a standard deviation of 15, which permits direct comparisons of the mental processing global scales with individual achievement areas.

PSYCHOMETRIC PROPERTIES OF THE K-ABC

Standardization

The K-ABC was standardized on a sample of 2,000 children, using primarily 1980 United States Census figures. The sample was stratified by age, gender, geographic region, race/ethnic group, parental educational attainment (used as a measure of socioeconomic status [SES]), community size, and educational placement (regular class placement versus placement in a variety of programs for exceptional children). In the past, exceptional children have been excluded from the standardization samples for individually administered tests (Kaufman & Kaufman, 1983c). The K-ABC authors included representative proportions of learning disabled, mentally retarded, gifted and talented, and other special populations in the standardization sample according to data provided by the National Center for Education Statistics and the U.S. Office of Civil Rights. Overall, the match of the sample to Census statistics is quite good, although high-SES minorities (specifically African Americans and Hispanics) were statistically significantly oversampled (Bracken, 1985). The effect of this sampling was probably rather small, however, resulting in an overestimation of African American and Hispanic populations' total scores by around two points on the Mental Processing Composite (MPC). (*Overestimation* here refers to the mean scores of these groups had their representation in the standardization sample been a perfect match to the 1980 U.S. Census Bureau statistics [Kamphaus & Reynolds, 1987].)

Reliability

Split-half reliability coefficients for the K-ABC global scales range from 0.86 to 0.93 (mean = 0.90) for preschool children, and from 0.89 to 0.97 (mean = 0.93) for children ages 5 to 12½. All of the K-ABC subtests show internal consistencies that are comparable to those of other measures save one—Gestalt Closure. This test had mean internal consistency coefficients of .72 for preschoolers and .71 for school-age children. These results suggest that this test has a relatively heterogeneous item pool. A notion that is consistent with clinical observations is children perform inconsistently on this test. A child may solve easy items incorrectly, and later, more difficult items correctly. The

Gestalt Closure subtest is also a good example of the difference between internal consistency coefficients and test-retest coefficients. The stability or test-retest coefficients are considerably higher for this test (.74 for preschoolers, .84 for early elementary grades, and .86 for later elementary grades) than the internal consistency estimates. These data suggest that although this test has a heterogeneous item pool, the overall scores obtained by a child are relatively stable over time.

The test-retest reliability study was conducted with 246 children retested after a two- to four-week interval (mean interval = 17 days). The results of this study showed good estimates of stability that improved with increasing age. For the Mental Processing Composite, coefficients of .83, .88, and .93 were obtained for each age group (for preschoolers, for early elementary grades, and for later elementary grades, respectively). Achievement scale composite reliabilities for these same age ranges were .95, .95, and .97, respectively.

A test-retest reliability coefficients for the global scales, and to a lesser extent the internal consistency (split-half) coefficients, show a clear developmental trend, with coefficients for the preschool ages being smaller than those for the school-age range. This trend is consistent with the known variability over time that characterizes preschool children's standardized test performance in general (Kamphaus & Reynolds, 1987).

Validity

The *K-ABC Interpretive Manual* (Kaufman & Kaufman, 1983c) includes the results of 43 validity studies, an impressive amount of prepublication research that at the time was all too uncommon in test manuals. Studies were conducted on aspects of construct, concurrent, and predictive validity. In addition, several of the studies were conducted with samples of exceptional children, including samples classified as hearing impaired, physically impaired, gifted, mentally retarded, and learning disabled.

Developmental Changes. The K-ABC yields satisfactory growth curves for most age groups (Kamphaus & Reynolds, 1987). It has, however, some problems with a lack of easy items for preschoolers (inadequate floor) and difficult items for older children (inadequate ceiling) (Kamphaus & Reynolds, 1987). At the preschool level, the K-ABC generally lacks difficulty for 2½- and 3-year-olds with below-average intelligence. Since children are usually referred at this age for developmental problems, a child will likely obtain at least one raw score of 0. A child who obtains more than one raw score of 0 has not been measured because the examiner does not know how far below 0 this child's skill or ability lies. When this situation occurs, it makes interpretation of the child's scores difficult and results in the examiner having to engage in a high level of inference. The examiner would do better to avoid such problems by choosing a test with more floor. The problem with this age group is that there are not many alternatives to the K-ABC with evidence of adequate floor (see Kamphaus, 1993, Chapter 12).

The parallel problem is the lack of ceiling for older age groups, which occurs for children beginning at about 10 years of age. The major problem here is on the Simultaneous scale on which a child may obtain a perfect score on tests such as Photo Series and Matrix Analogies. If this eventually occurs then, again, the child has not been measured. These findings suggest that the K-ABC is not the test of choice for gifted children 10 years old or older.

In summary, age differentiation validity is an issue of greater relevance to the K-ABC than to the WISC-III. The K-ABC introduces new tests at a variety of ages and spans the preschool- and school-age ranges, and both of these factors make the scale more prone to 0 and perfect raw scores than the WISC-III. Clinicians have to keep knowledge about age differentiation validity clearly in mind in order to use this test effectively.

Item Bias/Content Validity.   The K-ABC is also unusual in that the Kaufmans went to great lengths to remove biased items. As such, the K-ABC has an extremely well scrutinized set of items. Many items were removed at various stages of the test development process due to concern over gender, regional, or racial/ethnic group bias. A more thorough discussion of this issue and more examples of biased items can be found in Kamphaus and Reynolds (1987). This complete examination of test items was emulated recently by the WISC-III.

Correlations with other Tests.   Despite the fact that the K-ABC differs in numerous ways from tests such as the WISC-III, overwhelming evidence shows that these measures correlate very highly (Kamphaus & Reynolds, 1987) (see Table 9–1). In a study of 182 children enrolled in regular classrooms, the Mental Processing Composite (MPC) correlated 0.70 with WISC-R Full-Scale IQ (FSIQ) (Kaufman & Kaufman, 1983c). Hence, the K-ABC Mental Processing scales and the WISC-R share a 49 percent overlap in variance. They correlate in a manner similar to the relationship between older versions of the Wechsler and Binet scales. The correlations between the K-ABC and WISC-R for numerous nondisabled and exceptional populations shown in the *Interpretive Manual* range from .57 to .74. The K-ABC overlaps with the WISC-R a good deal, and yet it also shows some independence.

This significant correlation between the K-ABC and major intelligence tests has been corroborated in numerous investigations (see Table 9–1). A study of the relationship of the K-ABC MPC with the Stanford-Binet IV Composite involving 175 children yielded a coefficient of .89. Similarly, the MPC was found to correlate .66 with the Kaufman Adult Intelligence Test (KAIT) Composite Intelligence score for a sample of 124 11- and 12-year-olds, and .75 for a sample of 27 children who were administered the Differential Ability Scale.

The correlations among preschool measures are slightly lower, which seems sensible given the lower reliabilities often associated with tests used

Table 9–1 Criterion-Related Validity Studies

	M	SD	Sequent Process	Simult Process	Mental Processing Composite	Achievement	Nonverbal
Nonhandicapped Preschool, Hartnett & Fellendorf,* N = 40							
WPPSI Verbal	94.8	10.7	0.37	0.28	0.37	0.64	0.17
WPPSI Performance	98.5	12.2	0.41	0.50	0.55	0.47	0.44
WPPSI Full Scale	96.1	10.7	0.46	0.47	0.55	0.66	0.36
K-ABC Mean	93.0		93.8		92.6	91.7	94.2
K-ABC SD	12.6		12.4		11.9	8.4	14.1
Mexican-American, Valencia, 1985, N = 42							
WPPSI Verbal	95.7	11.2	0.33	0.52	0.52	0.52	0.35
WPPSI Performance	109.2	14.1	0.24	0.68	0.59	0.52	0.62
WPPSI Full Scale	102.4	12.4	0.31	0.68	0.62	0.58	0.56
K-ABC Mean	100.1		106.5		104.1	90.6	106.9
K-ABC SD	10.5		13.2		11.6	9.1	10.2
Nonhandicapped Children, WPPSI-R Manual, Wechsler, 1989, N = 59							
WPPSI-R Verbal	94.4	12.5	0.41	0.31	0.42	N/A	N/A
WPPSI-R Performance	100.4	13.5	0.31	0.37	0.41	N/A	N/A
WPPSI-R Full Scale	96.8	12.6	0.43	0.41	0.49	N/A	N/A
K-ABC Mean	104.4		101.3		103.1		
K-ABC SD	14.3		13		13.1		
5- to 7-Year-Olds, DAS Manual, Elliot, 1990, N = 27							
DAS Verbal Ability	106.2	10.5	0.18	0.35	0.32	0.64	
DAS Non-Verbal Reasoning Ability	101.6	13.1	0.24	0.68	0.56	0.72	
Spatial Ability	100.6	14.1	0.62	0.74	0.81	0.39	
GCA	102.8	11.1	0.46	0.78	0.75	0.78	
Special Non-Verbal	100.3	12.0	0.49	0.82	0.80	0.64	
K-ABC Mean	110.6		110.5		111.9	110.5	N/A
K-ABC SD	13.8		12.1		12.5	7.4	N/A
Nonhandicapped, Cuccio, Devine, & Mollner; Swerdik & Lewis; Tolman, Zins & Barnett, 1984,* N = 182							
WISC-R Verbal	115.40	15.1	0.49	0.51	0.59	0.78	0.54
WISC-R Performance	114.60	14.5	0.30	0.68	0.61	0.51	0.63
WISC-R Full Scale	116.70	14.3	0.47	0.68	0.70	0.76	0.67
K-ABC Mean	110.0		113.1		113.6	112.8	113.6
K-ABC SD	15.1		12.9		13.6	12.5	13.6

Continued

355

Table 9-1 *Continued*

	M	SD	Sequent Process	Simult Process	Mental Processing Composite	Achievement	Nonverbal
Naglieri, 1985, N = 34							
WISC-R Verbal	105.5	12.1	0.73	0.73	0.79	0.90	N/A
WISC-R Performance	109.9	11.5	0.65	0.84	0.81	0.75	N/A
WISC-R Full Scale	108.3	11.9	0.74	0.83	0.85	0.89	N/A
K-ABC Mean			108.8	107.4	108.8	104.3	N/A
K-ABC SD			10.6	10.1	9.8	10.1	N/A
Sapp & Hritcko, 1984, N = 58							
WISC-R Verbal	94.8	27.3	0.78	0.82	0.85	—	N/A
WISC-R Performance	93.9	22.9	0.77	0.90	0.90	—	N/A
WISC-R Full Scale	94.2	26.2	0.81	0.90	0.91	—	N/A
K-ABC Mean			95.7	93.8	94.1	89.8 (N = 25)	N/A
K-ABC SD			21.5	22.7	23.5	28.1	N/A
Sioux, Brokenleg, and Bryde, N = 40*							
WISC-R Verbal	91.4	14.6	0.34	0.39	0.44	0.85	0.40
WISC-R Performance	103.6	11.8	0.28	0.74	0.65	0.48	0.67
K-ABC SD			21.5	22.7	23.5	28.1	N/A
Sioux, Brokenleg, and Bryde,* N = 40							
WISC-R Verbal	91.4	14.6	0.34	0.39	0.44	0.85	0.40
WISC-R Performance	103.6	11.8	0.28	0.74	0.65	0.48	0.67
WISC-R Full Scale	96.8	12.6	0.36	0.62	0.61	0.80	0.59
K-ABC Mean			99.6	101.3	100.6	93.3	100.2
K-ABC SD			12.4	10.7	10.7	12.8	12.0
Navajo, Naglieri,* N = 33							
WISC-R Verbal	74.9	13.5	0.36	0.40	0.43	0.84	0.26
WISC-R Performance	102.8	11.8	0.46	0.55	0.60	0.47	0.42
WISC-R Full Scale	86.9	11.1	0.46	0.53	0.57	0.80	0.38
K-ABC Mean			87.7	99.8	94.2	81.7	99.1
K-ABC SD			11.3	10.2	10.3	11.2	10.7
African-American, Naglieri, 1986, N = 86							
WISC-R Full Scale	92.3	11.8	—	—	—	0.77	N/A
K-ABC Mean			93.0	92.4	91.5	92.0	N/A
K-ABC SD			9.6	11.6	10.6	9.6	N/A

Gifted Minority, Mealor & Curtiss, 1985, N = 53

WISC-R Verbal	105.6	13.8	0.38	0.55	0.57	0.84	N/A
WISC-R Performance	105.2	11.6	0.13	0.64	0.54	0.33	N/A
WISC-R Full Scale	105.9	12.6	0.32	0.67	0.64	0.71	N/A
K-ABC Mean			107.5	104.8	104.7	105.6	N/A
K-ABC SD			12.3	13.2	12.5	10.3	N/A

Gifted, McCallum, Karnes & Edwards, 1984, N = 41

WISC-R Verbal	132.0	9.7	0.06	0.34	0.31	0.40	N/A
WISC-R Performance	126.1	13.4	-0.05	0.74	0.60	(0.09)	N/A
WISC-R Full Scale	132.4	10.5	0.03	0.67	0.58	0.16	N/A
K-ABC Mean			114.8	118.2	119.2	120.2	N/A
K-ABC SD			11.0	11.1	10.3	6.8	N/A

Gifted, Naglieri & Anderson, 1985, N = 38

WISC-R Verbal	131.9	11.6	0.40	0.35	0.50	0.63	N/A
WISC-R Performance	129.7	10.3	0.41	0.36	0.54	0.05	N/A
WISC-R Full Scale	134.3	8.9	0.54	0.47	0.70	0.50	N/A
K-ABC Mean			122.4	122.8	126.3	124.4	N/A
K-ABC SD			10.1	6.2	7.4	6.7	N/A

Seriously Emotionally Disturbed, Pommer, 1986, N = 59

WISC-R Verbal	76.7	18.1	0.33	0.54	0.45	—	N/A
WISC-R Performance	74.8	20.2	0.16	0.66	0.51	—	N/A
WISC-R Full Scale	73.8	18.5	0.31	0.68	0.58	—	N/A
K-ABC Mean			89.5	82.5	83.2	—	N/A
K-ABC SD			12.3	13.1	12.0	—	N/A

Hearing-Impaired, Courtney, Hayes, Watkins, & Frick,* N = 40

WISC-R Verbal	90.1	18.2	—	0.64	—	—	0.63
K-ABC Mean				90.5			88.6
K-ABC SD				15.8			17.2

Learning-Disabled, Klanderman, Anselmo, & Kaplan;* Naglieri & Pfeiffer;* Obrzut & Obrzut;* Snyder, Leark, Golden, Allison, & Grove,* N = 138

WISC-R Verbal	92.8	13.9	0.50	0.51	0.60	0.74	0.55
WISC-R Performance	96.3	15.2	0.31	0.76	0.68	0.46	0.73
WISC-R Full Scale	94.0	13.5	0.47	0.73	0.74	0.71	0.73
K-ABC Mean			92.3	93.1	91.8	86.2	91.8
K-ABC SD			14.5	14.3	13.7	12.0	13.6

Continued

Table 9-1 *Continued*

	M	SD	Sequent Process	Simult Process	Mental Processing Composite	Achievement	Nonverbal
Learning Disabled, Smith & Lyon, 1986, N = 32							
WISC-R Verbal	94.4	11.4	0.76	0.65	0.74	0.88	N/A
WISC-R Performance	100.8	15.3	0.65	0.85	0.82	0.69	N/A
WISC-R Full Scale	97.2	13.0	0.77	0.81	0.85	0.86	N/A
K-ABC Mean			90.0	98.1	94.1	89.8	N/A
Learning-Disabilities Referrals, Gunnison, Masunaga, Town, & Moffitt,* N = 60							
WISC-R Verbal	93.7	15.0	0.31	0.47	0.47	0.80	0.52
WISC-R Performance	96.6	15.2	0.32	0.71	0.63	0.39	0.60
WISC-R Full Scale	94.7	14.5	0.36	0.66	0.62	0.70	0.64
K-ABC Mean			89.2	93.7	90.8	89.0	91.0
K-ABC SD			12.9	11.9	11.7	11.4	11.6
Learning Disabilities Referrals, Smith & Lyon, 1986, N = 67							
WISC-R Verbal	—	—	0.76	0.65	0.74	0.88	N/A
WISC-R Performance	—	—	0.65	0.85	0.82	0.69	N/A
WISC-R Full Scale	—	—	0.77	0.81	0.85	0.86	N/A
Educable Mentally Retarded, Bolen, Childers, Durham, & Benton;* Naglieri;* Obrzut & Obrzut, 1987* N = 69							
WISC-R Verbal	61.8	9.4	0.48	0.43	0.50	0.54	0.48
WISC-R Performance	67.8	12.9	0.58	0.75	0.76	0.34	0.71
WISC-R Full Scale	62.0	10.5	0.64	0.73	0.77	0.51	0.72
K-ABC Mean			69.7	70.8	67.9	65.0	70.0
K-ABC SD			13.3	11.1	10.8	9.5	11.3
Behaviorally Disordered, Nelson,* N = 43							
WISC-R Verbal	94.6	18.6	0.48	0.64	0.65	0.87	0.63
WISC-R Performance	97.3	17.8	0.54	0.76	0.75	0.68	0.74
WISC-R Full Scale	95.4	18.1	0.56	0.75	0.76	0.85	0.74
K-ABC Mean			92.1	92.5	91.5	93.1	90.6
K-ABC SD			14.4	14.4	14.5	16.2	15.2
Prelingually Deaf, Phelps, & Branyon, N = 48							
WISC-R Verbal	70.0	11.8	0.31	0.70	0.64	N/A	0.67
WISC-R Performance	76.7	15.7	0.51	0.77	0.76	N/A	0.72
WISC-R Full Scale	71.2	13.0	0.46	0.83	0.79	N/A	0.78
K-ABC Mean			76.5	84.9	79.3	N/A	81.1
K-ABC SD			13.0	14.9	13.8	N/A	12.0

	Mean	SD	(1)	(2)	(3)	(4)	(5)
Nonhandicapped School-Age, Devine & Mollner;* Swerdik & Lewis;* Zins & Barnett,* N = 121							
Stanford-Binet L-M IQ	116.5	17.3	0.53	0.50	0.61	0.78	0.53
K-ABC Mean			110.4	114.1	114.5	113.5	114.2
K-ABC SD			15.5	13.4	14.1	13.0	14.3
Nonhandicapped, Kindergarten, Durham, Bolen, Childers, & Smith,* N = 38							
Stanford-Binet L-M IQ	94.3	16.2	0.63	0.65	0.72	0.79	0.70
K-ABC Mean			93.5	94.6	93.3	93.0	93.1
K-ABC SD			14.7	18.2	16.7	13.2	18.1
Nonhandicapped Preschool, Klanderman, Brown, Stranges & Page,* N = 39							
Stanford-Binet L-M IQ	109.6	18.2	0.58	0.58	0.65	0.74	0.31
K-ABC Mean			109.9	115.1	114.8	113.8	113.9
K-ABC SD			19.9	16.3	18.5	17.6	17.3
Nonhandicapped Preschool, Durham, Childers, & Bolen,* N = 38							
Stanford-Binet L-M IQ	117.2	14.9	0.39	0.15	0.36	0.57	0.44
K-ABC Mean			105.9	107.6	107.8	117.0	105.4
K-ABC SD			15.3	11.5	12.0	11.4	15.9
High-Risk Preschool, Klanderman, Wisehart, & Alter,* N = 28							
Stanford-Binet L-M IQ	88.9	15.4	0.56	0.54	0.66	0.52	0.62
K-ABC Mean			91.5	90.4	89.6	89.6	93.8
K-ABC SD			15.5	15.4	14.7	12.8	15.2
Gifted Referrals, Barry, Klanderman, & Stipe,* N = 50							
Stanford-Binet L-M IQ	137.3	13.1	0.27	0.50	0.47	0.55	0.46
K-ABC Mean			129.0	123.3	130.5	126.5	125.8
K-ABC SD			11.2	10.2	11.7	7.0	11.6
Gifted, McCallum, Karnes, & Edwards, 1984,* N = 16							
Stanford-Binet L-M IQ	130.9	8.5	0.09	0.53	0.46	0.42	N/A
K-ABC Mean			114.8	118.2	119.2	120.2	N/A
K-ABC SD			11.0	11.9	10.3	6.8	N/A
Normal Preschool, Hendershott, Searlight, Hatfield, & Rogers, 1990, N = 36							
Stanford-Binet IV Test Composite	110.5	12.4	0.55	0.46	0.65	0.74	N/A
K-ABC Mean			116.7	114.7	112.8	118.2	N/A
K-ABC SD			13.2	13.3	14.5	13.2	N/A

Continued

Table 9–1 *Continued*

	M	SD	Sequent Process	Simult Process	Mental Processing Composite	Achievement	Nonverbal
Nonhandicapped Children, Stanford Binet IV Manual, 1986, N = 175							
Verbal Reasoning	110.6	21.8	0.77	0.71	0.80	0.87	N/A
Abstract/Visual Reasoning	110.2	19.7	0.68	0.77	0.78	0.75	N/A
Quantitative Reasoning	111.2	18.9	0.73	0.72	0.78	0.75	N/A
Short-Term Memory	110.7	20.1	0.82	0.73	0.83	0.83	N/A
Composite	112.7	21.6	0.84	0.82	0.89	0.89	N/A
K-ABC Mean			109.7	111.5	112.3	107.4	N/A
K-ABC SD			21.0	18.9	21.6	19.9	N/A
Learning Disabled, Stanford Binet IV Manual, 1986, N = 30							
Verbal Reasoning	99.1	10.9	0.54	0.33	0.53	0.70	N/A
Abstract/Visual Reasoning	95.6	13.8	0.28	0.50	0.51	0.45	N/A
Quantitative Reasoning	88.6	11.1	0.31	0.47	0.55	0.64	N/A
Short-Term Memory	90.9	12.6	0.55	0.43	0.63	0.72	N/A
Composite	92.5	11.8	0.50	0.51	0.66	0.74	N/A
K-ABC Mean			91.1	97.5	94.2	93.2	N/A
K-ABC SD			11.8	12.2	12.0	13.2	N/A
At-Risk Preschool, Lyon & Smith, 1986, N = 72							
McCarthy Verbal	90.3	15.2	0.54	0.36	0.53	0.72	N/A
McCarthy Perceptual-Performance	87.2	14.1	0.43	0.32	0.43	0.38	N/A
McCarthy Quantitative	86.5	12.7	0.30	0.17	0.27	0.38	N/A
McCarthy Memory	84.1	13.6	0.56	0.33	0.52	0.64	N/A
McCarthy Motor	84.1	15.8	0.30	0.26	0.33	0.18	N/A
General Cognitive Index	86.3	16.6	0.57	0.44	0.59	0.59	N/A
K-ABC Mean			86.6	88.0	85.9	88.5	N/A
K-ABC SD			11.0	13.2	11.8	12.6	N/A
Naglieri, 1985, N = 51							
McCarthy Verbal	50.9	10.7	0.38	0.30	0.38	0.72	N/A
McCarthy Perceptual-Performance	54.4	10.4	0.21	0.42	0.37	0.35	N/A
McCarthy Quantitative	46.4	9.9	0.55	0.55	0.63	0.76	N/A
McCarthy Memory	49.0	10.9	0.58	0.47	0.59	0.63	N/A
McCarthy Motor	49.5	13.0	0.20	0.52	0.43	0.28	N/A
General Cognitive Index	101.3	15.0	0.46	0.50	0.55	0.79	N/A
K-ABC Mean			100.5	103.2	102.4	103.6	N/A
K-ABC SD			15.2	13.4	14.0	14.8	N/A

Nonhandicapped Preschool, McLaughlin & Ellison, 1984, N = 32							
PPVT-R	110.4	12.1	—	—	—	0.66	N/A
K-ABC Mean			—	—	—	113.5	N/A
K-ABC SD			—	—	—	13.3	N/A
Learning Disabled, Klanderman, Perney, & Kroeschell, 1985, N = 44							
PPVT-R	87.5	15.3	0.48	0.43	0.54	0.79	N/A
K-ABC Mean			92.7	92.3	—	87.8	N/A
K-ABC SD			12.4	13.5	—	9.1	N/A
Referrals, Grimm, & Allen, 1985, N = 40							
Woodcock-Johnson Reasoning	95.0	10.8	0.35	0.33	—	—	N/A
Woodcock-Johnson Perceptual Speed	90.4	11.2	0.53	0.40	—	—	N/A
Woodcock-Johnson Memory	92.2	14.6	0.69	0.51	—	—	N/A
Broad Cognitive Ability	89.4	10.9	—	—	0.80	0.94	N/A
K-ABC Mean			92.6	94.5	92.8	88.9	N/A
K-ABC SD			12.6	11.6	11.4	10.3	N/A
11- to 12-Year-Olds, KAIT Manual, 1993, N = 124							
KAIT Crystallized	99.8	14.1	0.46	0.53	0.57	0.81	0.52
KAIT Fluid	99.3	13.6	0.44	0.62	0.62	0.64	0.61
KAIT Composite Intelligence	99.6	13.4	0.50	0.63	0.66	0.82	0.62
K-ABC Mean			102.7	103.5	103.6	104.1	101.1
K-ABC SD			12.2	14.8	14.0	13.1	14.5

*This study is taken from the K-ABC Interpretive Manual (Kaufman & Kaufman, 1983) with younger children (Kamphaus, 1993). A study from the WPPSI-R manual produced a correlation of .49 between the MPC and FSIQ, and a McCarthy study produced a coefficient of .59 for the composite scores (see Table 9–1).

Predictive Validity.   Predictive validity evidence for the K-ABC is generally comparable to that of the WISC-R (Kaufman & Kaufman, 1983c). Murray and Bracken (1984), for example, evaluated the predictive validity of the K-ABC over an 11-month interval for a group of 29 children. They found the MPC to predict PIAT Total Test scores at a .79 level over this time period. The Achievement Scale composite from the K-ABC was an even better predictor with a validity coefficient of .88. In a 6-month predictive validity study by Childers, Durham, and Bolen (1985), the MPC was found to correlate .65 with the total score on the California Achievement Test. The relationship of the K-ABC Achievement Scale to the CAT was .77. These studies, along with those in the *K-ABC Interpretive Manual* (Kaufman & Kaufman, 1983c), suggest good predictive validity evidence for the MPC and exemplary predictive validity evidence for the K-ABC Achievement Scale.

Factor Analysis.   The K-ABC initially sparked a flurry of factor-analytic investigations. These studies are helpful for understanding the K-ABC better and, because of similar results, they have the potential to enhance interpretation of the WISC-III and Binet 4. The factor structures of these three measures are looking more similar with each new factor-analytic investigation.

A first point to consider is the "g" or unrotated first factor loadings of the K-ABC in comparison to the WISC-R. Initially, researchers thought that the K-ABC, particularly the Sequential scale, was a more diluted measure of "g" and that the mental processing subtests measured more simple memory and spatial skills than high-level intellectual abilities (Jensen, 1984; Sternberg, 1984). Subsequently, these researchers have been proven wrong as the "g" factors of the K-ABC and the WISC-R have proved strikingly similar (Kamphaus & Reynolds, 1987). Also of interest is the finding that the Sequential and Simultaneous scales measure "g" to the same extent (Kamphaus & Reynolds, 1987). This is a somewhat surprising finding, given that for most children the Simultaneous scale has two more tests than the Sequential scale and is slightly more reliable. In addition, the Sequential scale subtests also have a distinct short-term memory component.

The first well-known factor-analytic evidence offered in support of the Sequential and Simultaneous scales was by Kaufman and Kamphaus (1984). These authors identified three factors for the K-ABC and labeled them as sequential, simultaneous, and achievement.

Some problems with the sequential/simultaneous model, however, were apparent even in this early investigation. Hand Movements had a split loading, particularly at the school-age level. Even though Hand Movements was consistently the third-best measure of the sequential factor, it had a consistent and significant secondary loading on the simultaneous factor. In addition, Photo Series loaded consistently higher on the simultaneous factor. As a result, after norming, this test was switched from its tentative placement on the Sequential Scale to the Simultaneous Scale (Kaufman & Kaufman, 1983c). There was, however, some support for the K-ABC theoretical model that emerged from the "nonloadings" in this investigation for Hand Movements and Spatial Memory. The Hand Movements subtest had an insignificant loading on the simultaneous factor for preschoolers. Similarly, Spatial Memory never had an important loading on the sequential factor. These two sets of loadings support the processing (versus content) distinction of the Kaufmans. Hand Movements has an obvious visual component and yet it never loads higher on the more visual simultaneous factor than it does on the sequential factor for preschool age groups. Spatial Memory, with its obvious short-term memory component (has a five-second exposure of the stimuli before their placement must be recalled), never joins the sequential factor. These two findings suggest that there may be problems applying hierarchical (memory versus reasoning) and content (verbal versus nonverbal) models to the K-ABC.

Kamphaus and Kaufman (1986) conducted an exploratory factor analysis for boys and girls. This investigation yielded similar results to the Kaufman and Kamphaus (1984) study finding virtually no differences in factor structure attributable to gender. There was a tendency for Hand Movements to have a higher simultaneous loading for girls at the school-age level than for boys. Again, however, Hand Movements and Spatial Memory remained aligned with their respective scales, providing some support for the Kaufmans' processing distinction.

In a series of studies, Keith and colleagues have called the K-ABC processing model into question by applying Wechsler-like content labels to the K-ABC scales (Keith, 1985; Keith & Dunbar, 1984; Keith, Hood, Eberhart, & Pottebaum, 1985). Keith (1985) has used labels such as nonverbal/reasoning (Simultaneous), achievement/verbal reasoning (Achievement), and verbal memory (Sequential) for the K-ABC factors, making the scales similar to the tradition of psychological assessment. In a study of a sample of 585 referred children (Keith et al., 1985), three factors emerged in an exploratory factor analysis. Virtually all of the factor analyses were similar to those found in previous studies, but their interpretation differed greatly. Hand Movements, for example, loaded highest on the "verbal memory" factor and Faces & Places, Riddles, and Arithmetic had substantial secondary loadings on the nonverbal/reasoning factor. The issue of what to call the K-ABC factors remains debated but unresolved (see, for example, Kamphaus, 1990).

Kaufman and McLean (1987) conducted a factor-analytic investigation for a sample of children with learning disabilities and obtained a factor structure that was similar to the model proposed by Keith. Findings of this nature suggest that the interpretive model applied to the K-ABC may depend on sample (child) characteristics. In this way, K-ABC interpretation is entirely consistent with Kaufman's (1994) intelligent testing model.

One confirmatory factor-analytic investigation has provided strong support for the two-factor sequential and simultaneous processing model (Willson, Reynolds, Chatman, & Kaufman, 1985), but less enthusiastic support of a distinct Achievement scale. The subtests of the Achievement scale do show their largest loadings on a separate factor, as Kaufman and Kaufman (1983b) proposed, yet each shows large secondary loadings on the two mental processing factors. This supports Anastasi's (1984) contention that the K-ABC MPC/Achievement distinction is more theoretical that practical, as there is a substantial correlation between the MPC and Achievement scales.

ADMINISTRATION AND SCORING

Administration and scoring procedures for the K-ABC are available in the *K-ABC Administration and Scoring Manual* (Kaufman & Kaufman, 1983b). One important aspect of K-ABC administration that deserves special mention, however, is the notion of teaching items. The first three items of each mental processing subtest (the sample and the first two items appropriate for a child's age group) are designated as teaching items. On these items, the examiner is required to teach the task if the child fails on the first attempt at solving the item. The phrase *teaching the task* means that the examiner is allowed the flexibility to use alternate wording, gestures, physical guidance, or even a language other than English to communicate the task demands to the child. The examiner is not allowed to teach the child a specific strategy for solving the problem, however. This built-in flexibility was designed to be particularly helpful to preschoolers, minority-group children, and exceptional children, who sometimes perform poorly on a task from a traditional IQ test, not because of a lack of ability but because of an inability to understand the instructions given. Kaufman and Kaufman (1983c) discuss the concept of teaching items in greater detail and note that this built-in flexibility has not adversely affected the reliability of the K-ABC. Sample items are now common fare, as they were subsequently embraced by both the Binet 4 and WISC-III.

The K-ABC basal and ceiling rules, referred to as starting and stopping points in the *K-ABC Administration and Scoring Manual* (Kaufman & Kaufman, 1983b), also differ from those of many existing intelligence tests. The first rule for administering the K-ABC subtests is very straightforward: Examiners are instructed to start and stop testing at the items designated as starting and stopping points for the child's age group. The set of items between the starting and stopping points are, therefore, designed based on standardization data, to represent a full range of difficulty for the child's age group. This first basal and ceiling rule is very straight-forward, but it is also rigid. Hence, several supplemental rules are given to allow examiners to find items of appropriate difficulty for children at the ends of the distribution of ability (Kaufman & Kaufman, 1983b). The K-ABC also incorporates a very simple discontinue rule that is the same for all K-ABC subtests.

The K-ABC Subtests

In contrast to the WISC-III, the K-ABC subtests are a rather unique collection. The WISC-III subtests, for example, were taken primarily from the early Army group tests. The K-ABC subtests are taken from a wider range of sources, including the WISC-III (Number Recall and Triangles), experimental cognitive science (Face Recognition), neuropsychology (Hand Movements), and early psychometricians such as Raven (Matrix Analogies), among other sources. In addition, some of the K-ABC subtests are novel, such as Magic Window and Faces & Places, with roots that are difficult to trace.

The K-ABC subtests, however, do have a common lineage in the K-ABC theoretical model, the division of the Sequential, Simultaneous, and Achievement scales. The K-ABC subtests had to show a great deal of consistency with the test's theoretical model in order to be retained. This philosophy is illustrated by the large number of tests that were discarded in the developmental process (Kaufman & Kaufman, 1983c).

The psychometric properties shown for each subtest are taken from the *K-ABC Interpretive Manual* (Kaufman & Kaufman, 1983c). Some of the factor-analytic results are from Jensen (1984).

Magic Window (Ages 2½–4)

Magic Window requires the child to identify a picture that the examiner exposes by moving it past a narrow slit, or "window" (making the picture only partially visible at any time). This subtest appears to be one of the few subtests that can justifiably be described as novel, as it has no clear counterpart in the history of intellectual assessment. This test is designed as the first measure of simultaneous processing and the first test to be administered to preschoolers. It appears to be appropriately placed as the first subtest for preschoolers, as viewing through the window to try to discover the object behind it is a genuinely intriguing task for young children.

It is also an interesting task from the standpoint that while the stimulus is visual, the response is clearly verbal, demonstrating again the relative independence of test content from the mental process used to solve the item. This task was found to be one of the best measures of simultaneous processing for preschoolers (Kaufman & Kaufman, 1983).

Psychometric Properties

Average reliability = .72
"g" loading = N/A
Loading on Sequential Factor = .24
Loading on Simultaneous Factor = .53
Loading on Achievement Factor = .23
Subtest Specificity = (.40) ample

Face Recognition (Ages 2½–4)

This test requires a child to select from a group photograph the one or two faces that were shown briefly in a preceding photograph. This task is also a good early task on the K-ABC, as children seem to have a natural curiosity about photographs. This test has its roots in neuropsychological assessment in which it has been used for the diagnosis of cerebral dominance (Benton, 1980). The Kaufmans (Kaufman & Kaufman, 1983c) chose this task not only because it was a good measure of simultaneous information processing but also because it was a measure that produced few group differences for children from disparate cultures (Kagan & Klein, 1973).

The Face Recognition subtest was excluded from the school-age level of the K-ABC because it switched factor loadings for older children. For older children, it became more of a measure of sequential processing, suggesting a developmental change in the way that children process these types of photographs. Perhaps young children process faces more as a whole and older children try to break them down into component parts and describe them verbally.

Psychometric Properties

Average reliability = .77
"g" loading = N/A
Loading on Sequential Factor = .24
Loading on Simultaneous Factor = .44
Loading on Achievement Factor = .33
Subtest Specificity = (.48) ample

Hand Movements (Ages 2½–12½)

For this test, the child has to imitate a series of hand movements in the same sequence as the examiner performed them. This test is taken directly from the work of Luria (1966), who used a similar test to assess motor function as part of his neuropsychological evaluation. This test also gives the examiner a clinical sense of the child's fine motor skills (Kaufman & Kaufman, 1983c) and eye/hand coordination.

Psychometric Properties

Average reliability—preschool = .78
Average reliability—school age = .76
"g" loading = .54
Loading on Sequential Factor = .46
Loading on Simultaneous Factor = .31
Loading on Achievement Factor = .18
Subtest Specificity = 2.5–4 (.49) ample
                                  5–12½ (.41) ample

Behaviors to Note

1. Inability of the child to form the three different hand movements adequately
2. Demonstrating all of the correct movements but failing the items primarily because of difficulty in sequencing
3. Vocalization or subvocalization being used as a strategy to solve the items correctly.

Gestalt Closure (Ages 2½–12½)

The child is required to name an object or scene pictured in a partially completed "inkblot" drawing. Not unlike some Rorschach items, this test requires a child to visually "complete" drawings. On the face of it, this test is another classic measure of simultaneous/holistic right brain types of processing. This is borne out by factor-analytic findings (Kaufman & Kaufman, 1983c; Kamphaus & Kaufman, 1984). This test has a very long history, dating back to the early 1930s (Street, 1931), and yet the Kaufmans were the first to include it in a major test of intelligence.

Psychometric Properties

Average reliability—preschool = .72
Average reliability—school age = .71
"g" loading = .47
Loading on Sequential Factor = .10
Loading on Simultaneous Factor = .49
Loading on Achievement Factor = .28
Subtest Specificity = 2.5–4 (.39) ample
                        5–12 (.38) ample

Number Recall (Ages 2½–12½)

This task is a familiar adaptation of Digits Forward from Wechsler's scales. Of course, this type of task has been part of intelligence testing since the days of Binet (Binet, 1905). This test is, however, different from Wechsler's in at least a few respects. Most importantly, this test includes only Digits Forward.

Psychometric Properties

Average reliability—preschool = .88
Average reliability—school age = .81
"g" loading = .55
Loading on Sequential Factor = .66
Loading on Simultaneous Factor = .16
Loading on Achievement Factor = .24
Subtest Specificity = 2.5–4 (.51) ample
                        5–12½ (.34) ample

Triangles (Ages 4–12½)

The Triangles subtest is also an adaptation of Wechsler's Block Design task, which is an adaptation of Kohs's (1927) Block Design test. As was the case with Gestalt Closure, this test, too, seems to be a clear measure of simultaneous processing. This supposition is also borne out by factor-analytical results (Kaufman & Kaufman, 1983c; Kamphaus & Kaufman, 1984; Kamphaus & Reynolds, 1987). Wechsler's Block Design task has also been used in split brain research investigations as a marker task of right brain processing (Reitan, 1974; see Chapter 2). Although the Triangles test is obviously related to Wechsler's Block Design test, the correlations between these two tests are moderate, generally in the 50s (Kaufman & MacLean, 1987), suggesting that these two tests, are not interchangeable.

Psychometric Properties

Average reliability—preschool = .89
Average reliability—school age = .84
"g" loading = .65
Loading on Sequential Factor = .21
Loading on Simultaneous Factor = .63
Loading on Achievement Factor = .27
Subtest Specificity = 4 (.51) ample
               5–12 .37 ample

Word Order (Ages 4–12½)

Word Order is the third and last sequential processing subtest on the K-ABC. It ranks behind Number Recall as the premier measure of sequential processing. This task requires a child to touch a series of pictures in the same sequence as they were named by the examiner. On more difficult items, a color interference task is used. The Kaufmans see this task as an auditory-vocal test of the McCarthy (1972) Verbal Memory I. This task is also similar to tests such as Memory for Sentences on the Stanford Binet Fourth Edition. The Kaufmans borrowed some aspects of this test, including the interference task component, from a clinical neuropsychological test used by Luria (1966).

The color interference task of Word Order may also provide some valuable clinical information. Denckla (1972) and Denckla and Rudel (1974, 1976) have found that children with reading disabilities perform more poorly than capable readers on rapid naming tests that include the naming of colors, letters, and objects.

Psychometric Properties

Average reliability—preschool = .84
Average reliability—school age = .82

"g" loading = .64
Loading on Sequential Factor = .68
Loading on Simultaneous Factor = .22
Loading on Achievement Factor = .29
Subtest Specificity = 4 (.33) ample
                           5–12½ (.28) ample

Matrix Analogies (Ages 5–12½)

The Matrix Analogies test requires the child to select a picture or abstract design that completes a visual analogy. In many ways, the Matrix Analogies test resembles Raven's Progressive Matrices (1956, 1960). As such, Matrix Analogies is one of the better measures of simultaneous processing skills. In fact, Raven's Progressive Matrices was used by Das, Kirby, and Jarman (1979) as part of their simultaneous/successive test battery.

One of the interesting aspects of this task is that it may also have a sequential component at older age groups. A separate factor analysis conducted for boys and girls in the K-ABC standardization sample found that, when the sample was divided by gender, Matrix Analogies began to take on more substantial loadings on the Sequential Scale for 11- and 12-year-olds, especially for girls. This result suggests that children may apply different, perhaps more sequential/analytic skills to solving the matrices at older ages. This occurrence may be inferred through observation of the child during testing.

Psychometric Properties

Average reliability = .85
"g" loading = .62
Loading on Sequential Factor = .30
Loading on Simultaneous Factor = .50
Loading on Achievement Factor = .26
Subtest Specificity = (.44) ample

Spatial Memory (Ages 5–12½)

Spatial Memory requires the child to recall the placement of pictures on a page that was exposed for a five-second interval. This test serves to round out memory assessment on the K-ABC, in that it provides for a nonverbal stimulus and response, like Hand Movements. This subtest, however, is somewhat unique from the other K-ABC memory tasks in that it shows a substantial loading on the Simultaneous Processing factor. This test, along with Face Recognition at the preschool level, makes it difficult to apply a memory versus reasoning type dichotomy to the sequential/simultaneous processing scales. This relatively large number of memory tests, however, provides the basis for a strong measure of children's memory.

Psychometric Properties

Average reliability = .80
"g" loading = .56
Loading on Sequential Factor = .26
Loading on Simultaneous Factor = .58
Loading on Achievement Factor = .15

Photo Series (Ages 6–12½)

Photo Series requires the child to place photographs of an event in chronological order. This test, on the face of it, looks similar to Wechsler's Picture Arrangement subtest. However, several investigations of these two batteries show modest to poor intercorrelations among these two subtests (Kaufman & Kaufman, 1983c; Kaufman & McLean, 1987). The Photo Series test also appears to have a distinctly sequential component. However, factor analyses of the K-ABC have shown that this subtest, along with Triangles, is a marker task of simultaneous processing ability (Kamphaus & Reynolds, 1987). One hypothesis is that in the case of Photo Series, the sequential response is anticlimactic to the holistic processing of the stimuli that is required prior to producing a response. In other words, a child has to first visually interpret and verbally label the series (e.g., a car backing up) before he or she can put the pieces in their correct sequence in the examiner's hand. Furthermore, the child is not allowed to rearrange the photos, which places great emphasis on the child's ability to *visualize* the relationships among the photos (an aspect of simultaneous processing).

Psychometric Properties

Average reliability = .82
"g" loading = .67
Loading on Sequential Factor = .25
Loading on Simultaneous Factor = .64
Loading on Achievement Factor = .26
Subtest Specificity = (.33) ample

Expressive Vocabulary (Ages 2½–4)

Expressive Vocabulary requires the child to name objects that are pictured in photographs. This test is the first one encountered by preschoolers on the achievement scale. The Expressive Vocabulary test is intended to follow in the tradition of Wechsler and Binet Vocabulary tests (Kaufman & Kaufman, 1983b). The Kaufmans propose that the assessment of verbal intelligence is essential as part of an intellectual evaluation, but they prefer that the "verbal intelligence" subtests on the K-ABC be included on the Achievement scale and not labeled intelligence as such (Kaufman & Kaufman, 1983c; Kaufman & Reynolds, 1987).

Psychometric Properties

Average reliability = .85
"g" loading = N/A
Loading on Sequential Factor = .25
Loading on Simultaneous Factor = .61
Loading on Achievement Factor = .77
Subtest Specificity = (.27) ample

Faces & Places (Ages 2½–12½)

Faces & Places involves having a child name a well-known person, fictional character, or place pictured in a photograph or illustration. This test is designed as an analog of Wechsler's Information subtest. It is sensitive, just as is the Information subtest, to factors such as linguistic and cultural background. This test is also sensitive to academic stimulation in school.

Faces & Places, however, presents general information items in a novel format. This format has led to considerable criticism of some of the items, the main complaint being that some of them are out of date (e.g., most notably Muhammed Ali) (Kamphaus & Reynolds, 1987). Although the content of the individual items is controversial, the test still correlates rather highly with Wechsler's Information subtest (Kamphaus & Reynolds, 1987). Also, African American children perform relatively well on Faces & Places (earning mean standard scores of 96–97, as reported in the K-ABC Interpretive Manual, Table 4.35), a finding that does not hold true for Wechsler's Information subtest.

Psychometric Properties

Average reliability—preschool = .77
Average reliability—school age = .84
"g" loading = .69
Loading on Sequential Factor = .21
Loading on Simultaneous Factor = .39
Loading on Achievement Factor = .67
Subtest Specificity = 2.5–4 (.27) ample
                      5–12.5 (.24) ample

Arithmetic (Ages 3–12½)

The Arithmetic subtest of the K-ABC requires a child to answer questions that assess knowledge of math concepts or the manipulation of numbers. This Arithmetic subtest resembles more the Arithmetic subtest of Wechsler's genre as opposed to pencil-and-paper subtests found on clinical measures of mathematics achievement. As such, Kamphaus and Reynolds (1987) recommend that this test should be considered as a measure of verbal intelligence or a screening measure of mathematics as opposed to a mathematics subtest per se. While designed as an analog of Wechsler's Arithmetic test, this test is somewhat unique because it is considerably longer and assesses a wider range of mathematics skills and content than Wechsler's. This test does show substantial correlations with more traditional mathematics achievement tests (Kamphaus & Reynolds, 1987).

Psychometric Properties

Average reliability—preschool = .87
Average reliability—school age = .87
"g" loading = .82
Loading on Sequential Factor = .46
Loading on Simultaneous Factor = .48
Loading on Achievement Factor = .49
Subtest Specificity = (3–4) (.28) ample
                      (5–12) (.20) adequate

Riddles (Ages 3–12½)

Riddles requires a child to name an object or concept that is described by a list of three of its characteristics. From a psychometric standpoint, it appears to be a close analogue of vocabulary tests that have always been a part of intelligence tests (Kamphaus & Reynolds, 1987). While this subtest does not require the eloquent multiword expression of the Vocabulary test of the WISC-III, it does seem to require a high level of vocabulary knowledge. This test mimics vocabulary tests from other batteries in other ways, including the fact that it is one of the premier measures of general intelligence ("g") on the K-ABC.

Psychometric Properties

Average reliability—preschool = .83
Average reliability—school age = .86
"g" loading = .78
Loading on Sequential Factor = .34
Loading on Simultaneous Factor = .42
Loading on Achievement Factor = .62
Subtest Specificity = (3–8) (.23) adequate
                      (9–12.5) (.19) inadequate

Reading/Decoding (Ages 5–12½)

This test requires a child to read words out of context. This is a simple word recognition task similar to those found on screening measures of academic achievement such as the Wide Range Achievement Test-Revised. This test is intended as a measure of basic reading skill. The test may not serve as a substitute for other clinical tests of reading achievement, in spite of its high correlations with these measures. This prohibition is primarily because of questionable content validity. There are, for example, a number of items with silent consonants. These items may lack "social validity" or utility since they may not be frequently used by children or appear regularly in their reading materials.

Psychometric Properties

Average reliability = .92
"g" loading = .79
Loading on Sequential Factor = .39
Loading on Simultaneous Factor = .26
Loading on Achievement Factor = .68
Subtest Specificity = (.21) adequate

Reading/Understanding (Ages 7–12½)

This task requires a child to act out commands that are given in words or sentences. While intended as a measure of reading comprehension, it is an extraordinarily novel way of assessing reading comprehension. In contrast to many academic achievement measures, this task requires a child to follow commands. While this approach makes the task somewhat controversial, it correlates in the expected fashion with other measures of basic reading skills and reading comprehension (Kamphaus & Reynolds, 1987).

This test also has the potential to yield some insights into the child's personality. A child's refusal to do the task or demonstration of no reluctance whatsoever may be used to corroborate findings from personality measures. This test should be interpreted cautiously if a child seems reticent and perhaps more so at the older ages (age 10 and above) since the reliability tends to dip somewhat.

Psychometric Properties

Average reliability = .91
"g" loading = .71
Loading on Sequential Factor = .37
Loading on Simultaneous Factor = .28
Loading on Achievement Factor = .76
Subtest Specificity = (.11) adequate

INTERPRETATION

The K-ABC is amenable to the integrative framework espoused by Kamphaus (1993). The following steps are advised for beginning the K-ABC interpretive process.

1. Offer apriori hypotheses.
2. Assign a verbal classification to the MPC (e.g., average).
3. Band the MPC with error (the 90 percent level of confidence is recommended).
4. Assign verbal classifications to the Sequential and Simultaneous scales.
5. Band the Sequential and Simultaneous scales with error.
6. Test the difference between the Sequential and Simultaneous scales for statistical significance (a reliable difference at the .05 level) using Table 10 of the *K-ABC Administration and Scoring Manual* (Kaufman & Kaufman, 1983b).
7. Test the difference between the Sequential and Simultaneous scales for clinical rarity (where a difference that occurred in 5 percent of the population or less is considered rare) using Table 5.12 (p. 193) of the *K-ABC Interpretive Manual* (Kaufman & Kaufman, 1983c).
8. Test apriori hypotheses.
9. Develop aposteriori hypotheses at the composite, shared subtest, and single subtest level.
10. Test aposteriori hypotheses.
11. Draw conclusions.

Apriori Hypotheses

In order to offer apriori hypotheses, one must know the cognitive and behavioral factors that affect K-ABC composite and subtest scores. The characteristics of subtests have already been discussed. Now the Sequential and Simultaneous scales will be considered.

Hypotheses for Sequential/Simultaneous (Seq/Sim) Differences

The relatively clear factor structure of the K-ABC Mental Processing scales makes a difference in Sequential and Simultaneous processing a necessity to investigate (Kaufman & Kamphaus, 1984). The major question regarding the K-ABC is in regard to the range of application of the Seq/Sim model. Just how many and what types of children have Seq/Sim discrepancies? The answer to this question is only recently becoming apparent. Children who are learning disabled or mentally retarded do not show clear patterns (Kamphaus & Reynolds, 1987). Hence, the meaning of a Seq/Sim discrepancy is going to be difficult to establish in many cases, thereby testing the clinical acumen of the examiner to the same extent as V/P differences does.

While the K-ABC is built around a fairly explicit theoretical stance, Kaufman's (1994) own intelligent testing philosophy would encourage examiners to entertain other possible reasons for Seq/Sim differences. Various explanations for Seq/Sim differences are offered next.

Linguistic Differences (Sim>Seq)

Two of the three Sequential scale subtests have English language content (Number Recall, Word Order). In contrast, the one test with obvious English language content on the Simultaneous scale (Gestalt Closure) makes up only 1/5 of that composite (versus 2/3 for the Sequential Scale) for school-age children. Consequently, where English language proficiency is in question, a Sim>Seq pattern is likely. A Navajo sample cited in the *Interpretive Manual* demonstrated this problem (Kaufman & Kaufman, 1983b). The Navajo sample spoke the Navajo language both at home and at school. They obtained a mean Sequential score of 88 and a mean Simultaneous score of 100. This pattern of Sim>Seq for a linguistically different group was also found by Valencia (1984) in an investigation of 42 Mexican American preschoolers. Here, the mean Sequential score of 100 was again lower than the Simultaneous score of 106.5. Another interesting finding from this investigation was the WISC-R Verbal score of only 96 compared to a Performance score of 109, indicating that Wechsler's Verbal scale is more sensitive to linguistic difference than the Sequential scale of the K-ABC.

Whether or not a Sim>Seq pattern can be attributed to a linguistic difference can be checked by the achievement scale. For that same Navajo group, the K-ABC analog of Wechsler's Vocabulary, Riddles, was the groups lowest Achievement score with a mean of 75.

These findings regarding linguistic differences on the K-ABC are also enlightening from a test design standpoint. The Kaufmans clearly wanted to limit the influence of cultural and linguistic factors on the K-ABC intelligence (mental processing) scales. As is clear from these data, the effects of language may be deemphasized on the K-ABC Mental Processing Scales, but its influence may still be felt, especially on the Sequential Scale.

Motor Problem (Sim<Seq)

Motor problems may adversely affect a child's performance on the Simultaneous scale of the K-ABC. While the K-ABC Simultaneous scale requires only minimal fine motor skill, it does require enough dexterity that children with substantial motor involvement may produce lower scores on this scale due to a motor problem as opposed to a simultaneous processing weakness.

A potentially difficult aspect of evaluating the potential effects of a motor deficit is teasing out the effects of visual problems or simultaneous processing problems. This "unmasking" or clarification process can be aided by administering additional tests. One case that the first author observed involved a child with cerebral palsy who obtained a whopping 55 standard score point discrepancy in favor of sequential processing. In order to determine if the simultaneous weakness was only the result of motor problems, the clinicians involved administered the Motor Free Visual Perception Test (MVPT) to assess visual perception skills relatively independently of motor skill. The

MVPT score was very similar to the Simultaneous score, suggesting that the child's visual perception problems were more important than the motor problem in determining the low Simultaneous score. This finding was also sensible in light of the K-ABC profile, which showed that even tests such as Gestalt Closure, which has a visual perceptual component but no motor involvement, was also depressed.

For some children with motor problems *both* the Simultaneous and Sequential scales may be well below the mean of 100. This possibility is exemplified by a study of hemiplegic children (Lewandowski & DiRienzo, 1985). In this study, a group of children with cerebral palsy (and documented congenital neurodevelopmental delays that were localized primarily to one of the cerebral hemispheres) were compared to a group of control children without neurodevelopmental problems. These children with obvious hemiplegia on one side achieved mean K-ABC Sequential and Simultaneous scores that were significantly below that of the control group that achieved means near 100. The mean Sequential scores of the two brain-injured groups with associated motor problems were 95 and 95, whereas their Simultaneous scores were 84 and 95. These data hint that the Simultaneous scale may be more sensitive to motor problems but they also suggest that the Sequential scale, with tests such as Hand Movements, may show some depression due to severe motor problems.

Auditory Short-Term Memory Problem (Sim>Seq)

This profile seems to be all too frequent and tests the interpretive savvy of clinicians (Kamphaus & Reynolds, 1987). It occurs relatively frequently because it is consistent with the factor structure of the K-ABC. The Hand Movements test "switches allegiance" because of its equivocal factor loadings for school-age children (Kamphaus & Reynolds, 1987). This test's loading on the Sequential factor is consistently *but not considerably* higher than its loading on the Simultaneous factor.

The often observed consequence of this factor structure is that the Number Recall and Word Order tests will yield similar scores that are both discrepant from the rest of the profile. The difficult call in this instance is to determine if these two tests are reflecting sequential processing or auditory short-term memory. Several suggestions for testing these hypotheses are listed next.

1. If a child's response on these two tests indicate good recall but poor sequencing, than a sequencing hypothesis is supported. For example, a child who responds to the stimulus "8-2-5-1" with "2-5-1-8" may have greater problems with sequencing in recall than memory span per se.
2. If Spatial Memory and Hand Movements scores are more in line (not necessarily strong or weak to the same degree) with Number Recall and

Word Order than with the Simultaneous scale subtests, then hypotheses related to a memory problem are more plausible.

3. Teacher reports can also help test an auditory short-term memory versus sequencing hypothesis. A child's teacher may produce evidence of sequencing problems from worksheets or other student products. The child's teacher should also be asked if examples of significant memory failure can be cited.

Verbal vs. Nonverbal Intelligence (Ach>Seq>Sim)

Factor analyses of all K-ABC subtests have consistently produced three factors similar to the Sequential, Simultaneous, and Achievement scales. Factor labels, however, are dictated to a large extent by the theoretical orientation of the test author or researcher conducting the investigation (Kamphaus, 1990). Kamphaus and Reynolds (1987) have taken this work one step further by developing new scores for the K-ABC that facilitate the application of a verbal/nonverbal intelligence dichotomy to the K-ABC. Use of the Wechsler model, however, is not only a change in labels but also a change from a process to a content distinction.

Kamphaus and Reynolds (1987) divide the Achievement scale into two components: Verbal Intelligence, which includes all of the Achievement scale subtests exclusive of the two reading tests, and a Reading Composite, which consists of the two reading subtests. Even without the use of these supplementary procedures (See Kamphaus & Reynolds, 1987) the verbal/nonverbal distinction may be of some value.

Two of the Sequential tests (Number Recall and Word Order) use verbal stimuli as do the Achievement scale subtests. A child with an oral expression deficit, speech problem, language processing problem, or similar difficulty that may adversely impact performance on verbal subtests may produce a profile of Ach<Seq<Sim. Similarly, a child with strong verbal skills may produce the reverse.

Apriori Hypotheses

Examples of apriori hypotheses for the K-ABC are given next.

Source of Hypothesis	**Hypothesis**
Jesse is a first-grader who is referred for a suspected reading disability. His teacher reports that he is slow to acquire phonics skills and he has difficulty sequencing.	Sim>Seq

Source of Hypothesis	Hypothesis
Jack is referred for language delays by his social worker. His native language is Navajo although he speaks primarily English at school. His mother is concerned because he spoke much later than her other children and his Navajo and English articulation is poor.	MPC>Ach
Peter was diagnosed with fetal alcohol syndrome shortly after birth. His mother used alcohol daily during pregnancy and she smoked one to two packs of cigarettes per day. His developmental milestones were delayed and he was retained in kindergarten for an additional year. His family is poor. His mother and father cannot read.	Below average Seq, Sim, MPC, and achievement scores
Monja is in the gifted class at her school. She was referred by her teacher for behavior problems in class and inattention.	Ach>Sim>Seq
Cheng was born with cerebral palsy.	Ach & Seq>Sim
Gina has missed 60 days of school this past year due to frequent relocations of her family. Arithmetic may be particularly low.	MPC>Ach

ASSESSING EXCEPTIONAL CHILDREN WITH THE K-ABC

Given that for most children the K-ABC correlates substantially with the WISC-R, it is likely that the K-ABC and WISC-III will covary to a great extent when evaluating exceptional children. Some groups of children, however, show substantial differences. For these groups, the selection of one test over another can be crucial in the diagnostic process. Moreover, the clinician has to be especially alert when dealing with individual cases where research does not apply or is lacking. This section summarizes research on the utility of the K-ABC for assessing exceptional children with special emphasis on its assets and liabilities, as identified by Kamphaus and Reynolds (1987).

Mental Retardation

There is a tendency for children who are mentally retarded to have higher K-ABC than WISC-R scores (Naglieri, 1985). K-ABC data for samples of previously identified (usually with the WISC-R) children with mental retardation (Kamphaus & Reynolds, 1987; see Chapter 13) show mean Mental Processing Composite scores ranging from the mid 60s to about 70. Naglieri (1985a) administered the K-ABC to 37 children who were diagnosed previously as mildly mentally retarded. When these children were reevaluated, the K-ABC and WISC-R were administered in counterbalanced fashion. The resulting WISC-R Full Scale mean was 58 and the K-ABC mean was 65. The correlation of the K-ABC and WISC-R for this sample was very high (.83), suggesting that the rank order of the children on these two tests was highly similar, but the K-ABC distribution of scores was tilted more toward the normative mean of 100.

The K-ABC has some practical limitations that examiners must consider in using the test to diagnose mental retardation. First is the issue of subtest floor. Kamphaus and Reynolds (1987) observed that the K-ABC lacks easy items for some children with developmental delays. In other words, a 5-year-old child who is mentally retarded may obtain too many raw scores of 0. This risk of a lack of floor, however, is less likely to occur for an 8-, 9-, or 10-year-old child who is mildly retarded. For children who are moderately to severely mentally retarded, however, there is a substantial risk of a lack of floor for most ages, as the K-ABC has new subtests introduced at virtually every age group from ages 2½ through 7. Second, the K-ABC composite score norms usually do not extend below a standard score of 55, which makes the K-ABC less useful for the diagnosis of moderate or severe levels of mental retardation. Tests such as the Stanford-Binet Fourth Edition and the DAS may be better suited for the purpose since their composite score norms often extend down below 55 (see Kamphaus, 1993, Chapters 10 and 11).

The availability of sample and teaching items and the intuitive nature of the K-ABC task demands are advantages for the assessment of delayed children. A potential benefit of the use teaching items is that they allow the examiner to see how a child responds to instruction. This opportunity to see how a child responds to instruction can be a primitive assessment of a child's zone of proximal development (ZPD; Vygotsky, 1962; see Kamphaus & Reynolds, 1987), where the ZPD is the difference in performance on a task with and without instruction.

Children with Learning Disabilities

Mean K-ABC global scale and subtest scores for a number of samples of children with learning disabilities suggest that such children tend to score in the below-average to average ranges, exhibit a "mild" Simultaneous greater than

Sequential profile (6 to 8 standard score points), and have their lowest scores on the Achievement and Sequential scales (Kamphaus & Reynolds, 1987, see Chapter 14). There is also a consistent trend for the average MPC to be greater than the average Achievement scale score. This is consistent with the operational definition of learning disabilities where a discrepancy between "ability" and achievement must be identified.

Fourqurean (1987) identified a substantial pattern of underachievement for a sample of limited-English-proficient Latino children with learning disabilities. These results support the hypothesis that the K-ABC Achievement scale is adversely affected not only by learning problems but also by cultural and/or linguistic differences. In addition, the MPC in this study appeared to be less influenced or confounded by linguistic or cultural differences. This study highlights the theoretical differences between the K-ABC and the WISC-R. The mean WISC-R Verbal IQ of 68.1 for these children, for example, was almost identical to their mean Achievement scale score on the K-ABC of 67.7. As a result, the MPC for this sample was considerably higher (82.9) than the Full Scale IQ (76.7). The K-ABC may prove valuable in cases where a clinician is trying to differentiate among intellectual, cultural, and linguistic influences on learning.

Children Who Are Intellectually Gifted

No typical global scale profile emerges for samples of children who are gifted (Kamphaus & Reynolds, 1987, see Chapter 13). Gestalt Closure is one of the worst subtests for these children. Relative strengths on Triangles and Matrix Analogies may suggest that the higher the "g" loading of the subtest, the more likely the gifted samples will score higher (Kamphaus & Reynolds, 1987). The K-ABC MPC is consistently lower than Stanford-Binet and Wechsler scores for these children. Naglieri and Anderson (1985), for example, obtained a K-ABC mean of 126.3 and WISC-R mean of 134.3

McCallum, Karnes, and Edwards (1984) obtained a mean Stanford-Binet L-M IQ (1972 edition) that was about 16.19 points higher than the mean K-ABC MPC. One explanation for the difference between the 1972 Stanford-Binet and the K-ABC for children who are gifted is that the 1972 Stanford-Binet may give higher bound estimates of intelligence for these children. This is suggested by a study by Zins and Barnett (1984), which showed an extremely high correlation (.86) between the 1972 Stanford-Binet and the K-ABC Achievement scale. In addition, a study in the Stanford-Binet Fourth Edition *Technical Manual* (1986) indicates that the 1972 Stanford-Binet produces much higher scores (mean IQ = 135.3) than the 1986 Fourth Edition (mean IQ = 121.8). It may be that the 1972 Stanford-Binet shared extensive overlap with measures of academic achievement.

When using the K-ABC to assess children who are gifted, Kaufman (1984) recommends that examiners use good performance on *either* the MPC *or* the achievement scale as evidence of giftedness. Relying on only the MPC unfairly penalizes children who are verbally gifted. The Kaufmans' goal in separating mental processing from achievement was to provide fairer assessment of the intelligence of children who are learning disabled and from a minority population; their goal was *not* to have the elimination of verbal and factual tasks from the MPC penalize children who are gifted.

Educational Remediation Research

The K-ABC is unique in that one of the test development goals was to produce a test that is helpful in the educational remediation process (Kaufman & Kaufman, 1983c). This is an ambitious goal that is similar to saying that a cure existed for low intelligence (i.e., mental retardation). Hence, the mere statement of intent to be useful for educational remediation was controversial and led to immediate attack (Salvia & Hritcko, 1984).

The K-ABC goes much further than its predecessors by including an entire chapter on educational translation of K-ABC scores in the *Technical Manual* (Kaufman & Kaufman, 1983b). Researchers reviewed some models of special education intervention, identified problems, and proposed solutions. They offered a "strength" model of redmediation (Reynolds, 1981) that borrows heavily from neuropsychological models of remediation. The Kaufman's model proposed that one should not try to remediate weaknesses (e.g., prescribe exercises that would improve a child's simultaneous weakness), but rather a child's cognitive strengths should be utilized to improve academic skills. This model is a familiar one in medical rehabilitation. A stroke victim, for example, may never regain the strength of his dominant hand that he used to dress himself. In cases such as this, an occupational therapist will teach the patient dressing skills that capitalize on the patient's strengths. The therapist may allow the patient clever ways to fasten fasteners partially before the garment is worn. Similarly, the Kaufmans propose that a child with reading problems and a sequential deficit not be taught sequencing skills (this would be nonsensical since sequencing is the predictor variable not the criterion variable), but rather be taught how to use simultaneous skills to compensate for sequential weaknesses in the reading process.

Recently, the whole idea of using intelligence tests with the goal of a *direct* link to intervention has been questioned (Kamphaus, 1990). As Kamphaus (1990) observes:

> I think that intelligence tests will never have *direct*, and I emphasize the word *direct*, effects on treatment planning. . . . Take, for example, measures of height, such as feet and inches. Do these measures have "treatment validity" for measuring height? (p. 366)

Kamphaus (1990) proposes that intelligence tests will be more likely to have *indirect* effects on treatment. Medical tests such as the MRI scan do not possess strong evidence of treatment validity, but they do allow for more sophisticated research on the disorder that may indirectly lead to treatment. This discussion calls into question the inclusion of a "remediation" chapter in the K-ABC manual. It also renders criticism of the K-ABC intervention model less important.

Some pilot data presented in the K-ABC *Interpretive Manual* (Kaufman & Kaufman, 1983c) suggest that the K-ABC may be useful for designing educational interventions. In direct contrast, studies by Ayres, Cooley, and Severson (1988) and by Good, Vollmer, Creek, Katz, and Chowdhri (1993) suggest that the K-ABC will not be useful for treatment planning. All of those pieces of research have methodological weaknesses. The Kaufman and Kaufman (1983b) and Good and colleagues' (1993) studies were based on small samples and were not well controlled. The Ayres and colleagues' (1988) investigation used criterion measures of sequential and simultaneous processing that had no strong evidence of validity. The question of whether the K-ABC remedial model is effective is still not answered. There are simply no large-scale, well-controlled studies available on this topic. Unfortunately, it does not appear likely that research on this issue will become available in the near future. This model of intervention, however, is perhaps not so important as far as the K-ABC goes but rather this approach to pedagogy for exceptional children deserves more research and consideration.

K-ABC SHORT FORMS

Kaufman and Applegate (1988) developed short forms of the K-ABC that may be useful when only general estimates of mental processing and achievement that can be administered in relatively brief amounts of time are needed. Examples of uses of short forms include preschool screening for identification of children who are "at risk" or who are potentially gifted, research, and certain clinical or educational circumstances. Although the administration of a short form can never replace the multiple scores and clinical evaluations obtained from administration of a complete battery, short forms of the K-ABC demonstrate excellent psychometric properties and offer useful estimates of functioning.

Extensive analysis of the reliability and validity of various combinations of subtests led to the selection of the following short forms for ages 4 through 12½ years. (Short forms were not developed for younger children because the K-ABC is already relatively brief for these ages.)

Mental Processing Dyad: Triangles, Word Order
Mental Processing Triad: Triangles, Word Order, Matrix Analogies
Mental Processing Tetrad: Hand Movements, Triangles, Word Order, Matrix Analogies

Mean reliability coefficients for the short forms are excellent and range from .88 to .93. Although the corrected validity coefficient between the Mental Processing dyad and the complete K-ABC is a marginal .80, the remaining short forms demonstrate excellent validity, with corrected coefficients of .86 for the Mental Processing triad, .88 for the Mental Processing tetrad, and .93 for an Achievement dyad. Kaufman and Applegate (1988) recommend using either the Mental Processing triad or tetrad along with an Achievement dyad (Arithmetic, Riddles) whenever a short form of the K-ABC is needed. Tables for computing *Estimated* Mental Processing Composites and Achievement standard scores (X = 100, SD –15) based on the sum of subtest scaled or standard scores are provided by Kaufman and Applegate (1988). The word *estimated* should be used whenever scores from short forms are reported.

NONVERBAL SCALE

The Nonverbal scale is intended for use with children for whom administration of the regular K-ABC (and virtually all other well-normed, standardized measures of intelligence) would be inappropriate: those who are hearing impaired, have speech or language disorders, other communication disabilities, or have limited English proficiency. The Nonverbal scale yields a global estimate of intelligence. Most well-normed intelligence tests that are applicable to children with communication problems are narrow and give a quite limited view of these children's intelligence (e.g., the Columbia Mental Maturity Scale) (Glaub & Kamphaus, in press). Although the K-ABC Nonverbal scale has limitations in this regard, of those tests of mental ability with adequate technical/psychometric characteristics, the K-ABC Nonverbal scale provides the broadest sampling of abilities and their development. The lack of adequately normed scales with any breadth of assessment has been a hindrance not only to clinical assessment of children with communication disorders but also to research in the area (Reynolds & Clark, 1983). The Nonverbal scale of the K-ABC is one of the best-normed, psychometrically most sophisticated nonverbal scales presently available.

K-ABC STRENGTHS AND WEAKNESSES

Strengths

1. The theory underlying the K-ABC is explicit, making it easier to understand why the test is organized as it is. The theory also yields a predictable factor structure that is the beneficiary of some research support.
2. The K-ABC is lawfully related to other intelligence measures. It does differ from other measures when language is an important variable for a child.
3. The K-ABC is relatively fun and easy to administer and score. The new "K-ABC Lite" (a more portable and lighter version) is also a boon to the mobile clinician.

4. The psychometric properties of the K-ABC, including norming, reliability, and validity, are strong.
5. From a neuropsychological standpoint, the K-ABC is helpful in that it assesses more memory functions.

Weaknesses

1. While the MPC may be easily interpreted, the meaning of the Sequential and Simultaneous scores is not as clear, making the test more of an interpretive challenge for clinicians.
2. The K-ABC suffers from floor and ceiling effects at a number of ages. This problem is compounded by changing subtests at various ages.
3. The K-ABC Achievement scale is enigmatic. It is a Wechsler-like verbal intelligence scale in some regards, but it also resembles clinical measures of achievement that are used for diagnosing learning disabilities. The Achievement scale then seems to require some experience in order to interpret it properly.
4. The Kaufmans' remedial model should be used cautiously until some research is available to support it.

CONCLUSIONS

The K-ABC is a unique contribution to the intellectual assessment scene, one that has led to polarizations—either you like it or not. The K-ABC has made some important contributions to children's intellectual assessment. The most important one is that the K-ABC has served as catalyst for research on children's intellectual assessment. The K-ABC has also been adopted by clinicians, suggesting that it has proven clinical value for some children in some settings, and its comprehensive, data-based manual has served as a model for manuals written subsequently for new tests and revisions of old tests. This is a well-known test because of all of its related research, which will likely foster its use for the foreseeable future.

SAMPLE CASE REPORT

The best way to summarize this chapter is to present a comprehensive case report written for a child referred for evaluation. The following report is for Tony B., with a chronological age of 8 years, 8 months.

Referral and Background Information

Tony was referred for evaluation by Mr. and Mrs. B., Tony's parents, and a psychologist whom Tony has seen in the past. Mr. and Mrs. B would like to gain further insight into Tony's intellectual and behavioral functioning. Mr. B. reports that Tony has been tested many times through the school system and that, in the past, he has been diagnosed with Attention Deficit Hyperactivity Disorder (ADHD) and Pervasive Developmental Disorder (PDD) with autistic features. Mr. and Mrs. B. are confused about the multiple diagnoses that have been given to Tony and they would like this testing to clarify the diagnostic picture. Additionally, Mr. and Mrs. B. want to ensure that Tony is getting his academic needs met in school and would like to know what type of learning environment would best suit him.

Tony lives with both of his parents, his 7-year-old sister and his half siblings from his father's previous marriage: a 22-year-old female and 19-year-old male. Mr. B. was unemployed for 13 months but he currently works full time as a computer programmer and Mrs. B. works full time as a human resources advisor. Tony attends school all day and is cared for by his older sister or a babysitter in the afternoons. Mr. B. reports that Tony gets along fairly well with his older siblings but that he has some difficulty with his younger sister. Mr. B. describes Tony's sister as "the opposite of Tony" and "manipulative." Mr. B. reports that Tony and his sister are not allowed in each other's room and that they are very competitive with one another.

Tony was carried for a full-term pregnancy and he weighed 7 pounds and 11½ ounces at birth. Mr. and Mrs. B. report that there were no complications during pregnancy and that Tony's delivery was normal. Tony is in fairly good health, although he does have asthma and was hospitalized at age 18 months for an inability to breathe. He also had ear infections from birth to 2 years of age, which resulted in having tubes placed in his ears and having his tonsils and adenoids removed. Tony currently wears glasses for reading and has had two eye surgeries for strabismus. The muscles in his right eye still appear to be weak, as his eye noticeably drifts. In addition to the physical difficulties, Tony has been diagnosed as having Attention Deficit Hyperactivity Disorder. He was placed on Ritalin but he reportedly did not do well on it and was then prescribed Cylert. Tony continues to take 56.25 mg of Cylert a day. Mr. and Mrs. B. report that Tony sat up at age 6 months, which is within the normal range of development, and that he walked at age 18 months, which falls within the low-average range. Tony's speech was also developmentally delayed. He said his first words at 2½ years of age and did not speak in full sentences until he was 4 years old. Mrs. B. describes Tony's speech as "okay" now, but reports that he has had a speech difficulty for 5 years.

Mr. B. sees Tony as a social individual who likes to interact with others. Tony enjoys putting puzzles together and playing with toy dinosaurs and computer games. Mr. B. also reports that Tony is very manipulative, stubborn, and obstinate. He also says that it is often difficult to motivate Tony to get him to pay attention. Tony's parents usually use money, food, and the computer as a means to motivate Tony; however, they also report that these rewards do not always work and that they often have to try several of them before they find the one that works best for that particular incident. When Tony does not comply, Mr. and Mrs. B. use the following approaches to discipline him: talking and reasoning, yelling at him, washing his hands, and putting him in a cold shower with his clothes on.

Tony has a quite complex and lengthy educational history. When he was 3 years old, he attended the Learning School in Los Angeles. The Learning School offers a special speech and language program for children who are communicatively disabled. His parents report that he cried for the first two weeks of school because he had difficulty separating from them. Tony attended preschool at Brentwood Gardens, a public special education school. Tony attended school five days a week for four hours a day. He then went to kindergarten at Chadbourne, which is another public special education school. Mrs. B. reports that Tony did not do well at Chadbourne, so they sent him to Spreckels. After Spreckels, Tony attended Valley for one year. Mr. and Mrs. B were very unhappy with Tony's lack of progress and what they felt was mismanagement of his case. They made the decision on their own to send Tony to Santa Monica Country Day, where he is currently in the second grade. Both Tony and his parents are happy with this school and Mr. B. reports that Tony is more interested in school and that he likes his teachers.

Throughout Tony's educational history, he has been identified as a student with special needs. He has had numerous Individual Education Placement (IEP) meetings to assess and address his special needs. In addition to these meetings, Tony has been tested many times with a variety of tests. Past testing has included the Wechsler Intelligence Test for Children-Third Edition (WISC-III), Peabody Picture Vocabulary Test-Revised (PPVT-R), Woodcock-Johnson Tests of Achievement, Draw a Person, Test of Auditory Comprehension of Language-R, Boehm Test of Basic Concepts-R, Expressive One-Word Picture Vocabulary Test, Test of Language Development-2, Vineland Developmental Inventory, Structured Photographic Expressive Language Test-II, and Arizona Articulation Proficiency Scale.

These tests revealed that Tony was approximately 2½ years behind in his ability to comprehend auditorily presented words, concepts, and sentences. Significant delays were also noted in his ability to define, label, and pronounce common words. Five years ago, the Vineland Adaptive Behavior Scales, administered by his teacher, indicated that Tony was 1 year 5 months below his age level in Communication Skills, 1 year 4 months below in his Daily Living Skills, 1 year 4 months below in Socialization, and 5 months below in Motor Development. Two years ago, Tony was given the WISC-III and received a Verbal IQ of 84, a performance IQ of 115, and a Full Scale IQ of 98. About three months ago, Tony was given the WISC-III again and received a Verbal IQ of 83, a Performance IQ of 110, and a Full Scale IQ of 95. Tony's scores on intelligence testing vary considerably, with overall scores from 79 on the Slosson Intelligence Test to 98 on the WISC-III. His scores on achievement testing are lower than his intellectual scores. On the Woodcock Johnson-Revised Tests of Achievement (WJ-R), Tony was at least one grade level behind where he should be on most of the subtest. In general, it appears that Tony is far below his age level in a variety of areas, especially verbal communication skills.

Tony was observed in the classroom and his behavior was assessed with the Student Observation System (S.O.S.) section of the Behavior Assessment

System for Children (BASC). The observer noted that Tony's teacher provided a very structured setting and that she taught at a quick pace, which, along with the small class size, did not allow for the children to lose focus. In the classroom, the majority of Tony's behavior fell under the adaptive behavior category of Work on School Subjects, as he was most often observed working on the worksheet in front of him. He also was observed, at times, responding to the teacher in an appropriate manner, answering all of the questions posed to him. He made some transition movements that were necessary when the boys were asked to turn in their math homework, which also falls under adaptive behaviors.

Overall, Tony appeared to be engaged in the classroom activity, was compliant with the teacher's requests, and seemed to enjoy working on his school subjects. He was frequently observed laughing or smiling in response to the teacher and seemed to put full effort into his performance. Tony did struggle in areas, especially with exercises that required retrieval from memory, and he was greatly aided by visual cues. The fast pace and constant structure provided by his teacher kept Tony focused and on task in the classroom.

Appearance and Behavioral Characteristics

Tony is a handsome, thin, small Caucasian boy. He presented himself as a neatly groomed and casually dressed young boy. He lacked color in his face and had dark circles under his eyes, characteristic of allergies. He wore reading glasses three of the four testing sessions, but they did not appear to affect or change his perception of test stimuli. He was eager to participate in the testing and put forth much effort during the entire testing sessions. Tony was attentive and motivated to perform the tasks given by the examiner. As testing continued and Tony interacted more with the examiners, he exhibited signs of inattention and "fidgetiness," such as slouching down in his seat, rocking back and forth in the chair, constant eye movements, staring off into the distance, and biting his clothing. Although his right eye was a "lazy eye," both eyes drifted at times when Tony became inattentive. He also supplied more spontaneous and appropriate speech as testing continued.

On the third day of testing, Tony did not take medication and his disruptive behaviors were more profound than previously observed. Testing that day was stopped, and continued on a later date because Tony was overactive and constantly moving/rubbing his head against his hand and elbows in his chair. In addition, he could not concentrate or focus on tasks for any extended period of time, staring at a hole in his jeans and licking it. During the rest of the testing, and despite difficulties with sustaining his motivation throughout tasks, Tony was cooperative, attentive, and hard working.

Although Tony typically showed persistence and motivation throughout the tasks, he performed best when he had a holistic/gestalt problem-solving approach or sense of what the entire task entailed, especially if it was a visual-perceptual task. He responded quickly, confidently, and in a loud voice to visual-perceptual tasks. Conversely, when tasks were presented auditorily,

Tony had difficulty understanding the holistic/gestalt of the task. For example, when he understood a task, such as identifying a picture given only part of the image, he would begin to respond quickly and anticipated future items. On the other hand, when items became more difficult, Tony would focus on parts of the question or on his previous responses, and perseverate. As a result, he appears to have problems with selective attention to stimuli. The perseveration results from him not being able to disengage from the information/stimuli provided. Consequently, when Tony cannot integrate the receptive/sensory information with already stored information, he gives his best guess at a response by using part of the question or part of a previous response, whichever is most accessible.

Due to this perseveration, seen across tasks, test results must be interpreted within Tony's behavioral set. On the incomplete image task, for example, he responded to one item as being "dinosaur bones" and continued incorrectly with that set, by responding "eagle bones," "elephant bones," and "sheep bones" to the next three items. Another example was when he was asked what holds convicts *inside,* he responded *sidewalk.* As a result of the perseveration, Tony would lose sight of the goal or expectation of the task. Although the perseveration was pervasive on many of the tasks, Tony was redirectable with training in most cases. He performed best on visual tasks when he verbalized, as well as touched and pointed to the visual stimuli. Thus, the use of multimodal integration and information aided Tony in problem solving when tasks were not too difficult. When tasks became more difficult, usually involving more integration of different modalities, Tony appeared to dampen his emotional and behavioral production and focus all energies on problem solving. Tony exhibited flat affect and appeared more sluggish.

This paragraph describes the interaction between Tony's affect and his need to focus when dealing with multisensory stimulation: At the beginning of the testing, Tony exhibited flat affect. He would put his face down in between his elbows, and rub his ears, face, and hair with his hands. As testing continued, Tony became more animated and laughed or smiled when items were funny or examiners made a joke. In addition, Tony's eye contact with the examiners increased as testing transpired. But when tasks required more involvement from different modalities, such as perceptual and tactile, his affect became very flat again when speaking. He became focused and absorbed in the task.

In general, Tony had a short attention span and tended to shift his attention constantly, while continuing to stay on the same mental set. Tony received sensory information auditorially but appeared to have problems integrating the auditorially presented stimuli, in order to respond to questions. As a result, he would selectively attend to details and perseverate on specific parts of the task. He would perseverate on one step, usually the first, of the problem-solving approach, something that was simple—such as an overlearned association. For example, when Tony had to provide a synonym for a word, he would access the definition but not the next step, another word. As an example, to the stimulus *look*, he responded *look both ways*. It is interesting to note that Tony did not appear to be impulsive in his physical behavior or his problem-solving approach unless he was very confident of the task format or his answer.

Tests Administered

Kaufman Assessment Battery for Children (K-ABC)
Kaufman Test of Educational Achievement (K-TEA): Comprehensive Form
Woodcock-Johnson Tests of Cognitive Ability—Revised (WJ-R): Nine Selected Subtests
Sentence Completion Test
Vineland Adaptive Behavior Scales: Expanded Edition (administered to both parents in the home)
Behavior Assessment System for Children: Student Observation Scale (BASC-SOS)

Test Results and Interpretation

On the Kaufman Assessment Battery for Children (K-ABC), Tony earned a Sequential Processing Standard Score of 71 ± 8, a Simultaneous Processing Standard Score of 86 ± 7, a Mental Processing Composite Standard Score (IQ equivalent) of 78 ± 6, and a Verbal Intelligence Standard Score (based on the three K-ABC Achievement subtests that were administered to Tony) of 69 ± 6. The 15-point difference between his Simultaneous Processing (18th percentile) and Sequential Processing (3rd percentile) standard scores is statistically significant and suggests that he performs better when solving problems that require a gestalt-like, holistic integration of stimuli (simultaneous) than when solving problems in a linear, step-by-step fashion (sequential). But even his highest score, on the Simultaneous Processing Scale, is probably an underestimate of his intellectual potential. The perseveration that he displayed throughout the evaluation was especially evident on a Simultaneous subtest that required him to sequence photographs in their appropriate chronological order. The 2nd percentile that he achieved on that task is not a valid indication of his ability; when that subtest is excluded, his prorated Simultaneous Processing standard score computes to 93 (32nd percentile) and his Mental Processing Composite Standard Score computes to 81 (10th percentile).

Within the Sequential Processing Scale, Tony's performance was a function of the degree to which auditory stimuli were involved. He performed poorest (well below the 1st percentile) when the stimulus and response were both auditory (repeating numbers spoken by the examiner); he performed at an intermediate level (9th percentile) when the stimulus was auditory and the response was visual-motor (pointing to pictures in the same order that the examiner named them); and he performed best (25th percentile) when the stimulus was visual and the response motor (copying a series of hand movements performed by the examiner).

His extreme difficulty in his ability to process and interpret auditory stimuli, therefore, seems to account in large part for his low (2nd to 3rd percentile) Sequential Processing and Verbal Intelligence scores on the K-ABC. In contrast to his Well Below Average to Lower Extreme ability on auditory/verbal tasks, he demonstrated an Average level of ability on tasks within the visual-motor channel. Similarly, he earned a strikingly lower WISC-III Verbal IQ (84) than Performance IQ (115) when he was tested about two years ago, and again about three months ago (VIQ = 83 and PIQ = 110).

Tony was administered nine subtests from the Woodcock-Johnson-Revised (WJ-R) Cognitive Battery to help pinpoint more specifically Tony's visual strengths and auditory weaknesses. Of greatest interest is the enormous scatter that he displayed. His best performance was on the Visual Processing Scale, as he earned a standard score of 114 ±, which indicates that his ability to interpret visual stimuli is Above Average and surpasses the visual-perceptual abilities of 82 percent of children Tony's age. Within the auditory-vocal channel of communication, by contrast, he earned a standard score of 72 ± 5 (3rd percentile) on Auditory Processing and 66 ± 5 (1st percentile) on Oral Vocabulary. He was unable to identify incomplete words presented auditorially (e.g., "eanut utter"), to connect spoken syllables and phonemes to form a word, or to provide the correct antonym or synonym to words spoken by the examiner. On the K-ABC, as noted, he could not repeat a series of numbers spoken by the examiner.

Tony also had considerable difficulty with long-term memory tasks requiring him to pair verbal stimuli, presented orally, with pictures or symbols; he earned a standard score of 71 ± 4 (3rd percentile) on the Long-term Retrieval Scale. He has clear-cut deficits, at the Well Below Average to Lower Extreme level of intellectual functioning, on tests of memory, sequential processing, and auditory processing. These areas of impairment very likely make it difficult for him to understand long or complex directions spoken by his parents and teachers, and they also make it inconceivable that a phonics approach to reading (such as Distar) will be successful. Despite his difficulty in learning the verbal-visual paired associations on their initial presentation, there is evidence that he is quite able to retain his learning over time. When he was retested on a set of word-symbol associations one week after they were taught, his retention was in the Average range (standard score of 95 ± 5 on the WJ-R Delayed Recall Visual-Auditory Learning subtest). Despite his memory problems, the use of visual stimuli seems to have a facilitating effect on his learning. Therefore, a technique for teaching reading such as Rebus Readers, which require the child to pair words with pictures, may be very successful with Tony.

Tony's problems with the processing of auditory stimuli make it hard for him to convey his knowledge base. On the WJ-R, he performed substantially better when naming pictorial stimuli (17th percentile on the Picture Vocabulary subtest) than when responding to auditory stimuli (1st percentile on the Oral Vocabulary subtest). Nonetheless, part of his difficulty on Oral Vocabulary concerns his problems with his memory. When he is required to solve verbal problems, as opposed to having to recall facts or words, then he is able to display Low Average mental ability. He earned standard scores in the 80s on a K-ABC test of riddle solving (83), and on the WISC-III administered two years ago (VIQ = 84) and about three months ago (VIQ = 83).

Tony's achievement on the Kaufman Test of Educational Achievement Comprehensive Form (K-TEA) was consistently low. His standard scores on the five separate subtests were all at or below the 5th percentile, ranging from 64 ± 9 on Mathematics Applications to 75 ± 6 on Spelling. His highest grade equivalents were 1.2 on Spelling and 1.1 on Reading Decoding; he scored below the first-grade level on Mathematics Applications, Mathematics Computation, and Reading Comprehension, failing every item on the latter subtest. On Spelling, Tony was able to spell *and, dog,* and *big,* but was unable to spell words such as *on* (he spelled it *ot*), *came* (*cam*), or *school* (*sac*). In Reading Decoding, he was able to identify upper-case and lower-case letters (except for reversing *b* into *d*), and he correctly read the words *to, in,* and *deep.* He was unable to decode words such as *four* (*funner*), *new* (*nee*), or *take* (*key*). In mathematics, he was able to identify numbers up to 12, but he could not identify higher numbers. He solved two easy computation problems (4 + 1 = 5 and 3 + 6 = 9), but confused subtraction with addition (9 − 2 = 11 and 4 − 3 = 7), and was unable to perform even the most basic addition or subtraction when the items were presented auditorially as word problems.

Tony's level of basic academic achievement on the K-TEA is entirely consistent with the scores he earned on the Wide Range Achievement Test-Revised, administered about two years ago, and with his WJ-R Achievement Battery standard scores on reading (67), mathematics (64), and written language (53) obtained from a previous administration about three months ago. On the WJ-R Achievement Battery, at that time, Tony performed relatively well on the Broad Knowledge Scale (87), which makes liberal use of visual stimuli, demonstrating his factual knowledge of science, art, music, and literature. That standard score is consistent with his performance on the WJ-R Cognitive Picture Vocabulary subtest and on tests of verbal reasoning. The past and present evaluations indicate that Tony has striking deficiencies in basic school skills such as reading and math, but that he has acquired a considerable knowledge base that he is best able to display when he is presented with pictorial stimuli.

In the present evaluation, the best (least contaminated) measure of Tony's intelligence is the prorated standard score of 93 on the K-ABC Simultaneous Processing Scale. From the recent administration of the WISC-III, Tony's Performance IQ of 110 provides the least contaminated estimate of his mental ability. His level of intelligence is somewhere between the low end and high end of the Average range; the midpoint of his K-ABC Simultaneous

Processing score and his WISC-III Performance IQ probably represents the best estimate of his current intellectual functioning. That midpoint of 102 is strikingly (more than two standard deviations) higher than the standard scores in the 50s, 60s, and 70s that he earned on the K-TEA and in basic academic skill areas on the WJ-R Achievement Battery. These test results suggest that Tony has not achieved up to his potential and may be considered learning disabled.

One may hypothesize that Tony's learning disability appears to be a direct function of apparent central processing deficits that dramatically affect his ability to process and recall auditory stimuli. His verbal, auditory, sequential, and memory deficits are consistent with neurological dysfunction primarily affecting the left cerebral hemisphere, and his visual processing and nonverbal reasoning strengths are consistent with integrities within the right hemisphere.

The Vineland Adaptive Behavior Scales, Interview Edition, Expanded Form, was administered during a home visit. On the Vineland Expanded form, Tony obtained an Adaptive Behavior Composite standard score of 56, and at the 90 percent confidence level, his true score is said to fall within the range of 51 to 61, which classifies his general adaptive functioning as low. Tony's standard scores in the adaptive behavior domains are as follows: Communication 60 ± 7, Daily Living Skills 57 ± 6, and Socialization 66 ± 8. His performance in the Communication, Daily Living Skills, and Socialization domains, which correspond to the percentile ranks of .4, .2, and 1, respectively, is classified as Low when compared with other children his age.

Tony exhibited a relatively consistent level of functioning in the different adaptive domains (communication, daily living skills, and socialization) and, overall, is perceived as performing well below average for his age group. These scores may not reflect his true adaptive behavioral functioning. Tony's high pain tolerance, coupled with other handicapping conditions, provide for restricted opportunity to perform certain tasks. Thus, his scores may not truly reflect his adaptive behavior abilities. For example, an item in the Daily Living Skills domain such as "uses stove or microwave oven for cooking" or "uses sharp knife to cut food" lowers Tony's score, because although he can probably perform these functions, he is not allowed to because his parents fear that he will hurt himself as a result of not feeling pain (e.g., if he leans on the hot stove and burns himself, he won't feel the burn). Items referring to the use of basic tools, materials, and so on, are also affected by this variable. His language weaknesses and deficits contribute in his low scores on the Communication domain, which inquires about functions such as his usage of plural nouns and verb tenses (e.g., "uses irregular past tense verbs correctly"). Tony has very little grasp on more complex language and has tremendous difficulties with reading and writing, all of which are measured within this domain. His Socialization domain score seems to reflect Tony's problems of separation from his parents, with items such as "stays overnight at friends' houses" and "has friends stay overnight" contributing to his low score.

Summary and Diagnostic Impressions

Tony is an 8-year-old Caucasian boy. He was referred for an evaluation by his parents and psychologist. The purpose of the referral was to assess Tony's level of cognitive and achievement functioning. Previous to this testing, Tony had received a diagnosis of ADHD and PDD with autistic features and his parents would like some clarification regarding the diagnosis. Additionally, Mr. and Mrs. B. would like information about what type of learning environment would best suit Tony's needs.

Tony is rather petite and he looks younger than his stated age. Initially, Tony was reserved and withdrawn with the examiners; however, as time passed, he became more animated and verbal. He was cooperative and motivated but when tasks became too difficult and demanding, he would disengage, perseverate, and engage in self-stimulating behavior. For example, Tony would bite and pull on the sleeves of his sweatshirt and then lick and chew on the knees of his pants. On the third day of testing, Tony had not taken his medication and as a result he was unable to sit still, focus, and cooperate with the examiners. Therefore, testing was discontinued for that day and was rescheduled for a later date.

Tony's pervasive language difficulties make it difficult to interpret his cognitive functioning. The K-ABC Mental Processing scores classify Tony's overall cognitive ability at the below-average level, corresponding to a percentile rank of 10. In general, Tony was able to solve problems significantly better when he relied on holistic, simultaneous information in comparison to linear, step-by-step problems. Tony appeared to have great difficulty with tasks that involved auditory-verbal skills and memory, but he demonstrated average ability with purely visual-motor tasks. This pattern suggests that Tony learns best when presented with visual and/or tactile information that minimizes the use of language.

On Achievement testing, Tony's scores were far below average across the different content areas. Tony scored highest on Spelling and Reading Decoding, performing at approximately the first-grade level. He scored lower on Mathematics Applications, Mathematics Computation, and Reading Comprehension, with scores below the first-grade level. His language difficulties significantly impeded his Achievement scores as well. Tony's Achievement functioning is commensurate with his overall scores on cognitive tests; however, it is difficult to provide a fair assessment of Tony because of his pervasive language difficulties, perseveration, and memory impairment.

The best indicator of Tony's overall intellectual functioning would be to look at all of the nonverbal tasks that he was given during this evaluation and previously. These tasks suggest that Tony's intellectual capacity falls within the average range. Tony's performance on achievement testing was consistently far below average even when language was minimized. These results are indicative of an individual who is exhibiting a learning disability, as well as Attention Deficit Hyperactivity Disorder. It also appears that Tony is not working up to his potential. At this time, Tony is exhibiting behaviors that are characteristic of individuals with Developmental Dysphasia or Developmental Receptive Language Disorder (315.31).

Even though Tony exhibits a generally consistent level of functioning in the different adaptive behavior domains (communication, daily living skills, and socialization) and, overall, performs well below average for his age, Tony's cognitive strengths reveal his potential in learning. Tony's Vineland scores may not reflect his true adaptive behavioral functioning because of (1) Tony's high pain tolerance, (2) his other handicapping conditions, and (3) his restricted opportunity to perform certain tasks. Therefore, Tony's adaptive behavior abilities are not a function of his cognitive ability, but rather a reflection of his need for socialization skills and his difficulties with separation from his parents.

Recommendations

1. Based on the test data and Tony's often disruptive behavior, it is recommended that Tony continue to take his prescribed medication consistently. Without his medication, Tony appears to have great difficulty controlling his impulsivity, perseveration, inattention, and overall behavior, which interferes with both his learning and interactions with others.

2. Tony has attended many different schools and has had many different teachers. It is believed that this inconsistency and instability have exacerbated his academic difficulties. Therefore, it is recommended that Tony be placed in one school that provides a stable and structured environment.

3. In the classroom, it is felt that Tony would benefit from the following:

   a. Tony learns best with visual techniques and he enjoys playing with computers. Therefore, whenever possible, computers and visual aids should be used as an aid in teaching Tony.

   b. Interactive materials should also be utilized when trying to teach Tony language skills.

   c. Phonics should not be used to teach Tony to read because of his difficulty with perseveration and discrimination of phonemes. A better technique would be to use a "sight word" reading method such as Rebus Readers.

   d. Tony has difficulty identifying and interpreting symbols such as numbers. Therefore, he should be taught basic math skills using a concrete and practical approach. For example, actual coins should be used when teaching him monetary value, but numerical concepts should be developed with blocks or sticks, such as Cuisenaire rods.

   e. Peer tutoring, with an older peer, may provide academic support as well as a role model for appropriate behavior.

   f. When Tony's perseveration is manifested, acknowledge the behavior and stop the task. Because this behavior is indicative of Tony's lack of understanding of the task at hand, it is important that (1) the task be explained using again simpler/shorter demands and (2) the instructor not continue until Tony understands the task. Modeling and shaping simpler forms of the task to meet Tony's level of understanding will best maximize learning.

4. Tony's behavior at home may be handled with consistent behavior modification. The behavior modification approach should include the following:

a. Discuss with Tony and specify what behavior is expected of him and establish reasonable expectations and limitation of his behavior. This might be accomplished by accompanying drawings, storybook pictures, or child videos on behavior (i.e., *Manners Can Be Fun*). Tony should be involved in determining what reinforcements will be used. Model the acceptable behavior for him and have him practice the behavior. In addition, provide feedback on the correctness of Tony's responses and, if necessary, practice again.

b. Establish specific rules (i.e., work/play quietly, remain on task, no talking back, etc). These rules should be discussed and reviewed on a regular basis.

c. Provide Tony with *consistent* praise and rewards for acceptable/appropriate behavior.

d. Create a visual chart (perhaps on the computer) that has simple symbols (e.g., stars) to keep track of Tony's behavior and overall performance on the behavior modification program. Making a large (2 feet × 3 feet) bar graph display to show Tony his accomplishments each week will be tangibly reinforcing, especially if displayed in a prominent place in the house.

5. Tony is a child who needs a considerable amount of order and structure in both his school and home environment. He becomes easily overwhelmed and confused when presented with too much stimuli. Therefore, it is important to provide him with consistent feedback and structure, and a predictable home environment.

6. Due to Tony's competitiveness in school and with his sister at home, a positive reinforcement plan must be incorporated into the behavior modification program. For example, using a visual chart (as mentioned previously) to monitor Tony's and his sister's good/positive behavior at dinner can be used by placing stickers for every positive behavior he exhibits during a set period of time. In school, a similar chart can be established for all the students in the class—for example for those who have finished their homework.

7. In order to implement the behavior modification program, Mr. and Mrs. B. should consult with Tony's psychologist for support and guidance. Behavior modification can be a rather intense and complex technique that may need to be revised periodically. Therefore, the psychologist may need to be consulted with on a regular basis.

PSYCHOMETRIC SUMMARY

Kaufman Assessment Battery for Children (K-ABC)

Sequential Processing = 71 ± 8 (3rd percentile)
Simultaneous Processing = 86 ± 7 (18th percentile)
Nonverbal = 84 ± 6 (14th percentile)
Mental Processing Composite (IQ) = 78 ± 6 (7th percentile)
Verbal Intelligence Standard Score = 69 ± 6 (2nd percentile)

Subtest Scale Scores

	Sequential			Simultaneous	
	Scaled Score	*Per-centile*		*Scaled Score*	*Per-centile*
Hand Movements	8	25	Gestalt Closure	10	50
Number Recall	1	.1	Triangles	9	37
Word Order	6	9	Matrix Analogies	8	25
			Spatial Memory	9	37
			Photo Series	4	2

Achievement Subtest Scale Scores

	Scales Score	*Per-centile*
Faces & Places	77 ± 9	6
Arithmetic	56 ± 9	.2
Riddles	83 ± 9	13

Kaufman Test of Educational Achievement (K-TEA)

Reading Composite = 71 ± 4 (3rd percentile)
Mathematics Composite = 65 ± 6 (1st percentile)
Battery Composite = 68 ± 3 (2nd percentile)

Subtest Scale Scores

	Scaled Score	*Per-centile*
Mathematics Applications	64 ± 9	1
Reading Decoding	71 ± 5	9
Spelling	75 ± 6	5
Reading Comprehension	74 ± 6	4
Mathematics Computation	69 ± 7	2

Woodcock-Johnson Tests of Cognitive Ability-Revised (WJ-R)

Standard

Cluster	Score and SEM	Percentile
Long-Term Retrieval	71 ± 4	3
Auditory Processing	72 ± 5	3
Visual Processing	114 ± 7	82
Comprehension-Knowledge	76 ± 4	5

Cluster	Subtest Scale Scores	Standard Score	Percentile
Long-Term Retrieval			
	Memory for Names	67 ± 4	1
	Visual-Auditory Learning	78 ± 5	7
	Delayed Recall: V-A Learning	95 ± 5	36
Auditory Processing			
	Incomplete Words	71 ± 6	2
	Sound Blending	80 ± 5	9
Visual Processing			
	Visual Closure	109 ± 8	72
	Picture Recognition	117 ± 7	87
Comprehension-Knowledge			
	Picture Vocabulary	86 ± 6	17
	Oral Vocabulary	66 ± 5	1
	Listening Comprehension	78 ± 6	7

REFERENCES

Anastasi, A. (1984). The K-ABC in historical and contemporary perspective. *Journal of Special Education, 18,* 357–366.

Ayres, R. R., Cooley, E. J., & Severson, H. H. (1988). Educational translation of the Kaufman Assessment Battery for Children: A construct validity study. *School Psychology Review, 17(1),* 113–124.

Benton, A. L. (1980). The neuropsychology of facial recognition. *American Psychologist, 35,* 176–186.

Binet, A., & Simon, T. (1905). New methods for the diagnosis of the intellectual level of subnormals. *L'annee Psychologique, 11,* 191–244.

Bogen, J. E. (1969). The other side of the brain: Parts I, II, and III, *Bulletin of the Los Angeles Neurological Society, 34,* 73–105, 135–162, 191–203.

Bracken, B. A. (1985). A critical review of the Kaufman Assessment Battery for Children (K-ABC). *School Psychology Review, 14,* 21–36.

Childers, J. S., Durham, T. W., Bolen, L. M., & Taylor, L. H. (1985). A predictive validity study of the Kaufman Assessment Battery for Children with the California Achievement Test. *Psychology in the Schools, 22,* 29–33.

Das, J. P., Kirby, J. R., & Jarman, R. F. (1979a). *Sequential and simultaneous cognitive processes.* New York: Academic Press.

Das, J. P., Kirby, J. R., & Jarman, R. F. (1979b). *Simultaneous and successive cognitive processes.* New York: Academic Press.

Denckla, M. B. (1979). Childhood learning disabilities. In K. M. Heilman & E. Valenstein (Eds.), *Clinical neurospychology.* New York: Oxford University Press.

Fourqurean, J. M. (1987). A K-ABC and WISC-R comparison for Latino learning-disabled children of limited English proficiency. *Journal of School Psychology, 25,* 15–21.

Good, R. H. III, Vollmer, M., Creek, R. J., Katz, L., & Chowdri, S. (1983). Treatment utility of the Kaufman Assessment Battery for Children: Effects of matching instruction and student processing strength. *School Psychology Review, 22,* 8–26.

Jensen, A. R. (1984). The black-white difference on the K-ABC: Implications for future tests. *Journal of Special Education, 18,* 377–408.

Kagan, J., & Klein, R. E. (1973). Cross-cultural perspectives on early development. *American Psychologist, 28,* 947–961.

Kamphaus, R. W. (1990). K-ABC theory in historical and current contexts. *Journal of Psychoeducational Assessment, 8,* 356–368.

Kamphaus, R. W., & Kaufman, A. S. (1986). Factor analysis of the Kaufman Assessment Battery for Children (K-ABC) for separate groups of boys and girls. *Journal of Clinical Child Psychology, 3,* 210–213.

Kamphaus, R. W., & Reynolds, C. R. (1987). *Clinical and research applications of the K-ABC.* Circle Pines, MN: American Guidance Service.

Kaufman, A. S. (1984). K-ABC and giftedness. *Roeper Review, 7,* 83–88.

Kaufman, A. S., & Applegate, B. (1988). Short forms of the K-ABC Mental Processing and Achievement scales at ages 4 to 12-½ years for clinical and screening purposes. *Journal of Clinical Child Psychology, 17,* 359–369.

Kaufman, A. S., & Kamphaus, R. W. (1984). Factor analysis for ages 2½ through 12½ years. *Journal of Educational Psychology, 76(4),* 623–637.

Kaufman, A. S., & Kaufman, N. L. (1983a). *Administration and scoring manual for the Kaufman Assessment Battery for Children.* Circle Pines, MN: American Guidance Service.

Kaufman, A. S., & Kaufman, N. L. (1983b). *Interpretive manual for the Kaufman Assessment Battery for Children.* Circle Pines, MN: American Guidance Services.

Kaufman, A. S., & McLean, J. E. (1987). Joint factor analysis of the K-ABC and WISC-R with normal children. *Journal of School Psychology, 25(2),* 105–118.

Keith, T. Z. (1985). Questioning the K-ABC: What does it measure? *Journal of Psychoeducational Assessment, 8,* 391–405.

Keith, T. Z., & Dunbar, S. B. (1984). Hierarchical factor analysis of the K-ABC: Testing alternate models. *Journal of Special Education, 18(3),* 367–375.

Keith, T. Z., Hood, C., Eberhart, S., & Pottebaum, S. M. (1985, April). *Factor structure of the K-ABC for referred school children.* Paper presented at the meeting of the National Association of School Psychologists, Las Vegas, NV.

Kinsbourne, M. (1975). Cerebral dominance and learning. In H. R. Mykelbust (Ed.), *Progress in learning disabilities.* New York: Grune & Stratton.

Kohs, S. C. (1927). *Intelligence measurement.* New York: Macmillan.

Lewandowski, L. J., & de Rienzo, P. J. (1985). WISC-R and K-ABC performance of hemiplegic children. *Journal of Psychoeducational Assessment, 3(3),* 215–221.

Luria, A. R. (1966a). *Higher cortical functions in man.* New York: Basic Books.

Luria, A. R. (1966b). *Human brain and psychological processes.* New York: Harper & Row.

McCallum, R. S., Karnes, F. A., & Edwards, R. P. (1984). The test of choice for assessment of gifted children: A comparison of the K-ABC, WISC-R, and Stanford-Binet. *Journal of Psychoeducational Assessment, 2,* 57–63.

McCarthy, D. (1972). *McCarthy scales of children's abilities.* New York: The Psychological Corporation.

Miller, T. L., & Reynolds, C. R. (1984). Special issue . . . The K-ABC. *Journal of Special Education, 18(3),* 207–448.

Murray, A., & Bracken, B. A. (1984). Eleven-month predictive validity of the Kaufman Assessment Battery for Children. *Journal of Psychoeducational Assessment, 2,* 225–232.

Naglieri, J. A. (1985a). Assessment of mentally retarded children with the Kaufman Assessment Battery for Children. *American Journal of Mental Deficiency, 89,* 367–371.

Naglieri, J. A., & Anderson, D. F. (1985). Comparison of the WISC-R and K-ABC with gifted students. *Journal of Psychoeducational Assessment, 3,* 175–179.

Obringer, S. J. (1988, November). *A survey of perceptions by school psychologists of the Stanford-Binet IV.* Paper presented at the meeting of the Mid-South Educational Research Association, Louisville, KY.

Reitan, R. M., & Davison, L. A. (1974). *Clinical neuropsychology: Current status and application.* Washington, DC: Winston.

Reynolds, C. R. (1981). Neuropsychological assessment and the habilitation of learning: Considerations in the search for the aptitude × treatment interaction. *School Psychology Review, 10,* 343–349.

Reynolds, C. R., & Clark, J. H. (Eds.) (1983). *Assessment and programming for children with low incidence handicaps.* New York: Plenum.

Salvia, J., & Hritcko, T. (1984). The K-ABC and ability training. *Journal of Special Education, 18(3),* 345–356.

Sperry, R. W. (1968). Hemisphere deconnection and unity in conscious awareness. *American Psychologist, 23,* 723–733.

Sperry, R. W. (1974). Lateral specialization in the surgically separated hemispheres. In F. O. Schmitt & F. G. Worden (Eds.), *The neurosciences: Third study program.* Cambridge, MA: MIT Press.

Sternberg, R. J. (1984). The Kaufman Assessment Battery for Children: An information-processing analysis and critique. *Journal of Special Education, 18,* 269–279.

Street, R. F. (1931). A gestalt completion test. *Contributions to education.* New York: Bureau of Publications, Teachers College, Columbia University.

Valencia, R. R. (1985). Concurrent validity of the Kaufman Assessment Battery for Children in a sample of Mexican-American children. *Educational and Psychological Measurement, 44,* 365–372.

Wada, J., Clarke, R., & Hamm, A. (1975). Cerebral hemisphere asymmetry in humans. *Archives of Neurology, 37,* 234–246.

Willson, V. L., Reynolds, C. R., Chatman, S. P., & Kaufman, A. S. (1985). Confirmatory analysis of simultaneous, sequential, and achievement factors on the K-ABC at 11 age levels ranging from 2 ½ to 12 ½ years. *Journal of School Psychology, 23,* 261–269.

Zins, J. E., & Barnett, D. W. (1984). A validity study of the K-ABC, the WISC-R, and the Stanford-Binet with non-referred children. *Journal of School Psychology, 22,* 369–371.

10

The Bender-Gestalt Test (BGT)

Arthur Canter

INTRODUCTION

The Bender-Gestalt Test (BGT), also referred to as the Bender Visual-Motor Gestalt Test or more simply as the Bender Test, has been one of the most widely used psychological tests since its development (Lubin, Wallis, & Paine, 1971). Brown and McGuire (1976) noted that the Bender-Gestalt is among the 10 most popular means of personality appraisal and among the 10 most popular cognitive appraisal techniques across all age groups in a survey of test practice preferences by clinical psychologists. Similar findings were reported in a survey of commonly used projective techniques for the period 1947 to 1965 by Crenshaw and associates (1969). A Psychology Database (Psychological Abstracts) provided for computer catalog searches for the period from 1967 through 1993 lists almost 400 entries of articles on the Bender-Gestalt Test. However, there has been a sharp decline in the literature on the BGT beginning around 1991, suggesting that the test may be losing its eminent position in the armentarium of clinical psychologists, in particular those whose practice is devoted to neuropsychological evaluations.

Until recent years, one could hardly read a case report of an adult or child who had undergone psychological test examination without some reference to the findings with the Bender-Gestalt Test. Despite the changes in neuropsychological test practice using specialized test batteries, the ubiquitous Bender shows up in both research and clinical test reports of various psychopathological groups, test interrelationships, diagnostic signs, cortical dysfunction, behavioral changes as a result of treatment or an experimental condition, and so on. This is especially true in reports of children with respect to their intellectual development, educational difficulties, and emotional status. For extensive reviews of studies of the Bender, the reader is referred to Tolor and Schulberg (1963) and Tolor and Brannigan (1980).

In practice, for many psychologists, the Bender becomes a clinical tool for sampling visual motor behavior. The clinician can make observations of the patient's behavior as well as study the performance of the patient. Based on clinical experience or the experience of other clinicians, as reported in the literature on case studies of clinical research, the examiner makes inferences and hypotheses about some aspect or condition of the patient. If, in fact, the BGT does give reliable data on both personality characteristics and cognitive integrity as claimed in much of the literature, it is no wonder that it is so popular. However, there also has long been a disenchantment with the claims made for the Bender Test. This has led to research, in particular the development of techniques in varying test administration and evaluating test performance such as objective scoring schemes (Tolor & Brannigan, 1980). However, new voices have appeared, suggesting that severe limitations be placed on the use of the Bender-Gestalt (Sola, 1983), even to the point of outright banning the test's use as a single neuropsychological technique (Bigler & Ehrfurth, 1981).

CONSTRUCTION

The original Bender-Gestalt test was developed by Lauretta Bender for her studies of the so-called gestalt experience of children and adults that were carried out in the early 1930s, culminating in her monograph published in 1938. She used nine figures that she adapted for her purposes from Wertheimer's patterns that were published in his 1923 paper on the theory of gestalt psychology. Bender's modifications of the Wertheimer figures consisted of accentuating or simplifying some features of the patterns. Her research goals were to examine the gestalt experience of children at different stages of maturation and adults suffering from various psychopathological or intellectual defects. What was meant by the gestalt experience was the response to a patterned visual stimulus as an integrated or whole perceptual experience. Whereas Wertheimer's data were based on the verbal reports of the subject's experience in viewing the "Gestalten," Bender had her subjects copy them with pencil and paper, giving rise to her calling the technique a Visual Motor Gestalt Test. The nine test figures she used were published later in a separate series, and she provided a simple instruction pamphlet in response to the demand for her test. It is this set of cards and instructions that constitute the standard Bender-Gestalt Test.

Bender's monograph made quite an impact on the psychological world, coming at a time when there would shortly thereafter be a tremendous upsurge in the demand for and training of clinical psychologists. It must be remembered that in the period of the 1940s and early 1950s clinical psychology had few accepted standard tools for its role in psychodiagnosis. These were the Wechsler Scales, the Binet tests, the Minnesota Multiphasic Personality Inventory, the Rorschach, and the Thematic Apperception Test. These tests and the Bender became the core instruments in the instruction of clinical appraisal techniques and were readily accepted by clinical psychologists. It mattered little that the original rationale for use of the Bender Test and its original purpose, centered about concepts of gestalt psychology, were being displaced by other movements in psychology. Based on the studies being carried out at the time, the Bender Test seemed useful as a technique for appraising organic brain damage and personality.

The use of the Bender as a projective personality test owes itself to the heightened interest of psychologists in all projective techniques during the same period. An analogous phenomenon had already taken place with the Rorschach test, which in its original development by Rorschach, was based on concepts that had gone out of favor and had been replaced by newer ones that were propounded by the projective test psychologist. At the same time, psychological sophistication demanded that the instruments used for diagnostic appraisal show evidence of reliability and validity using modern statistical and experimental design techniques. The projective test psychologist in particular felt vulnerable to the criticism that was mounting. It was natural, then, that the Bender-Gestalt also began to receive research attention to develop objective criteria for the evaluative statements made in its clinical use and quantification of performance characteristics, neither of which was provided for Bender's original publication. Numerous methods for scoring Bender Test protocols, both for children and adults, were developed for various purposes. The major methods will be taken up in detail in subsequent sections. Similarly, research studies of alterations in administration procedures, and the use of the Bender Test figures as a visual memory test, multiple-choice matching test, sorting tasks, and so forth appeared in the literature and were more or less adopted by practicing clinicians (see Tolor & Brannigan, 1980).

It is interesting to note that Lauretta Bender herself, in the foreword to Tolor and Schulberg's first comprehensive review of the Bender Test (1963), rather decried some of the developments that had taken place "some 30 years and 300 research papers" after her own work. As she pointed out, the test arose from her clinical experience and not from controlled experiments. The major concern she expressed was that the "original meaning and values of the Gestalt test has been lost sight of by many of these investigators and their followers" (Bender, 1963, p. x). This is in reference to the application of principles of gestalt psychology as particularly developed by Wertheimer, which she claimed were of basic importance in understanding the test. To Bender, the subjective global evaluation of the patient's responses and reproductions of the test figures would be "more reliable and meaningful than any scoring method."

The fate of the Bender Test, as with Rorschach's original test and the Thematic Apperception Test, has been that it changed as it became employed by psychologists in an era when there were different approaches to examining psychological phenomena and evaluating human behavior than existed at the time the test was proposed. Whether the original theoretical basis for the Bender-Gestalt can be supported or not, or is even valid, is not a necessary condition for its continued use. This is an empirical matter and depends on what kinds of inferences one wishes to make on the basis of the data and the operations defined to obtain the data. If the Bender Test works, it is justifiable even if those who make it work use different criteria than did the originator of the test. It is not unusual for clinical practice to outstrip its theory with changes in the former often causing changes in the latter rather than vice versa.

RELIABILITY AND VALIDITY

Until objective scoring schemes and rating procedures for the Bender Test came into being, there was no evidence provided for the test reliability. Establishing reliability in a clinical instrument has its problems even where the instrument yields an objective index of some kind. Here we are concerned with the capacity of the instrument to yield approximately the same values for equivalent states of the individual under identical conditions. We would expect that as the individual's state varies the index will vary. To the extent it is possible to reproduce this state, we should be able to reproduce the index, if we had a reliable instrument. Test-retest methods of determining reliability thus may not be appropriate (Wagner & Flamos, 1988), depending on what state is being measured, its variability over time, and its interaction with more stable properties of the person (e.g., the state-trait distinction).

In clinical practice there is a tendency to be less concerned about apparent low statistical reliability of a test as long as there is some reason to believe that the test is a valid measure of the state. Translated to Bender Test terms, if a Bender sign or combination of signs is interpreted to indicate the presence of psychosis or an organic brain disorder, the evidence that such signs are highly predictive of the disorder is more convincing than being able to demonstrate that the individual will give the same signs on another testing at another time. The important issue is that the sign not mean one thing at one time and another thing at another time. Yet this is exactly what seems to take place in sign interpretation in projective tests and in global interpretations and increasingly complicates the task of determining the validity of the instrument.

In the history of clinical assessment techniques used by psychologists, validity procedures have varied from case history matchings with test interpretation and correlation techniques to sophisticated statistical experimental design techniques. Their purpose is to demonstrate that singular or combination of test characteristics will correctly identify characteristics of individuals or groups of persons bearing the same characteristic. The bulk of the Bender-Gestalt's validation is based on studies of the test efficacy in detecting organic brain disorder and not personality appraisal (Tolor & Brannigan, 1980).

Lubin and Sands (1992) more recently carried out a review of studies examining the psychometric properties of the Bender Test (i.e., reliability, validity, factor analyses, and scoring systems and norms) and have made available a bibliography of these studies.

BENDER TEST MATERIALS

The Bender Test that is currently available through various psychological test suppliers bears the copyright 1945 by Lauretta Bender and the America Orthopsychiatric Association, Inc. The test consists of nine cards, each 15.2 cm. by 10.1 cm. (4 × 6 inches). Each card has a design or pattern on its face side and a number from 1 to 8 on the opposite side, and, in the case of one card, the letter A instead of a number. The designs may be noted in Figure 10–1. The pattern in design A, the circle and diamond shape figure, covers a span of approximately 5 cm. across. Design 2 has dots spaced approximately 1.2 cm. apart with each dot being a little over a millimeter in diameter. Design 2 con-

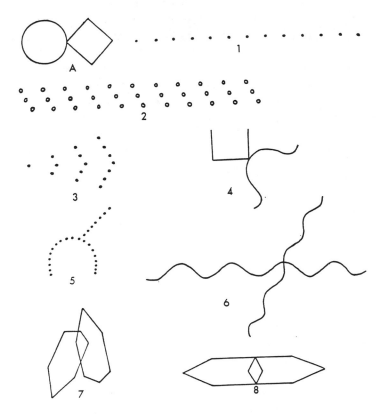

Figure 10–1   The Nine Designs of the Bender Visual Motor Gestalt Test (BGT) Figures

tains rows of loops arranged in 11 columns of three. The loops are elliptical in shape, approximately 2 × 3 mm in diameter, and the array covers a horizontal span of approximately 14 mm. Design 3 contains dots in a figure that fans out left to right. The horizontal span of the figure is approximately 4.5 cm. and the vertical span at its extreme height is approximately 2.7 cm. Design 4 has a rectangular figure approximately 1.8 cm. for each side. The combined figures occupy an area approximately 4.5 × 4.5 cm. Design 5 has an array of dots that form a little more than half of the top of a circle with a tail running out at a slant. The figure is approximately 2.7 cm. in diameter. Design 6 has two intersecting sinusoidal curves. The horizontal one extends about 12.2 cm. and the vertically oriented curve which is slightly smaller extends approximately 7.3 cm. Design 7 is made up of overlapping hexagonal figures, each about 4.2 cm. in length and 1.3 to 1.4 cm. in width. Design 8 is a horizontally oriented hexagonal figure 7.6 × 1.4 cm.

There have been a number of variations in the test figures developed for use with special populations (see Tolor & Schulberg, 1963). In the Hutt adaptation of the Bender Test (Hutt, 1985), the Bender figures have been redrawn to enhance their vividness.

ADMINISTRATION OF THE TEST

There is no single standard procedure for administering the Bender Test. In Bender's own use of the test, Design A served as an introductory figure with the designs on cards 1–8 given in a sequence. In a number of current techniques, Design A, while leading off the test, is included as an integral part of the test for both scoring and interpretation. The procedures of administration that conform closely to Bender's instructions (Bender 1946) will be referred to subsequently as traditional administration. The subject is given a sheet of plain white unlined paper 8½″ × 11″ on which to copy all nine figures but additional sheets are provided where needed, as may be the case for intellectually defective or confused subjects. A pencil with eraser is provided. No other aids (e.g., rulers, coins by which to trace circles, etc.) are provided.

The cards are presented one at a time correctly oriented before the subject (i.e., each card has an up position as identified by the location of the letter or numbers and names on the back of the card). The card is placed above the sheet of paper on the work surface. The subject is told simply to copy each design free hand. Variations in the wording are used but in essence the subject is advised to copy the designs the way they are seen. Card turning is discouraged. Any attempt to turn the cards during copying despite instructions not to is finally permitted, but note is made of the fact by the examiner who also notes when the paper is rotated, erasures are made, reworking of designs takes place, and so on. In the traditional procedure, the subject is free to do much but is not encouraged to do any more than simply copy the designs. Questions by the subject as to how to proceed (e.g., if dots should be counted, etc.) are answered by "It is not necessary, but do as you like." The traditional procedures do not make use of time limits but some examiners do record times taken by the subject to copy each design and/or the latency from the design presentation to the initiation of drawing. Notes are made of anything unusual that may aid the examiner in scoring the protocol or in the interpretation of the performance.

VARIATIONS IN ADMINISTRATION

It is necessary for the examiner to be clear as to the purpose for which the Bender Test is to be used. What scoring scheme and interpretative system are to be employed? These matters will determine the mode of administering the test, the types of observations made, and what records of performance are kept. It should always be noted somewhere on the test protocols or accompanying data whether the traditional administration had been used or a variation. For example, if a time limit was set for the subject, this should be indicated. If the subject was instructed to "copy the designs *exactly* as they are," this should be noted. Any restrictions placed on the subject that depart from the rather unstructured traditional approach may alter the interpretations of test products, especially those based on projective test concepts. Where scoring schemes are used that measure degrees of departure from the actual design models, methods of administration that loosely guard against paper and/or test card positions may be affected. For many objective scoring methods, the scoring and/or interpretation of the test need not be done by the same person who administers the test as long as the administration method is known. A review of various methods of Bender Test administration may be found in Chapter 2 of Tolor's and Brannigan's book (1980).

The test cards lend themselves to experimentation in administrative techniques apart from any scoring system. The cards or the paper may be oriented in different positions during presentation. Group administration is possible using slide projections of the design cards (Freed, 1964) or multiple individual sets of cards (Adams & Canter, 1969). The author's variation of the Bender Test included the use of a specially prepared sheet of paper on which to copy the designs (Canter, 1966). Where the Bender is used as a memory-for-designs test, the technique of administration may vary accordingly, as is the case where the test is used as a recognition task with or without tachistiscopic presentation. A number of research studies have been carried out to determine what, if any, effects variations in administrative procedure would have on the subjects responsiveness (Tolor & Brannigan, 1980).

SCORING METHODS

As noted earlier, the traditional Bender Test was not scored in the sense of being subjected to a specific set of criteria for measuring or rating the various parameters of the subject's reproductions of the test figures. However, in the period since the publication of the original test, many scoring methods have been developed to objectify measures or rate Bender performances. Some of these involved minor adaptations of the test figures and/or techniques of administration. The various scores proposed were developed as indices of developmental stages in visual motor ability, or as measures of specific and/or global manifestations of visual-motor disturbances that would be more reliable than the usual subjective scrutinizing methods employed by clinical psychologists. Also, the objective scores lend themselves to validation studies of the predictive and/or diagnostic power of the Bender Test (Tolor & Schulberg, 1963; Tolor & Brannigan, 1980).

Controversy has always accompanied the development of new scoring methods, whether on the basis of the inadequacy of the validation studies, the failure of the methods to yield accurate individual diagnoses, or on the scheme's apparent violation of basic gestalt precepts. In any event, there is no widely accepted standard method for scoring Bender Test protocols although several methods have achieved a fair degree of popularity. Which method should one choose? This will depend on the applicability of the scores to the goals of the examiner, the suitability of the normative data for the types of subjects tested, the adequacy of the validation criteria supporting the particular scoring methods used, and the ease with which the method can be reliably used.

Another factor that seems to play a role in whether a scoring method will be used with the Bender is the amount of effort required by the clinician to yield the interpretation he is inclined to use. The more cumbersome or apparently cumbersome the method seems to be, the more likely the clinician is inclined not to use it. Some scoring methods are easily carried out by a test technician with little clinical experience. Other rating or scoring procedures require considerable clinical experience. In the following, only a few methods of scoring the Bender Test will be described. These have been chosen for their current availability, their degree of acceptance, and their promise for future research and clinical use. For complete descriptions of the scoring of the Bender Test by any one of these methods, the reader will be required to secure a copy of the particular manual or detailed publication of the method.

THE PASCAL-SUTTELL METHOD

Pascal, in his early work with the Bender Test in the 1940s, noted that the Bender productions could be graded in terms of neatness and accuracy of reproduction to the extent that one could distinguish between psychiatric patients and nonpatients. His experience led to a series of studies that culminated in the publication of a method (Pascal & Suttell, 1951) of quantifying Bender Test productions that has stood the test of time and has proven to be valuable in a variety of research studies with the test. Pascal and Suttell proposed that the subject's performance in copying the Bender figures be regarded as a work sample that involves not only the capacity to perceive the designs and to reproduce them but also the subject's attitude during the performance. If the task is regarded as a bit of reality with which the subject has to cope, the greater the attitude toward reality is disturbed, the greater the deviations in perception, reproduction, or both in response to the test stimuli. Thus, the scoring system they developed provides a continuum of scores ranging from accuracy in production (low scores) to extremely deviant reproductions (high scores), which is said to be correlated with a progression from low to extreme psychological disturbance. In turn, the progression in scores is "correlated with decreasing ability to respond adequately to stimuli in the environment" (Pascal & Suttell, 1951, p. 9).

The method of scoring was empirically derived with tryouts on different types of patients using different types of drawing deviations until the authors could achieve the best discrimination between patient and nonpatient. Slight alterations in test administration are required by the method: (1) the subject is told there are nine designs to copy and (2) the subject is told not to sketch the design but to make single line drawings. In other respects, the instructions follow traditional lines. No time limits are used nor is time recorded as part of the scoring. Design A as in the traditional approach is not scored. For Designs 1–8, the scorable deviations are defined with examples for each.

Each deviation carries a weighted score ranging from 1 to 8. The types of deviations determined by the authors to be the more serious as pathogonomic indicators were given higher weights. For example, on Design 1, deviation #1 is called "wavy line of dots," which refers to an obvious departure from the straight line of dots presented on the design card. If a subject's reproduction meets the criteria for the deviation, a score of 2 points is given. On the other hand, deviation #6, which is called double row, requires that, if the subject reproduces the design on two lines as described in the criteria, a score of 8 points be given. The scorable deviations for the eight designs include such errors in reproduction as the drawing of circles or loops for dots and vice versa, dashes for dots or circles, overworking elements of lines, dots, or loops, distortions, rotations, parts of designs missing, use of guidelines, failure to join lines where appropriate, second attempts, extra angles, asymmetries, and so on.

Design 1 has 10 scorable deviations, Designs 2, 3, 4, 5, and 6 each have 13 scorable deviations, Design 7 has 11, and Design 8 has 12 scorable deviations. There are seven other scorable deviations for what the authors call configuration. These include different weighted scores for (1) placement of design A, (2) overlapping of the designs, (3) compression (using only half the sheet of paper for all designs), (4) lines drawn to separate the designs, (5) order (mild departure from a logical order in placement of designs), (6) no order (haphazard or confused design placements), and (7) relative size of reproductions. The manual provides illustrations as examples of each type of deviation and a large sample of scored records for instruction and practice in scoring. A summary score sheet is provided for noting and recording the scorable deviations. The raw scores (i.e., the total of weighted deviation scores) may be converted to a standard score (Z-score) based on the authors' normative population.

Their tables provide cumulative frequencies and ogives plotted from these frequencies for the Z-scores of patients and nonpatients. The patients are divided into psychoneurotic and psychotic. The authors propose a range of cutoff points in the scores to screen individuals in need of psychiatric help (Pascal & Suttell, 1951).

Scorer reliability was tested by blind scorings of 120 records by both authors independently. They report a correlation coefficient of .90. Other studies support their findings that higher scorer reliability may be obtained with practice. That is to say it is important for any scorer to achieve a high level of accuracy and proficiency in the scoring as a necessary condition before one can obtain higher reliability. Studies have been carried out on the test-retest reliability, influence of intelligence, sex differences, drawing ability, age, and education on the Pascal-Suttell scores (Pascal & Suttell, 1951, Tolor & Brannigan 1980, Wagner & Flamos (1988).

HAIN SCORING METHOD

Hain's method (1964) is an example of a simple system of scoring the Bender Test reproductions that approaches the test performance as a whole in contrast to the Pascal-Suttell card-by-card method. By the time of its appearance, several studies using the Pascal-Suttell scoring system failed to demonstrate clinically useful diagnostic precision, although significant discrimination could be made between groups of organic and nonorganic patients. Hain proposed his method in the hope of achieving greater diagnostic precision. He noted which types of errors seem to be frequently made by brain-damaged patients, nonbrain-damaged psychiatric patients, and normal subjects. He carried out studies, including cross-validation groups, of the discriminating power of 31 signs or errors he noted to be frequently made by patients.

The final scoring system contains 15 signs or errors that appeared to discriminate between organic and nonorganic patients. Each sign was weighted in relation to the degree that it discriminated between the patient groups. Any single instance of an error was scored for the category, and no category was scored more than once. The signs and their weights are as follows: Perseveration, Rotation or Reversal, and Concretism are given 4 points each; Added Angles, Separation of Lines, Overlap, and Distortion are given 3 points each; Embellishments and Partial Rotation are given 2 points each; Omission, Abbreviation of Designs 1 or 2, Separation, Absence of an Erasure, Closure, and Point of Contact on Figure A are given 1 point each. The range of scores is from 0 for no scorable errors to 34 when every type of error is made at least once.

In practice, scoring can proceed more rapidly with the Hain than the Pascal-Suttell method. Once an error category is noted, the scorer need not look for any more instances of it. Hain has a manual available for defining the categories and their application (see footnote in Hain, 1964). In a sense, Hain's method is more in keeping with Bender's notion of treating the test performance as a whole, although her objections to quantifying alterations in the Gestalten still apply. Cutoff scores for discriminating organic from nonorganic patients are offered. Subsequent studies have yielded mixed results that suggest there are weaknesses in the scoring method in that it produces a relatively high number of false negatives (i.e., failure to reflect presence of brain damage) despite relatively few false positives (Tolor & Brannigan, 1980; Pardue, 1975).

THE KOPPITZ DEVELOPMENTAL BENDER TEST SCORING SYSTEM

The Koppitz scoring method (1963) is probably the most widely used system for evaluating children's records; it comes close to being a standard method in this area. The Pascal-Suttel, Hain, and other systems were developed primarily for adults but have been applied to children's records with less than satisfactory results. The Koppitz system has been subjected to much research to evaluate its efficacy, but even more so has been the major means by which children's Bender productions have been evaluated in studies of the properties of Bender performance that correlate with or differentiate among other parameters of children's performances, status, and capacities. For a review of these studies, see Koppitz (1975) and Tolor and Brannigan (1980).

The Koppitz system was designed to assess typical stages of visual-motor integration as manifested by copying the Bender Test figures in children from ages 5 to 10 years. It is noted by Koppitz that by age 10, most normal children can copy the figures accurately. The system has been standardized for ages 5.0 to 10.11 at six-month intervals. Beyond age 10, the test is no longer regarded as a developmental test for normal children and any use of the system for normal teenagers is actually decried by Koppitz. She does accept the possible use of this system for children older than age 10 who show marked immaturity or malfunction in visual-motor perception.

The Koppitz system contains 30 scoring items defined with a variety of examples in the 1963 manual. Her 1975 monograph contains a revised scoring manual that includes the same 30 items of the original manual. The criteria for scoring have not been changed but rather clarified and sharpened to reduce confusion and error in scoring. The original admonition for scoring is retained: "Only clear cut deviations are scored. In case of doubt an item is not scored" (Koppitz, 1975, p. 172). The use of a protractor and a ruler facilitates scoring of some items as it does in the Pascal-Suttel method.

The Koppitz method of administration of the Bender Test to children follows the traditional lines very closely. The child is advised that there are nine cards from which he or she is to copy the figures on a blank sheet of paper. Extra paper is available if needed and a pencil with eraser provided without specific instructions beforehand that erasures are permitted. The types of deviations scored include (1) Rotations of designs from a central axis, integration, usually referring to omission of parts or marked deviations in spacing of elements; (2) Distortion, usually referring to converting dots to circles or alterations in configurations; (3) Perseveration (i.e., the repeating of rows or columns of elements beyond certain limits); and (4) some other deviations unique to particular designs. The scored items are applied design-by-design and each receives a weight of 1 point, making a maximum possible Developmental Score of 30. Each deviation is identified by its index number and summarized by this index number when scored, allowing the results of groups to be compared not only by total scores but also by distribution of types of items.

For example, one child has a Developmental Score of 8 formed by deviation items 1a, 4, 10, 14, 18a, 21b, 22, and 23. Another child with the same Developmental Score of 8 may have deviations noted on items 1a, 3, 8, 12a, 13, 17a, 17b, and 24. The two records, while developmentally equivalent by total score, are qualitatively dissimilar. One child may be noted also to have different Emotional Indicators than another. In addition to the deviation item, the protocols are scored for the presence of up to 12 emotional indicators (EI). The original 10 items from the 1963 manual were augmented by two more (Koppitz, 1975). The Emotional Indicators are identified on the summary of scores by a Roman numeral, and they include the following: I, confused order (comparable to Pascal-Suttel's notion); II, wavy line in figures 1 and 2; III, dashes substituted for circles in figure 2; IV, increasing size of figures 1, 2, or 3; V, large size (compared to stimulus card); VI, small size; VII, fine line; VIII, careless overwork or heavily reinforced lines; IX, second attempt; X, expansion; XI, box around design; XII, spontaneous elaboration or addition to design. Each of the foregoing is said to be associated with some emotional factor (e.g., withdrawal, anxiety, acting-out behavior, impulsivity, low frustration tolerance, etc.).

Brief summaries of research studies in support of the interpretations given to the emotional indicators are provided in the more recent Koppitz manual (1975, Chapter 10). She also provides a large number of plates of children's records scored for the Developmental Score and the Emotional Indicators to help the scorer learn and become more proficient in the method. There is an extensive listing of normative data by grade level (see Koppitz, 1975, pp. 39–41). The widespread use of the Koppitz method has led to a number of studies relating ethnic background to the performance of children on the BGT which may affect the interpretation of scores (Taylor & Partenio, 1984; Sattler & Gwynne, 1982).

BRANNIGAN AND BRUNNER MODIFIED VERSION

The Modified Version of the Bender-Gestalt Test (Brannigan & Brunner, 1989) makes use of only six of the Bender cards (A, 1, 2, 4, 6, and 8), which may be administered to children, individually or to a group, by slide projector. The cards are presented one design at a time and the children are required to copy all designs on a single sheet of paper, as in the standard administration of the Bender Test. The procedures take about five minutes. The protocols are scored by a Qualitative Scoring System that focuses on the child's overall reproduction of each design. A 6-point rating scale (from 0 to 5) for each design and a total score for all six designs provide the quantitative indices for the performance. General scoring and specific scoring guidelines, with examples, are provided for the individual design rating scores in the test manual. The overall score can range from 0 to 30.

In essence, the ratings are based on judgments of the degree to which the child's reproduction resembles the design as to configuration, design elements, and lack of distortion. The more perfect the representation, the higher the rating score. This is in contrast to error scoring systems where high scores represent poor performance. Interscorer reliability has been noted to be .95 and test-retest reliability, over a short interval, to be .80 (Brunner & Brannigan, 1991).

The authors have carried out a number of studies demonstrating significant correlations between the Qualitative Scoring System for their Modified Version of the Bender-Gestalt Test, the Metropolitan Reading Readiness Test, and the Metropolitan Achievement Test scores of children from kindergarten through the second grade. (Brannigan & Brunner, 1989). Comparisons of the Modified Version with the Koppitz Developmental Scoring System have indicated the two systems yield comparable results, with the Modified Version slightly superior to the Koppitz in predicting scores on the Otis-Lennon School Ability Test (Brannigan & Brunner, 1990, 1993). The range of norms for the Modified System has been extended to include third- and fourth-grade children (Brunner & Brannigan, 1991). In summary, it would appear that the Modified Version of the Bender Gestalt Test is shorter and simpler than the Koppitz system and lends itself to the study of the very young child and the developmentally delayed child. In particular it may be efficacious in identifying children at risk for reading and other academic problems (Brunner & Brannigan, 1991).

THE HUTT ADAPTATION OF THE BENDER GESTALT (HABGT)

Max Hutt's approach to the Bender Test is probably the best-known example of the use of the test as a projective technique in a systematic and organized manner. At the time of this writing, Hutt's method is in its fourth edition (Hutt, 1985). The historical development of the HABGT is presented in this edition and is of interest in its coverage, not only of Hutt's own work but also of the projective and nonproductive uses of the Bender as a means to study what he calls "perceptual-motoric behavior." The Hutt adaptation refers not only to the method of evaluation and interpretation of a subject's copying of the test figures but also to the subtle differences in the test designs themselves. The same nine Wertheimer figures are used but the line quality and spacing characteristics of elements in the designs have been altered to give smooth lines and more sharply delineated features that reproduce more evenly than the original Bender figures. The test cards for the HABGT are available from the publisher of the manual (Grune & Stratton, Inc., New York).

The HABGT is usually administered in three phases: (1) copy, (2) elaboration, and (3) association. For the copy phase, the subject is not told how many cards there are and has access to a stack of paper. The instructions are to the effect that the cards will be shown one at a time, that each will have a simple drawing on it, and that the task is to copy the drawing as well as the subject can. "Work in any way that is best for you." It is pointed out that is not a test of artistic ability but that the subject is to try to copy the designs as accurately as possible, working as fast or as slowly as the person desires (Hutt, 1985). Questions by the subject are answered by paraphrasing the instructions or by a noncommittal phrase, "Do it any way you think it best" or "That's entirely up to you."

The examiner then takes a single sheet of paper from the stack, presents it vertically oriented to the subject and places the first card (A) oriented "up" with the instruction repeated "Copy this as well as you can." The availability of the stack of paper is to permit choice of using a single sheet or more for the test without advice. Thus, if the subject chooses to use one sheet for each design, he or she is allowed to do so. The stack of design cards is visible for the subject to plan, if the subject wishes, how to proceed with the size. If the subject asks how many cards there are, the response is, "Just this stack of cards." Rotation of the paper is permitted, but note is made of this fact. Initial attempts to rotate the test cards are interrupted by the examiner who then states, "You are supposed to copy it this way." However, if the subject insists on shifting the cards, it is permitted and notation is made of the fact. As with the traditional method, the cards are presented in a sequence A through 8. Spontaneous remarks and all relevant test behaviors are noted for later study.

With the HABGT, it is important to observe and make notes about the subject's method of work, apparent planning, impulsive actions, frequent erasures, direction, and order in which the subject attacks each design (e.g., from bottom up), use of sketching movements, apparent blocking on any figures, and so on. Extreme variation in time is also noted. After the copy phase is completed, the subject's drawings are removed from sight and the elaboration phase is then undertaken to be followed by the association phase. Both of these procedures exemplify the projective use of the test. For the elaboration phase, the subject is instructed to modify or change the figures on the cards in any manner desired. The emphasis is placed on making the changes more pleasing to the subject and any wording appropriate to this intent may be used (e.g., more aesthetic, better looking, etc.). The cards are presented again in sequence and the subject recopies the designs in keeping with these new instructions. If time considerations require reducing the total testing time, Hutt suggests the examiner use only cards A, 2, 4, 6, 7, and 8 as an abbreviated elaboration procedure.

The association phase follows closely after the elaboration phase and makes use of the subject's drawings resulting from it. The subject is asked to look at the design card and the modification made of it during the elaboration procedure and to verbalize associations to each: "What could they be?" "What do they look like?" In this respect, the association phase is much like the free association technique used in inkblot tests and other ambiguous stimulus tests. Various other projective test procedures have been employed by clinical psychologists using the Bender. One may have the subject sort the cards according to preference. A test-of-limits procedure may be used, where certain responses or associations are suggested by the examiner and the degree of acceptance or rejection of them by the subject is evaluated. Where peculiar or abnormal responses are noted during the copy or association phases, the examiner may carry out a type of inquiry or, as Hutt refers to it, "an interview analysis" (see Hutt, 1985, p. 52).

A global measure of the degree of psychopathology manifested on the copy phase of the test is provided by the Psychopathology Scale (PS). The PS consists of 17 factors, each defined objectively (see Hutt, 1985, Chapter 4). Scoring is facilitated by the use of a scoring template provided with each package of the HAGBT revised record forms. Sixteen of the PS factors are scored on a scale from 1 to 10. These include: Sequence, Use of Space I, Collision, Shift of Paper, Closure Difficulty, Crossing Difficulty, Curvature Difficulty, Change in Angulation, Perceptual Rotation, Retrogression, Simplification, Fragmentation, Overlapping Difficulty, Elaboration, Perseveration, and Re-Drawing of Total Figure. The one other factor scale, scored from 1 to 3.25, is the Position on First Drawing. Scores may range from a minimum of 17.0 to a maximum of 163.25. The sum of the scale values constitutes the Psychopathology Scale Score.

Hutt also provides an Adience-Abience Scale as an attempt to measure a personality characteristic said to be related to the subject's perceptual *openness* or *closedness*. This is thought of as a perceptual personality style related to the openness of the individual to new learning experiences or the tendency to block out such experiences. The Adience-Abience Scale includes factors relating to space and size, organization, change in form of Gestalt, and distortion. In his latest edition, Hutt offers a rapid procedure for differentiating patients with organic brain syndrome from other psychiatric patients and normals based on this Configurational Analysis. However, he emphasizes that *screening* is not *diagnosis* and should not be confused with psychodiagnosis (see Hutt, 1985, Chapter 5).

CANTER'S BACKGROUND INTERFERENCE PROCEDURE FOR THE BENDER TEST

The Background Interference Procedure (BIP) proposed by Canter (1963, 1966, 1968) is an innovation that makes use of a two-phase administration of the Bender Test. In the first phase, the subject copies the usual Bender figures on blank paper, but in the second, the background interference procedure phase, the test is carried out on specially prepared interference paper. This sheet is printed with a randomly placed array of intersecting curved black lines that the subject has to ignore in copying the test figures. The BIP sheet, as it is called, may have a carbon paper as an interleaf between it and a blank sheet of paper.

The BIP Bender is administered with some modifications of the traditional method to accommodate the BIP sheet itself and to permit precision in the scoring of deviations from the stimulus figures on the design cards. For the standard phase administration of the Bender Test, the usual blank sheet of paper, pencil with eraser, and stack of design cards are presented to the subject. The subject is advised that there are nine designs to be copied and all are to be placed on one side of a single sheet of paper. The instructions convey the idea of drawing the figures freehand without sketching and to make the figures about the same size as they appear on the cards. To reduce the opportunity for casual or deliberate paper rotations, the author recommends use of a test board that clamps the paper in a fixed position relative to the stimulus card. If the board is rotated, the cards are rotated with it. When the board is rotated severely, the examiner interrupts the action and states, "You are to work on the paper held this way," returning the test board and paper to its proper orientation to the subject. Erasures are permitted as are retests, but notations are made of same.

The design cards are exposed in the usual sequence A through 8. Questions regarding counting and procedural matters are answered in the usual fashion, "Make your copy as much like the one on the card as you can." If the subject asks for more paper because he or she is running out of room (e.g., overly large designs), he or she is given one more sheet. However, if there is sufficient space left on the sheet, the examiner suggests it be used. When the standard sheet phase of the test is completed, the copies of the design cards and the board are removed from sight and some other type of task is given to the subject. This may be a brief test or subtest, when a battery of tests is being used, or a rest period of at least 10 minutes.

Then the BIP phase is introduced with the design cards, pencil, and test board all brought back into view and a BIP sheet clamped in position on the test board instead of a blank sheet of paper. The instructions given to the subject indicate that the same figures are to be copied and that they are to be done exactly as they were before, "Only this time the drawing is to be done on this special paper." The subject is encouraged to attempt the task even if it seems difficult or impossible. If the initial drawing of Card A results in a very small reproduction, representing an obvious attempt to fit an empty space on the BIP sheet, the subject is stopped, the paper is withdrawn, and a fresh BIP sheet is provided. The instruction is given to draw the figures the same size as was done before even if the subject has to go over the printed lines. If the subject appears to ignore the examiner's instructions, he or she is permitted to continue with the test and notation is made of the fact.

The purpose of the BIP sheet is to produce an interference effect and the scoring measures the differences in deviations in copying the test figures to both standard and BIP presentations. It was reasoned that a repeat copy procedure would provide a means for correcting for drawing defects due to lack of skill, mental defect, autism, and so on. It was felt that such idiosyncratic errors would be repeated, thus having a canceling effect. New errors appearing only on the BIP sheet could be more safely attributable to the effects of the distraction lines. The major hypothesis was that interference-induced errors were more likely to occur in patients with organic brain disorder than in nonorganic psychiatric patients. The research findings in support of the hypothesis are summarized in Canter's manual (1983).

The procedure requires that both phases of the test be scored by the same method. The author's modification of the Pascal-Suttell scoring method (Canter, 1968, 1983) was chosen as the preferred method. The modification includes redefinition of a number of the Pascal-Suttel deviations, omission of others, altered weights for some, and the use of a Maximum Deviation Score for each design. The latter is applicable to copies too distorted to be recognizable or containing an overly large number of errors in various combinations. If the subject is unable to carry out the task even after an attempt is made, or the standard phase is successfully copied, the Maximum Deviation Score may be used for each design. The scores derived in the Canter method include: (1) a Total Error Score for a standard procedure copy; (2) a Total Error Score for the BIP copy; (3) a Difference Score (D score)—the algebraic difference between the standard and BIP total error scores; and (4) a Number Positive—the total number of designs in which the error score for BIP exceeded that for the standard on that design by 2 points.

From the size of the Total Error Score for standard phase administration, the Base Level of performance is indexed, ranging progressively from a Level I to a Level VII, using cutoff points provided in the test manual. A Base Level I indicates an error range from 0 to 15. Base Level II represents a range from 16 to 29, and successively each Base Level has a range of 20 error points until Base Level VII. This is used to represent Total Error Scores on the standard performance of 100 points or more. The maximum Total Error Score for either standard or BIP performance is 180. A matrix using the Base Level, the D Score, and the Number Positive or NP value is provided in the manual for classifying the BIP performance as: A, no organic brain disorder; B, borderline or equivocal; and C, organic brain disorder. There is a score for the presence of Design Overlap (Collision, in other systems) but this is not entered into the matrix classification.

The matrix to classify BIP Bender records was determined by a cross-validation study carried out by the author as part of the development of the technique (Canter, 1968). The matrix is applicable only to ages 15 and older, although the scoring system (i.e., the adapted Pascal-Suttell method) appears suitable for children as young as age 8. However, as has been determined in a study by Adams and Canter (1969), there is a maturational development in the capacity to cope with the BIP analogous to the development in perceptuomotor ability to copy the Bender figures themselves. By age 12 to 13, normal children are able to deal with the BIP effect as effectively as adults do. While Canter's scoring method was used in the development of the indices used to classify organic brain disorder among psychiatric patients, the BIP itself does not preclude the use of any other scoring scheme applicable to Bender Test performance. Hain's method has been used with the BIP (Pardue, 1975), as has the Koppitz (Hayden et al., 1970), and, more recently, Schlange's method, as used in a German study comparing it to the Koppitz and Canter scoring methods for children (Wallasch & Moebus, 1977).

For any objective scoring scheme it is possible to use a D score to indicate the difference in deviation scores on the standard and BIP phases of the test as a measure of BIP effect. The D score concept permits examination of three possible effects attributable to the BIP: (1) the positive BIP effect indicative of impaired function, (2) a zero BIP effect indicative of no change due to the interference procedure, and (3) a negative BIP effect, indicative of actual improvement under interference conditions. Although the focus of attention has been on the positive BIP effect and its efficacy in detecting brain damage, it is conceivable that the study of negative BIP effects in known cases of organic brain damage may be useful in evaluating the capacity of a brain-damaged person to adapt to stress and/or arousal.

INTERPRETATION

General Considerations

The interpretation of Bender Test results is complicated not only by the availability of different scoring systems but also by the use of the test for different purposes based on varied concepts of personality formation and psychopathological functioning. Much of what is interpretable on the Bender Test stems from three sources: (1) reports of clinical case studies and observation of patient records, (2) validation studies supporting a particular scoring system, and (3) correlational studies, generally of Bender Test scores, Bender item characteristics, and extra-test parameters such as IQ, educational achievement, learning disability, cultural status, psychiatric diagnosis, maturational status, and scores on other psychological tests.

As Tolor and Brannigan (1980) have indicated, the bulk of Bender interpretations has been directed toward the diagnosis of organic brain pathology, whether by score cutoff points or signs (i.e., specific type of deviations in design copies). The validation of personality diagnosis and types of psychopathologies by the Bender Test has received very little controlled research. Yet the clinical use of the Bender Test is heavily saturated with interpretation based on invalid or poorly validated psychodynamic and projective test concepts. As long as this state of affairs exists, Bender interpretation will be more art than science and will require apprenticeship training under the supervision of an experienced clinician for one to learn the art. In actual practice, the Bender is most likely to be only one of a number of other tests used to evaluate a patient or a school child. Under such circumstances, the additional data from the other tests may not only temporize overinclusive interpretations, but may contribute to the analysis of the Bender results themselves. Even when the Bender is used primarily as a screening test, it is ordinarily not good practice to use it as the sole examination technique.

Interpretation of Bender Scores

If Bender Test scores are used, it is important to keep in mind the purpose of the scoring system as set forth by its developer and the criteria for their interpretation. Thus, for example, if a high score is said to be representative of pathology, as is usually the case, the question to ask is: What kind of pathology? The normative data supplied for different score ranges may indicate only a high probability of psychopathology without differentiating between cortical damage, so-called functional psychoses, emotional instability, low intelligence, or even drawing ineptitude. It is necessary to look beyond the size of the score and into correlative data that will support or deny one or more of the possibilities: age, educational status or background, cultural/ethnic factors, occupational factors, intelligence, and perhaps features of the test performance and test behaviors themselves (e.g., apparent inattentiveness, clumsiness in handling materials, content of spontaneous speech, obvious hand tremors, observable visual acuity problems, etc.).

Are there any features in the subject's known background, scores on other tests (e.g., IQ), or behavioral manifestations that would lead the examiner to have certain expectations? Are the results in keeping with these expectations? A person with an educational history, occupational status, and premorbid estimate of intelligence all consistent with above-average intelligence is expected to produce a fairly low error score on the Bender. If it is high, the implication is that there is a pathological process in evidence. One proceeds to delineate the possibilities or, lacking the data to do so, to indicate which possibilities are the most likely and which the least likely. If the particular scoring method provides rather circumscribed indices supported by validation studies (e.g., a score or index representing organic brain damage), the task for the examiner may be to find evidence in support of cognitive defects from other tests used in the battery and known case history data. Thus, an adult patient who has complaints of memory problems, episodes of confusion, deterioration in behavior without obvious symptoms of psychosis, and who scores in the organic range of the Bender Test, may be presumed to be correctly identified by the test.

Additional test data may be used in this case to help delineate the extent of cognitive impairment. If, on the other hand, this same patient scored in the nonorganic range on the Bender Test, the examiner may conclude that the apparent cognitive impairment is functional or that the Bender result is a false negative, depending on the strength of other data and results of specialized neurological examinations (e.g., computerized axial tomography). One may then use the Bender score as a means of detecting pathology or disorder and the other test data to give greater specificity to the nature of the disorder. For adults, the use of the Bender may be not only used as a screen for organic brain disorder but, following Koppitz's scheme, may be used to define a feature of developmental retardation that is correlated with learning disability. According to Koppitz's system, it may also be used to detect emotional disturbances that interfere with school adjustment (see case examples in Koppitz, 1975).

Interpreting Features of Bender Test Protocols

In this section we shall consider commonly occurring deviations in copying Bender figures that are considered to be signs of pathology specific to certain personality/psychodynamic characteristics. The approach is basic to the use of the test as a projective technique. For a more detailed representation, the reader is directed to Hutt's work (see Hutt & Briskin, 1960; Hutt, 1985) and to the examples found in DeCato and Wicks (1976) and in Lacks (1984).

The way the reproductions on the sheet of paper are organized is taken to indicate something about the subject's planning and organizational attitudes. Thus, sequence in the placement of drawings on the sheet of paper is noted as to its regularity or orderliness, ranging from a rigid, overly methodical sequence to an apparently confused or haphazard one. An overly methodical sequence is considered to be indicative of rigid impulse control, while irregular sequence is indicative of poor impulse control. Noting the point in the record at which a shift in sequence has taken place may be used to call attention to the particular design and its potential symbolic value. If the sequence is orderly but the subject appears to have run out of room and has to fit in subsequent designs, it may be considered as evidence of poor planning. The compression or expansion of the drawn figures relative to the test stimuli is considered to reflect modes of expressive behavior. Constricted use of space (e.g., small figures cramped together) is said to be indicative of fearfulness, withdrawal, or avoidant behavior, while expansive use of space is related to assertiveness, boldness, and manic mood.

On adult protocols, the actual overlapping of one design by another, referred to as Collision in several scoring systems, is taken to indicate a marked disturbance in ego function. It is considered to reflect poor anticipatory planning, difficulty with figure-ground relationships, and extreme impulsivity (Hutt, 1985). As such, it is found frequently in people with organic brain damage who often display a loss in ego control. The phenomenon appears to be found frequently in normal, very young children (under 8 years of age), but in older children and adolescents it is taken to indicate ego control problems.

Difficulty in joining parts of the designs or in having the parts touch each other (e.g., in Designs A, 2, 4, 7, and 8), referred to by Hutt as closure difficulty, is a problem commonly noted in pathological level records, but is considered a normal developmental problem in children. Closure difficulty in the adolescent and adult is thought to be related to fearfulness and interpersonal relationship but generally indicative of some form of emotional maladjustment.

The rotation of the copied designs when the stimulus card and the test paper are in the normal position is another obvious drawing deviation that appears to be correlated with pathology. The degree and frequency of such rotation have to be considered. The more severe the rotation of any design, the more likely it is considered to be a pathological indicator. Originally thought to be pathognomic of psychosis, rotation has not been demonstrated by research studies to have differential diagnostic value. However, rotations occur more frequently in varied disorders, including organic brain damage, schizophrenia, neuroses, reading disabilities, and mental retardation (Tolor & Brannigan, 1980). It has been suggested that the direction of the rotation (i.e., clockwise versus counterclockwise) may be indicative of behavioral tendencies: counterclockwise—oppositional behavior, clockwise—depressive mood.

The counting and recounting of elements of the designs containing dots or loops (i.e., Designs 1, 2, 3, and 5), as noted in the examiner's observation of the copied performance, are taken to indicate perfectionism. Work-over, which refers to going over drawn lines, thickening them somewhat extensively, is taken to reflect anxiety or lack of self-confidence. Irregularities in curve reproduction (e.g., Designs 4 and 6) reflect changes in emotional expression, with the increase in curvature said to be associated with emotional lability and acting-out behavior, whereas decreased or flattened curvature is reflective of decreased or inhibited emotionality, as may be found in depressive patients.

Distortions in the reproduction of designs where there is a substitution with more primitive gestalt forms (e.g., dashes for dots, open loops for circles) are taken to reflect regression. Here, the nature subject produces a result comparable to that obtained from the immature. Gross configural distortion, where the essential character of the design figure is destroyed, is representative of more severe disturbances in perceptual-motor functioning. Alteration of designs or parts of designs relative to the stimulus card representation may provide inferences about psychodynamic issues. For example, Design 4, with its open square and a touching curve, is often taken as a symbol of potential male-female relationships. In this view, decreasing the axis of the square, while flattening the curve, may be taken to reflect problems in heterosexual relationships. The tail of Design 5 also may be regarded as a phallic symbol and problems in its reproduction or attachment may be reflective of problems in masculinity. Design 8, with its central diamond, may be regarded as a symbol for female sexuality. The overlapping hexagonal figures of Design 7 may be thought of as representing phallic symbols or interpersonal interactions (e.g., aggressiveness).

The symbolic interpretation of Bender protocols is more likely to come into play in those instances where the copies are not overly distorted or disrupted. Extreme disintegration of the gestalt forms is more likely to indicate organic pathology, severe mental defect, or psychopathology. In a sense, there is too much noise in the system for differential interpretations.

It should become apparent that the projective test approach is based on conceiving the Bender Test as a microcosmic representation of the subject's real world of experience, motivational systems, attitudes, and the like. There is a certain amount of dualism represented in the interpretative concepts. If the general quality of anxiety is in its vagueness or diffuseness, then any apparent expression of this vagueness (e.g., hesitancy in drawing, lightly drawn lines) may be said to represent this quality. If the quality of impulsiveness is to be boundless (i.e., going beyond controls), then the failure to place controls during the drawing (e.g., running figures together or making them overly large) are the microcosmic representations of the quality of impulsiveness. This approach to the task on a projective test is widespread but rarely examined for its validity. There is a sort of logic or psychologic to these notions that is taken to be almost self-evident. One has to assume that styles of behavior manifested on one level have their direct representations on another. Supporting these notions with research data is another matter and not easily done.

CASE EXAMPLE

The case that follows was chosen to illustrate the use of the Bender Test as part of a screening battery of tests to aid the diagnostic work-up of a patient seen in a psychiatric clinic. The case also illustrates the sensitivity of the Bender to changes in the mental status of the patient, even when there is only minimal change in linguistic-cognitive function in the early progression of the neurological disorder finally accepted as the diagnosis: Alzheimer's disease.

The patient is a married white female in her early 50s (age 50 when first tested) who had been sent to the clinic because of complaints of depression, memory problems, and poor concentration dating back at least one year. She had a college degree in the arts and drama and had been able to maintain an active interest in her social, recreational, and family pursuits without difficulty until recently. Six months prior to the admission to this clinic, she had been treated for a depressive syndrome by a local psychiatrist. She showed improvement in mood but then later complained of the return of her depression and continued memory problems. The current psychiatric work-up revealed mild depressive symptoms, anxiety, and an apparent memory deficit on the mental status examination in an otherwise intellectually intact woman. She was referred for psychological testing with the question of cortical dysfunction. A screening battery was chosen, consisting of the complete Wechsler Adult Intelligence Scale; the Wechsler Memory Scale, Form 1; and the Canter BIP Bender Test.

The patient was generally pleasant and cooperative, demonstrating a good sense of humor, even joking about her apparent deficiency. However, the examiner noted her to be nervous and unsure of herself, constantly seeking reassurance about the correctness of her answers on the intelligence test. It was also noted that she tended to give up easily, becoming overtly upset when experiencing difficulty and at one point even getting angry at her failure. During the testing she was noted to exhibit a hand tremor that increased under apparent stress (e.g., on timed tasks on the WAIS). The WAIS yielded a verbal IQ of 108, performance IQ of 106, and a full scale IQ of 108, with relative deficiencies noted on Block Design, Digit Symbol, and Picture Arrangement. The WMS yielded a Memory Quotient of 67, corrected for her age, with marked deficiencies noted in the Logical Memory subtest, Visual Reproduction, and Associate Learning. The Bender was administered by Canter's two-phase method. The BIP phase was carried out after completion of the WAIS verbal tests. Canter's scoring method yielded an error score for the standard paper phase of the test of 32 (see Figure 10–2). This falls into a Level III, or moderate degree of pathology noted to be frequently found in all types of psychiatric patients. If scored by the Pascal-Suttel method, the results are comparable: a raw score of 43, for an adult with college background corresponds to a Z-score of 83, which is above the cutoff for psychiatric disorder.

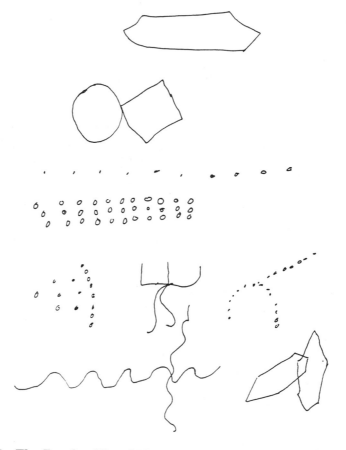

Figure 10–2   The Bender Visual Motor Gestalt Test as Completed by a Married White Female in Her Early Fifties Who Was Referred for Testing Because of Complaints of Depression and Memory Loss

At this point, the Bender, judged solely by the objective scores, indicates undifferentiated psychopathology. We can rule out mental retardation because of the history and the IQ test results. The differential diagnosis would be between nonorganic psychotic disorder or one primarily attributable to cortical dysfunction. In trying to rule in cortical dysfunction, we can look to clues from the cognitive tests, the history and psychiatric examination, as well as delve further into the Bender results themselves. If we examine the results of the BIP copy phase (not illustrated), we find that the patient made significantly more errors on Designs A, 2, 3, and 7, yielding a BIP error score of 44. The difference in error scores (standard minus BIP), the D-score, is found to be +12, which according to Canter's norms is a significant BIP effect, which, for a Level III record with the NP of 4 (the 4 designs significantly worse), is taken to indicate a positive index for organic brain dysfunction. This finding lends support to interpreting the cognitive deficits noted on the WAIS and the WMS as due to brain disorder rather than a severe anxiety disorder, mood disorder per se, or thought disorder. A qualitative analysis of the standard Bender copy results along the lines set forth by Hutt was also carried out. Hutt's complete system would not be applicable because of the more restrictive method of administration used and the lack of an elaboration and inquiry phase as described earlier.

The sequence of the design placement is mildly irregular with two shifts noted, one from the vertical downward placement to a horizontal ordering, and the second, shifting back to the vertical in an apparent effort to fit Design 8 on the sheet (see Figure 10–2). It may be conjectured that had Hutt's directions been followed, the patient might have used a second sheet of paper for Design 8 or might have followed the downward placement altogether. Be this as it may, it does indicate failure to plan adequately for the space limitations set by the examiner's instructions. The fact that Design 8, being out of order, also is the only design to contain a gross disruption (fragmentation or distortion) of its gestalt by the omission of the inner diamond. The possibility this raises is that under the intensification of stress or emotional disturbance there is a primary breakdown of perceptuo-motor function. The patient becomes forgetful and even lacks awareness of this.

We already know the patient tends to overreact to stress by her behavior on the WAIS. On the BIP phase, she drew the inner diamond but showed a haphazard sequence (i.e., a greater disruption of planning and judgment). The tendency for increased compressed use of space going from Design 1 onward is suggestive of tension, anxiety, and even withdrawal tendencies. There is also a decrease in the size of the designs at the same point, which not only suggests withdrawal but also an inhibiting or lowering of mood. It is as if she first approached the test with enthusiasm and expansiveness but then quickly retreated and began to experience a constriction of mood, as might be the case for a depressed patient. The irregularity in curvature noted on Designs 4 and 6 and the angulation problems apparent from the start (the square on Design A), and reappearing on Design 7 and 8, are suggestive of disturbances in emotional behavior and/or perceptual processes independent of emotional reactivity.

What Hutt calls retrogressive signs are evidenced by the substitution of loops and dashes for dots in Designs 1 and 3. The fact that the patient is able to reproduce the desired dots indicates she retains the capacity to do so but lacks the control to keep from resorting to the more primitive response. Considering the maturity of the patient, her intelligence, and her educational background (including art training), this type of error is unexpected and signals a true disruption in perceptuo-motor functioning, slight as it may seem. On the BIP copy phase not shown here, the added stress of the interference lines disrupted perceptuo-motor functioning to a more marked degree. Angulation errors increased, as did the primitivization of loops formed for dots. Closure difficulty, which was not evident on the standard sheet copy, is present on the BIP copy. Ordinarily, this deviation is interpreted in the Hutt system to indicate emotional maladjustment, but, considering the nature of the BIP sheet in this instance, the error is more likely to reflect a mild breakdown of visual tracking.

In summary, the evidence of the Bender BIP combination is strongly indicative of cortical dysfunction due to organic brain disease. In view of the other test results—in particular the marked memory deficiencies, visual constructional and visual tracking speed defects, with a relative intactness of other cognitive-intellectual functions (abstract reasoning, language functions, general judgment), and the age of the patient (50)—the most likely diagnosis is early Alzheimer's disease or some other diffuse cortical disease.

In response to the psychological test findings, a CAT (computerized axial tomography) scan and EEG examinations were ordered. The CAT scan revealed dilated ventricular structures and prominent cortical sulci consistent with mild cortical atrophy. The EEG indicated bilateral slow activity over both temporal areas with no evidence of focal lesion or stroke and was considered consistent with diffuse organic brain disease. The standard neurological examination was negative except for the defective mental status. Serological, blood chemistry, thyroid studies, and so on were all negative. The tentative diagnosis offered by both neurology and psychiatry was early Alzheimer's disease. It must be pointed out here that Alzheimer's disease is a diagnosis by exclusion. The depression/anxiety symptoms were considered by the psychiatrist to be secondary phenomena.

Follow-up studies were carried out over the next four years in the course of which it was possible to repeat cognitive tests and the BIP Bender. Figure 10–3 illustrates the obvious deterioration in perceptual motor functions on the standard copy phase two years after the original testing.

The Canter method yielded scores on the standard copy of 71 for the total error score (Level V, extreme pathology) and a D-score of +31 (with six of nine designs showing significant deterioration on BIP over standard). Thus, as poorly done as the standard Bender is, the BIP copy is even worse. In other tests there are only minor changes in intellectual functioning, chiefly in abstract reasoning. Memory impairment remained prominently de-

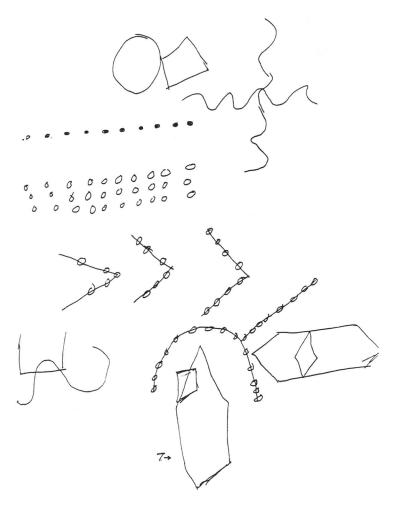

Figure 10–3   Completed Two Years After the Original Testing (see Figure 10–2) and Illustrates the Obvious Deterioration in Perceptual Motor Skills (She Was Diagnosed as Having Alzheimer's Disease)

fective. Testing carried out two years later than the second series, or four years after the initial testing, revealed relative stability of the verbal IQ (104) but a marked deterioration in the patient's ability to do the Bender Test. She was barely able to complete the standard copy with some semblance of recognition of designs, and she was totally unable to carry out the BIP, exhibiting a catastrophic reaction when confronted with the BIP sheet. Similar reactions have been noted by the author to occur on the BIP in cases of senile dementia and in some cases of multiple sclerosis where diffuse cortical dysfunction is in evidence.

As the patient was confronted in her daily living more and more with her memory impairment and perceptual motor difficulty, she became increasingly depressed, as might be expected. Throughout the follow-up period of the four years, the standard neurological examinations were essentially negative except for a defective mental status. However, both the CAT scan and EEG were repeated with the results consistently indicative of diffuse brain damage. The patient was treated several times for acute depression, each time resulting in improved mood but without ameliorating effect on her memory deficiencies or on behavior dependent on visual-perceptual orientation. For example, she had to give up driving her car around her hometown because she would frequently get lost. The patient and her family refused to accept the initial diagnosis, leading to diagnostic work-ups in another major medical center where the diagnosis of early Alzheimer's disease was confirmed.

ASSETS AND LIABILITIES

Assets

- The Bender Test is relatively inexpensive as formal psychological tests go. It is also highly portable when used in the traditional manner: a stack of design cards, sheets of blank 8½″ × 11″ paper, and #2 grade pencils with erasers.
- It is a fairly simple, straightforward test requiring very little skill and training to administer as a copy test, even when augmented with a memory phase. The addition of elaboration and inquiry phases as in Hutt's adaptation is another matter, requiring an appropriate professional background and training. However, the Bender generally is a relatively brief test, taking only 10 to 15 minutes for most subjects.
- It is applicable to a wide range of subjects, children, adults, the aged, the mentally retarded, the psychologically or neurologically impaired, and the hearing impaired.
- In the hands of a trained and experienced clinician, depending on technique used, the Bender can serve as a broad-band test to provide measures of perceptual-motor, cognitive, and personality functioning.
- It is a fairly innocuous-appearing test and is rarely perceived as a threat to self-esteem or as a challenge of one's personal integrity. As such, it is facilitative of rapport and often serves well as the initial test of a battery containing more exciting or detailed procedures. It also serves well as a vehicle for observing work habits, effort, and cooperation under untimed and benign conditions, but can be used to judge the effect of performance under pressure conditions by use of appropriate instructions and/or timing procedures.
- When objective scoring schemes are used, the test does not require a background of professional training in clinical psychology and clinical experience to administer and score. This approach increases the cost effectiveness in the use of the test by freeing up the clinician to spend more time and effort in more involved techniques. The test appears to be

highly sensitive to subtle impairments of perceptual-motor functions that might go undetected in more complex tasks.

Liabilities

- There is no single accepted method of scoring Bender Test protocols that one can refer to as the standard method.
- There is no alternate or parallel set of designs available to test subjects who are overly familiar with the original set.
- Systematic research to support the commonly held relationships between Bender performance and personality dynamics is lacking.
- There is a significant positive correlation between error scores and IQ that have to be taken into account. The BIP D score method overcomes this problem with its lack of correlation with IQ (Yulis, 1969).
- The test cannot be used with the blind and its valid use with persons having severe visual acuity problems not correctable with lenses is most doubtful. Similarly, the motor handicapped, not having use of the preferred hand, cannot complete the traditional test. Such cases require multiple-choice or recognition methods.
- The role that drawing skill plays in the production of scorable deviations or elaborations is not known. Yet psychological interpretations are made of copy production characteristics that may be merely a function of drawing ineptitude as well as personality dynamics. Tolor and Brannigan (1980) correctly point out that this problem is a pivotal one for research in understanding Bender Test productions and their bases.

CONCLUSIONS

The Bender Gestalt test is a fairly straightforward-appearing examination procedure that, in its simplest use, merely requires the subject to make freehand copies of the nine figures chosen by Lauretta Bender from Wertheimer's study of visual perception and gestalt psychology. As a specific test, the Bender has a long history of use as a tool to study the deviations in perceptual-motor functioning that reflect changes in childhood maturational development, intellectual status, cortical function, and psychological health. The problem of how to measure and evaluate the responses produced by the test procedure has been subjected to considerable research leading to the development of different objective scoring and rating methods. The typical scoring involves operational definitions of certain types of errors in the subject's reproduction of the test figures—for example, overcrowding, overlapping, failing to join lines accurately, errors in reproducing angles and curves, and so on. The greater the amount and degree of errors in reproduction, the more likely the record will be considered indicative of psychopathology or cognitive impairment in the adult. Children's records are scrutinized with reference to the expected improvement in accuracy of reproduction of design features as a function of maturation.

Other methods of evaluating responses to the Bender Test stimuli are based on concepts applicable to projective and/or expressive techniques for personality appraisal. Such approaches to the Bender Test are often used in combination with an objective scoring method. However, there is relatively little research support for the validity of the projective use of the Bender. There is an increasing amount of criticism directed toward the use of the Bender Test as a single examination procedure for the comprehensive personality appraisal or for its simple use as a screening test for cortical dysfunction. As with any other singular examination procedure, good clinical practice demands that the Bender be considered in the context of other formal examinations, history, and clinical examination data. This is as true of the individual tests that make up the typical neuropsychological test battery, the EEG, the various radiologic imaging systems, and other single laboratory examinations, as it is for the Bender Test.

Further research may help establish ways of adapting different procedures to the original Bender Test and to analyze the responses to the test stimuli to increase its usefulness for differential diagnosis. However, the question of the sensitivity of various scoring methods may be examined not so much for their diagnostic efficiency but rather as measures of neuropsychological functioning before and after special conditions. Research may be directed at the causes of subtle changes in Bender performance apart from the idiosyncratic errors in drawing. In any event, there is a need for a parallel set of figures.

REFERENCES

Adams, J., & Canter, A. (1969). Performance characteristics of school children on the BIP Bender Test. *Journal of Consulting and Clinical Psychology, 33,* 508.

Bender, L. (1938). *A Visual Motor Gestalt Test and Its Clinical Use.* American Orthopsychiatric Association Research Monograph, No. 3. New York: American Orthopsychiatric Association.

Bender, L. (1946). *Instructions for the Use of the Visual Motor Gestalt Test.* New York: American Orthopsychiatric Association.

Bender, L. (1963). Foreword. In A. Tolor & H. Schulberg (Eds.), *An Evaluation of the Bender-Gestalt Test.* Springfield, IL: Charles C. Thomas.

Bigler, E. D., & Ehrfurth, J. W. (1981). The continued inappropriate singular use of the Bender Visual Motor Gestalt Test. *Professional Psychology, 12,* 562–569.

Brannigan, G. G., & Brunner, N. A. (1989). *The Modified Version of the Bender-Gestalt Test for Preschool and Primary School Children.* Brandon, VT: Clinical Psychology Publishing.

Brannigan, G. G., & Brunner, N. A. (1990). Relationship between two scoring systems for the modified version of the Bender-Gestalt Test. *Perceptual and Motor Skills, 72,* 286.

Brannigan, G. G., & Brunner, N. A. (1993). Comparison of the qualitative and developmental scoring systems for the Modified Version of the Bender-Gestalt Test. *Journal of School Psychology, 31,* 327–330.

Brown, W. R., & McGuire, J. M. (1976). Current assessment practices. *Professional Psychology, 1,* 475–484.

Brunner, N. A., & Brannigan, G. G. (1991, November). *Identifying Children At Risk for Academic Failure: An Update on the Modified Bender-Gestalt Test.* Paper presented at the National Academy of Neuropsychology, Dallas.

Canter, A. (1963). A background interference procedure for graphomotor tests in the study of deficit. *Perceptual and Motor Skills, 16,* 914.

Canter, A. (1966). A background interference procedure to increase sensitivity of the Bender-Gestalt Test to organic brain disorder. *Journal of Consulting and Clinical Psychology, 30,* 91–97.

Canter, A. (1968). The BIP-Bender Test for the detection of organic brain disorder: Modified scoring method and replication. *Journal of Consulting and Clinical Psychology, 32,* 522–526.

Canter, A. (1983). *The Canter Background Interference Procedure for the Bender Gestalt Test.* Los Angeles: Western Psychological Services.

Crenshaw, D., Bohn, S., Hoffman, M. M., Matthews, J., & Offenbach, S. (1969). Projective methods in research: 1947–1965. *Journal of Projective Techniques and Personality Assessment, 32,* 3–9.

Decato, C. M., & Wicks, R. J. (1976). *Case Studies of the Clinical Interpretation of the Bender Gestalt Test.* Springfield, IL: Charles C. Thomas.

Freed, E. X. (1964). Frequencies of rotations on group and individual administrations of the Bender-Gestalt test. *Journal of Clinical Psychology, 20,* 120–121.

Hain, J. D. (1964). The Bender-Gestalt Test: A scoring method for identifying brain damage. *Journal of Consulting Psychology, 28,* 34–40.

Hayden, B. S., Talmadge, M., Hall, M., & Schiff, D. (1970). Diagnosing minimal brain damage in children: A comparison of two Bender scoring systems. *Merrill-Palmer Quarterly of Behavior and Development, 16,* 278–285.

Hutt, M. L. (1985). *The Hutt Adaptation of the Bender-Gestalt Test* (3rd ed.). New York: Grune & Stratton.

Hutt, M. L., & Briskin, G. J. (1960). *The Hutt Adaptation of the Bender-Gestalt Test.* New York: Grune & Stratton.

Koppitz, E. M. (1963). *The Bender Gestalt Test for Young Children.* New York: Grune & Stratton.

Koppitz, E. M. (1975). *The Bender Gestalt Test for Young Children* (Vol. II). *Research and Application, 1963–1973.* New York: Grune & Stratton.

Lacks, P. (1984). *Bender Gestalt Screening for Brain Dysfunction.* New York: John Wiley & Sons.

Lubin, B., & Sands, E. W. (1992). Bibliography of the psychometric properties of the Bender Visual-Gestalt Test 1970–1991. *Perceptual and Motor Skills, 75,* 385–386.

Lubin, B., Wallis, R., & Paine, C. (1971). Patterns of psychological test usage in the United States: 1935–1969. *Professional Psychology, 2,* 70–74.

Pardue, A. M. (1975). Bender-Gestalt test and background interference procedure in discernment of organic brain damage. *Perceptual and Motor Skills, 40,* 103–109.

Pascal, G. R., & Suttell, B. J. (1951). *The Bender-Gestalt Test: Quantification and Validity for Adults.* New York: Grune & Stratton.

Sattler, J. M., & Gwynne, J. (1982). Ethnicity and Bender Visual Motor Gestalt performance. *Journal of School Psychology, 20,* 69–71.

Sola, S. A. (1983). On "testing for organic brain damage": A critique of traditional methods. *Clinical Neuropsychology, 5,* 47 (abstract).

Taylor, R. L., & Partenio, I. (1984). Ethnic differences on the Bender-Gestalt Relative effects of measured intelligence. *Journal of Consulting and Clinical Psychology, 52,* 784–788.

Tolor, A., & Brannigan, G. G. (1980). *Research and Clinical Applications of the Bender-Gestalt Test.* Springfield, IL: Charles C. Thomas.

Tolor, A., & Schulberg, H. C. (1963). *An Evaluation of the Bender-Gestalt Test.* Springfield, IL: Charles C. Thomas.

Wagner, E. E., & Flamos, O. (1988). Optimized split-half reliability for the Bender Visual Motor Gestalt Test. *Journal of Personality Assessment, 52,* 454–458.

Wallasch, R., & Moebus, C. (1977). Validierung und Kreuzvalidierung des Goettinger Form reproduktionstests von Schlange et al. (1972) und der Background Interference Procedure von Canter (1970) zur Erfassung von Hirnschaedigungen bei Kindern zusammen mit zwel auderen Auswertungssystemen fur den Bender Gestalt test sowie weiteren Verfahren. *Diagnostica, 2,* 156–172.

Yulis, S. (1969). The relationship between the Canter Background Interference Procedure and intelligence. *Journal of Clinical Psychology, 25,* 405–406.

The Halstead-Reitan Neuropsychological Test Battery (HRNTB)

Stephen N. Macciocchi
Jeffrey T. Barth

Neuropsychology focuses on the interface between psychology and the neurosciences with a firmly established role in each discipline. Clinical neuropsychology is intimately concerned with the identification, diagnosis, and documentation of the effect of neuropathological processes on psychological functions. To view neuropsychology only as a diagnostic process is somewhat misleading and suggests a singular purpose typically undertaken by medical specialties such as neurology and neuroradiology. Although clinical neuropsychology began as a neurodiagnostic endeavor, it is far from being at odds with other neuroscientific disciplines, and in fact, creates a communication vehicle that bridges the gap between the neurologist and the behavioral scientist or clinical psychologist. For this reason, clinical neuropsychologists are considered best prepared if they have training both as clinical psychologists and in specialty areas such as neuroanatomy, neuropathology, and neurophysiology.

The primary purpose of neuropsychological assessment is to evaluate the neurologically impaired patient's cognitive, behavioral, and psychological strengths and weaknesses. Psychologists are specialists in the observation and analysis of behavior and cognition, and, as such, play a significant complementary role to the neurologist, neuroradiologist, and neurosurgeon in the evaluation of patients suspected of demonstrating cerebral dysfunction. In most cases, neurodiagnosis is secondary to the assessment of cognitive abilities, but sometimes the neuropsychologist must be able to relate cognitive and behavioral test results to neuropathological disorders in order to help confirm a diagnosis or establish the possibility of related disorders. Neuropsychologists must use their backgrounds and training in neuroanatomy and neuropathology, as well as knowledge of brain-behavior relationships in order to facilitate communication among health care professionals, coordinate treatment planning, initiate rehabilitation, and promote development of coping behaviors (Barth & Boll, 1981; Boll, 1977).

Neuropsychological assessment is also vital for assessing level and rate of improvement for both clinical and research purposes. For example, if a patient has experienced a moderate to severe closed head injury, there is an expected recovery period (after coma) during which substantial cognitive/behavioral restitution takes place. If neuropsychological evaluations are initiated at regular intervals following trauma, recovery can be objectively documented and estimates concerning degree and quality of improvement over time can be established. Neuropsychological assessment can also provide similar indexes of recovery following neurosurgical, radiologic, and chemotherapeutic interventions.

In the past, neuropsychological assessment has been practiced within teaching hospitals and medical settings where patients with serious neuropathological conditions are evaluated by a variety of health care specialties, and where treatment may include neurosurgery, chemotherapy, radiation, and other highly invasive techniques and procedures. As stated earlier, neurodiagnosis is seldom necessary in such settings but confirmation of pathological process and prognosis, documentation of decline or improvement in functioning, delineation of cognitive, behavioral, and psychological strengths and weaknesses, implications for everyday functioning, and recommendation for rehabilitation and other therapeutic interventions is important. Neuropsychological evaluation in other settings, such as community mental health centers, inpatient psychiatric facilities, or school systems, although oriented to similar issues, may also be concerned with whether a particular patient or student demonstrates cognitive impairment significant enough to suggest a disturbance in neuropsychological functioning and referral for further medical/neurological assessment.

If neuropsychological deficits are due to a neurological disorder, the need for a neurological examination usually will be quite obvious from acute physical deficits such as incoordination, visual, tactile and/or auditory problems, headaches, seizures, and the like. Neurological symptoms should be red flags that indicate the need for medical (neurological) intervention rather than a neuropsychological examination. If any health care specialist suspects a central nervous system disorder, he or she should make an appropriate referral to a primary care physician. On some occasions, a neuropsychologist will be asked to determine whether a medical referral is necessary, particularly when there are questionable data regarding physical or suspected neurologic symptomatology. A neuropsychological evaluation can be helpful in this regard; however, the primary purpose of this assessment remains a clear definition of cognitive, behavioral, and psychological strengths and weaknesses related to brain function and pathology. This information can then be utilized to plan further assessment, psychotherapeutic and behavioral intervention, and educational placement and remediation, as well as to develop discharge plans, assessment of daily living needs, and vocational adjustment and rehabilitation.

Another typical and appropriate referral question is a request for information regarding how a particular past neuropathological condition, such as closed head injury, has affected cognitive and behavioral functioning for a specific patient. In this case, the neuropsychological examination can be of great value, as well as in more vague situations where there are behavioral abnormalities or difficulties in learning with no known associated neuropathological conditions. Again, relating cerebral functioning (as defined by test data) to the more salient issue of a comprehensive assessment of cognitive and behavioral skills and applying these findings to intervention strategies and coping behavior is of great importance.

Although many authors have advised against using neuropsychological tests solely as neurodiagnostic tools (Barth & Boll, 1981; Boll, 1978, 1981; Golden, 1978; Jarvis & Barth, 1994; Lezak, 1983; Ranseen, Macciocchi, & Barth, 1983; Reitan & Davison, 1974; Swiercinsky, 1978), on occasion this process has been extremely useful and a necessary step in the overall learning process. Until recently, many physicians and even some psychologists believed there were single tests, such as the Bender-Gestalt, capable of determining whether a person suffered from cerebral dysfuntion or "organicity." Aside from the fact that the term *organicity* is extremely vague, the supposition that one test (any test) can identify all forms of cerebral impairment suggests that the consequences of cerebral dysfunction present uniformly regardless of etiology, lesion location, lesion momentum, and so on. Neuroscientists have known for decades that cerebral dysfunction may be the consequence of many disease processes that have differing etiology, progression, severity, and neuropsychological consequences. As is well known, the brain is complex, systemically organized, and variable in response to neuropathological disorders. In order to evaluate a representative sample of brain-behavior relationships and to delineate cognitive and behavioral strengths and weaknesses associated with cerebral impairment, a *battery* of psychometric tests must be utilized that assesses major abilities and skills and that complement each other in order to build a comprehensive picture of functional cerebral integrity. The Halstead-Reitan Neuropsychological Test Battery (HRNTB) is traditionally considered to be the most well-validated set of test procedures that meet these criteria.

DEVELOPMENT OF THE HALSTEAD-REITAN NEUROPSYCHOLOGICAL TEST BATTERY (HRNTB)

In 1935, Ward Halstead developed his neuropsychology laboratory at the University of Chicago, where he pursued interests in the psychometric aspects of adaptive human abilities, or biological intelligence (Halstead, 1947). Although his four-factor theory of biological intelligence received minimal empirical attention over the years, he continued to develop tests to assess these abilities in normal subjects and patients with brain damage. Halstead's work has become the foundation of present-day human quantitative neuropsychological research. Using factor-analytic methods, Halstead identified eight tests (and 10 test scores) that he believed would measure biological intelligence and separate normal from brain-damaged subjects (Russell, Neuringer, & Goldstein, 1974). These tests included the Halstead Category Test, Seashore Rhythm Test, Speech-Sounds Perception Test, Tactual Performance Test (Total Time, Memory, and Localization), Finger Oscillation Test, Critical Flicker Frequency, Critical Flicker Fusion, and Time Sense Test.

Subsequently, Ralph Reitan, one of Halstead's students, further refined the test measures by applying them to a variety of neurologic populations and analyzing individual test's ability to discriminate neurologic patients from normal controls (see Reitan & Davison, 1974). Reitan found most of these tests to be extremely sensitive to the integrity of the cerebral hemispheres, but Critical Flicker Frequency, Critical Flicker Fusion, and the Time Sense Test demonstrated lower levels of significance and, consequently, were eventually excluded from the formal battery.

Since both Halstead and Reitan's research endeavors required the evaluation of cognitive and behavioral abilities associated with biological intelligence, a battery of tests was considered necessary to define such a construct. The battery eventually modified by Reitan included five tests (seven test scores) adapted from the original Halstead measures (plus the Halstead Impairment Index, which will be discussed later), as well as the Trail Making Test A & B, the Reitan-Indiana Aphasia Screening Test, the Sensory-Perceptual Examination, and two allied procedures: the Wechsler Intelligence Scales (originally the Wechsler-Bellevue) and the Minnesota Multiphasic Personality Inventory (MMPI-2). Other tests are often added to this battery in order to assess additional areas of functioning. These tests include the Strength of Grip Test (Hand Dynommeter), Grooved Pegboard Test, academic achievement testing, memory evaluation (Wechsler Memory Scale-Revised, Benton Visual Retention Test, Rey Auditory Verbal Learning Test, Rey Osterreith Complex Figure Test, or Selective Reminding Test), and lateral dominance assessment (see Lezak, 1983). In complete form, this battery assesses a wide range of cognitive, behavioral, and psychological abilities.

Reitan's modification of Halstead's original work led to many validation and cross-validation studies focused on diagnosis of cerebral dysfunction, lateralization of cerebral impairment (left or right hemisphere), and the impact of neuropathological process (see reviews in Boll, 1978; Hevern, 1980; Reitan & Davison, 1974). A wide range of criterion measures were utilized in these early studies, including neurologists' and neurosurgeons' reports, autopsies, physical and neurological examinations, skull x-rays, EEGs, pneumoencephalograms (PEG), angiograms, brain scans, blood flow studies (BFS), and, more recently, MRI and CT scans. As Boll (1981) points out, such validational efforts were necessary in the early development of the neuropsychological battery in order to demonstrate clinical utility and validity as well as "to determine whether the behavioral variations between patients reflected underlying neurologic status rather than other variables such as systemic illness, drugs, hospitalization, and so on" (p. 582). He goes on to state:

> It is unfortunate, but understandable, that what one does first is often assumed to be the issue of greatest or even sole interest. . . . It is understandable that (these) impressive validity demonstration(s) would be seized on by applied clinicians as the development of a neurodiagnostic procedure . . . [however] it remains a fact that the goal of neuropsychological assessment is not now, and never has been, diagnosis or the creation of bigger and better neurodiagnostic techniques. (p. 582)

As stated previously, this battery of neuropsychological test procedures was principally designed to study brain-behavior relationships by assessing a wide range of cognitive abilities. This remains a major goal that has been expanded to include the application of these findings to treatment and rehabilitation issues as well as to theoretical considerations in neuroscience. In keeping with this purpose, the succeeding discussion describes the HRNTB in some detail with particular attention to test description and administration. This chapter was written as an introduction to the HRNTB rather than an advanced guide to application and interpretation which other more extensive manuals address in great detail (see Reitan & Wolfson, 1985; Jarvis & Barth, 1994).

HALSTEAD-REITAN NEUROPSYCHOLOGICAL TEST PROCEDURES FOR ADULTS (AGE 15 AND ABOVE)

The Halstead-Reitan Neuropsychological Test Battery (HRB) is technically comprised of 10 tests, 2 of which are considered allied procedures. The Category Test, Speech-Sounds Perception, Seashore Rhythm, Tactual Performance Test (TPT), Finger Oscillation, Trail Making A & B, Aphasia Screening, and Sensory-Perceptual Examination constitute the main battery, with the Wechsler Intelligence Scales (WAIS or the preferred WAIS-R) and MMPI (or MMPI-2) also contributing to the comprehensive nature of the assessment. Since these last two procedures are reviewed in separate chapters of this book, they will not be described here.

The Halstead Category Test

The Halstead Category Test is composed of 208 color and black-and-white slides of geometric figures that are divided into seven subsets of 8 to 40 slides per set. Each slide is projected onto an opaque screen within a self-contained viewing apparatus that is placed directly in front of the patient. Beneath the screen is a box with four lights numbered 1 to 4, and four levers (or buttons) directly below the lights. The patient is instructed to watch the slides presented on the screen, determine which number between 1 and 4 is suggested by each slide, and then pull the lever corresponding to that number. Patients hear a bell sound if they choose the correct number, and a buzzer if their choice is incorrect. Patients are allowed only one choice per slide. The examiner controls the rate of slide presentation with an instrument panel attached to a clipboard, and patients are typically allowed as much time as necessary to make each individual choice. Patients are told that each set of slides represents only one principle. They are also informed, at the beginning of each subset, that another group of slides will be presented in which the idea or principle may remain the same or be different from the previous set. Patients then must decide what principle can be used to obtain the correct responses. It is imperative that patients never be told the principle being used in any of the subsets, since retesting (or using the same slides) may be necessary to document decline or improvement in cognitive condition.

The first subset of slides requires the patient to identify Roman numerals and pull the lever corresponding to the correct number. There are eight of these relatively easy items that are designed to help the patient understand the task and experience success. The next subset begins with a slide of a four-sided figure similar to that shown in Figure 11–1. Responses for this slide may include a 4 (for a four-sided object) or a 1 (for one object). If the fourth lever is pulled, the patient will hear the buzzer, signifying an incorrect response. Since only one response per slide is allowed, the next slide is presented (see Figure 11–2). This one shows three similar four-sided figures, which usually stimulates the patient to choose lever 3 (for three objects). This is a correct response generating a bell sound. All of the slides in that subset (2) require the patient to respond to the number of items shown on the screen. In the third subset, the patient is required to identify the position of different items on each slide. Identification of the quadrant in which an item is missing, or the quadrant that is missing, is the principle required in Subset 4. Sub-

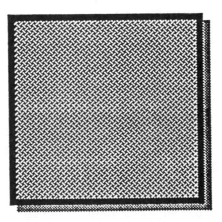

Figure 11–1   Halstead Category Test: Slide 1, Subset 2

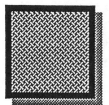  

Figure 11–2   Halstead Category Test: Slide 2, Subset 2

sets 5 and 6 involve the same principle, which is the proportion of the figure that is composed of solid lines. The last subset is made up of slides from the previous subsets, and the patient is instructed to make his or her choice based on experience with the previous principles.

Difficulties during testing generally arise from problems motivating the patient to perform at his or her best, which is essential to data gathering for all of the HRNTB measures. Description of the test procedures in order to minimize test anxiety as well as a friendly, yet firm and professional attitude, are always necessary. Since Subset 3 is much more difficult than the first two subsets, it is important for the examiner to offer any necessary reassurance and to encourage the patient to expend maximum effort at that point. Prompting the patient to look at the slides and how they change is useful throughout the testing, as long as the principle is never divulged. It is also quite common for patients to attempt to choose more than one response per slide. Since this is not permitted, such behavior must be anticipated and discouraged (if necessary, by reminding the patient before each slide that only one choice is allowed). Finally, even though this test is not timed, the patient should not be allowed to spend too much time on each item. From 15 to 20 seconds should be quite sufficient.

Scoring is quite simple for this test and requires only a record of the total number of errors (range = 0–208). Profile analysis may one day prove useful in determining specific patterns of problem-solving impairment, but at the present, limited empirical evidence is available to establish such relationships. The Halstead Category Test is a learning task requiring a high level of new problem-solving skills. Individuals who demonstrate impairment on this assessment measure often exhibit deficits in abstract learning, concept formation, and judgment, as well as mental flexibility and mental efficiency.

Speech-Sounds Perception Test

The Speech-Sounds Perception Test involves a taped presentation of 60 nonsense words, all of which contain the "ee" sound. The patient listens to each word and is then required to identify that word from a printed list of four similar words on the answer sheet. For each of the 60 nonsense words on the tape recording, there are four choices on the answer sheet, only one of which is correctly matched with the stimulus word. The first taped stimulus word is *theets,* and that word must be identified from the first four words on the answer sheet, which are *theeks, zeeks, theets,* and *zeets.* The next word is *weej,* and the choices are *weech, yeech, weej,* and *yeej.* The scoring for this test is simply the total number of errors (range = 0–60). This is a relatively slow-paced task requiring a moderate level of attention and concentration as well as verbal/auditory perception and language processing.

The Seashore Rhythm Test

This test, which was adapted from the Seashore Test of Musical Talent, requires the patient to listen to a taped presentation of 30 sets of auditory tones and determine whether the second set of beats is the same or different from the first set. This is recorded as an "S" or "D" on the answer sheet. The following are two written examples of what might be heard on the tape:

1st Example Pair

(line 1)   bop – bop, bop – bop – bop
(line 2)   bop – bop, bop – bop – bop

2nd Example Pair

(line 3)   bop, bop, bop – bop – bop, bop
(line 4)   bop – bop, bop – bop, bop – bop

In the first example, the answer would be "S," or same, since the second set of beats (line 2) is identical to the first (line 1). Different, or "D," would be the appropriate response to the second example since the second set of beats (line 4) is different from the first (line 3). Scoring is based on the number of correct responses (range = 0–30), which is traditionally converted to a ranked score (range = 10–1; impaired to nonimpaired). In contrast to the Speech-Sounds Perception Test, this task is quickly paced and requires focused and sustained attention and concentration, since it is quite easy for the patient to lose his or her place when marking the answer sheet.

The Tactual Performance Test

The Tactual Performance Test (TPT) uses a wooden board with spaces for 10 geometrically shaped blocks (a variation of the Seguin-Goddard Form Board). This board is mounted on a support stand and placed on a table in front of the seated patient, who is blindfolded throughout the test and is never allowed to see the board or blocks. The blocks (square, circle, triangle, star, cross, rectangle, etc.) are placed on the table between the patient and the form board. The examiner runs the patient's dominant hand over the blocks and the corresponding spaces in the board to briefly acquaint the patient with the location and dimensions of the initial task, which is to place the blocks in their proper space on the board as quickly as possible using only the dominant hand. The task is timed and at the end of the first trial with the dominant hand, the blocks are removed from the board and replaced on the table. The patient is then instructed to go through the same procedure, this time using only the nondominant hand. Once this trial is timed and completed, a third trial is performed using both hands. The board, blocks, and stand are removed from the patient's view after the third trial, following which the blindfold is removed. The last step in this assessment procedure is to ask the patient to draw a picture of the board on a plain white sheet of paper, including replications of all blocks remembered, and their location on the board. If the patient can remember the shape of a block, but not the location, the block should still be drawn on the paper wherever desired.

This test is one of the two most difficult procedures in the battery to administer and requires significant observational and practice experience to avoid pitfalls. The first problem the examiner may encounter is an inadequate blindfold. If a patient is able to see through or underneath the blindfold, data collection and interpretation become meaningless. Therefore, most neuropsychology laboratories suggest the use of sterile eye patches held in place by a standard black "sleep mask" type of blindfold. Sometimes patients attempt to use both hands to place the blocks on the board during the first two trials, so the examiner must be attentive throughout the testing and prevent this rather natural behavior. Having the patient place the hand that is not being used under the table can be helpful. In addition, certain patients will lose their orientation to the top of the form board and only place blocks on the bottom two-thirds. They may have forgotten about the top of the board, and, under these circumstances, it is permissible to remind them to feel the entire board. Elderly patients in particular will become tired during the trials and will need to take a break. In these cases, stop the clock (stopwatch), tell them to keep the blindfold on, and take a short break. If the blindfold must be removed for any reason, throw a blanket or sheet over the form board or remove it from sight. Patients who are completely unable to utilize one of their upper extremities may still be tested by using the intact arm for all three trials to determine whether learning and memory have been affected.

The scoring for this test is also more complicated than for most of the others, and there are essentially six pertinent scores. Timed scores include those for dominant hand, nondominant hand, both hands, and total time for all three trials. Since some patients will be unable to complete this task within a reasonable time period, there is a 15-minute time limit for each trial (unless the patient is on the verge of completing the task at that cutoff time, at which point a little more time may be given). The patient must be given the same opportunity and time to complete each trial so that the performance of both upper extremities may be compared on an equal basis. For example, is the patient is given over 15 minutes to complete trial 1 (dominant hand) because he or she was close to completion at 15 minutes, the same amount of time must be allowed for the nondominant hand and both hands. The number of blocks placed in their correct location on the board is also recorded for each trial.

In addition to the four timed scores, number of memories and localizations are recorded based on information provided by the drawing of the board. The memory score is calculated by counting the number of figures the patient draws that accurately represent form board blocks. Since not all patients have a flair for art, when in doubt as to what shape has been drawn, ask the patient to name the design. If the block is accurately named or described, it may be considered an acceptable memory (range = 0–10). Localization is determined by the placement and juxtaposition of the block drawing. The blocks should be drawn in their approximate position on the board and in appropriate relation to other correctly placed blocks. Localization is then calculated as the number of blocks correctly placed (drawn) on the sheet of paper (range = 0–10). The TPT is a measure of right-left differences in tactile, kinesthetic, and motor abilities in the absence of visual cues. It is a problem-solving task requiring intact spatial analytic ability and incidental memory.

The Finger Oscillation Test

The Finger Oscillation Test requires the patient to use the index finger to quickly tap a lever connected to a mechanical counter. Five consecutive 10-second trials are attempted, first with the dominant hand, then with the non-dominant hand. If the scores for each hand are all within a five-point range of each other, no further finger oscillation testing is necessary, but if patients are inconsistent, as many as 10 trials with one or both hands may be necessary to obtain appropriate tap variation (≤ 5) range. If five consecutive scores within a five-tap range are not obtained within a maximum of 10 trials, most laboratories suggest dropping the highest and lowest scores and averaging the remaining eight.

The most typical problem in the administration of this test is patient hand fatigue, and this can usually be remedied by allowing for short breaks after several trials. Scoring is simply the average number of taps per 10 seconds for dominant and nondominant hands (range = 0–75 per hand). The Finger Oscillation Test is a measure of right-left differences in motor speed and gross motor manipulation skills in the upper extremities.

The Trail Making Test

The Trail Making Test is a two-part assessment procedure that requires the patient to draw lines to connect circles that are printed on an 8½ × 11-inch piece of white paper. On Part A, there are 25 circles, each with a number on it from 1 to 25. The patient uses a pencil to consecutively and as rapidly as possible connect the circles, starting at 1 and ending with 25. A short practice run is completed and then the patient is timed while performing the main task. If the patient makes a mistake by connecting any circles out of order, he or she is stopped, asked to correct the mistake, and then allowed to continue. The clock continues to run during corrections. Part B is quite similar but on this task, the circles have either numbers (1 to 13) or letters (A to L) in them.

The task is to consecutively connect the circles beginning with 1 and alternating between a number and a letter in a sequence which begins 1 to A, A to 2, 2 to B, B to 3, and so on. There also is a practice session prior to beginning this trial. Part B is considerably more difficult than Part A, so the patient must be urged to concentrate on the task.

Scores consist of the time needed to complete Parts A and B (up to 300 seconds for each) and the number of errors on each trial (range = 0–25 for each). Trail Making A & B is a measure of ability to sustain attention to two aspects of a problem-solving task simultaneously. The test requires visual scanning, verbal and numeric processing, as well as sequencing skills.

The Reitan-Indiana Aphasia Screening Test

In this task, the patient is asked to complete 32 relatively simple tasks requiring receptive and expressive language functions as well as visuo-constructional abilities and simple mental arithmetic skills. Items include (1) drawing (copying) simple geometric designs such as a square, triangle, Greek cross, and a skeleton key; (2) naming designs and objects such as line drawings of a fork and a baby; (3) spelling simple words and writing words and phrases; (4) writing the names of objects presented in pictures; (5) reading letters, words, and sentences; (6) articulating word combinations such as "Methodist Episcopal"; (7) describing the meaning of phrases; (8) carrying out simple mathematical computations; and (9) demonstrating the use of objects (key) and following commands associated with sequential movement of body parts. This test is not typically scored, but rather evaluated from a qualitative standpoint to delineate gross communication deficits and language processing impairment.

The Sensory-Perceptual Examination (Reitan-Klove)

This evaluation is quite similar to the sensory evaluation that is a standard part of the traditional physical neurological examination. The sensory examination is a difficult test to administer because it requires a high level of motor coordination and attention to the patient's threshold for tactile, auditory, and visual stimulation. The original Sensory-Perceptual Examination included eight subtests of tactile, auditory, and visual processing, but many laboratories no longer administer one of the tests for astereognosis (tactile recognition of a penny, nickel, and dime) or the complete visual field examination. The tactile subtest involves lightly (just above tactile threshold) touching the back of the patient's hand and asking the patient to identify which hand is being touched, while keeping his or her eyes closed.

First, unilateral stimulation (touching one hand at a time) is attempted with bilateral simultaneous stimulation (touching both hands at once) being interspersed among unilateral trials shortly after baseline tactile thresholds are established. Four unilateral right, unilateral left, and bilateral simultaneous stimulation trials are attempted. The score consists of the number of errors on the right and left sides, with special note being made of suppression errors (where only one side is reported as being touched during bilateral simultaneous stimulation). This unilateral and bilateral stimulation procedure is also carried out for hand-face stimulation (right hand and left cheek, or left hand and right cheek). The patient is not told (in this subtest or others) that both sides may be stimulated together (bilateral simultaneous stimulation).

The auditory subtest is quite similar to the tactile procedure. The examiner stands behind the seated patient and makes a slight noise (just above auditory threshold) next to the patient's ear by rubbing the thumb and index finger together lightly. Unilateral and bilateral simultaneous stimulation are also required and the patient is asked to indicate which ear is being stimulated. Scoring is identical to the tactile subtest. Like the auditory subtest, the visual subtest involves the same stimulation format; but the examiner extends his or her arms approximately three feet in front of the patient out to the sides and equidistant between patient and examiner. The patient is asked to focus on the examiner's nose (midline) and report whether the examiner's right or left fingers move in the patient's peripheral vision. Unilateral and bilateral simultaneous stimulation are initiated and this procedure is performed at three different levels of peripheral vision (high, middle, and low).

The assessment of finger agnosia requires the patient to identify which finger is being (lightly) touched on each hand, while keeping eyes closed. Fingers are usually numbered (1 to 5) so that responses are defined and the order of stimulation is random. The score reflects the number of misidentifications per hand out of 20 trials. Fingertip number writing perception follows naturally from the finger agnosia subtest and asks the patient to identify numbers that are written on their fingertips with a stylus or empty ballpoint pen, while keeping eyes closed. The numbers used are 3, 4, 5, and 6, and each of these numbers is written on the patient's palm at the beginning of the test to familiarize him or her with the particular number formation. There is a prearranged order of presentation so that each number is written once on each finger of each hand. Scoring is based on the number of errors for each hand out of 20 trials.

The last subtest is tactual form recognition involving the identification of plastic geometric shapes (circle, square, triangle, and cross) that are placed in the patient's hand after it is inserted through an opening in a board, so that no visual feedback will be available. The patient's responses are nonverbal and are made by pointing with the free hand to identical plastic shapes attached to the top of the board facing the patient. Each of the plastic shapes is presented twice to each hand, with the scores being the time required to identify each shape and the number of errors per hand out of eight presentations.

Comprehensive neuropsychological assessment utilizing the Halstead-Reitan Battery requires a high level of technical expertise, objective data collection, and a dedication to obtaining the best possible performance that the patient can offer. Instructions are typically memorized so that the examiner may focus full attention to patient observations and appropriate motivational techniques. During the 1940s, Halstead was one of the first to recognize that such testing requirements were ideally suited to administration and scoring by highly trained technicians (Boll, 1981). Although these assessment procedures are sometimes given by doctoral-level professionals, neuropsychological laboratories and assessment centers often employ technicians in this important duty. Well-trained technicians can accurately and reliably administer and score this test battery.

THE HALSTEAD-REITAN NEUROPSYCHOLOGICAL TEST BATTERY FOR CHILDREN (AGES 9 TO 15)

The older children's (or intermediate) neuropsychological assessment battery is similar to the adult battery with the following changes being developed by Reitan:

1. The Category Test is reduced from 208 slides to 168 slides that are subdivided into six subsets (rather than seven). The fourth subset from the adult battery is eliminated and there are no colored slides.
2. The Speech-Sounds Perception answer sheet has been changed to reflect only three nonsense word choices per trial. The tape, correct responses, and number of trials (60) remain the same.
3. The TPT form board has only six cut-outs and blocks (four cut-outs and blocks were eliminated from the adult version).
4. The number of circles on the Trail Making Test for both Parts A and B have been reduced from 25 to 15, while the two tasks remain the same.

All other tests and all instructions from the adult battery are identical in the older children's evaluation with the possible exception of substituting the WISC-R (or WISC III) for the WAIS-R and the elimination of the MMPI (or MMPI-2).

THE REITAN-INDIANA NEUROPSYCHOLOGICAL TEST BATTERY FOR YOUNG CHILDREN (AGES 5 TO 9)

The modification of the adult and older children's battery to meet the needs and level of understanding of young children required more extensive changes in specific presentation and instructions, as well as the elimination of several tests (Speech-Sounds Perception, Seashore Rhythm, and Trail Making A & B). The following changes have been made to the children's battery for application with 5- to 9-year-olds:

1. The Category Test stimulus slides are reduced from 168 to 80 (in five subsets) and the numbers above the levers have been replaced with colors (blue, red, green, and yellow) since number concepts may not be de-

veloped in the 5-year-old. The slides are all colored and the principles behind each subset of slide presentation involves different aspects of color (placement of color, quantity of color, uniqueness of color, and absence of color). The last subset of 10 slides is a memory section consisting of previously presented slides.

2. The TPT utilizes the children's six-block form board turned on its side so that it is within easy reach of a young child's short arms.

3. The Aphasia Screening Test has been reduced from 32 items to 22 items that essentially reflect evaluation of the same language processing and usage areas, but at a level that is appropriate for young children. For example, they are not asked to spell *triangle;* however, they are asked to name objects such as a fork.

4. The Sensory-Perceptual Examination is similar to the adult and older children's versions with the exception of fingertip number writing in which symbols (Xs and Os) are substituted for the numbers.

5. Age-appropriate Wechsler Intelligence Scales (the WISC-R, WISC-III, or WPPSI) are used.

Additional other tests—such as the Marching Test, Color Form Test, Matching Pictures, Progressive Figures, Matching Vs, and Target Test—that are described by Reitan (1959) and Reitan and Davison (1974) have been recommended to supplement the young children's battery; however, few neuropsychology laboratories consistently apply these measures to their young, impaired populations. Other developmental and academic tests should be added to these core evaluation procedures in order to broaden the range of assessment of adaptive cognitive abilities.

In order to accurately administer and score the adult, intermediate, or young children's neuropsychological test battery, the examiner must take sufficient time to study the manual and practice the procedures under appropriate supervision. The manual and test procedures may be ordered from several sources. Material can be ordered from Dr. Ralph M. Reitan, Reitan Neuropsychology Laboratory, 2920 South 4th Avenue, Tuscon, Arizona.

INTERPRETATION

Interpretation of neuropsychological test data is predicated on the organization and understanding of assessment scores, the relationship of these data to normal and impaired functioning, the delineation of basic questions to be answered, the use of several methods of inference as well as consideration of patient history, environmental variables, and behavioral observations. The organization of assessment data may be accomplished in many ways; however, the most straightforward method is to transfer individual test scores to a summary data sheet (see Figure 11–3). Based on these scores, a Halstead Impairment Index (HII) is calculated. The HII is a summary score reflecting general level of cerebral dysfunction computed from seven scores

Case Number: _____ Age: _____ Sex: _____ Education: _____ Handedness: _____

Name: _____ Employment: _____ Date of Testing: _____

WAIS or WAIS-R

 VIQ

 PIQ

 FS IQ

         Scaled Scores

 Information

 Comprehension

 Digit Span

 Arithmetic

 Similarities

 Vocabulary

 Picture Arrangement

 Picture Completion

 Block Design

 Object Assembly

 Digit Symbol

MINNESOTA MULTIPHASIC PERSONALITY INVENTORY

   T Scores

 ?

 L

 F

 K

 Hs

 D

 Hy

 Pd

 Mf

 Pa

 Pt

 Sc

 Ma

 Si

IMPAIRMENT INDEX

CATEGORY TEST

TACTUAL PERFORMANCE TEST

        Time _____ # of Blks. In

 Dominant hand:

 Nondomin. hand:

 Both hands:

  Total Time:

  Memory:

  Localization:

TRAIL MAKING TEST

 Part A: seconds   errors

 Part B: seconds   errors

SEASHORE RHYTHM TEST (correct)

 Raw Score:

SPEECH-SOUNDS PERCEPTION TEST

 Errors:

FINGER OSCILLATION TEST

 Dominant hand:

 Nondominant hand:

STRENGTH OF GRIP

 Dominant hand: kilograms

 Nondominant hand: kilograms

REITAN-KLØVE TACTILE FORM RECOGNITION TEST

        Errors Seconds

 Dominant hand:

 Nondominant hand:

SENSORY SUPPRESSIONS

 Dominant:

 Nondominant:

APHASIA SIGNS:

Figure 11–3   Data Summary Form Results of Neuropsychological Examination

Reproduced by special permission of Psychological Assessment Resources, Inc., from *The Halstead-Reitan Neuropsychological Battery: A Guide to Interpretation and Clinical Application* by Paul Jarvis, Ph.D., and Jeffrey Barth, Ph.D. Copyright 1994. Further reproduction is prohibited without permission from PAR, Inc.

Table 11–1   Halstead Cutoff Scores Suggesting Brain Damage*

Tests	Halstead Cutoff Scores	
Category Test	51	or more errors
TPT Total Time	15.7	minutes or more
Memory	5	or less correct
Localization	4	or less correct
Seashore Rhythm	25	or less correct
Speech Sounds Perception	8	or more errors**
Finger Oscillation (Tapping) (Dominant hand)	50	or less taps in 10 seconds
Impairment Index	5	or above

Normal	Mild	Moderate	Severe
0.0–0.2	0.3–0.4	0.5–0.78	0.8–1.0

The following test, while not contributing to the Halstead Impairment Index, has established cutoff scores

Trail Making		
Part A	40	seconds or more
Part B	91	seconds or more

Reproduced by special permission of Psychological Assessment Resources, Inc., from *The Halstead-Reitan Neuropsychological Battery: A Guide to Interpretation and Clinical Application* by Paul Jarvis, Ph.D., and Jeffrey Barth, Ph.D. Copyright 1994. Further reproduction is prohibited without permission from PAR, Inc.

*(From Reitan, 1955; 1959; and based upon Halstead, 1947)
To calculate the Halstead Impairment Index, one divides the number of scores from Table 1 which are in the impaired range, by the total number of tests given which contribute to the Halstead Impairment Index (maximum 7). This results in a decimal value between 0 to 1.0. If none of the scores were in the impaired range the Impairment Index would be 0.0, while if all of them were in the impaired range (7 divided by 7, and 6 divided by 6, etc.), the Impairment Index would be 1.0. Since it is traditional to round all the results of this to the nearest 1 decimal place, the number of tests in the impaired range and the resulting impairment indices are listed on the prorated schedule in Table 2.

**Reitan and Wolfson (1985) suggest a cutoff score of 11 or more errors on the Speech Sounds Perception Test based upon analysis of more recent data.

on the Halstead-Reitan Neuropsychological Test Battery for Adults including the Category Test, Speech-Sounds Perception, Seashore Rhythm, Finger Oscillation, TPT Total Time, Memory, and Localization (the Impairment Index is not computed for the intermediate or young children's battery). Based on initial interpretive guidelines, each of these seven scores is evaluated against Halstead's cutoff scores norms (see Table 11–1) to determine whether they will contribute to the Impairment Index. Recent development of normative data for age, education, and gender have been invaluable in assisting interpretation of HRNTB scores (see Heaton, Grant, & Matthews, 1991). The greater the number of test scores falling in the impaired range, the larger the Impairment Index (see Table 11–2). An Impairment Index of 0.0 to 0.3 is considered to reflect normal functioning to mild cognitive im-

Table 11–2   Calculation of the Halstead Impaiment Index Based on Number of Tests Used and Number of Test Scores Which Fall Within the Brain-Impaired Range

	Number of Halstead Tests Utilized		
	7 Tests	6 Tests	5 Tests
Number of tests in Impaired range	1 = 0.1	1 = 0.2	1 = 0.2
	2 = 0.3	2 = 0.3	2 = 0.4
	3 = 0.4	3 = 0.5	3 = 0.6
	4 = 0.6	4 = 0.7	4 = 0.8
	5 = 0.7	5 = 0.8	5 = 1.0
	6 = 0.9	6 = 1.0	
	7 = 1.0		

Reproduced by special permission of Psychological Assessment Resources, Inc., from *The Halstead-Reitan Neuropsychological Battery: A Guide to Interpretation and Clinical Application* by Paul Jarvis, Ph.D., and Jeffrey Barth, Ph.D. Copyright 1994. Further reproduction is prohibited without permission from PAR, Inc.

pairment; 0.3 to 0.5, mild; 0.5 to 0.7, moderate; and 0.8 to 1.0, severe dysfunction.

A comprehensive neuropsychological examination should be designed to answer a number of questions directly influencing the understanding of cognitive and behavioral functioning, as well as influence treatment and rehabilitation. These questions include but may not be limited to:

1. Does the patient demonstrate neuropsychological impairment consistent with cerebral dysfunction?
2. How severe is the impairment?
3. If there is evidence of a neurological condition, does neuropsychological dysfunction appear to be progressive?
4. Is there impairment that is lateralized to the right or left cerebral hemisphere or located in the anterior or posterior portion of the brain?
5. Are the neuropsychological data consistent with the diagnosed neuropathological process?
6. What are the cognitive and behavioral strengths and weaknesses associated with this condition?
7. What are the implications for everyday functioning or prognosis?
8. What treatment and rehabilitation efforts should be made?

As stated earlier, the answers to the first five questions are usually viewed as secondary to the primary function of the neuropsychological examination, particularly if these questions have already been answered prior to referral. Nevertheless, the first five questions are an important foundation for developing a comprehensive assessment and establishing appropriate intervention strategies. In any case, in order to answer these eight questions, a systematic approach to the data and the use of at least four traditional methods of inference (interpretation) are required. These methods of inference include level of performance, pattern of performance, pathognomonic signs, and right-left differences (Boll, 1978; Golden, 1978; Reitan & Davison, 1974).

Assessment data are typically analyzed first to determine whether the patient has done well or poorly on a particular test measure. This interpretive schema allows for comparisons of individual test scores to normative and pathological populations (Boll, 1981). *Level of performance* is a limited interpretive method generally reflecting standard quantitative measurement in the absence of qualitative assessment. Although level of performance can be an important issue, use of only one method of inference to evaluate test results is not recommended.

Pattern of performance is a familiar method of data analysis to most psychologists, in part due to similar strategies learned in the application of the Wechsler Intelligence Scales and Minnesota Multiphasic Personality Inventory. Pattern analysis involves evaluating relationships among and within tests (scores) on the neuropsychological test battery. Since the Halstead-Reitan Neuropsychological Test Procedures were developed to be a comprehensive battery of tests, many of the measures demonstrate related features that allow a dovetailing and stepwise building of one result on another. The TPT, for example, provides right, left and both-hand time scores that can be analyzed together to provide information reflecting on tactile-kinesthetic learning across trials. This pattern of scores within the TPT can then be related to other motor (Finger Oscillation) and sensory (Sensory-Perceptual) test findings to determine the probable interaction of these skills and how they affect the TPT results.

Neuropsychological test data must be inspected for dramatic signs of neuropathology. Such signs or evidence of pathology are referred to as *pathognomonic indicators* and are often quite specific to a particular disorder. Pathognomonic signs may be found on the Aphasia Screening Battery and may include saying "a spoon" when naming a picture of a fork, and responding "red cross" when naming a black and white drawing of a Greek cross. These answers are considered pathognomonic for a type of aphasia or communication disorder referred to as *dysnomia*. This method of inference can be critical in the refinement of a diagnosis so that specific and appropriate intervention may be initiated.

The last method of inference, *analyzing right-left differences,* is directly related to pattern of performance and is usually applied to those tests measuring motor and sensory functions on each side of the body. In most instances, upper extremity dominance implies approximately 10 percent more efficient motor functioning on the dominant side than on the nondominant side (Finger Oscillation and Strength of Grip), although recent studies have challenged this degree of expected dominance (Thompson, Heaton, Matthews, & Grant, 1987). Moreover, this relationship does not generalize to sensory systems (Sensory-Perceptual Examination) where functions on both sides of the body should be intact and identical. If aberrant relationships between the right and left sides are discovered, impairment of cerebral functions in the contralateral cerebral hemisphere is often suggested. Such information can help to clarify brain-behavior relationships as well as diagnostic issues.

In addition to formal tests, pertinent patient history, environmental information, and behavioral observations are gathered as part of the neuropsychological evaluation. These data are critical to accurate test interpretation and development of appropriate intervention strategies. Since technicians frequently are employed to carry out many of the assessment duties, it may be assumed that the clinician does not see the patient and that blind analysis of test scores is a typical clinical practice. Despite advocates of this actuarial method of test interpretation (Foust, 1990), we do not recommend this approach since important clinical data may be lost if a comprehensive interview is not performed by the clinician in order to supplement the assessment data and behavioral notes gathered by the technician.

The interview and history gathering should include information regarding present circumstances (age, education, occupation, and family history); level of functioning in school and occupation; family dynamics; extrafamilial relationships; medical history; developmental history; recent cognitive, behavioral, psychological or physical changes or symptoms; past or present psychological or medical evaluation results; and other professionals' documentation. These data, combined with the extensive notes provided by the technician regarding behavioral observations during testing, can have a significant impact on the interpretive process. For example, as in any other psychological assessment, age plays an important role in developing adjusted scores and in our understanding of level of everyday functioning. This is certainly quite clear in certain tests that have age-correction factors (or age-appropriate scaled scores as on the WAIS-R), indicating that our expectations are different for a 65-year-old, as opposed to a patient in his or her 30s. When evaluating level of impairment, it is important to use corrected scores or norms when assessing the difference between normal aging effects and suspected neuropathology such as dementia.

Under similar circumstances, the same holds true for academic or vocational success as well as other variables. The patient's school and job-related performance (premorbid abilities) are also important because the issue of possible decline from a previously higher level of functioning as well as prognosis and treatment strategy determinations are often required. Family ties and general relationships with others are important in understanding test data, particularly if extended support systems appear necessary for rehabilitation success. Finally, knowledge of previous evaluation results and professional interventions can clarify diagnoses, reduce redundancy in test procedures, assist in team-oriented treatment planning, and facilitate professional communication.

Halstead-Reitan neuropsychological test data can best be interpreted by attempting to systematically answer the previously mentioned eight questions by using the four methods of inference and rules or hypotheses for test analysis arising from these methods (see Jarvis & Barth, 1994). Although every clinician has his or her own unique perspective and schema for inspecting data, the following outline is typical of the general process employed by many neuropsychologists. In the following discussion, test interpretation is described in a generalized manner and the conclusions are used for illustration rather than an attempt to provide definitive decision rules.

1. First, review demographic information and history, and evaluate the scores on Halstead's four most sensitive tests of brain damage (in order of sensitivity). These tests are the Halstead Impairment Index, the Category Test, TPT, Localization, and Trail Making B. Level of performance and normatively based scores are important here. This step can help answer question 1, "Is there evidence of neuropsychological impairment?" and question 2, "How severe is the impairment?" If all or most of these test scores are significantly beyond Halstead's cutoff scores or impaired by normative standards, cerebral impairment is highly probably.

2. Speech-Sounds Perception and Seashore Rhythm can be analyzed next to help determine the basic level of concentration and attention and to aid in answering question 3, "Is this a progressive neurological condition?" Good scores are usually not compatible with space-occupying, progressive lesions. Poor scores may indicate cerebral dysfunction; but impairment on SSPT and SR are not always compatible with progressive conditions. Of course, the optimal method for determining whether a condition is progressive is to search the recent history for indications of acute, physical, or mental decline, and to initiate serial testing over a 6- to 12-month period.

3. Lateralization and location of lesion (question 4) can be evaluated next through the inspection of test scores that lend themselves to pattern analysis and right-left comparisons (e.g., TPT time for dominant, nondominant, and both upper extremities; Finger Oscillation [and Strength of Grip]; Sensory-Perceptual Examination; and Wechsler Adult Intelligence Scale-Revised Verbal and Performance IQs). Since TPT is a learning task, the expected relationship is one of improvement in test scores (less time) from trial to trial (dominant, nondominant, both hands). Normal test scores for Finger Oscillation and Strength of Grip generally reflect better performance on the dominant side of the body than on the nondominant side. Few sensory deficits should be found and in most cases Wechsler Intelligence Scale VIQ and PIQ scores are expected to have less than a 20-point differential. Deviations from these motor and sensory relationships can suggest dysfunction in the contralateral cerebral hemisphere from the side exhibiting the impaired function. Impaired VIQ may indicate left hemisphere dysfunction, while poor PIQ scores sometimes reflect deficits in right hemisphere function. If sensory test scores are more impaired than motor skills, posterior cerebral hemisphere dysfunction may be suspected, and if the reverse is found, anterior cerebral hemisphere deficits are likely.

4. The Aphasia Screening Battery, WAIS-R subtests, and other allied procedures should finally be evaluated through the use of all of the methods of inference. A full analysis of all test scores and the responses to the previous four questions should enable the examiner to develop certain hypotheses (see Jarvis & Barth, 1994) regarding pathological process (question 5). A knowledge of neuroanatomy and neuropathology, along with the neuropsychological data, demographics, history, and so forth, will help eliminate many neuropathological entities and confirm the likelihood of others. A determination can then be made if the neuropsychological assessment is consistent with diagnoses that have been made by neurologists or other related professionals.

5. The next step is the most important and is reflective of the utility of a neuropsychological examination. All data must be reevaluated to determine the cognitive and behavioral strengths and weaknesses and how these variables will impact on the patient's everyday functioning (questions 6 and 7). This is accomplished by understanding the abilities and skills necessary to perform each of the tasks in the battery (described in test procedure sections). A profile of strengths and weaknesses, along with pathology prognosis, can then be developed and applied to the individual patient's life situation to begin to speculate on the changes taking place in daily living skills and on what interventions should prove useful (question 8).

The preceding outline for test interpretation is extremely limited, particularly since it suggests that the clinician is constantly developing and testing hypotheses concerning the integrity of neurologic, cognitive, and behavioral functioning, yet the reader is not exposed to all of these possible hypotheses. This ambiguity is intended, since this chapter would develop into several volumes if allowed to present to the reader the information, hypotheses, and interpretive rules necessary to immediately begin independent evaluation of test data. In fact, it would be misleading to suggest that this chapter could sufficiently prepare students for complex data analysis; however, it is hoped that this basic approach to the understanding and organization of test data can be an important beginning to further study in the field of neuropsychological assessment (see Reitan & Wolfson 1985; Jarvis & Barth 1994).

INTERPRETIVE CASE EXAMPLE

To concretize the interpretive procedures, the following will systematically review one patient's data and attempt to clarify the process of data analysis, hypothesis testing, and the basic information to be presented in a report. Instead of illustrating results from an obvious and serious medical disorder—such as a neoplasm or major cerebrovascular accident, which often result in profound neuropsychological dysfunction—this case example will describe and analyze a more subtle condition where neuropsychological assessment can be extremely useful.

Mr. William G. is a 32-year-old corporate tax attorney who has been employed by a large tax-consulting company for the past four years. He is married with no children, and he reports that his family life has always been a stable and happy one. He is an active, personable, and successful young man who is well liked in his community, and his past medical and psychological history (including that of his parents and family) is unremarkable.

The reason for Mr. G.'s referral for neuropsychological assessment was due to symptoms he began to experience following a head injury incurred three weeks earlier as a result of falling 10 feet from a ladder while painting his house. Mr. G. struck his head and experienced a period of unconsciousness lasting approximately 10 minutes. He was taken to the medical center emergency room where he was examined by a neurology resident who ordered a skull series. The x-rays were negative, but Mr. G.'s pupils were slightly dilated and he complained of a headache. His speech and thought process appeared relatively normal, but he did demonstrate mild dysnomia (word-finding difficulty). These results convinced the medical staff to admit him. An EEG and a CT scan were obtained, revealing no abnormalities.

Within 24 hours, his headache had decreased, his pupils were symmetrical and normal, and his mild dysphasia had almost entirely disappeared. He was released that day and returned six weeks later as part of a routine follow-up. At that time, Mr. G. continued to complain of headaches and dizziness, as well as difficulties in word finding, vague feelings of anxiety and depression, and memory problems. His wife reported a personality change characterized by his "losing some control over his temper," which was not typical of Mr. G prior to his accident. A repeat EEG and CT scan were both unremarkable. Since subtle changes (at the histological levels) can occur in mild and moderate head injuries but not be evident on radiologic procedures (CT/MRI), he was referred for neuropsychological assessment in order to delineate the cognitive and behavioral components of his present disorder and to relate these to his present functioning, prognosis, and need for treatment.

Mr. G. was extremely cooperative throughout the test process. He produced maximum effort and was genuinely concerned about his test results. He informed the examiners that he was worried about these "strange symptoms" he was having since they were disrupting his work and family life. He clearly wanted to know what was wrong with him and how to correct it. His neuropsychological results are presented in Figures 11–4 and 11–5.

An Halstead Impairment Index of 0.3 places him in the normal to mildly impaired range of adaptive cognitive abilities, and his Category score of 54 errors, TPT localization of 4, and Trail Making B of 105 seconds all indicate low average to mildly impaired functioning when utilizing Halstead and Reitan's cutoff scores or Heaton and colleagues' (1991) normative projections. These scores are generally consistent with mild cerebral dysfunction. There are no indications of severe impairment in these data or from other scores, but the Category score (54 errors) can be considered indicative of significant dysfunction. For example, a bright, active attorney should be capable of producing considerably less than 35 or 40 errors. Since both Speech-Sounds Perception and Seashore Rhythm performance are well within normal limits and given the history of a mild to moderate head trauma, there is no reason to believe his symptoms are due to a progressive neurologic condition. Nevertheless, in

Case Number: __001__ Age: __32__ Sex: __M__ Education: __20+__ Handedness: __R__

Name: __William G.__ Employment: __Attorney__ Date of Testing: _____

WAIS or WAIS-R	
VIQ	1 2 4
PIQ	1 1 2
FS IQ	☐

	Scaled Scores
Information	1 5
Comprehension	1 5
Digit Span	1 0
Arithmetic	1 4
Similarities	1 4
Vocabulary	1 5
Picture Arrangement	1 0
Picture Completion	1 4
Block Design	1 0
Object Assembly	1 4
Digit Symbol	1 0

MINNESOTA MULTIPHASIC PERSONALITY INVENTORY

	T Scores
?	0 0 0
L	0 4 0
F	0 5 2
K	0 6 9
Hs	0 6 5
D	0 7 0
Hy	0 5 6
Pd	0 6 2
Mf	0 5 1
Pa	0 5 4
Pt	0 6 8
Sc	0 5 1
Ma	0 6 9
Si	0 5 3

IMPAIRMENT INDEX 0 . 3 *

CATEGORY TEST 0 5 4 *

TACTUAL PERFORMANCE TEST

Time _____ # of Blks. In

Dominant hand:	5 . 2 – 1 0
Nondomin. hand:	3 . 1 – 1 0
Both hands:	2 . 6 – 1 0
Total Time:	1 0 . 9 *
Memory:	0 7 *
Localization:	0 4 *

TRAIL MAKING TEST

Part A: 0 2 8 seconds 0 0 errors

Part B: 1 0 7 seconds 0 0 errors

SEASHORE RHYTHM TEST (correct)

Raw Score: 2 8 *

SPEECH-SOUNDS PERCEPTION TEST

Errors: 0 2 *

FINGER OSCILLATION TEST

Dominant hand: 5 2 . 5 *

Nondominant hand: 4 7 . 2

STRENGTH OF GRIP

Dominant hand: 4 7 kilograms

Nondominant hand: 4 2 kilograms

REITAN-KLOVE TACTILE FORM RECOGNITION TEST

	Errors	Seconds
Dominant hand:	0	1 3
Nondominant hand:	0	1 7

SENSORY SUPPRESSIONS

Dominant: 0 0

Nondominant: 0 1

APHASIA SIGNS: Mild dysnemia
Mild dysarthria

Figure 11–4 Data Summary Form Results of Neuropsychological Examination

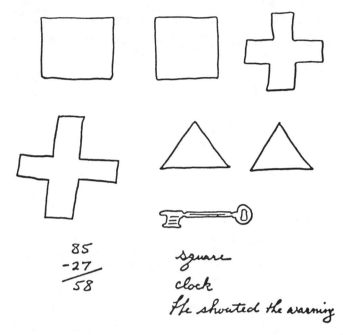

Figure 11–5   Illustrative Results of Mr. William G.'s Aphasia Screening Test

Reproduced by special permission of Psychological Assessment Resources, Inc., from *The Halstead-Reitan Neuropsychological Battery: A Guide to Interpretation and Clinical Application* by Paul Jarvis, Ph.D., and Jeffrey Barth, Ph.D. Copyright 1994. Further reproduction is prohibited without permission from PAR, Inc.

some cases behavioral and cognitive disruption may be exacerbated over time due to a rise in the level of frustration when impaired abilities are recognized and work or family functioning is affected.

No lateralized deficits are noted on TPT, Finger Oscillation, Strength of Grip, Sensory Perceptual Examination, or WAIS-R VIQ and PIQ. Learning has occurred on the TPT as evidenced by the decreasing time scores across hand trials and, as expected, there is approximately a 10 percent difference between dominant and nondominant hands on Finger Oscillation and Strength of Grip (dominant hand being faster and stronger). The absolute speed of dominant index finger tapping is also within normal limits on Finger Oscillation, thus it does not contribute to the Halstead Impairment Index. The Sensory-Perceptual Examination is unremarkable, except for one nondominant side suppression when stimuli were presented in a bilateral, simultaneous fashion, and since there are no other indications of sensory or motor impairment, little significance will be attached to this finding. WAIS-R Verbal and Performance IQ scores were discrepant by 12 points, which is unlikely to have a diagnostic significance; however, the Performance subtest scores are generally lower and less evenly developed (intertest higher variability) than the Verbal scores, which might suggest impairment of abilities mediated by the right cerebral hemisphere (evidence for a lateralized finding), or, more probably, an indication of difficulty solving new problems (PIQ) as opposed to accessing overlearned and stored verbal knowledge (VIQ). Nevertheless, it is important to note that Mr. G.'s Performance subtest variability may reflect premorbid cerebral organization often associated with high verbal/analytic achievement in educational and vocational pursuits.

The Aphasia Screening Test was performed quite well, including constructional items (Figure 11–5), yet there were mild indications of dysnomia (in naming the cross, he first called it a "plus sign"), and some mild difficulty repeating "Methodist Episcopal" (dysarthria). Such findings cannot be considered normal for an individual with Mr. G.'s education and profession; however, they are consistent with profiles from similar individuals who have experienced mild to moderate closed head injuries. The possible disruption of Performance subtest scores on the WAIS-R, difficulties in abstract reasoning and concept formation solving (Category Test), deficits in two-step problem solving, and attention and concentration (Trail Making B) in the absence of major motor and sensory deficits are all typical neuropsychological test findings following cerebral trauma. Test findings are consistent with the medical history and indicate that most of Mr. G.'s present problems seem related to his recent trauma and his emotional reaction to associated cognitive deficits.

To describe Mr. G.'s cognitive and behavioral strengths and weaknesses and to determine their implications for everyday functioning, the examiner must again review the test data, focusing on abilities and skills necessary to successfully complete the tasks and then apply those findings to Mr. G.'s particular requirements for successful living. This necessitates a familiarity with the patient's lifestyle and occupation as well as a thorough understanding of the relationships between the tests and cognitive/behavioral skills and abilities. In this particular case, the patient exhibits reasonably intact general cognitive abilities with his general fund of information and verbal skills being above average (WAIS-R Verbal) and his visuo-spatial new problem-solving abilities appearing somewhat unevenly developed (WAIS-R Performance). His mental flexibility, mental efficiency, abstract reasoning, and concept formation (Category Test) are somewhat impaired, as is his ability to concentrate simultaneously on two aspects of a complex problem-solving situation (Trail Making B).

Basic, attentional skills seem generally intact (Speech-Sounds Perception and Seashore Rhythm). Sensory and motor testing revealed no deficits in bilateral upper extremity motor speed and strength (Finger Oscillation and Strength of Grip), and no significant sensory deficits were noted (Sensory-Perceptual Examination). His abilities in the area of psychomotor problem solving were generally intact when tactile and kinesthetic cues were substituted for visual feedback (TPT), but he demonstrated some difficulties in remembering spatial relationships when incidental memory was required (TPT Localization). Aphasia screening revealed no true aphasic symptomatology; however, he did exhibit mild deficits in naming common designs and in articulation. Objective psychological assessment indicated a mild yet clinically significant level of depression and anxiety, as well as a concern with physical symptomatology, typical sequelae of closed head trauma. Follow-up memory testing (Wechsler Memory Scale-R) indicated mild impairment of immediate and short-term verbal and visuo-spatial recall, possibly related to attentional deficits.

The preceding information regarding cognitive and behavioral functioning should comprise the majority of the neuropsychological report with only a small section devoted to neurologic implications, and the remainder focusing on how the deficits are affecting the client and what intervention will be necessary. In Mr. G.'s case, these deficits, although generally mild, are significantly disruptive to his everyday functioning. A corporate tax attorney undoubtedly requires a high level of concentration and attention, as well as new problem-solving skills, memory abilities, and mental flexibility to successfully compete and fulfill his vocational duties. Recognizing his impairment and the impact on his occupational functioning may increase his level of frustration and anxiety, which may begin to strain his relationship with others. His reported personality change and lowered frustration tolerance are indirectly, if not directly, related to these factors.

Since these results are quite commonly found following cerebral trauma, the examiner might expect restitution in functioning to occur over the next 6 to 18 months. Immediate benefits can be realized by informing Mr. G. and his family that his symptoms are quite normal for CHI and that he should experience significant recovery in function over the next several months. He should also be informed that these specific deficits, although relatively mild, can become quite frustrating if they are not understood, and that it will be important for him, his family, and his employer to realize that recovery from such an injury is not immediate and that a reduction in workload stress and responsibilities is highly recommended. Other rehabilitative interventions such as cognitive therapy, changes in organization of work environment, and psychotherapy may also be helpful. Finally, follow-up neuropsychological evaluation is suggested in six months to chart recovery and reassess the need for outpatient therapies.

ASSETS AND LIABILITIES OF THE HALSTEAD-REITAN NEUROPSYCHOLOGICAL TEST BATTERY

The Halstead-Reitan Neuropsychological Test Battery is a comprehensive, well-validated, and reliable set of assessment procedures measuring a variety of cognitive abilities and behaviors. This battery has been used for many years and, as such, a tremendous amount of data have been collected, which adds to its clinical and research application. Most recently, the development of age, education, and gender-based normative scores allows for transformation of results into T scores for comparison purposes (Heaton et al., 1991).

As described, the HRNTB represents only one model of contemporary neuropsychological assessment. A fixed battery approach provided by the HRNTB has several assets. First, procedures are standardized, which allows for comparison of scores among patients with similar and dissimilar disorders. Second, interpretive guidelines are clear and qualitative interpretation of data can be undertaken as the clinical situation dictates (Benton, 1992). Conversely, fixed battery methodology has several limitations. First, fixed batteries are usually lengthy and expensive. In many cases, patients who have complicated medical and/or neurologic conditions are unable to complete extensive testing due to reduced endurance, cognitive disorganization, or physical limitations. The issue of cost is complicated, but in today's capitated health care system, extensive assessment is often refused and/or truncated.

Fixed battery approaches also assume, possibly erroneously, that all diagnostic and prognostic questions can be answered by the tests administered (Benton, 1992). This is usually not the case, and despite having numerous tests and extensive observation of patients during an examination, the tests utilized may not be sensitive to particular behavioral disturbances secondary to central nervous system disorder. For example, fixed batteries, including the Halstead-Reitan Neuropsychological Test Battery, are subject to false-negative findings, particularly when patients have anterior cerebral lesions that do not disturb language, memory, motor, or sensory systems (Eslinger & Damasio, 1985).

A final criticism of the HRNTB relates to the long-standing concerns that the battery is empirically derived rather than based on a theory of cerebral organization reflecting hierarchical neuropsychological functions. As mentioned previously, the HRNTB empirical foundations are both a strength and a weakness. Because the HRNTB was validated using the criterion of cerebral dysfunction, the battery has not proven useful in predicting everyday functioning (Heaton et al., 1988; Durham et al., 1992). In addition, recent studies suggest some tests in the HRNTB (Speech-Sounds; Rhythm) may not adequately measure theoretical constructs (attention) or contribute diagnostically when attempting to discriminate among patients with and without cerebral dysfunction (Sherer, Parsons, Nixon, & Adams, 1991). Despite the weaknesses mentioned, similar criticisms can be aimed at most neuropsychological batteries regardless of orientation.

SUMMARY

As discussed previously, this chapter was designed to serve as an introduction to the Halstead-Reitan Neuropsychological Test Battery. In contemporary neuropsychology, a single approach to assessment during the learning process does not always facilitate comprehensive learning and evaluation of existing measurement strategies. Therefore, both coursework and application in a variety of models of assessment appear important to developing clinical skills and a sound basis in understanding how assessment may be applied to patients suffering from neurologic disorders.

REFERENCES

Barth, J. T., & Boll, T. J. (1981). Rehabilitation and treatment of central nervous system dysfunction: A behavioral medicine perspective. In C. K. Prokap & L. A. Bradley (Eds.), *Medical psychology: Contributions to behavioral medicine.* New York: Academic Press.

Benton, A. (1992). Clinical Hemopsychology: 1960–1990. *Journal of Clinical and Experimental Hemopsychology, 14,* 3, 407–417.

Boll, T. J. (1977, February). A rationale for neuropsychological evaluation. *Professional Psychology,* 64–71.

Boll, T. J. (1978). Diagnosing brain impairment. In B. B. Wolman (Ed.), *Clinical diagnosis of mental disorders.* New York: Plenum.

Boll, T. J. (1981). The Halstead-Reitan neuropsychological battery. In S. B. Filskov & T. J. Boll (Eds.), *Handbook of clinical neuropsychology.* New York: John Wiley & Sons.

Dunn, E. J., Searight, H. R., Grisso, T., Margolis, R. B., & Gibbons, J. L. (1990). The Relation of the Halstead-Reitan Neuropsychological Test Battery to functioning living skills in geriatric patients. *Archives of Clinical Neuropsychology, 5,* 103–117.

Eslinger, P. J., & Damasio, A. R. (1985). Severe disturbance of higher cognition after bilateral frontal lobe abation. *Neurology, 35,* 1731–1741.

Faust, D. (1990). Research on human judgment and its application to clinical practice. *Professional Psychology: Research and Practice, 17* (5), 420–430.

Golden, C. J. (1978). *Diagnosis and rehabilitation in clinical neuropsychology.* Springfield, IL: Charles C. Thomas.

Halstead, W. C. (1947). *Brain and intelligence: A quantitative study of the frontal lobes.* Chicago: University of Chicago Press.

Heaton, R. R., Grant, I., & Matthews, C. G. (1991). *Comprehensive norms for an expanded Halstead-Reitan Battery.* Odessa, FL: Psychological Assessment Resources.

Hevern, V. W. (1980). Recent validity studies of the Halstead-Reitan approach to clinical neuropsychological assessment. *Clinical Neuropsychology, 2,* 49–61.

Jarvis, P., & Barth, J. T. (1994). *A guide to interpretation of the Halstead-Reitan Battery for Adults.* Odessa, FL: Psychological Assessment Resources.

Lezak, M. D. (1983). *Neuropsychological assessment* (2nd ed.). New York: Oxford University Press.

Ranseen, J. D., Macciocchi, S. N., & Barth, J. T. (in press). Neuropsychological assessment: Issues in its clinical applications. In J. R. McNamara (Ed.), *Clinical Issues, Developments and Trends in Professional Psychology 2.*

Reitan, R. M. (1969). *Manual for administration of neuropsychological test batteries for adults and children.* Unpublished manuscript, University of Washington, Seattle.

Reitan, R. M., & Davison, L. A. (Eds.). (1974). *Clinical neuropsychology: Current status and applications.* Washington, D.C.: V. H. Winston & Sons.

Reitan, R. M., & Wolfson, D. (1985). *Halstead-Reitan Neuropsychological Test Battery: Theory and clinical interpretation.* Tucson, AZ: Neuropsychology Press.

Russell, E. W., Neuringer, C., & Goldstein, G. (1970). *Assessment of brain damage: A neuropsychological key approach.* New York: John Wiley & Sons.

Sherer, M., Parsons, O. A., Nixon, S., & Adams, R. L. (1991). Clinical validity of the Speech Sounds Perception Test and the Seashore Rhythm Test. *Journal of Clinical and Experimental Neuropsychology, 13* (5), 741–751.

Swiercinsky, D. (1978). *Manual for the adult neuropsychological evaluation.* Springfield, IL: Charles C. Thomas.

Thompson, L. L., Horton, R. J., Matthews, C. G., & Grant, I. (1987). Comparison of preferred and nonpreferred hand performance on four neuropsychological tests. *The Clinical Neuropsychologist, 1* (4), 324–334.

Author Index

Subject Index